Sport Psychology:
from Theory to Practice

Related Benjamin Cummings Kinesiology Titles

Bishop, *Fitness through Aerobics*, Fifth Edition (2002)

Darst/Pangrazi, *Dynamic Physical Education for Secondary School Students*, Fourth Edition (2002)

Darst/Pangrazi, *Lesson Plans for Dynamic Physical Education for Secondary School Students*, Fourth Edition (2002)

Freeman, *Physical Education and Sport in a Changing Society*, Sixth Edition (2001)

Fronske, *Teaching Cues for Sport Skills*, Second Edition (2001)

Fronske/Wilson, *Teaching Cues for Basic Sports Skills for Elementary and Middle School Children* (2002)

Harris/Pittman/Waller/Dark, *Social Dance from Dance a While*, Second Edition (2003)

Hastie, *Teaching for Lifetime Physical Activity through Quality High School Physical Education* (2003)

Horvat/Eichstaedt/Kalakian/Croce, *Developmental and Adapted Physical Education*, Fourth Edition (2003)

Housh/Housh/Johnson, *Introduction to Exercise Science*, Second Edition (2003)

Lacy/Hastad, *Measurement and Education in Physical Education & Exercise Science*, Fourth Edition (2003)

Mosston/Ashworth, *Teaching Physical Education*, Fifth Edition (2002)

Pangrazi, *Dynamic Physical Education for Elementary School Children*, Thirteenth Edition (2001)

Pangrazi, *Lesson Plans for Dynamic Physical Education for Elementary School Children*, Thirteenth Edition (2001)

Plowman/Smith, *Exercise Physiology for Health, Fitness, and Performance*, Second Edition (2003)

Powers/Dodd, *Total Fitness and Wellness*, Third Edition (2003)

Powers/Dodd, *Total Fitness and Wellness*, Brief Edition (2003)

Schmottlach/McManama, *Physical Education Activity Handbook*, Tenth Edition (2002)

Silva/Stevens, *Psychological Foundations of Sport* (2002)

Check out these and other Benjamin Cummings kinesiology titles at: www.aw.com/bc.

Sport Psychology: from Theory to Practice

Fourth Edition

Mark H. Anshel

Middle Tennessee State University

Benjamin
Cummings

San Francisco   Boston   New York
Cape Town   Hong Kong   London   Madrid   Mexico City
Montreal   Munich   Paris   Singapore   Sydney   Tokyo   Toronto

Publisher: Daryl Fox
Acquisitions Editor: Deirdre McGill
Assistant Editor: Michelle Cadden
Managing Editor: Wendy Earl
Production Editor: Leslie Austin
Copy Editor: Anna Reynolds Trabucco
Proofreader: Martha Ghent
Compositor: Marian Hartsough
Cover Designer: Yvo Riezebos
Manufacturing Buyer: Stacey Weinberger
Marketing Manager: Sandra Lindelof

Library of Congress Cataloging-in-Publication Data

Anshel, Mark H. (Mark Howard), 1948–
    Sport psychology : from theory to practice / Mark H. Anshel.—4th ed.
       p. cm.
    Includes bibliographical references and index.
    ISBN 0-8053-5364-X (alk. paper)
       1. Sports—Psychological aspects. I. Title.

GV706.4 .A57 2003
796'.01—dc21   2002031447

ISBN 0-8053-5364-X
1 2 3 4 5 6 7 8 9 10—06 05 04 03 02
www.aw.com/bc

CONTENTS

(Continued)

I couldn't believe what I was seeing. The coaches of the team that I was observing during the season were screaming obscenities into the faces of their athletes; making promises to players they couldn't (or wouldn't remember to) keep; punishing team members for the slightest "infractions"; refusing to explain to players the reasons for team decisions, policies, and strategies; teaching skills ineffectively, if at all; and generally treating team members in a negative and disrespectful manner. I was not surprised that team morale was poor. And so was the season record. For me, these observations signaled the need for a book in applied sport psychology. Despite their expertise in the sport that they were coaching, these coaches had much to learn about the psychological needs of athletes.

My experiences as a consulting sport psychologist for several U.S. collegiate teams and individual athletes and as a "mental skills coach" for a professional rugby team in Australia indicate that coaches and competitors often do not apply even the most basic, commonsense elements of effective leadership and performance. Ignoring (or perhaps unaware of) revelations by sport psychology research over the past two decades, many coaches use strategies for teaching skills, motivating athletes, and planning for competitive events that are no different than those used decades ago. Sadly, I have seen leadership strategies that consist of intimidation, disrespect, and the virtual absence of effective communication and empathy. Athletes, especially those exhibiting classic signs of pregame anxiety, often are not aware of mental techniques used to optimize psychological readiness and sport skill execution. Under these conditions, the sport experience is rarely enjoyable to the participants, and their disappointing competitive performance often shows it.

On the other hand, many fine coaches in sport have the insight, skills, and personality to genuinely care about other people and help each athlete reach his or her performance potential. The teams of these leaders are typically successful, and their members are often very satisfied. What coaches do and how they do it can have a significant impact on the athlete's attitude, feelings, and performance. Helping athletes be mentally and physically prepared to play their best is what coaching is all about. The effective coach takes the time to help a player learn, improve, and contribute to team success.

The primary purpose of this book is to help coaches and sport participants alike reach a higher, more sophisticated level of expertise, and thus, make the sport experience a more satisfying and successful one. This text fills a need for an applied sport psychology text based on credible, published research. Many sport psychology publications do a fine job of explaining the theoretical framework and social–psychological foundations of this discipline. Others offer a handbook approach to using psychological strategies as a sport participant. This text addresses both needs. A deliberate attempt is made to base application on theory while avoiding scientific and statistical jargon so that persons at various levels of education, past experience, and expertise may comfortably absorb the book's content. Sport examples from media publications and from my own experiences as a sport psychologist nurture the connection between the professional literature and real-life sport experiences.

I begin the book (Chapter 1) with an explanation of the field of sport psychology, which also encompasses the related field of study, exercise psychology. Researchers in the new and emerging area of exercise psychology are concerned primarily with the links between psychological factors (e.g., personality, emotion, and motivation) and exercise behavior. That is, what are the psychological benefits of exercise and how does a person obtain them? What are the best ways to improve exercise participation and to help individuals maintain their exercise habits? Many tasks performed by sport psychologists may be applied in both sport and exercise settings.

The following are just a few chapter highlights of the rest of the text. Chapter 5 explains the underlying causes of an athlete's emotions, particularly anxiety, just prior to the contest and what one can do about them. For example, anxiety and arousal are common in sport and influence performance both directly and indirectly; both coaches and players can learn to control these emotions. How coaches and athletes interpret and explain the causes of contest results plays an important role in future participation, which is the focus of Chapter 4. For instance, players may be less motivated if they feel that a lack of ability caused an error or loss. On the other hand, players who recognize that enhanced effort will help ensure their future success typically have increased motivation and self-image.

This text also includes two chapters uncommon in sport psychology literature: Chapter 9 discusses communication and counseling. Although communication and counseling are typically covered in counseling and educational psychology texts, they are not commonly applied to sport psychology contexts. Effective communication is the ability to listen and respond to a person's feelings with the appropriate compassion and empathy and with valid information. In sport, the collective purpose of communicating and counseling is to have a positive effect on the athlete's feelings and behaviors, both in and out of the sport domain. Achieving this is much more of a science than most people realize. Chapter 11, a new chapter in this fourth edition, addresses the area of applied exercise psychology—the application of performance and sport psychology in exercise settings. This area represents an important area of future research and practice in the field of sport psychology.

To lend additional credence to the application of cited research studies, Chapter 12 includes portions of my conversations with many athletes. As these conversations show, ideas believed to be widely held "truths" in the coaching profession often are considered myths by athletes themselves. For example, basketball and football coaches frequently give a pregame talk that is meant to motivate and "psych up" the team. But many athletes contend that a loud, assertive message has the opposite effect; they are more apt to get "psyched out" than "psyched up." These interviews provide a valuable source of information for effective coaching—through the athletes' eyes.

To further familiarize the reader with sport psychology literature, a brief explanation about how to read and interpret sport science research is presented in Appendix A, a feature unique to this sport psychology text. A wealth of information exists in the research literature about the factors—good and bad—that influence performance and about what coaches and athletes can do to promote the good and reduce or eliminate the bad. Having the skills to read published research studies helps practitioners access and apply this information, bridging the gap between research and application.

The following represent highlights of the significant changes to this edition:

- In keeping with current thinking, the chapter on "The Female Athlete" has been eliminated. The material has been refocused to present gender distinctions and has been integrated in appropriate areas of the text.

- Chapter 1 includes a new section on ethics in sport psychology that discusses such issues as the clarification of the sport psychologist's role, the importance of respecting individual needs and differences among athletes, the appropriate use of psychological interventions, and cautions about making performance enhancement claims.

- Chapter 11, the new material on applied exercise psychology, offers an in-depth review of theories in this area, yet goes the extra step in describing ways to apply these theories in exercise and rehabilitation settings. Application strategies not only address ways to assist exercisers to participate in physical activity, but to prevent the all-too-common problem of quitting exercise programs, an area of research and practice called adherence. Also included is the proper use of mental skills typically used by athletes to enhance sport performance, but often ignored in exercise settings.

- A new section on the use of qualitative research in sport psychology has been included in Appendix A.

One underlying theme of this book is that success in athletics is not necessarily spelled W-I-N. Despite the pleasure that comes with competing against and beating an opponent, sometimes athletes can derive far more enjoyment from their sport or exercise experiences if the quality of their performance during the contest is as important (and for child athletes, even more important) to themselves and to their leaders as the final outcome. As depicted in Chapter 10, children drop out of athletics if it is not fun; their own or their team's winning percentage rarely has anything to do with it. Truly, coaches and parents have a wonderful opportunity to make a significant contribution to the lives of many individuals in athletics. The message to the participant should be: "If you are going to make the effort to compete, do everything you can to reach your performance potential."

Acknowledgments

I would like to thank the several individuals who reviewed previous editions and offered constructive suggestions toward its improvement: Mary Duquin, University of Pittsburgh; Robert E. Stadulis, Kent State University; Steven J. Petruzzello, University of Illinois, Urbana-Champaign; Bob Shillinglaw, University of Delaware; Robert P. Pangrazi, Arizona State University; Bradley L. Rothermel, University of Nevada, Las Vegas; Dale P. Toohey, California State University, Long Beach; Milledge Murphey, University of Florida; and Wendel H. Gatch, University of Southwestern Louisiana. I especially would like to thank the following reviewers for their work on this edition of the text: Robert Baker of Ashland University; Bradley L. Rothermel of University of Nevada, Las Vegas;

Patricia Sullivan of George Washington University; Richard Stratton of Virginia Tech University; and Lance Green of Tulane University. The book is greatly improved as a result of their help.

I would also like to thank the many coaches who have given me the opportunity to interact with them and their players. Without firsthand experience, this book could not have been written with credibility. Finally, my deepest appreciation goes to the staff at Benjamin Cummings Publishers—Deirdre McGill, Leslie Austin, Sandra Lindelof, and Michelle Cadden—for their time, talent, and warm support in completing this fourth edition of the book.

I dedicate this book to my father, Bernard, and to the memory of my mother, Rochelle, for providing me with the opportunity to learn, the drive to achieve, and the desire to care about others. They gave to me what I always try to give to my students and to the coaches and athletes with whom I consult—100 percent.

Mark H. Anshel

About the Author

Dr. Mark H. Anshel is a professor in the Department of Health, Physical Education, Recreation, and Safety at Middle Tennessee State University in Murfreesboro, Tennessee. He has consulted with sports teams, ranging from youth sports to professional levels, and has applied the sport psychology literature in both medical and corporate settings. For example, he consulted with cardiac and pulmonary patients undergoing exercise rehabilitation in hospital settings, consulted with exercisers to enhance exercise performance and adherence in fitness programs, and applied performance psychology concepts in helping corporate clients to reach and sustain high performance under pressure. From a scholarly perspective, Dr. Anshel has an international reputation as a leader in the field of sport psychology. He has a prolific publication record, including scientific journals and book chapters. He is the author of *Aerobics for Fitness* (5th ed.) and editor of the *Dictionary of Sport and Exercise Sciences*. He has been an invited international speaker in at least 12 countries. Dr. Anshel is a reviewer for numerous scholarly journals. He is most widely published in the area of coping with acute stress in sport, and has expanded his research interests to include perfectionism in sport and intervention effectiveness to improve exercise adherence. He is an active member of the American Psychological Association, Division 47 (Exercise and Sport Psychology), the Association for the Advancement of Applied Sport Psychology, and the Stress and Anxiety Research Society. Dr. Anshel received his Bachelor of Science degree in physical education at Illinois State University. After working for five years as a director of physical education in the community recreation field, he returned to graduate school, earning a Master of Arts degree from McGill University in Montreal, and a Doctor of Philosophy degree in psychology of motor performance from Florida State University.

The Science of Sport Psychology

What Is Sport Psychology?

S port psychology involves properly selecting and motivating athletes so that each participant competes at his or her capacity. To do this, the athletes must use strategies to "psych out" opponents, reduce or cope with extraordinary levels of stress, prevent drug abuse, develop successful team strategies, and learn skills. Clearly, psychology is a central component of sport competition. Studying and using psychology in a sport situation gives one the ability to describe behavior ("athletes on teams that win consistently are more friendly toward one another than athletes on teams that consistently lose"), to explain behavior ("the upset may have occurred because the favored team was underaroused; the underdogs were up for the game and ready to prove that they could beat a worthy opponent"), and to predict behavior ("if a coach teaches in an angry manner, the athlete will not retain the information because of anxiety and the inability to concentrate on the information").

Since the mid-1980s, sport psychology has become increasingly linked to areas that go beyond sport performance. The most notable areas of study have been *psychophysiology* and *exercise psychology*. Whereas traditional sport psychology research and practice have been concerned with psychological inventories and performance outcomes, psychophysiological research examines the physiological (somatic) responses that influence or accompany cognition (thinking and emotion) and performance. For example, if poor performance is attributed to heightened anxiety, it would be of interest to know if the source of that anxiety was somatic (e.g., changes in muscle tension, heart rate, or other somatic responses) or cognitive (e.g., negative self-talk, poor concentration, or internal attentional focusing). Such information allows sport scientists and educators to suggest the use of certain mental techniques (e.g., relaxation or imagery) to reduce the effect of these undesirable changes in bodily processes. Published research in recent years often includes physiological measures that help explain possible cause and effect relationships between a person's thoughts or emotions and his or her physical performance (e.g., Hardy & Rejeski 1989; Petruzzello et al. 1991).

The area of exercise psychology has received increased attention in the sport psychology literature. Rather than examining sport performance, exercise psychology focuses on cognitive, psychophysiological, and situational factors that influence exercise behavior (see Anshel 1990a; Buckworth & Dishman 2002; Berger, Pargman & Weinberg 2002; and Seraganian 1993 for reviews of this emerging field). Examples of topics studied in this area include effects of physical activity on the exerciser's emotions and certain psychological dispositions, reasons for engaging in exercise programs and the causes for dropping out of them, changes in personality due to improved physical fitness, positive and negative addiction to exercise, factors that influence an exerciser's perception of his or her physical exertion, the effects of cognitive techniques on exercise performance, and others (see Chapter 11).

What has become increasingly certain to educators, researchers, and coaches is that the field of sport psychology is a science. It is the study of human behavior in the context of participating in sport and of how behavior (performance) is affected by three primary sources: the athlete, the team leader (i.e., the coach), and the environment in which these individuals interact. (See Figure 1.1.)

The Athlete

Sports fans show a genuine interest in "their" teams through attending, watching, listening to, and reading about contests. The media devotes considerable time to describing the events and the players who perform them. Reporters and announcers have become more sophisticated in their analyses of the factors that underlie performance. They often venture beyond describing someone as a good "game player" to explain the possible reasons for superior play in competitive situations. However, most sports fans do not consider important psychological factors when they are observing, or trying to understand, sport performance.

For example, former professional tennis player John McEnroe received considerable criticism for losing his temper on the court. However, McEnroe has admitted that at times he used anger as a mental technique to get "psyched up." To sport scientists, this is no surprise; however, no sport psychology consultant would endorse using anger to change one's mental state. Athletes don't want to become too aroused, just stimulated

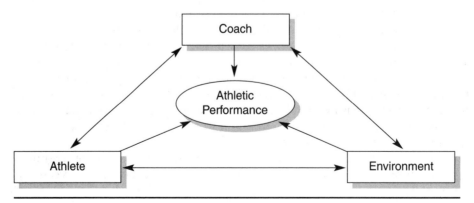

Figure 1.1 Factors that affect sport performance.

enough to play their best. The actions of football players on the sideline before and during the game, such as "high fives," pregame team cheers, and other warm-up activities performed by the athletes, all serve the purpose of establishing the desired emotional effect before the contest. Self-induced arousal strategies are an integral part of mental preparation and maintaining optimal performance for many competitive athletes.

Another important psychological factor in athletic achievement is *personality*: Is there a "personality type" that is predictive of high quality in sport performance? Can the coach predict sport success from a paper-and-pencil personality inventory? Do personalities differ between athletes and nonathletes, between male and female players, and among athletes in different sports? Sport psychologists have devoted considerable research to the topic of personality in sport. The answers to the above questions, which might surprise you, are provided in this book.

Individual differences is another popular subject of research concerning the reasons athletes differ in performance even when they have similar skills. Why do some players succeed under pressure in sport while others do not? What psychological factors separate the consistently successful competitor from his or her less successful counterpart? One could write a book on this last question alone. For example, this is what former heavyweight boxing champion, Mike Tyson, had to say in explaining why he would wake up at 4 A.M. to run in his prefight training regimen: "Because the other guy doesn't. I've got to prove to myself that I'm more disciplined than the other guy" (*Newsweek*, June 20, 1988, p. 56).

In the area of *youth sports*, in which participants typically range in age from 8 to 13 years old, sport psychologists are studying the effects of competitive activities: Should child athletes compete for awards? Do younger athletes have different psychological, emotional, and social needs than older, better-skilled players? If so, how can these needs be met through "healthy" sport involvement?

Another psychological factor to be considered is *motivation*: Why are some athletes more motivated than others, and what are the sources of their motivation? Why do some individuals participate in sport because it's fun or desirable, while others are motivated by external factors such as awards, recognition, or money? What are some of the psychological factors that help to motivate athletes, and which ones demotivate them?

The Coach

American author Henry Miller once wrote, "The real leader has no need to lead—he is content to point the way." And so it is with effective coaches in sport. Given the resources of player talent and their knowledge of the game, the team leader's primary goal is to develop the physical and mental skills of athletes so that they, individually and as a team, can achieve consistent success. In team sports, how can the coach facilitate the interaction of all team players to promote group identity, player satisfaction, and group cohesion? Hold on! Does it really matter? Does meeting the players' needs for affiliation and group "togetherness" have much connection to whether or not the team succeeds? Is a player's performance affected by that player's satisfaction in being a team member or by whether he or she has close friends on the team? If winning is the coach's only objective in sport, should he or she care about the athlete's social and emotional needs? Considerable sport psychology literature is devoted to why sport leaders *should* care about issues that go beyond player performance if they want a successful team.

But not all coaches are aware of these important psychological issues. In fact, if we can agree that, in general, coaches learn their trade by observing and listening to other coaches (the modeling effect or, more to the point, "monkey see, monkey do"), the athlete's personal needs are not often taken into account prior to, during, and following the contest. For example, Kirschenbaum, Wittrock, Smith, and Monson (1984) cite literature in which coaches publicly and frequently extol the virtues of criticism in sport. I have confirmed from my own experiences as a team consultant (Anshel 1989a) that many coaches tend to reject the interventions of others who attempt to modify coaching behavioral patterns.

For instance, one national survey of high school and college coaches indicated that 75 percent were not aware of the *Journal of Sport Psychology*, now called the *Journal of Sport & Exercise Psychology* (Silva 1984). However, although 80 percent of the coaches surveyed said that they had "never" worked directly with a sport psychologist, 68 percent indicated a desire to do so—on a volunteer basis, that is. Would they be willing to pay for such consultation? "No," said almost 65 percent. Perhaps they should. However, this skeptical attitude appears to be changing. In a more recent study of 75 national-level coaches and 123 elite athletes from New Zealand, Sullivan and Hodge (1991) found that the importance of sport psychology in training athletes is rated very highly. In addition, psychological skills are rated as very important for elite sporting success. However, Coté, Salmela, and Russell (1995), in their study of 17 expert gymnastic coaches in Canada, found that "properties considered crucial in the sport psychology literature, such as developing an athlete's self-confidence or developing concentration skills, were not discussed extensively by the expert coaches" (p. 93). The coaches indicate more traditional, extensive use of skill-instruction techniques and involvement in the athletes' training. Thus, in the absence of a sport psychologist, at least some coaches remain skeptical—or uninformed—about implementing mental skills. It appears that the lack of attention given to sport psychology information may be due to a lack of awareness about it.

On a more positive note, journal articles and media reports in more recent years indicate increasing acceptance by coaches and sport organizations of the need for psychological interventions in competitive sport. For example, the complete December 1990 issue of *The Sport Psychologist* was devoted to the experiences of sport psychologists who consult with elite sports teams in the United States, Canada, Great Britain, and Australia. Biddle, Bull, and Seheult (1992) report "a substantial increase in the demand for sport psychology services in Britain over the last few years" (p. 68). Tasks included the education of coaches and participants in mental training programs and in the psychological aspects of sport. Clinical sport psychologists are trained to address more personal problem behaviors among athletes. Finally, the sport psychology research and applied literature is filled with examples of programs worldwide that include sport psychology specialists as an integral part of preparing elite athletes for the Olympic Games. The specialists often accompany the team to provide on-site mental preparation and crisis management. Hopefully, one positive outcome from the increased involvement of sport psychology specialists will be to change selected behaviors of coaches.

Research findings in sport psychology do not support some of the common practices of coaches. Some of these practices may even be harmful, as shown in the following examples.

The Pregame Pep Talk. Many coaches, particularly in contact sports, give an exciting, emotionally charged talk just before game time. Sport psychologists and some of the more successful coaches argue *against* a hyped-up pregame talk (see Chapter 8). Researchers have found that athletes are already anxious or "pumped up" for the contest. An arousal-inducing talk before the game tends to excite the players above optimal levels; they become too excited (see Chapter 2). A low-key approach in which a review of information is presented may be more effective. Promoting enthusiasm for the contest should begin at practice.

"Winning Is the Only Thing." Feelings of anxiety and fear of failure already exist in players before the contest. The coach's job is to help the athlete to manage (i.e., to cope with) these feelings; their total elimination is unrealistic and even counterproductive. Pregame messages that express the need to win only heighten this anxiety. To review skills and strategies and then to tell players to go out and have fun or do the best they can is preferable to emphasizing winning.

Criticism. The effect of criticism on sport performance is clear: Sometimes it is helpful, but at all times its effectiveness is dependent on the manner in which it is communicated. As the late psychologist Haim Ginott recommended in his book *Between Parent and Child* (1965), authority figures should criticize behavior ("Jim, you're not keeping your eye on the ball"), not personality or character ("Boy, Eric, that was a dumb play"). The same goes for anger. Ginott claims that anger per se is normal, and its free expression should be allowed. But when anger is expressed through abusive and destructive messages that serve no other purpose than to destroy a person's self-image and to promote feelings of guilt, then its potential benefits are void.

Punishment. How often have you heard a coach yell, "OK, that's 10 laps around the field (or court)," because a player committed some infraction or failed in a contest or skill test? Considerable evidence indicates that punishing an individual with exercise reduces that person's desire to be physically active and a well-conditioned sport participant. An association between exercise and punishment is undesirable. A far better tool for punitive purposes is the short-term denial of participation in physical activity or sport, not additional (exercise) activity.

Many other examples of common, yet incorrect and unethical, coaching practices, some leading to the emotional destruction of the player, are offered throughout this text, including some forms of punishment. Coaches are required to fulfill the demands of many different roles and to deal with numerous psychological issues. Some of these issues include:

- motivating individual athletes and the team before, during, and after the season, and before, during, and after the contest
- positively affecting player attitudes either to increase anxiety as a precaution against complacency and overconfidence, or to reduce anxiety and promote feelings of excitement and loyalty to the coach and team
- promoting self-confidence and self-esteem in each athlete

- developing team leadership and morale *among the athletes*
- understanding and meeting the needs of younger athletes
- identifying the potential and promoting the development of each athlete
- enhancing performance consistency
- helping players to cope with stresses, disappointments, and other problems both within and away from the sport arena
- conducting practices and preparation for the contest that result in learning and mastering skills and strategies

Each of these issues is of significant importance to successful sport participation, and all of these areas are directly tied to meeting the psychological needs and fostering the mental skills of each player. The coach has direct control over, and must take primary responsibility for, helping each athlete to address these issues.

The successful management of a team is a complex and sophisticated skill. To make everyone in the group feel that he or she contributes to team success, and to promote desirable behaviors (e.g., developing quality player leadership, showing team loyalty, and building internal motivation) while inhibiting inappropriate ones (e.g., cheating, exhibiting hostility toward other team members, taking banned drugs, forgetting skills and strategies, or quitting the team) is a difficult task. Coaches are asked to achieve the most difficult of human objectives: to change the attitudes, feelings, perceptions, and behaviors of others for the good of a team. How? Now *that* is what effective coaching and sport psychology are all about. One way to meet these objectives is to create the proper environment for sports participation.

The Environment

The sport environment refers to the *situations* and *features* of sport competition and the *interactions* between athletes, other sport participants, and observers. For example, media reports have shown that players are almost "paranoid" about making fools of themselves in front of thousands (in the stadium) or millions (on television) of fans. Playing on synthetic turf and using newly developed equipment also influence the athletes' mental state. As a visiting team, competing in front of hostile fans may concern athletes and affect their concentration.

One environmental issue in sport psychology is a concept called *team cohesion*, the "togetherness" of group members. Effective coaches try to foster a team atmosphere in which athletes offer mutual support of one another's efforts, improvement, and performance. It is also desirable for team members to feel group satisfaction and a sense of pride in being on the team representing their school, club, or community. Strong team affiliation strengthens athletes' commitment to go "all out" to meet the team's needs.

Other environmental issues that are the focus of sport psychology include:

- Is there research support for the popular conception of a home-field advantage, or is it a myth?
- Does the cheering or booing of the crowd influence performance? Are quality athletes really affected by crowd reactions?
- Does the effect of environmental conditions on performance depend on the sport? For example, would golfers practicing on a different course experience a

significantly greater environmental effect than basketball players playing on a different basketball court?

- What is the effect of social team cohesion on player performance? Does it matter if teammates do not spend time together away from the sport scene? Is team success possible only if the players interact socially and enjoy one another's company off the field or court?

- Is it a good idea to tell athletes that their parents, a college recruiter, professional scout, or some other evaluator of their performance is observing them play?

- When are anger and criticism appropriate, and when are they likely to be damaging to player development and performance? How can anger and criticism be communicated to players in a way that can improve rather than hurt performance?

- Was the late newspaper columnist Sydney Harris right when he wrote, "Even the behaviorists concede that praise works twice as well as criticism in providing the incentive to improve—but it is also twice as hard for most people to praise as it is to point out defects"?

These are only some of the many questions concerning how environment can influence the outcome of competitive events in sport. One or more psychological factors are present in each of these examples to a significant degree as depicted in Figure 1.2 (on page 8). It should be obvious to the reader that participating in and coaching competitive athletics is a far more sophisticated endeavor than most spectators, journalists, and even the participants themselves realize.

Over the past 30 years or so, sport psychology has grown to be a legitimate academic discipline (or subdiscipline of physical education) and field of study. As with any academic area, interests among learners, researchers, and practitioners vary, and so do the directions in which interested parties move. Researchers in the area of sport psychology have devoted considerable energy to disseminating scientific findings through journals and have begun to receive appropriate recognition from the academic community. These researchers have generated and tested theories and models from the behavioral sciences and have published their findings in reputable journals such as the *Journal of Sport & Exercise Psychology*, the *Journal of Sport Behavior*, *Research Quarterly for Exercise and Sport*, the *Journal of Applied Sport Psychology*, the *International Journal of Sport Psychology*, the *Journal of Sports Sciences* (U.K.), the *Australian Journal of Science and Medicine in Sport*, and *The Sport Psychologist*. The individuals who have attempted to apply the results of this research (and who, in fact, conduct their own research typically in "real world" sport settings) are a group of scientists/practitioners called *sport psychologists*, *sport psychology specialists*, or *consultants*.

A Brief History of Sport Psychology

The late U.S. Senator Adlai Stevenson said, "We can chart our future clearly and wisely only when we know the path which has led to the present." Indeed, understanding the current status and future directions of sport psychology requires information about its history, which is far older than most students and scholars in the sport sciences realize. As early as 1897, Norman Triplett, a psychologist at Indiana University, published (in the *American Journal of Psychology*) what is believed to be the first experiment directly related to sport psychology. Triplett investigated a phenomenon that we now call *social*

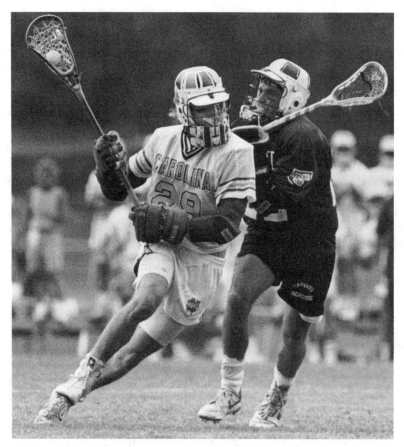

Figure 1.2 Situational demands in competitive sport often require sudden shifts in emotional intensity, the ability to process information quickly and accurately, and the competence to formulate and carry out strategy and tactics—all occurring simultaneously or in rapid succession.

facilitation, the favorable effect of observers on one's performance. He noticed that cyclists performed faster when competing against other cyclists, and faster with other cyclists on a tandem bicycle than when cycling alone. Triplett explained that the presence of others (i.e., competitors, co-actors, audience members) results in the release of energy and incentive for increased effort. In another study (published in *Popular Science Monthly* in 1899) E. W. Scripture, a psychologist at Yale University, concluded that participating in sport could lead to desirable personality traits. The contemporary view that competitive athletics builds character has its roots in Scripture's research. But the recognized pioneer of sport psychology, at least in the United States, is Coleman Roberts Griffith. Referred to as the "father of sport psychology in America," Griffith is acknowledged as the first person to conduct systematic and frequent sport psychology experimentation over a period of several years (Kroll & Lewis 1970; Wiggins 1984).

Griffith developed the first sport psychology laboratory—the Athletic Research Laboratory—at the University of Illinois in 1925, but his research on the psychological factors that affect sport performance began as early as 1918 (Gould & Pick 1995). His primary areas of interest included psychological and environmental factors that influence the learning and performing of motor skills, and personality in sport. He developed equipment for his laboratory that measured awareness of skilled movements; mental alertness; reaction times to sight, sound, and pressure; steadiness; muscular coordination; muscular tension and relaxation; and learning ability (Kroll & Lewis 1970). He was the first scientist to acknowledge, based on an interview with football great Red Grange, that better athletes perform sport skills automatically, with no or minimal thinking. He wrote the first sport psychology texts in 1926 (*Psychology of Coaching*) and 1928 (*Psychology of Athletics*) and taught the first sport psychology college course, at the University of Illinois in 1923. In a task that today's sport psychologists would truly envy, Griffith was hired by the Chicago Cubs major league baseball club to be the team's consulting sport psychologist for the 1938 season. He administered various motor tests and psychological inventories to determine each player's current psychological status, ability, and potential as a competitive athlete from spring training to the season's end. Gould and Pick (1995) provide an in-depth review of the role of Griffith's contributions to the development of sport psychology from 1920 to 1940.

Sport psychology research was at a virtual standstill in the 1940s and 1950s, with the exception of the occasional doctoral dissertation. More common during this time was the establishment of motor learning laboratories, including those founded by John Lawther at Pennsylvania State University, Clarence Ragsdale at the University of Wisconsin, C. H. McCloy at the University of Iowa, and, perhaps most notably, the late Franklin Henry at the University of California at Berkeley. This movement provided the field of physical education with a more sophisticated, scientific approach to research in motor behavior. Subsequently, all sport scientists learned from the improvement in research design, equipment, statistical techniques, and more frequent publications of information pertaining to the psychomotor processes that underlie learning and performing skilled movements. Despite the "striking void . . . between Griffith's productive years and the work of more contemporary researchers in sport psychology" (Wiggins 1984, p. 14), the field of sport psychology has benefited from these initial attempts in motor behavior research.

It wasn't until the mid-1960s that sport psychology made great strides toward becoming the scientific discipline that it is today. A number of factors contributed to the development of this academic area. Textbooks were more readily available. Examples include Bryant Cratty's *Movement Behavior and Motor Learning* (1964), Bruce Ogilvie and Thomas Tutko's *Problem Athletes and How to Handle Them* (1967), Robert N. Singer's *Motor Learning and Human Performance* (1967), and Joseph Oxendine's *Psychology and Motor Behavior* (1967). A subsequent book by Singer, *Coaching, Athletics, and Psychology* (1972), was among the first college textbooks in sport psychology. These books provided an impetus for prolific research and publication in scientific journals, most notably *Research Quarterly* (now called *Research Quarterly for Exercise and Sport*), the official research publication of the physical education profession in the United States. But even more important to the advancement of sport psychology and motor behavior scholarship was the proliferation of courses and university graduate programs in the 1970s, becoming increasingly common in the 1980s, that led to the emergence of our most prestigious scholars in sport psychology. (See Landers 1995 for an in-depth review of the formative years in sport psychology, 1950–1980; and Gill 1995 for a review of women's roles in sport psychology during this period.)

The final component in the growth of sport psychology was the establishment of several professional associations. The first annual meeting of the North American Society for the Psychology of Sport and Physical Activity (NASPSPA) was held in 1967. Its Canadian counterpart, the Canadian Society for Psychomotor Learning and Sport Psychology (CSPLSP), was founded in 1969. At first, this organization was affiliated with the Canadian Association for Health, Physical Education, Recreation, and Dance (CAHPERD), but it became an independent society in 1977. In 1975, a subdivision of the American Alliance for Health, Physical Education, Recreation, and Dance (AAHPERD) was created to promote sport psychology within the academic framework of physical education. It was called the Sport Psychology Academy. The purpose of the academy was to promote theory and research that could be applied in a physical education or sport setting. In 1986, the Association for the Advancement of Applied Sport Psychology (AAASP) came into existence to promote a more "hands-on" approach in sport psychology. AAASP, with one of the largest memberships of sport psychology professionals and students in the world, comprises three subdisciplines: health psychology (e.g., studying the psychological effects of physical activity), intervention (i.e., sport counseling and studying the effectiveness of using psychological and behavioral techniques on sport performance), and social psychology (i.e., examining the influences of environmental factors on emotions and behaviors of athletes and coaches). Although the field of sport psychology is rooted in the area of physical education, it has gained increasing recognition by and affiliation with the field of psychology in recent years. This is due partly to the legal use of the word *psychologist*, which should reflect academic training in psychology. Understandably, considerable debate currently occurs among scholars and practitioners about which discipline—physical education and sport science or psychology—should coordinate programs for training sport psychologists.

The American Psychological Association includes Division 47 (the Division of Exercise and Sport Psychology), an "interest group" comprised of researchers who examine psychological factors linked to human performance. However, the purpose of this group is to promote a field of study rather than to develop certification criteria. The link between sport psychology and psychology is also strong in Australia, where a national organization, the Australian Psychological Society (APS), has included sport psychology as an integral component. The importance of this status is based on the development of standards for licensure (called registration in Australia) to use the title of and practice as a sport psychologist. Other national sport psychology organizations exist either independently or as subdivisions of their respective psychology associations throughout Europe, South America, India, Asia, and Africa. Finally, sport psychology is best recognized around the world through the International Society for Sport Psychology (ISSP).

The purpose of these organizations is to provide scholars and practitioners in sport psychology with their own national and international identity as a scientific discipline. They also allow members an opportunity to meet annually (1) to exchange ideas, (2) to communicate their research experiences, (3) to hear and interact with established scientists and practitioners whose work and expertise is well-known in areas applicable to sport behavior, (4) to debate and perhaps make decisions about controversial issues, and (5) to bring back to their respective departments' programs and classes new and exciting ideas in the field. From these organizations have come additional scientific journals to meet the needs of an expanding field of study.

Finally, sport psychology is compatible with the growth of computer information technology. In addition to CD-ROM library search programs (e.g., PSYCHLIT, SPORTS-DISC), the listserve SPORTPSY@LISTSERV.TEMPLE.EDU provides opportunities to interact through electronic mail (e-mail) via computer. Discussion of professional issues, exposure to recent articles and events, job placements, and seeking professional advice or assistance have become increasingly popular and simplified in recent years with advanced computer technology that is accessible to many people.

Sport Psychology Is Multidimensional

Clearly, sport psychology is a multidisciplinary area of study and practice. It is derived from, and therefore includes, many of the traditional disciplines of psychology, such as social psychology (the study of group behavior and environmental/situational factors that affect a person's emotions and actions), developmental psychology (changes in cognition and behavior with age), cognitive psychology (the link between thoughts, emotions, and performance), educational psychology (factors that influence learning and remembering sport skills and strategies), clinical psychology (examining personal issues that require professional guidance in order to gain individual satisfaction in sport and approach optimal performance), and many others. These subdisciplines of psychology— exercise psychology is the only area that is not a traditional area of study in psychology, although it is linked closely with health psychology—are illustrated in Figure 1.3.

Social Psychology of Sport. Components of social psychology that are studied and applied in sport psychology include leadership theory and styles, the psychological aspects of effective coaching, understanding the factors that influence group cohesion (a group's sense of togetherness) and group dynamics (interactions among group members), effects of audience characteristics (e.g., size, evaluative role, passive presence

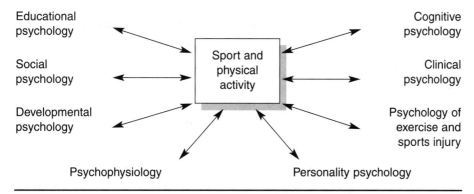

Figure 1.3 Multidimensional components of the field of sport psychology.

versus interaction with the athlete) on athletic performance, aggression, cultural factors that explain psychological characteristics and behavior, and effects of gender, usually studied as cross-gender comparisons, on an array of psychosocial and behavioral factors that influence sport performance.

Developmental Sport Psychology. As we grow and develop with age, so does our ability to perform sports skills. Developmental sport psychology is concerned with the psychological factors that accompany these changes with age and skill. It is no secret that child athletes have unique psychological needs that separate them from older, more mature individuals, both in life and in the context of competitive sport. How do coaches and parents recognize and respond to these unique needs? Why is there such a high dropout rate—about 80 percent—among youthful athletes (under the age of 13 years), and what can be done to create a more enjoyable, fulfilling sport experience for these younger athletes? Less emphasis on training and competitive outcomes (i.e., winning and losing) and more emphasis on skill development and enjoyment are typical suggestions coming from youth sport research. Other areas of study include socialization factors that contribute to participation in sport, and ways in which we can encourage sport participation (recreation) and other forms of physical activity among the elderly.

Cognitive Sport Psychology. Cognition is the technical term for thinking. In sport psychology, researchers and practitioners want to know the ways in which the timing and content of the athlete's thoughts and emotions influence performance quality and outcome. Sources of intrinsic and extrinsic motivation, the manner in which an athlete explains performance success and failure (causal attributions), and the influence of an array of mental (e.g., imagery, psyching up, thought stopping, self-expectations, confidence, coping, self-talk) and behavioral (e.g., goal setting, planning, self-regulation) strategies on performance are primary areas of study and application. Helping athletes to manage anxiety, for example, is a common requirement for successful competition, and an area where much intervention research has been conducted. Surprisingly, coaches are often the source of an athlete's anxiety rather than a source of comfort and confidence. How can coaches (and parents, too) communicate information that will facilitate confidence rather than instill feelings of worry and threat (i.e., anxiety) among their players? This is addressed in Chapter 5.

Educational Sport Psychology. Good coaches are good teachers. Improved athletic performance often reflects the coach's ability to communicate skills and strategies effectively. This area of sport psycholgy is concerned with examining the processes of learning and remembering sports skills, often referred to as information processing, the study and application of ways to increase motivation and other desirable emotions and feelings while reducing anxiety and related undesirable thought content, and the proper use of instructional techniques. Educational sport psychology is related to other disciplines of sport science called sport pedagogy and applied motor learning.

Clinical Sport Psychology. Perhaps the most popular and well-known area of sport psychology concerns addressing the psychological issues that impede the athlete from reaching and sustaining high-level performance. One common, related aspect of clinical issues is the use of mental skills that help athletes overcome obstacles to high performance and to achieve desirable outcomes. Researchers in this area often concentrate on developing and testing the effectiveness of instruments that measure certain psychological dispositions that may predict the athlete's thoughts, emotions, and performance, while practitioners use this information to counsel athletes (see Figure 1.4) about the sources of certain problems and suggest interventions to overcome them.

One real dilemma in clinical sport psychology is in understanding the different roles of clinical psychologists, who are licensed by their state board and may use the title "psychologist," and sport psychology consultants, individuals whose education in sport psychology is extensive and who know the sport psychology literature, though they are not trained in clinical psychology, may not refer to themselves as "psychologists," and deal primarily in performance enhancement techniques. This dilemma goes far beyond the purpose of this section, which is to describe components of sport psychology. However, it is important to know that both sets of skills, clinical and performance enhancement, are needed to address the whole spectrum of issues that athletes present in taking advantage of mental skills training.

Personality Sport Psychology. Through the use of psychological inventories, can we predict who will become a successful athlete? Who will achieve champion status and who will not? Who is best suited to achieve success in a particular sport? Who is most likely to reach his or her potential? Who is most resilient to pressure and the expectations of others? Personality assessment in sport received considerable attention in the 1970s and 1980s, then began to wane in the 1990s, and is less popular today. The

Figure 1.4 Sometimes sport psychology interventions can be most effective when consultants work with athletes at the practice venue rather than in office settings.

reasons for this decreased popularity are addressed in Chapter 2. Instead of using personality tests to predict an athlete's future, researchers have focused more recently on examining the extent to which an athlete's style—a stable disposition (not an entrenched personality trait)—and thoughts—more situational and unstable—affect athletic performance. Attempting to predict an athlete's future by using a psychological inventory, without considering the roles of growth, development, coaching, training, motivation, and a vast array of other factors, is obsolete thinking.

Psychophysiology of Sport. Psychophysiology is formally defined as the inference of psychological processes, emotional states, and performance outcomes from examining physiological measures. What, exactly, goes on beneath the surface of human performance? For example, is an athlete's anxiety due to muscle tension (somatic anxiety) or to worry and thoughts of possible future harm or failure (cognitive anxiety)? How do we train athletes in archery, shooting, bowling, and other sports that demand reduced arousal, the mental skills needed to lower heart rate, and other physiological processes that will optimize performance through mental skills training? Researchers want to know the mechanisms of the muscles and the nervous system that are associated with performance quality.

Psychology of Exercise and of Sports Injury.   Two relatively new, emerging areas of research and practice are called exercise psychology and psychology of sports injury. Exercising psychology is defined, according to the *Dictionary of Exercise and Sport Sciences* (Anshel et al. 1991), as "the study of psychological factors underlying participation and adherence in physical activity programs" (p. 56). Other components of exercise psychology include examining the effects of physical activity on mental health and emotion, determining the reasons why certain individuals voluntarily engage in a structured exercise program and why some of them continue to exercise (called adherence) while others decide to stop exercising (dropping out), determining how a person's perception of their exertion (called ratings of perceived exertion) influences exercise intensity and duration, and studying the phenomenon of positive and negative exercise dependence, or addiction.

Exercise psychology is gaining extensive attention by researchers, practitioners, and graduate students in sport psychology programs. This is partly because the same concepts that explain and improve sport behavior are similarly valid in exercise settings. In addition, graduates and practitioners are finding that there is a professional market for applying exercise psychology in fitness clubs, weight loss clinics, and rehabilitation settings.

Psychology of sport injury addresses the reasons that some athletes become more seriously or frequently injured than others and why selected competitors are unable to regain previous performance levels after injury rehabilitation despite all test data indicating full recovery; ways of determining differences in pain detection and pain tolerance among athletes, and of how athletes' pain perception influences their recovery from injury and subsequent performance quality; and methods for identifying the effectiveness of psycho-behavioral interventions that improve rehabilitation from sports-related injuries. A team's athletic trainer and sports medicine staff have an important role in helping athletes recover mentally, as well as physically, from injury.

What Do Sport Psychologists Do?

One approach for examining the roles of sport psychologists is derived from the United States Olympic Committee (USOC). At their meeting in August 1982, in Colorado Springs, Colorado, the USOC's Sport Psychology Advisory Committee divided into three broad areas the services of sport psychologists: clinical services, educational services, and research services (see Clarke 1984).

Clinical Services

This area includes helping athletes who experience severe emotional problems (e.g., depression, anorexia, panic) and who need treatment over an extended period of time. Although laws vary among states and countries, persons should not practice clinical sport psychology unless they have full membership in their national psychological, psychiatric, or clinical association; a current license to practice clinical counseling; and for professional, though not legal, reasons, some academic preparation in the sport sciences.

Educational Services

The teaching component of sport psychology occurs most often on university campuses, in community seminars, and in consulting with teams and individual athletes. It usually involves helping performers develop the psychological skills to realize their athletic potential. Relaxation, concentration, imagery, and coping strategies to handle stress are examples of these cognitive skills. Many university faculty members who teach sport psychology tend to lecture and provide counseling services simultaneously. Because such persons are perceived by constituents to possess up-to-date knowledge and expertise in this area, they must read the most recent professional research literature and have the academic skills to translate this information into applied form. Without the ability to bridge the gap from theory to practice, the educator continues using antiquated, perhaps unproven and ineffective, techniques. Imagine being the patient of a physician whose practice is based on medical education of 10 or 20 years ago. For this reason, an educational sport psychologist or consultant should have earned at least a master's degree in psychology or have completed graduate study in sport psychology.

Research Services

A doctorate in psychology or a related field (e.g., sport science), evidence of scholarly research activity applied to sport or exercise, and letters of reference from reputable research institutions that recognize one's research attempts and contributions to the field qualify one to provide research services. The research sport psychologist has three major responsibilities: to conduct research, to publish his or her research findings in a professional (refereed) journal, and, if possible, to present these results to colleagues at professional conferences. A scientist who lacks the skills to communicate about his or her work is effectively mute and literally goes unrecognized in the scientific community.

The types of research services that are conducted by sport psychologists include the effects of certain mental techniques on the athletes' psychological state (e.g., arousal or anxiety levels, readiness to perform, or self-confidence) and performance. Other popular research areas include examining effects of various personal and situational factors on the individual's psychological or physiological status and on physical performance. Sometimes the participant is asked to complete a psychological inventory, which may "describe" a current mental state or psychological disposition (e.g., self-esteem or trait anxiety) or point out certain mental strengths and weaknesses of the performer. The effectiveness of certain cognitive or behavioral strategies on altering the subject's mental status and athletic performance may be evaluated. How certain leadership styles influence the team or individual players forms yet another area of research.

In examining the roles of sport psychologists as counselors, educators, and researchers, the question that has often been raised in the literature and at conferences is "Are sport psychologists really psychologists?" The answer is, it depends. Various national and state professional organizations in psychology around the world mandate certain criteria related to academic training, supervision, and field experience before a person can describe and advertise himself or herself as a "psychologist." The purpose for screening members of this profession is to prevent unqualified, poorly trained, or unethical charlatans from abusing the proper professional standards and training to practice clinical or counseling psychology (Nideffer 1981; Sachs 1993). Although the issue of licensure for sport psychologists is still unsettled, many professionals prefer using the terms "mental skills coach," "sports counselor," "consultant," or "educator" for persons without appropriate qualifications.

AAASP has generated criteria for becoming a "certified sport psychology consultant" (*AAASP Newsletter*, Winter 1990, no. 1, pp. 3, 8). In addition to an extensive amount of education and supervised training in psychology, the guidelines require that consultants possess adequate knowledge in the sport and exercise sciences. Many psychologists who work with athletes have never taken a university course in sport psychology, the biomechanical and/or physiological bases of sport, motor learning/control, motor development, the sociology of sport, physical education, or the biological bases of behavior. Virtually no professional preparation program in psychology favors inclusion of the sport and exercise sciences as a *required* area of training and expertise in order to be an effective sport psychologist. The type and extent of educational experience deemed necessary for certification as a sport psychology consultant remains an area of contention between trained psychologists—persons with a graduate degree in psychology—and persons with a background in physical education or the sport and exercise sciences. These recommendations concerning the roles and qualifications of sport psychologists are not law. They are merely guidelines toward a clearer understanding about the credentials and expertise of individuals who practice sport psychology. They are an attempt to recommend standards for quality control in a relatively new area of practice that unfortunately lacked a public image of respect and integrity for many years. Whereas some individuals (e.g., Anshel 1992a, 1993) claim that even the process of certification in sport psychology is flawed, the only certainty at this time is that only persons trained and certified in counseling or clinical psychology and licensed by their state board may call themselves psychologists—including *sport* psychologists. For more information about the AAASP certification program, see *AAASP Newsletters* (Winter 1990, vol. 5, no. 1, and Winter 1991, vol. 6, no. 1). See also Zaichkowsky and Perna (1992) for a spirited defense of the AAASP criteria for certification as a sport psychology consultant.

Ethics in Sport Psychology

The rapid growth of sport and exercise psychology has been accompanied by ethical issues concerning the practice of sport psychology. Issues addressed here include the debate about the qualifications of the sport psychologist, clarification of the sport psychologist's role, claims about performance enhancement techniques, sensitivity to individual needs, confidentiality, use of psychological inventories, and the need for updating knowledge in the field.

Who Is a Sport Psychologist? The contention from the psychology profession is that only individuals educated and university-trained in the field of psychology may refer to themselves as *psychologists*, and state licensing boards have traditionally supported this position. On the other hand, individuals with university training and experience in sport psychology have come from departments of physical education, sport and exercise science, and human movement studies, and are not qualified to use the title *psychologist*. According to the laws and regulations of most states, in the United States and other countries, an individual who wishes to practice as a sport psychologist and counsel athletes must be a counseling or clinical psychologist. The field of psychology legally "owns" the title of psychologist. The dilemma is this: The field of sport psychology has its traditions, history, and research in the sport sciences, not in psychology. Yet, only trained psychologists may legally use this title. It is this issue that defines the ethical boundaries of this field of study.

First, let's clarify the term *ethics*. Ethics provide the moral component of professional practice, forming a system of principles that suggest a particular code of conduct (Singer 1993). This code is communicated as a set of guidelines that describe acceptable actions or procedures a person may use to work at a level of expertise that has been predetermined by a professional body (e.g., usually a country's legally established psychological organization or a state's psychology licensure board). This works well when it comes to using the title *psychologist*. The rule is clear: If practitioners are not legally recognized as psychologists, they may not use this title to describe the type of service they provide. Does this mean that all psychologists who possess expertise and knowledge in sport psychology need to refer to themselves as *sport psychologists*? Not according to Dr. Michael Sachs, licensed sport psychologist and academic from Temple University (Philadelphia).

Sachs (1993) contends that "Just as psychologists trained in marital and family counseling would not ethically note themselves as having expertise in substance abuse counseling (unless, of course, they were trained in this area), psychologists who do not have training in exercise and sport should not be calling themselves 'sport psychologists'" (p. 922). While many licensed psychologists may be excellent clinicians or counselors, sport psychology may not be an area within their field of expertise. As Sachs notes, "clinical or counseling excellence does not necessarily transfer to the exercise and sport setting" (p. 922). Still, Singer (1993) contends that "in reality any licensed psychologist can claim to be a sport psychologist [even though] that person may never have had a course in sport psychology or have experienced athletic competition directly" (p. 99). On the other hand, individuals trained in the sport sciences but not in psychology can refer to themselves by other titles that exclude the term psychologist, such as sport psychology consultant, mental skills coach, and sports performance consultant, among others.

Clarification of the Sport Psychologist's Role. One common ethical dilemma faced by sport psychologists or sport psychology consultants is determining their primary loyalty. Is it to the athlete, to the coach, or to the organization that hired the psychologist? Although loyalty is not an issue in private practice, consultants who are hired by teams and organizations have a wider array of individuals to whom they are accountable. For whom does the consultant work? There are no set guidelines, but Sachs (1993) offers what is probably the safest approach: "Whatever arrangement is entered into must be clearly specified in advance, preferably in writing, and explained and understood by the athletes and team" (p. 923). All nonathletes associated with a sport organization, including members of the governing board, need to know that without confidentiality, there is no trust. Athletes who do not feel certain that issues discussed in sessions will remain private are not willing to disclose personal issues and, in fact, will refrain from even approaching a sport psychology consultant.

There are three common strategies taken by sport psychologists for sharing privileged information with coaches or other team personnel. Perhaps the ideal approach is to work with the athlete to initiate contact with the coach (or any other person who is the subject of conversation), thereby dealing with the issue directly. Another technique is first to get the athlete's permission to disclose and obtain *specific* information to and from a predesignated person. For example, athletes may feel uncomfortable approaching their coach to ask why they are not receiving more playing time. The counselor may then ask an athlete's permission to solicit this information from the coach, but keeps other issues confidential.

A third approach, one that has worked very effectively in my own practice, is to help the coach plan the content of at least one private meeting with each team member early to midseason for the purposes of (1) offering positive feedback on past performance and effort, (2) providing input on one or two areas for further improvement, and (3) asking athletes to disclose any feelings, questions, or wishes they may have about their experiences up to that point. To overcome the athlete's hesitation about being candid, the coach could ask this question: "Without my making any promises, what is one thing that you would like to see changed or improved to be more satisfied or more productive?"

Claims about Performance Enhancement Techniques. Perhaps among the most frequent criticisms of applied sport psychology, even from members within the profession (e.g., Landers 1988; Morgan 1988), is the exaggerated claims of treatment effectiveness. Sometimes the scientific evidence simply does not support verbal arguments of consistent improvements in psychological and performance measures based on certain techniques or programs. Other doubts exist about the validity of specific inventories to provide highly accurate psychological profiles about the client's mental "strengths and weaknesses" or predictions of future performance. In short, sport psychology practitioners must be prudent about claiming credit for *anything* about the athlete's success. Professionals in sport psychology, as in all areas of psychology, have a professional and ethical obligation to know the research evidence supporting a particular technique or treatment before making such claims. In fact, due to the inability to prove cause and effect between using a mental skill and performance outcomes, it would be best if such claims were not made at all. There currently exists an array of cognitive and behavioral strategies and mental skills programs in the academic and applied literatures from which to choose. Consultants should take a conservative approach in using and interpreting the results—positive or negative—of these treatments.

Use of Psychological Inventories.   Despite the widespread use of psychological inventories in sport psychology, researchers (e.g., Schutz & Gessaroli 1993) and practitioners (e.g., Orlick 1989) have questioned the validity and usefulness of scores derived from many of these measures. Ethical considerations arise when a sport psychology consultant either uses an inventory without knowledge about how to interpret its results or does not understand the limitations of certain inventories, especially those that were not originally developed for sport (Gauvin & Russell 1993). Still other omissions in proper ethics occur when the consultant provides the athlete with a score without properly interpreting its meaning, or does interpret inventory scores but fails to probe for more information in order to validate or invalidate the objective measure (Anshel 2000). After all, athletes have the right to say, "Your interpretation of my score doesn't sound like me."

The use and *misuse* of psychological inventories in sport psychology consulting is potentially more complicated, unproductive, and even damaging to experiencing desirable outcomes in consulting than most people (including practitioners) think. Though a vast array of self-report inventories is often an integral part of the process of conducting research, there are different criteria when using an inventory for consulting or clinical purposes. Anshel (2000) and Gauvin and Russell (1993) have addressed these issues.

Preliminary Issues.   Questions that consultants should ask before using an inventory include: (1) Is an inventory necessary when consulting in this situation? (2) What will the inventory score tell the consultant that a personal interview will not disclose? (3) Does the inventory have a diagnostic purpose, perhaps to disclose a limitation in a psychological characteristic, psychopathology, or dysfunction (e.g., depression, chronic anxiety, neuroticism), or is the inventory meant to describe some characteristic (e.g., confidence, self-control, perfectionism)? (4) What can be done with the information obtained? Will it be useful in the consultation process to improve performance, or to reach an issue that might explain a deeper, more complicated problem that prevents or inhibits athletic success? Finally, (5) does the consultant have the credentials—educational, legal, and experiential—to interpret and apply the inventory's findings in a clinical or consultative setting? Although athletes are not immune to the advantages of counseling, either for clinical or performance enhancement purposes, the focus of these questions should help consultants focus on the selective and cautious use of inventories with the athletic population whose trust and willingness to engage in the counseling process is marginal.

Use of the Term "Test."   The term "test" has been widely, but incorrectly, used in sport psychology consulting. Gauvin and Russell (1993) provide a superb overview of this issue. Briefly, a "test" infers a "right" or "wrong" answer, an amount or degree of a characteristic, and a quantitative comparison with some standard, an outcome that is quite rare for the purpose of most inventories with athletes. To the authors, "tests are designed to classify respondents on a given attribute in comparison to a normative group, whereas a scale can distribute subjects along the quantity of an attribute only within the limited sample under investigation" (p. 892). A scale or questionnaire lacks the competitiveness of a test. Finally, it is reasonable to surmise that, to an athletic population, at least, the terms "inventory" or "scale" would be perceived as less threatening than responding to items labeled "test," a word that reminds most of us of educational settings, evaluations, and grades.

Using the Correct Inventory. It is important that the inventory be used with the appropriate population. That it is not is a widespread problem. Too often, the data on which the inventory was developed—often nonathletes—came from respondents with a different set of psychological characteristics (e.g., culture, gender, age, skill level). This is one reason that there have been many articles in sport psychology research journals in recent years devoted to validation of inventories constructed for the athletic population, including scales that focus on a particular sport or age group.

Psychometric Scrutiny. Inventories that are published in research journals receive different levels of statistical validation, depending on the inventory's purpose. An inventory that is meant for diagnostic or predictive purposes will be expected to have greater predictive power and have more extensive statistical validation than an inventory that serves to describe or categorize a specific sample within the study. Consultants should be cautious about using an inventory incorrectly. Because the inventory was published in a journal article does not automatically mean it can provide valid information about a particular client in a counseling or clinical setting.

Developing Trust. To be effective, the counseling process requires building trust between the consultant and the client (athlete). Developing the client's feelings of security about disclosing personal issues, reducing client anxiety about being in a potentially unfamiliar environment, and determining the client's psychological needs all require time. Often, visiting a sport psychology consultant is unfamiliar and is threatening to most athletes. For some athletes, the use of inventories before the consultant-client relationship has matured sufficiently prevents them from revealing very personal thoughts, particularly in writing. It is one thing to ask an athlete to disclose information about behavioral tendencies, such as whether he or she has developed any precontest routines. It is an entirely different level of disclosure, however, to ask the athlete about the extent to which they feel nervous or pressured before confronting an opponent, or about their feelings toward authority figures such as a coach or team administrator. These issues can be exacerbated by cultural differences: Some cultures simply do not allow a person to answer such personal questions.

Sachs (1993) offers five guidelines for using psychological inventories. (Incidentally, these are not labeled "tests" because, unlike tests, which ascertain "right" and "wrong" answers, the purpose of inventories used in sport psychology is to obtain an individual's feelings or emotions without regard to correctness.)

1. *Know the inventory's psychometric properties.* Users of an inventory should know its validity and reliability in order to ensure that the results are meaningful and accurately reflect the consultant's reason for using this particular inventory. This information is usually published in the manual that accompanies most inventories or in the journal article that includes a copy of the inventory.

2. *Know for whom the inventory is intended.* To expand on an issue that was addressed earlier, most inventories were developed for adults, unless otherwise noted. The Sport Competition Anxiety Test has both adult and child versions, for example. Other inventories were developed only for individuals with certain characteristics (e.g., an abnormal condition such as chronic depression or a personality disorder) and may not be valid for clients who do not have this condition. It is also necessary to know if the inventory was developed for athletic participants as opposed to nonathletes. Sport psychology consultants must be sure that a given inventory is used prudently to improve the accuracy of interpreting the results.

3. *Beware of false interpretations.* The consultant must restrict the interpretation of measures to the types of personal characteristics the inventory is intended to obtain. For instance, a certain personality profile does not mean the athlete needs to use certain mental skills. Thus, a poor score for the trait "stability" does not necessarily mean the athlete lacks self-confidence, at least not until additional measures are collected or a personal interview is conducted. Similarly, athletes whose favorite color is red are not necessarily more aggressive than athletes whose favorite color is pink. It is now generally accepted by researchers that inventories not designed for athletes, especially if they reflect abstract interpretations of the responses (e.g., linking color and aggression), have little validity in predicting sport-related emotions and performance. Feedback from athletes themselves ought to be considered necessary for validating psychological inventories. Finally, many inventories are intended for use and interpretation by individuals with special training (e.g., a licensed psychologist). If the consultant does not have this training, then the test is being administered and interpreted unethically. If the client's health or well-being is endangered, the consultant may face legal action.

4. *Avoid inventories for exclusionary purposes.* Perhaps the greatest abuse of psychological inventories is to select members for a team or to determine playing time. This concept is often called *talent detection* or *talent identification*. Sport psychology consultants should refrain from using inventories for this purpose at all times. Not a single measure has yet been devised that is capable of accurately predicting future performance or ability. See Régnier, Salmela, and Russell (1993) for an excellent review of the problems associated with talent detection.

5. *Maintain confidentiality of results.* All scores obtained from psychological inventories and the interpretation of results should be available only to the client, unless there is a written agreement using a standard consent form that is signed prior to the inventory being administered and indicating the athlete's permission to share this information.

Sensitivity to Individual Needs and Differences.   Like everyone else in society, athletes differ in culture, gender, ethnicity, previous experiences, and personal needs. The ethical sport psychologist is aware of individual differences, tries to understand and be sensitive to these differences, and does not allow the uniqueness of each athlete to interfere in their perceptions of and judgments about the person. Athletes from some cultures, countries, or ethnic groups may be more hesitant to seek or be receptive to consulting with a sport psychology consultant or to use mental skills techniques than a person more familiar with this service or with these techniques. This may be particularly true if there is a language barrier (e.g., English is not the athlete's first language in an English-speaking country). Ethical practice also includes sensitivity to the unique needs of athletes of color, such as African Americans, Hispanics, and so on. For example, Anshel (1990c) interviewed 26 African American football players from a university in the southwestern United States about racial issues in competitive sport, with particular reference to their own experiences on the team. The athletes reported a general lack of sensitivity on the part of coaches to individual and sociocultural needs of African American team members. Particular concerns reported were a perceived lack of fairness and a general lack of psychological support from white coaches. In another study, Anshel and Sailes (1990) attempted to identify racial differences among 64 white and African American team sport athletes from universities in the northeastern and southwestern United States. Results from their inventory indicated several racial differences among the players. For example, African American players, in contrast to their white peers, perceived their coaches as too authoritative, were more likely to become upset upon receiving critical feedback from the coach, preferred more independence in controlling their pregame preparation, felt more accountability for performance and game outcomes, and perceived interracial relationships as less pleasant and more disruptive. These studies, taken together, indicate that sport consultants should be sensitive to ethnicity in providing effective counsel.

The issue of male consultants who work with female athletes is another area of consideration. Sport psychologist Keith Henschen (1991) from the University of Utah indicates that he works differently with female athletes than he does with males. He stresses the importance of particular professional approaches in gaining the trust and confidence of athletes of the opposite sex. For example, Henschen suggests that male consultants strive to maintain ethical practice by consulting in a semiprivate atmosphere, in which the office door remains partially open; staying in constant communication with the athlete's coach and sometimes her parents; avoiding physical contact (e.g., hugs and other physical contact common among female athletes) so as to avoid misunderstandings; and even avoiding traveling with female athletes in some cases.

Issues concerning athletes' sexual orientation also require great sensitivity among sport psychology consultants. Homosexuality in sport has gone virtually unrecognized in the sport psychology literature. One rare professional article on this topic has addressed homophobia in sport, defining homophobia as "the irrational fear and/or intolerance of homosexuality" (Rotella and Murray 1991, p. 356). The authors offer superb recommendations to coaches and to sport psychology consultants for ensuring that sexual orientation is respected, that it is not viewed as a predictor of athletic performance, and that the individual is viewed as equal to other team members.

The Need to Update Knowledge.   Is it ethical for a doctor to diagnose an illness and then prescribe drugs based on his or her knowledge from medical school without consulting recent journals and incorporating more current information? A specialist who fails to offer clients information about the most recent advances in the field may be considered unethical. Sport psychology is a field of rapidly advancing knowledge. Content of the sport literature, in part testing theories and examining the effectiveness of performance enhancement techniques, is unique and differs starkly from the general psychology literature. Therefore, sport psychologists must keep current with the literature to be effective in their diagnosis and prescription.

Knowing When to Provide a Referral.   Inherent in proper ethical practice is determining when an issue with a client goes beyond the consultant's training and expertise. However, too often, consultants overstep the bounds of their expertise and become involved with clients in areas for which they have no training or certification. For example, counseling and clinical psychologists are trained in different types of interventions for clients with different types of problems. *Clinical* psychologists, on the one hand, work with individuals with severe psychological dysfunction (e.g., chronic depression, eating disorders), while *counseling* psychologists, on the other hand, are legally restricted to work within the "normal" population, which includes most athletes. Training in psychology provides instruction on when to recognize certain types of psychological disorders that require referral to a clinician with specialized training. Sport psychology consultants who are not licensed psychologists need to practice similar referral services. Failure to do so may result in misdiagnoses and inappropriate treatments, potentially placing the client at risk. For example, an athlete with an eating disorder, chronic sleeplessness, or relationship problems with family members usually requires consultation with a person trained and registered as a counseling or clinical psychologist. An athlete who requests help to manage pregame anxiety or to overcome a slump in performance may obtain the necessary knowledge and techniques offered by a person trained in sport psychology through a university sport science or physical education program. Proper ethics dictate that consultants assist the client by acknowledging limitations in their own knowledge and training, and by knowing when to refer the client to a colleague with superior expertise.

SUMMARY

How important is sport psychology for success in competitive sport? According to all-star Chicago Bulls basketball player Michael Jordan, it's essential. Referring to his athletic peers, Jordan claims that "these young guys don't realize how much of the game is played in your head. There are a million ways to mentally compensate when one of your physical skills starts to diminish . . . the young guys don't know how to play now. They don't even know how to practice" (*USA Today* 1995).

The media are filled with stories about skilled athletes and coaches who attribute individual and team success to psychological factors. Improving concentration, increasing or reducing arousal level (i.e., psyching up and psyching down, respectively), managing stress and anxiety, and maintaining high self-confidence are examples of what athletes must do to approach their optimal performance. The importance of sport psychology is also shown in two other, very different, ways. At the elite sport level, more countries now include sport psychologists as part of their teams' preparation for the

Olympic Games. At the other end of the spectrum, sport psychology educators have uncovered the reasons why young athletes drop out of sport. These educators are actively working with sport organizations, coaches, and parents to improve continued sport participation and reduce the dropout rate by young competitors. This is accomplished by helping athletes have more fun and experience less stress, improve their sport skills and fitness, meet new friends, experience success and achievement, and develop self-esteem. Sport psychology educators also lead seminars for coaches on improving leadership skills, including heightened sensitivity to the performer's individual needs; on sport skill instruction; and on implementing mental skills and strategies to improve the athlete's psychological readiness. The value of sport psychology reaches athletes of all age groups and skill levels. Understanding the psychological factors that influence sport participation is what sport psychology is all about.

The primary goals of sport psychology are to describe, explain, and predict the attitudes, feelings, and behaviors of sport participants—including athletes, coaches, and even crowd members. Persons who are familiar with the psychological factors that underlie sport competition are sport psychologists, or, if not licensed psychologists, are referred to as sport psychology specialists, educators, consultants, or mental skills coaches. Clinical sport psychologists, i.e., persons with a graduate degree in clinical psychology, apply research findings by interacting directly with athletes to help them to deal with issues that may impede reaching their performance potential. Educational sport psychologists, on the other hand, teach psychological skills to inform athletes, coaches, and students about resolving these issues. Research sport psychologists/specialists examine the effects of various treatments and environmental situations on the competitor's mental status, ability to execute sport skills, or both. New areas of study include psychophysiology and exercise psychology, both of which offer more extensive and sophisticated approaches to the study of human performance.

There are numerous ethical considerations in the practice of applied sport psychology. As a growing area of research, education, and practice, the field of sport psychology is open to unethical conduct. Examples include inappropriate claims about the usefulness of performance enhancement techniques, the misinterpretation of research findings, improper training for counseling, and misuse of the title *sport psychologist*. There is currently debate among professionals concerning the proper training of sport psychologists and consultants to help enhance ethical practice and treatment effectiveness.

Currently, numerous professional publications and organizations exist to promote and disseminate new information on the research and practice of sport psychology. Persons interested in learning more about this area may wish to become members of a professional organization, attend conferences, and read the professional scientific and applied literature.

REVIEW QUESTIONS

1. Describe the ways in which the coach's leadership, environmental factors, and the athlete's personal characteristics and behaviors favorably and unfavorably influence sport performance.

2. Sport psychology consists of and reflects different areas of general psychology. What are these areas? Provide an example of how each area is represented and studied in sport psychology.

3. Name some of the different specializations in sport psychology and describe the various roles they play.

4. Who may be called a sport psychologist? In other words, what are the criteria for being a sport psychologist, as opposed to a sport psychology consultant or specialist?

5. Why is it important to have a separate set of criteria and training for sport psychologists and sport psychology consultants? In your opinion, is an individual trained in psychology more qualified to counsel athletes than one trained in the sport sciences, or is it the other way around? Support your views with examples.

6. How has the field of sport psychology become a recognized and respected scientific discipline and field of professional practice over the past 30 years?

7. Describe three examples of unethical behavior in sport psychology and how each of these behaviors can be prevented or changed.

8. If you are not a trained, registered psychologist, can you still use psychological inventories with athletes? Are there inventories that a sport consultant who is not a psychologist can use? On a related issue, how should the athlete's inventory scores be used or not used during the consultation? Are there right and wrong ways to use inventory measures with a client?

9. Describe the case in favor of and the case against using a psychological inventory in assessing an athlete's personality, emotions, or other mental characteristics.

CHAPTER 2

Characteristics
of Successful Athletes

How do they do it? How do the best, most consistent sport performers make it to the top and stay there? Is it their total commitment to excellence? An extremely high need to achieve? Is it the incentive to meet more meaningful long-term goals rather than needing the reinforcement of meeting short-term goals like most of us? How do these competitors withstand the physical stress of constant conditioning and practice and the mental stress of performing at optimal levels before thousands, sometimes millions, of spectators? Sometimes they don't. In order to stay competitive, some athletes feel compelled to take artificial and illegal substances. Given the pressures to succeed, especially in elite sport, perhaps it is not surprising that ingesting banned drugs is so common. For this reason, the topic of drug abuse will be explored in this chapter.

While spectators observe and appreciate the finesse and skill of elite athletes, researchers study the underlying causes of, and factors that contribute to, their quality performances. Although research on examining the unique qualities of elite athletes is surprisingly scant, the available studies that help identify and explain these factors will be reviewed here. Psychological differences between the best athletes and less successful competitors and nonathletes will also be explored. After reading this chapter, you should be able to identify these unique traits, personal dispositions, mental processes, and behavioral tendencies.

Personality Traits and Psychological Dispositions

It would be appealing to delve into the sport personality research and derive a list of ingredients that, when mixed together, form a champion athlete. For example, selected characteristics such as competitiveness, confidence, and self-control would appear to be strongly linked to performance success. Early attempts at assessing the personality of athletes resulted in promises of finding such an ideal athlete. It was thought that a person's answers on a questionnaire could be used to predict successful performance. Coaches were at first ecstatic about the possibility of selecting their players based on the ability of a psychological inventory to predict success. As it turned out, the preliminary data from these inventories were not interpreted and used appropriately by coaches or by researchers. In fact, some inventories have been shown to be invalid and unreliable for use with sport competitors (Vanden Auweele et al. 1993).

Before examining the issues surrounding personality testing and research, it is important to point out that many researchers and educators disapprove of the term test when discussing personality assessment. The term *test* is synonymous with "right" and "wrong" answers, according to this thinking. A description of someone's personality is void of value judgments; that is, there are no "good" or "bad" traits. Therefore, rather than administering a personality "test," the document that examines any type of psychological trait is more accurately described as an *inventory*, *scale*, or *profile*. In keeping with this view, these terms will be used interchangeably in this chapter and throughout the book.

An additional point of clarification concerns the difference between the terms *psychological dispositions* and *personality traits*. *Traits* are commonly regarded as "properties of persons that dispose [them] to react in certain ways in given classes of situations [and] are usually narrower in scope [than dispositions]" (Lazarus & Folkman 1984, p. 121). *Dispositions*, on the other hand, are "broad, pervasive, encompassing ways of relating to particular types of people . . . or situations" (p. 120). For example, the Type A behavior pattern is a *disposition*—a chronic, never-ending drive to achieve more and more, often under time restraints, sometimes self-imposed. Personality traits that are linked to the Type A disposition include dominance, need for achievement, internal locus of control, and trait anxiety. Dispositions may be more predictable in sport situations than traits and, therefore, are relevant here.

Personality, in contrast to psychological dispositions, can be defined in terms of traits possessed by an individual. Traits are considered enduring and stable. This means (1) that individuals have a predisposition to act in a certain way in most, but not all, situations and (2) that their actions are consistent, that is, predictable under various conditions—in sport or otherwise. However, traits derived from personality inventories have not been shown to be consistent from sport to nonsport situations (Vealey 1992).

Personality assessment has been limited in recent years. Students of sport psychology, consultants, and coaches need to take a critical look at the personality issue in sport based on the reviews of sport scientists such as Vealey (1992) and Vanden Auweele et al. (1993). These authors have identified a number of weaknesses associated with personality inventories and have expressed reservations concerning their use in sport, issues that are examined in the next section.

Using Personality Inventories

One way in which personality scales have been used inappropriately is to examine changes in personality traits over time (e.g., before versus after the season). This is incompatible with the design of any instrument that examines personality because, by definition, traits are stable and enduring. Consequently, results cannot be interpreted to measure personality change.

Often personality profiles have been used to predict the *probability* that an individual will achieve sport success. However, researchers have shown that inventories can predict athletic behavior and success only 10 percent of the time (Fisher 1977).

Sometimes the terms and factors used in personality scales are not universally defined. For example, who is an athlete? *Athletes* to one researcher might be participants in *recreational sport* while in another study the term may refer to competitors who represent a school or who perform at more elite levels. In addition, sociability, ego strength, shrewdness, dominance, and other traits are defined differently in various inventories.

Further, different scales are used to measure the same thing, but the results of these scales differ (Morgan 1980). Thus, the comparison of results from different scales is invalid.

Some personality traits are better predictors of success than others. Personality inventories such as Cattell's Sixteen Personality Factors Questionnaire (16 PF) and the California Personality Inventory (CPI) inherently assume that each of many factors is interpretable in sport situations. But how would a coach interpret a high relationship between dominance and reaction time? Wouldn't traits related to one's anxiety be better predictors of success in sport performance? Morgan (1980), for example, accurately predicted which athletes would participate on the U.S. Olympic wrestling team in 1972 based on measures of anxiety and a few other traits using the Profile of Mood States (POMS).

Another concern is that answers to questions on a personality inventory can be faked. Most respected inventories, especially those used for clinical diagnosis and treatment, have built-in lie scales. Lie scales include questions inserted in the inventory that are either discarded when the results are computed or used to detect response inconsistencies. Researchers sometimes include in their studies the Social Desirability Scale (Hays et al. 1989), which detects biased self-reported responses. The SDS is intended to screen for "favorable self-representation," that is, when a subject's answers on a scale falsely reflect a "more desirable" personal characteristic. These subjects must be omitted from the study.

The traditional personality inventories used in sport personality research were not created for sport participants. For example, the Minnesota Multiphasic Personality Inventory (MMPI) was originally meant to diagnose mental illness. The CPI requires a reading comprehension level equal to about the tenth grade, making younger athletes or persons with poor reading skills ineligible for this assessment tool. In addition, personality inventories such as the MMPI, CPI, and Cattell's 16 PF do not include a single item related to thoughts, emotions, or behaviors in competitive sport situations. Thus, such inventories may not be interpretable and valid as predictors of sport performance, for which they have been used—or misused—in past years.

Vanden Auweele et al. (1993) have extensively reviewed the previous research on personality in sport and offer several additional limitations. The primary shortcoming, cited in most review articles on this topic, is the lack of a conceptual (theoretical) framework. That is, there is no defined body of literature on which to base comparisons between athletes and nonathletes, male and female, or elites and nonelites. This failure to define a conceptual framework has been termed the "shotgun" approach; investigators administer various personality inventories to a group of athletes, hoping to find something of "significance" or importance that makes the sample unique. Properly conducted scientific studies do not happen in this way. The failure to approach the many research questions about personality in sport has been the primary limitation. Another limitation is poor sampling techniques, in which whole teams or categories of sports (e.g., team vs. individual sports) are examined in the same study without controlling for skill level, age, gender, and cultural differences. Improper use of statistical procedures is an additional problem: certain types of statistics are more valid than others. Finally, some studies rely on anecdotal, or single-subject, data, which may not represent any other athlete than the individual being questioned. Although the purpose of examining personality in sport is to generalize the results to large groups of athletes, these research limitations severely hinder this capability.

Despite the above problems, certain personality traits of successful athletes have been identified, albeit not conclusively, in the literature. Evidence does support the existence of a consistent psychological profile of highly successful performers that differs from the profiles of less successful competitors. An example is Morgan's (1979a) attempt to predict members of the U.S. Olympic wrestling team using the Profile of Mood States (discussed later in this chapter). Whether these traits are inherited, developed, or both is not clear. What *is* apparent, however, is that the results of a personality profile cannot predict sport success perfectly and therefore should *not* be used as a way to identify talent and eliminate those who score low on certain "desirable" traits.

Personality and Gender Roles

Are females who engage in physical activity, particularly competitive athletics, more "masculine" than their inactive counterparts? Are female nonathletes more "feminine" than female athletes? One area of considerable study over the years has concerned the measurement of individual differences in a personality characteristic called *gender role orientation*. According to Bem (1974), who popularized this research by generating the Bem Sex Role Inventory, these characteristics are defined as *masculine, feminine,* and a mixture of both called *androgynous*. Examples of stereotypically feminine items include affectionate, cheerful, yielding, and sensitive to the needs of others; while independent, self-reliant, athletic, and willing to take risks are examples of masculine items.

Bem found that these personality characteristics, labeled "traits" rather than "dispositions" by the Bem study, were not linked to biological sex or sexual orientation. Thus, women who scored high on masculine traits did not necessarily possess a male personality nor did they prefer female companionship. Further, nonathletes were not always more feminine than athletes. In addition, masculinity and femininity are not opposite ends of the same personality continuum. Rather, masculinity and femininity are separate clusters of personality traits.

Gill's (1992) review of Bem's research indicated that "there is no reason why males should possess only masculine characteristics or females only feminine characteristics. . . . The most mentally healthy and adaptable individuals possess both feminine and masculine characteristics" (p. 145). This combination of both masculine and feminine traits is called androgyny. Bem contends that androgyny is desirable because these individuals, in possessing both types of traits, have greater flexibility of behavior than do persons who are gender-typed toward the perceived male or female extremes.

Gill's (1992) review of the sport psychology research examining gender role orientation of female athletes indicates that "female athletes possess more masculine . . . personality characteristics than female nonathletes" (p. 147). This does not surprise Gill, who acknowledges that sport, the area for much of this research, is an achievement activity that demands assertive behavior. She surmises that the higher masculine scores of female athletes probably reflects an overlap with other dispositions studied in sport psychology called competitiveness or sport achievement orientation. The fact that female athletes possess more masculine personality traits than female nonathletes does not mean that athletes are less feminine, but rather that certain traits Western society designates as masculine are inherent in any individual who has high motivation in achievement activities. Nevertheless, this finding has implications for the type of female who is more likely to participate in, and persist at, competitive sport.

Based on their review of the gender role literature, LeUnes and Nation (1995) conclude that females who score markedly higher on perceived feminine traits than perceived masculine traits will experience a higher degree of gender role conflict and be less comfortable in competitive sport situations than females with high androgynous and masculine scores. The authors also conclude, similarly to Gill (1992), that (1) female athletes do not express a feminine gender role orientation, citing relatively low feminine rates in various studies ranging from 13 percent to 22 percent and (2) female athletes respond with more of an androgynous orientation than a masculine orientation. They conclude, in support of an earlier study by Friedman and Berger (1991), that "the androgynous or masculine female should succeed in sport without experiencing the sex [gender] role conflict that the feminine scorer would feel. . . . Androgynous and masculine females would find sport to be a great outlet for their expressive . . . energies" (LeUnes & Nation 1995, p. 333).

Friedman and Berger (1991) examined the effects of three stress reduction techniques on stress reduction as a function of gender, masculinity, and femininity. The stress reduction programs included jogging, relaxation training, and group (social) interaction. Among their findings is that psychological masculinity influences the effectiveness of the stress reduction activities, whereas psychological femininity does not. In particular, perceived masculine traits of both sexes are associated with joggers' short-term mood improvement. This finding supports an earlier study (McCutcheon & Mitchell 1984) which shows that established women runners tend to have more androgynous or masculine traits than feminine traits. Psychological masculinity was also related to decreases in perceived fatigue as measured on the POMS inventory. Thus, it appears that physical activity is, indeed, a constructive outlet for female athletes. Taking into consideration the results of studies and the well-known benefits of exercise on one's health, one could conclude that perceived masculine personality traits are highly desirable for mental and physical well-being in both males and females.

The Elite Athlete: A Profile

Elite, or champion, athletes have been defined in recent literature as "athletes who are eligible for competition at the national, international, or Olympic level, or who are professional sportspersons" (Vanden Auweele 1993, p. 257). For many years, researchers have shown a keen interest in the psychological dispositions and personality traits of those who are consistently in the upper echelon of their sport.

Early Sport Personality Research

Far more studies have been conducted on elite male than on elite female athletes. In one study, Williams (1980), in her review of research examining the personality characteristics of successful female athletes, concluded that:

- Women on the 1964 U.S. Olympic team who engaged in individual sports were more dominant, aggressive, adventurous, sensitive, independent, self-sufficient, and introverted than women who engaged in team sports.
- Female competitors in general tend to be assertive, dominant, self-sufficient, reserved, achievement oriented, and intelligent, and have average to low emotionality.

In other early studies, Reilly (1979), Paige (1973), and Rasch and Kroll (1964) reviewed the personality research of champion male athletes in soccer, football, and wrestling, respectively. In Reilly's review, the soccer athletes were assessed almost uniformly with the Cattell 16 PF questionnaire and were found to be stable, extroverted, tough minded, and highly efficient. Researchers using the MMPI across nine European countries found most male soccer players to be aggressive and dominant, especially the Germans and Italians. Brazilian players scored higher in intelligence than the other groups. But in general, elite soccer players scored significantly higher on each of these traits than less skilled participants and nonathletes.

According to Paige (1973), American football athletes differ from competitors in other sports. He concluded, based on his review, that football athletes "are outstanding for their roughmindedness, extroverted tendencies, and self-control. There is some indication that despite the footballer's extroverted traits, he is not as sure of himself as his actions indicate . . . winners are less sportsmanlike than losers which reflects the 'win at all cost' attitude sometimes found in winning teams" (p. 12). Kroll and Peterson (1965) compared personality traits between winning and losing football teams of 176 players (six teams). The most common difference between the teams was that players on teams with winning records were less sportsmanlike than participants on teams who lost more games than they won. However, not every personality study of football players has revealed unique personality attributes. For example, Rushall (1976), using the 16 PF inventory, failed to find differences among collegiate players competing in different sports at a large university, and he concluded that personality was not an important factor in football performance. However, in most instances, at least at the elite level, studies indicate that success in football requires extensive tenacity to overcome the skill and effort of opponents, to tolerate pain and play with injuries, and to maintain vigorous conditioning. Because of the physical nature of all contact sports, players must maintain high self-confidence, even to the point of bravado. Similarly, based on anecdotal evidence, boxers tend to brag and to appear very self-confident—even conceited—prior to a fight. For the football athlete whose commitment to excellence and whose pain threshold are high, but whose tolerance for failure is low, the chance of being successful increases measurably.

Another group of competitors who have received considerable attention is wrestlers. In Rasch and Kroll's (1964) review, the personality profile of wrestlers was less than conclusive. Generally, these athletes tend to score high on sociability, enthusiasm, love of adventure, and group dependency, at least according to the 16 PF inventory. Gould, Weiss, and Weinberg (1981) compared successful and unsuccessful wrestlers participating in the 1980 Big Ten championship tournament, and Highlen and Bennett (1979) studied the top 10 percent of all Canadian wrestlers. In both studies, successful participants scored statistically higher on measures of self-confidence, perceiving their skills as closer to their maximum wrestling potential, and on their ability to focus attention on task-related issues. Finally, Morgan (1979a) found, using the Profile of Mood States (POMS) inventory, that wrestlers on the 1972 and 1976 U.S. Olympic wrestling teams were "uniformly low on tension, depression, fatigue, and confusion, but well above average on vigor" (p. 184). The shape of the curve that illustrates these results resembles an iceberg and, therefore, has become known as the "iceberg profile" (see Figure 2.1).

Olympic Wrestlers: Who Made the Team

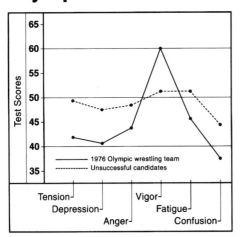

Average scores on the Profile of Moods States (POMS) test given during tryouts for the U.S. Olympic wrestling team in 1976. The eight candidates who didn't make the team display a profile close to the average score (50) for the general population. The eight wrestlers selected exhibit the Iceberg Profile typical of elite athletes: well above average in vigor and below average on tension, depression, confusion, and fatigue.

Figure 2.1 Example of iceberg profile.

One important limitation of Morgan's study is that the POMS is a measure of subjects' mood within one week of completing the scale. It is not a measure of stable traits associated with personality. Thus, it is more accurate to conclude that the iceberg profile reflects the *consequences* of competition among elite competitors rather than acting as an antecedent or predictor of skilled performance.

Recent Advances in Sport Personality Research

Terry (1995) has criticized the concept of an iceberg profile in sport. According to Terry, sports—and the individuals who play them—vary markedly concerning the mood state that is most "desirable" or predictable for their own successful performance. For example, he cites other research in which tension and anger, undesirable mood states in the iceberg profile, are linked to performance success in cross country running and karate. Similarly, the needs and tendencies of individual athletes are very different. As Terry concludes, citing his own earlier research, "it is not uncommon for athletes to perform well despite having theoretically 'negative' profiles" (p. 313). He concludes that mood states best predict performance when preperformance conditions include short-duration events, competing against previous personal standards rather than against opponents, and when opponents have similar levels of ability and conditioning.

The POMS has also been criticized for use in competitive sport. For example, according to its instructor's manual, POMS was developed as a measure of mood for psychiatric outpatients, specifically individuals with mental illness who are about to be discharged from the hospital. Any inventory that is not used with a population for which it was originally developed is invalid (Thomas & Nelson 2001). In defense of the use of POMS as a personality measure, Vanden Auweele et al. (1993) contend that POMS scores resemble a traitlike concept and, in fact, have been effective in predicting success among highly skilled athletes. Vanden Auweele and his colleagues reviewed 11 published studies totaling 308 elite athletes using the POMS to predict sport success. They report that "only one group . . . of 16 lightweight wrestlers had scores entirely not consistent with Morgan's iceberg profile" (p. 263). The authors warn, however, that these studies consist solely of American, mostly male, elite athletes, thereby limiting generalizations of these conclusions to females and to people in other cultures.

Despite flaws in research tools and other limitations, sport psychologists generally acknowledge that highly skilled athletes score relatively low in neuroticism, tension, depression, anger, fatigue, and confusion. They tend to score very high in self-confidence, self-concept, self-esteem, vigor, need achievement, dominance, aggression, intelligence, self-sufficiency, mental toughness, independence (autonomy), sociability, creativity, stability, and extroversion. A composite of psychological profiles of elite athletes reveals a person who is mentally healthy, physically and psychologically mature, and committed to excellence. Certainly, these are traits that serve as a model toward which all athletic participants should strive. However, some authors (e.g., Landers 1983; Singer 1988) question the value of applying these findings in sport, and many others (see Vealey 1992 and Vanden Auweele et al. 1993 for reviews) do not support using these personality characteristics as the basis for athlete selection, promotion, or elimination.

Psychological Dispositions

The purpose of this section is to review selected personal characteristics of elite sports competitors. These characteristics are not depicted here as personality traits but rather as styles or tendencies of thinking. I've selected these particular dispositions based on their examination in the literature and their commonality among quality sports competitors. For instance, Vanden Auweele et al. (1993), in their review of the sport personality literature, conclude that relative to their less skilled counterparts, elite athletes possess more self-confidence; less anxiety, both prior to and during competition; more effective techniques for managing anxiety; greater concentration on task-specific goals and movements; better ability to cope with unexpectedly poor performance; and more positive thought content.

Risk-Taking. One characteristic of highly successful competitors is risk-taking. The term *risk* is defined in most dictionaries as a dangerous element or factor, possibility of loss or injury, hazardous speculation, danger, or peril. In sport, risk has been associated with physical injury during competitive athletics. Risk-taking is a function of narrowing the margin of safety, both physically in terms of bodily harm and psychologically in terms of the probability of success or failure. Malone's (1985) review of literature on risk-taking in sport concludes that the athlete's perception of danger creates excitement and a desire to master the environment. Sport scientists have studied the tendency of highly skilled athletes to engage in more risk-taking behaviors—actions that can lead to bodily harm or failure—compared to less skilled competitors. However, skilled competitors will rarely perform tasks for which they are not well trained and physically fit. As much as high-quality athletes want to win, they also realize that it's only a game. No one wants to get hurt, because there is always another game to play.

Sport competition is, of course, inherently risky for all performers. But the elite athlete, more than others, seems to thrive on and to prefer the excitement of engaging in risk-taking behaviors. These behaviors occur most often during situations that require solving problems and making decisions. The quality defensive back in football will guard his opponent (the receiver) more closely than his conservative, less skilled counterpart. Champion divers, skaters, skiers, and gymnasts all tend to "go for it" in attempting very complex coordinated movements, and they usually succeed.

The question becomes "Why do elite athletes take greater and more frequent performance risks than others in improving their chances for success?" The answer to the question, although still open to further scientific inquiry, might be found in the areas of stimulus-seeking, competitiveness, self-confidence, attentional style, expectations for success, strategies for developing mental toughness, and ability to regulate stress.

Stimulus-Seeking. A psychological disposition of elites that is similar to risk-taking is called stimulus-seeking, or sensation-seeking. Athletes enjoy the challenge presented in competitive sport. Zuckerman (1984) was the first to classify individuals who desire situations that foster tactile and other forms of sensory stimulation as high stimulus-seekers. Stimulus-seeking is a motivational factor to participate in sport and to engage in risk-taking behaviors (Malone 1985). Stimulus-seeking appears to be based on a chronic level of activation (high excitation) that is easily and quickly rewarded by taking risks in sport. Indeed, the elite athlete thrives on it.

Straub (1982) studied the sensation-seeking disposition of hang-gliders, automobile racers, and bowlers. Hang-gliders scored highest on the sensation-seeking scale for *thrill and adventure seeking* and *experience seeking*, whereas racers scored highest for *disinhibition*. Not surprisingly, bowlers scored lowest on all sensation-seeking dimensions. Thus, it may be an overgeneralization to conclude that all athletes are higher sensation-seekers than nonathletes. But it appears that this disposition is associated with engaging in high-risk sports.

Competitiveness. Naturally, all athletes want to win. Researchers Gill and Deeter (1988) generated the Sport Orientation Questionnaire (SOQ) to measure the extent of this desire to win along three dimensions: competitiveness (desire to strive for success in competition), win orientation (focus on winning and avoiding losing), and goal orientation (focus on personal goals). When athletes and nonathletes are compared using the SOQ, athletes score higher on all three dimensions, with competitiveness being the major discriminator. In addition, Gill and Dzewaltowski (1988) found that males tend to score higher on the SOQ than females. Contrary to expectations, however, the researchers found that elite athletes did not score uniformly high on win orientation but were more oriented toward the quality of their performance than toward the contest's outcome. Gill's extensive work in this area over the years has shown that highly skilled athletes enjoy and optimally strive for success in competition but tend to measure their success by performing at their personal best (performance goals) rather than by only winning or losing (outcome goals). The implication for coaches is that quality performance deserves at least as much recognition as the contest's outcome.

Self-Confidence. Sport psychologists, coaches, and researchers agree that self-confidence is one of the most important mental states for success in sport competition. Self-confidence, also called *sport confidence* (e.g., Vealey 1986), is the athlete's belief about his or her ability to be successful in performing a desired skill. Feltz (1988) defines self-confidence as "the belief that one can successfully execute a specific activity rather than a global trait that accounts for overall optimism" (p. 423). Whether confidence exists in both state (i.e., this moment) and trait forms (i.e., stable and permanent) is unknown. However, Vealey (1986) has developed trait and state scales of sport confidence. *State sport confidence* is "the belief or degree of certainty individuals possess *at one particular moment* about their ability to be successful at sport," whereas *trait sport confidence* is depicted as their *usual* belief about their sport success (p. 223). Thus, in its trait form, self-confidence in sport is a component of the athlete's personality that he or she brings to the sport venue. Highly confident athletes are more likely to have high self-expectations and to anticipate successful performance outcomes.

Maintaining high confidence is accompanied by positive emotions (e.g., elation, excitation, vigor), improved concentration, increased effort, lower susceptibility to mental distractions, reduced muscular tension, improved ability to remember and use game strategies, and more rapid and accurate decision making (Weinberg & Gould 1995). Successful athletes possess—and maintain consistently—a high degree of confidence. However, this mental state does not occur automatically. Coaches, and the athletes themselves, must employ mental and behavioral strategies that induce self-confidence. The boxes on pages 37 and 38 list at least some of these strategies.

Self-efficacy, a concept often associated with confidence, is a situationally specific form of self-confidence—the athlete's conviction to perform successfully skills that are required to produce a certain desirable outcome. Self-efficacy combines state confidence with self-expectations (Bandura 1977). Athletes should maintain a high degree of both self-confidence and self-efficacy.

Attentional Style.   Attentional style, a concept developed for sport by Nideffer (1979), is defined as a "predisposition to attend to the environment in a certain personalized manner; depicted as internal, external, broad, or narrow" (Anshel et al. 1991, p. 13). Nideffer's model of this cognitive tendency is that each person possesses a unique manner of attending to environmental stimuli, and that efficient task performance is a function of the compatibility between the person's attentional style and the attentional demands for the specific task and situation.[1] Heightened anxiety, for example, results in a narrowed, internally focused attentional state that is rarely desirable. The important issues in depicting elite performers are their ability to shift attention as the situation demands and that their attentional style is compatible with the types of skills they most often perform (e.g., open and closed skills in which environments are unpredictable and predictable, respectively, thus requiring different attentional strategies).

Expectations for Success.   One reason for upsets in sport is that the more successful teams—athletes who are expected to win easily—do not perceive their opponents as

---

[1] Although the instrument for measuring attentional style, the Test of Attentional and Interpersonal Style (Nideffer 1979), has been criticized by researchers for its poor validity (e.g., Summers et al. 1991), some applied sport psychologists (e.g., Bond & Nideffer 1992) use this instrument as an additional source of information for counseling purposes.

Building Confidence: Coaching Strategies

1. *Have high, positive expectations of all of your athletes.* Studies on self-fulfilling prophecy indicate that high expectations by teachers and coaches result in better performance by students and athletes, respectively. In addition, if athletes do not perceive their coach's high expectations, performance may suffer.

2. *Ensure early sport success in each athlete.* A primary source of self-confidence is performance accomplishments. Structure the environment whereby each athlete is given the opportunity to succeed at a skill, no matter how elementary.

3. *Offer positive feedback.* Athletes will feel more assured if their coach offers verbal information about the quality of their performance. This type of input also reinforces desirable skill execution.

4. *Maintain a positive precompetition environment.* Emotional arousal is an important component of self-confidence. A person cannot be enthusiastic and unhappy at the same time. Be sure athletes maintain an upbeat mood before the contest. This does not necessarily mean using "psyching up" techniques, because athletes differ in their preferred precontest thoughts and behaviors. But research evidence strongly suggests that positive moods are linked to self-confidence, desirable attention focus, and favorable performance outcomes (Prapavessis 2000).

5. *Teach skills and strategies.* Self-confidence and performance jointly improve when athletes continue to learn new skills and strategies. Good coaches are good teachers. Be sure athletes continue to acquire skills and overcome deficiencies. As indicated earlier, let them know quickly when they have improved on a given task.

6. *Be a proper role model.* Weinberg and Jackson (1990) find that coaches foster higher self-confidence in their athletes when they exhibit this same quality. Players look to their coaches for guidelines on desirable feelings and actions.

7. *Make accurate causal attributions.* Coaches should teach athletes to explain the causes of performance outcome—good or bad—accurately. Perhaps the most important strategy is to avoid concluding that failure, or the *perception* of failure, is explained by a lack of ability—this is a leading cause of decreased confidence and influences athletes to quit participating (see Chapter 4). Low effort and/or high task difficulty attributions appear more helpful in response to failure. On the other hand, high ability and optimal effort following successful performance are confidence builders and improve motivation.

threatening to their continued success. Their expectation of success is too high and the amount of effort they give is too low. Success expectations and athletes' motive to achieve are influenced by the perceived ability of their opponents. In many cases, low expectations of success become self-fulfilling prophecies. In the opposite direction, quality athletes have a very high expectation of success: they expect to win—and they often do. Competitors are optimally motivated when they feel that they have about a 50 percent chance of success (Atkinson 1957). In high-risk sports such as high jumping or pole vaulting, which require explosive muscular effort as shown in Figure 2.2, expectations of success must be as high as possible.

Building Confidence: Athletes' Strategies

1. *Determine and emulate positive role models.* Modeling fosters desirable emotional states and improves performance if athletes can easily identify with a highly skilled competitor who possesses characteristics that are similar to their own.

2. *Use cognitive strategies.* Mental techniques such as positive self-talk, mental imagery (see Appendix B), thought-stopping, and many others have been used for building confidence. Thought-stopping serves to prevent athletes from engaging in negative self-talk, a response that should not be allowed.

3. *Reflect on previous successes.* All athletes have a history of quality sport performance. If you have self-doubts about the present situation, reflect on those past successes, even if they occurred in practice.

4. *Interpret anxiety as a sign of enthusiasm and readiness, not fear.* Virtually all quality athletes feel anxious before the contest. It is the interpretation and management of this feeling that separates successful from less successful competitors. Rather than pretending you do not have anxiety, interpret

it as a positive sign, a display of readiness and confidence.

5. *Be ready.* Nothing builds self-confidence like good preparation. Athletes should practice hard, *be in good physical condition*, listen to their coach, learn from past mistakes, remember skills and strategies already learned and practiced, and always do their best.

6. *Have fun.* One of the most effective pregame thoughts an athlete can have, especially prior to "high-pressure" contests or in tense situations, is the thought of enjoying the competitive experience. I've seen athletes play their best games against their most superior opponents when their coach reminded them to "go out there and have some fun."

7. *Know your opponent's strengths and weaknesses.* Fear, intimidation, and threat about the *perceived* superiority of opponents is a major obstacle to self-confidence. All opposing players and teams have weaknesses. Athletes should know them, and through their competition plan, exploit them.

Mental Toughness.   Sport psychologist Dr. James Loehr (1982, 1991, 1994) generated the term "mental toughness" in sport to mean reaching and sustaining high performance—the athlete's ideal performance state—under pressure by expanding capacity physically, mentally, and emotionally. Loehr contends that mental toughness is learned, not inherited. One common, but false, view of many athletes (and coaches) is that we are born with the right "competitive instincts," and that not being able to handle failures is due to lacking the genetic predisposition to be mentally tough. Loehr contends that holding this view—the belief in a "mental toughness gene"—is very tempting because it absolves the athlete of feeling responsibility for failure. This is self-destructive thinking, because the athlete is more likely to feel helpless, lose self-control about developing this skill, and lack the self-motivation to learn the proper mental skills to become more competitive.

Mentally tough competitors are self-motivated and self-directed (their energy comes from internal sources; it is not forced from the outside), positive but realistic (they are

Figure 2.2 Performing at one's capacity requires having high, realistic self-expectations, the ability to control emotions, and the willingness to deal constructively with inevitable performance setbacks.

builders and optimistic, not critics, fault-finders, and pessimistic), in control of their emotions (they have "tamed the lion inside" in response to frustration and disappointment), calm and relaxed under fire (rather that avoiding pressure, they are challenged by it), highly energetic and ready for action (capable of getting themselves pumped up and energized for optimal effort and performance), determined (they have a strong will to succeed and are relentless in the pursuit of goals), mentally alert and focused (capable of long and intensive periods of full concentration), dogged self-confident (have a high belief in their ability to perform well), and fully responsible (take full responsibility for their own actions). The box on page 40 contains an overview of the mentally tough athlete, including Loehr's (1982) recommendations for building mental toughness in sport.

Ability to Regulate Stress.   Based on his extensive experience with counseling elite athletes, Canadian sport psychologist Terry Orlick (1986, 1990) claims that the ability to remain cool under situations of tension and stress is the true sign of a champion. To take risks in sport when one feels uptight, anxious, or too aroused is very difficult. The key is not to eliminate stress, however, but to regulate it by using proper coping techniques. Coping will be covered later in this chapter.

The ability to cope with failure is another trait of the successful athlete (Orlick 1980, 1986). Coaches should be careful not to overreact to an athlete's mistakes. Especially during competition, the player may improperly concentrate more on not making further errors than on feeling in control and focusing on the proper cues. The participant will be overly cautious in order to avoid further mistakes, and risk-taking will be the last thing on his or her mind. To succeed, athletes must have the confidence and skills to

Building Mental Toughness in Athletes

Definition: The ability to ignore elements of interference during competition.

Personal traits of mentally tough athletes: High self-esteem, commitment, self-discipline, strong desire to succeed, personal accountability (responsible for performance outcomes), competitive, high but realistic self-expectations, no (or controlled) fear of failure, high goal orientation (motivated by setting and meeting goals), and hardiness/resourcefulness.

Thoughts and actions of mentally tough athletes: Mental plan (pregame and game), emotional control, optimal arousal, confidence, intrinsic motivation, optimism, controlled anxiety, concentration and attentional control (alert and mentally focused), performs automatically, proper situational appraisals (challenge, not threat), good coping skills (deals effectively with adversity), projects a positive attitude (positive body language), sense of enjoyment in the competitive setting.

Strategies for Building Mental Toughness

1. Increase fitness (strength and endurance).
2. Work hard to improve mental skills.
3. Set realistic, but challenging, goals.
4. Think positively and create enthusiasm.
5. Repeat positive affirmations to yourself.
6. Increase self-discipline (be in control).
7. Use positive visualization.
8. Review film/video of best performances (or recall them).
9. To prevent choking, think practice.
10. See competition as a challenge, not a threat.
11. Be confident in your ability and preparation.
12. Think before, not during, execution.
13. Stay externally focused on the task at hand.
14. Ignore negative feelings and other distractions.
15. Take responsibility; use failure and coach feedback as motivators (sources of learning).
16. Attribute success to internal causes.
17. Remain in control; dismiss thoughts of helplessness and hopelessness.
18. Say to yourself "stop" when having a negative thought.
19. Remember your successes, present and past.
20. Have positive role models.
21. Keep learning.

take risks. The better players learn from their mistakes, then put them out of their thoughts until after the contest.

Behavioral Tendencies

How are elite athletes different from other athletes in how they approach competitive events? Here is what Ahmad Rashad, former all-pro receiver for the (U.S. football) Minnesota Vikings, has to say:

> *If you're any good as a receiver, you scout fields. You look for dead spots. I found out long ago that the best footing is often where they paint the lines. I learned to make my cut on the lines. You leave a lot of cornerbacks that way. . . . At the opposite end (of the field), very near the end zone, there was a low, slushy spot, and I could run a post route in there and—literally—give my man the slip. I loved that old place.*

Rashad's knowledge of the characteristics of the playing surface serves as an example of the type of intense commitment and dedication that most elite athletes give to game preparation and performance. The hours, weeks, months, and even years of conditioning, practicing, preparing, and struggling to reach their potential is what ultimately separates the elite performers from all others. Sometimes an athlete's pregame preparation can take the form of superstitious behaviors. Three-time American League baseball batting champion Wade Boggs of the New York Yankees, like many other elite athletes, is noted for his obsession with certain rituals carried out on a specific and detailed schedule on the day of a game.

Sport psychology researchers such as Rushall (1979), Orlick (1986), Mahoney et al. (1987), Vanden Auweele et al. (1993), Anshel (1995b), and Weinberg (1988) have studied extensively the behavioral patterns of elite athletes before and during the event. They noted the following pre-event and event behavioral tendencies:

- Many elite athletes put less effort and intensity into practice than they do into the competitive event. Apparently they do not hold true to the adage "You play as you practice." They seem to produce a level of energy and skill during serious competition that exceeds their achievement in practice, in training, or during less challenging competitions.

- However, when it comes to physical training, elites go all out; they get in top shape and maintain it during the season.

- Athletes feel increasingly confident with more detailed competition plans. Therefore, coaches should use competition plans that are specific and detailed. Highly skilled athletes feel comfortable and capable handling a sophisticated approach to contest preparation and implementation.

- Elite athletes have contest contingency plans to implement if things do not go as expected. As discussed in Chapter 5, Orlick (1986) refers to this strategy as "the mental plan," in which the athlete's actions and thoughts are predetermined and extensively rehearsed for months before the competitive event—*what* they will do and think, and *when* they will do it and think it prior to and during competition. Athletes feel capable of coping and adapting to unusual situations that arise during the contest. Their confidence about dealing with the unexpected is enhanced by a secondary set of alternatives, which Orlick (1986) calls "the refocus plan," that they can use during the contest if necessary.

- They often prefer to be alone or remain silent immediately before the contest. Elite athletes tend to use relaxation techniques, review individual and team strategies, image successful performance, and verbalize positive self-statements to promote confidence.

- Elite athletes prefer to have a coach present during the warm-up period, perhaps as a source of inspiration or to obtain information. The athletes feel less competitive anxiety when surrounded by supportive personnel.

- They don't worry about other competitors before a contest. There is a difference between acknowledging the strengths, weaknesses, and tendencies of an opponent and being consumed with these thoughts and worrying about them.

- They are nervous and tense. Mahoney et al. (1987) found elite athletes are not unlike their nonelite peers in their precontest emotions, but are far better at managing these emotions. Nervousness and tension translate into high levels of controlled arousal. This is desirable. They use self-statements that reflect their readiness and eagerness to compete. Elite athletes sometimes use behavioral techniques, such as jogging in place or even throwing tantrums, to manage high arousal levels. For example, professional tennis player Martina Hingis slammed her racquet on the court 6 times in one winning match. She explained her actions by saying, "When I throw my racquet, it helps me concentrate" (*Sydney Morning Herald*, October 21, 1996, p. 26).

- They are capable of regaining composure if they become troubled, stressed, or too excited. The performers know their optimal level of arousal and have trained themselves to control it.

- They engage in numerous mental rehearsals. Quality performers expect to be successful, and they review images of their successful performance before the contest. This builds confidence and promotes mental practice.

- They can concentrate totally on the upcoming event during preparation (warm-up). They focus intently on the demands of their upcoming performance instead of observing and being preoccupied with their opponents during this time.

- They can accurately assess how well they will do during the competition. Skilled athletes are keenly aware of their physical and mental status before the event and, therefore, are able to make mental or physical adjustments for meeting performance demands.

- They can deal with unusual circumstances and distractions before and during the event. Top athletes do not allow unpleasant or unexpected circumstances to break their mental preparation. Examples include enduring a delay in the contest, a change in weather conditions, pre-event harassment, waiting for transportation to escort them to the event, or lacking appropriate warm-up and locker-room facilities.

- They are relatively unaffected by unfamiliar competitive environments. Practicing in an unfamiliar environment before the contest is beneficial to deal with specific features of the area. However, they are able to perform skills competently regardless of the uniqueness of their surroundings. In fact, research on the home field advantage has shown that the presence of supportive others may actually be more harmful than helpful in some situations. For example, Baumeister and Steinhilber (1984) found that the home team won more baseball and basketball games than they lost in early games in the playoffs but lost disproportionately more games in the games that determined the final winner.

- They prefer to "play their own contest" and to regulate their own effort levels. This means that elite performers would like to use certain strategies and skills in the contest without having to react to or be put on the defensive by opponents. For example, top runners and swimmers prefer to regulate the pace of the event.

- When fatigue sets in, they concentrate on technique and effort rather than outcome. Such concentration serves the purposes of distracting them from sensations of fatigue, reducing the possibility of injuries (which occur more often near the end of contests, when fatigue has set in), and helping them to maintain proper form and performance quality. Elite performers will fight pain and fatigue rather than succumb to it.

- They are able to overcome the physical demands—even abuse—that are a part of being a participant. In fact, contact sport athletes actually enjoy the physical aspects of the contest.

- They compete even when they are injured. True, some athletes have a higher tolerance, or threshold, of pain than others, but typically, successful elite athletes can focus their attention externally on the task and opponents rather than be preoccupied with physical discomfort.

- There is no "giving up." Elite competitors are reluctant to give less than their best efforts because they are proud of their ability and past accomplishments.

- They can withstand poor officiating. Poor calls may temporarily upset top performers, but not for long. They may express their feelings and then get on with the task at hand.

- They prefer that time-outs be used for productive purposes. Skilled athletes use a pause in the contest (1) to focus their attention on certain aspects of the game, (2) to gather information that can be used to improve their status, or (3) to relax and reduce physical fatigue. However, sometimes time-outs slow their psychological momentum and induce temporary failure (Silva, Hardy, & Crace 1988).

- The skilled athlete handles the pressure of a contest's final stages. According to Rushall (1979, p. 27), "This is an index of confidence that elite athletes have in their own abilities." Orlick's (1986) mental plan helps prevent "choking" in high-pressure situations.

- They can concentrate on using aspects of a strategy throughout the contest. Anshel's (1995b) study of elite swimmers indicated greater use of self-regulation strategies compared with nonelites. The best players know what they are supposed to do in great detail and when they are supposed to do it.

- They learn and later use information gained from each contest. This information may come from coaches, teammates, and even from spectators, in some cases. They engage in debriefing and self-evaluation to formalize the feedback process, which sometimes changes their strategies in future contests.

A person's capacity to perform motor skills may be genetically fixed, but what separates the elite athlete from those who are less successful is the willingness to make mental and physical efforts to reach that capacity.

Routines

Routines are thoughts and behaviors that are automatically integrated into our day. We have routines before we go to sleep, when we wake up in the morning, and, yes, just before the event in competitive sport. In sport, as in life, routines serve many valuable purposes. These include reducing the amount of in-depth thinking (e.g., creating, decision making, problem solving) that must be done, which saves a good deal of time, maintaining emotional control (particularly under pressure), and regulating our physical, mental, and emotional performance preparation, both before and during competition. Finally, rituals help athletes move from the cognitive stage to the automatic stage of performing sport skills. The cognitive stage is characterized by a considerable amount of thinking (e.g., planning, decision making), typical of novice performers. The automatic stage is more advanced, in which sport skills are performed with minimal thinking. Rituals help the competitor maintain self-control and concentration under conditions of high duress and pressure, not uncommon in competitive sport. One of the best examples of using rituals in elite sport comes from Dr. James Loehr (1990), who developed the "16-second cure," a set of rituals that has been adopted by most of the top professionals in tennis. According to Loehr (1994), "repetition of the right physical, mental, and emotional habits eventually brings them under automatic control" (p. 184).

The 16-Second Cure. Imagine what it feels like to lose a point in tennis by hitting an "easy" shot into the net, or by double faulting (hitting two consecutive serves into the net or out of bounds), or by having a "bad" call go against you. In professional tennis, you have all of 20 seconds to get the ball back in play. No time to lose your concentration or emotional control, or to have a temper tantrum. Yet, many fine athletes are incapable of regaining their composure and "letting go" of past unpleasant events while focusing on the task at hand. Sport psychologist Dr. Jim Loehr has developed a set of four mental and physical routines performed in sequence between points for competitive tennis players which many professional players have adopted. The routines, performed over a period of 16 seconds, allow the player to respond to the pressure of being mentally and physically ready for the next serve—performing under pressure on demand. Loehr describes the sequence as stages.

Stage 1 is called "The Positive Physical Response." Its purpose is to help the athlete maintain positive emotion, and to reduce the chance of anger, disappointment, and frustration that might disrupt performing the next task. Stage 1 consumes 3–5 seconds, beginning as soon as the point ends. Physically, the athlete should make a quick, decisive move (e.g., a pumping action with the arm, clap using the hand and racket, moving away from the mistake). Mentally, the athlete's self-talk is "no problem," "come on," or "nice shot," depending on who won the point.

Stage 2 is "The Relaxation Response," which allows the athlete's body to recover from physical and emotional stress of the previous point and to return the athlete's arousal to optimal level. Stage 2 endures for 6–15 seconds. According to Loehr, "the more stressful the previous point or the more important the next point, the more time (the athlete) should take in this stage" (p. 110). Here, the athlete thinks calming thoughts, such as "settle down," "relax," or "everything is fine." Physically, the athlete should keep his or her feet moving (e.g., walk back and forth across the baseline area, engage in mild stretches, bounce the ball a few times, spin the racket).

Stage 3, "The Preparation Response," takes 3–5 seconds, and consists of a pre-serve preparation period for what the athlete intends to do before the next serve. Physically, the athlete should project a very confident, aggressive image. The athlete looks at his or her opponent and verbalizes the score out loud. The self-talk might consist of something like "I have full confidence in winning this point." Mentally, the player plans his or her strategy—what where, and how to play the next serve.

Stage 4, "The Automatic Ritual Response," lasting 4 seconds, deepens concentration and produces an instinctive, automatic form of play. Physically, the player bounces the ball 2–3 times prior to the serve. Loehr claims that this delay in serving reduces the tendency to rush the next serve under pressure. If receiving the serve, the player may be jumping up and down, swaying back and forth, or blowing into one's hands. The receiver's eyes should be fixed on the ball, now being held by the opponent. Mentally, the player avoids thoughts of technique and even self-talk. Instead, the serve should be mentally rehearsed. The same rituals should be repeated on the second serve if the first serve is missed.

Dr. Loehr's 16-second between-point routine provides a good example of how athletes enter and remain in their "zone" for maintaining concentration and attention focus on important information in the competitive environment, and manage anxiety and other distracting thoughts that interfere with optimal performance. Routines are used by elite athletes.

Cognitive Strategies

Numerous attempts have been made by researchers to ascertain the thoughts and feelings of elite, consistently successful athletes before and during the contest in contrast to less successful competitors and nonathletes. What do highly skilled athletes think about, when do they think it, and what effect does this have on their mental preparation and performance?

A cognitive, or mental, strategy is a technique a person uses (1) to improve the processing of information and enhance learning and remembering or (2) to affect one's emotions favorably, such as to reduce anxiety, focus attention, maintain concentration, and cope with stress (Singer 1980).

One issue of *The Sport Psychologist* (1990, vol. 4, no. 4) was devoted to the experiences of sport psychology consultants who worked with professional and Olympic-level athletes. One consistent observation was that athletes often lack knowledge about the existence of mental skills and how to apply them correctly. It was apparent from the various articles in this issue that the awareness and use of cognitive strategies varies greatly among athletes and between sports. The experiences of these consultants also revealed the difficulty of deriving a psychological profile, or model, of the mental techniques by all elite athletes or the best method to apply them. Even frequent users of mental skills differ widely on which techniques work best for them and when they should be employed. For example, some athletes find that self-talk actually hinders their concentration and ability to respond automatically during the contest, while others find that self-talk has very favorable effects on their emotions and physical reactions.

A potential pitfall for sport psychology consultants is overprescribing cognitive strategies. In attempting to follow a consultant's advice, an athlete may get so caught up in using the mental skill that he or she becomes distracted or less coordinated in performing the task at hand. As briefly discussed in Chapter 1, this problem is called "paralysis by analysis" in the sport pedagogy literature. It is important, therefore, to remember three things. First, mental skills *are skills*, and, like any sport skills, need to be learned and mastered over time. Second, athletes can be burdened by learning and using too many skills; sometimes responding automatically before or during the contest with only a minimum of conscious thinking is more desirable. And third, athletes differ in their need to use certain types of cognitive strategies. Some mental techniques are applicable to many different sports while others are effective for certain specific sports only. One primary role of a sport psychology consultant is to help athletes select and learn the strategies that best meet their needs. See Table 2.1, which details some commonly used cognitive strategies among elite athletes.

Let's look at some other mental strategies employed by successful athletes.

Table 2.1 Cognitive strategies commonly used by skilled athletes before and during the contest.

Strategy	Purpose
Anticipating	Improve speed of reactions and decision making
Association	Thinking about bodily sensations during performance execution
Automating	Performing skills with little or no thinking (just let it happen)
Boxing	Placing negative thoughts in a mental "box" before the contest to avoid distractions
Chunking	Reducing a series of movement or team strategies to only one unit of information to improve retention and movement speed (e.g., "Let's run 'A-blue' to the left")
Coping	The conscious use of thoughts and actions for reducing chronic or acute stress
Approach coping	Attempts to get at the stressor's source and to deal actively with it (e.g., seeking information, venting feelings)
Avoidance coping	Attempts to ignore or reduce the importance of the stressor
Cueing	Focusing on a particular aspect of the sport environment to improve speed and accuracy of player reactions and decisions
Dissociation	Ignoring bodily sensations (e.g., effort, fatigue, sweating) during performance execution, and instead, focusing externally on more pleasant sights and sounds
Distracting	Focusing attention on harmless or meaningless sights or thoughts to "take a mental break" (i.e., reducing tension, regaining composure)
Focusing	Attending to the most meaningful information about the task at hand
Imagery	Thinking about an aspect of sport competition experienced before, during, or after the game that simulates actual game conditions, attempts to replicate the same sensations (visual, auditory, tactile, even smell if relevant) as vividly as possible, and in which the outcome of these images results in improving one's disposition (e.g., self-confidence), emotions (e.g., reduced anxiety), and performance
Labeling	Using a clock face to point out locations of body parts ("Your racket should strike the ball pointing at two o'clock") and bodies in the field of play ("On this play, the passed ball and receiver meet simultaneously at nine o'clock")
Mental planning	Knowing in advance your thoughts and actions 12 to 24 hours before, as well as during, the game
Mental practice	Mentally rehearsing a motor skill and replicating its physical characteristics; unlike imagery, does not include thinking about performing in gamelike conditions
Organizing input	Selectively filtering out meaningless or unpleasant information (e.g., crowd booing, hostile coach comments), while taking in important input (e.g., instructions, constructive feedback)
Planning	Thinking about to-be-performed skills and strategies prior to execution
Positive self-talk	Internal statements (e.g., "I feel good," "I'm ready") that enhance positive feelings (e.g., self-confidence, optimism) and emotions (e.g., excitation), while reducing unpleasant mood states (e.g., anxiety, tension, pessimism); self-talk also regulates thought processes that help focus attention (e.g., "Focus!") or prevent unpleasant, distracting thoughts (e.g., "Stop!"), as described below
Precueing	Looking or listening for a stimulus before it occurs, which allows the athlete to anticipate an upcoming event
Psychological distancing	A technique of avoidance coping in which the athlete feels detached from the source or cause of an unpleasant (stressful) event (e.g., the fans are booing because they are frustrated, have had too much alcohol, or are just having a good time)

Table 2.1 Cognitive strategies commonly used by skilled athletes before and during the contest. *(continued)*

Strategy	Purpose
Relaxation	Using one of several different techniques (e.g., biofeedback, progressive, centering) to reduce somatic processes such as heart rate, muscle tension, or blood pressure
Self-monitoring	Attempting to observe and regulate one's thoughts (e.g., avoid self-doubt, stay optimistic), emotions (e.g., maintaining optimal arousal), efforts (e.g., maintaining a certain pace), and behaviors (e.g., regulating food intake two hours before practice and contests) for maximal benefits in training and competitive performance
Thought-stopping	Telling oneself "STOP!" when having undesirable thoughts that breed a negative mood state or reduce a desirable disposition such as self-confidence

Relaxation.   Relaxation is the reduction or complete absence of muscular activity in the voluntary muscles (Harris & Harris 1984). Relaxation techniques are popular among athletes and sport psychologists because they help reduce anxiety and stress, which are common problems in sport (see Appendix B for examples of imagery scripts). There are various types of relaxation strategies, each serving different purposes and meeting individual needs. Examples include progressive relaxation, autogenic training, biofeedback, imagery, centering, and hypnosis. Though full descriptions of these techniques go well beyond the scope of this chapter, all of them serve similar purposes in reducing muscular tension and improving thought processes. However, it is important to note that relaxation is not always the proper response to unpleasant thoughts, emotions, and muscle tensions. Some athletes would rather use other cognitive or behavioral strategies, such as exercise or self-talk. Others find relaxation very difficult and stressful in itself. Further, many situations are not compatible with relaxation strategies (e.g., just before or during the contest). However, used correctly, relaxation training is a valid and proven means of preventing or reducing muscular tension and anxiety, while improving the athlete's concentration and self-confidence (Harris & Harris 1984; Orlick 1986).

Positive Self-Talk.   One of the best ways to maintain self-confidence is to engage in positive self-talk. This is a universal practice among champs. The purposes of self-talk strategies vary. When the technique is used to gain or to maintain self-confidence, focusing inwardly and thinking about one's strengths rather than about one's opponent can generate a sense of self-control and responsibility for a contest's outcome.

Another reason to engage in self-talk is to analyze the movement positively. According to Orlick and Partington (1986), Sue Holloway, 1984 Canadian Olympic silver medalist in the kayak pairs competition, engaged in a postrace analysis by asking herself, "Did this work? Did we do this? Or did we forget about it? How are we going to remember this?" For competitors to take the time to reflect upon their performances and the possible causes of the outcomes—whether or not they are successful—is important. This self-reflection should be done in a positive manner. See the boxes earlier in this chapter for techniques for building self-confidence.

The box on page 48 provides examples of positive self-statements.

Examples of Positive Self-Statements

Self-encouragement

"I'm doing great."

"Keep going."

"Keep on schedule, stay with it."

"This is my chance to dominate."

Effort control

"Concentrate on flowing movements."

"You have prepared for this, so execute your strategy."

"Others are hurting just as much, but they do not have a strategy."

"Let's go do it; give 100 percent."

Segment goal

"The pace is good. Lengthen the stroke."

"Make bat contact."

"Force a turnover on this set of downs."

Positive self-talk

"Great work."

"I feel good!"

"I'm in control."

Attentional Focus.   Quality performers know where and when to focus their attention. This allows them to exclude information that might slow their responses or interfere with their sensations. Orlick (1986) found that championship-caliber competitors do not focus on outcomes while they're performing. Instead, their attention is directed to the task at hand. As Orlick describes it, "The problem with thinking about winning or losing within the event is that you lose focus of what you need to do in order to win. In that sense it is self-defeating" (p. 10).

Arousal Regulation.   Getting psyched up for the contest is more than a matter of a few "rah-rahs." Superior athletes, more than their less successful counterparts, know two things about the process of psychological arousal: (1) their optimal level of arousal (remember, that's *optimal*, not necessarily *maximal*) and (2) when and how to begin the psyching techniques (see Chapter 3).

Making Accurate Attributions.   As will be discussed in Chapter 4, attributions consist of a person's attempts to explain the causes of an event, specifically in response to a performance outcome. Elite athletes more often than not accurately explain the causes of and tend to feel responsible for their performance results.

Performance Expectations

In the 1960s and 1970s, heavyweight boxing champion Muhammad Ali shocked a world that was (and is) very uncomfortable with self-centeredness and conceit with his brash proclamation, "I am the greatest." Ali gained notoriety by not only predicting that he would win boxing matches but also announcing before the fight the round in which his opponent would fall. What the world did not realize was that Ali's exercise in apparent vanity may have been a mental strategy that served three purposes: (1) to raise his expectations of success, (2) to lower the expectations of his opponent, and (3) to eliminate or mask his fear. Boxers realize, as much as if not more than many spectators, the level of violence and possible injuries and pain that may be sustained in a boxing match. Such self-defeating thoughts have no place in the boxer's mind, hence the need to eliminate these thoughts. No doubt skill had much to do with Ali's success in boxing, but Ali serves as a salient example of the relationship between expecting to do well in competition and actually doing it. Ali simply said aloud what all quality athletes should say to themselves.

The one essential quality that describes the thoughts of a champion is that they are positive. Denis Waitley, who wrote *The Psychology of Winning* (1978), confirmed the importance of positive expectations when he did extensive interviews with "winners" from various fields of endeavor, including sport. He grouped the characteristics of these individuals into categories of six "attitude qualities."

Positive Self-Expectancy.   Winners have an overall attitude of personal optimism and enthusiasm. They realize that a person usually gets what he or she expects. The self-talk of a winner is, "I was good today; I'll be better tomorrow," while losers lament, "With my luck, I was bound to fail."

Positive Self-Image.   Self-image acts as a subconscious device that governs behavior. Waitley contends that we cannot do what our self-image does not allow us to do. Imagining success begets real-life success. The positive self-talk of winners is, "I can see myself growing, achieving, improving, and winning." Losers say, "They're my hang-ups, faults . . . and I'm stuck with them." To Waitley, *it's not who individuals are that holds them back, but who they think they are not.* Winners, he contends, give themselves a preview of coming attractions. What you envision is what you get, and who you feel is who you are.

Positive Self-Control.   If a winner expects success, he or she is also capable of accepting responsibility for causing the actual outcome. Taking control of the events in one's life is characteristic of winners (Orlick 1980). Winners take the credit or the blame for their performance. Losers say, "I can't understand why this happened," or "It was someone else's fault, not mine."

Positive Self-Esteem.   Winners are inner-directed. They recognize their unique qualities and develop and maintain their own high standards. They also tend to choose models who exemplify the high goals and achievements to which they aspire. Despite very normal feelings of fear and anxiety, winners do not give in to these emotions. They are secure enough as individuals and as athletes to respect themselves as well as their peers and opponents. Losers are far less secure and, consequently, need to criticize and undermine others.

Positive Self-Direction.   Winners have an action plan to turn fantasy into fact, and to achieve success. They have a game plan for life, called the power of purpose. It's comprised of knowing what they want to accomplish on a day-to-day basis. Goals drive us; we are goal-seeking by design, Waitley contends. Having a purpose for life allows us to survive and to feel fulfilled. Individuals who are programmed with vague, random thoughts wonder aimlessly through life. Positive self-direction is about finding your purpose, your contribution to life to feel satisfied. Whereas those who fail or feel dissatisfied in life are helplessly adrift, probably every successful athlete has been committed to goals, has had a dream, and has been drawn to make the dream come true.

Positive Self-Awareness.   Cratty (1984) reports that "most superior athletes prefer to know all they can about themselves" (p. 6). Waitley agrees; winners know who they are and their potential both as individuals and as athletes. They have learned through experience and through having the security and maturity to ask for and to accept the feedback and judgments of others. Winners say, "I know who I am and where I'm going," whereas losers say, "If I only had the chance."

Peak Performance

One aspect of competitive sport that clearly separates elite from nonelite athletes is the experiencing of a peak performance, "a state of altered consciousness" (Ravizza 1984, p. 453). The athlete's mental state just prior to and during peak experiences is characterized by complete absorption in the task at hand. This allows for the proper internal attentional focus; that is, the necessary preoccupation with mental and physical readiness and effort. Ravizza claims that the quality of the athlete's experience is heightened in that there is a quicker and clearer focus on movement cues. This results in faster reaction and movement times in a controlled, skillful manner. Sometimes the athlete can actually anticipate the speed, direction, and timing of a stimulus. A person's peak performance does not necessarily exceed that of other persons, but rather surpasses what could be anticipated for that individual in a particular situation. However, such effects are apparently not long term.

Ravizza describes peak sport experiences as being temporary, nonvoluntary, and unique. They are temporary in that the person's altered mental state is short term. They are nonvoluntary, not susceptible to any intervention techniques; neither an athlete, a coach, nor anyone else can "make it happen." And they are certainly unique in that their occurrence is rare. Thus, achieving a championship victory, breaking a performance record, competing on a beautiful day, playing after signing a professional sports contract, and other circumstances or aspects of the sport environment that may have attended a peak experience are not prerequisites of this phenomenon. The only prerequisite to a peak experience is the athlete's mastery of the basic sport skills. There is almost an absence of thinking during skill execution. And the feelings that accompany peak performance are quite pleasant.

Emotionally, peak performers report an extremely fulfilling and happy psycho-emotional state. Fears, insecurities, and inhibitions dissipate. Brewer et al. (1991), in a series of three experiments examining factors associated with peak performance, concluded that *focused attention* and feelings of confidence were the most apparent mental states. Factors *not* linked with peak performance include lack of concern with outcome, effortless performance, and perceptions of time slowing. Two limitations in their study were inclusion of nonathletes (college psychology majors) and use of laboratory tasks rather than field activities, with which this phenomenon is more closely identified. These limitations would be particularly important if peak performance contains a significant *physiological* component, a factor not taken into account by Brewer et al. In fact, there is evidence that such feelings of euphoria during vigorous physical activity have a physiological basis (Morgan 1985).

Some athletes refer to their experience of performing in an emotional high as "being in the flow." The concept of *flow* has been interpreted differently in various situations (see Csikszentmihalyi, 1990, for an extensive review of this concept). Athletes are in a state of flow when they are "totally involved in an activity and experience a number of positive (feelings), including freedom from self-consciousness and great enjoyment of the process (Jackson & Marsh, 1996, p. 18). Their Flow State Scale is located in Figure 2.3.

Cratty (1984) has classified flow states into four categories:

1. *Anxiety or arousal.* A flow state can be unpleasant or can affect performance negatively. For example, athletes can become so upset that they lose self-control. Getting too psyched up may also overexcite the athlete.

2. *Extremely good feelings.* Cratty refers to this state as a "positive in-performance phenomenon," in which the well-prepared athlete develops very positive feelings during most of the competitive period. The athlete is "into" the event, both mentally and physically, but tends to come out of it when an opponent takes the upper hand.

3. *Mental escaping.* Instead of feeling "in sync" with performance demands, the athlete is mentally escaping from them. This can be favorable, such as the "runner's high," in which performers can dissociate themselves from the physical demands, even pain, of prolonged, arduous physical activity. However, this form of escape can be counterproductive. Cratty argues that the athlete should be attending to the immediate task demands, and perhaps even to any pain that accompanies performance (negative in-performance state), instead of mentally "floating." Injured athletes should not totally ignore their discomfort because they may incur further injuries.

4. *Postcontest mental break.* Immediately after intense physical competitive activity, athletes need to take a mental break. They are usually—and normally—unresponsive to questions from the media and tend just to sit and stare or move very slowly and deliberately. They need to recuperate from the physical and psychological demands of the contest, from preparation stages to the event's conclusion. Players report a "buzzing out" or "coming down" period. This is why the immediate postcompetition period is not the time for coaches to communicate thought-provoking statements and analyses of the contest.

The box on page 53 contains a list of various feelings that accompany peak performance (Garfield & Bennett 1984).

Garfield and Bennett (1984) assert that the most important factor for experiencing peak performance is "letting go." Other phrases that describe this feeling include "going on automatic pilot" or "playing in a trance." But they all mean performing in the virtual absence of calculating and thinking. Play must be automatic, natural, and spontaneous. To let go, the athlete must relax his or her mind and body and use mental pictures to develop concentration "by holding the mental picture of the desired end result for a few seconds" (p. 181). And, if the athlete wishes to succeed, the end result imaged must be a successful one.

So far, our discussion about flow states and peak performance has been based on theory and interviews with athletes. Attempts to measure the psychological state of flow

Figure 2.3 The Flow State Scale.

Please answer the following questions in relation to your experience in the event you have just completed. These questions relate to the thoughts and feelings you may have experienced during the event. There are no right or wrong answers. Think about how you felt during the event and answer to questions using the rating scale below. Circle the number that best matches your experience from the options to the right of each question.

Rating Scale:

Strongly Disagree 1	Disagree 2	Neither Agree nor Disagree 3	Agree 4	Strongly Agree 5

1.	I was challenged, but I believed my skills would allow me to meet the challenge.	1	2	3	4	5
2.	I made the correct movements without thinking about trying to do so.	1	2	3	4	5
3.	I knew clearly what I wanted to do.	1	2	3	4	5
4.	It was really clear to me that I was doing well.	1	2	3	4	5
5.	My attention was focused entirely on what I was doing.	1	2	3	4	5
6.	I felt in total control of what I was doing.	1	2	3	4	5
7.	I was not concerned with what others may have been thinking of me.	1	2	3	4	5
8.	Time seemed to alter (either slowed down or speeded up).	1	2	3	4	5
9.	I really enjoyed the experience.	1	2	3	4	5
10.	My abilities matched the high challenge of the situation.	1	2	3	4	5
11.	Things just seemed to be happening automatically.	1	2	3	4	5
12.	I had a strong sense of what I wanted to do.	1	2	3	4	5
13.	I was aware of how well I was performing.	1	2	3	4	5
14.	It was no effort to keep my mind on what was happening.	1	2	3	4	5
15.	I felt like I could control what I was doing.	1	2	3	4	5
16.	I was not worried about my performance during the event.	1	2	3	4	5
17.	The way time passed seemed to be different from normal.	1	2	3	4	5
18.	I loved the feeling of that performance and want to capture it again.	1	2	3	4	5
19.	I felt I was competent enough to meet the high demands of the situation.	1	2	3	4	5
20.	I performed automatically.	1	2	3	4	5
21.	I knew what I wanted to achieve.	1	2	3	4	5
22.	I had a good idea while I was performing about how well I was doing.	1	2	3	4	5
23.	I had total concentration.	1	2	3	4	5
24.	I had a feeling of total control.	1	2	3	4	5
25.	I was not concerned with how I was presenting myself.	1	2	3	4	5
26.	It felt like time stopped while I was performing.	1	2	3	4	5
27.	The experience left me feeling great.	1	2	3	4	5
28.	The challenge and my skills were at an equally high level.	1	2	3	4	5
29.	I did things spontaneously and automatically without having to think.	1	2	3	4	5
30.	My goals were clearly defined.	1	2	3	4	5
31.	I could tell by the way I was performing how well I was doing.	1	2	3	4	5
32.	I was completely focused on the task at hand.	1	2	3	4	5
33.	I felt in total control of my body.	1	2	3	4	5
34.	I was not worried about what others may have been thinking of me.	1	2	3	4	5
35.	At times, it almost seemed like things were happening in slow motion.	1	2	3	4	5
36.	I found the experience extremely rewarding.	1	2	3	4	5

Source: Published in the *Journal of Sport and Exercise Psychology,* Vol. 18, March 1996, pp. 17–35.

Cues of Peak Performance Feelings

1. *Mentally relaxed.* Inner calm; time slowing; able to focus clearly on details in the present.
2. *Physically relaxed.* Muscles loose throughout the body; feelings of warmth; movements fluid; body seems to respond directly and precisely to volition.
3. *Confident/optimistic.* High expectation of success; recognition of challenge and excitement in response to the idea of accepting that challenge; feelings of strength and control.
4. *Focused on the present.* Sense of harmony—that is, of body and mind working together as a unit; no thoughts of past or future; a sense of body performing automatically, without conscious or deliberate mental effort.
5. *Highly energized.* Associated with feelings of joy, ecstasy, intensity, and of feeling "charged" or "hot."
6. *Extraordinary awareness.* An acutely sharp sense of one's whole body and its movements (perceived as physical sensations rather than as thoughts or ideas); acute awareness of other players' movements, size, physical presence, and of how these players think and feel (mental impressions rather than analysis); ability to know what other players are going to do even before they do it; a sensation of being completely in harmony with one's environment.
7. *In control.* Body seems to be automatically doing exactly what one wants it to do; mind seems to respond to the environment and to process all information from it in the most efficient and appropriate ways possible; no sense of exerting or imposing control, though everything is happening as one wishes it to.
8. *In the cocoon.* Feelings of being in an envelope, with complete access to all of one's powers and skills; feelings of detachment from external environment, even though acutely aware of everything associated with one's performance; a feeling of euphoric awareness and of containment of one's skills and power; a feeling of invulnerability.

using a statistically validated inventory have been absent from the literature—until very recently. The development of the Flow State Scale by Jackson and Marsh (1996) represents the first objective attempts to measure statistically an athlete's flow state. Briefly, their studies identify nine components of flow, each with a set of questions that measures it. These components, each followed by a sample item, include: challenge–skill balance ("My abilities matched the high challenge of the situation"), action–awareness merging ("Things just seemed to be happening automatically"), clear goals ("I knew clearly what I wanted to do"), concentration on the task at hand ("My attention was focused clearly on what I was doing"), sense of control ("I was not concerned with how I was presenting myself"), loss of self-consciousness ("I performed automatically"), transformation of time ("At times, it almost seemed like things were happening in slow motion"), and autotelic experience ("The experience left me feeling great"). One limitation of this study, which is very difficult to overcome in survey research, is that subjects were asked to reflect upon previous experiences and feelings, which may be partially inaccurate. Flow is a "now" type of experience, and the Flow State Scale should be used immediately after performance in order to ensure accurate and immediate feelings. As Jackson and Marsh indicate, further research is needed to validate the scale. Still, the items are consistent enough with the various concepts of flow that have been previously published to justify use of the scale by coaches and athletes. An attempt to validate two scales that measure flow experiences in various types of physical activity—the Flow State Scale-2 and the Dispositional Flow Scale-2—have been published more recently (Jackson & Eklund 2002).

Preparing an Athlete for Peak Performance

One way in which highly skilled athletes approach their performance potential is to structure and formalize their contest preparation. Athletes who closely attend to meeting their unique needs in preparing for each contest will be ready, both mentally and physically, to perform at their best. Routines that are conducted on the day of, and immediately before, the event also help athletes regulate their stress, anxiety, and arousal levels (Hackfort & Schwenkmezger 1989; Orlick 1986). One method for ensuring optimal event preparation is to use a checklist that lists all of the required behavioral and cognitive strategies to be performed at some point, usually within one week of the competition. Based on my experience as a sport psychology consultant, I have found the mental game checklist in Figure 2.4 to be very helpful in preparing the athlete for competition.

Using the mental game checklist consists of the athlete reviewing each item that pertains to his or her unique needs and situation. All items the athlete deems relevant and useful should be reviewed at the start of each week prior to the competition. This review process sets in motion a self-expectation that each point is necessary for success and, therefore, will be followed. The athlete should attempt to engage in each strategy, then review the list as the event approaches. Finally, the list should be reviewed at some convenient time after the event to determine which aspects could be improved before the next competition. Each item is worded so that *higher scores are more desirable*. In this way, the athlete can compare scores during the season, perhaps from week to week, to work toward increasing the final score. The athlete is invited to add his or her own items that are not listed here if the item reflects an area of preparation and performance that is viewed as desirable and a natural part of the athlete's routine during a particular time period from week to week. Examples might include using a certain mental technique (e.g., relaxation training the night before the contest), having a desirable attitude or emotional intensity (e.g., a particular level of anxiety or aggression), or engaging in a specific action (e.g., certain intake of food or liquid; taking a walk). This inventory is not intended for comparing the scores of different athletes; its purpose is to ensure that an athlete's current score is as high as or better than previous scores.

Anxiety about Failure and Success

Athletes of all ages are often under great pressure to succeed. Their need for approval and to meet the expectations of others, together with their tendency to link self-esteem to positive performance outcomes, may cause heightened anxiety about the possibility of performance failure. Conversely, anxiety may also be experienced due to the pressures and expectations following success (e.g., "they're not as good as they used to be"). The psychological outcomes of these dilemmas are called fear of failure and fear of success, respectively.

Clinical sport psychologist Ronald Smith (1984), from the University of Washington in Seattle, states, "In my experience, the most common sources of anxiety in athletes

Figure 2.4 Athlete's mental game checklist.

The purpose of this checklist is to assist you in examining the psychological and physical factors that help maximize your performance. Rate yourself on each of the following statements from 1 (strongly disagree) to 5 (strongly agree). Then try to change or work on the lower-rated items before the next competition. Since the items reflect desirable mental and physical states, the higher your score, the closer you are to performing at your potential.

1 **Strongly Disagree**	2 **Disagree**	3 **Not Sure (yes and no)**	4 **Agree**	5 **Strongly Agree**

Event Preparation

1. I train (strength, aerobic) with enthusiasm.   1   2   3   4   5
2. I am looking forward to the next event.   1   2   3   4   5
3. I view my next opponent as a challenge, not as a threat.   1   2   3   4   5
4. I am happy to receive instruction and feedback from the coach.   1   2   3   4   5
5. I feel very confident in my ability against the next team.   1   2   3   4   5
6. I encourage at least one other teammate to give 100 percent toward   1   2   3   4   5
    game preparation.
7. I look carefully at the videotape to examine my performance in the previous   1   2   3   4   5
    game or to review my next opponent.
8. I try to learn something from each video session.   1   2   3   4   5
9. I attend volunteer training sessions.   1   2   3   4   5
10. I set at least one performance goal for the next event.   1   2   3   4   5
11. I remind myself of my goal(s) during the week.   1   2   3   4   5
12. I maintain a healthy lifestyle during the week.   1   2   3   4   5
13. I sleep well the night before the event.   1   2   3   4   5

Pre-Event (Game Day)

1. I awaken in the morning feeling well rested and ready to play.   1   2   3   4   5
2. On the morning of the event, I look forward to competing.   1   2   3   4   5
3. I anticipate the event on game day with enthusiasm.   1   2   3   4   5
4. I view the upcoming game as exciting, as a challenge.   1   2   3   4   5
5. I eat a good breakfast.   1   2   3   4   5

Pre-Event (At the Venue)

1. I arrive at the competitive event with a sense of enthusiasm.   1   2   3   4   5
2. I remember my game goals and plan to meet them.   1   2   3   4   5
3. As I get dressed, I feel ready to play.   1   2   3   4   5
4. I feel good during the warm-up.   1   2   3   4   5
5. I find myself looking forward to the match—almost impatient.   1   2   3   4   5
6. As I walk from the locker room to the field/court to compete, I feel energetic   1   2   3   4   5
    and ready to play.
7. I use positive self-statements, such as, "I'm ready and well prepared";   1   2   3   4   5
    "I can do this"; "I'm in good shape."

(continued)

Figure 2.4 Athlete's mental game checklist. *(continued)*

1 Strongly Disagree	2 Disagree	3 Not Sure (yes and no)	4 Agree	5 Strongly Agree

8. I feel arrogant toward the event; I deserve to win. 1 2 3 4 5

During the Event

1. I am giving 100 percent effort. 1 2 3 4 5
2. I talk during the event, giving support, encouragement, or instruction. 1 2 3 4 5
3. I support my teammates; I recognize them for doing a good job or help them overcome a problem. 1 2 3 4 5
4. I feel I am playing to my capability. 1 2 3 4 5
5. During halftime or time out, I appreciate receiving the coach's feedback on my performance. 1 2 3 4 5
6. After I make an error, I move on to the next task quickly. 1 2 3 4 5
7. I don't let mistakes discourage me and ruin my confidence. 1 2 3 4 5
8. If I receive a penalty, I move on to the next task quickly. 1 2 3 4 5
9. I feel up to the challenge of my opponent. 1 2 3 4 5
10. I feel very confident during the event. 1 2 3 4 5
11. I ignore the unpleasant comments of others, including spectators and opponents. 1 2 3 4 5
12. I feel my aggression level is about right. 1 2 3 4 5
13. If the other team scores, I continue to concentrate on task and give 100 percent. 1 2 3 4 5
14. I feel in full control of my emotions; I'm not too uptight or upset during the event. 1 2 3 4 5
15. I find myself anticipating what I'm going to do next. 1 2 3 4 5
16. I can recover quickly from unpleasant occurrences. 1 2 3 4 5
17. When I'm tired, I take some deep breaths, take a short rest, then quickly regain my composure and stay on task (no social loafing). 1 2 3 4 5
18. Regardless of the score, I'm trying my best. 1 2 3 4 5
19. I am not overly critical of myself; my self-image as an athlete remains high regardless of the game outcome. 1 2 3 4 5

After the Event

1. I take responsibility for my performance, good or bad. 1 2 3 4 5
2. I feel I have contributed to the game's outcome, win or lose. 1 2 3 4 5
3. I listen to and learn from performance feedback. 1 2 3 4 5

List any additional personal items here that form your weekly routine:

Total Score: _____

(Higher scores from week to week show marked improvement in your mental preparation and mental game performance. You want to work toward 4s and 5s for each item).

are fears of failure and resulting social disapproval or rejection" (p. 160). One of the less fortunate aspects of sport competition is the pressure that athletes feel to meet the expectations of others—especially persons whose opinions the athletes value. The more an athlete succeeds, the more those expectations rise, and the more the pressure increases. In an interview with Canadian sport psychologists Terry Orlick and John Partington (1986), Canadian 1984 Olympic double gold medalist swimmer Alex Baumann reported "a tremendous amount of pressure on me . . . because everybody expected me to win, and everybody expected me to break the world record . . . The pressure came from Canada in general, and then from the whole Canadian team . . . My heart was pounding because of the pressure and I was unable to sleep between heats and finals . . . I thought, 'Here goes 11 years of work, and here I come and get a silver medal.' I really wondered if I could ever win feeling that bad" (pp. 13–14).

Fear of Failure (FOF)

Fear of failure (FOF), also referred to as the motive to avoid failure, was initially defined by Atkinson (1966) as "a disposition to avoid failure and/or a capacity for experiencing shame or humiliation as a consequence of failure" (p. 13). More recently, researchers and practitioners tend to view FOF as a form of performance anxiety. Failure provokes fear to the extent that its consequences are perceived as aversive. As Conroy (2001) notes, in his development of an instrument that measures FOF, "an adequate measure of [fear of failure] should assess how strongly individuals believe or anticipate that certain aversive consequences will occur when they perceive that they are failing" (p. 433). Thus, FOF will be high for athletes whose self-esteem is firmly entrenched in successful sport performance or successful outcomes (e.g., winning), while for others whose self-esteem is derived from multiple sources (e.g., fitness and health, family, social relationships, academic success, religion), FOF in sport contexts will be reduced.

Not surprisingly, most athletes are afraid to fail (Passer 1984). This fear comes not from the fact that the potential for losing a contest is inherent in competitive sport, but from the individual's personal history. For instance, when young children fail or lose in competitive situations, adults may respond in ways that have negative emotional and psychological consequences. Following failure, the child begins to expect a negative evaluation. The individual then associates failure with more intense feelings of shame, guilt, and other unpleasant emotions. Passer concludes that fearing failure is one primary cause of competitive trait anxiety. Even professional and Olympic athletes have this trait to some extent. Most are able to control it. Less effective performers feel, perhaps subconsciously, "If I don't try, I can't fail." This is the worst possible result from FOF. The athlete may decide to withdraw from the competitive situation, either physically by quitting the team or mentally by reducing the effort needed to compete at the level of his or her capability.

The following are some recommendations for coaches and parents to help prevent or reduce FOF in the athlete (Cratty 1983; Passer 1984).

- *Regardless of the outcomes, be supportive of the individual's attempts to perform at his or her best.* A good example of parental support comes from 1984 Olympic Canadian diving champion Sylvie Bernier, who revealed the following personal story (Orlick & Partington 1986):

  My parents had an important effect. My mother always put a little note in my baggage when I went to competitions. One time I found it in my shoe. The note said, "You are our champion, no matter what happens." Then it said, "Bring me home some chocolates." I laughed and cried . . . but this helped keep things in perspective.

- *Emphasize better effort.* Athletes need to feel that winning is associated with more practice and other forms of physical and mental preparation. Avoid informing an athlete that losing was due to low ability. Persistent feelings of low competence bring on a sense of helplessness, depression, and low self-esteem. Quitting becomes the best alternative, whether or not it is justified.

- *Define success and failure broadly.* Success in sport is more than winning and losing. Even when an athlete or a team loses a contest, the individual or the entire team may have performed successfully. One's definition of failure should be restricted to specific events or unmet goals, such as missing a particular basketball free throw or failing to break a personal record in track. Every contest comprises numerous successes and failures, and even competitors with poor skills may be complimented on improvement or effort.

- *Have reasonably high expectations of the athlete's performance.* As indicated earlier in this chapter, athletes (and most people, no matter what their field of endeavor) tend to perform in accordance with what others expect of them.

- *Look for signs of FOF.* Examples include chronic complaining (the player is looking for excuses to explain anticipated failure), excessive talking, continued boasting (a cover-up for anxiety), inability to sit still (a display of nervous energy), crying (a stress-release mechanism), frequent absenteeism from practices and games ("if I don't try, I won't fail"), a quick temper (a sign of considerable fear or insecurity), frequent injury or abnormal recovery time from an injury, and the tendency to avoid taking risks during contests.

- *Avoid asking the athlete about his or her emotions.* Questions such as "Are you uptight (scared, anxious)?" tend to invite, not reduce, stress. The athlete thinks that the coach expects these types of thoughts. Or such questions may further direct the athlete's attention toward such feelings.

Fear of Success (FOS)

Do athletes, whose prime objective in sport is to be successful, actually fear achieving that success? In some cases, they might. Where does FOS originate? Based on his training and experience in both clinical and sport psychology, Dr. Bruce Ogilvie (1968) has proposed five syndromes that may explain the source or antecedents of FOS.

- *Athletes' fear of social and emotional isolation that accompanies success.* An athlete may feel that performing at a level far superior to that of teammates or peers will result in social discomfort, even ostracism.

- *Athletes' guilt from self-assertion in competition.* Some athletes are uncomfortable about exhibiting aggressive behavior, especially at the "expense" of an opponent's feelings or "losing image." Such athletes would likely score low on any measure of competitiveness.

- *Athletes protect themselves from competition because they fear discovering their true potential.* In this case, fears about succeeding are derived from fearing failure: FOS and FOF are two sides of the same coin. Why should this athlete even engage in competition? That's the point. Perhaps they shouldn't. According to Oglivie, withdrawing from competition is a defense against this fear.

- *Athletes may feel anxiety about surpassing a previous record established by an admired performer.* It is unlikely that Barry Bonds, who hit a record 70 home runs in the 2001 baseball season, was concerned that the previous home run record holder, Mark McGwire, might be offended. Some athletes, however, might be intimidated by breaking a record previously held by a highly respected or admired athlete. They may also feel that others (fans, teammates, coaches, media) may also resent the broken record.

- *Dealing with the pressure to constantly match or exceed one's previous best performance.* In the absence of published research, my own experience in counseling athletes and my conversation with coaches of elite athletes (depicted in my interview, described later in this section, with the late major league baseball coach, Charlie Lau) points to this latter explanation as the most valid. Trying to live up to the expectations of fans and the media can place an extensive amount of pressure on athletes to reach or exceed their previous best performance. Failing to achieve this standard may be perceived as disappointing or even performance failure.

Cratty (1983) reports that clinicians observing this fear in athletes have hypothesized that "the individuals involved simply were afraid of being the best, thus creating a situation in which others would direct their energies toward defeating them. Moreover, the success-phobic athlete may also fear winning, since spectators and fans might not be as solidly behind him or her in the future, preferring to cheer for the underdog rather than the top dog" (p. 125).

The late Charlie Lau, a well-known major league batting coach, told me in an interview (Anshel 1986) that one reason why many hitters with major league skills do not become consistently successful at hitting is their fear of performing well. Incredible as this may sound to some people, Lau cites anecdotal evidence from his personal experiences that some athletes are fearful of living up to the expectations of others after they have demonstrated competent performance. They feel too much pressure to maintain high standards and are not able to deal with criticism from others, notably the media and fans, after performing below previous achievements. So, what happens? They retain, sometimes unconsciously, their mediocrity as athletes. For them, this is a safer, less risky approach.

Two studies have explored FOS in sport situations. McElroy and Willis (1979) tested female athletes from five different sports and failed to find the FOS dimension. Silva (1982) found that male athletes had less FOS than female athletes.

Although a few elite participants may be uncomfortable with the notion of attaining and maintaining high performance standards, Orlick and Partington's (1986) interviews with 16 Olympic and World Champion athletes failed to reveal a single incidence of fearing success. Perhaps it's the drive to succeed that truly separates winners—at least those who compete at the national and world levels—from others. This is an area in need of further research.

Although this psychological state has not been supported by the fear of success literature, performance failure under high expectancies of success by observers may be at least partly explained by research on choking in sport.

Choking

Performing under pressure is inherent in competitive sport. The ability to perform according to one's skill level and in accordance with previous performance quality often creates anxiety (worry; threat) and pressure that is thought to be responsible for the phenomenon in sport called choking. Choking in sport contexts has been defined as reduced performance quality under pressure circumstances (Baumeister 1984); the inability to perform up to previously exhibited standards (Leith 1988); suboptimal performance despite incentives for optimal performance (Lewis & Linder 1997); and performing more poorly than expected given one's level of skill (Beilock & Carr 2001). To many sports fans, any player or team that does not perform to their own expectations have been labeled "chokers." Examples, based on media reports, include the 1998 San Diego Padres or the 1990 Atlanta Braves baseball teams, each of which lost four games in a row to the New York Yankees in their respective World Series. Yet, whether these major league baseball players, teams that won the National League pennant, actually succumbed to pressure in the World Series is far from certain. The only way to measure if sports competitors choke is to determine their perceived level of pressure, among other feelings and emotions, and the quality of game performance during each game. Therefore, ostensibly, players with high perceived pressure and anxiety who also perform poorly ("poorly" have to be operationally defined, in such a study, such as striking out with men in scoring position, pitching poorly, making mental and physical errors) might have choked. But wait a minute. Perhaps the 1998 and 1999 Yankee teams had superior pitching and better talent than their opponents. Rather than choking, the opposing national league teams simply lost to a more talented team—at least during the World Series. Can choking be identified and explained? Researchers have proposed a few interesting explanations.

For example, Baumeister (1984) conducted six experiments in an attempt to understand the causes of choking. Briefly, he found that two factors, high pressure to succeed and a heightened state of self-consciousness, strongly contributed to a "choking" response. This outcome was further exacerbated when the subject's disposition of self-consciousness (SC) was low. Subjects with low SC dispositions placed in self-conscious situations brought on by the expectations of the observers cope *least* well under pressure; pressure creates high self-consciousness. This needs an explanation.

Intuitively, it seems strange to conclude that highly self-conscious persons would actually be *less* likely to choke than persons who are habitually less self-conscious, since being self-conscious focuses one's attention on pressure and other undesirable thoughts and emotions. As Baumeister contends (1984), if self-consciousness hurts performance, then low-self-conscious persons should perform better than highly self-conscious persons in low-pressure conditions. However, if pressure causes self-consciousness, then habitually high-self-conscious persons should be able to deal with high-self-consciousness situations because they are accustomed to performing while self-conscious. Strangely, then, choking is greater among those habitually low in self-consciousness—who are less accustomed to dealing with high-pressure conditions—then among habitually highly self-conscious persons. Thus, the results of Baumeister's study partially confirms Lau's observations, reported by Anshel (1986), that the athlete's inability to cope with the pressure, that is, to choke, may be partly created by an evaluative (high expectancy) audience.

How Spectators Affect an Athlete's Performance

Top athletes like an audience. Psychologist Abraham Maslow, in his theory on personality and motivation, contends that one of our greatest needs on our way to self-actualization (fulfilling one's inherent potential) is the need for recognition from others. Athletics provides an important outlet for this need to be met. As Alderman (1974) explains, "Athletic success to satisfy the needs for self-esteem also receives massive reinforcement from society via the media and spectators at sports events" (p. 168).

Spectators are, of course, inherent in athletic competition. One could not be a successful athlete while feeling uncomfortable about having others watching. Elite athletes are not only comfortable with being observed by others, they prefer it. This characteristic is best attested to by the popular concept of the home-court advantage.

Swartz and Barsky (1977) examine the extent to which the home-team advantage—playing in front of one's own fans—is related to game outcome. Based on information obtained from thousands of professional baseball, football, and ice hockey events, and collegiate basketball games, they conclude that the home team won only 53 to 64 percent of the time. They surmise that the home team may have had a slight advantage because audience support generated more offensive production by the host players. Jay Triano, captain of the Canadian men's basketball team in the 1983 World Student Games held in Edmonton, Canada, agrees: "The crowds were great for our games, and the guys were feeling great about themselves because they got a chance to play in their home town against Yugoslavia, and it was really a powerful feeling" (Orlick & Partington 1986, p. 189). However, Swartz and Barsky find evidence of a home team disadvantage when examining game outcomes that determine the championship. The home team lost more high-pressure home games, at least in basketball and baseball, than they won.

In their extensive review of related literature, Courneya and Carron (1992) confirm evidence of a home-team advantage. They surmise that other possible explanations for better performance at the home arena might include higher arousal and aggression levels by the home team, factors related to the visitors' travel, such as a change in time zone, the players' "biological clocks," different patterns or arrangements in sleeping and eating, subjective decisions by officials against visiting teams, and unfamiliar surroundings. To conclude that the mere presence of an audience is always sufficient to affect athletic performance would be simplistic and, as discussed later, not supported by research. Other factors partly determine how the competitor is influenced by spectators.

Zajonc (1965) recognizes the effect of an audience on sport performance in his model of *social facilitation*. According to Zajonc, the critical factor that decides whether an audience will improve or inhibit performance is whether the performer's dominant response is correct or incorrect (see Figure 2.5). What decides the correctness of a response? One or more of three factors: (1) task difficulty, (2) the person's skill level, and (3) the type of audience. The presence of observers who the athlete believes are qualified to assess performance (an evaluative audience—judges or scouts, for instance) might inhibit performance if the task is complex for the athlete. Conversely, an evaluative audience may actually improve performance if the individual finds the task relatively simple. But what if a skill is being performed in front of a passive audience or one in front of which the athlete feels unthreatened? In this case, simple tasks are not performed as well, while responses to complex tasks tend to improve measurably. Take, for example, the influence of the Seattle Seahawks' and Minnesota Vikings' football fans on their players and, for that matter, on their opponents' performances. According to media reports, the noise volume in their respective enclosed stadiums, the Kingdome and the Metrodome, seems to excite the home team. The Seahawks and Vikings traditionally

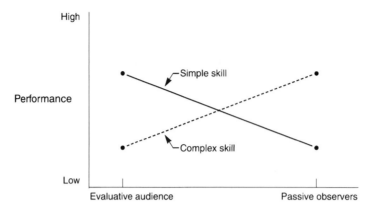

Figure 2.5 Effect of skill difficulty and type of audience on performance.

win far more games at home than on the road. Visiting players and coaches complain that the noise makes communicating difficult. Some opponents have admitted to feelings of intimidation prior to competing against these teams.

The degree to which an athlete perceives and reacts to the makeup of an audience is referred to as its *evaluative potential*. If this perception hurts performance—perhaps due to heightened anxiety, inappropriate arousal level, poor concentration, or focusing attention improperly, among other possible reasons, then the condition is known as *evaluation apprehension* (Cottrell 1972). Reflecting the results of past studies, Figure 2.5 shows that less complex skills are better performed in the presence of an evaluative audience than with passive observers. On the other hand, more difficult skills are likely to be better performed in the presence of passive observers than under the scrutiny of evaluators.

What can athletes and coaches do about this apprehension? First, athletes should focus their attention on the immediate task, not on the observers, especially when performing complex skills. An example of the *wrong* way to increase player motivation (though coaches do it all the time) is to inform the player about the presence of an important audience member. This often backfires: The result is poorer, not better, performance. True, athletes do enjoy, sometimes even need, the presence of spectators so as to perform at their potential. But the players may not perceive fans—even their own family and friends—with the same evaluative potential as they do scouts for professional teams, college recruiters, or judges who subjectively rate performance.

Second, the athlete who is learning a complex skill should practice until the skill is mastered before performing it in a competitive event. Elite athletes do exactly that. For hours and hours, they practice a new skill or technique so that the presence of judges, the media, opponents, and other spectators will not inhibit their concentration. In fact, highly skilled gymnasts, a champion boxer, and intercollegiate athletes in football, golf, and swimming have indicated to me that they usually ignore members of the crowd. Instead, they concentrate on the task at hand. Basketball, volleyball, and wrestling athletes say that the crowd gets them psyched up, but once the event begins (when the ball is in play or when the match begins), they become oblivious to the crowd.

Perhaps the final word—at least for now—on the effects of an audience on performance comes from an analysis of 241 studies involving about 24,000 subjects (athletes and nonathletes) performing sport skills and cognitive tasks (Bond & Titus 1983). The authors—using a statistical technique called meta-analysis in which the results of all topic-related studies, published and unpublished, are combined and then summarized—find that, in general, the effect of an audience can predict performance outcome only 3 percent of the time. Nevertheless, for many athletes, especially nonprofessionals, performance is affected by who's watching. Research in this area needs to be updated.

Coping with Stress

All those who participate in competitive sports must have the ability to deal with criticism, pain, losing, physical and mental errors, and other sources of stress. Elite athletes, like the tennis professional seen competing in the U.S. Open in Figure 2.6, have the

Figure 2.6 Professional athletes have more demands on them than other athletes, such as dealing with crowd behavior, performance expectations of the public and from sponsors, fan mail, and media scrutiny.

additional ability to quickly recover from, or ignore, these less pleasant aspects of competitive sports. Instead of maintaining a hostile, frustrated disposition, winners are capable of redirecting their energies in a productive manner. Failure to quickly adapt to unpleasant experiences often results in performance failure. For example, Krohne and Hindel (1988) found that "vigilant coping strategies" (e.g., "focusing attention on threat-relevant information," p. 227) are significantly more harmful to the athlete's emotional and performance responses to acute stress than "cognitive avoidance strategies" (e.g., "avoiding threat-relevant information," p. 227). Thus, the successful elite competitor says, "Time to put (the unpleasant experience) behind me and go for it." See Krohne (1996) and Anshel et al. (2001) for several reviews of literature on the coping process with implications for sport.

Coping with Competitive Situations

How do elite athletes prevent or cope with stress? Unlike the unskilled performer, top competitors (1) plan each aspect of their performance, whether it will occur before or during the event, and (2) have at least one alternative behavior for every planned action (Orlick 1986; Rushall 1979). An example is the basketball or ice hockey player who, after shooting, approaches the net in anticipation of a rebound. Quality players and teams calmly plan and correctly execute changes in strategy in response to an opponent who is experiencing success. Orlick (1986) refers to the mental plan as "focusing" and to the anticipation of sudden change as "refocusing." Anger responses are either inhibited or expressed and then quickly extinguished.

Orlick (1980) suggests that the best way to prevent panic situations and anxiety is to begin thinking about and implementing solutions before problems get out of hand. "Ideally, you anticipate and prepare to solve problems before they arise" (p. 187). Thus, in order to institute elaborate alternative techniques rapidly, elite competitors plan, practice, and master secondary or coping strategies in practice or in exhibition games.

Coping with Pain

One unpleasant aspect of sport competition is sustaining an injury and enduring the accompanying discomfort. Experiencing pain is an inherent feature of participation in sport (see Figure 2.7). Athletes differ in the degree to which they perceive pain (called *pain threshold*) and tolerate it (referred to as *pain tolerance*). These differences among participants have been studied in clinical settings in an attempt to understand why some players can cope with sport-related pain better than others.

Ryan (1976) and his colleagues at the University of California at Davis studied pain threshold. They found no difference in the pain thresholds of three groups: athletes who engaged in contact sports, noncontact sport participants, and nonathletes. However, differences were noted in pain tolerance. Contact sport athletes tolerated the most pain, followed by noncontact athletes. Nonathletes tolerated the least amount of discomfort. The authors surmised that one's pain threshold appears to be related to one's physiological makeup, whereas pain tolerance may be more dependent on psychological and environmental factors.

How do elite athletes respond to physical discomfort? According to Rushall (1979), "In fatiguing events, better athletes generally know at what stage they become stressed

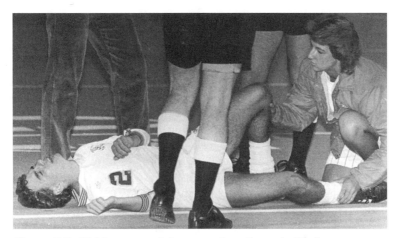

Figure 2.7 Athletes are one injury away from the end of their career, a thought that creates considerable anxiety.

by the pain or discomfort of fatigue" (p. 96). The top performers follow some or all of these four steps in coping with the onset of pain:

1. *They use cognitive strategies*. Top athletes prepare for pain by developing self-statements and mental imagery that allow them to handle it. Examples include, "Stick with my plan to handle it," "Concentrate on my opponent," and "Focus on technique."

2. *They confront and handle the pain*. To overpower the feelings of discomfort, athletes use self-statements such as, "You will get through this," "Ignore my body, and concentrate on my opponent (playing assignment)," "Focus on performance efficiency"; or they use pain as a cue to get "psyched up," the cognitive technique called *association*.

3. *Elite athletes cope with pain at critical moments*. Competitors may "allow" themselves to feel discomfort only at certain times. For instance, players may focus on their injuries only between plays, but will ignore those injuries when executing movements on the field or when concentrating on their opponents.

4. *They use reinforcing self-statements*. When the stressful activity ceases, they assess the coping strategy by asking: "Was it better to keep my feelings inside?" "Should I communicate my discomfort to the coach or to a friend?" "Am I capable of using a more effective technique, or could I have used this strategy more effectively?"

As discussed earlier, elite athletes tend to use one of two mental techniques in coping with physical discomfort, *association* and *dissociation*. The objective of association is to be "in touch" with one's body and to maintain the necessary effort and motivation to meet challenges and personal goals. This technique demands an internal focus. For example, elite distance runners might concentrate on planting each foot with every step. Weight lifters "associate with" the muscles used for optimal effort during the lift. Elite long-distance runners and weight lifters, among others, consciously use an association strategy (Iso-Ahola & Hatfield 1986; Morgan 1985).

Association, however, can backfire. Athletes focusing internally on an injury may be misfocusing their attention. Sport psychologists have found that one reason injured athletes do not return to their former performance quality despite an apparent full physical recovery (as determined by a physician) is that their attention is incorrectly aimed toward the injured area rather than on environmental factors such as teammates, opponents, and objects (Nideffer 1979). Monitoring internal bodily functions may be contrary to past habits and not compatible with task demands.

Dissociation entails being mentally preoccupied with external events as opposed to internal feelings and sensations. Exercising in synchronization to music, for example, serves a dissociative function that focuses the performer's attention externally on the musical input and away from the physical responses to vigorous exercise (Anshel & Marisi 1978). This technique can also help injured players to keep discomfort from interfering with the cognitive demands of the contest. The box below describes some of the issues that should be addressed when developing an injury rehabilitation program.

Athletic Injuries Have Psychological Consequences

Injured athletes have more than bones and muscle that need mending. A recent study indicates that self-esteem may get injured as well—making depression and anxiety an unwelcome part of recuperation.

Leddy et al. (1994) found that at the time of the injury as well as two months later, injured athletes suffered more depression, anxiety, and lower self-esteem than athletes who were not injured. In fact, within a week eight percent of the injured athletes showed emotional reactions as strong as those in people receiving outpatient psychotherapy. And four percent of the injured athletes continued to show moderate to severe clinical symptoms even after two months.

What does this mean for the rehabilitation of injured athletes? The authors recommended the use of a more comprehensive rehabilitation training program—one that deals not only with the physical aspects of the injury, but also its psychological effect on the athlete. They offered the following guidelines for persons involved in developing such a treatment program:

- Be aware that injury can have serious psychological consequences for athletes.
- Let athletes know that psychological effects are a part of the recuperation process.
- Know an athlete's injury history, and find out what emotional reactions they may have had to injury; then act accordingly.
- Have athletes assessed by a competent mental health professional following an injury.
- Offer injured athletes alternatives for channeling physical energies, such as swimming, weight lifting, or cycling.

Adapted from Leddy, Lambert, & Oles. (December 1994) "Psychological consequences of athletic injury among high-level competitors." *Research Quarterly for Exercise and Sport* 65, 347–354.

Coping with Sport-Related Stress

Stress, both chronic (long term) and acute (short term), is inherent in competitive sport. Examples of chronic stress include communication problems with coaches or other team members, low team member satisfaction, chronic injury or pain, and prolonged poor performance (slumping). Making mental and physical errors, an opponent's success, receiving a "bad" call from the referee or umpire, experiencing pain or injury, and performing in poor weather are examples of stressful events (acute stress sources). To perform effectively, athletes must be able to initiate a mental process called *coping* in order to deal with and overcome all sources of stress. Coping has been receiving more and more attention by sport psychology researchers in recent years in an attempt to understand it and find ways to improve it.

Coping is usually defined as "conscious psychological and physical efforts to improve one's resourcefulness in dealing with stressful events . . . or to reduce external demands" (Anshel et al. 2001, p. 45). From their extensive review of the coping literature, Anshel et al. have noted two important characteristics of coping that are often misunderstood or ignored by writers and practitioners. First, coping is a *conscious* and *effortful* process. In a sport context, the athlete is aware of the stressor and uses a learned strategy, mentally or physically, to manage external demands (i.e., reduce the stressor's intensity) or enhance internal resources (e.g., self-control, optimism, confidence, discounting the stressor's importance). An angry outburst or ignoring an unpleasant comment both occur automatically and in the virtual absence of thinking. These responses, therefore, are not considered coping (Anshel et al. 2001). Coping, then, is a learned skill. It is not considered a personality trait.

The second misunderstood characteristic about coping is that it is not necessarily performed effectively. Coping can be adaptive (effective in reducing perceived stress) or maladaptive (have ineffective properties) in reducing the stressor's intensity. For instance, smoking, drug-taking, and excessive alcohol use are behavioral examples of coping, yet would be considered maladaptive. They do more harm than good. Thus, while an athlete may engage in a coping strategy, the outcome of that strategy might be counterproductive to reducing stress, actually producing more stress and anger, or lead to another undesirable outcome (e.g., being dismissed from the contest, receiving a penalty, being fined, or even arrested).

Before moving on to suggested ways to deal with sport-related stress, it is important to separate an athlete's coping *style* from the use of coping *strategies*. *Coping style* is a disposition. It refers to the athlete's preference, or tendency, to use a certain category of coping strategy following chronic or acute forms of stress (Krohne 1996). Examples of paired coping styles common in the sport psychology literature include approach and avoidance, attention and distraction, monitoring and blunting, and problem focused and emotion focused. *Coping strategies*, on the other hand, are state or situational measures consisting of the athlete's use of one or more cognitive or behavioral methods of overcoming chronic or acute stress. Examples include seeking information, thinking about and trying to resolve the issue, seeking social support, and discounting the source of the stressor. An athlete's consistent use of a certain coping strategy would reflect the individual's coping style, especially in response to a particular type of stressor. For instance, persistently seeking to resolve the situation, mentally or physically, would reflect an approach coping style (Anshel et al. 2001), while forgetting about or reducing the importance of the stressor would be categorized as an avoidance coping style. One important implication for identifying and athlete's coping style is to assist coaches and sport psychology consultants in teaching coping strategies to athletes that are compatible with their style of coping. This should improve the effectiveness of coping interventions, an area to which we now turn.

Coping Interventions

Better competitors use techniques to handle stress both during and between contests. Stress in sport can be long term or short term. Chronic stress programs, those that can be implemented between and immediately preceding competitive events, include Gauron's (1986) cognitive self-regulation program. It is based on the athlete's ability to control attitudes, perceptions, thoughts, and "internal dialogue," the potential agents that may interfere with performing at optimal levels. Another program is Meichenbaum's (1985) stress inoculation training, which focuses on strategies to circumvent the unpleasant effects of stress. The COPE model (Anshel 1990b) describes cognitive-behavioral strategies to handle acute (immediate) forms of stress caused mainly by negative input from others, primarily coaches. As an intervention, use of the COPE model has assisted athletes to overcome unpleasant verbal feedback on performance in tennis (Anshel 1990b), baseball (Anshel et al. 1990), gymnastics (Anshel 1991c), and dart throwing (Anshel et al. 1993).

COPE is an acronym that describes four cognitive and behavioral strategies that can be used to handle unpleasant input from others. Athletes implement these techniques immediately upon receiving the undesirable input.

C = Control Emotions. The immediate reaction of an athlete's mind and body upon exposure to hostile input might be to feel uptight and tense. This response is known as the "fight-or-flight" reflex in the sympathetic nervous system, and the athlete feels the rush of adrenaline being pumped into the bloodstream. The model requires taking a few deep breaths and regaining composure. By controlling emotions at this stage, athletes can remain aware of and receptive to any important information that will contribute to better subsequent performance, while reducing muscular tension. This is not the time to use relaxation techniques that slow somatic processes and inhibit rapid thinking and reacting.

O = Organize Input. The objective here is for the athlete to deal rationally with the stressful episode. One trait of skilled performers is that they know the difference between important and unimportant (or redundant) information. A coach who yells, "You fool! How many times do I have to tell you. . . ." is providing an important message: "Don't do 'such and such' in certain situations." But the coach is also including a less constructive message when using name-calling and ridicule. To maintain the proper mental and physical readiness after exposure to uncomplimentary input, the athlete must be able to decide what is worthy of attention.

Author John Feinstein, in his best-selling book *A Season on the Brink* (1986), depicts how members of Bobby Knight's basketball team were able to cope with unpleasant input from their well-known coach when he was angry.

Other Indiana players . . . knew that Knight would say almost anything when he was angry and that the only way to deal with that was to ignore the words of anger and listen to the words of wisdom. . . . When he's calling you an _____, don't listen. But when he starts telling you why you're an _____, listen. That way you'll get better (p. 5).

Another approach to organizing input is to integrate all of it and then decide what has validity ("I can use this information") and what does not ("The person is angry; the message, if there is one, is inaccurate or based on the person's emotions, so ignore it"). Psychologist Alfred Korzybski (1933) refers to this technique as language discrimination. Although simply to ignore stimuli that serve no purpose to the listener would be very efficient, it is also very difficult to do. A more practical approach is to hear all of it and then develop skills to integrate what is desirable and try to forget undesirable input quickly. The best ways to do this are (1) stop thinking about the stressful episode, at least temporarily during the contest, and (2) quickly refocus on environmental task demands.

P = Plan Response. At this point, the coach's hostilities or other forms of stress are history. The last thing an athlete should do is to focus on his or her own unpleasant feelings. This prevents him or her from maintaining a state of optimal readiness for the next response. Instead, the performer must quickly begin to plan upcoming actions based on recent feedback and experiences. He or she might acknowledge certain strengths, strategies, or tendencies of the opponent or concentrate on correcting his or her own performance. At this stage, the athlete's thoughts must go from integrating information to using it.

E = Execute. All skilled athletes move with the appropriate precision and speed almost automatically and without thinking. This is especially important after experiencing an unpleasant event. An athlete who has been intimidated or upset by the discouraging remarks of others will hesitate, take fewer risks, and lack self-confidence in subsequent performance. The objective at this stage is to execute purposeful movements with the appropriate level of assertiveness, arousal, and concentration.

The sport psychology literature contains a vast array of cognitive techniques that help athletes overcome sudden—and chronic—stress. For example, *discounting* is a mental strategy athletes use to reduce the importance of undesirable messages (e.g., an angry coach's remarks) or experiences (e.g., making a performance error). This technique helps organize information as meaningful and nonmeaningful. Although examining these strategies goes beyond the scope of this book, readers may review the reference list at the back of this book for additional information.

Psychology of Drug Abuse

Desperate people sometimes do desperate things. One salient example of the desperation of competitive athletes to succeed in sport—or cope with the pressure—is the use of banned substances. Attempts by sport organizations to prevent drug use by athletes has peaked in recent years. Sport administrators, coaches, and even parents have attempted to eliminate the problem of drug use primarily through threats and punitive responses.

However, relatively little effort has been made to understand the psychological causes of drug use in sport. Of course, the term *drug* means different things to different people. Competitors who take anabolic steroids are attempting to enhance their performance, whereas those who use recreational drugs (e.g., cocaine, marijuana) actually inhibit their performance. Indeed, the goal of the recreational drug user is often altering his or her psychological state. If we can determine the underlying cause of drug use in sport, then cognitive and behavioral techniques can be used to inhibit or eliminate the problem.

One particularly popular, and misunderstood, drug in recent years has been creatine (see Anshel 2001 for a brief review). It's popularity is partly due to its admitted use by many professional athletes, most notably retired baseball player Mark McGwire, who said he used it during the 1998 season in which he hit a then-record 70 home runs. Creatine is not yet banned in many sports because it is categorized as a nutritional, physiological sports ergogenic. Ostensibly, creatine increases muscular power and speed in sport events. Its increased popularity is because it is not considered an anabolic steroid and is legally available over the counter. Whether or not it is effective as a performance enhancer appears to depend on the type of sport in question. In reviewing this literature, Anshel concluded that "even if creatine improves lean body mass and muscular strength, it may help performance only in sports that require repetitive, high-intensity, very short-term tasks with [a] brief recovery period" (p. 421). Given the uncertain long-term effects of prolonged creatine use, athletes should either avoid this substance or take it under the close supervision of a physician.

In one study that attempts to examine the causes of drug use, 126 intercollegiate athletes were interviewed about their perceptions of the reasons that they or other athletes were taking drugs (see Anshel 1991a). Questions were categorized under the headings of "performance-enhancing drugs" and "recreational drugs." The answers to the questions were further divided into physical, psychological/emotional, and social causes of drug taking. Examples of quoted responses for each cause of taking drugs for purposes of performance enhancement or recreation are listed in the accompanying box. An important feature of this study was not asking the athletes about their own behavior because past research has shown extensive underreporting of self-reported drug use (see Anshel 2001 for a review of this literature). Instead, athletes were asked to respond to their "impressions" and "perceptions" of drug taking on their team or among players they know.

The results of this study (Anshel 1991a) indicate that males took performance-enhancing drugs to "be competitive" more than for any other reason. Over 72 percent of the male subjects acknowledged that athletes they knew took steroids, whereas 64 percent of females knew of steroid ingestion among other female athletes. The most common reason for taking recreational drugs was to reduce tension and anxiety (48.9 percent for males and 49.2 percent for females). A summary of the athletes' responses from this study is in Table 2.2. Based on the results of this study and others, it is apparent that drug taking is primarily a function of coping with the pressures to succeed in sport—even to the possible detriment of the athlete's health. Anshel (1991b) provides cognitive and behavioral strategies that coaches can use to help combat drug abuse on their team. Indeed, it may be that the pressure to "be competitive," leading to drug taking in the first place, comes at least partly from the coach. Clearly, more research is

Quoted Responses to Questions about Drug Use

Performance Enhancement

Physical

(a) Pain/injury: "The drugs help me recover faster."

(b) Improve strength: "Steroids will help me bulk up."

(c) Be more competitive: "All of my opponents take them, so I have to stay competitive."

(d) Weight control: "I take pills so I can 'make' (not put on) weight."

Psychological/emotional

(a) Expectations of others: "The coach expects me to overpower my opponent. I need to be stronger." "My sponsor expects me to win or I lose a lot of money."

(b) Superman complex: "I'm strong; nothing is going to hurt me."

(c) Build self-confidence/self-esteem: "I feel on top of the world by using them."

(d) Fear of failure: "What if the other team takes them and I don't? Who do you think will have the advantage?"

(e) Get psyched up: "Steroids make me feel mean."

Social

(a) Modeling: "All the pros do it and it doesn't hurt them."

(b) Improve appearance: "Steroids will improve my physique."

Recreational Purposes

Physical

(a) Pain/injury: "A joint helps me forget the pain. I don't hurt as bad."

(b) Improve performance: "Drugs help me play more aggressive."

Psychological/emotional

(a) Boredom/stimulus-seeking: "I've got plenty of time to have fun." "I just wanted to do something different." "All of us get bored of doing the same thing all the time. Drugs give us a lift."

(b) Cope with stress or personal problems: "They get my mind off the pressure."

(c) Fear of success: "I don't want to play over my head or the coach will expect me to play that way all the time." "I've met my (performance) goals, so I'm happy."

Social

(a) Peer pressure: "It's the 'in' thing to do at a party." "All the guys do it."

(b) Experimentation/fun: "I just wanted to see what it was like." "It relaxes me at a party."

From the *Journal of Sport Behavior*, Vol. 14, no. 4 (203–308). Copyright © 1991 by University of South Alabama: Mobile, AL. Reprinted with permission.

needed to determine the extent to which elite athletes, particularly those who are highly successful, ingest steroids and other drugs for either recreational or performance enhancement purposes.

Table 2.2 A summary of the number and percentage of athletes' responses about their perceived causes of drug use in sport as a function of drug type and gender.

Perceived Causes of Drug Use	Male Total	(N = 94) Percent*	Female Total	(N = 32) Percent*	Combined Total	(N = 126) Percent**
Performance-Enhancing Drugs						
PHYSICAL						
Reduce pain	24	25.50	18	56.20	42	33.30
Injury rehabilitation	17	18.10	7	22.00	24	19.40
Increase energy/arousal	27	28.70	2	.06	29	23.00
Relaxation	1	.01	1	.03	2	.01
Weight control	19	20.20	17	53.10	36	28.50
Be competitive	61	64.80	11	34.30	72	57.10
PSYCHOLOGICAL/EMOTIONAL						
Fear of failure	27	28.70	14	43.70	41	32.50
Self-confidence	24	25.50	7	21.80	31	24.60
Superman complex	9	.09	1	.03	10	.08
SOCIAL						
Models	21	22.30	11	34.30	32	25.30
Social support	0	.00	4	12.50	4	.03
TOTAL USE	63	72.30	13	40.00	81	64.20
Recreational Drugs						
PHYSICAL						
Improve performance	12	12.70	1	.03	13	10.30
Control pain	8	4.10	4	4.70	12	4.30
PSYCHOLOGICAL/EMOTIONAL						
Reduce anxiety/tension	46	48.90	16	50.00	62	49.20
Boredom	21	22.30	11	34.30	32	25.30
Low coach loyalty	5	.05	3	.09	8	.06
Personal problems	6	.06	10	31.20	16	12.60
SOCIAL						
Peer pressure/acceptance	4	.04	3	.09	7	.05
Experimentation/fun	28	29.70	16	50.00	44	34.90
TOTAL USE	**61**	**64.80**	**18**	**56.20**	**79**	**62.60**

* Represents the percentage of subjects for each gender.

** Represents the percentage of total number of subjects (N = 126).

From the *Journal of Sport Behavior*, 14, no. 4 (203–308). Copyright © 1991 by University of South Alabama: Mobile, AL. Reprinted with permission.

SUMMARY

Successful athletes differ markedly from their less successful counterparts in several ways. Despite flaws in personality research, studies have shown that successful participants tend to be self-confident, have a high need to achieve, maintain a relatively high self-image, at least in the sport environment, and score low on personality inventories in trait and state anxiety, tension, depression, mental fatigue, confusion, and anger. They often score relatively high in mental toughness, intelligence, sociability, creativity, stability, dominance, aggression, and extroversion. Still, personality scales should not be used to predict the level of any athlete's future success, the type of sport for which a person is best suited, or other sport-related measures.

Successful athletes have unique habits that they perform before and during the contest. Before the contest, they use the warm-up as a means to reduce tension and anxiety; although they prefer to be alone immediately before the contest, they prefer to have a coach present during the warm-up period; they use mental imagery to build confidence and rehearse performance strategies; they have alternative plans to execute during the contest if their original strategy falters; they do not worry about their opponent before the contest and instead concentrate on correct skill and strategy execution; and if their opponent is gaining the upper hand, they are capable of recovering the necessary confidence, composure, and proper skill execution to be successful, either during the same contest or in a subsequent one.

Top performers experience a type of short-term mental state called peak performance in which they are "absorbed" in the task at hand. The performer is in a state of euphoria, especially during vigorous physical effort, while fear, insecurity, and inhibition dissipate. Also referred to as an emotional high or a state of "flow," athletes in this condition experience improved anticipation, faster reaction and movement time, and a more focused attention to environmental cues.

Not surprisingly, elite athletes prefer the presence of big crowds for emotional support, yet tend to ignore spectators while concentrating on performing their skills and strategies. Research and anecdotal evidence indicates that supportive spectators (e.g., judges or the home crowd) tend to enhance the athletes' arousal and aggression to favorable levels. Performance outcomes are favorable particularly when the person's skill level is relatively high and the task complexity somewhat low. Other factors, however, can inhibit correct skill execution. The spectators' high expectations for team or player success, performing complex skills in the presence of evaluative audience members (e.g., judges or the home crowd), and/or the athlete's perception of a highly skilled opponent may hinder rather than promote sport performance. Still, a perusal of the literature related to audience effects is far from conclusive. The ability to predict performance success based on audience and situational characteristics is quite low.

Elite athletes cope better with competitive events, pain, and sport-related stress than nonelite competitors. They understand that stress is an integral part of sport competition and are more likely to move on to the next task at hand rather than to dwell on the past. Consequently, they anticipate stress and do not allow it to prevent them from performing optimally. They often invoke the use of mental strategies to cope with these stressors. One likely reason for their superior coping ability is the high degree of self-confidence that top-quality competitors bring to the event.

REVIEW QUESTIONS

1. What are some of the limitations of using personality inventories to identify traits of athletes and nonathletes?

2. Despite the limitations you may have described in the first question, researchers have noticed a few personality tendencies in skilled athletes. Describe some of these, particularly those that seem to separate athletes from nonathletes.

3. How are personality traits of both elite and nonelite female and male athletes similar? How are they different?

4. Why are top athletes risk takers and stimulus seekers? How would a coach detect and promote these tendencies in an athlete?

5. Elite athletes have certain habits (routines) that they conduct before the contest. Describe these habits. What purposes do they serve, both psychologically and physically?

6. What are some of the unique tendencies of good athletes performed during the event in addition to executing the skills? What psychological and physical purposes do they serve? Why is Loehr's 16-second between-points routine in tennis effective?

7. This chapter discusses athletes' use of cognitive (mental) strategies that are initiated in preparation for and during the contest. What general purpose do these techniques serve? Describe five of the strategies, and indicate *why* and *when* each should be used.

8. How would you describe peak performance? Can peak performance be planned or anticipated? Why, or why not?

9. Various factors in sport influence the behaviors of elite athletes differently than those of nonelite athletes during competition. These include the presence of an audience, the use of aggression, and the fear of failing and succeeding. Describe each of these factors, and indicate how successful athletes handle them to maximize performance either before or during the contest. How can the coach favorably influence the performer for each of these factors?

10. How do successful athletes cope with pain and other sudden stressors? Provide an example of an acute stressor in sport and describe the techniques you recommend for effective coping.

11. Why is the ability to cope with sport-related stress important to success? How do elite athletes generally cope with stress in sport? How do they differ from their nonelite counterparts in their ability to handle fatigue, pain, competitive situations, and performance failure?

12. Why do athletes use performance-enhancing drugs? What are the potential "costs" of using banned drugs in sport? What can coaches, parents, and sport administrators do to reduce drug taking in sport?

CHAPTER 3

Motivating Athletes: Dos and Don'ts

How many professions actually require a person to alter another individual's thoughts, feelings, attitudes, and behaviors, sometimes very rapidly, and to maintain the changes over a prolonged time period? No easy task. Yet this is a primary responsibility of coaches in sport. However, coaches cannot meet these job expectations alone. Unless the athlete is motivated to learn skills and strategies and to perform them consistently well, often in stressful situations, the coach's ability to compel these behaviors will be restricted. Although motivating athletes may not appear to be a very difficult task, it is far more sophisticated than many individuals believe. After reading this chapter, you should be able to understand the theoretical bases of motivation; to become aware of and avoid the many mythical practices used in coaching to motivate competitors (which often have the opposite impact); and to apply effective principles of motivation in a sport context. Consider the following typical examples of "motivation" in sport.

- *Intimidation.* During team tryouts, the coach tells the participants, "Most of you aren't good enough to make this team. You're going to have to go out there and show me you deserve to play for me." Or an athlete makes an error, and the coach threatens, in front of team members, to kick that athlete off the team unless the player can "get it together."
- *Threats.* The coach grabs an athlete who has just made an error and, eyeball to eyeball, makes a physical threat if he doesn't "do it right."
- *Criticism.* "That's the worst performance I've ever seen. If you can't do better than that, then you can leave this team."
- *Criticism and sarcasm.* "Hey, rubber hands, try using a basket to catch the ball," or "My grandmother can pass the ball better than that."
- *Guilt.* "I'm really surprised at you guys. I can't believe what I'm seeing. You guys should be ashamed of yourselves. You call yourselves athletes?"
- *Physical abuse.* The coach requires the athletes to run ten 40-yard sprints in 90-degree heat after the regular practice session. Or, athletes are awakened at 5 A.M. for a five-mile run as punishment for being late for practice the previous day. Or the coach deprives the athletes of water (for whatever reason), which deteriorates performance at best and at worst is life threatening.

In these examples, the coach is attempting to induce short-term changes in the behavior of another individual. In doing so, the coach is assuming that the athlete will, in fact, respond favorably to harsh treatment. But what many coaches do not realize is that such forced changes in behavior have only short-term benefits, if any, and that more desirable long-term effects will not be reached. The strategies so commonly used by coaches to motivate athletes can do more harm than good. The purpose of this chapter is to offer a scientific basis for motivation and to recommend strategies that will favorably influence the athlete's feelings and actions.

What Is Motivation?

Because writers and scientists have defined motivation in different ways, the use of this concept in a sport-related context needs clarification. The term *motivation* is derived from the Latin word *movere*, meaning "to move." Motivation is typically defined as the tendency for the direction and selectivity of behavior to be controlled by its connections to consequences, and the tendency of this behavior to persist until a goal is achieved. To give this academic definition some life, let's review a few key words and phrases to determine their implications in sport.

The *direction of motivation* refers to the purpose and the desired actions of the activity. The motivated athlete is energized to engage in a purposeful and meaningful task. Deciding which task(s) to perform is *selectivity of behavior*. At times, coaches need to solicit input from athletes as to what they find important and then provide the individual with the proper direction. Except to meet biological needs (e.g., hunger or thirst), motivation is rarely automatic.

"You mean if I don't show up to practice on time, I have to get up the next morning at 5 A.M. to go jogging?" "If I don't attend weight-training sessions, I'll be dismissed from the team?" These are also examples of behaviors that are controlled by their *connections to consequences*. However, these threatening statements are examples of aversive control of behavior and represent a negative approach to motivation (Smith 1993). More desirable, long-term consequences include linking physical training to improved fitness, which, in turn, should lead to better sport performance. In the second example given, the coach should state the importance of punctuality to practice as a way to use practice time most efficiently.

Of what value is motivation in sport unless the athletes continue to perform the desirable behaviors (i.e., unless they persist)? The purpose of motivation is to prolong desirable feelings and actions of athletes. Many coaches and, for that matter, managers in business and industry fail to understand the long-term advantages of positive motivational strategies rather than being satisfied with any possible short-term "benefits" of negative, critical, or threatening motivational techniques.

For example, being in top physical condition (preferably year-round) is an important objective of coaches and players. To use coaching strategies that make physical conditioning fun and enjoyable (such as exercising to music, organizing relay races, and creating an atmosphere free of tension) certainly makes sense. What, then, is the rationale of using physical conditioning as a vehicle for punishment, as so many sport leaders and physical education teachers do? Should athletes be asked to run laps or wind sprints as a consequence of inappropriate behavior? The unintended result may be that athletes will be *less*, not more, inclined to exercise and stay in shape on their own, especially during the off-season or after they retire from sport due to an unfavorable attitude toward physical activity.

For persons to feel motivated, they should be involved in an activity in which they can achieve short-term and long-term *goals*. Goals provide direction for effort and the incentive to persist at a task until a new skill or performance mastery has been achieved. The individual's anticipation of meeting some goal is called a motive. It is a function of how important the athlete considers the consequences of certain actions and how strongly the performer desires (*approach motive*) or resists (*avoidance motive*) these ramifications (White 1959). For example, anticipating certain responses from spectators, teammates, or the coach based on one's performance serves as a motive to succeed or to avoid failure.

Perhaps one of the most challenging motivational tasks is for coaches to motivate every team member, and athletes to motivate themselves, by feelings that the performer's efforts will lead to meeting desirable goals (*expectancy*). Athletes who toil every week during practice, yet are not allowed to appear in any of the contests, or whose goals far exceed their capabilities, will not likely be motivated to persist at the activity. In both examples, the athletes will be less motivated to give 100 percent.

As indicated earlier, the coach can foster *incentive* in an athlete by pointing out the specific ways in which certain behaviors can lead to goals and outcomes that the performer finds meaningful. Athletes can also improve their incentive by engaging in activities they find pleasant and about which they have realistic expectations for at least some degree of success. Anticipating a career in professional sport, for example, is not a realistic goal for most athletes, whereas starting, improving performance, and even making the team are far more realistic and achievable.

Sources of Motivation

Where does motivation come from? Why are some people more motivated than others, and what factors contribute to motivated states? These are important questions, not only for participation in sport, but also in business and industrial settings and for maintaining proper healthy habits. Researchers have concluded that motivation is not simply a matter of personality type. Rather, there are likely a set of personal characteristics and situational factors that foster motivation, separately and jointly. To examine several reviews of this literature, see Duda (1993), Roberts (1992a, 1993), and Weinberg and Gould (1995).

Participant-Centered View

One approach to understanding sources of motivation in sport is to examine the personal dispositions that researchers have found are closely linked to high motivational states. Referred to as the participant-centered, or trait-centered, view (Weinberg & Gould 1995), it is thought that high—or low—levels of motivation reflect individual characteristics. This view holds that if individuals do not have what it takes to reach goals and perform at their best, there is nothing anyone can do to "make" this happen. Individual desire is the first and foremost characteristic of motivation. For example, just *some* of the personal attributes that separate highly motivated persons from their less motivated peers include high levels of need achievement, goal orientation, self-confidence, competence, optimism, positive expectancies, and, among skilled athletes in particular, competitiveness.

Situational View

The situational view holds that personal attributes are insufficient predictors of motivation. Individuals with a high propensity to be motivated will not exhibit this characteristic unless the situation or environment fosters it. Thus, the circumstances that produce motivation are far more important than merely possessing certain personal dispositions. In support of this view, one has to think only about situations or environments that have either increased or decreased the person's motivation level, changing original thoughts and emotions. Situations anticipated to be exciting or interesting, but that turn out to be disappointing, or conversely, situations that promise little or no excitement and that turn out to be very satisfying, are examples that explain the importance of situational factors that enhance motivational states. Other situational examples include teacher/coach behaviors, the team's win/loss record, and the type of environment in which the contest is being played (e.g., home versus away, weather conditions, crowd reactions).

The main limitation of the situation-centered view of explaining motivation is that situations do not always influence a competitor's motivation. Some situations are quite unpleasant and demotivating, yet some athletes remain motivated despite negative experiences or unpleasant environments. Furthermore, athletes do not usually quit their team because of the loss of a single game, a reprimand from the coach, or making an error. Even after being injured, many athletes become highly motivated to return to competition.

Interaction View

Because people are more complicated than two-dimensional characters, there exists a third explanation for motivation, the interaction view. The contention here is that motivation results from the combination of personal and situational factors, rather than from each factor alone. Therefore, it is the combination of personal characteristics and the situation that fosters—or destroys—motivation. For example, my study with elite and nonelite male Australian swimmers (Anshel 1995b) indicates that the combination of personal characteristics such as high need achievement, intrinsic motivation, and extreme commitment with situational factors such as a positive and trusting relationship with the coach, use of coach feedback, and strong parental support is unique to the elite group. Thus, motivation is more likely if athletes, exercisers, and workers possess certain characteristics that compel them to want to achieve something and if they are in a situation that is supportive of and nurtures their desires.

One might ask, what about feelings of motivation that accompany threat? Certainly an athlete will tend to increase his or her effort if the coach threatens expulsion from the team or some other consequence. (Remember that exercise as punishment is undesirable because it reduces the athlete's natural desire for and positive attitude toward physical activity and keeping in good condition). Negative reinforcement, or short-term threats and punishments, usually in the form of withholding positive messages or experiences, does have motivational effects. It is also true that sometimes this type of treatment from an authority figure is desirable, even required, to increase the athlete's incentive to change his or her behavior. However, reliance on this motivational technique has two shortcomings. First, it has only short-term effects. Usually the athlete's behavior changes just until the source of threat is removed (e.g., not being allowed to participate with the team until the athlete completes a predetermined exercise regimen). After the threat is removed (performing the exercises), the incentive to persist in this activity (either when the coach is not monitoring the exercise session or during the off-season to stay in shape) is minimal. The second shortcoming is that threat creates extrinsic, not intrinsic, incentive (discussed later in this chapter). That is, the reason for the activity is based on achieving some external reward (e.g., recognition, participating on the team, not being punished). Intrinsic rewards related to pleasure and satisfaction derived from performing the activity are rare. Only if the athlete views exercise and keeping in top physical condition as beneficial to his or her athletic performance and success will some intrinsic value be derived.

In summary, motivation in sport is dependent on meeting the athlete's personal needs and objectives while pursuing a certain predetermined course of action, responding to the coach's leadership, and possessing necessary feelings and attitudes associated with performance success.

Theories of Motivation

Theories in psychology help scientists and practitioners to understand the causes of certain actions, which in turn helps them to predict when these behaviors might occur. Particular strategies can then be implemented to affect performance favorably. The theories reviewed in this chapter were chosen based on their application to sport and the extent to which they have received attention in the sport psychology literature.

Need Achievement

According to most personality studies (see Chapter 2 for a brief review), one characteristic of successful athletes is their high need to achieve (Cox 1995). This need is commonly referred to as *achievement motivation*. The central focus of this theory is that some individuals derive tremendous satisfaction from success in achievement activities. However, it is important to note that "success" is in the mind of the beholder. That is, each individual is responsible for determining his or her own achievement behavior. According to Roberts (1992b), "success and failure are psychological states based upon the interpretation of the effectiveness of that person's achievement striving" (p. 14). Thus, if the performance outcome is viewed as a result of the person's effort and skill, then the outcome is interpreted as successful. However, if the outcome is perceived as a result of some undesirable personal quality such as poor effort or lack of talent, then the outcome will be interpreted as a failure. What is success for one person may be failure for another person. Of course, in reality, life is a bit more complicated. For example, some athletes do not even try because they predict that they do not have a chance to succeed when playing against a superior opponent. According to achievement motivation theory, these competitors will not necessarily interpret losing as failure because they didn't even try. "Blame" for losing usually rests with low effort, not with poor ability or skills. Still, high need achievers give extra effort in achievement-oriented conditions as depicted in Figure 3.1. It is this optimal level of effort that is interpreted

Figure 3.1 An athlete's need to achieve is often
a source of energy, commitment, and long-term
motivation to give 100% during competition.

as success, not always the outcome. Effort and performing one's best are associated
with mastery goal orientation, whereas performance outcome (winning) is linked to
ego goal orientation.

To identify athletes' interpretations of their successes and failures and to determine
their goal orientation as based on mastery of skills or on competitive outcomes, Roberts
and Treasure (1995) have developed the Perceptions of Success Questionnaire (POSQ).
The POSQ is based on comparing mastery-oriented with ego-oriented athletes. Because
ego orientation is related to competitiveness and a greater need to win (Duda 1993),
ego-oriented athletes experience a higher dropout rate as compared to mastery-oriented athletes, as this need is often not met. Mastery-oriented competitors, on the
other hand, are more satisfied with the sport experience than ego-oriented athletes
(Roberts 1993). This difference in goal orientation is one reason high need achievers,

who tend to be mastery-oriented, drop out of sport *less* often than low need achievers, whose satisfaction from sport is more dependent on event outcomes, an ego orientation. The POSQ focuses on separating these orientations. Athletes are asked to complete the following partial sentence: "When playing sport, I feel most successful when:" Examples of completions that reflect an ego orientation include "I beat other people," or "I outperform my opponents." Items that represent mastery orientation are "I perform to the best of my ability" or "I reach a goal."

Persons who are relatively high need achievers (as determined by paper-and-pencil inventories) (1) usually experience more pleasure in success, (2) have fewer and weaker physiological symptoms of arousal, such as increased heart rate, respiration rate, or sweating, (3) feel responsible for the outcomes of their own actions, (4) prefer to know about their success or failure almost immediately after performance, and (5) prefer situations that contain some risk about the result (McClelland 1961; Roberts 1993).

Typical high need achieving athletes are usually fully conscious of the fact that they alone are responsible for how well they perform, they know immediately (through their own perceptions and the feedback from teammates and spectators) whether they have failed or succeeded in their particular endeavor, and there is always present in sport settings an element of risk as to the outcome of their performance. However, some athletes do not consider sports competitions as "pure" achievement settings in that the individual may be largely motivated by reasons other than achievement (Roberts 1993).

For example, children may engage in competitive sport to have fun; winning is of relatively minor importance (Gerson 1978). Certainly elite athletes want to win, but many are motivated by the inherent danger of participating in a risky sport such as ski jumping or motorbike racing. Others derive pleasure from physical contact, as is the case with some ice hockey players who compile penalties for fighting and enjoy a "defensive" team role. Still others enjoy being in top physical condition (e.g., distance runners), relish the attention of an admired physique (e.g., weight lifters), or enjoy the peer affiliation available in team sports.

In each of these examples, the individual acts to bring about pleasurable experiences. These are referred to as *approach motives*. But if one's actions serve to prevent something unpleasant from happening, an *avoidance motive* explains behavior (McClelland 1961). An example would be an athlete who participates in sport due to pressure from parents, peers, coaches, or, in some countries, the government (Vanek & Cratty 1970). The importance and the anticipation of success make the approach motive far more common with successful competitors than with their less skilled counterparts.

Duda (1993) and Roberts (1993) separate the concept of need achievement from motive for achievement. A person can have a high need to achieve but, due to a past history of failure, have a low motive to achieve. They suggest that children with a past history of failure in sport should not be expected to possess a high motive for achievement in competitive sport situations. In fact, their expectancy for success would probably be quite low. This does not mean, however, that their need to achieve is also low. Unless the high need achiever with a low approach motive finds a sport in which he or she is successful, the person will tend to stop participating in sport altogether. This is the heart of the fear-of-failure (avoidance motive) phenomenon so common in younger or less successful athletes.

Separating the High and Low Need Achiever. The best-known researchers in this area, the late John Nicholls (1984), Joan Duda (1993), and Glyn Roberts (1993) have been able to derive a psychological profile of individuals with high and low need achievement, particularly related to the conditions of competitive sport. Their research covers the areas of motivational orientation (i.e., the person's disposition to feel motivated to achieve), attributional tendencies (see Chapter 4), type of preferred goals (performance versus outcome), task choice (easy versus difficult), and performance outcomes in evaluative conditions. Over numerous studies, based on scores from psychological inventories (which categorize individuals according to their level of need achievement), the researchers have found very clear differences between high and low need achievers, using the symbol for achievement, *Nach*.

On *motivational orientation*, individuals with high *Nach* have high motivation to achieve success, low motivation to experience failure, and possess great pride in their success. Low *Nach* subjects, on the other hand, have low motivation to achieve success, are far more comfortable with—and sometimes even desire—failure, and focus on shame and worry that may result from failure (e.g., "What will my friends, or parents/coach, think of me?"). Regarding *causal attributions*, high *Nach* subjects tend to explain their success as due to high ability/skill (stable, internal factors), and attribute failure to bad luck or high task difficulty. Low *Nach* subjects, however, attribute success to an easy task or good luck, and failure to poor ability.

Differences between groups also exist in the types of *preferred goals*. Persons with high *Nach* adopt performance goals relating to the level of task mastery, whereas low *Nach* persons prefer outcome goals (the final product). With respect to types of *tasks preferred*, high *Nach* performers seek out challenges and prefer to compete against opponents. Low *Nach* performers prefer to avoid challenges, performing relatively easy tasks against lower-skilled competitors (although Roberts [1993] contends that low *Nach* subjects will also prefer very difficult tasks, thereby avoiding responsibility for performance failure). Finally, differences in *performance outcome* suggest that high *Nach* individuals perform well in evaluative conditions, whereas low *Nach* persons perform rather poorly under such conditions. It is no wonder that successful athletes are high need achievers while low *Nach* individuals are more likely to drop out of sport, especially following consistent perceived failure (i.e., losing contests) (see Duda 1992 for a review of related literature).

Reinforcing Achievement Motivation. Achievement motivation can and should be fostered by coaches and parents. The need to achieve should be reinforced by (1) creating challenging goals ("Let's try to contact the ball more than 50 percent of the time"), (2) teaching skills that lead to performance improvement and success ("In today's practice, we're going to learn a new blocking technique"), (3) giving positive and constructive feedback on performance while avoiding negative and derogatory remarks ("Janice, I liked how you used your body to block out Martha from getting the rebound"), (4) allowing for risk-taking behaviors and learning from the outcomes— good or bad—rather than responding in a punitive manner ("Jim, you took the shot a bit early; we had eight more seconds to set up the play"), (5) creating situations in which the athlete feels successful, such as emphasizing improvement, skill development, and effort, and (6) ensuring that at the end of a practice or an event, the person feels a sense of competence—that he or she has achieved something or is closer to doing so. See Chapter 10 for a discussion on achievement motivation in youth sports.

Competence Motivation

White (1959), who pioneered the theory of competence motivation, proposes that behavior is directed, selective, and persistent owing to "an intrinsic need to deal (effectively) with the environment" (p. 318). He argues that the need for competence is an inherent part of life starting in childhood. We habitually attempt to master our surroundings, and when we're successful, we feel pleasure. Children in particular are motivated by mastery, curiosity, challenge, and play to satisfy their urge toward competence. Their rewards for achieving competence are feelings of internal pleasure: it's fun, pleasurable, and satisfying.

Harter (1981), in her competence motivation theory, claims that individuals are motivated by, and attempt to exhibit, skill mastery in achievement situations such as sport. If they are successful, their mastery experiences result in pleasant emotions and heightened self-confidence. In turn, these feelings will lead to continued incentive to engage in competitive sport. Central to Harter's theory is that individuals high in perceptions of competence and degree of self-control in the sport environment will exert more effort, persist longer at tasks in achievement situations, and experience more positive feelings than individuals lower in perceived competence and self-control. These predictions have been confirmed in sport situations (Vallerand & Reid 1984). Another factor that influences the motivation for competence and achievement is goal orientation.

Goal Orientation.   Embedded in the dispositions of achievement and competence motivation is another disposition, called *goal orientation*, that refers to the extent to which an athlete is motivated by setting and then meeting goals (Duda 1992, 1993). Goal orientation in a sport context reflects two thought processes, the athlete's achievement goals ("What do I need to do to feel I have accomplished something meaningful and challenging?") and his or her perceived ability ("Do I have the skills needed to meet this goal?"). The answer to these two questions will affect self-evaluations of demonstrated ability. Therefore, an athlete with high goal orientation will: (a) set a challenging, yet realistic and achievable, goal, (b) feel a moderate to high degree of certainty about meeting this goal based on his or her high perceived ability, (c) will select a task, and (d) persist at that task with optimal effort until this goal is achieved. Because goal orientation is a disposition, not a personality trait, it can be more apparent in some situations than in others, it can be learned, and it is affected by previous experiences, particularly past experiences of perceived success and failure. This means that goal orientation can become stronger or weaker for a given time period, for a specific task or goal, or within a given context (e.g., sport, academic, work, or social settings). The thought process that drives an athlete's goal orientation—that provides the "fuel" for the need to feel competent—is called task involvement or ego involvement.

An important objective of competence motivation is the individual's perception of his or her own ability (i.e., perceived competence). This perception is influenced by improving one's ability in one of two ways: (a) improvement over time rather than improving current ability, a concept called *task involvement*, or (b) demonstrating competence based on proving current ability by outperforming others (or performing similarly with less effort), a concept called *ego involvement*. Because ego-involved performers are concerned with the adequacy of their ability level, perceived competence theory predicts that ego involvement increases the probability of feeling incompetent. This is especially the case with individuals who already doubt their ability (Duda 1992).

This prediction is supported by a study by Burton (1989), who compared male and female university swimmers on their perceived ability following a five-month goal-setting program. One group received goal-setting training that encouraged perceived competence based on performance (i.e., improved times) rather than outcome goals (i.e., winning or losing). A second (control) group from another university did not receive the goal-setting program. The no-treatment group determined their own competence by the outcome of their race. Burton found that swimmers in the goal-setting program perceived their ability as higher and felt more successful following competition than did those in the control group. Duda (1993) has concluded from her extensive review of studies in this area that severe decreases in competence motivation are most likely to occur in situations combining perceptions of low ability with performing in ego-involving situations (i.e., when the performer assesses competence based on outcome).

Competence motivation can be increased if competitors feel good about their participation in sport regardless of the outcomes. Effort and improvement should be emphasized rather than—or at least in addition to—winning or losing. In addition, sport performers should be taught to formulate accurate perceptions of their ability within "achievement contexts." Does the athlete possess the necessary skill to succeed? What must he or she continue to work on? Adults should do everything possible to persuade young athletes to think positive thoughts about their future involvement in sport. This is why learning new skills and having an opportunity to perform them are so important in maintaining motivation. At the same time, always having an excuse for failing is not productive. If the demands of a sport are too great for an individual, perhaps more time for instruction and practice is needed before the individual is placed in a pressure-filled competitive situation.

Cognitive Evaluation Theory: Intrinsic and Extrinsic Motivation

Cognition and motivation theory is about understanding the connection between a person's thoughts and how these thoughts influence his or her actions. The cognitive approach to motivation involves making choices about goal-directed behaviors. These choices are based on the main reasons individuals decide to engage in physical activity: pleasure and enjoyment. This is the basis of Deci's (1975) cognitive evaluation theory and its application in sport and physical activity settings by Deci and Ryan (1985).

Deci's theory is predicated on two primary drives (or *innate needs*) that provide the person with the energy for goal-directed behavior. These are *to feel competent* and *to be self-determining* in coping and interacting with one's environment. A person who experiences success tends to attribute it to high ability. The activity is enjoyable—even fun—and participation continues. A person who participates in activity for its enjoyment and without an external reward is said to be intrinsically (internally) motivated. *Intrinsic motivation* (IM) is highly desirable in sport because it forms the individual's motives for participating in sport. According to Duda (1992), ". . . task involvement should foster intrinsic interest in an activity, [whereas] ego involvement is assumed to lead to a decrease in intrinsic motivation" (p. 71). The factors that affect IM and the reasons for engaging in sport are illustrated in Figure 3.2.

Actions that are performed voluntarily, without coercion, and that are perceived as pleasant are intrinsically motivating. Typical research on IM includes (1) a measure of each person's initial (baseline) level of motivation for performing a task, (2) the introduction of some treatment, perhaps various types of rewards, offered to one group but not to another (control) group, and (3) a follow-up (posttreatment) attempt to assess each person's IM toward the task. The measurement can be conducted with a questionnaire or through a

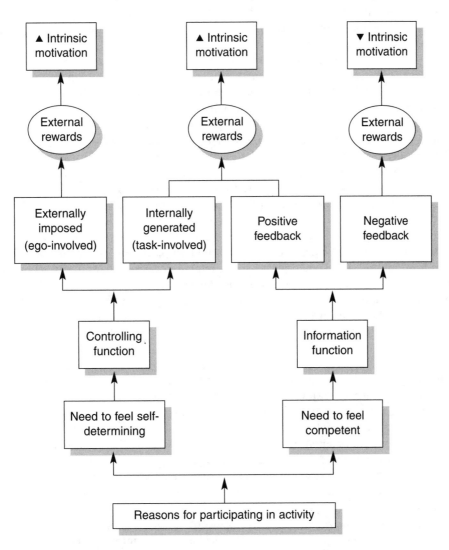

Figure 3.2 The effect of internal and external factors on intrinsic and extrinsic motivation and reasons for sport participation.

planned analysis of the subjects' behaviors. IM may be measured by the Intrinsic Motivation Inventory (Ryan et al. 1983) and has since been validated for sport by McAuley (1989). A more recent inventory, called the Sport Motivation Scale (SMS), was developed by a group of Canadian researchers (Pelletier et al. 1995). The behavioral analysis approach consists of recording the extent to which subjects continue to practice a task to which they were earlier exposed without any external demand or reward for so doing. Persons who persist in practicing a task are said to be intrinsically motivated. For example, Martin and Hall (1995) examined the effect of "successful imagery" on subjects' intrinsic motivation while learning a golf putting task. Length of time practicing the task served as the primary measure of IM. They found that the imagery group performed golf putting significantly longer than the (control) subjects who did not use imagery when all subjects were given the option of resting. The researchers reasoned that mentally rehearsing successful performance increased subjects' expectancies of success and self-confidence, both of which are associated with IM (Ryan et al. 1983). Practicing successful imagery, then, may produce self-evaluations that are both higher and more realistic. *Extrinsic motivation* (EM), on the other hand, is the desire to perform an activity due to the anticipation of some external reward such as money or a trophy (Deci 1975).

Researchers have found, as one might expect, that intrinsically motivated behaviors are more persistent, more enjoyable, and enhance the person's self-image as compared to extrinsically motivated actions. An excellent example of an intrinsically motivated person was the renowned scientist Albert Einstein, who said, "I am happy because I want nothing from anyone. I do not care for money. Decorations, titles, or distinctions mean nothing to me. I do not crave praise. The only thing that gives me pleasure, apart from my work, my violin, and my sailboat, is the appreciation of my fellow workers."

But what happens to a person's IM when he or she is offered extrinsic rewards such as money or a trophy? Why, for instance, do children participate in playground games for the fun of it and then, when placed in a competitive sport situation, care about the score and who wins and loses? Why do kids play sports "to have fun," yet drop out of competitive sport at alarming rates? And why is receiving a trophy so important if having fun is the main reason for participating? Deci's theory proposes two processes by which extrinsic rewards can affect IM: the *controlling function* and the *information function*. The ways in which rewards affect motivation are depicted in Figures 3.2 and 3.3.

Controlling Function.   Persons are intrinsically motivated to engage in an activity under conditions of high enjoyment and self-control. That is, the decision to engage in an activity is their own. However, external rewards can shift the person's reasons for participation from internal (e.g., fun, pleasure, or competence) to external (e.g., trophies, recognition, or gifts). EM may override IM when the source of control is no longer within the person, that is, the performer engages in an activity for the purpose of obtaining approval, recognition, or financial gain (e.g., a raise in salary) rather than for the activity's inherent enjoyment. Some common forms of EM include trophies, ribbons, money, parental or peer pressure, need for approval, and other awards that recognize success. However, without the "reward" of pleasing others or receiving an award, the intrinsic incentive to continue participating may not be strong enough.

The effects of a sport program that relies on a selective reward system whereby some athletes receive tangible rewards and others do not are even more potentially damaging

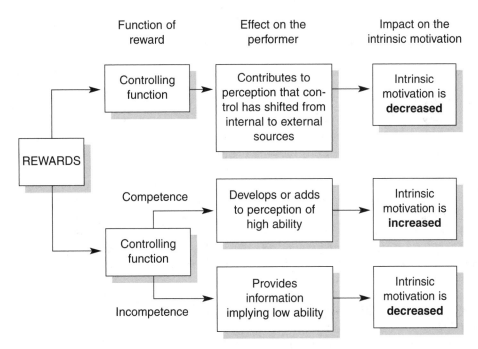

Figure 3.3 The impact of rewards on intrinsic motivation.

to IM. Does this mean that trophies should never be used? Not necessarily. Rewards may be used in a positive way to convey information about an individual's competence. For example, athletes can receive an award for their effort (e.g., "Most Motivated" or "Best Effort"), improvement (e.g., "Most Improved"), support of other teammates (e.g., "Best Team Player"), leadership (e.g., "Mr. [Ms.] Leadership"), skill ("Strongest Arm"), and so on. In each of these examples, the recipient should feel rewarded for accomplishing a task, meeting a goal, or demonstrating competence. The trophy serves to reinforce this recognition. Or all team members can receive the same award, such as a "Good Job Award" or "Achievement Award." Coaches and parents must stop assuming that young athletes possess a high need for trophies and other external awards in order to derive satisfaction from sport. Recognition and approval can successfully replace rewards *if* used often and consistently over time, as indicated by the information function of this model.

Information Function.   Feelings of competence and self-determination are other factors in the extent to which extrinsic rewards can affect IM. Deci (1975), in support of White's competence motivation theory (1959), contends that people are attracted to activities in which they feel successful (in which they perceive *competence*). Performers who have high perceived ability will likely be intrinsically motivated. Rewards can have the same favorable effect on IM if they increase the person's feelings of competence and self-worth. In this way, rewards can actually foster IM if they provide all participants with some recognition for demonstrating success, be it improvement in performance, high effort, or showing competent skill execution.

Self-determination, the second component of the information aspect, is concerned with the extent to which the individual perceives that he or she controls the reason(s) for engaging in the activity. Self-determination theory (Ryan & Deci 2000) focuses on the extent to which behaviors are purposeful, volitional, or self-determined. The theory is based on human needs for competence and autonomy. High self-determination accompanies high IM. In addition, the intrinsically motivated person feels responsible for earning any rewards from this activity. For instance, a team member who does not feel that he or she contributes to the team's success will feel less self-determination and, therefore, will be less intrinsically motivated in contrast to feelings of high contribution. As shown in Figure 3.4, coaches can foster the players' feelings of self-determination and personal responsibility for outcomes by consulting players for suggestions about a few team policies, codes of player behavior, and game strategies and plans. Examples include asking team members to take turns leading warm-up exercises or voting for team captains. Central to promoting self-determination (and IM) is encouraging "full engagement" by athletes and preventing feelings of alienation. The athlete's perceptions of excessive externally based control and feelings of helplessness foster alienation and markedly reduce or extinguish IM.

In their revision of Deci's (1975) cognitive evaluation theory, Deci and Ryan (1985) have proposed a third primary component, *functional significance of the event*. Most events include both controlling and informational functions, possibly influencing the individual's perceived control of the situation (locus of causality), perceived ability, and IM. However, the aspect of the situation perceived as most important or obvious by the individual,

Figure 3.4 Developing friendships and positive social interactions among team members provides sources of satisfaction, enjoyment, and intrinsic motivation.

that is, having high functional significance, will influence feelings of self-control (internal or external), feelings of perceived ability (high or low), and, eventually, intrinsic or extrinsic motivation. According to Deci and Ryan (1985), choice (self-control), perceived competence, autonomy (self-determination), and positive feedback result in the *informational aspect* receiving the most importance. Rewards, time deadlines, and being observed by significant others result in the *controlling aspect* being most salient.

An example of the functional significance component on IM is derived from my personal experience with a 13-year-old elite (nationally ranked) swimmer whose international stardom was predicted. Despite performing admirably at swim meets and receiving a great deal of positive feedback and media attention on his performance, his coach was confused about this athlete's lack of effort, positive mood, and enthusiasm for swimming. The competitor was chronically late for practice, gave minimal energy to training, and often complained of not feeling well. Only in the presence of his father did the swimmer give 100 percent and appear to be "back on track." After a couple of conversations with the swimmer and observations of his practice sessions in the presence of his father, I realized the problem. The swimmer's motive to compete was not his own, but rather his father's pressure. "My dad wants 'this,' and my dad wants 'that,'" the swimmer would often tell me. "But what do *you* want from swimming?" I asked. "I don't really like swimming," the athlete responded. "It keeps me away from my friends." It was obvious that the controlling aspect was most important to this swimmer. The result was the swimmer's perception of low self-control (i.e., an external perceived locus of causality), the undermining of IM, heightened EM, and defiance. When the swimmer's father (the extrinsic motivational source) was absent from practice, there was minimal satisfaction from the activity and, hence, no incentive to maintain optimal effort. This swimmer never achieved the stardom predicted for him and dropped out of swimming by age 16.

Application of Deci's Theory.   The cognitive evaluation model has several components that interact and are predicted to create IM or EM. At this point, let's reexamine the components of this model, then attach examples of sport behaviors to each component.

These factors and conditions seem to facilitate IM, as shown previously in Figure 3.2.

1. *Reason for participation.* Which is better for athletes, task involvement or ego involvement? If the athlete is *task-involved*, IM increases because sport is experienced as an end in itself. One's motivation to perform a task is derived from its intrinsic properties, enjoyment, fun, and so on. If, however, the person's self-worth is based on good performance, and when failing to meet an internal standard is a possible threat to self-esteem, the person is ego-involved; IM decreases. Ego involvement results in attempts to meet a performance standard rather than focusing on the task at hand, resulting in less IM as compared with task involvement. To Frederick and Ryan (1995), "coaches who think that 'winning is the only thing' are likely to induce ego involvement in their players and undermine their long-term participation in sports" (p. 15).

   Example: An athlete wants to learn sport skills and play his or her best, without comparing performance outcome against a standard or being evaluated by others. However, even if the athlete *is* being evaluated, IM will not decrease if the athlete views such evaluations as having *low* functional significance. Thus, the first question parents should ask their child athlete is *not* who won, but rather, "Did you have a good time?" If the response is "no," parents should try to find out the reasons and help their child resolve the issue by encouraging him or her to reappraise the experience in a more favorable light; a parent might say, for instance, "Winning is more fun than losing, but if you gave it your best, I'm still proud of you," or "Even if you lost, did you *learn* something from the game?" Roberts (1992b) contends that creating the right motivational climate includes communicating to athletes that one criterion of success is improvement, even in the practice setting, as opposed to relying on performance outcome as the only means to improve IM.

2. *Controlling function.* The question here is whether the athlete is participating in sport due to his or her own personal satisfaction and volition—internal, self-determining factors—or due to external factors, such as trying to satisfy others, receiving money, or earning a trophy. IM is closely associated with self-determination. Another controlling factor is *task involvement.* As indicated earlier, IM is higher if athletes are task-involved than if they are ego-involved. EM, on the other hand, is fostered if the athlete is *ego-involved.* At least in the early stages of sport competition, ego involvement is less likely to result in "fun" experiences and more likely to increase anxiety (perceived threat) before and during the contest.

Example: As discussed earlier, IM is not possible if Mom and Dad (or anyone else) attempt to coerce a child into competing in sport unless the child *wants* to compete. Coaches and parents of athletes of all ages should emphasize the fun aspect of playing and, for that matter, of practicing and staying in top physical condition. Ideally, competitors should view all aspects of their participation as enjoyable and see that they are capable of handling task demands. Playing sport should include the goal of improving skills.

3. *Information function.* Researchers call it *perceived ability,* and it is a very powerful factor in IM theory. Starting with White's theory of competence motivation in 1959, it has been well-known that feeling good about our skills, or at least about our ability to learn and improve skills over time for better performance, is a basic need. Hence, it is not surprising that almost central to IM is the perception of high ability. Athletes will rarely continue to engage in a task that they are not performing well, at least according to their own perception.

Example: One goal of every coach and parent, indeed, every teammate, should be to offer encouraging remarks regardless of the actual outcome. Positive feedback should reflect performance effort and improvement, as well as (or, in the case of unsuccessful outcomes, instead of) actual performance. Feedback can actually increase IM *if* it serves to reinforce the performer's feelings of competence, that is, to provide useful information. For instance, if the coach compliments the athlete about performing a skill or strategy correctly, or exhibits some other form of desirable behavior (e.g., cheering or supporting teammates), the athlete's feelings of competence will likely rise. A similar increase in IM can also follow negative feedback if it is accompanied by a positive message (e.g., "You still have to improve the speed of your throw, Carla, but I see nice improvement"). However, repeated negative feedback can reduce IM if the message indicates reduced competence, since the athlete feels less confident about his or her ability and performance success. The amount of pleasure received from the activity is markedly reduced.

Finally, receiving an award (e.g., a trophy, certificate, or any other form of tangible reward for participating) is another form of feedback and is common in youth sports. Awards can either reduce or increase IM depending on how athletes perceive the message. Awards are intrinsic motivators if athletes perceive them as representing their success (e.g., improved performance, contributions to the team, winning). The award, then, has positive information value; the information reflects high competence and achievement (Duda 1993). However, if athletes engage in sport primarily to receive an award, rather than for the fun, pleasure, and perceived competence sport brings, and if they expect and even depend upon receiving the award as one reason for engaging in sport, then the award is an extrinsic, not an intrinsic, motivator (Roberts 1993). One way to determine if the athlete is extrinsically or intrinsically motivated to compete in sport is to ask him or her this question: "If there were no awards given for being a member of this team—no trophies, no ribbons, no certificates, no prizes—would you still want to participate?" If the answer is "yes," then IM (pleasure, feelings of competence and achievement, and so on) is likely the primary incentive to participate. An answer of "no," on the other hand, would indicate that the individual's sport involvement is based on EM. One good example of the influence of awards on EM can be seen in Olympic athletes, who often claim that their motive to train is to receive a medal at the Games, then retire (discontinue their participation in competitive sport) immediately after the Games have ended.

The best suggestion for using the information function to increase IM is to keep the message positive. This means either (a) give token rewards, such as certificates or a small trophy to everyone on the team (even for different reasons, such as "best fielder," "best hustler," "best supportive team member," and so on) in response to a desirable action or attitude, or (b) offer verbal recognition to all players for their effort, but give special rewards to no single individual. The objective here is to avoid making rewards the reason to participate, and instead, to make rewards a reflection of success. As Duda (1993) concluded, "individuals are less likely to perform up to their potential and maintain their involvement in achievement activities when they do not feel competent" (p. 426). Therefore, it is very important that coaches and parents do everything they can to help athletes *avoid* feelings of low ability and to search for and recognize any form of desirable behavior exhibited by the participant. Some suggestions for improving IM are given in the box on page 92.

The Hierarchical Model of Intrinsic and Extrinsic Motivation

Dr. Robert Vallerand (1997) of the University of Quebec in Montreal, Quebec, Canada has constructed a model of intrinsic motivation with direct implications for sport that recognizes several factors that contribute to understanding human motivation. Though a full description of the model goes beyond the scope of this chapter, an overview of the model and its connections to sport will be provided here. For greater in-depth description of the model in a sport context, readers may consult two book chapters, Vallerand and Perreault (1999) and Vallerand and Rousseau (2001).

Vallerand and his colleagues make four primary points about the concept of motivation. First, humans are motivationally complex. Rather than talk about motivation, in general, to describe a person, there are several types of motivation that vary in *types and levels of generality*. An athlete can be intrinsically motivated toward academic or social environments (e.g., the gratification derived from learning or being with friends), yet be

Suggestions for Improving Intrinsic Motivation

Although coaching suggestions to improve motivation are offered later in the chapter, strategies to improve IM, in particular, are offered here.

- *"Guarantee" success.* This may sound difficult; little in life is guaranteed. Yet coaches can structure player activities, both individually and as a team, that can virtually ensure success. Lowering the height of a basket when taking shots (in youth sports), using improvement or effort as goals rather than performance outcomes or winning, or giving repeated opportunities to perform skills during practice are examples.

- *Give athletes a role in goal setting and decision making.* Feelings of self-control directly improve IM. Input from all athletes, particularly older or more experienced team members, to guide the development of younger, less skilled peers is an excellent way to improve feelings of team member satisfaction.

- *Praise performance, not personality or character.* The late child psychologist, Haim Ginott (1965, 1969, 1972), extolled the virtues of praise in both home and school settings. But at the same time, he urged parents and teachers to use praise correctly: to address the individual's *behaviors—his or her efforts and accomplishments*—that warranted praise, not the individual's character or personality. Correct methods to offer praise (and criticism) are extensively reviewed in Chapter 8. With respect to improving IM, praising a person's actions offers tangible and concrete information about competence. This, in turn, offers significant positive social reinforcement and enhances positive self-evaluation. In sport, the athlete feels more competent based on specific, performance-based information. The results

are improved perceived competence and participation satisfaction.

- *Facilitate perceptions of competence.* One approach to ensuring perceived competence is to set realistic goals. Rather than set unrealistic, lofty standards as the definition of success, use individual comparisons as more reliable sources of competence (Gill & Dzewaltowski 1988). These feelings promote IM. As Duda (1992) and Roberts (1993) suggest, the use of rewards may improve IM *if* the reward is interpreted as providing information related to feelings of self-competence at the task. Conversely, not receiving a reward due to low competence is predicted to decrease IM.

- *Use variable, not constant, positive reinforcement.* Behavioral psychologists (e.g., Rushall & Siedentop 1972) assert that the benefits of positive feedback are prolonged if performance is reinforced intermittently—on an interval basis—rather than constantly, perhaps after reaching a particular goal or demonstrating desirable performance. Variable reinforcement allows time for the effects of learning, practice, and training to be demonstrated as improvement, thereby improving IM.

- *Vary content and sequence of practice drills.* Boredom is one enemy of sport participation and IM because it is the antithesis of fun. The lack of fun is a primary reason for dropping out of sport. Practice sessions can be pleasant and exciting, filled with opportunities to learn, demonstrate new skills, engage in simulated competition, or even perform tasks for fun, such as obstacle or relay races, or playing different games for conditioning and variety. My college baseball team played soccer games every other week. Taking trips or engaging in nonsport

(continued)

Suggestions for Improving Intrinsic Motivation (continued)

tasks are other examples. For example, one college team went on a camping trip during a break in the season.

The source and type of evaluations received by the individual seem to dictate whether intrinsic or extrinsic motivation prevails. According to Halliwell (1980),

> rewards can either increase or decrease a person's intrinsic motivation. If . . . the controlling aspect is more salient, the rewards will decrease intrinsic motivation. But, if the informational aspect is more

salient and provides positive information about one's competence and self-determination, intrinsic motivation will be enhanced. . . . Receiving trophies should increase an athlete's intrinsic motivation because they provide him with information about his competence as an athlete. (However) . . . the controlling aspect of these rewards may be more salient than the informational dimension if the reward recipient perceives that his sports involvement is controlled by the pursuit of trophies and other tangible rewards (p. 87).

---

extrinsically motivated in sport (e.g., participating to receive a reward). A second issue is that motivation is both intrapersonal—reflecting a person's predisposition to feel motivated—and social—determined by the context, or setting, within which the person is motivated (e.g., sport, recreation, exercise) and by specific situations (e.g., asking the athlete to select his or her own exercise routine or strategy in the sport contest). Therefore, motivation can be evident at one of *three levels of generality: global, contextual, or situational.*

The third issue concerning motivation in Vallerand's model is that motivation leads to important consequences, each of which may occur at the three levels of generality. At the global level, an athlete may feel an inherent need to be physically active or to be competitive. At the contextual level, an athlete may feel intrinsically motivated (i.e., satisfied, competent) in certain types of sports but not others, or in a preferred context, such as low pressure, recreation focus rather than strongly competitive, not keeping score, or the absence of an organized league or team. Each of these contexts may bring great joy, happiness, and perceived success to an athlete who thrives under low-pressure, nonthreatening conditions. The athlete may not feel intrinsically motivated in the context of sport that requires a significant commitment to time, physical training, and pressure to succeed.

The fourth issue is that instances of situational intrinsic motivation (e.g., swimming a fast race, getting a base hit in pressure situations) will facilitate contextual intrinsic motivation (e.g., the sport in which high skills are demonstrated). Thus, if an athlete gets a hit with the bases loaded to win the game, the high competence shown in this situation will transfer into higher contextual intrinsic motivation toward the sport, in general. The model in sport posits that motivation results from an ongoing transaction between the athlete and the sport environment. If the athlete fails to see the connections between outcomes and actions, the athlete is neither intrinsically nor extrinsically motivated. The athlete is said to be nonmotivated, referred to in the model as *amotivated*. The amotivated

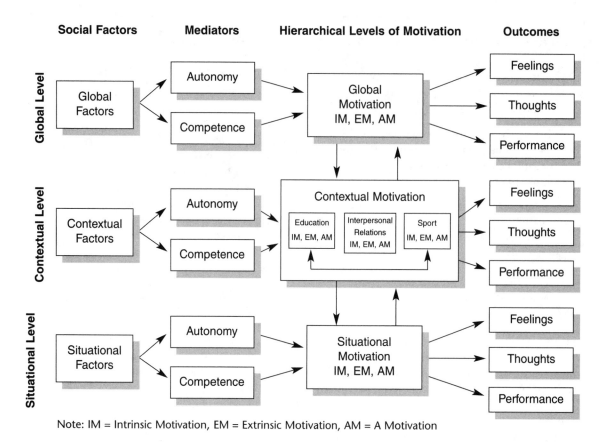

Note: IM = Intrinsic Motivation, EM = Extrinsic Motivation, AM = A Motivation

Figure 3.5 Adapted version of *The Hierarchical Model of Intrinsic and Extrinsic Motivation* (Vallerand & Perreault, 1999).

athlete perceives his or her actions as caused by forces out of his or her own control and begins to experience feelings of helplessness. Consequences are decreasingly positive from intrinsic motivation to amotivation. The result may be burnout, mental withdrawal, and eventually, quitting the activity. Figure 3.5 illustrates an *abbreviated* and *adapted* version of the hierarchical model of intrinsic and extrinsic motivation. The complete, published model is available in the chapters authored by Vallerand and Rousseau (2001), page 391, and Vallerand and Perreault (1999), page 195.

In summary, Dr. Vallerand and his colleagues have provided an interesting and insightful view of the complex dynamics that comprise and reflect IM and EM. The authors provide a conceptually solid framework within which to conduct future research on the model—Vallerand and Perreault (1999) offer several suggestions—and provide guidelines for ways to improve IM in different contexts and situations. *For example, perhaps one of the most salient implications for building IM is to ensure that athletes not only experience, but also are given proper recognition for, early success on an aspect of their participation.* IM begins in small, observable units, perhaps in executing a skill properly, completing a task that contributes to a desirable outcome, improving performance, being recognized for contribution to the team, and so on. Another implication is that some sports present conditions and physical demands that are more compatible with some individuals than with others. Not every child can demonstrate competence at every sport, nor meet high performance expectations in every situation with which he or she is presented. If parents want to encourage their child to compete in sport, they should allow the child to experiment with different sports and to learn various sports skills that will be compatible with the youngster's needs and psychological dispositions. For example, a child may not thrive under pressure, making team sports somewhat less threatening than individual sports. According to the hierarchical model, building IM takes *autonomy* (the youngster decides his or her area for participation, called self-determination), *competence* by receiving uplifting messages from parents, peers, and, most important, from coaches, and *social factors* (support from and positive interactions with friends and teammates with whom the athlete feels comfortable and secure). Perhaps heeding the implications of this model will reduce the extensive dropout rate in youth sport, a topic extensively addressed in Chapter 10.

The Science of Goal Setting

Goal setting is an aspect of motivation aimed at focusing the performer's effort and providing a means to monitor progress or success (Burton 1992). Not only do most quality competitors tend to set goals but they also use correct guidelines for doing so. Elite athletes correctly set higher, more challenging, yet more realistic goals than their less skilled counterparts (Orlick & Partington 1986). Orlick (1986), who based his findings on personal interviews with highly successful Canadian athletes, asserts that when setting goals, athletes should "dream a little. . . . Goals that are unimaginable are unachievable—not because they really are unachievable, but because they were never dreamt of" (p. 6). Elite competitors do not tend to sell themselves short.

The effectiveness of goal setting was examined statistically by Kyllo and Landers (1995). The researchers used meta-analysis, a statistical technique that analyzes the results of numerous studies simultaneously to obtain an overall (generalized) result. Based on the outcomes of 36 scientific studies, the researchers concluded that setting even moderate goals led to significant performance improvement in performing sport skills or other motor tasks. Performance was optimal when goals were (1) set in absolute (observable) terms, (2) short term as well as long term, (3) set with the participation of the subjects, and (4) made public.

According to Burton (1992), every goal includes two basic components: direction and amount or quality of the product. By direction, Burton means focusing one's behavior. Amount or quality indicates a minimal standard of performance that is anticipated and desired. Thus, goals have been used primarily to motivate the person to take direct action by focusing attention, increasing effort and intensity, and encouraging new strategies to solve problems and foster persistence, especially after experiencing failure.

Goals have also been used to describe personality traits. This role implies dispositions for participating in an activity based on an underlying motive for what the person wants to attain (Burton 1992). Because the tendency is stable and long term rather than short term, while changing from situation to situation, this disposition has been referred to as *goal orientation*. For example, as described earlier, some individuals are motivated by a high need to achieve and engage in achievement-oriented situations (Nicholls 1984). Burton (1992) links the dispositions of need achievement with goal orientation in his generation of the concept of *goal-setting styles* (GSS).

The foundation of GSS is that (1) perceived competence or ability is the critical factor responsible for motivational behaviors, and (2) a person's goal orientations are thought to influence how perceived ability develops and how it affects achievement behavior (such as the need to become involved in and excel at a sport). He further contends that individuals possess one of two goal orientations, performance and outcome.

A *performance* goal orientation reflects an athlete's increased perceived ability, mastery of new tasks, or skill improvement. Success is defined in terms of internal ("self-referent") standards; success is a function of comparing present with previous performance. The process is more important than the final product. An *outcome* goal orientation concerns maintaining positive views of one's ability and avoiding negative judgments about one's ability. This is accomplished by proving, validating, or documenting one's skill level, typically through social comparison processes. Winning or positive social comparisons are essential in order to maintain high perceived ability. Thus, task mastery and improvement are only a means to an end (winning), not ends themselves (Weinberg 1992). The challenge to coaches and parents of athletes is to determine the athlete's individual needs and preferences and then provide some goal-setting strategies that meet these needs.

According to scientific literature on goal setting (see Weinberg 1992, Burton et al. 2001, and Gould 2001 for excellent reviews of this literature), goals may be applied both in practice and during competition for improving self-confidence, and in both short-term and long-term forms. Athletes should use the following goal-setting strategies:

1. *Use performance, not outcome.* Goals should be performance-based rather than dependent on the contest's outcome. Goals that relate to winning (an outcome goal) are not under the athlete's control. This reduces the purposes of goal setting, which is to focus effort and improve motivation. As Orlick (1986) claims, "If you start to assume responsibility for what is beyond your control you are inviting trouble. . . . You should assume responsibility for only that which is within your direct control" (p. 8). *Good examples of performance goals:* (a) "I will relax and feel confident before the meet"; (b) "I will make contact with over 50 percent of the pitches thrown." *Poor examples of performance goals:* (a) "We will win the game"; (b) "I will be a starter on the team." Neither of these goals is under the player's control and, therefore, will more likely undermine motivation and focused effort.

   Another advantage of performance-based goals is that they are observable and measurable. How would a competitor know if a goal was attained—if performance was successful—unless the executed movements could be seen or measured? In this way, meeting goals becomes motivating to the performer and forms the basis to define future goals.

2. *Be realistic.* If one purpose of a goal is to provide incentive, then it has to be within the athlete's perceived reach. Otherwise the performer will tend to view the goal as unmeaningful—perhaps even reduce effort due to feelings of helplessness or discard the goal altogether. One way to be sure a goal is realistic is to base it on past experience. The athlete's recent history of performance should indicate what he or she will be able to do in the near future.

3. *Negotiate.* One of my students was a collegiate swimmer who became despondent after her coach told her to swim at a speed that, in the swimmer's view, was totally unrealistic. She became so depressed and upset about this unattainable goal that she could not continue to give a 100 percent effort. If her coach would have negotiated the goal based on past performance with input from the performer, the goal-setting strategy would have had its intended benefits.

Many coaches believe that athletes should be involved in the setting of future performance expectations (Mechikoff & Kozar 1983). They set goals with their athletes individually, and then the athletes set their own personal goals in the presence of the coach. This approach makes sense. If the players refuse to identify with a goal (presumably set by an external agent such as the coach or a parent), then it may not be supported; the player will tend not to feel committed to attaining it, and the necessary effort to meet the expectations will not be made.

4. *Make goals challenging.* Top athletes enjoy—even need—a challenge in order to reach their potential. The suggestion that goals should be realistic and negotiated between player and coach does not mean that they should be easy to attain. On the contrary, goals that are viewed by the performer as too easy do not increase motivation.

5. *Make goals specific to the type and demands of the task.* Challenging goals are even more effective when they are specific (Weinberg 1992). Asking athletes to improve their performance speed by 5 seconds, a particularly difficult goal in all-out tasks such as swimming, is more effective than "do your best" or "try to improve" types of goals. In one study, Anshel et al. (1992) found that setting specific, difficult goals—an improvement of 100 percent on a juggling task—markedly increased subjects' intrinsic motivation, as compared to setting easy or no goals.

O'Block and Evans (1984) have developed a formula called *interval goal setting* (IGS) that allows the competitor to derive goals that are challenging and based on objective criteria—the person's past performance scores. Guesswork should not be the basis for setting proper goals. An example using the IGS model is shown in Figure 3.6 on page 98. O'Block and Evans used the last five performances of a swimmer performing the 50-yard freestyle. The times were 26.48, 26.43, 27.12, 27.82, and 26.69.

A = 26.91 (average of 5 performances)

B = 26.43 (best time out of 5 performances)

C = 0.48 (difference between average and best time) (26.91 – 26.43)

D = B (26.43) (lower boundary of interval; performer's best time out of 5 performances)

E = 25.95 (interval midpoint) (26.43 – 0.48)

F = 25.47 (upper interval boundary) (25.95 – 0.48)

The authors contend that the interval midpoint (E) is realistically higher than the performer's best attempt (D). The upper limit (F) of the interval gives the competitor a target for exceptional performance. The result of any attempt that falls within the interval's boundaries can be called successful no matter what the contest's outcome.

If higher scores are better, as with frequency/accuracy (such as the number of contacts or points) or length (the shot put or pole vault, for instance) rather than speed, the IGS model is adjusted in these ways:

Average	Previous Best	Midpoint	Upper Boundary
A	D	E	F
26.91	26.43	25.95	25.47

Where *speed* is the criterion:

    A = Average over the last 5 performances
    B = Best time within the last 5 performances
    C = Difference between average and best performance (A minus B)
    D = Lower boundary of interval
    E = Interval midpoint (D minus C)
    F = Upper interval boundary (E minus C)

Figure 3.6 The IGS model, in which speed of performance is the criterion.

$C = B - A$ (the difference between the best and average scores)
$E = D + C$ (the interval midpoint)
$F = E + C$ (the upper interval boundary)

6. *Ensure goal "ownership."* The concept of setting goals based on previous performance appears to form a rational basis for determining reasonable, yet challenging expectations about future performance and is understandably appealing. However, a few words of caution about the IGS are warranted. First, the validity of any model is tested by scientific examination; at present, there is an absence of published research that supports the IGS. This is an ominous sign, considering that the IGS was first published in 1984. The second note of caution focuses on the exclusive use of performance outcome to determine success or failure. As noted earlier, effort and improvement are other determinants of success, in addition to the end result. Goals also have value when they reflect performance in practice settings or mastery of subskills and learning, rather than exclusively on competition outcomes. The IGS excludes these other factors. A third limitation is the model's reliance on optimal levels of achievement (e.g., the "best" performance level), which may have been due to luck or to a favorable environment or situation. Skill may have had little or nothing to do with the outcome, yet the IGS assumes that the high performance level reflects skill mastery and performance consistency. This is especially true when performing tasks "all-out," in which speed is essential. For this reason, the likelihood of *not* meeting the goals provided by the IGS may be quite high. Thus, the IGS may be used as one vehicle to determine future performance, but not as the only measure. In addition, the coach should directly communicate IGS results to the athlete, rather than merely posting the individual's outcome in the absence of the coach's interpretation, instructional messages, feedback, and emotional support. Goals are motivating when athletes have input into their development. The athlete will then feel accountable for meeting the goal. Goals that are set by outside sources, such as coaches and parents, may not have the same incentive value because the competitor may not endorse, or "own," the goal.

7. *Make goals short term and long term.* Elite athletes know at what level they want their performance to be on both a long-term (several weeks or months away) and short-term (today, tomorrow, or next week's performance) basis. The short-term goal serves the purposes of providing immediate incentive to perform at optimal levels and, predictably, to experience early success. It is important for athletes to feel that their efforts will soon lead to the achievement of some desirable outcome or that success was due to such effort. Short-term goals allow us to meet these needs.

Examples of short-term goals used by top competitors include to run or swim at a particular speed, lift a particular weight in power lifting or weight training, make a given number of tackles, or score a predetermined number of points.

Long-term goals allow a competitor to evaluate the quality of his or her performance when compared with (1) goals that were established or outcomes that occurred before the season or last season, and (2) the performance of opponents. Ideally, a series of short-term goals should lead to a realistic, yet challenging long-term performance goal. Here's an example:

Long-term goal: I will bat .300 at the end of this baseball season. *Series of short-term goals:* (1) I will practice my batting 30 minutes at each practice at least three days a week. (2) 1 will make solid bat contact with at least 50 percent of the pitched balls. Other examples of short-term goals based on subcomponents of skilled tasks are listed in the box on page 100 (Locke & Latham 1985).

8. *Teach goal-setting techniques to coaches and athletes.* Despite frequent use of the term "goal" by athletes and their coaches, it is false to assume that these individuals are aware of proper goal-setting techniques. Gould (2001) reviewed several studies in which researchers examined athletes' actual goal-setting practices. Among the findings was that many athletes rate their goal setting strategy as only moderately effective, and were least successful with goals that were set too high (difficult). Goals of moderate difficulty were reported as most effective and rewarding. One important feature of athletes who reported more effective goal setting was their use of different types of goals (e.g., practice and competition, fitness and skill development, short term and long term) and more frequent use of goal setting than athletes reporting less effective goal setting. Gould concluded that "coaches and athletes underutilize goal setting and need further goal-setting education" (p. 193).

Team Goals

Carron and Hausenblas (1998) conducted an extensive review of literature on the extent to which athletes set team goals in addition to individual goals, whether individual and team goals were compatible, and the effectiveness of team goal setting on individual and team sports performance. One of their conclusions was that "coaches and athletes do not tend to establish team goals that are specific and measurable" (p. 273). This would mean that goals do not have their intended favorable result on team performance. The authors contend that "team goal setting can serve to improve performance in targeted indices" (p. 274). Thus, if one goal of a basketball team is to increase field goal shooting percentage, it is likely that the motivation, effort, teammate support, and practice time devoted to this aspect of the game will increase, and that performance in this area will improve. The authors also warn, however, that sometimes pursuing

Examples of Goals for Subcomponents of Skills Tasks

Tennis

10 backhands in a row down the line

10 volleys in a row alternating left and right corners

5 first serves in a row in left third of service court; 5 in middle third; 5 in right third

5 returns of serve in a row deep to the ad court

Football

Wide receiver: catch every ball thrown to me accurately (reaches my hands)

Defensive back: 5 interceptions in a row with receiver using preannounced route; do not allow a receiver to get behind me

Kicker: 10 field goals in a row from 40-yard line

Any defensive player: make at least 5 tackles per game

Baseball

Infielder: 10 grounders in a row fielded without error

Outfielder: 20 fly balls caught on the run without error

Hitter: 5 curve balls in a row hit out of infield; make solid contact with pitch on at least 3 at bats per game

Basketball

15 out of 20 foul shots

10 rebounds per game

5 of 10 jump shots

5 out of 10 jump shots from 40 to 50 feet

9 of 10 successful passes to teammates

Soccer

10 shots on goal from 30 feet or longer

Accurate passing percentage of 90%

Field or Ice Hockey

Goalie: stop 10 of 15 shots from 20 feet

Forward: pass successfully 8 out of 10 times to open player

Defense: do not allow offensive player to skate/run past me

Lacrosse

Similar to soccer and hockey

Golf

8 of 10 drives over 200 yards and landing on fairway

2 putts (or less) on the green at every hole

---

individual goals detracts from team goals. If, for instance, a player's goal is to maintain a game average of 15 points in basketball, the player might be less willing to make the effort to play defense, or more likely to take the shot rather than pass to an "open" teammate. Group goal setting appears to be optimally effective when the tasks are highly interdependent. Sports such as basketball, field hockey, ice hockey, and soccer are examples. In such cases, group goals are likely to enhance player cooperation and communication as opposed to individual goal setting.

Carron and Hausenblas also contend that individual and team goals may be not only compatible, but also actually mutually beneficial. Remaining with the basketball example, individual goals could be set for different team members that improve the chance of meeting the team's goal (e.g., the number of shots taken, number of rebounds, time of ball possession). Different individual goals might include points scored for the team's best shooter, number of assists for the team's playmaker, number of offensive and defensive rebounds for the team's forwards and center, and so on.

Finally, the authors reported on several studies that examined consequences of team goal setting. First, Carron and Hausenblas note that team goals are effective under practice conditions as well as in actual competition. Among other findings of previous studies was that player satisfaction with team goals was higher with improved clarity of the goals, and when the players believed that the goal could be achieved. In addition, teams that possessed better task and social cohesion (discussed in Chapter 7) felt greater satisfaction with the team's goals. This favorable outcome was enhanced further when athletes perceived that team goals produced improved performance. Finally, the players' participation in team goal setting was related to improved task and social team cohesion. It is important, then, for coaches to allow team members to have a primary role in setting challenging, yet realistic, performance-based goals to obtain the optimal benefits of team goal setting.

How *Not* to Motivate Athletes

Earlier in this chapter, examples were given of how coaches typically "motivate" athletes, using tactics that make sport psychologists cringe. Many of these techniques do not have their intended effect, especially with younger participants, and many generate only short-term incentives for athletes. In the long run, their influence may actually wane or have the opposite of their intended effect. Where's the common sense? Do people tend to respond positively to abusive treatment? Do they give optimal effort on behalf of insensitive, unpleasant leaders? Over the long term, don't people usually respond with more enthusiasm and energy toward others who have earned their respect and trust?

The following is my list of 10 of the most common, but erroneous, beliefs and practices used by sport leaders (professionals and volunteers) in their attempts to motivate athletes. They are myths because coaches use these techniques and believe in their effectiveness, yet an array of sport psychology literature indicates that they tend to hinder more than improve motivation.

Myth #1: Exercise for Punishment. "OK, Jones, that will cost you four laps for being late to practice." "If you guys had won on Saturday, practice would have been over. But you didn't, so we're running an extra 10 laps." Many athletes (and physical education students) are very familiar with perhaps the most common form of punishment used by coaches and gym teachers—physical exercise. Whether it's push-ups, sprinting, pull-ups, or jogging, exercise has been used for years as a tool to punish and control the behavior of students and athletes. Here are three reasons why this approach should be *avoided*:

1. If coaches want their athletes to be in good physical condition, athletes should not be taught to associate physical activity with punishment. Isn't it more desirable to promote the enjoyment and advantages of staying in shape?
2. The purpose of punishing a person is to prevent the recurrence of certain undesirable behaviors; therefore, the punishment should be an unpleasant experience that is understood to be a direct consequence of the inappropriate behavior. Don't athletes, in general, especially children, actually enjoy being physically active?

Nonparticipation in competition would probably be a more effective form of punishment for those who have failed to train appropriately.

3. This technique does not motivate the individual. The person is not likely to behave more positively or to have more incentive after performing the required activity.

Myth #2: The Pregame Pep Talk. Age, skill level, the type of sport, and the athlete's personality jointly dictate how an athlete will respond to various pre-event communication styles. Some participants prefer a boisterous, aggressive pregame talk, but others want as little noise and distraction, verbal and nonverbal, as possible. Some coaches use the occasion to review game strategies. The purpose and content of the pregame talk is of less importance than most leaders think, especially at the professional level. Of more importance is the emotional tone and the level of arousal elicited by the message (see Chapter 5). For the most part, game preparation, including the "mental game," occurs at practice.

Myth #3: "Cut 'em Down to Build 'em Up." Most players are uncomfortable hearing the coach's derogatory remarks about opponents, for several reasons: (1) The remark might not hold true in the upcoming event since the opponent may prove far better than the coach has indicated. (2) If the opponent *is* poorly skilled and the coach's team still loses, the athletes will feel more humiliated than if they lost to a more skilled opponent. If the coach's team wins, they may attribute the victory to an easy task, which is not very reinforcing. Athletes may want to think that their success was due to their skills and effort, not because the opponent was weak. Past performance might not be a good predictor of the future outcome for this opponent. (3) It's unrealistic to think that an opponent has weaknesses but no strengths. Every competitor is capable of winning, and every athlete wants to know the strength of that capability. And (4) athletes typically have a great deal of empathy and mutual respect toward one another. Some athletes believe that criticizing another sport competitor is stepping on common ground; it's unethical and disloyal.

Myth #4: "Our Goal Is to Win."   In recent years, much has been written in the professional literature about proper goal-setting techniques. One finding that makes most coaches uncomfortable is that winning should not be a competitor's primary goal. All sport participants want to win. But focusing on the individual's *performance* rather than exclusively on the contest's outcome is more productive. Researchers are convinced that a goal such as "I want to win 10 games" will not be as effective as "I will make 60 percent of my free throws."

Myth #5: Treating Team Players Differently. Athletes become incensed when the coach is not consistent in his or her interactions with all team members. I asked a few former successful professional athletes—Jean Beliveau (ice hockey), Rusty Staub (baseball), and Johnny Robinson (Canadian football)—what single trait stands out in their minds about the best coaching they've experienced. They all agreed that the ability to treat everyone with the same respect and maturity was most important. They said that favoritism and inconsistency as coaching behaviors did more to *demotivate* players than anything else.

Myth #6: "If They Don't Complain, They're Happy."   Coaches often assume that a quiet player is contented. Not necessarily! An unhappy player may be consumed by his or her own unpleasant thoughts. Instead of focusing on the actions and tendencies of opponents and remembering skills and strategies, dissatisfied players are thinking about issues that interfere with preparing for and participating in the contest. It's wrong, therefore, to assume that team members who say nothing to the coach in fact have nothing to say.

Myth #7: "What Do Athletes Know, Anyway?"   No one can argue with the claim that most coaches have a sound knowledge base about the technical aspects of their sport. By the time a person becomes the head coach of a team, he or she tends to feel "in control." But just as good teachers stay in touch with learners throughout the skill acquisition period, researchers (e.g., Fisher et al. 1982) have found that good coaches monitor and communicate constructively with their athletes during practices and games. Is there a reason why a certain play didn't work? Does the other team have a certain weakness or tendency that we can use to our advantage? Do we have certain weaknesses that we need to work on immediately? Was the official correct in calling that penalty? Why not ask the players for at least some of the answers?

Myth #8: The Postgame Rampage.   The contest is over, and the athletes are emotionally and physically drained. At this time, the coach sets the mood in the locker room. What the coach has to say and how he or she says it will leave a lasting emotional impression on the athlete. Certainly successful outcomes of competition should be reinforced with verbal recognition and adulation reflecting what went right. A far more difficult, but effective, task is to behave in a rational, mature, and professional manner after losing the contest. As discussed earlier, this is not the time to discuss the details of strategy or to have a temper tantrum. The athletes may be too exhausted to absorb technical information.

Myth #9: The Napoleon Complex.   Some team leaders put a lot of energy into reinforcing the "boss" role with loud, aggressive, and often angry remarks. Coaches who motivate athletes successfully, however, are perceived as secure, knowledgeable, intuitive, and sensitive. They know how to share their power so that all members of the team (including players and assistants) have a sense of ownership and responsibility for team activities and outcomes. Coaches who appear to thrive on and enjoy the power of their position are likely to be personally insecure and lacking in self-confidence.

For example, I personally knew a new head university baseball coach who was well-liked as an assistant with the team for two years. He had a friendly manner and a low-key, sincere style of communication. Soon after becoming head coach, however, he became aggressive, demanding, and hostile. He threatened to dismiss any player who committed even the slightest infraction. Conditioning exercises were grueling. In fact, he told the team of his intention to "weed out the weak links" on the team. His general communication style went abruptly from humanistic to autocratic. This coach greatly disappointed his players. They became increasingly depressed and began to lose interest in the team's success. The team's low morale was accompanied by a poor win-loss record. A month after the season, the coach resigned to become an assistant coach at another, smaller school.

Myth #10: Fear! Some coaches want their athletes to fear them so that they can easily induce their athletes' arousal as well as improve and maintain their motivation. Athletes who view their coach as an authoritarian or father figure are particularly susceptible to being afraid of a coach who uses fiery speeches, threats, harsh criticism, and insults to psych them up. Fear is relatively easy to bring about in subordinates. But, in fact, coaches who are perceived as threatening invoke anxiety rather than motivation in athletes. And fear breeds resentment and disloyalty toward the coach. As British writer Thomas Fuller once said, "He that fears you present will hate you absent." Thus, fear is likely to diminish the athletes' motivation to provide optimal effort and to persist at the activity.

Strategies for Motivating Athletes and Teams

Former Oakland Raiders (U.S.) football coach John Madden said in an interview, "I only had three rules for my players: Be on time, pay attention, and play like heck when I tell you to." Madden had a profound influence on his team because his demands were realistic, focused on game-related tasks, and sincere. He had tremendous player loyalty. Thus, the challenge for any coach is to find the goals of each athlete—what he or she really wants from participation—and to convince the individual of what he or she must do to reach them.

The ability of a coach to affect the behaviors, feelings, and attitudes of the competitors begins with the coach–athlete relationship. Some of the most important ingredients of this relationship, derived from Hoehn (1983) and Fuoss and Troppmann (1981), include:

- Communicating effectively
- Teaching skills
- Rewarding players with praise and encouragement
- Dwelling on strengths instead of weaknesses
- Appearing organized and in control
- Inserting occasional times for fun and humor
- Developing mutual respect between coach and athlete
- Knowing when to take a break and when to give the athletes a day off
- Developing leadership skills among players
- Supporting the athletes after errors and losses as well as upon making good plays and winning
- Setting limits fairly and consistently on inappropriate behaviors
- Not embarrassing, intimidating, or criticizing the character of an athlete

Some effective techniques for motivating athletes to reach their potential, that is, the "dos" of coaching success, include the following:

Get to Know Each Performer. Knowing each team member starts with learning and using each athlete's first name. This promotes trust between coach and athlete. Players who are addressed by their first names become less intimidated by the authority figure. The nonverbal message is "the coach knows and recognizes me. He may even like me." The next step is developing a relationship with the athlete that supersedes the sport arena. This does not include socializing with the players (many of whom are uncomfortable spending their "free time" with their coach), but rather, means making an effort to listen to the players' feelings on team-related issues, discussing topics unrelated to the team (e.g., academic experiences, movies, or current events), and showing a genuine concern for the athlete *as a person*.

Plan It Out. Influencing the thoughts and actions of others doesn't usually happen by itself. Effective coaches anticipate using certain techniques that enhance player motivation. Examples include structuring a practice session to improve team morale, using a particular strategy during the contest that was recommended by the players, building self-confidence, bringing in a guest speaker to address the team, taking a break from the daily grind of practice, changing the content of practice sessions, and attending to injured athletes to let all team members know that no one is forgotten and that everyone is appreciated for his or her contribution.

Agree on Future Directions and Actions. American philosopher Eric Hoffer said, "The only way to predict the future is to have power to shape the future." The coach's ability to create and plan for the athletes' future aspirations is dictated by his or her ability to convince players of two things: (1) the worthiness of these aspirations and (2) the athletes' ability to act upon and to achieve them. In order to move in the same direction, the performers must be able to share the coach's vision.

Develop Skills. There is no greater motivator in sport than success. But success does not happen accidentally. It requires constant effort and determination as shown in Figure 3.7. If coaches expect athletes to learn skills, improve their performance, and eventually succeed, they *must* teach skills and strategies.

Figure 3.7 One goal of every coach should be to recognize at least one contribution that each player brings to the team—and to personally inform that player of it.

Everybody Needs Recognition. The need for prestige, status, dominance, attention, importance, appreciation, and recognition are firmly based in human nature; they underlie human motivation (Weinberg & Gould 1995). These needs may even be greater in elite athletes than in nonathletes (Cratty 1983; Vanek & Cratty 1970). An occasional pat on the back, literally and figuratively, gives the athletes deserved recognition and a reason for continuing their efforts.

Discipline Is Not a Four-Letter Word. There's nothing wrong with setting limits on inappropriate behaviors. In fact, many athletes test the coach's ability and willingness to carry out team policies and disciplinary measures. Testing is the individual's way of making sure that the adult guardian (e.g., the parent, coach, or teacher), cares about him or her. According to Ginott (1965), "They feel more secure when they know the borders of permissible action." In fact, as Ginott states, "When a [person] is allowed behavior that he knows should not be tolerated, [the person's] anxiety mounts" (pp. 114–115). The coach who sets limits and responds quickly and appropriately when tested communicates sincerity and credibility.

Perceptions Are Everything.   As an old adage says, "An ounce of image is worth a pound of performance." The athlete's perception of his or her role on the team, the interpretation of a coach's actions and statements, and other personally held views are reflections of "the truth" through the athlete's eyes. For example, an athlete may attribute a lack of playing time to a poor relationship with the coach. "The coach just doesn't like me," he or she might complain. If an athlete feels that the coach "does not like me," it's this perception that the coach must react to rather than how the coach really feels. This is especially important if the athlete's perception is wrong. Coaches must deal with reality as their players interpret it.

Make It Fun.   Undoubtedly, the coach wants to win, but it's dangerous to produce a team climate that is continuously submerged in a sea of hard work, seriousness, and redundant, time-consuming preparation. In human motivation, more is not always better. Having fun and adding some humor promotes intrinsic motivation while it reduces the onset of mental fatigue.

Consistency and Sensitivity Are Signs of Strength.   Coaches, male and female, should exhibit similar behaviors and attitudes whether interacting with male or female participants. Crying, disclosing personal feelings, and showing aggression should be perceived as normal types of expression for all athletes. Motivation is also an emotion that is virtually blind to gender differences. All coaches, male and female, are more effective when they encourage male and female athletes to share feelings and exhibit sensitivity (Officer & Rosenfeld 1985).

Winning Is Not the Only Thing.   At least it shouldn't be. There are so many experiences in sport to feel good about. It's sad to think that the only pleasant experiences are associated with the final outcome. Why dismiss opportunities for satisfaction just because the final outcome was not in the participant's favor? Given the rarity with which most teams win consistently, total reliance on victory as the sole criterion for success in sport will make a lot of athletes—and coaches—feel very unsuccessful. The performer's effort and improvement are examples of other reasons to "celebrate" success.

Beware of the Self-Fulfilling Prophecy.   As indicated earlier, it's important to perceive and respond to each athlete in a manner that promotes confidence in his or her capability. Not only do coaches with higher expectations of their players elicit better performance but they also offer more—and better—instruction (Horn & Lox 1993). To paraphrase the poet Longfellow, athletes should be judged by what they are capable of doing, not on what they have already done.

Motivating the Child Athlete

Children are not miniature adults. They participate in sport for different reasons than older competitors do and, therefore, do not have the same needs as those of more mature athletes. Older players have superior skills, are better at coping with sport-related stress, and consider winning to be a primary goal of competition. Children, on the other hand, often do not have adequate sport skills, are easily upset by and unable to cope with the pressures put upon them by impatient and insensitive adults, and play sports to have fun and to learn new skills (Gould 1984). Chapter 10 includes specific strategies for motivating child athletes.

Motivating the Nonstarter

Making the starters happy and keeping them motivated is easy compared to having the same effect on the substitutes. The psychological problems that beset the "bench-warmer" include frustration, alienation, futility, and a loss of self-confidence (Tutko & Bruns 1976). Ultimately, the coach's task is to help every substitute feel that he or she is an important team member. Group identity depends on the coach's ability to define and to communicate each person's role in the group and on the athlete's perception of his or her role as an important contribution to team success. Motivation will be a natural outcome of this process.

How can coaches motivate athletes who have limited playing time? This is where coaching really *is* a science. First (and foremost), avoid labeling anyone a "substitute." Every athlete should feel that he or she is contributing to the team's welfare. This means that starters should not have more privileges than substitutes, even though the coach may put more time into preparing the starting team. A second important suggestion is to provide nonstarters with opportunities to learn and demonstrate skills, particularly under practice conditions that simulate actual competition. No one should feel that he or she is "wasting time" practicing for the contest, a frequent complaint of nonstarters. Such opportunities should include a liberal dose of positive verbal and nonverbal cues that indicate admiration, respect, and trust in the nonstarter's ability. Many substitutes erroneously feel that the reason they don't play is because their coach doesn't like them. This is particularly destructive for athletes who want and need a positive relationship with their coach.

In general, strategies for motivating nonstarters should aim toward the following:

- giving them feelings of importance to the team
- indicating that they are contributing in some meaningful way
- providing them with opportunities to learn, improve, and eventually demonstrate their skills in competitive situations
- promoting positive and challenging future aspirations

The coach should never be dishonest about his or her intentions or in evaluations. Examples of dishonesty in coaching, intentional or unintentional, include promising a date on which an athlete may enter the contest and then reneging on that promise, giving verbal praise of skills without supporting these statements with more playing time, and being less than honest about the reasons why an individual is not playing more often or starting (e.g., "We need a strong bench"). One possible outcome of dishonesty will be to reduce the player's willingness to remain a team member. Just because the playing time of nonstarters is limited at present doesn't mean that they won't eventually perform at acceptable levels and, perhaps, even start. That may be sooner than coaches think if a starting player is injured. Substitutes should be treated as potential first-string players.

Team Motivation

Clearly, promoting friendship, trust, mutual admiration, respect, and harmony on the team is important. Common sense dictates that athletes who like one another will also tend to support one another. They will be more motivated to be part of a group that meets the goals of its members. Some recommendations for the coach are discussed below.

Compatible Group and Personal Goals.   Be sure that the individual's goals are compatible with team goals. The coach should first discuss the team strategy before players develop their own personal goals so that their performance expectations will be realistic and compatible with the team strategies and aspirations. Agreement on team objectives will enhance the individual's incentive to develop and attempt to meet personal goals.

Agreement on Team Goals.   The team should feel a sense of ownership toward group goals. Even when group goals are initially set by the coach, the competitors must identify with them, or they will hardly be motivated to achieve them. Coaches should explain the basis and reasons for group goals and what it will take to reach them. Although the athletes' "permission" to have these goals is not needed, the coach should allow players to express their feelings about the goals.

Dealing with Group Heterogeneity.   Teams will usually be comprised of athletes with different needs, different ethnic and racial backgrounds, and different personalities. The coach's role is to ensure that dissimilarity among team members does not distract from the team's purpose and erode group solidarity. Whether team members spend their free time together may be unimportant, but it is quite important that all members get along in preparing for and participating in the contest.

Awareness of Role. One way to improve the quality of team interaction is to be sure that every member is aware of his or her role in the group (Carron 1984a). For instance, a high school baseball coach realized that one of his athletes was not a good hitter but had excellent speed on the base paths. This individual was very proud to be known as the team's leading substitute runner.

Planning Interaction. To prevent cliques and social isolation on the team, Carron (1984b) suggests the use of mandatory interaction. The objective of this approach is to ensure personal communication among team members. Examples of preplanned events and situations that require players to interact include the rotation of roommates, preselection of seating arrangements at team meals and on road trips, equal representation in team leadership positions such as co-captains and committee heads, and the organization of team committees to serve various specifically defined roles. A player without at least one friend on the team is usually not a happy participant.

Allowing for Team–Coach Communication. Only the naive coach thinks that the absence of a player's complaint automatically signals satisfaction. Not dealing with unpleasant issues is to pretend that they don't exist. Nothing can be further from the truth. Players who are bothered by certain feelings are less able to concentrate on contest-related tasks, especially in the mental preparation for competition. Providing some vehicle to voice these concerns is healthy because it facilitates confronting issues and dealing with them in a constructive manner to everyone's satisfaction. It's important to "clear the air."

Before the Contest. Pep talks were discussed earlier. The issue here is what to say to the team before competing that will provide incentive regardless of the anticipated outcome. According to Yukelson, an underdog (i.e., an athlete or team widely predicted to lose the contest) might be addressed this way (1984, p. 234):

> *If my team were a decided underdog, I would provide information that we are not as bad as people claim, and that the opposing team has weaknesses and can be beat if we play to our potential. If our team were a decided favorite, I would want to place the probability of success at the intermediate range of difficulty in order to avoid complacency. I would focus on our opponent's strengths rather than our own strengths. Thus, I would provide proximal short-term goals for the team as an incentive or standard of excellence to shoot for.*

After the Contest. Motivating athletes does not end on the field or court. The coach's comments after the contest will affect team motivation. Most athletes recommend that coaches just "be themselves and speak sincerely." Athletes are uncomfortable with hostile tirades following a loss. At this time, an honest, but sensitive, reflection of the team's performance should be offered. Postgame speeches should be kept short. Usually the players are tired, sweaty, and generally not mentally receptive to a long, drawn-out monologue. The coach's postgame talk also should be honest and constructive and always end with a positive statement.

SUMMARY

Motivation is both an art and a science. The art of motivating others means having a communication style—verbal and nonverbal—that offers a mixture of credibility, knowledge, and sensitivity. Associated with motivating athletes are numerous myths and practices of coaches that have been handed down over the years with no scientific basis. Often, these techniques do more harm than good. Intimidation, threats, physical abuse, and hostile criticism are examples. Motivation is also a science in that the leader must know when to say something and how to say it.

Sources of motivation may be derived from personal factors, situational factors, or a combination of both, called the interaction view. The personal view holds that motivation reflects the individual's characteristics, such as individual desire or a high need to achieve. The situational view is that motivation is fostered primarily by situational characteristics, such as anticipating or experiencing excitement, achievement, and satisfaction. According to the interaction view, the combination of personal and situational characteristics best predicts and describes motivation.

Different types of motivation have been identified. Achievement motivation, intrinsic and extrinsic motivation, and competence motivation are based on a person's strong desire to achieve and to deal effectively with his or her environment for a prolonged period of time. Motivation models by Deci and Ryan (1985) and Vallerand and his colleagues illustrate the numerous factors that underlie intrinsic motivation in sport, and suggests how team leader athletes can implement strategies to enhance intrinsic motivation. Child athletes, nonstarters, and teams require various motivational techniques of which the coach should become aware.

Finally, one effective method of motivating athletes is to set goals. For best results, goals should be challenging yet realistic, based on previous performance, both short term and long term, performance-based rather than outcome-based, and observable and measurable. Coaches and athletes should work jointly to set goals and, based on ongoing assessments of performance, should agree to alter them if necessary.

REVIEW QUESTIONS

1. The definition of motivation includes key words or phrases that have implications for athletic behavior. For each of the following, explain what the coach should do to promote the athlete's motivation: (a) direction of behavior, (b) selectivity of behavior, (c) persistence, (d) goal achievement.

2. Describe five unique characteristics of athletes who have a high need to achieve. What approaches should a coach take to motivate athletes with high need achievement? In contrast, what tactics might be used with low need achievers?

3. Do you agree with White that the need for competence as a motivator is inherent? Defend your answer. How does Harter expand White's theory? What are the implications for coaches in the use of competence motivation in sport?

4. Deci, in his cognitive evaluation theory (updated by Deci & Ryan), contends that a person's attempt to meet goals is directed by controlling and information aspects.

What are they? Describe how a coach can increase intrinsic motivation by influencing each of these aspects.

5. How does intrinsic motivation (IM) differ from extrinsic motivation (EM)? How could a person argue in favor of using awards to increase IM? How could someone argue that the use of awards actually decreases IM and, instead, increases EM?

6. What is the role of self-determination (and self-determination theory) in the IM model? How can coaches improve an athlete's self-determination?

7. How do task involvement and ego involvement influence IM? Which is preferred to increase IM, and why?

8. Briefly describe Vallerand's Hierarchical Model of IM and EM. List 3 implications from the model to improve an athlete's IM.

9. What should a coach of youth sports do to motivate younger performers? In what ways would these motivational techniques be *similar to* and *different from* the motivation of older athletes?

10. What are three advantages of goal setting in sport? Are there any disadvantages? If so, describe at least one situation or condition in which setting a goal is not advisable. Finally, list five examples of goals that incorporate the guidelines listed in this chapter.

11. More sport competitors are substitutes than starters. Sustaining the motivation of these nonstarters is probably one of the more challenging tasks in coaching. Describe (a) why nonstarters are such an important part of the team and (b) how coaches can keep them motivated.

CHAPTER 4

Attributions: Explaining the Causes of Performance and Contest Outcomes

How do elite athletes assess their performance? According to Orlick and Partington (1986):

If the performance was excellent, they will note the mental factors associated with that best performance. In this way, they integrate important lessons into their plan for subsequent competitions. If the performance was "off," they will try to assess why, paying particular attention to their mental state or focus, before and during the competition. They are extremely good at drawing out the important lessons and then letting the performance go, especially if it was less than their best. Many of the best athletes use their diaries, logs, or some other post-competition evaluation procedure to write down the lessons learned. Some go back to these notes to help direct their focus for subsequent competitions (p. 7).

Perhaps all coaches and athletes should remember the words of nineteenth-century American scholar and politician Booker T. Washington, who said, "Success isn't measured by the position you realize in life, but by the obstacles you overcome to reach it."

After the contest, or upon completing segments of the contest, athletes collect their thoughts about the preceding event and its outcome. They also reflect on the quality of their own performance. Of course, coaches are involved in the same thought processes, but with one difference. They often play a more important role than the players in assessing the causes of these contest and performance outcomes. If coaches conclude that winning or losing was the result of the players' high effort and high competence or poor effort and poor competence, respectively, the participants will evaluate the contest in one way. If, however, the victory or loss is labeled "a lucky (unlucky) break," if the other team or opponent is portrayed as poorer or better, or the task is viewed as very difficult or easy, then the players may make a different interpretation. It has been said that "to err is human; to blame it on someone else is even more human." And so it seems in sport.

The ways in which individuals (including athletes) explain or interpret their performance directly affects their intrinsic, extrinsic, achievement, and competence motivation. The purpose of this chapter is to look at the athlete's feelings *after* the contest or following sport performance and to examine how the athlete's explanations of performance outcomes influence their motivation, emotions, and expectations of success. The power-ful role of the coach in influencing how athletes formulate their causal explanations of performance outcomes will also be addressed.

Theoretical Basis

The theoretical basis for making causal attributions in sport is that people—coaches, players, parents, spectators, the media—speculate about the probable causes of winning and losing or success and failure. In his initial model back in 1971, psychologist Bernard Weiner and his colleagues suggested that we perceive and explain success and failure in terms of four categories: ability, task difficulty, effort, and luck. Weiner's (1985a, 1986) reformulation of his earlier attributional model is a more in-depth and realistic (i.e., externally valid) explanation of an individual's interpretation of achievement outcomes. These explanations of performance outcome are called *causal attributions*.

What is important about causal attributions is that the content of these explanations often influences the athletes' future motivation and their performance effectiveness. For instance, researchers have shown that when players are told that they made an error owing to poor ability, they will more likely reduce their effort, or even quit the team, than if they interpret the error as due to task difficulty ("That was a tough ground ball"), low effort ("Let's work harder in practice to get those"), or even luck ("The ball took an unlucky bounce") (Roberts 1984). As indicated in Table 4.1, the four explanations are categorized into two dimensions, stability and locus of control.

Stability

Stability is a function of changes in attributions from situation to situation. Factors that are stable are *ability* and *task difficulty*. They are relatively consistent; the performer's ability is either present for a given task or outcome or it is not. Task difficulty also does not tend to change very rapidly. True, prolonged practice and skill development will improve perfor-mance and reduce task difficulty. But central to the stability dimension is that stable attributes—ability and task difficulty—are more predictable than unstable ones—effort and luck. Whereas a performer can offer high or low effort or be "lucky" or "unlucky" at a given moment, both unstable attributes, an attribute of high or low ability or perceiving the task at hand as relatively difficult or easy is more long term and unchangeable.

Table 4.1 Attribution model based on the four causal explanations of performance outcomes.

		LOCUS OF CONTROL	
		INTERNAL	EXTERNAL
	Stable	Ability	Task difficulty
STABILITY			
	Unstable	Effort	Luck

Locus of Control

Locus of control, first popularized by Rotter (1966), explains the extent to which a person (1) feels responsible for his or her performance and (2) is reinforced by performance outcomes. The main issue, then, is the extent to which individuals perceive the results of their performances as under their own control. These feelings seem to persist across different situations and, thus, are viewed as a personality trait. Rotter developed a questionnaire designed to categorize persons into one of two classes: those who have *external* or those who have *internal* dispositions.

Externals perceive—and perceptions may or may not be based on reality—relatively little control over events in their lives. Consequently, positive experiences (e.g., successful sport performance) have relatively little reinforcement value to externals as compared to internals. Internals, on the other hand, tend to believe that their experiences are attributable to their own actions. Hence, the internal or external dispositions of athletes predict whether they feel responsible for their own success or failure. As reviewed later in this chapter, male and female nonathletes may differ on making causal attributions, in general, and on locus of control, in particular. However, such differences among skilled athletes are far less certain.

Weiner's Attribution Model

The theoretical framework for Weiner's model is that individuals search to find the reasons why a particular performance outcome occurred. Whereas the causal explanations of ability, effort, task difficulty, and luck were included in his earlier model, Weiner (1985a) later added a third dimension, "controllability." Although Weiner does not discount his original two-dimensional model (stability and locus of control), he has since contended that identifying components that are common to, and underlie, all causal attributions may be a more accurate and realistic predictor of future performance (Weiner 1985a, 1986). Three causal dimensions have been identified: locus of causality, stability, and controllability. Table 4.2 depicts these new dimensions.

Table 4.2 Weiner's reformulated causal attribution model, including the three dimensions of *locus of causality, stability,* and *control.*

		LOCUS OF CAUSALITY			
		INTERNAL		EXTERNAL	
STABILITY		Stable	Unstable	Stable	Unstable
CONTROL	Controllable	Individual's Stable Effort	Individual's Unstable Effort	Others' Stable Effort	Others' Unstable Effort
	Uncontrollable	Ability	Mood	Task Complexity	Luck

Not unlike Weiner's earlier model, the *locus of causality* refers to whether the cause of the performance or achievement outcome is perceived to reside within or is external to the performer. Again, the *stability* dimension concerns the relative change of the cause over time. The additional component, *control*, determines whether the cause is under the performer's control or is controlled by other people. According to Biddle (1993), this third dimension makes it "possible to distinguish between elements that are internal but not under a great deal of personal control, such as 'natural ability,' and internal factors that are more controllable, such as personal effort" (p. 440).

Weiner's reformulated model adds one other factor that is missing from his earlier model—the role of emotions and expectations that come into play between making the causal attribution and future behavior. For example, following a performance outcome, the individual will react emotionally in a manner that Weiner has labeled *outcome dependent*. If a performance is successful, the individual will feel relatively good, whereas an unsuccessful performance will likely be followed by relatively bad feelings. Then the individual engages in a *causal search* to help explain the reasons for this outcome. After the causal attribution has been made, it is processed according to its placement among one of the three dimensions—locus of causality, stability, and control. The combination of these dimensions with the performer's emotional reactions and future expectations jointly determine future behavior. Each of the dimensions is related to emotions. Weiner's (1985a) new model is illustrated in Figure 4.1.

To summarize Weiner's updated causal attribution model, the individual is assumed to experience one or more "automatic" emotional responses immediately following the performance outcome. These emotions primarily consist of positive (pleasant) feelings after experiencing success and negative (unpleasant) feelings upon experiencing failure—or at least one's own perception of failure. The performer then attempts to explain the cause(s) of the outcome. After a causal attribution is derived, such as making a successful free throw in basketball due to many hours of practice, it is thought about with

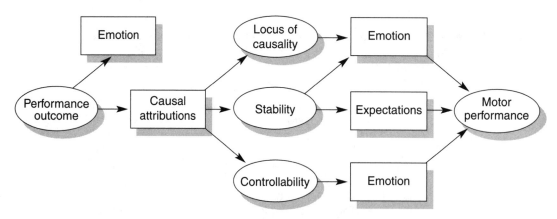

Figure 4.1 Weiner's model illustrating the relationships among performance outcome, emotion, attributions, and performance.

respect to the model's other dimensions: locus of causality ("Should I take responsibility for this outcome?"), stability ("Is the outcome due to something that will be consistent over time, such as my ability level, or due to rapidly changing factors, such as my effort?"), and control ("Do I control the cause of this outcome?"). The performer's subsequent behavior is based on the interaction of these factors.

For example, Weiner's model predicts that an athletic competitor will drop out of sport under the following conditions: he or she (1) experiences consistent failure (or, perhaps more accurately, *perceives* performance outcomes as unsuccessful, regardless of what others think), (2) feels unhappy about these experiences rather than viewing the lack of success as a learning experience, (3) takes responsibility for, and feels he or she is the cause of the lack of success, and (4) perceives this problem as relatively long term. However, persistence at sport participation is not necessarily linked to the opposite of these processes. For example, perceived failure can still occur as long as the competitors view at least *some* aspect of their sport experiences as successful (e.g., serving well despite losing the tennis match). In addition, positive feelings can still follow unsuccessful outcomes if the performer concludes that he or she has benefited from the experience or that he or she was unable to control the outcome (e.g., because of a superior opponent or bad luck). In this way, one important advantage of Weiner's new model is its flexibility in explaining and predicting future performance based on the multitude of emotions and thought processes inherent in sport situations. However, it is important to note that in a review of 17 published attribution studies, Weiner (1985b) found that attributions are more likely when a goal is not attained or when an outcome is unexpected. Following these guidelines for sport, athletes who lose unexpectedly, and/or are unhappy about their performance, will more likely make causal attributions than athletes who do not fit this profile.

McAuley and Duncan (1989) suggest that perceived success that is attributed to internal causes results in feelings of pride, whereas the person will likely feel gratitude if performance success is attributed to external causes. Failure that is explained by internal causes will induce guilt, and failure explained by external causes will result in anger and/or surprise.

McAuley and Duncan (1989) tested Weiner's model by examining the effects of success and failure outcomes and subjects' expectations on emotional responses and causal attributions. They asked subjects to ride a bicycle ergometer all-out for 15 seconds in a competitive situation. The researchers manipulated success (winning) and failure (losing) outcomes in order to influence the subjects' future expectations (e.g., "How many trials will it take to win in future competitions?") The failure condition was ensured by altering one of the ergometers so that it recorded only 60 percent of the actual pedaling revolutions. Subjects were assigned to one of four groups: (1) high expectancies–successful outcome, (2) high expectancies–failure outcome, (3) low expectancies–successful outcome, and (4) low expectancies–failure outcome. Russell (1982) created a scale, the Causal Dimension Scale (CDS), which was used to measure subjects' causal attributions based on Weiner's updated model.

McAuley and Duncan found that subjects with low expectations who had successful outcomes (Group 3) reported more positive emotions (e.g., highly satisfied, grateful, proud, and confident) and highly stable attributions. On the other hand, subjects with initially high expectations who had failure outcomes had the most intense negative emotions (e.g., depressed, displeased, guilty, angry, ashamed).

Attributions: Are There Gender Differences?

Blucker and Hershberger (1983) conclude, in their review of related literature, that although differences on causal attribution exist between men and women in general, "there has been very little published research comparing the causal attribution of men athletes with women athletes or women athletes with women nonathletes" (p. 357). Studies, even those published after Blucker and Hershberger's article appeared, generally suggest that females are more external in making causal attributions than males.

More recently, researchers have attempted to overcome this limitation in addressing gender differences in causal attributions among sport participants. In one laboratory study, Anshel and Hoosima (1989) compared male and female athletes and nonathletes on their attributions and quality of motor performance on a visual tracking task, using the pursuit rotor apparatus, in response to positive feedback. They found that although no gender differences existed in causal attributions, males performed better than females after receiving positive, but not negative, feedback. One possible explanation for this outcome may be that males, particularly male athletes, are more motivated than females to achieve success, especially after receiving positive feedback. According to Rejeski (1980), females tend to make external causal attributions after experiencing success (an easy task or good luck) in achievement situations. Rejeski says that this tends to "reduce task satisfaction and implies that female athletes may have lower expectancies for success than males" (p. 34).

Horner (1968) was among the first to recognize that *nonathlete* males and females did not react to performance outcomes—nor did they approach tasks—in a similar manner. She identifies fear of success (FOS) as a personality trait more prevalent among women than men and that influences females' success and failure. The results of her research show that (1) women, much more often than men, feel uncomfortable when they are successful in competitive achievement situations because of the inconsistency with expectations of "feminine" behavior, (2) the motive to avoid success differs among women, and (3) the motive to avoid success is more prevalent in competitive achievement situations (competing directly against other people) than when a female competes against an impersonal standard. Thus, the fear-of-success motive, discussed briefly in Chapter 2, is believed to be a feminine characteristic.

Have Horner's conclusions about nonathlete subjects, based on information collected in the mid-1960s, remained valid in more recent years? Not likely. Reis and Jelsma (1978) acknowledge that fear of success among female nonathletes "still remains a valid concept to describe a pattern of taking the blame (lack of ability) and denying credit for success (luck, easy task)" (p. 186). However, in a critique of over 100 studies, Tresemer (1976) found insufficient evidence to support gender differences in fear of success.

It appears that FOS is not common among skilled female athletes. For instance, McElroy and Willis (1979) found no evidence for FOS in female athletes and that achievement attitudes of female competitors are similar to those of male athletes. A relatively recent review of this literature by Gill (1992) confirms the results of McElroy and Willis. According to Gill, "The research does not point to any unique gender-related personality construct as an explanation [of gender influence on sport achievement and competitive sport behaviors]." She suggests that more probable explanations of gender differences and sport achievement FOS are factors associated with cultural influences, socialization (childhood) experiences, and other personal dispositions. Thus, similar to other personal dispositions, gender differences in locus of control among highly skilled athletes are almost nonexistent (Biddle 1993; Gill 1992). From his review of this literature, Biddle concluded that the "assumption that males and females attribute success and failure in different ways in sport has not been supported with confidence" (p. 455).

The likely reasons for lack of gender differences among athletes, as opposed to nonathletes, may reside in understanding the antecedents and consequences of causal attribution selections. In sport, success is closely linked to confidence and a high degree of certainty about positive expectations (Biddle, Hanrahan, & Sellars 2001). In explaining cause of performance outcome, outcome expectancy is dependent on the attribution's stability (e.g., ability, task difficulty). Thus, if an athlete concludes that his or her success reflects high ability, a stable cause, then the (successful) outcome will be anticipated with increased certainty—a positive expectancy. According to Biddle et al., successful outcomes attributed to stable causes (i.e., ability) "will be anticipated to be repeated in the future with greater certainty than outcomes attributed to unstable causes" (p. 456). In addition, the authors also concluded that internal explanations, especially following perceived success, result in positive emotions and heightened self-esteem. Highly skilled athletes of both genders bring to the event a history of successful experiences, and, as the review in Chapter 2 revealed, similar personality profiles—particularly those related to high intrinsic and achievement motivation and high self-efficacy. Another gender similarity includes positive emotions about competitive sport events. Thus, it seems plausible to expect both male and female athletes to reflect similarly on the likely (stable) causes of successful performance.

In past years, the single most important factor that explains the different patterns of causal attributions between males and females was their respective expectations of success. In 1984, Deaux hypothesized that if men have higher perceptions of competence and more positive expectations in achievement settings than women, then men will be more likely to attribute success to stable and internal factors (e.g., high ability and effort). On the other hand, if women have lower expectations of success than men, they will be more likely to explain success based on unstable and external causes (e.g., good luck) and attribute failure to internal, stable factors (e.g., lack of ability). However, given similar expectation levels, men and women should not differ in explaining performance outcomes. This is exactly what has occurred in more recent years, at least among competitive athletes.

In research settings, expectations for success may be related to the type of task being performed and situational factors (e.g., competition, presence of feedback) that accompany performance. For example, a motor task perceived as "masculine," as is the case with many types of sport skills, performed under competitive conditions and accompanied by critical feedback (characteristics of a high achievement context) will likely result in the disparity in explanations of success between males and females, as described earlier. However, if expectations for success and perceived competence in performing the task are similar for both males and females, then no gender differences should exist. As described in Chapter 2, female athletes, particularly at elite levels, tend to exhibit similar personal characteristics (e.g., perceived competence, need for achievement, positive expectations, self-confidence) to their male counterparts.

Changing Locus of Causality

One area of interest among researchers is the extent to which locus of causality can be shifted, preferably to a more internal state. Researchers disagree about whether a person's locus of causality (referred to as locus of control by writers before Weiner's reformulated model) can be changed. Are one's beliefs about self-control over the events in one's environment a stable personality trait, as some scientists (e.g., Phares 1976) contend? Or are these beliefs inferred from momentary feelings that can be assessed by a questionnaire, and are those feelings susceptible to sudden change, as proposed by Lefcourt (1976)? In the latter view, a person might feel one way about mastery of his or her environment on one day or in certain situations but feel differently on another day or in different situations. Attempts to alter one's locus of causality, at least after performing a motor task, have not been successful with children (Anshel 1979) and college students (DiFebo 1975). Table 4.3 compares and contrasts the feelings and behaviors of internals and externals (Anshel 1979; Lefcourt 1976; Phares 1976).

Table 4.3 Differences in characteristics of persons with an internal versus external locus of control.

INTERNALS	EXTERNALS
Perceive positive and negative events as a consequence of their own actions	Do not connect the events in their lives with their own actions
Feel they can regulate and be held responsible for most events in their lives	Feel that events are beyond their control
Are markedly affected by environmental factors such as external feedback or performance outcomes	Are not affected physically or emotionally by external feedback or outcomes (which they explain as being caused by luck, chance, or high skill difficulty)
Are easily upset from criticism in skill situations	Are relatively impervious to outside criticism
Prefer situations in which they can employ skill, rather than chance situations	Prefer luck or chance to skill situations
Are very concerned about performance outcome	Are relatively less concerned about outcome
Set relatively high performance goals	Set relatively less challenging goals
Have higher self-confidence and self-esteem	Are lower in self-confidence and self-esteem
Contract for and earn higher grades in school	Are less academically successful
Are relatively more common among older people	Are more common in younger age groups
Depend more on recognition for increasing their chances of future success	Recognition for performance is less important because they do not tend to take responsibility for their success
Success has more reinforcement value	Success has less reinforcement value
Persist longer at tasks	Have relatively short persistence
React more adversely to continued failure	Are somewhat less upset by failure
More common in males	More common in females

Based on my review of related literature (Anshel 1979), I have concluded that one or more of four factors must be present if locus of causality is to be altered. First, the person must be exposed to certain environmental conditions over a prolonged period of time (e.g., prolonged attribution training that emphasizes the link between effort and successful outcomes). Second, the person must have frequent experiences with the condition (e.g., positive feedback received at every practice session and after each competition). Third, the task being performed in this environment should be perceived by the subject as meaningful; the person must be interested in the results from the experience(s). And fourth, because locus of causality is often based on the information that a person receives about performance, it is important that the source of that information be perceived by the performer as credible and given by someone whose opinions the individual respects. For example, the coach's views carry far more credibility and respect than the views of spectators—in fact, often more credibility and respect than parents, teammates, and sport psychologists. The length and intensity of a coach's involvement with competitors makes a shift in locus of causality not only desirable but possible. A few strategies that coaches can implement to help athletes to become more internal are discussed below. Also see the section on attributional retraining later in this chapter.

Environmental Conditions. Shifting to an internal locus of causality means offering feedback to athletes that is positive; that is based on behaviors ("Good kick, Dan"), not character ("Good thinking, Jill"); and that is consistent (avoiding a "Jekyll and Hyde" change in personality and behaviors toward the players). In addition, the effect of such feedback is long term; it may take weeks, months, or even years to alter players' feelings about their mastery over performance outcomes or situations in the environment. Athletes need to go from "It's not my fault" to "It's my responsibility." In many cases, it takes a long-term commitment by the coach, as well as by parents and teammates, to help get them there.

Frequent Experiences. Feelings, particularly if they reflect long-held views about oneself or others, do not change quickly. How we feel about ourselves begins in early childhood and is reinforced throughout life. Persons who feel that they can make a difference in their life events likely have been nurtured to feel this way for years. Similarly, if a youngster has never been made to feel responsible for his or her behavior, he or she will maintain this tendency for a long time—perhaps always. In order for persons' negative feelings about their influence over the events in their lives to change, they need to experience frequent successes based on their own effort and ability. Only when this mastery is reinforced consistently will their perceptions change about "being in charge" of their destiny.

The coach's role is to provide feedback that reinforces positive performance (even if "positive" means the player's high effort and improvement rather than the final outcome), yet is appropriately critical when necessary. Athletes should not be fed a steady diet of compliments and praise. As Dweck (1975) and others have found, exclusively positive feedback is less productive than exposing a person to instructional input of a critical nature at least occasionally.

Task Meaningfulness.   Does the athlete find playing this particular sport very important? How does the participant define *success*? Is it defined as merely "getting a chance to play," or is it defined at a more advanced level, such as reaching a particular performance plateau? After all, not all sport participants consider being a successful athlete of significant importance in their lives. Does the performer feel concerned about the performance outcome? Is it of any concern to the person whether he or she succeeds? To alter a person's locus of causality, the information feedback should be based on a task or sport experience that has meaning to the individual, or the person is likely to conclude, "Who cares?"

A Credible Information Source.   Coaches cannot influence attitudes, feelings, and actions of athletes if the coaches' messages are not believed. If players are to accept information that provides them with the incentive to improve and to feel responsible for their performances, the source of the information must be viewed as credible— someone whom the athletes believe, trust, and respect. Only this perception will allow players to feel secure and interested in environmental mastery.

Shifting locus of causality to an internalized state takes an extensive, long-term commitment. Athletes must come to realize the advantages of feeling in control of and responsible for the events and outcomes in their lives, including athletic performance. The alternative might be feelings of powerlessness and an inability or unwillingness to reach goals or to successfully cope with stress. In extreme cases, a person might feel virtually helpless about influencing the direction of his or her life—a condition called *learned helplessness*, discussed later.

Attributions and Skilled Athletes

Sometimes, skilled athletes offer more than one attribute that explains the causes of a performance outcome. Here is retired professional tennis player Jimmy Connors's interpretation to the media of why he lost a match at Wimbledon in the first round to then newcomer Robert Seguso: "He was serving bomb after bomb (high task difficulty). I was waiting for him to falter just one inch, and I was going to be all over him (Connors's high ability). But he just kept going boom, boom, boom (superior opponent)." Notice that Connors never suggested that he did not have the ability to win against Seguso. Top athletes almost never say, "I'm not good enough." The box on page 123 lists typical examples of attributions based on the four categories of the Weiner et al. (1971) original model that incorporate features of his reformulated model.

Skilled, habitually successful athletes focus on internal causes (ability and effort) to explain their performances (McAuley & Gross 1983). According to Roberts (1984), elite athletes see outcomes as being not necessarily limited to outcomes of events, but also as referring to meeting goals or demonstrating competence. In such cases, skilled athletes do not always feel responsible for a team loss. Instead, they will attribute the lack of team success to teammates while viewing their own performance as successful, or at least not contributing to the undesirable outcome. One primary reason for this tendency is the skilled player's history of success.

The tendency to explain performance in a manner that protects self-esteem while retaining motivation in the task is termed *attributional bias*. Researchers have found that

Examples of Common Causal Attributions

Ability attributes

"We weren't mentally ready."

"I felt good out there."

"I was terrible today."

"I've been kicking (throwing) the ball well lately."

Difficult task or opponent attributes

"No one could hit that guy today."

"Her timing was excellent."

"We played a better team."

"The other team played better today."

"We weren't able to stop the big play."

"Injuries have really hurt us."

Effort attributes

"I've been working hard in training."

"We weren't aggressive enough out there."

"We weren't able to make the big play."

"I gave it my best."

Luck attributes

"We didn't get any breaks."

"The ref didn't let us play our game."

"We couldn't 'find' the basket."

"The weather 'killed' us."

certain situations or personalities encourage acceptance of personal responsibility for successful outcomes and discourage externalization of failure. For example, Brawley and Roberts (1984) contend that the motive to maintain or enhance self-esteem results in a *self-serving attributional bias*. This occurs when positive events are ascribed as due to internal factors (e.g., high ability or high effort) and negative events to external factors (e.g., high task difficulty, superior opponent, or bad luck). Thus, when an athlete is penalized by the referee, he or she may explain the event as due to a "bad" call rather than admitting to a mistake. Elite athletes often attribute injury (an unstable, external cause) to explain poor performance, especially if the lack of success persists. Quality competitors almost never explain disappointing performance as due to low skill (ability) level. This is because better athletes possess a sufficient amount of past success on which to base positive expectations for future performance. They realize that failure is temporary, resulting in unstable causal attributions. However, less talented competitors are more likely to make low-ability attributions, perhaps due to a lack of previous success and low future expectations. The combination of persistent failure and low ability attributions often leads athletes to drop out of sport. Thus, because the underlying cause of attributional tendency is to maintain motivation to persist at the task with optimal effort, a self-serving attributional bias is more likely when the task *creates* high motivation and enjoyment, and improves self-esteem.

A strong relationship exists between consistent performance outcomes and the causal attributions of athletes, especially children. Roberts (1975), in a study of 200 Little League baseball players, found that the teams that consistently won made high ability attributions. However, athletes on these winning teams did not attribute a lack of ability to explain an occasional loss. Instead, the players thought that low effort or a tougher opponent (task difficulty) was responsible for the team's lack of success. If, however, they performed successfully when their team lost, they attributed their performance to high effort. On the other hand, teams that consistently lost contests attributed these outcomes to poor personal ability or low team ability. Brawley (1984) also concludes that athletes—at least those below the collegiate (elite) level—who consistently fail (or *perceive* themselves as failures, which is even more important) consider themselves to have low ability. This means that they have little hope for future success and are less likely to respond to failure with increased effort. Even worse, they tend to drop out of their sport or resort to attention-getting (negative) behaviors such as clowning, breaking team rules, and so on. Quitting sport as a result of not anticipating future success is a phenomenon called *learned helplessness*.

Learned Helplessness

The *Dictionary of Sport and Exercise Sciences* (Anshel et al. 1991a) defines learned helplessness (LH) as a "condition descriptive of individuals who demonstrate maladaptive achievement patterns such as avoidance of challenging tasks, low task persistence in the face of obstacles, and feelings of low ability, low pride, and low satisfaction under unsuccessful conditions" (p. 86). The failure to gain control over the situation often results in lowered motivation, cognitive limitations, and depression. Carol Dweck (1980), a respected specialist in this area, contends that LH individuals believe that their actions will not influence the course of negative events. Learned helplessness can be a debilitating and harmful mental state, particularly in achievement situations such as competitive sport.

Linking attributions to LH, Prapavessis and Carron (1988, p. 191) found in their study that attributions to causes that are internal (ability or effort), stable (ability, task difficulty, or superior opponent), general (across situations), and important maximize the severity of LH. The researchers conclude that high LH subjects do not feel that they have the ability to control and/or change factors that contribute to unsuccessful performance. Abramson et al. (1978) contend that LH is more likely when the reason for failure is uncontrollable (perceived low ability, negative mood state, high task difficulty, or bad luck) and when attributions are made to internal (ability or effort), stable (ability or task difficulty), and global (helplessness across a variety of situations) factors.

Conditions of LH can be created in a laboratory. In one study (Marisi & Anshel 1976), subjects were asked to contact a handheld instrument with a rotating metal disc about one inch in diameter. On a pretest, each subject's pain threshold was determined in response to electric shock to the fingertips. For one group (related stress), subjects were given an electric shock if their "time-on-target" did not equal or exceed the best score from the previous four trials (every four trials resulted in a new standard of future performance). Subjects in the unrelated stress group, however, were given electric shock on a random basis, regardless of their performance. A third (control) group performed the same task without electric shock. Results of the study showed that subjects who had no control over receiving the shock (unrelated stress group) performed poorest among the three groups. The related stress group was superior to the others. This study is an example of a common response when a person feels unable to reduce or eliminate an unpleasant event. An individual's perception that people have no or little control over the effects of their actions leads to a sense of helplessness. Sadly, this condition is responsible for causing significant psychological harm to sport participants, especially less skilled and younger players.

The theory of LH in humans stems from the work of Dweck (1975), who examined the reasons why children refuse to participate, or make a brief attempt and then quickly give up, in an activity—especially in sport. Such children refuse to stay with, or persist at, an activity because they have little or no control over the outcome, as did the subjects in the unrelated stress group in the Marisi–Anshel study described earlier. These children probably have LH.

To understand the condition of LH, remembering that this is a *learned* phenomenon is important. This condition is not hereditary. Feeling inadequate, being a "failure," and feeling unable to alter an unpleasant situation or outcome is based on past experiences, usually of a prolonged nature. Examples of situations in sport that promote LH include the athlete's perception of several "wrong" calls by the referee (umpire) over a prolonged time period, the belief of no improvement in sport skills, or no positive feedback from the coach, particularly after interpreting one's own performance as effective. What creates LH? What is responsible for how a person perceives the cause of his or her success or failure?

Dweck and Reppucci (1973) were interested in determining why children attributed outcomes to high or low ability rather than to high or low effort. As described earlier, ability attributes are relatively fixed (stable). Kids drop out of sport if they feel that failure is due to low ability, especially beginning at about age 11 or 12 years (Roberts 1984). Effort attributes are not fixed and, therefore, can be used to connect successful outcomes with effort or motivation. The researchers found that children who persist longer at the task are more likely to attribute their performance outcomes to effort than are helpless children. The more persistent child also tends to perceive the causes of his or her performance as due to effort ("If I try harder, I'll get better"). On the other hand, helpless children, those with less persistence, were more likely to attribute failure to their lack of ability rather than to lack of effort. Diener and Dweck (1978) found that to performance-oriented individuals (i.e., persons who are concerned with and perceive success based on performance improvement rather than outcome), effort is the most critical attribution. This is because individuals assume that they have the ability to learn and improve which is highly desirable in avoiding a helpless mental state.

In a sport context, self-appraisals of low ability after lower-than-expected performance or failure outcomes increase the likelihood of dropping out. Hence, it is advisable that in most cases athletes attribute poor performance to a lack of effort. Such performance can be improved if they try harder—which is an unstable attribution (changeable over time) and under the performer's control. However, feeling in control of an outcome and interpreting that outcome as success or failure depends on the individual's perception. As Dweck and Reppucci (1973) have shown, two children may receive exactly the same number and sequence of success and failure experiences yet react quite differently according to whether they *interpret* the failure to mean that the situation is within or beyond their control.

What is responsible for differences in this perception, which in turn influences helplessness? Dweck and Reppucci (1973) and Anshel (1979) describe the presence of at least one of four factors: (1) the person's history of success and failure (greater frequency of success inhibits feelings of helplessness more than failure), (2) the manner in which information feedback is offered ("Nice try, John, but . . ." as opposed to "That was a dumb mistake. Can't you do anything right?"), (3) the frequency with which feedback is offered (perception is more influenced by frequent input), and (4) the source of the information (credible sources—that is, significant others or models such as coaches, elite athletes, parents, and friends—have more influence than persons with less credibility). One reason LH field research in sport is lacking and difficult is because many persons experiencing LH will already have dropped out of sport (Biddle 1993).

Reducing Learned Helplessness: Attribution Retraining

The good news about this condition is that it is amendable, especially in childhood. If children can learn to be helpless, they can also be taught to overcome it by changing attributional patterns (i.e., tendencies of explaining the causes of performance outcomes). To Biddle et al. (2001), attributional retraining programs "seek to alter attributions that are deemed unsuitable and that may lead to cognitive, emotional, or behavioral deficits, and then seek to develop more appropriate attributions that might suggest positive and future-oriented thoughts" (pp. 462–463). The purpose of Dweck's (1975) attributional retraining program is to reinforce the importance of effort for successful performance, as opposed to less controllable perceptions such as luck or high task difficulty. At the same time, feelings of low ability are extinguished. Directing the attributional patterns of performers toward the unstable variable of effort increases the chance of persisting at a task.

Attributional retraining has received research support. In one study, Dweck (1975) identified children who lacked persistence or tended to be "quitters." These "helpless" children were given one of two treatments: (1) one group was offered constant reinforcement for success to develop self-confidence and to overcome a negative reaction to failure, and (2) the other group received effort attribution training while experiencing both success and failure. After each trial, subjects were encouraged to attribute their success or failure to their personal effort. Thus, Dweck tried to repattern the children's perception of their performance outcome to a personal factor that could be controlled, an effort attribute. She found that children who received effort attribution training (Group 2) were more persistent, more willing to attribute their performance to effort, experienced less anxiety in an achievement situation, and rated themselves as better performers than did the children who received constant reinforcement (Group 1).

Dweck concludes that subjects who are trained to recognize the need for more effort and not the lack of ability as the reason for "failing" respond more productively in subsequent trials; they don't give up. She surmises, "If a child believes failure to be a result of his [or her] lack of motivation, he [or she] is likely to escalate his [or her] effort in an attempt to obtain the goal" (p. 683). To increase effort, Weiner's (1985a) attribution theory would suggest creating and maintaining positive emotions and high expectations for future success following both positive and negative performance outcomes. Attributions of low ability after failure should also be avoided. The key objective in attributional retraining is the subject's perception of control following any outcome (Dweck 1975). Biddle et al. (2001) suggest that attributional retraining should incorporate positive emotional states and expectancies after success and failure. As indicated earlier, low ability attributions after failure should be especially avoided.

In summary, then, helpless individuals, including athletes, have some of the following characteristics. They

1. persist less at, withdraw earlier from, or do not even attempt an activity, especially if it is a new one
2. attribute failure primarily to a lack of ability
3. perceive themselves as consistent failures
4. do not feel that greater effort will result in success
5. consider luck or low task difficulty to be possible causes for their success
6. tend not to risk failure, which means that they are less comfortable in learning situations and in attempting new skills
7. do not feel control over performance outcomes and interpret failure as beyond their control
8. tend to have an external locus of control (causality) disposition, usually attributing performance to factors not under their control
9. misinterpret or misunderstand the actual causes of their poor performance; helpless persons feel that trying to overcome failure is fruitless, whereas nonhelpless performers view failure as a temporary skill deficit

Attributions and Helplessness: The Coach's Role

It is important for coaches to know the factors that underlie an athlete's causal attributions. Why, for example, would one player claim that the main reason for his or her failure was an injury—very common in professional sports—while another competitor explains losing as due to a tough opponent? Why do some coaches claim that their team lost because the opponent was better, while other coaches contend that their own team played poorly? What effect do these different attributions have on team and player performance? And, finally, how do individual sport athletes, such as wrestlers (see Figure 4.2) differ in making causal attributions from team sport athletes?

Figure 4.2 Knowing when—and when not—to take responsibility for performance outcomes is the key factor linking causal attributions to motivation.

The key factor between making accurate causal attributions and motivation is *emotion*. From his review of this research literature, McAuley (1992) concludes that the benefits derived from explaining performance outcomes (e.g., more incentive and effort, reduced helplessness) are due primarily to the competitor's emotional reactions to these explanations. In McAuley's terms, "Causal dimensions do indeed mediate affective reactions to achievement outcomes" (p. 106).

McAuley makes three recommendations about the influence of attributions on emotion. First, athletes must care about their performance by being emotionally influenced by performance and contest outcomes; they must care about their success and failure (which is not necessarily the same as winning and losing). Second, successful outcomes elicit more intense emotional responses than failure outcomes. Therefore, coaches must ensure that athletes interpret their participation as at least partially successful. Third, the causality dimension of Weiner's theory (i.e., making internal causal attributions) is most responsible for producing an emotional reaction. The performer's ego involvement in competitive sport produces feelings of "ownership," that is, taking personal responsibility for one's performance. Taken together, these three ingredients are essential for producing improved motivation and performance in applying attributional theory.

The Coach's Comments

In sport settings, the coach has tremendous power over the athlete's perception of the situation. The manner in which a player's actions are assessed often dictates how the player explains his or her own playing skills and ability. In fact, comments by parents and others whose opinion is valued has a similar effect (Cratty 1983). The content of the coach's comments before and after performance, either in a game or during practice, not only affects the player's performance but also markedly contributes to whether the athlete continues to participate with the team. For example, Roberts (1975, 1984) asserts that child athletes who ascribe the causes of failure to low ability tend to drop out of sport.

How, then, should the coach go about reducing or, better yet, preventing feelings of helplessness in sport? Certainly the coach's objective is to use strategies that will help players maintain sport participation with the motivation to continue learning and improving. Rejeski and Brawley (1983) concluded in their review of related literature that athletes usually evaluate their own abilities higher than do their coaches. Specifically, the authors found that the players' self-esteem was directly linked to their expectations and perceived ability concerning future performance. Competitors with high self-esteem were more confident in their ability and had higher expectations of future performance than did persons with lower self-esteem. Thus, it comes as no surprise that one very important goal of every coach is to raise and maintain heightened self-esteem of each team member. It makes no sense to make statements to athletes that tear down their positive feelings. In addition, because skilled athletes tend to have an internal (rather than external) locus of causality (Rejeski & Brawley 1983), they tend to feel responsible for their performance success—or failure.

Therefore, coaches have two responsibilities regarding the internal–external disposition of their athletes. First, coaches need to know the extent to which each player is willing to take responsibility for his or her own performance. Second, coaches should promote their athletes' internal disposition. This may include using techniques to shift a player's locus of control from external to internal. Athletes with an external locus of causality do not usually feel responsible for their actions and are less reinforced by the coach's responses to their performance. Neither of these tendencies is desirable for long-term motivation in sport. Table 4.4 summarizes Carron's (1984b) depiction of the influence of each causal attribution on a person's emotional feelings and expectancies.

One approach to fostering an internal locus of causality and positively influencing the competitor's motivation before the contest (or during practice) is giving instructions that emphasize effort. A study by Yukelson et al. (1981) illustrates the effect of instructional content, referred to by the authors as *attributional instructions,* on performing a sport skill. In their study, college students, all high achievers, engaged in an overhand ball-tossing task. They were told that the scores would be compared to a "standard of excellence" set by other subjects in the study. Thus, the subjects thought that they were competing against others but, in fact, these comparisons were fictitious. The subjects were then told, after a few contrived calculations, that they were either five points ahead of or five points behind the norms established by their classmates. They were given one of two sets of instructions before continuing the ball-tossing task to induce them to attribute their performance primarily to ability or effort. The instructions (similar to what a coach might say to a player) were as follows:

> *Ability-oriented instructions:* "We've found that the amount of ability an (athlete) has for this (skill) is by far the most important determinant of how well one will perform. This (skill) is pure in the sense that it is relatively unaffected by effort. Your performance is highly dependent upon the ability you possess; some (athletes) just seem to be good at the (skill) while others are not. You will now be given 10 more throws at the target. Concentrate before each throw for it is the accuracy of your throws that will determine your score" (p. 49).

Table 4.4 Factors that affect motivation for future participation in sport.

Initial Expectancy	Performance Level	Causal Attribution	Emotional (Affective) Reaction	Expectancy
High[1]	High	Ability or other stable, internal factors	Maximum pride and satisfaction	Higher
High	Low	Bad luck, difficult task, lack of effort, or other unstable factors	Minimum shame and dissatisfaction	High
Low[2]	High	Good luck, special effort, or the relative ease of the task	Minimum pride and satisfaction	Low
Low	Low	Lack of ability, difficulty of the task, or stable internal factors	Maximum shame and dissatisfaction	Lower

[1]Associated with males

[2]Associated with females

From Carron, A.V. (1984). Cohesion in sport teams. In J. M. Silva & R. S. Weinberg (Eds.), *Psychological foundations of sport* (pp. 340–351). Champaign, IL: Human Kinetics.

Effort-oriented instructions: "We've found this (skill) to be heavily influenced by the amount of effort a person puts into the (skill), that is, the motivation one has to do well. There are some slight differences in ability, but they are minor. No one can do well unless they try hard. You will now be given 10 more throws at the target. Remember to concentrate and try to do your best" (p. 49).

The best results occurred when subjects attributed their performance to effort rather than ability. As their perception of task difficulty increased, so did intended effort and subsequent performance. The subjects reported that they tried harder when receiving effort instructions. Therefore, informing an athlete that effort is the most important factor in skill development and success will be more motivating and will more likely result in better performance than indicating that ability ("either you have it or you don't") is most important. Effort attributions are especially important to sport participants with relatively low skills and little past success. In fact, the lack of ability attribute results in the highest incidence of withdrawal from sport compared with the other attributes, especially starting at about age 10 to 12 years (Roberts 1984). As indicated earlier, an unfortunate but common result, especially in children, is LH.

Attributions for Motivation in Sport

The following are some coaching suggestions to prevent, reduce, or eliminate learned helplessness and to use causal attributions to motivate athletes.

1. *Know when to use internal and external attributions.* Usually, coaches should not promote the use of external attributions (task difficulty or luck) to explain the lack of goal achievement or not meeting expectations (Brawley 1980). A better approach is to indicate that future effort must be increased—or maintained if the effort was sufficient—for success, rather than blaming the official, bad luck, skill difficulty, or a superior opponent. External attributions for failure might promote LH, whereby the player feels that he or she can do little to change present or future outcomes. Thus, an athlete who has just struck out against a "hittable" pitcher needs to know that greater effort toward skill development and concentration are needed (internal attributes). Telling the player that the umpire's calls were inaccurate (external attributes) or that performance was due to bad luck may not provide the needed incentive for improvement. As Branch Rickey, the late American baseball owner and Hall of Famer, said, "Luck is the residue of design" (Will 1990, p. 246). Also not helpful are comments that degrade the player's self-esteem (e.g., "You messed up") or release the player's accountability (e.g., "Don't worry about it").

2. *Know when to use task difficulty attributions.* Attributing failure to a difficult task is common among good athletes. Researchers generally agree that task difficulty attributes, similar to superior opponent explanations, are useful in preventing low self-confidence, poor self-esteem, and low ability attributes. However, if the athlete's expectations of success toward the opponent or task are high, or if the high task difficulty or superior opponent explanations are frequent and of long duration, then feelings of low ability or helplessness may occur.

3. *Teach skills.* Nothing is more important than learning the skills and performing them proficiently. Skill development improves performance and reduces feelings of helplessness for athletes of all ages. Poor skills promote continued failure. Quality

educational attributional statements inform; they give a player feedback on ways to improve performance.

4. *Create sport situations that foster success.* Try to match opponents based on age, skill, and physical maturity. For example, a 120-pound athlete should not attempt to tackle a 160-pounder. Athletes should practice the skill as soon as possible after receiving instruction and practice. As discussed in Chapter 10, some controversy exists about the rule that all athletes must play in every game, regardless of their skill. Some participants need additional development during practice before they are ready to compete.

5. *Avoid comparing athletes.* Statements such as "Why can't you dribble the ball like Marge?" or "If you could only run as fast as Bill" reduce feelings of self-competence. There's nothing wrong with telling a player about the superior skills of an older, more experienced team member, however, the emphasis should be placed on using objective criteria based on standards and reasonable expectations. For instance, explaining to a player the reasons for not starting ahead of another athlete are based on performance ("Darlene is playing ahead of you, Fran, because she is aggressive in getting rebounds") helps the less-skilled performer to understand what he or she must be able to do competently and consistently in order to play. However, players of lesser ability might view the superior skills of a teammate as impossible to overcome, fostering feelings of helplessness. General, subjective statements such as "He's a better player" or "You don't move as quickly as Joan" might promote feelings of inadequacy and LH.

6. *Offer supportive verbal and nonverbal messages.* This is probably the most important recommendation. Athletes need to feel accepted, even liked, by their coach. Verbal support such as "Good effort, Susan" or "Your dribbling is looking better today, Phil" and nonverbal cues such as a thumbs-up, smile, or a pat on the back communicate a sense of acceptance, recognition, warmth, and performance approval of the individual regardless of athletic ability. Coaches should avoid messages that induce guilt ("I'm ashamed of you and the way you played today") or insult ("You guys can't hit your way out of a paper bag"). Definitely avoid "gallows humor" and sarcasm ("Nice performance, folks. Next time I'll get volunteers from the crowd to take your place"). Chapter 9, which discusses communication techniques, offers several specific suggestions on promoting motivation and self-confidence while eliminating learned helplessness, boredom, and unhappiness.

7. *Be positive when evaluating external factors.* Achievement in sport is difficult enough without the coach downplaying an athlete's or the team's success. All success must be positively reinforced with a measured degree of compliments and encouragement. Attributing success to luck ("We were lucky to win today") or an inferior opponent ("The other team had a bad game") is an insult to the players' efforts and skills. External attributes can be used selectively after failure, however. For example, an effective luck attribute might be "We played well today but the other team had a few good breaks and won. Keep up the good work." An example of an effective task difficulty attribute after losing is "Don't feel bad. The other team has outstanding talent. It's good to know how good we have to be to win. We learned something today. Stay with it."

8. *Reflect reality in attributions.* Athletes respect and want honesty from their coaches. Therefore, in addition to avoiding character-destroying comments, coaches (and

parents) should "tell it like it is." This means that if a player in fact misjudged a ball (that is, the ball should have been caught), regardless of whether the error affected the score, internal attributions (effort and ability) are appropriate. An example might be "Melissa, we have to work harder during practice on catching fly balls. This is a weak area, but you can do it, as long as you are prepared to work hard at it." A statement such as "Oh, that was an unlucky break, Richard" about a skill that should have been performed flawlessly may be perceived by the athlete as dishonest and might reduce the coach's or parent's credibility in the player's eyes.

9. *Avoid effort attributions for failure when the outcome is based on physiological parameters*. For instance, if a distance runner is not successful (in whatever way "success" is defined by the coach or player), the coach who says "You didn't try hard enough" may be inaccurate. Full effort may be observable. In fact, Biddle et al. (2001) contend that low effort attributions after failure may backfire, causing the athlete to make low ability explanations (e.g., "I gave 100% and still failed. I guess I just don't have the ability.") Athletes whose performance is based on physiological measures (e.g., strength, speed, and cardiovascular endurance) tend to avoid effort attributions for failure because there is no doubt about the effort they expended. According to Rejeski (1980), "Most sport events provide direct perceptual information regarding effort expenditure. Thus, it may be informationally inappropriate for athletes to perceive that failure was caused by a lack of effort" (p. 34). Not winning the contest or task requiring optimal effort might be correctly attributed to external causes such as the quality of opponents (task difficulty) or, if accurate, some other luck-related causes, such as poor weather, illness, or a referee's inaccurate call.

SUMMARY

How does a person explain the causes of an event in his or her life or, in sport, a performance outcome? Most often, the outcomes of events are attributed to one of four causes. Was success or failure due to ability? To effort? The difficulty of the task experienced, perhaps due to a superior opponent? Or was the outcome interpreted as a matter of luck? The individual's perceptions in using any of these causal explanations are the basis of attribution theory. This area has received much attention by sport psychology researchers and practitioners because of its effect on the athlete's motivation and desire to maintain participation in sport. For example, attributions can affect a competitor's interpretation of a contest outcome as success—"Our team lost but I feel good about my effort"—or failure—"I accept the blame for my team's loss today." Athletes who chronically perceive their performance outcomes as failures and attribute these failures to their own lack of ability or bad luck tend to drop out of sport sooner and more often than performers who attribute undesirable outcomes as a function of low effort. In other words, the two key issues in helping athletes make appropriate causal attributions are accuracy and controllability.

Coaches can help players to perceive more of their participation as successful (a superb technique for improving motivation) and can explain the causes of most events as a result of high or low effort. In addition, the athlete's feelings of little or no control over performance outcomes can lead to learned helplessness. Such feelings are typically accompanied by mental and then physical withdrawal from further sport participation. Thus, the coach's comments following an event, either a particular play or the complete contest, can strongly influence the performer's subsequent emotions, attitudes, and future participation in sport.

REVIEW QUESTIONS

1. Describe *learned helplessness*. Why is it so potentially harmful, especially in sport? How is it nurtured in sport situations? What can a coach do to reduce or to eliminate it?

2. Based on either of the Weiner et al. (1971, 1985a) attribution models, what would be the proper causal explanations for the following situations? (a) A team that consistently wins has just lost a game; (b) A team that tends to lose has just won the game; (c) A player made a physical error on a relatively easy play; (d) The underdog team won; (e) A player failed to catch a pass after slipping on the field; (f) The team, despite making several physical and mental errors, beat a poorly skilled opponent; (g) A batter just struck out against a "poor" pitcher; (h) The referee called a penalty that disallowed your team's goal; and (i) The team just lost to an opponent with inferior skills.

3. What are two advantages of having an internal disposition? Can you think of a condition in which being a strong internal could hurt more than help the athlete?

4. Describe the conditions in which having an external disposition might actually be desirable.

5. Describe four ways in which a coach can induce more internality in athletes.

6. Have researchers found gender differences in making causal attributions in sport? Discuss the factors that may or may not lead to gender differences in the way highly skilled male and female athletes explain performance outcomes.

7. What guidelines would you use in constructing an attribution retraining program to optimize an athlete's motivation?

CHAPTER 5

Regulating Stress, Anxiety, and Arousal

Emotions are an integral part of being a competitive athlete. Of constant concern to participants (and to coaches) is reaching and maintaining the proper emotional state that will allow them to perform at their potential. To reach this objective, they must regulate three emotions that play primary roles in performance: stress, anxiety, and arousal. After reading this chapter, you should be able to understand state and trait anxiety, how anxiety differs from arousal, the underlying causes of these mental states, and what coaches should and should not do to help athletes manage, but not eliminate, stress, anxiety, and arousal.

Given the importance of stress, anxiety, and arousal in sport, it is ironic that coaches and athletes understand relatively little about them. Perhaps this is why coaches use such a diversity of methods in their attempts to "psych up" without "psyching out" their players. For example, coaches disagree on the effectiveness of a forceful pregame talk, even in sports that demand a high level of energy and aggression. Many leaders foster an exciting atmosphere before the contest, but others use a low-key approach, as confirmed by media reports.

For example, in defense of reduced pregame enthusiasm, former National Football League head coach Ron Meyer claims that "there was a lot of emotion at the Alamo, and nobody survived." Meyer's point, confirmed by sport psychology researchers (e.g., Gould & Krane 1992), is not that high emotion is unnecessary for success, but that the individual's needs, the situations, and sport type each partially dictate the "proper" emotional level for optimal performance. As suggested by Walter Alston, the late and very successful manager of the Los Angeles Dodgers baseball team, the athlete's "ideal" emotional status and the coach's actions to help the individual reach it are often dependent on the sport. For example, a football coach has to fire up the players. Football is that kind of sport. Baseball is another kind of sport. You can only play baseball relaxed, Alston contended. You have to stay loose and maintain relatively low excitement before and during the game. To Alston, if the manager is low key, the players will more likely relax.

Should coaches psych up their teams with excitement and tension? Or should they aim for a more relaxed and subdued mental set? What are the purposes—and validity— of some of the more common pregame techniques that coaches use to prepare their players mentally? What is the purpose and proper content of a pregame talk? What is the coach's role in fostering an appropriate emotional state for each player, and when should these strategies be implemented? In this chapter, we will (1) examine the properties and underlying causes of stress, anxiety, and arousal, beginning with the premise that they are not the same thing, and (2) suggest using strategies for coaches and athletes that will regulate (increase and decrease) and maintain the "proper" level of each of these emotional states.

Stress

Stress is probably one of the most misunderstood concepts in sport psychology. For example, stress tends to be viewed as undesirable, unhealthy, and negative; something to be avoided at all times. This is not true, especially when examining the definitions associated with stress. Schafer (1996) defines stress as "arousal of mind and body in response to demands made on them" (p. 6). A *stressor* is "any demand on mind or body [while] a *distressor* is any demand resulting in harm to mind or body." Thus, while most demands—physical, mental, or emotional—that are made on us are harmless, even positive, these demands can turn negative. Stressors can become distressors. When an athlete, for example, perceives a stressor as predictable and manageable (e.g., physical contact, successful performance by an opponent, booing from the crowd), they become less threatening, producing less anxiety. Stress, then, should not be avoided. It is both desirable and necessary in life—and in sport competition.

Shafer's (1996) definition of stress differs from the often-cited definition of Lazarus and Folkman (1984), which focused primarily on the negative features of stress. To Lazarus and Folkman, stress is "a particular relationship between the person and the environment that is appraised by the person as taxing or exceeding his or her resources and endangering his or her well-being" (p. 19). Two main features of this definition warrant attention in sport contexts. First, the environment plays an important role in experiencing stress, rather than presuming that athletes experience stress in isolation or independent of anything around them. This means that managing stress includes attending to environmental factors that cause or contribute to it. Second, the concept of appraisal is a prominent feature of this definition. This means that stress is controllable, since the athlete must first perceive a stimulus or situation as taxing or exceeding their resources to deal with the stressor. In other words, if the athlete perceives a situation as challenging or harmless, rather than as threatening or harmful, ostensibly the athlete should feel no, or little stress. Successfully managing stress, then, primarily consists of three processes: managing the environment, building resourcefulness (e.g., confidence, optimism, self-control, mental toughness, coping skills), and influencing the athlete's interpretation (appraisal) of situations from harmful or threatening to challenging, harmless, or positive. The ways in which stress differs from anxiety will be discussed later in this chapter in the anxiety section.

The Concept of Positive Stress

To many people, especially athletes, the term "positive stress" is an oxymoron. Based on how we typically view the concept of stress, the two words simply do not seem compatible. However, as discussed earlier, stress can be positive, productive, and even desirable. According to Shafer (1996), "stress can be helpful as well as harmful. Positive stress can provide zest and enjoyment, as well as attentiveness and energy for meeting dead-lines, entering new situations, coping with emergencies, achieving maximum perfor-mance, and meeting new challenges" (p. 16). Sport psychologist Dr. Jim Loehr has generated the concept of positive stress based on his perusal of the research literature and from over 30 years of consulting with athletes, particularly at the elite level.

Loehr (1994) contends that "stress is anything that causes energy to be expended . . . physically, mentally, and emotionally" (p. 67). Stress, then, is a form of "positive energy," because it produces growth and achievement. Stress is experienced physically, mentally, and emotionally. For example, physical stress occurs when exercising; mental stress occurs in response to thinking and concentrating (cognition), emotional stress is energy expenditure following certain negative feelings (e.g., anger, fear, sadness, frus-tration, anxiety). Emotional stress, however, can also consist of more positive content (e.g., happiness, relaxation, enthusiasm).

There are two important points about positive stress. First, without taxing the sys-tem—physically, mentally, or emotionally—the athlete cannot reach nor maintain his or her ideal performance state. Growth takes place in response to stress, that is, the expenditure of energy. Second, the problems associated with stress can easily be allevi-ated when stress is balanced with "voluntary recovery." Recovery is anything that causes energy to be renewed or recaptured—physically, mentally, or emotionally. Vol-untary recovery is planned in content, time, implementation, and duration. Involuntary recovery, on the other hand, consists of the biological breakdown of the human organ-ism. Sickness, disease, and depression are examples of involuntary recovery.

Recovery consists of two characteristics. It has a reenergizing effect, so that after the recovery period, the person feels more invigorated, and the recovery strategy distracts the performer from the task at hand. Thus, a baseball/softball player would not recover from batting practice by immediately taking ground balls. Instead, he or she would "discon-nect" physically, mentally, and emotionally by drinking water, having an informal con-versation, or thinking about anything *except* the next task. Loehr (1994) contends that "balancing stress and recovery is fundamental to becoming a tough competitor" (p. 67).

Examples of *physical stress* include running, hitting, jumping, walking, weight lifting, and exercising. Examples of *physical recovery* are eating, drinking, sleeping, reducing muscle tension and respiration, and napping. Examples of *mental stress* are thinking, con-centrating, focusing, visualizing, imaging, analyzing, and problem solving. Examples of *mental recovery* are calmness, increasing fantasy and creativity, and decreasing focus. Finally, examples of *emotional stress* are anger, fear, sadness, depression, frustration, and feeling "negative." Examples of *emotional recovery* are emotional relief, increased positive feelings, personal fulfillment, fun, enjoyment, security, and decreased fear, anxiety, and anger. Thus, increased exposure to stress, followed by voluntary (planned) recovery periods, a process called "oscillation" (Loehr, 1994; Loehr & Schwartz, 2001), prolongs the athlete's ability to sustain high performance on demand under pressure.

As indicated earlier, Shafer (1996) agrees with the concept of positive stress. He defines positive stress as "helpful arousal—arousal that promotes health, energy, satis-faction, and peak performance" (p. 11). The key word, for Shafer, is "moderation." When stress (or anxiety, he adds) is experienced occasionally and in moderation, per-formance can actually improve. Examples include preparing for an upcoming difficult task, remaining alert over time, concentrating on the task at hand, not being distracted by extraneous, irrelevant thoughts, and overcoming obstacles. Stress, then, can be desirable—even necessary—in sport, and in life.

In summary, there appears to be widespread agreement among writers and researchers in the vast stress literature. First, an external stimulus or event appraised as threatening will be stressful and change psychophysiological and behavioral responses. The so-called "good news" about this conclusion is that stress is controllable. To feel stressed, a person must interpret (i.e., appraise or perceive) a stimulus or event as unpleasant or threatening. Second, and more ominously, failure to cope properly with stressful events will lead to chronic stress, which in turn, will lead to burnout, demotivation, poor performance, and eventual withdrawal (first mental, then physical) from the activity. Thus, prolonged exposure to stress will have very unpleasant consequences to the person's performance and psychological well-being. Third, stress can be positive, even desirable, in promoting necessary mental and emotional readiness to reach and sustain high performance, particularly in pressure conditions. This is a welcomed, yet less recognized, component of stress. The key issues are to maintain stress at a moderate level, and experience it only intermittently.

Anxiety and Arousal in Sport

Understandably, two sets of terms, *anxiety* and *arousal* and *stress* and *anxiety*, have been used interchangeably—and incorrectly—by writers, both in the media and in the scientific literature. Iso-Ahola and Hatfield (1986), for example, use the term *anxiety* in virtually the same context that Bird and Cripe (1986) and Landers and Boutcher (1993) apply the term *arousal*. However, in more recent years, writers and researchers in sport psychology have recognized that anxiety and arousal are not synonymous. They are measured differently and, in fact, require different techniques to regulate them. In addition, stress refers to *present* bodily or cognitive responses to an environmental demand. This demand can be interpreted as positive or negative. Anxiety, on the other hand, reflects negative feelings of worry or threat about a *future* event.

Perhaps one primary cause of using each of these terms interchangeably is that they have been examined as having somatic and cognitive properties. Traditionally, arousal has been interpreted and measured strictly as a physiological process on a continuum ranging from sleep to high excitation (Duffy 1957). Even in current literature, arousal is often determined by changes in heart and respiration rate, extent of sweating, and other physiological measures. However, Oxendine (1970) and Anshel (1985) have measured emotional aspects of arousal, including positive feelings (e.g., excitement, happiness) and negative feelings (e.g., fear, embarrassment, and depression). Such emotions may or may not correlate highly with physiological responses. Anxiety has also been measured in terms of somatic and cognitive properties. Iso-Ahola and Hatfield (1986) take a "multidimensional view of anxiety," asserting that it has "both a physiological and a psychological basis" (pp. 193–194). Recent attempts at measuring state anxiety in sport have incorporated cognitive and somatic components (see Gould et al. 1992a for a review). Cognitive anxiety consists of negative concerns about performance and other unpleasant feelings, whereas somatic anxiety includes symptoms of autonomic reactions such as stomach upset, sweating, and increased heart rate. At least one research study supports the independent nature of cognitive and somatic anxiety. For example, Anshel et al. (1993) examined the effectiveness of coping strategies on subjects' dart-throwing performance, emotions, and muscular tension immediately after receiving critical verbal feedback. Whereas the intervention strategies resulted in significantly better performance and fewer unpleasant feelings (i.e., cognitive anxiety), muscle tension (somatic anxiety), as measured by electromyography, was uninfluenced by the strategies.

Landers and Boutcher (1993) consider state anxiety an extension of high arousal. To these authors, "When arousal levels become extremely high, you experience unpleasant emotional reactions . . . This maladaptive condition is often referred to as stress or state anxiety" (p. 165). Essentially, then, anxiety is the unpleasant emotional reaction when the autonomic nervous system (i.e., uncontrolled physiological responses such as heart rate, breathing rate, and sweating) is stimulated (aroused). More recently, Gould and Krane (1992a) contend that "anxiety can be considered the emotional impact or cognitive dimension of arousal" (p. 121). From the literature, then, we can conclude that arousal is *essentially* a physiological response and that anxiety is *primarily* a cognitive process. However, both arousal and anxiety contain psychological and physiological components and manifestations.

For the purposes of this book, and to remain compatible with recent literature, *anxiety* is defined here as an emotion—in two words, *perceived threat*. A person who is worried about an upcoming exam and consequently has trouble sleeping is anxious. In sport, anxiety reflects the performer's feelings that something may go wrong, that the outcome may not be successful, or that performance failure may be experienced (Figure 5.1). Perhaps the performer views an opponent as superior or knows that a member of the audience—a judge, family member, friend, teammate, or the coach—is evaluating the quality of his or her performance. This can be threatening, particularly for individuals with relatively low self-confidence, low self-esteem, or a lack of previous success. Such individuals are sometimes referred to as "practice players" or "chokers." They have a tendency to "freeze up" and to perform more poorly during the contest, especially in pressure situations, than in practice. They rarely experience their performance potential. This is not to say that anxiety is always undesirable. To succeed in sport, athletes must be aware of potentially threatening situations. Upsets are often caused by an underexcited, less than optimally ready team that was favored to win but "forgot" that the opponents wanted to win too. Anxiety levels must be controlled, not eliminated.

Whereas anxiety is traditionally defined as an unpleasant emotion, arousal, on the other hand, can be either physiologically or psychologically based. This is because, according to Weinberg and Gould (1995), "arousal is not automatically associated with either pleasant or unpleasant events. You might be highly aroused by learning you have won 10 million dollars [or] be equally aroused by learning of the death of a loved one" (p. 92). The key issues concerning arousal for coaches and athletes are (1) determining the level of arousal that is optimal in a given situation to establish the point of diminishing returns and (2) learning the proper techniques for controlling it. When it comes to feelings of excitation in sport, more is not always better. Let's look at anxiety and arousal more extensively.

Anxiety

Spielberger (1972) was probably the first to categorize anxiety as having either state or trait qualities. *State anxiety* (A-state) is transitory in that it fluctuates over time. Martens et al. (1990) define competitive state anxiety as conscious feelings of apprehension and

Figure 5.1 High-quality sport performance requires optimal arousal—being psyched up, not being psyched out.

tension due mainly to the individual's perception of the present or upcoming situation as threatening. Often, though not always, anxiety is accompanied by activation of the autonomic nervous system, which is why it is confused with arousal. Still, researchers commonly measure state anxiety by its somatic (physiological) and cognitive (psychological) properties.

Trait anxiety (A-trait), on the other hand, is a relatively stable and acquired behavioral disposition, often depicted as a personality trait. A-trait predisposes an individual to perceive a wide range of nondangerous circumstances as threatening or dangerous. Further, the individual with high A-trait tends to demonstrate A-state reactions beyond what is necessary, given the present sense of danger. Thus, high A-trait athletes are more susceptible to state anxiety before a competitive event than low A-trait performers.

It is often reported in the sports media that some athletes become literally sick to their stomachs before every game (so much for the value of a proper pregame meal). It is likely that athletes who experience acute illness before a contest, a sign of extreme state anxiety, have high A-trait. Pregame nausea or vomiting is an example of why high A-state is not desirable. In addition to negative emotional and physiological ramifications, anxiety has also been shown to have a deleterious effect on motor performance. Weinberg and Hunt (1976) and Anshel et al. (1993) have shown through electromyography, a measure of muscle tension, that muscular coordination in skilled movements decreases with high A-state.

In summary, athletes with high A-state interpret a present situation as threatening, while high A-trait individuals have an underlying tendency or disposition to react in a certain way when confronted with sufficiently stressful information. Trait and state anxiety tend to be moderately to highly correlated, usually about .60 or above (Gould & Krane 1992). Thus, A-trait affects an individual's appraisal of the situation, increasing the likelihood that an athlete will view the situation as threatening.

As indicated in Figure 5.2, the individual takes in external stimuli that are perceived as unpleasant or potentially threatening (box 1). This input, along with the person's

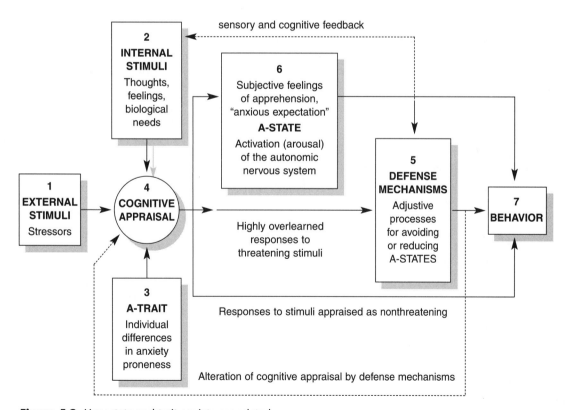

Figure 5.2 How state and trait anxiety are related
Source: From "Theory and research on anxiety" (1966). In C. D. Spielberger (Ed.), *Anxiety and Behavior* (p. 17). New York: Academic Press. Reprinted with permission.

internal psychological and biological signals (box 2) and his or her personal disposition toward anxiety (A-trait) (box 3). Individual differences in A-trait determine which stimuli are appraised as threatening, and the intensity of these appraisals (box 4). After appraisal, the individual makes mental and physical adjustments to eliminate, reduce, or prevent the onset of state anxiety (box 5). Relaxation techniques, imagery, positive self-statements, and physical removal from the immediate environment are examples of such adjustments, which are collectively referred to as *defense mechanisms*. Often these techniques are learned and mastered over a long time period. They can then be initiated very quickly and automatically. These defense mechanisms, combined with the resultant level of A-state (box 6), jointly affect the person's behavior or performance (box 7).

Probably the most important factor that contributes to feeling anxious or worried in a sport situation is *cognitive appraisal*. Appraisal consists of the athlete's interpretation of a given situation or event and directly influences his or her psychological and physiological responses. For example, using the appraisal model of Lazarus and Folkman (1984), a stress appraisal will elicit a different set of mental and somatic responses than an appraisal considered irrelevant or positive. Stress appraisals are further categorized as harm/loss, threat, or challenge. A coach's reprimand may cause considerable anxiety if the event is appraised as threatening to the athlete's self-esteem. Similarly, experiencing pain or injury will likely elicit an appraisal of harm or loss. However, if stressful events, such as remarks by others, are interpreted by the athlete as a challenge, then they provide incentive to improve performance. The result is less anxiety and greater arousal. Similarly, the success of an opponent may elicit an appraisal of *irrelevance* early in the game, but may be interpreted as far more *stressful* near the game's end with a close score. Each of these appraisals usually elicits different types of coping responses. Personal dispositions, such as trait anxiety, self-confidence, optimism, performance expectancies, and the motivation to achieve and feel competent, also influence the individual's appraisal.

Skill level is another factor that contributes to an anxiety appraisal. For example, Jones and Swain (1995) found that elite British cricket players interpret their anxiety levels as significantly more beneficial and less debilitative to their performance than their less-skilled counterparts. The key finding in this study was not the absence of differences in state anxiety between elites and nonelites. Rather, elite competitors revealed more positive *interpretations* of their anxious feelings about their future performance (i.e., higher positive expectations). Therefore, an intervention to improve the management of anxiety should include cognitive techniques that create more accurate and productive appraisals of the situation or event.

In sport, coaches and athletes want to regulate A-state at manageable levels so that it helps rather than hinders performance. To do this effectively, anxiety has to be measured and monitored. This is done primarily by psychological, physiological, and behavioral methods.

Psychological Techniques.   Measuring anxiety in this manner is usually accomplished with a standardized paper-and-pencil questionnaire. Several have been published (see Anshel 1987a and Ostrow 1996 for a list of these surveys). Very few anxiety inventories, however, were created for athletic participants and sport situations. For example, Taylor's (1953) Manifest Anxiety Scale (MAS) is used to ascertain chronic (trait) anxiety. However, it does not adequately predict differences between high- and low-anxiety persons with respect to learning and performing sport skills (Martens 1971). A more precise measure of A-trait and A-state is the State–Trait Anxiety Inventory (STAI) (Spielberger 1970). It is used less often in more recent sport psychology literature than in the 1970s and 1980s because the STAI was not developed for, and does not ask respondents about, their thoughts and feelings in sport situations. The second reason for not using the STAI is due to the emergence of a newer inventory developed specifically to measure state anxiety for sport situations, the Competitive State Anxiety Inventory-2 (CSAI-2, Martens et al. 1990).

Trait anxiety in sport has been typically measured by the Sport Competition Anxiety Test (SCAT) and, more recently, by the Sport Anxiety Scale (SAS; Smith et al. 1990). Upon reading the SCAT's questions, it is easy to see why it could not be used as a measure of state anxiety. Martens (1977) and Martens et al. (1990) point out that measures of A-trait predict heightened anxiety only in specific types of stress situations (a school classroom versus a sport competition, for example). This means that a person might have a disposition to feel anxious before school exams but not necessarily in sport-related situations or vice versa. Yet, the person's subjective feelings about how he or she views the competitive situation is the single most important issue in measuring and in experiencing anxiety. The CSAI-2 remains the most common measure of state anxiety in sport research.

The SAS is an improved measure of A-trait because, unlike the SCAT, it measures both cognitive and somatic components of sport-specific trait anxiety. For example, SAS includes items such as, "My body feels tense," "My heart races," and "My stomach gets upset before or during competition," all responses to somatic anxiety. SCAT, on the other hand, addresses only cognitive forms of A-trait. Smith et al. correctly reflect the sport anxiety literature in claiming that "cognitive and somatic anxiety have differential effects upon performance, depending upon the nature of the task" (p. 264). In addition, each component of anxiety requires different approaches to treatment. Somatic anxiety, for instance, should respond best to treatments that decrease physiological arousal, such as various relaxation techniques, whereas cognitive anxiety is best treated with cognitive approaches, such as self-instructional training and thought-stopping. The SAS brings a much-needed new measure of sport-specific anxiety, not only for use by sport psychologists to treat athletes but also for researchers in studying the best ways to predict and to treat anxiety in sport. Whether somatic anxiety can actually be measured as a trait, as opposed to a state condition, is far from certain. After all, athletes react physiologically to *situational* demands that may be independent of traits. If those demands are perceived as threatening, then certain physiological processes (e.g., heart rate, sweating) will be affected. Thus, to contend that these processes reflect a trait rather than a state response is questionable. In fact, Smith et al. found that the somatic component of the SAS was not a strong predictor of performance, due in part to cognitive and physical situational demands—a state, not a trait—that jointly dissipate somatic anxiety. As the authors conclude, "It seems highly likely that the influence of the various components of sport anxiety are a function of the nature of the momentary task demands and the extent to which the anxiety components are operative" (pp. 277–278).

Physiological Techniques. Despite previous attempts to measure and treat somatic anxiety in both state (CSAI-2) and trait (SAS) forms, anxiety is not usually measured physiologically. This is for several reasons. First, there is no single physiological response to the anxiety state (Sonstroem 1984). Second, anxiety is typically viewed as a feeling—a person's perception or appraisal of a situation. The individual's somatic response (e.g., heart rate) to appraisals of joy may be similar to appraisals of threat, harm, or challenge. As Hackfort and Schwenkmezger (1989) point out, "An increase in heart rate can occur both in the context of the emotion anxiety and in reactions of joy or anger" (p. 59). Third, the relationship (correlation) between any two measures that are typical physiological measures of anxiety (heart rate and palm sweating, for instance) is quite low, about .10 (Hackfort & Schwenkmezger 1989). Fourth, the nervous system response to anxiety differs among individuals. While some persons sweat profusely when nervous, others don't sweat at all.

The final argument against using physiological measures of anxiety, at least in recent years, is the attempt by scientists to separate emotional from physiological responses to stress (Hackfort & Schwenkmezger 1993). An individual may experience feelings of stress without experiencing the harmful physiological effects often associated with stress. This is important because an athlete, sport psychologist, or coach may incorrectly assume the athlete is anxious if the conclusion is based on the performer's heart rate rather than the person's self-reported feelings. Further, the techniques for reducing somatic anxiety (e.g., progressive relaxation) and cognitive anxiety (e.g., positive self-talk) often differ. Anxiety is now viewed as a mental state based on feelings about a situation. The person's heart rate, blood pressure, or other physiological measures might not necessarily be affected. This is especially true if the person is or has recently been physically active, which would markedly affect physiological responses. Nevertheless, measuring physiological processes such as heart rate, muscle tension, sweating, and breathing rate is still considered an important source of information for determining the presence of state anxiety and the effectiveness of anxiety management techniques.

Behavioral Techniques.   We all tend to act somewhat differently in response to a stressful situation. Twitching; pacing; urinating frequently; talking a lot, sometimes in a loud, obnoxious manner; and exhibiting an unfriendly temperament are behavioral examples of anxiety. A coach may suspect that a player is anxious when that athlete's actions are unlike his or her usual behavioral patterns. This measure, however, is subjective based on the observer's own interpretation, and therefore questionable. Martens et al. (1975) have shown that SCAT is a better predictor of competitive anxiety in athletes than the coaches' observations. More recent research has confirmed this finding.

For example, Hanson and Gould (1988) examined the ability of coaches to estimate their athletes' trait and state anxiety levels. The 33 college coaches in this study rated their awareness of athletes' anxiety levels and their effort in discerning this information as very high. The cues most often cited to detect athlete anxiety were a change in communication level and a change in behavior pattern. However, a comparison of the athletes' trait and state anxiety scores with their coaches' ratings indicated that the coaches were not accurate estimators of their athletes' A-trait and A-state levels. Coaches of women's teams were more accurate than coaches of men's teams on these measures.

Still uncertain among researchers and coaches is the ability of any single means to measure A-state accurately. For example, Deshaires (1980) found that volleyball players who score similarly on A-state differ significantly in their perceptions of the importance of the sport situation and in the uncertainty of the game's outcome. Endler (1977), Klavora (1978), and, more recently, Martens et al. (1990) suggest that it may be necessary to isolate the components of each situation that causes an individual to feel anxious. Another factor that decreases the predictability of anxiety measures is the athlete's ability to adapt to potentially anxiety-producing situations in sport. Identifying anxiety level and predicting performance based on a single measure apparently has its limitations. In fact, some psychologists contend that merely labeling a person's feelings or behaviors as "anxious" and communicating this observation to the competitor might actually provoke additional, more intense feelings of anxiety. In sport, this might further erode performance quality.

Much additional research is needed in order to understand the ways in which cognitive and somatic anxiety affect sport performance. In his review of the anxiety literature, Anshel (1995c) recommended several areas for future study. However, these issues remain understudied and still warrant further examination. First, what are the internal mechanisms that explain the ways in which anxiety inhibits sport performance? This is a particularly important issue, because there is great uncertainty about how an athlete's thoughts influence his or her performance. As Jones and Swain (1995) have found, anxious thoughts can either facilitate or inhibit sports performance. A second area in need of more study is the extent to which an athlete's dispositions (e.g., confidence, self-esteem, optimism, coping style) affect perceptions of stimuli as threatening, and how the individual responds to those thoughts. The ability to predict state anxiety based on personal and situational factors remains a third area for additional study. To date, predictors of A-state have centered on A-trait, and, to a lesser extent, on confidence, skill level, and experience (see Burton 1998 for a review). Situational factors related to choking, for instance, include perceptions of high pressure and self-consciousness (Baumeister 1984), sport type, gender, and task complexity (Burton 1998). Researchers remain uncertain about the manner in which these variables "ignite" thoughts of worry and threat.

The fourth recommendation for future study concerns examining effective means for anxiety management. In fact, intervention research in this area is vastly underreported in the scientific literature. A fifth area requiring future attention is determining the athlete's optimal anxiety level. Whereas the concept of optimal arousal has been studied extensively, the thought that a modicum of anxiety is actually desirable—anxiety has life-saving properties when driving a car, for instance—has escaped most scholars. The exception to this tendency, of course, would be Jones and Swain's (1995) work on facilitative anxiety and Kerr's work on reversal theory, in which the content and interpretation of thoughts can actually improve cognitive efficiency and performance. Determining optimal state anxiety and understanding the cognitive strategies and situational factors that can control it and facilitate its occurrence remains an area for future research.

Arousal

As indicated earlier, whereas anxiety has a psychological basis, arousal has been more often defined physiologically as the intensity of behavior on a continuum from sleep to extensive excitement. Arousal, often synonymous in the literature with the terms *drive, activation, readiness,* or *excitation,* is a requisite for optimal sport performance. Reacting, thinking, and moving in sport at efficient speeds can be achieved only if the performer has established an appropriate level of physical and psychological readiness. The intensity of this readiness, or arousal, has been measured by skin conductance (sweating on the palm or fingertips), muscle tension, brain waves, pulse or respiration rate, and blood pressure (Duffy 1957).

Earlier, we discussed briefly that arousal has an emotional component. Oxendine (1970) was perhaps the first to note the importance of positive and negative feelings associated with being psyched up. Examples of positive affective arousal include joy, elation, ecstasy, interest, happiness, and love. Negative emotions include fear, anger, anxiety, jealousy, embarrassment, disgust, boredom, or rage (Figure 5.3). Anshel (1985) developed the Children's Arousal Scale, in which female gymnasts, aged 9 to 14 years, identified adjectives that described positive and negative feelings of arousal. Positive terms included *happy, relaxed, excited,* and *eager,* while negative feelings were *scared, worried, sad, upset, nervous,* and *frightened.*

Figure 5.3 Preshot routines help athletes control their emotions during performance.

Research on measuring emotional arousal has been scarce, perhaps partly because arousal has been traditionally measured as a physiological process. However, Oxendine (1970), based on his observations and interactions with competitors, has intuitively speculated about the level of arousal that is optimal for various sports and sport tasks (see Table 5.1). Clearly, sport tasks that require more relaxed, fine-motor skills (such as golf putting or bowling) need markedly less arousal than relatively more powerful, gross-motor behaviors, as found in contact sports or sprinting, for instance.

Several theories have been developed over the years to partially explain how arousal influences sport performance.

Drive Theory. Hull's (1943) drive theory, later revised by Spence (1956), was the first (see Figure 5.4). According to this theory, performance (P) is dependent on two factors, drive (D) and habit strength (H), illustrated by the formula $P = D \times H$. To Hull, *drive* is a general, nonspecific activation of all behavior. *Habit strength* is the dominance of correct and incorrect responses in motor performance. The theory predicts that arousal increases the dominant response, whether or not the dominant response is the correct

Table 5.1 Optimal arousal level for some typical sport skills.

Level of Arousal	Sport Skills
#5 (extremely excited)	football blocking and tackling running (220 yards to 440 yards) sit up, push up, or bent arm hang test weight lifting
#4	running long jump running very short and long races shot put swimming races wrestling and judo
#3	basketball skills boxing high jumping most gymnastic skills soccer skills
#2	baseball pitchers and batters diving fencing tennis U.S. football quarterback
#1 (slight arousal)	archery and bowling basketball free throw field goal kicking golf putting and short irons skating figure eights
#0 (normal state)	

From J. Oxendine (1970). Emotional arousal and motor performance. *Quest*, 13, 23–30. Reprinted with permission.

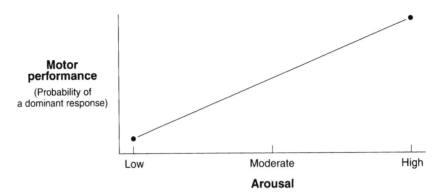

Figure 5.4 Hull's drive theory, in which performance and the probability of a dominant response—correct or incorrect—increases with higher arousal level.

one. Thus, if the dominant response is correct, as in well-learned or simple skills, then higher arousal will result in better performance. If, however, the proper response has not been mastered or if the performed skill is relatively complex, then more arousal will elicit the incorrect response; quality performance will be inhibited.

This "more is better" approach to explaining the drive/motor performance relationship has not been supported in research literature or in practice. Sport skills are typically very complex. The rapid actions and responses of gymnasts, divers, figure skaters, goaltenders in soccer and hockey, and skiers, to name a few, take hundreds of hours of practice, conditioning, and learning. Sports that demand less arousal (such as golf, archery, and bowling) also require extreme precision for success. The various positions and demands within each of these sports require different levels of arousal. Perhaps the behavior of a contact sport athlete or of a weight lifter might support the drive theory. But invariably, arousal must be controlled if sport skills are to be performed with optimal effectiveness.

Inverted-U Hypothesis. In contrast to the direct relationship between arousal and the dominant response as seen in Hull's drive theory, the inverted-U hypothesis, also called the Yerkes-Dodson law (1908), assumes a curvilinear relationship between arousal and performance (see Figure 5.5). Thus, the effect of arousal on performance is based on the optimal level given the particular skill. Remember that "optimal" does not necessarily mean "maximal." For instance, golf putting requires far less arousal than baseball batting, but each has its own arousal requirement for optimal performance. Not only is this optimal level defined differently for each skill, but for each performer's needs and the particular situation as well.

Frank Shorter, 1976 Olympic gold medal winner in the 26-mile marathon, and other marathon runners since then claim that an important key to success in distance running is total relaxation prior to the race. The runner doesn't want to burn up calories needlessly through nervous tension. And an athlete who is relatively unskilled or younger likely generates high excitation and needs to feel lower arousal than his or her more mature and higher skilled counterpart who are better able to control their emotions.

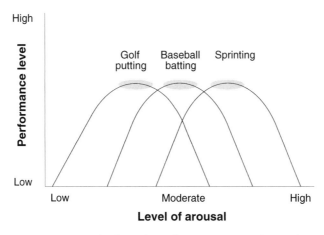

Figure 5.5 Inverted-U hypothesis illustrating optimal arousal level for golf putting, baseball batting, and sprinting.

Landers and Arent (2001) have provided an extensive review and critique of the inverted-U hypothesis. While not discarding the concept of optimal arousal, the authors contend that the idealized curve associated with the inverted U, located in Figures 5.5 and 5.6 in this chapter, is rare when analyzing actual research data. This is due to relatively small sample sizes and relatively few levels of arousal measured. Instead, the curve usually resembles an unsymmetrical inverted V. For example, Sonstroem and Bernardo (1982) supported the inverted-U hypothesis—which, in fact, was actually an inverted V (consistent with Landers and Arent's conclusions)—in a study of 30 university female basketball players. The researchers measured the state anxiety (using a self-report inventory) and performance quality (based on a compilation of performance statistics) of each player over three consecutive games. They found that "across the three games subjects achieved their own best performance during individually low and moderate state anxiety levels. When confronted by relatively higher state anxiety conditions, performance dropped off noticeably" (pp. 241–242). Landers and Arent conclude that "the relationship between arousal and performance is curvilinear with best performance occurring at an intermediate point within the range of arousal being examined . . . arousal is a factor influencing performance" (p. 214).

A more recent attempt at explaining the arousal–performance relationship is Hanin's (1980) proposed *zone of optimal functioning* (ZOF). Hanin contends that extensive differences among subjects' state anxiety in field studies casts doubt on the inverted-U hypothesis. In particular, he believes that rather than identifying a single optimal level of state anxiety, athletes possess a *zone*, or range, of optimal functioning just prior to competition. This zone consists of the performer's averaged state anxiety score on Spielberger's STAI, plus or minus four points. Hanin predicted that athletes whose state anxiety level falls within their ZOF would perform better than athletes whose state anxiety was outside their ZOF. Hanin cites research with weight lifters supporting his ZOF hypothesis but is unable to explain this state anxiety–performance link. Although the

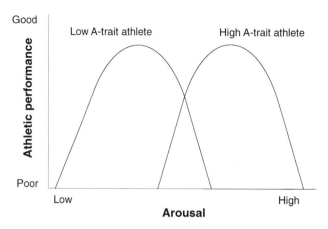

Figure 5.6 High trait-anxious athletes tend to perform best at a relatively higher arousal level than low trait-anxious athletes.

ZOF has recently received increased attention by researchers, additional research is needed to examine and validate this phenomenon further.

Catastrophe Theory. Hardy (1990) has contended that the inverted-U hypothesis describes the relationship between stress and performance but does not reflect anecdotal evidence in sport that this relationship should not be symmetrical. Thus, contrary to the inverted-U hypothesis, overexcited athletes suffer a rapid, not a gradual, drop in their performance; they are not able to return quickly to desirable performance levels. The inverted-U hypothesis and catastrophe theory share the prediction that higher A-state will improve performance up to an optimal level. However, whereas the inverted-U predicts that further increased arousal or anxiety will impair performance in an *orderly, curvilinear manner,* catastrophe theory predicts that further physiological arousal and cognitive anxiety will result in a *large and dramatic decline* in performance. Thus, the relationship between physiological arousal and performance depends on the performer's level of cognitive anxiety; only when cognitive anxiety is high in combination with high physiological arousal will there be "catastrophic" changes in performance. A "choking" response may result. The strengths of catastrophe theory, according to Gould and Krane (1992), are that it addresses the effects of both physiological and cognitive dimensions of arousal on performance, and that it reflects actual sport conditions more realistically; sport is not usually perfectly symmetrical and predictable. However, Gould and Krane also contend that catastrophe theory is overly complex and requires numerous assessments of the same athletes over time to test it. The validity of catastrophe theory awaits further scrutiny by researchers.

Reversal Theory. Reversal theory (Kerr 1985) is based on the premise that a person is capable of interpreting his or her arousal level as excitement (pleasant) or anxiety (unpleasant); low arousal may be interpreted as relaxation (pleasant) or boredom (unpleasant). The concept of psychological reversal stems from the person's shift in interpreting his or her feelings. For example, engaging in a dangerous, risk-taking task such as rock climbing or downhill skiing induces heightened arousal, called anxiety in this theory. However, when the dangerous task or situation is mastered, the anxiety suddenly "reverses" and becomes excitement. These psychological reversals alter a person's emotional state significantly. The athlete's interpretation of arousal states is viewed as central to the ability to explain and predict the effect of emotion on sport performance. Kerr (1990) provides a review of several studies that support his theory.

The Arousal/Performance Relationship.   One cause of poorer performance when arousal is too high is psychological. Individuals with either high arousal or anxiety tend to exclude too much information when performing. Overly excited competitors may not use all of the information available in scanning the field before making a decision to react. An inaccurate judgment could result. This is referred to as an overnarrowing of attention (Landers 1980).

This attentional-narrowing process could best be described by Easterbrook's (1959) cue-utilization theory. The sport environment is filled with signals (cues) that are available to athletes for optimizing performance. These cues provide information about features in the environment such as the speed and direction of objects in flight, the actions of opponents and teammates, and other input that allows the performer to anticipate movements, make accurate and rapid decisions, and respond appropriately to task demands. However, some of these cues are unnecessary and irrelevant—even harmful—for performance. Increased arousal narrows the athlete's attentional focus until, at some optimal point, all unnecessary cues are eliminated. The athlete is now able to concentrate only on the most important information. However, if attention narrows beyond this point, relevant as well as irrelevant information is excluded. This will tend to harm performance. Thus, Easterbrook's cue-utilization theory predicts that arousal will narrow the range of using these environmental cues, resulting in an inverted-U performance response.

Narrowed attention is often a good strategy in "closed" skills in which the performer initiates the response and the sport environment remains stable, such as in golf, archery, or bowling. Here, filtering out extraneous or unimportant input is desirable. But in skills that demand reacting to opponents and making decisions about movement direction, speed, and strategy, narrowed attention tends to hinder performance.

Another factor that interacts with the athlete's arousal is precompetitive trait and state anxiety. Athletes who have high A-trait also have relatively higher A-state (Martens et al. 1990). This combination can raise arousal levels beyond desirable limits. From their reviews of related literature, Iso-Ahola and Hatfield (1986) and Hackfort and Schwenkmezger conclude that (1) both high and low trait-anxious athletes need similarly moderate elevations of A-state prior to competition, but that (2) high A-trait athletes might need higher arousal to perform at their best as compared to low A-trait athletes. This is apparently because highly anxious athletes are usually at a chronically higher level of arousal in all conditions, as illustrated in Figure 5.6.

High arousal may not be desirable for child athletes, however. Gould (1984) concluded that child (or relatively low-skilled) athletes are less able to control their anxiety and, consequently, are more apt to be overly aroused. Further, high trait-anxious children do not cope well with high state anxiety and perform less well because of it. Consequently, youngsters who become easily threatened in evaluative situations—in which someone of "importance" is assessing their performance—or who are classified as highly trait anxious may choose not to participate in the activities (Simon & Martens 1979). One possible reason for the tendency to drop out of sport is the finding that high trait-anxious athletes in general do not often use efficient strategies for coping with stress. They are unable to regulate and maintain proper anxiety and arousal levels, and they tend to "choke" in high-pressure sport situations, performing better in practice—where the pressure is relatively low—and less effectively in games.

Poorer performance from high arousal is also dependent on muscular tension. Weinberg and Hunt (1976), in a study mentioned earlier, assessed movement coordination in high and low trait-anxious subjects when throwing darts. They created psychological stress in all participants by informing them that their performance was below average using bogus (fake) information feedback. Electromyography data, a measure of muscle tension, indicated that the high-anxious group lacked timing and coordination in the muscle groups used for throwing. Although not a recent study, it is rare in that it actually cites lack of neuromuscular coordination as a cause of poorer performance in relation to the subjects' anxiety or arousal. This partially explains why muscular relaxation is an effective technique to reduce tension when used prior to performance.

Determining Optimal Arousal.   What is the "best" arousal level for a particular situation or for a given individual athlete? How can the appropriate or customary level of arousal be ascertained? These are challenging questions for sport psychology researchers and practitioners. What *is* known is that generalizations are rarely valid for all participants. To individualize the prescription and treatment for optimal arousal for each competitor would be more desirable. According to Klavora (1979), an athlete's customary performance quality is associated with his or her customary arousal level.

Klavora suggests that the player's current (state) arousal level immediately prior to and during the contest should be compared with his or her subsequent performance. Then, after the contest, the coach and athlete should jointly determine whether changing the arousal level before or during future contests is desirable.

To test this strategy, Klavora examined senior (grade 12) high school basketball players, comparing their pregame arousal with the quality of their game performance. The participants completed the STAI just before the game. After the game, the coach evaluated each player's performance on a three-point scale indicating 1 (poor or below performance ability), 2 (average or close to performance ability), or 3 (an outstanding performance). The pairings of pregame arousal and game performance for each athlete were plotted. Examples of two players are illustrated in Figure 5.7.

From these data, Klavora concludes that:

- The two curves conformed to the inverted-U model of the arousal-sport performance relationship. This indicated that the players may have performed poorly or at least below their capability, owing either to a lack of psychological readiness or to overexcitation.

- The curves are positioned at different levels "indicating that Player 2 is generally a more excitable person than is Player 1" (p. 160).

- Both players have to be psyched up if they are to perform according to the coach's expectations. Marked differences in the arousal levels of the players exist initially. But both need a motivational "boost" prior to the game.

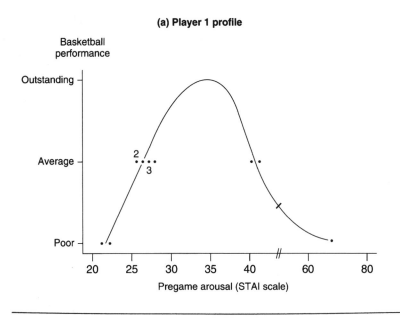

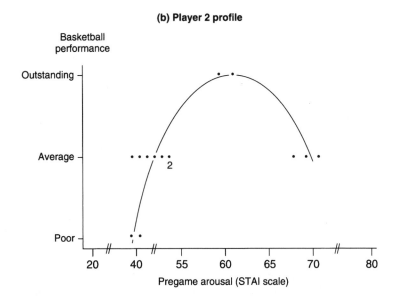

Figure 5.7 Raw score profile of two basketball players showing pregame arousal–game performance relationship.

One concern about Klavora's study was the method by which arousal was measured. The STAI measures anxiety, not arousal. As indicated earlier, contemporary scientists now acknowledge that anxiety and arousal are not the same (Anshel 1985; Weinberg & Gould 1995). Further, Klavora's assessment of arousal was not corroborated with physiological measures such as heart or respiration rate, blood pressure, galvanic skin response (a measure of sweating), or other available somatic measures as suggested by Martens et al. (1990). Since arousal has been traditionally measured as a physiological response (Duffy 1957), it might be argued that the players in Klavora's study felt some other unpleasant emotion, such as anxiety (perceived threat), rather than more positive feelings such as excitement or happiness. Nevertheless, Klavora addresses not only an area in need of further research but also a topic that has direct application in determining the athlete's optimal arousal level. This issue has received far more theoretical than applied study.

One possible approach to determining optimal arousal—the difference between feeling "up" as opposed to feeling "uptight"—is to pose questions that help the performer to identify certain feelings. Athletes can use these questions (1) to self-monitor feelings and physiological responses prior to and during competition, (2) to identify their feelings accurately, and (3) to remind them to use appropriate physical and mental strategies that can favorably affect mental status. Counseling sport psychologists typically ask athletes to identify the time or game in which they felt they performed at their best and at their worst, to describe these performances as accurately as possible, and to describe their feelings and mental attitudes during this time. Specific questions include: "What were you thinking about during this event, if anything?" "Was your concentration easily attained, or did you have to work hard to concentrate?" "Were you relaxed or tense, and why?" "Describe your focus of awareness: to what were you directing your attentions?"

Based on an athlete's responses to these questions, coaches or sport psychology consultants suggest mental strategies that the performer can use to alter levels of arousal and anxiety to improve his or her mental preparation for competition. The consultant's or coach's objective in asking these questions is to identify the feelings associated with desirable and undesirable performance and to recall the athlete's perceptions of his or her physiological responses at the time of competition.

This approach was used by Orlick (1986) in his respected and popular "mental plan" model. Briefly, Orlick asked athletes to identify certain feelings (e.g., self-confidence level) and emotions (e.g., anxiety, arousal) on a scale from 1 (very low) to 10 (very high). This self-monitoring technique encourages athletes to become more aware of their mental status at any given time. But perhaps more important, this increased awareness allows athletes to compare the kinds and levels of feelings/emotions that accompany good performance outcomes with the feelings/emotions linked to poorer performance outcomes. In this way, when conducted over several contests, the athlete's best (optimal) arousal state can be identified.

Perhaps the most extensive description of factors that affect the arousal–performance relationship comes from an extensive review of this literature by Landers and Arent (2001). These factors are: (1) the athlete (skill, fitness level, personal experience, and personality), (2) the sport situation (task difficulty and task demands), (3) cognitive appraisal (of demands, of resources, of consequences, of meaning of consequences, and of bodily reactions), (4) emotional or physiological responses (heart rate, muscle tension, brain waves, and skin conductance), and (5) behavior (motor performance, decision making, perception, and retention of learned material). Although a complete description of these factors goes beyond the scope of this section, the important points here are that the concept of optimal arousal is derived from numerous sources, and that an optimal level in one situation or for one athlete would likely be very different in other situations and for other athletes. The issue of why coaches should recognize individual differences among athletes in creating and sustaining optimal arousal level is addressed in the next section.

The Coach's Role in Game Preparation

The team leader cannot reach into the heart and mind of each athlete and cause the performer to feel a certain way. Each player has a different mental approach to the contest, and to affect every athlete in the same manner is impossible. This, by the way, is the problem with the so-called "T-E-A-M" approach, which many coaches support. In this strategy, everyone on the team goes through the same mental and physical preparation before the contest. My own experiences with athletes, supported by sport psychology literature, do not support this approach. While some precontest tasks must be conducted by all team members at the same time, athletes, particularly at the more advanced levels, prefer to prepare mentally for the contest in their own way; some players would rather be alone, while others prefer the company of their teammates, for instance. Let's look at some general suggestions that coaches can use in group settings and with individual athletes to help them to manage arousal and anxiety.

Anxiety and Arousal Reducers

Sometimes coaches must help their players to "psych down." Although arousal and anxiety are not identical and often warrant different techniques, several approaches to reducing both mental states can be used.

1. *Release stress and anxiety through physical activity*. Precontest emotions are often stressful. Stress is the body's way of preparing for "flight or fight." The athlete is in a physical state that urges him or her to move, yet the athlete remains sedentary. Brisk movement, with accompanying increases in physiological arousal, may relax the athlete because psychological, thought-induced stress is "converted" to physical stress. This stress-reducing technique is particularly effective with high state-anxious athletes (Morgan 1979b). Low-arousal sports such as golf, fencing, or tennis usually require less intense physical activity (walking, for instance) to relax the performer than do high-energy activities such as soccer, wrestling, and football.

   A warning about this technique seems warranted. Some debate as to the overuse of physical activity during warm-up has occurred. Often, teams seem to exert a game's worth of energy before the contest even begins. There is support in the physiology literature—although more research is needed—that an intensely physical and emotional pregame warm-up might do more harm than good by depleting players' energy.

2. *Avoid giving the "relax" command*. Coaches commonly tell their players to relax, especially just before the contest. Sometimes this actually *increases* tension. "The coach knows I'm uptight," the athlete thinks. Or, athletes may need to feel a degree of tension as preparation for a superior performance, and the coach's request to take it easy may be contradictory to the player's preferred mental state. For the coach to say nothing may be more helpful than using verbal messages that try to alter the player's state of mind.

3. *Promote task familiarity.* Tasks that are familiar to athletes are less anxiety-provoking than novel actions. This is why effective coaches have the players follow a regimented and familiar pregame warm-up routine. On the day of the contest, athletes should engage in activities that are comfortable and in relaxed or familiar company. The potential for anxiety is heightened when athletes are less certain about the precontest schedule, planned activities, and competition venue on the day of a contest. Of course, the activities of game day differ from other days. But coaches can decrease the athletes' nervousness derived from this different schedule by conducting game day rehearsals. Activities and schedules should simulate the anticipated routine, including the times of day that meals are consumed, the same opportunities for practice, and other conditions similar to the actual contest.

4. *Simulate games in practice.* Athlete anxiety will be reduced if skills and strategies that will be used in the contest are rehearsed in practice sessions until they are mastered. During the game is not the time to teach new, unrehearsed skills.

5. *Individualize mental strategies.* Athletes differ markedly in the ways that they prepare for competition. Some players prefer a sedate atmosphere that allows for self-reflection, mental imagery, and relaxation. Others desire a more vocal, exciting locker room atmosphere. The key coaching strategy here is, whenever possible, to allow each player to prepare mentally for the contest in the way that he or she finds most comfortable.

6. *Build self-confidence and high but realistic expectations.* Anxiety is heightened by personal insecurity, low self-esteem, and the player's perception of the sport situation as threatening. Coaches can increase player confidence, not with trite comments ("You'll do fine" or "Go after 'em"), but rather with informative messages that are based on performance. Reviewing a player's strengths, weaknesses of opponents, game strategies, and articulating the coach's confidence in the player's skill and effort will promote positive thoughts and reduce negative ones.

7. *Keep errors in perspective.* Physical mistakes are an integral part of performing physical tasks. The coach's response to mistakes directly affects the athlete's stress level. Keeping an error in perspective means: (a) remembering that the error is unlikely to affect the contest's outcome directly, (b) keeping the player focused on present and future events and, for the moment, forgetful of past mistakes, and (c) helping the athlete to cope with the error (see Chapter 2) so as to avoid negative self-statements, decreased self-confidence, and undesirable emotions and feelings.

8. *Avoid discussing the team's record.* Thinking about records and outcomes tends to decrease concentration and to increase anxiety. Reviewing the team's losing record or the pressures of maintaining a winning record are counterproductive. The best advice is to concentrate on performance, not outcome, and to let winning take care of itself.

9. *Respond to an injury.* Coaches should be calm, yet attentive, to the injured athlete. In addition to the pain, injured players must deal with their fear of possible surgery and with their fear that the injury will end their season or career. The coach's (or athletic trainer's) response to the player's injury will significantly affect the athlete's anxiety level. A supportive, empathetic coach will relax the player, whereas an angry, disappointed coach who ignores or inflicts guilt on the player, even during the rehabilitation period, induces anxiety and resentment.

Former successful cross-country and track head coach Dick Abbott, at Western Illinois University, considered it part of his job to "supplement the medical first aid that the training room provided with his own brand of emotional first aid" (Mechikoff & Kozar 1983, p. 82). After the athlete received proper training-room attention, Abbott would step in with concern and reassurance that the injury would heal on schedule. Then he would consult with the athlete on almost a daily basis.

10. *Minimize self-focusing.* Carver and Scheier (1981), based on a series of studies, suggest that persons who feel anxious and have unfavorable expectations about an outcome should not focus internally on these thoughts. Negative thinking tends to exacerbate anxiety and to disrupt future performance. Sometimes such thinking leads to the individual completely disengaging from further activity. Instead, the uptight individual should think about external events, focusing instead on the task at hand, or location of opponents and teammates. On the other hand, persons who have confident, positive feelings and expect favorable outcomes can focus internally on their thoughts. These individuals are likely to persist on tasks longer and feel more confident and in control.

11. *Acknowledge possible sources of stress and anxiety.* Sometimes it is a good idea for athletes to ignore stressful feelings and experiences. In fact, ignoring can be an effective coping technique. However, it is not as constructive for coaches to ignore the athletes' stressful feelings. It is often helpful to help athletes directly address sources of stress. One technique is called *disarming*, in which the coach verbally recognizes the athletes' possible stressful feelings. The coach's identification of sources of stress or anxiety (a) informs the athletes that their feelings are normal and understood, which, by itself, is a stress reducer for many competitors, and (b) begins the coping process by addressing any concerns that may be causing these undesirable feelings and working toward resolving them. The following is an example based on my experiences as a consultant for a professional rugby team.

One day before the game, players learned that a highly respected starting player had been unexpectedly injured in practice and would not play. The news of losing such an important teammate was upsetting to the other players. Individual player discussions revealed reduced team confidence and lower expectations for winning the game. In addition, there was no time to practice with the substitute player. The head coach and I agreed to use a disarming strategy in his pregame talk. He acknowledged that "all of us are disappointed that Paul is unable to play today. He's one of our best players and is a team leader." The coach also recognized the difficulty of receiving such news when it is such a surprise and comes so late in the week. He "disarmed" his team—that is, reduced the intensity of their anxiety—by recognizing a possible drop in their self-confidence about winning. The coach then advised the team that Paul's replacement, Jon, also had excellent skills and that Jon had the talent to give the necessary support. Finally, he informed them that they were capable of winning this game if they played at 100 percent effort. "This is not the type of sport," he reminded the players, "in which the loss of one individual separates success from failure. You can do it; just play the game using your talent." The team—and Jon—went on to play a superb game. Sometimes putting issues "on the table" is a good antidote to unpleasant feelings.

Precontest Arousal Raisers

Athletes cannot be effective if they're half-asleep or uninterested in competing. Their reactions will be slowed and their coordination reduced. The nervous system has to be in an optimal state of readiness. Sometimes the coach must bring the team "up" to ensure proper effort and concentration. This is more difficult than most people realize. A few guidelines follow.

First, the coach must consider each player's skill level, age, psychological needs, playing position, and task. Younger players, for instance, require less psyching up than older, more skilled participants. Less skillful players should focus on form, concentration, and planned maneuvers; therefore, levels of activation that are too high are more likely to disrupt their performance (Fisher & Motta 1977). Further, the ability to control both positive and negative emotions improves with age. Younger athletes are more susceptible to the deleterious effects of disapproval and negative feedback from significant others (e.g., coaches, parents, peers) than are their older counterparts (Passer 1983). Emotional control in sport is a function of the person's self-perceptions, personal feelings, and causal attributions following sport experiences (Roberts & Treasure 1995). Each of these factors tends to be more accurate and productive in older, more experienced, and better skilled athletes. Hence, younger athletes may become more anxious when they are scolded or exposed to the pressures of winning the contest than their older counterparts, who can keep these pressures and expectations in better perspective.

A second important feature of increasing arousal is acknowledging that some positions and tasks require higher levels of activation than others. As Oxendine (1970) suggests, sports that involve gross-motor movement can use higher activation levels than tasks that are highly complex in nature (refer back to Table 5.1 to determine arousal categories for different sport tasks). Sprinters should be more psyched up than long-distance runners, for instance.

Another important factor related to increasing arousal is timing. For example, it is not a good idea, contrary to popular practice, to get the team excited the night before a game. This only disturbs sleep and concentration. The late Woody Hayes, former football coach at Ohio State University, disagreed with coaches who have their athletes view commercial films that are high in aggression the night before a football game. After all, the game isn't played until the next day. Therefore, watching a film to increase aggression the night before a contest is ill-timed and may disturb sound sleep.

Visual aids, however, can be effective motivational tools. Some coaches show the film of last year's contest. Former college football coach and athletic director Dick Tamburo suggests, "If you are going to face a team at the end of the week that humiliated the team the year before, you may want to show the film of last year's humiliating defeat prior to the start of the game" (in Mechikoff & Kozar 1983). Rather than forgetting past failures, Tamburo's suggestion might have some merit if the present players are confident and want to prove that they are a better, improved team.

A different approach to visual input is to provide videotapes of the athletes' best previous performances. The purpose of this strategy is to model correctly executed skills, a concept that supports Bandura's (1977) self-efficacy theory. To increase precontest arousal, coaches want to instill a sense of self-confidence in each player. Athletes have a greater need to be reminded of their good qualities than many coaches acknowledge. To remind athletes of their past successes enhances feelings of reassurance, self-confidence, and expectations for success (Figure 5.8). Examples include "Based on how I saw you perform in practice this week, I know you're ready" or "This is a better team than our opponents." Think about what you can do well, and be proud of it. Let's prove

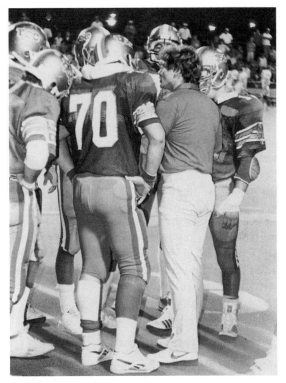

Figure 5.8 Coaches have an important role in helping to regulate emotions before, during, and following competition.

we're the better team." If, however, the opponent is commonly acknowledged as superior, the coach might remind the athletes: "This is a good opportunity to compare your skills to theirs." "How good are you? Let's find out!" I was present when a coach simply said: "Go out there and have fun" just before competing against a nationally ranked, far superior team. The team played their best game of the year.

Finally, although arousal has an emotional component, certain techniques are used to increase the athlete's physiological arousal level. An aroused athlete experiences increased physiological processes such as heart rate, sweating, respiration rate, muscular tension, and brain wave activity. Of course, measuring any of these processes prior to a contest is neither necessary nor desirable. But coaches can institute certain techniques that predictably increase their players' physiological arousal, again to *optimal, not maximal,* levels. Examples include (1) increasing voice intensity, (2) using bright indoor lighting, (3) generating loud noises such as clapping, foot stomping, or fast-paced music, (4) using nonverbal cues such as hand or facial gestures, especially in close proximity to the athlete, (5) contacting the athletes physically, such as holding a player's arm or shoulder (but be careful; abusive physical contact raises anxiety to the detriment of performance), (6) using the players' first names, especially when providing verbal recognition for quality performance, (7) setting immediate (short-term) performance goals, (8) introducing the players—at least the starting lineup—to the crowd before the contest, and (9) having players engage in light physical exercise, which is customary during the precontest warm-up.

If you think that this list of arousal-raisers is too much for one coach to do, you're absolutely right. Often, teams include a leadership role for people called assistant coaches or team captains. Less effective head coaches appear to forget that coaching assistants and selected players can have a valuable role in regulating the athletes' emotions before and during the contest. Payton Jordan, head coach of the 1968 U.S. Olympic track team, asserts, "If athletes hear you (the head coach) all the time, they will shut you out after a while" (Mechikoff & Kozar 1983). My own experience and research as a sport psychology consultant supports this view (Anshel 1989a). With time, the content of the head coach's message loses meaning; athletes "tune out" the person who is constantly offering verbal input. They become "coach deaf." Further, assistant coaches typically establish positive relationships with players, which increases their influence. In fact, in one study (Anshel & Straub 1991), American college football players indicated a preference for greater input by and the more effective use of the team's assistant coaches to improve team leadership. Head coaches would be wise to delegate some leadership responsibilities, at least occasionally.

Coaching Strategies for Half-time and Time-outs

Half-time is a period often used for adjusting, regrouping, reviewing plans and strategies, relaxing, and exchanging information. Athletes should be allowed to remain quiet and to calm down from their first-half efforts and to prepare mentally for the second half (or next period), even in isolation if they so choose. They have special physiological and psychological needs during this time to which coaches must be sensitive. For instance, liquid refreshment is essential to replenish energy and body resources, not only between periods but also during the contest. Sensitivity to their psychological needs will also better prepare them for postrest performance.

For example, as soon as the athletes enter the locker room during a break in game play, some coaches tend to shower them with information feedback. After vigorous physical activity, fatigue, and heightened arousal, the human system needs to relax for a short time before it can efficiently process and retain additional information. Researchers (e.g., see Wrisberg 2001 for a review of literature) maintain that a disruption in attentional processes may occur if internal/external factors (e.g., fatigue, high arousal) cause an imbalance between an athlete's ability to process information and task demands. Therefore, two suggestions for the coach are warranted: First, delay offering input to the players for several minutes at the start of a long rest period (half-time, for instance). The players need a little time to relax and to allow their information processing systems to focus and concentrate on new input. Second, limit the amount of information that is provided. Coaches may (and often do) have "a thousand things" to tell their players based on their observations. Unfortunately, much of this information will not be remembered and, hence, not used later in the contest. Ignoring the coach's input is not intentional but rather due to information overload, fatigue, and a limited ability to incorporate new, perhaps complicated, information. Effective teachers of athletes (1) make only two or three key points, (2) try to communicate visually (with a chalkboard or physical demonstration) as well as verbally, (3) summarize their points at the end of the session, and (4) include positive comments about earlier performances and have reasonably high expectations about the quality of subsequent performances (see Anshel 1990c and 1990d for additional teaching suggestions).

And, speaking of expectations, coaches should use criticism constructively and selectively without losing control (see Chapter 9 on techniques for offering critical input). Obviously, critical feedback is essential for learning and altering performance. But too much criticism is like too much of any type of information—it is soon forgotten. Also, critical input should not be communicated in a manner that intimidates or embarrasses the player—criticism in front of teammates, for example. A statement such as "You guys were terrible" has less impact on improving later performance than "We're waiting too long before taking the shot" or "We're playing too loose on defense; stay closer to your opponent."

In addition, coaches who "lose their cool" are communicating ineffectively. Players get caught up in the coach's anger rather than in the message. True, even psychologists contend that anger is a normal emotion of humans (Ginott 1965). But demonstrating a loss of emotional control and maturity (for example, name-calling, destroying equipment, physically abusing athletes, or making threats) is counterproductive. For successful coaches, the most effective approach is to accentuate the positive when the team is behind at half-time. The message typically is, "We are better than this; fortunately, we have 30 minutes left to show it." When a coach comes into the locker room and is visibly upset and projects anger and hostility toward the team, he or she is taking a fifty-fifty chance on positive motivational results.

Incorrect Coaching Strategies That Increase Anxiety and Arousal

Some anxiety is a good thing. Mature, higher-skilled players need a sense of concern—even urgency—before and during the contest (Mahoney et al. 1987). When Mahoney and his colleagues examined the psychological characteristics of elite and nonelite athletes, they found that both groups of competitors experienced anxiety. However, the elite athletes were better able to manage their anxiety than nonelites were. In this way, anxiety was far less disruptive to performance. Still, coaches do not want their players to be more anxious than necessary. Sometimes a coach will use a technique that has the opposite of its intended effect; it unintentionally promotes, rather than reduces, anxiety. Here are some examples of what coaches often do in the mistaken belief that they are helping the athletes:

1. *Teaching before or during the contest.* Studying minutes before an exam is fruitless because the learner is too tense to retain information. Information cannot be internally rehearsed during moments of high stress, so it is quickly forgotten. The same process occurs in sport. The emotions of high arousal and anxiety prevent learning to any significant degree, and the absence of physically practicing new skills dooms

initial attempts to failure. Coaches must avoid presenting new skills, complicated changes in strategy, and sophisticated explanations. New, unrehearsed plays should be saved for the next practice session and mastered before being included in competition plans.

2. *Maintaining that "We must win this game."* Don't the players already know that? Players are usually quite nervous before the contest. Statements that indicate the vital importance of a contest increase the participants' nervousness, not their excitation. Effective coaches focus on reviewing skills and strategies before the contest or between periods—or they say nothing at all. Reminding the players of the importance of winning psychs them out, not up.

3. *Using criticism as a motivator.* Why do some coaches believe that they can bring a player "up" by putting him or her "down"? Athletes need self-confidence in order to succeed; they need to feel good about their ability to perform at their best and win. Criticism of an athlete's character or sarcastic remarks tend to have the opposite effect. Wait a minute! What about the player who "rises to the occasion" in response to his or her coach's harsh remarks? True, some players may react with vigor, aggression, and determination, and perhaps succeed. Their reaction is "I'll show him!" But the long-term effect is often another story. Verbally abused players will feel resentment, anger, and less loyalty toward the coach. The recommendation to coaches is to base criticism on specific performance and not to use it to "play games" with an athlete's mind.

4. *Saying "Don't do . . . "* The adage "Never say never" can be translated in this context as "Don't say don't." Coaches who tell their players what not to do are actually reinforcing the wrong behaviors. The players mentally rehearse what they are told *not* to do and become preoccupied with these thoughts instead of thinking what they *should* do. In addition, scientists have found that we tend to remember positively stated information better than negative input. Coaches should help athletes to focus on future correct behaviors.

5. *Setting goals incorrectly.* Sometimes a coach will "require" an athlete to meet what the athlete feels is an unrealistically difficult goal. True, players should find challenging goals motivating. But goals that are too difficult, that are set exclusively by the coach without input from the athlete, and that are based on outcomes (over which the player often has no control) rather than performance, will tend to raise anxiety and inhibit performance. In fact, many athletes will give up or drop out rather than attempt to meet a goal that they consider to be far beyond realistic expectations. The competitor's belief is "If I don't try, I can't fail" or "Why even bother?"

6. *Inducing guilt.* A common error in coaching is to make athletes feel guilty about their performance. Statements such as "You guys should feel ashamed of yourselves" or "You mean to tell me that the other team is better than you?" do not motivate athletes or enhance player loyalty to the team and coach. According to Kroll (1982), "Guilt can contribute to heightened anxiety and it would appear that guilt is one of the causes of anxiety in the precompetitive situation" (p. 4). Another cause of guilt is asking the athlete to do something that is contrary to the athlete's wishes or character. Examples include instructing a player purposely to injure an opponent or to cheat.

7. *Blaming the referee.* Coaches often become antagonistic toward game officials,

especially if the team is losing. Essentially, the umpire or referee often becomes the scapegoat for the team's loss. Sometimes the coach feels that arguing with the arbiter will motivate the team. The potential problem with this approach is that when athletes feel that the outcome of a contest is not under their control (i.e., bad luck due to a "poor" official), they feel helpless. Consequently, players mentally give up and do not maintain optimal effort. In extreme cases, they stop trying. Coaches have a right and responsibility to communicate with game officials. But when the interaction is negative and persistent, players feel embarrassed ("I expect my coach to behave in a mature manner"), guilty ("I caused the argument"), or helpless ("We can't win because the ref doesn't like us").

8. *Reminding players who's watching.* Although athletes love a crowd, they seldom respond enthusiastically to being evaluated by persons whose opinions may influence their future success. Judges, scouts, and recruiters are potentially threatening to players (Cottrell 1972). Consequently, awareness of their presence might cause more harm than good by increasing anxiety (which, as you remember, is defined as "perceived threat"). Coaches would be doing players a favor by not mentioning who is watching.

9. *Maintaining that "I don't have to justify nothing to nobody."* So said an assistant college football coach upon hearing my suggestion that some players would benefit from understanding the reasons behind certain coaching decisions. Let's face it, the coach is in the driver's seat. He or she is the decision maker, and the athletes can either follow or leave the team. But this does not diminish the fact that players often feel more anxious and even less supportive of the decision when asked to do something without an explanation. Why do players have a particular training regimen? Why was a player removed from the game, a certain play called, or a particular strategy used?

   Perhaps the term *explain* is more palatable to the coach than *justify*, which may suggest sacrificing power, control, and authority. Of course, coaches don't have the time to explain all (or even most) decisions to the participants. But on some issues and in certain situations, to ask for the athletes' opinions before a decision is made and to explain the decision before any action is carried out makes sense.

10. *Applying the starter/nonstarter double standard.* One way to *decrease* player loyalty to the team and coach is to treat players differently based on their team status. Mistreating the players who are less central to the team's success negatively impacts all team members because athletes need to support one another regardless of their positions. The team leader may necessarily spend more time with starters than with substitutes, especially on larger teams. But ignoring substitutes or allowing starting players to follow one set of rules and policies while the nonstarters follow another is upsetting and may diminish team loyalty and motivation. Coaches should remember that substitutes are only one injury away from starting.

11. *Using exercise for punishment.* This practice is one of the great myths in coaching and physical education. Exercise serves the very important purpose of improving one's physical status so that maximal performance can be reached and maintained. For competitors to find conditioning to be meaningful and even pleasant is important. Exercise should be desirable, not something that is a tool to invoke pain or discomfort. In this way, administering exercise as a form of punishment to athletes is a con-

tradiction in terms. Using exercise as punishment turns the athlete away from the very activity that is necessary to promote good performance and health. Coaches should want to keep exercise enjoyable.

The Choking Phenomenon

As discussed briefly earlier in this chapter, athletes differ in their ability to overcome the intense pressures of sport. Competitors who demonstrate competence in practice but fail to perform at similar levels during the contest are often accused of "choking." According to the *Dictionary of the Sport and Exercise Sciences* (Anshel et al. 1991), choking is defined as the inability to perform up to previously exhibited standards. This decreased performance occurs in pressure situations. Roy Baumeister (1984), a leading researcher on choking in sport, defines pressure "as any factor or combination of factors that increases the importance of performing well on a particular occasion" (p. 610).

The causes of choking are both internal and external. Internal causes of choking include overarousal, appraising situations as highly stressful, the loss of self-control, and expectations of failure. External causes of choking include crowd pressure (high expectations of spectators and low to moderate expectations of the athlete) and fear of success (the pressure to maintain what the athlete perceives as unrealistically high quality of performance). Other external causes are expectations and actions of the coach (expressing the importance of winning or attaining a certain performance level) and peer pressure (demands and expectations of teammates).

Choking may result in heightened narrowing of attention and slower processing of information. A narrowed attentional focus, similar to high state anxiety, is undesirable when task demands require the athlete to scan the competitive environment, looking for the location of opponents and teammates and planning strategy. Slower information processing is manifested by being easily distracted from the task at hand, poor attentional shifting between internal (thinking) and external (scanning) directions, slower and less accurate decision making, more thinking and less reliance on automatic responses, and making performance errors.

Choking can also be accompanied by physiological changes such as increased muscle tension, sweating, higher heart rate, nausea, and stomach cramps, any of which can directly influence performing sport skills.

Are some athletes more likely to choke than others? Is there a "choking personality" type? Baumeister (1984) examined the extent to which individuals differ in their susceptibility to choking on a disposition called self-consciousness (SC), the tendency to focus attention on oneself. He theorized that pressure increases SC, possibly by means of heightened arousal, and that this focus of attention disrupts skilled performance. He predicted that persons who are habitually self-conscious would find it easier to cope with situations that promote self-consciousness (i.e., pressure situations). Low SC persons, on the other hand, were predicted to choke more easily in pressure situations. This is because going from low to high pressure situations is more extensive and uncomfortable for low SC persons who, in turn, do not cope easily with pressure. His findings supported these predictions. Choking, then, may be partly dependent on at least one personality trait, a finding that awaits confirmation by additional research.

Strategies for Overcoming "The Choke"

Choking in sport is not inevitable. Athletes can use mental and behavioral techniques to prevent and overcome the tendency not to meet expectations. Here are a few suggestions:

1. *Practice under gamelike conditions.* This allows the athletes to learn to adapt to real pressure in realistic conditions experienced during the contest.

2. *Improve the athlete's self-confidence.* This is the coach's job. Teaching and mastering fundamental skills and strategies, together with positive information feedback on performance quality, improves self-confidence.

3. *Keep expectations realistic.* Choking is partly due to external pressures that, in turn, are generated by high expectations of coaches and other observers. Keeping expectations in accordance with past performance will reduce pressure and lessen the likelihood of choking.

4. *Put the game—and sport—into perspective.* As indicated earlier, sport is not a life or death situation. Athletes compete to win, but it's also true that sport should be fun to play. This is a cliché, but nevertheless it's only a game.

5. *Coach, avoid pressure statements.* "We have to win this game," "The game is now in your hands," "We're counting on you," and other statements that induce guilt coming from coaches and to a lesser extent from parents, teammates, and spectators add considerable pressure for success and contribute to choking.

6. *Focus externally.* Choking is a reaction to aversive thoughts. Athletes should reduce the time spent thinking and, instead, focus on external features in the sport environment. I know one elite athlete who focused on advertisement signs in the stadium before the game; it relaxed him. Talking with teammates about topics that have nothing to do with the contest also relaxes the athlete.

7. *Develop performance routines.* Linked to external focusing is engaging in one or more thoughts and actions that prepare the athlete for action. As discussed earlier, Orlick (1986) refers to this as a "mental plan." Many other sport psychology researchers have suggested using specific mental and physical routines prior to skill execution or before the contest that will act as a tension reducer and confidence builder. Examples include specific thoughts and actions before and immediately after entering the batter's box, between tennis serves, or just prior to a golf swing. These routines should be automatic to avoid external distractions.

Guidelines for Managing Anxiety

Responsibility for controlling an athlete's emotions rests with the individual competitor. There are many books, chapters, and magazine articles that address the proper use of cognitive techniques for reducing undesirable feelings before and during the contest. Certainly some techniques will work better for one person than another person, and not all of these strategies are valid under all sport conditions. The following recommendations for anxiety management are derived from applied sport psychology researchers.

1. *Focus on what you can control.* One primary source of anxiety is worrying about uncontrollable factors such as sustaining an injury, playing a superior opponent, or

a successful game outcome. Athletes whose thoughts center on "what ifs" or "I hopes" are candidates for heightened anxiety. Quality competitors focus on their performance and reflect on the strategies they practiced in preparation for the contest. Anxiety lies in fear of the unknown. By focusing on what one can control, athletes become task oriented and concentrate on immediate performance demands. Focus on strengths, not weaknesses, and what you can do, not what you can't do.

2. *Think practice*. As a sport psychology consultant, I have found these two words to be the most concise yet powerful message I can give a competitor. If high anxiety is due to the performer's perception of a threatening situation, it makes sense to reflect on the times when sport skills were executed without these unpleasant thoughts. These times are practice sessions. When athletes "think practice," they are reflecting on a relatively relaxed, nonthreatening environment in which their sport skills were performed successfully. If, according to researchers, our bodies cannot tell the difference between real and imagined stimuli, why not play a mental videotape that reflects success, accompanied by positive, desirable thoughts, rather than the "nightmare" videotape?

3. *Remember the worst-case scenario*. The worst-case scenario reflects this simple question: "What is the worst that can happen?" If you were to walk across the street blindfolded, the worst-case scenario is death if you were struck by a car. Consequently, this sort of behavior is unthinkable. Fortunately, not since the early Romans has sport been a matter of life and death. The reasons for competing in sport is the enjoyment and pleasure it brings its participants. If it's not enjoyable, perhaps it's time to think of doing something else for recreation, or changing the situation (e.g., a change of team, coach, or sport type).

For many athletes, the worst-case scenario is losing the contest or playing poorly. Losing need not be linked to failure. What can you learn about your skills from the contest? How would you assess your skill level when compared with that of your opponent? Certainly losing the contest and performing poorly are undesirable. However, losing does not necessarily mean the sport experience need be unpleasant. More likely it means you competed against a superior opponent, at least on a given day. Remember that the contest's outcome is not always under the performer's control, so in thinking of the worst-case scenario, you are placing sport in perspective. Sport should be fun. If you give it your best shot—a reasonable and fair expectation—then let the sport experience be pleasant. With very few exceptions, sport competition is not about making the Olympic team.

4. *Keep active*. Researchers, most notably William Morgan from the University of Wisconsin, have shown that engaging in physical activity reduces anxiety. This relaxing effect is one reason for the pregame warm-up. Although the physiological basis of this response goes beyond the scope of this book, exercise (a) provides a physical outlet for heightened emotions, such as anxiety, rather than "bottling them up" and (b) focuses the person's attention externally on performing a physical task rather than internally on undesirable emotions.

5. *Use cognitive strategies*. Finally, the sport psychology literature suggests numerous cognitive techniques for managing stress and anxiety. Mental imagery, various relaxation techniques, thought-stopping, positive self-talk, and numerous mental

skills packages have been used successfully to reduce unpleasant emotions. Not unlike sport skills, these cognitive strategies are skills that require practice and eventual mastery over a period of time. The athlete's "obligation" in using them is to believe in the effectiveness of these techniques and to learn and practice them regularly. Appendix B offers guidelines for using progressive relaxation (one type of relaxation) and mental imagery.

SUMMARY

Stress, anxiety, and arousal are inherent in competitive sport. The proper mental preparation of sport participants to regulate these states before and during the contest is among the most complex skills in coaching. The "best" strategies used to accomplish this objective differ from sport to sport. In fact, rarely do two coaches use the same mental approaches in a given contest. When or how to increase or decrease arousal or anxiety is a matter of timing, knowing the needs of each athlete, and understanding the demands of a given sport, task, and position. Ultimately, only the athlete can control his or her own emotions. The coach plays only a supporting role. The purpose of this chapter was to suggest ways in which this role can be carried out more successfully.

Anxiety and arousal, although often used interchangeably, are not synonymous. Whereas anxiety is an emotional condition reflecting overworry or extreme perceived threat of a situation, arousal can be either emotional or physiological. It is caused by positive feelings of excitation and confidence or by negative feelings of fear or sadness. Physiologically, arousal is indicated by an increase in the body's level of activation. Sport psychology consultants use a variety of means to measure anxiety and the emotional and physiological aspects of arousal. The SCAT and SAS were developed to measure trait anxiety, whereas the STAI and CSAI-2 measures state anxiety. Most athletes experience mild anxiety, but when it becomes disruptive to the athlete's performance or to life satisfaction, treatment may be needed.

Each individual athlete, sport, position on the team, and sport situation has a level of arousal (and, to a lesser degree, anxiety) that will produce optimal performance. Theories that attempt to explain and predict an athlete's optimal arousal level include the inverted-U hypothesis, catastrophe theory, and reversal theory. Drive theory, the oldest, has not been supported by researchers.

An important role of the coach is to help athletes determine the level of arousal at which they function best in sport. Before and during the contest, coaches can enact strategies to reduce, maintain, or increase their athletes' arousal so that they reach and maintain an optimal state. Coaches can also markedly reduce the usually undesirable state of competitive anxiety. Unfortunately, many coaches ignore the recommendations supported by sport psychology consultants and often use techniques that are actually counterproductive in establishing the proper pregame and between-period mental set. The recommended dos and don'ts in this chapter are based on the sport psychology literature and anecdotal evidence accumulated by my interviews with athletes of all age groups and skill levels, including professionals.

REVIEW QUESTIONS

1. Define state and trait anxiety. How do they differ? What types of measures would a coach use to determine an athlete's level of trait and state anxiety?

2. How are anxiety and arousal similar and different, both physiologically and psychologically?

3. Is anxiety ever desirable for athletes? If so, under what conditions?

4. What are some causes of state anxiety in sport? Describe five coaching strategies to reduce it.

5. What is the inverted-U hypothesis? How does it vary among athletes, sports, and skills?

6. Briefly describe catastrophe theory and reversal theory. How might each be applied to describe or explain an athlete's optimal level of arousal?

7. How can a coach determine whether an athlete is overaroused? Underaroused? Playing at optimal arousal level?

8. Under what conditions would a coach want to increase an athlete's arousal? When is it desirable to lower it?

9. What should the coach do to raise and lower the player's arousal level?

10. Describe three *incorrect* strategies that coaches use in the mistaken belief that they are raising arousal.

11. What is choking? How can the athlete prevent its occurrence?

CHAPTER 6

Aggression in Sport

I tell you that in the arts of life man invents nothing; but in the arts of death he outdoes Nature herself, and produces by chemistry and machinery all the slaughter of plague, pestilence, and famine. The peasant I tempt today eats and drinks what was eaten and drunk by the peasants of ten thousand years ago. But when he goes out to slay, he carries a marvel of mechanism that lets loose at the touch of his finger all the hidden molecular energies, and leaves the javelin, the arrow, and the blowpipe of his fathers far behind. In the art of peace, man is a bungler. Man measures his strength by solely, it seems, his destructiveness.

(George Bernard Shaw, *Man and Superman*)

For many coaches and athletes, aggression is an important feature of performance success. Indeed, in several sports (e.g., ice hockey, wrestling, American football), aggressive behavior is required. Perhaps it is not surprising, then, that on numerous occasions, athletes are penalized by game officials for overstepping the boundaries of fair play in exhibiting behavior that can be labeled hostile or physically abusive. Examples abound of media reports of severe injury—even death—of competitors due to aggressive play. It is an easy matter for researchers and educators to suggest banning hostile actions in sport that are viewed as dangerous and unethical. But given the encouragement of such abusive actions by spectators (who often cheer when fights break out during the game), coaches (who have been known to bench or dismiss a player for *not* fighting or demonstrating hostile actions), and team owners and administrators (who benefit from the income generated by fans who are entertained by the aggressive actions), it is no wonder that attempts to discourage aggression in sport continues to be an uphill battle. The purpose of this chapter is to gain a better understanding of aggression, one of the most common, yet least understood, aspects of human behavior in competitive sport.

Many coaches, under the false belief that "more is better," encourage athletes to be increasingly aggressive. As we'll see later in this chapter, aggression is the wrong strategy when it is used in a blind and irrational manner. Silva (1980) and others have argued that sport aggression may decrease athletic performance rather than help it. Specific sports, skills, and situations require different levels of aggression. Often, in fact, even the slightest aggressive act is inappropriate (e.g., in golf putting, bowling, or shooting). But in many sports, aggression is an integral part of the competition and is an important component of player and team success. Of primary importance to the athlete is the extent to which aggressive behavior leads to success.

In addition to defining the concept of aggression, in this chapter we will (1) review aggression theory to understand and explain the possible causes of aggressive behavior in humans, (2) examine the relationship between aggression and sport performance, (3) examine differences between aggressive and assertive behavior in sport, and (4) discuss the implications of aggression and assertiveness in sport for the coach and the competitor.

What Is Aggression?

Sometimes to understand a concept, it helps to know what it is not. For example, contrary to popular opinion, thinking negative thoughts or expressing a desire to hurt someone is not aggression. Aggression is not defined by feelings such as anger or any other emotion. Aggression is behavior. *Aggression* is usually defined as the intention of a person to inflict pain or harm on another person. This definition is contrary to the concept of what Husman and Silva (1984) call *proactive assertion*—forceful yet acceptable behavior. For instance, blocking in football, checking in ice hockey, maintaining a defensive position for rebounding in basketball, and breaking up a double play in baseball are assertive behaviors if executed without malice and as integral parts of the contest. These acts, however, become aggressive when the player's intention is to injure the opponent or to behave in a more hostile manner than is necessary in meeting the performance objective.

A second characteristic of aggression, in addition to its behavioral content, is that it is intentional. Aggression does not happen by accident. The aggressor must desire or threaten to harm or injure the intended victim, a factor inherent in boxing, hunting, and most contact sports. A third dimension is that harm or injury must actually occur. The unpleasant outcome need not be physical, however. Acts that intimidate, embarrass, or deprive another person of something are also aggressive. And fourth, aggression must involve interacting with another living being. Hurting a person or animal is aggression; kicking a chair is not.

Aggression has been categorized as being either *instrumental* or *hostile/reactive*. The purpose of instrumental aggression is to achieve some goal. Harm to another person might occur, either accidentally or not accidentally, in the process of attempting to reach a goal. As Widmeyer et al. (2002) contend, ". . . even though the ultimate goal of instrumental aggression is not injury, the intent to harm remains an integral facet of the aggressor's motivation in performing the action" (p. 330). Instrumental aggression differs from Husman and Silva's concept of proactive assertion in that the latter does not usually result in harm or injury to an opponent. Although an athlete exhibiting instrumentally aggressive behavior may not seek to injure an opponent, such an outcome is still viewed as an integral part of the game. For instance, baseball or softball pitchers may want to throw the ball inside to a batter for strategic reasons. This is an example of a proactive assertive action. An instrumentally aggressive act would be to throw the ball inside at a fast speed to intimidate the batter; if the batter is hit, this is viewed as part of the game. Next time, the hitter will not likely stand as close to the plate and will be more vulnerable to strikes on the outside corner.

Hostile/reactive aggression, on the other hand, has as its purpose injury or harm to another person. Intentionally hitting a batter with a pitch is an example. The "brush-back" pitch in baseball serves as a good example. Skilled pitchers, however, might intentionally throw the ball inside either to intimidate psychologically or to "jam" the hitter to prevent solid bat contact with the ball, thereby reducing the opponent's success. This is an example of *instrumental aggression.*

Typically, the type of aggression most commonly associated with sport is instrumental (Figure 6.1). This may be for three reasons. First, purposely injuring another player is often met with some punitive measure by the sport arbiter, the umpire or referee. Penalties effectively prevent or stall the meeting of performance goals. As one coach put it, "I tell my players, 'In the end you lose when you abuse.'" The second reason comes from laboratory research findings in which athletes, both males (Figler 1978) and females (Finn 1978; Thirer 1978) have been found to react less aggressively to violent visual stimuli than nonathletes. In fact, even when they are provoked, athletes tend to react with less hostility than nonathletes (Zillman et al. 1974) and usually refrain from intentionally injuring an opponent. And third, based on their interviews with the 1984 Canadian Olympic team, Orlick and Partington (1986) find that highly skilled athletes want to perceive their success as due to their high ability rather than to an opponent's injury (in which case the outcome is perceived as a function of luck or lower task difficulty; see Chapter 4).

Figure 6.1 Successful sport performance, especially in contact sports, often requires frequent use of instrumental aggression.

Because sport, by its very nature, is competitive, some degree of aggression will need to occur from time to time to overcome an opponent. From the perspective of applied sport psychology, it's in the athlete's best interests to exhibit aggressive behavior when the time and situation are appropriate. Widmeyer et al. (2002) introduced the concept of a *legitimate act* when a behavior is viewed as acceptable in a given circumstance or context. To label an act as legitimate requires that the observer compare the act in question with appropriate normative standards. According to the authors, an act is legitimate when there is no need to justify the reasons for that behavior and the acceptability of the act is clear. To get to this point requires the observer to compare the act in question with appropriate normative standards. Clearly, receiving a body check in ice hockey, a hard slide in baseball, or a vigorous hit in U.S. football fall into the category of acceptable and legitimate. In baseball or softball, however, there are more complex scenarios.

As indicated earlier, throwing a pitch inside is considered an integral part of game strategy. If the batter is struck by the ball, it is assumed that the ball "got away" from the pitcher and the batter was hit unintentionally. This would certainly be true if the bases were loaded, allowing a run to score. In a different context, however, hitting a batter with the pitch could be considered hostile (reactive) aggression and unacceptable if, for example, the same batter had hit a home run off the same pitcher in an earlier at-bat, or if one of the pitcher's teammates had been struck by a pitch earlier in the game, thereby suggesting an act of revenge. Though appalling and morally repugnant to many observers, intentionally hitting a batter under such circumstances might be *justifiable* in the culture of professional baseball. As Widmeyer at al. (2002) explain, "justifications are used as a means to avoid the dissonance felt when one perceives an aggressive act to be antinormative yet acceptable" (p. 332).

Apparently, despite some aggressive moments during the contest, skilled athletes respect one another. For example, even in contact sports, such as boxing, wrestling, and football, players will interact with one another immediately after the contest in a warm and sincere manner. According to media reports, the objective of their actions during the contest was not to hurt or to maim their opponents but rather to win the contest. In fact, athletes are generally uncomfortable with deliberately trying to injure an opponent. As a consultant with a collegiate football team, I would hear the coach, in his pregame talks, urge the players to "hurt" the opposing team (Anshel 1989a). "Break their legs," he said before one game, which was subsequently lost by a large margin. The athletes did not respond enthusiastically to the suggestion. After practice sessions, I asked the players about the directive to injure an opponent. Not a single team member indicated his willingness to hurt another player consciously.

Theoretical Bases of Aggression

To explain or predict behavior, it is necessary to understand its probable causes. For many years, scientists have offered biological and psychosociological explanations for aggressive behavior in humans. These theories suggest how to control and to direct the expression of aggression in a productive and positive manner if, in fact, it can be controlled and directed. For example, observing and participating in sport competition has been viewed as an outlet for a person's innate need to express his or her aggression. Some individuals, however, seem to need this outlet more than others. This leads to an important question: Is aggression genetically determined? If so, is it possible to predict a person's tendencies to aggress and, subsequently, to anticipate such behavior and to channel it in a productive direction? Or is aggression a reaction to some psychological phenomenon such as frustration ("I have to get tougher with my opponent to beat him [her]") or learned social behavior ("You mean I can't fight in ice hockey just like the pros?")? The areas that have received most attention in the scientific literature include the biological (or instinct) theories, the catharsis hypothesis, the frustration-aggression hypothesis, and the social learning theories.

Biological/Instinct Theories

The claim that human behavior is genetically programmed is not a popular or acceptable theory to some people. This is because it implies that environmental and social factors have a minimal role in explaining or predicting a person's actions. In sport, for example, the role of proper training and skill acquisition would be neglected if coaches and athletes assumed that elite athletes were "born and not made." It may also be assumed in genetic theory that aggressive behavior is inevitable and a "normal" response in sport. Biological/instinct theories assume that aggression is a natural, innate characteristic of all persons and that this characteristic developed through evolution. The "proof" of this assertion, originally postulated by Konrad Lorenz (1966) in his famous book *On Aggression*, is the tendency of living beings to fight for survival, especially for territory. Territory is a foremost objective after the primary needs of food and procreation have been fulfilled. In fact, the birth and rearing of offspring provide a fundamental purpose for territorial possession, especially in animals. Another "innatist," Robert Ardrey (1961), has originated the concept of the *territorial imperative* to explain aggressive behavior as a means for survival. He asserts, "If we defend the title to our land or to the sovereignty of our country, we do it for reasons no different, no less innate, no less ineradicable than do the lower animals. . . . All of us will give everything we are for a place of our own" (p. 161). However, to Montagu (1968) and Morris (1967), the extrapolation of animal behavior to humankind is a fatal flaw in the biological/genetic explanation for aggression in humans. As Montagu asserts, "With the exception of the instinctoid reactions in infants to sudden withdrawals of support and to sudden loud noises, the human being is entirely instinctless" (p. 11). And Morris reminds us that not all animals, even primates, are territorial and that the interaction among primate groups is less defensive and less aggressive than among carnivores.

Still, more recent studies, particularly at the Minnesota Center for Twin and Adoption Research and at the University of Southern California, have shown that personality in general, and aggressive—even criminal—behaviors, in particular, follow striking hereditary patterns. For example, scientists have found that children whose biological parents were convicts are much more likely to become criminals themselves. They agree that child rearing and other social factors certainly help to determine who becomes a criminal, but they contend that a strong hereditary component makes some individuals more likely to behave in socially unacceptable ways. Some scientists firmly believe that aggression, criminal tendencies, and intellectual ability may be biologically inevitable.

Suppose Lorenz, Ardrey, and other proponents of the biological basis for aggressive behavior are right. The implications of such thinking worry social scientists. Do we "throw away the key" rather than rehabilitate people whose heredity "hard-wires" them to become aggressive? Should so-called predictive tests be used to diagnose certain personality types, particularly those with a predisposition toward aggression? Would society respond to the "future aggressor" in a manner that might actually cause or facilitate the occurrence of undesirable behaviors, in a type of self-fulfilling prophecy? In other words, would a person who was "diagnosed" as aggressive tend to become so? We know, for example, that people often act according to the expectations of "significant" others—people whose opinions and impressions they care about (self-fulfilling prophecy). And, in a worst-case scenario, would some cultures and races be perceived as superior to others under such a testing program?

On the other hand, if a genetic/biological basis for aggression were confirmed and accepted, perhaps the small percentage of children with genetic traits likely to predispose them to aggressive behavior could be screened out and given special attention, diverting these children from criminal activities to more productive and happy lives. Perhaps all members of society would benefit if a genetic predisposition to aggress were recognized.

Another indictment of the biological/innate explanation of aggression is that it does not contribute to explaining the phenomenon. Most scientists assume that aggressiveness is a universal instinct and innate. This explains very little about the construct and provides us with no new information.

Alderman's argument is similar to the position of persons who think that the nature-versus-nurture debate regarding other characteristics (such as intelligence, personality, and motor ability) is pointless. If each person has a predetermined genetic disposition and their capacity cannot be altered—we differ on some genetically determined characteristics, such as aggression—why not use every social and psychological means available to influence the person's environment—in this case, managing aggressive tendencies in sport? The one thing that scientists (naturists and nurturists) do agree on is that certain situations or stimuli seem to trigger aggression.

The Catharsis Hypothesis

According to Bushman, Stack, and Baumeister (1996), the view that acting aggressively, or even viewing aggressive behavior, is effective in reducing anger and aggressive feelings (i.e., the catharsis hypothesis) is based on Freud's *hydraulic model* of anger, or anger catharsis. The hydraulic model suggests that frustrations lead to anger, and that anger, in turn, builds up inside an individual like hydraulic pressure inside a closed environment until it is released in some way. From their review of related literature, Bushman et al. strongly contradict the hydraulic model. Rather than "releasing" pent-up emotions and reducing angry feelings, opportunities to view or express anger actually increase it. They also contend that media messages advocating catharsis encourage people to vent their anger through aggressive action, and may foster the displacement of aggression toward new, innocent third parties. The effect of advocating catharsis may actually increase aggressive behavior. The authors conclude that observing violence or "ventilating" anger to get rid of hostilities has virtually never been supported by research. One of the most common emotions that initiates an aggressive response is frustration.

According to innate theory, there is a natural build-up of aggression that requires its release through productive, acceptable channels (that must be why they invented ice hockey). Thus, daily activities could be structured that would allow the "release" of tension. Purging of the need to aggress is called *catharsis* (from the Greek word *katharsis*, "to cleanse or purify").

The catharsis hypothesis was derived from the work of Leonard Berkowitz at the University of Wisconsin (1970). He suggested that the buildup of anger, tension, and other unpleasant feelings does not subside unless these emotions can be discharged in aggressive action. Berkowitz concluded that engaging in various activities, including competitive sports, lowers the person's inclination to attack others. In partial support of Berkowitz, psychologist Jack Hokanson and his colleagues (1962, 1963) found that the systolic blood pressure of male subjects returned to normal more rapidly after being allowed to apply electric shock to a frustrator (group 1) than it did in subjects who were rewarded for their participation (group 2), subjects who did not have an opportunity to respond after experiencing frustration (group 3), or subjects who were not exposed to the frustrator (group 4). However, according to Husman (1980), this conclusion assumes, perhaps erroneously, that blood pressure is the best measure of arousal (especially in the absence of measuring an emotional counterpart such as anger or frustration). Theoretically, then, a sport performer should demonstrate less aggressive behavior than nonparticipants and observers. Right?

Wrong! The research literature does not support the catharsis hypothesis. On a global basis, scientists know that children who watch great amounts of violent television programs tend to show more hostility than infrequent viewers (Larsen 1968). In sport, Cox (1995) reports several studies that do not support the cathartic effect upon the observation of athletic contests. In fact, pre- and postmeasures of aggression, using paper-and-pencil inventories, show that state aggression tends to rise after the observance of competitive sporting events.

Frustration-Aggression Hypothesis

The English poet John Keats said, "There is no fiercer hell than failure in a great attempt." Most skilled sport competitors would agree. Because of their intense desire to achieve in sport, athletes are probably more susceptible than most others to making "great attempts" and suffering unpleasant emotions when they don't succeed at them. The frustration of not meeting goals and not satisfying personal needs can make a person angry. This is the basis for the frustration-aggression hypothesis developed by Dollard and his colleagues at Yale University (1939). The authors contend that aggressive behavior is a logical and expected consequence of frustration.

Take, for example, two basketball players attempting to rebound the ball. Both are positioning themselves near the basket, which sometimes leads to pushing and shoving. The player who does not get the rebound is frustrated and will likely be more assertive the next time. This frustration can build up and lead either to goal aggression (for the purpose of hurting the opponent) or instrumental aggression (the opponent might get injured accidentally while the frustrated player is legally pursuing the ball). Thus, if the player intentionally shoves the opponent to get better floor location and the rebound, instrumental aggression has occurred. If, however, repeated attempts to rebound the ball are constantly unsuccessful, resulting in a buildup of frustration, the frustrated athlete is more likely to attempt to injure the opponent. This would be an example of goal aggression. This is exactly what happened when, in 1982, Washington Bullets (basketball) forward Kermit Washington severely injured opponent Rudy Tomjanovich of the Houston Rockets with a punch to the face. Washington's action was in direct response to repeated physical contact under the basket while awaiting the rebound. Washington was heavily fined and suspended from the league for his action.

But what happens when you can't retaliate directly against the frustrating opponent; for instance, when a soccer or hockey goalie continually prevents shot after shot from going into the net? If other conditions prohibit the destruction or removal of the source of frustration, aggression may be carried out on other objects. This behavior is called *displaced aggression*. Thus, teammates of this skilled goalie might experience heightened aggression by opponents in the frustrated attempts to score a goal. In another common example, baseball pitchers who have just given up a home run have been known to hit or pitch inside to the next batter due to their frustration. Retaliation is yet another example of displaced aggression. When an opponent injures one of your teammates, someone on your team might attempt to injure one of the opponents. Staying with our baseball example, it's common to see a pitcher hit an opponent with a pitch in retaliation for one of his or her teammates being struck by the opposing pitcher. If the umpire concludes that the action was intended to be hostile (retaliatory, not accidental), the pitcher is immediately removed from the game and later fined by the league, at least in professional baseball.

It is more than mere frustration that dictates an aggressive response. The strength and intensity of a person's frustration, the frequency of occurrence, and the degree of interference associated with the frustration response directly influence aggressive behavior. A scenario that will likely lead to aggression in sport might involve a player who has repeatedly attempted to meet a desirable performance goal and has been repeatedly thwarted by the opponent; perhaps an athlete is unable to overpower his or her opponent. The coach then urges the player to "get tough or you won't continue to play." The intensity of a contact sport, the frequency of failure to meet performance goals, and the low degree of punishment anticipated as a response to aggression (i.e., the coach is condoning aggression) all work together to maximize an aggressive response.

The frustration-aggression hypothesis is not without its critics. Detractors argue that not all frustration leads to aggression. For instance, many frustrated individuals, especially persons with low self-esteem or low ability, tend to withdraw from the activity or to reduce their efforts in it (i.e., they mentally drop out). Another limitation is the assumption that if aggression is the response to frustration, then the release of this frustration, through competing in sports or watching a violent movie, should have a cathartic effect. Yet, as was indicated earlier, this outcome has not been supported in the literature. In fact, research has shown that aggression often increases rather than decreases after subjects observe others engaging in aggressive activity.

Another example in which athlete aggression is supposedly increased due to frustration is through sexual abstinence. For many years coaches directed their athletes to abstain from sexual activity for days—even weeks—prior to the competitive event. It was thought that sexual behavior reduced the athletes' aggression and even led to premature physical fatigue. Conversely, abstaining from coitus would increase the athletes' frustration, which, in turn, would be redirected at the opponent (i.e., higher frustration equals higher aggression). In my review of related literature (Anshel 1981), not one study was conducted to support this view nor has there been any recent test of this strategy. In fact, many individuals tend to withdraw emotionally under conditions of frustration. Still, some coaches and athletes in many contact sports follow this tradition at some point—days, weeks, or in boxing even months, before the contest.

Another limitation of the frustration-aggression theory is one of definition. As Husman and Silva (1984) point out:

> *Is frustration interference with a goal response, task failure, lack of reinforcement, internal arousal, or continued failure resulting in low self-esteem? With the acceptance of (social) learning as an intervening variable influencing the frustration-aggression relationship, frustration itself has become harder to define. Today the frustration-aggression hypothesis is of more interest as a historical document than a definitive statement about aggression (p. 254).*

Reformulation of the Frustration-Aggression Hypothesis.

The frustration-aggression hypothesis, first published in 1939, was reformulated most recently and extensively by Berkowitz in 1989. Rather than contending that all frustration leads to aggression or that all aggression is the result of frustration, Berkowitz now recognizes that the links between frustration and aggression are more complicated. For example, frustration could lead to withdrawal or some other behavior, and there are many causes of aggression other than frustration. In fact, while frustration often produces anger, acts of aggression may not follow. Rather, a readiness to aggress is a possible, even likely, outcome. In addition, the extent to which frustration produces anger and other negative feelings may be dependent on the person's cognitive evaluation of the situation. If, for instance, an opponent is using aggression to prevent the athlete from performing successfully, the athlete's cognitive evaluation of low competence may lead to a state of rapid and intense frustration, thereby producing an aggressive response to overcome the opponent's strategy of aggressive behavior. The single most important factor that appears to link frustration and aggression is anger.

The more frequently opponents compete against each other, the more likely frustration will lead to aggression—but only in the presence of anger, a mediating variable in the frustration-aggression relationship. In their Canadian study of aggression in ice hockey, Widmeyer and McGuire (1997) found that players felt less animosity (anger) toward an opponent when competing every two months as compared to facing the same opponent every three weeks. This suggests that the likelihood of frustration leading to animosity and aggression in sport might be cumulative, especially if the opponent was successful.

In their extensive review of the aggression in sport literature, Widmeyer et al. (2002) concluded that the greatest sources of frustration consisted of "losing by a large margin, losing to an opponent you are outplaying and/or an opponent who is inferior, along with not being allowed to perform one's skills, and playing poorly . . ." (p. 361). Still, while these events may have led to frustration, they may or may not have induced anger. As indicated earlier, according to the reformulated frustration-aggression hypothesis, frustration may lead to anger, but anger may or may not lead to aggression. Future research examining the frustration-aggression hypothesis now recognizes that anger is an important factor in attempts to understand the relationship between frustration and aggression in sport. Ostensibly, then, though frustration may be inevitable in competitive sport, an athlete's ability to manage his or her anger might result in greater self-control of thoughts, emotions, and performance.

Social Learning Theory

Is aggression a learned social behavior similar to other behaviors? In Albert Bandura's (1973) social learning theory, aggressive behaviors are acquired and maintained by two modes: modeling and vicarious processes. The *modeling* effect is based on a person's tendency to imitate the actions of the observed individual. Thus, according to the theory, observing an individual perform aggressive acts will likely lead one to demonstrate similar behaviors. *Vicarious* processes occur when observers are exposed to models who are rewarded for aggressive behavior as opposed to models who are punished for aggressive behavior. The observers are more likely to aggress after watching persons who are rewarded rather than punished for acting aggressively. When a child hears the crowd cheer after an athlete has injured an opponent, observes the success of the more "aggressive" team, or is offered adulation after performing an aggressive act ("Way to knock his block off, son"), vicarious processes through the direct reinforcement of this behavior are encouraging future aggressive actions.

Early research, much of it by Bandura and his colleagues, has supported the social learning theory explanation of human aggression. Two studies were concerned with the effect of modeling adult aggression on children's aggressive behavior. Bandura and Huston (1961) asked adult models to demonstrate aggressive behaviors in reaction to solving problems. When the children were asked to solve a problem, they imitated the adults' aggressive reactions even though they were unrelated to the solution. Bandura et al. (1963) asked children to observe four groups under different conditions: (1) a live adult modeling aggressive behavior, (2) adult aggression on closed-circuit television, (3) aggression as performed by an animal (cat), and (4) nonaggressive behavior of a model during play. The researchers found that exposure to aggressive models increased both the verbal and physical aggression of the young observers. Further, watching television aggression influenced behavior similar to watching adult behavior in person. The animal model had less effect.

Other studies have been concerned with the effect of the home environment on aggression. Bandura and Walters (1959) interviewed 26 delinquent white adolescent males and compared them to a random group of nondelinquent males of similar race, age, and family socioeconomic status. They concluded that both groups had similar affectionate feelings toward their mothers, but that the delinquent group exhibited considerable hostility toward their fathers. Mothers of the delinquent group often displayed a lack of warmth for their spouses, and this feeling was usually reciprocated. Delinquent boys showed less guilt for wrongdoing, and their behavior was maintained by fear rather than by moral standards. The researchers characterized delinquent boys by a lack of appropriate modeling after their father and a failure to develop a personal conscience.

McCord (1962), in a study of 174 male adolescents and their parents examined over a five-year period, found direct correlations between degree of aggressiveness of the adolescent and aggressiveness in the family environment. Aggressive males had parents who were aggressive, punitive, rejecting, and inconsistent in their guidance. Also, the parents were characterized as being often hostile with each other and as often undermining each other's values. Nonaggressive boys were reared in a warm, far less punitive environment. Their parents were consistent in providing guidance and displayed mutual respect for all family members.

The examination of social learning on aggressive behavior in competitive sport has received relatively scant attention in the literature. Mugno and Feltz (1985) compared high school (aged 15 to 18 years) and youth league (aged 12 to 14 years) football athletes and nonathletes on the extent to which they learned about, and subsequently practiced, illegal aggressive actions through observing college and professional football. Among other results, they found (1) that athletes consumed more football through the media than nonathletes, (2) that significant correlations existed between the number of illegal aggressive acts that players observed and the number of those acts used in their own games for both high school ($r = .62$) and youth league ($r = .50$) participants, and (3) that high school and youth league athletes were similarly aware of illegal aggressive acts and the use of those acts in their games. In support of social learning theory, then, the authors found a modest relationship for young players between learning about illegal aggressive behaviors through observing collegiate and professional football athletes and using those actions in games.

Perhaps nowhere is social learning theory more validated in real-life sport situations than in ice hockey. Canadian sport psychologist Michael Smith (1980) contends that violence in hockey is inevitable because it's an integral part of the "system." "One of the most important (professional standards to be promoted in hockey) is the willingness and ability to employ, and withstand, illegal physical coercion," he asserts (p. 188). Further, youngsters who play organized hockey in Canada know what type of behavior is required to succeed. Smith reported that 76 percent of 274 players in a survey agreed that the following statement applied to their leagues: "If you want to get personal recognition in hockey, it helps to play rough. People in hockey look for this." And 68 percent of the players agreed that, in their leagues, "To be successful most hockey teams need at least one or two tough guys who are always ready to fight." Apparently, aggression, particularly in sport, is indeed a learned phenomenon and is practiced in some situations and by certain individuals more than others.

Which situations? Which individuals? Schneider and Eitzen (1986) hypothesize that a competitor's violent behavior in sport is related to (1) the amount of scoring in the particular sport, (2) the amount of body contact allowed within the rules of the sport, (3) the amount of retaliatory power players have in the sport, and (4) whether the structure of the sport has high or low rewards throughout the contest. These characteristics, they contend, work in combination to help to explain the rationale for illegitimate violence by sport participants. But whether aggressive behavior hurts or helps sport performance is less certain.

Aggression and Sport Performance

When examining the issue of how aggression affects performance, it is important to recall how aggression is defined. The question becomes whether inflicting harm or injury to another person (a sport opponent, in this case), either intentionally (goal aggression) or accidentally, while pursuing successful performance (instrumental aggression), is desirable. Is there an optimal threshold of aggression beyond which success is less likely? And to what extent does the type of sport and specific skills being performed in certain situations warrant a particular aggressive response?

Unfortunately, research on the effect of aggression on sport performance is not abundant. Coaches, however, are in general agreement that in certain situations, aggressive acts are warranted. For example, several collegiate football coaches indicated in the media (and confirmed in personal interviews) that the primary means of deciding whether a player with "good size" plays on the offensive or the defensive line is the degree of aggression he exhibits in drills. Big, angry, hostile types are usually asked to play defense, while less assertive players of about the same size are assigned to the offense. It's no secret that coaches often advise their athletes to "get physical" with opponents. Smith (1980) reports the pregame words of one hockey coach: "Look, if this character starts anything, take him out early. We can't have him charging around hammering people. Somebody's going to have to straighten him out. Just remember, get the gloves off and do it in a fair fight" (p. 189).

Does such an aggressive approach to competition help or hinder performance? We will attempt to answer this question with a brief look at the arousal-performance (inverted-U) relationship and at the pros and cons of aggressive sport performance.

Arousal, Aggression, and Sport Performance

In Chapter 2, the relationship between arousal (both physiological and emotional) and sport performance was discussed. Performance improved as the person's arousal level increased and then deteriorated when the athlete became over-aroused. Every sport, and every skill and situation within that sport, has an optimal arousal level and aggression level that results in the individual's best performance.

Silva (1979) tested the arousal-aggression-performance relationship, asking actors (called confederates) to provoke hostility in subjects competing in a laboratory motor task and in subjects playing basketball. The provoked participants exhibited less concentration and poorer performance than unprovoked individuals for both tasks. Silva concluded that the players' level of concentration and their performance were impaired owing to their hostile reaction and an arousal level that was likely too high for the given task. He surmised that the players' hostility led to heightened arousal, both of which combined to inhibit performance.

Hostile aggression is more likely to occur when the person is excited, or aroused. For example, Zillman et al. (1972) found that arousal created by physical activity promoted aggressive behavior. Further, the successful expression of aggression led to an increase in aggressiveness, at least in a laboratory study. Although field research is needed to confirm these findings in actual sport situations, this study partially explains the athlete's motivation to act more aggressively than is required for performance success (Figure 6.2). As Husman and Silva (1984) conclude, "The reward for violent play is often higher than the penalty for such an act" (p. 257). Apparently, observers are also influenced by player aggression.

Russell (1981) studied the effect of violent behavior by ice hockey players on the emotional arousal level of spectators in Alberta, Canada. Adult spectators completed a mood-state test after each of two games, one high in hostility (142 minutes in penalties) and the other with relatively little violence (46 minutes in penalties). The spectators scored significantly higher in aggression and emotional arousal (both measured by an inventory) after the game that featured more hostility.

Figure 6.2 Heightened arousal often combines with aggression to meet performance demands.

How much aggression is required for successful performance? The answer might lie with the same paradigm documented in the arousal literature, the inverted U. This makes sense if we agree that aggression and arousal are highly related. Every sport and sport skill probably includes a desirable level of aggression—high or low. Too little aggression will not allow the athlete to compete with the necessary energy, speed, and "mental toughness." And too much aggression will lead to penalties, misdirected attention, and reduced concentration, especially when the purpose of aggression is to retaliate against and injure opponents. The trick is to find the level of aggression that is optimal for a given sport situation. While the inverted-U hypothesis has been rebuked in contemporary sport psychology research (see Gould & Krane 1992) for a brief review), to date, no studies have been conducted testing the inverted-U hypothesis with respect to optimal aggression level.

Pros and Cons of Aggressive Performance

Certainly not all coaches promote aggressive behavior in competition, nor does every sport warrant it. In fact, many coaches prefer (and many sports warrant) a rather sedate, relaxed environment, one that is as low in hostility as possible. Golf, bowling, archery, tennis, swimming, and even baseball come to mind. Presently, there are apparently no guidelines in the literature indicating desirable aggression levels for optimal performance. In the literature on arousal, for example, Oxendine (1970) suggests a range of desirable arousal levels for optimal performance (e.g., 1 = archery and basketball free throw shooting, and 5 = football blocking or tackling and weight lifting). No such guidelines exist for aggressive behavior.

Widmeyer (1984) suggests three reasons that explain the difficulty in deriving such a scale for aggression in sport:

1. Aggression cannot be directly measured. Its partial definition, "the intent to do harm," is not observable and, therefore, must either be inferred from the athlete's behavior or determined by asking the athletes to describe and interpret their actions. The most common means of determining aggression has been measuring rule infractions observed by game officials.

2. There is no consensus about what constitutes an aggressive penalty. Not all infractions indicate the athlete's intended harm to an opponent.

3. In examining the aggression-performance relationship, how is performance distinguished from performance outcome or success? Widmeyer defines performance as overt goal-directed behavior, whereas performance outcome is the consequence of such behaviors. Success is subjective in that each athlete makes his or her own decision as to what constitutes success for the particular situation.

Common sense dictates that in some sports and in certain situations, aggressive behavior is desirable, at least if it is within the rules. The basketball or hockey player who shuns body contact will not be successful. On the other hand, athletes who break the contest's rules are likely to be penalized for it, and this will hinder rather than lead to success. Further, the aggressive act is often a reflection of or leads to heightened arousal levels that reduce concentration, misdirect the player's attention, and diminish performance quality. Silva (1980), based on his review of related literature, concluded that "anger or heightened hostility directed toward the self or another can often create an attentional conflict for the performer. Thoughts about anger or injuring an opponent compete with and distract the player from fully focusing upon the skill task. In most sports this situation tends to create a skill decrement" (p. 184). A more appropriate approach to competition would be focusing on, even fostering, assertive behavior.

The Assertive Athlete

The aggression literature draws a clear distinction between behavior that is intended to harm another person (goal or hostile aggression) and behavior in which harm or injury occurs in the act of performing competitively (instrumental aggression). However, some writers (e.g., Connelly 1988) prefer to designate all aggressive action as motivated by hostile intentions and refer to actions that reflect "appropriate levels of performance intensity" as assertive behavior. According to Connelly (1988), "Assertive players do not let opponents take advantage of them, nor are they easily dominated or pushed around, yet they are also respectful of opponents' skill and personal safety" (p. 256). Assertive athletes are intense, confident, never give up, and constantly challenge themselves to reach optimal performance. Nonassertive athletes, on the other hand, "allow themselves to be pushed around on the field or are easily dominated by their opponents" (p. 257).

Because nonassertiveness in sport is associated with or leads to diminished performance effectiveness, Connelly recommends the teaching of assertiveness through cognitive and behavioral intervention. Assertiveness is a skill that must be learned and practiced. See Connelly (1988) for a description of a sample intervention program for heightened assertiveness.

To what extent should aggression be tolerated in sport? If we consider aggression to be inflicting physical harm or injury on another athlete, then perhaps no level of aggression should be acceptable. Aggression is of particular concern in youth sports, in which participants closely monitor and imitate the behaviors of older, more skilled athletes. Sport leaders should concern themselves with helping children to learn sport skills and to develop mental skills to control anxiety and enhance self-esteem. In addition, all athletic participation should occur in an environment that stresses fair play and effort. It is also important to remember that athletes of all ages are generally uncomfortable with their own aggressive behaviors. They often feel guilty after exhibiting hostile aggression, losing their temper, or "playing dirty" (Kroll 1979).

Implications for Coaches and Athletes

To suggest that aggression should not occur in competitive sport would be unrealistic, perhaps even incorrect. It would be more appropriate to discuss controlling goal-aggressive acts and promoting proactive assertion or instrumental aggression (Figure 6.3). Here are some guidelines on the appropriate and selective use of proactive assertion or instrumental aggression in sport (according to Cox 1995; Silva 1980; Widmeyer 1984; Widmeyer 2002).

1. If winning is an important goal, aggressive behavior, if used at all, is more effective early in the contest.
2. If the athlete is already psyched up, to provoke him or her to "get tough" or to be more aggressive is unwise. This will likely reduce performance quality.
3. Coaches have to state their expectations of appropriate athlete behaviors at the first meeting period. If the object of the program is to have fun and to learn skills, the participants should understand that hostility is out of place.
4. Athletes who abuse rules and aggress when such behaviors are not sanctioned must be immediately reprimanded. If such acts recur repeatedly, the threat of dismissal from the team is indicated.
5. If aggression is desirable, then instrumental rather than goal aggression should be promoted. Injury to an opponent should not be the objective. Aggressive behavior is more acceptable when seen as a way to enhance performance.
6. Expose athletes to models, or examples, of individuals who have succeeded without hostility by using good skills.
7. The game arbiters—umpires and referees—have an important role in controlling the aggression of players and spectators. They can reduce the embarrassment an athlete feels after committing an infraction. Often, the official will point at the athlete and loudly vocalize the penalty. For example, a boisterous "Stri-i-i-ke three-e-e-e, you'r-r-re ou-u-u-t!" by the umpire can embarrass and anger the batter. A less dramatic technique that still communicates the message effectively might be desirable.

Figure 6.3 High-skilled sport performance is accompanied by controlling emotions, including aggression, in order to maintain attentional focus and physical energy.

Also, an official who responds to an angry coach in a relatively relaxed manner will tend to reduce the aggressor's hostility.

8. Teach athletes to cope with failure and abusive treatment, especially when it's of a nonphysical nature. For example, an opponent who says terrible things about the player's family or team should be ignored. Or the athlete can be taught to "retaliate" with heightened arousal directed toward productive performance (e.g., by swinging hard at a pitch, leaping for the rebound, making a solid tackle in football, and always giving full concentration to the task). Above all, athletes should learn that physically abusing an opponent will reduce performance effectiveness and diminish team success.

9. Coaches should provide positive reinforcement to athletes who control their temper, especially in highly emotional situations. Widmeyer (2002) correctly asserts

that the combination of praising restraint and the ability to overcome the aggression of opponents (positive reinforcement), and reducing rewards for and discouraging aggression (e.g., not cheering and praising aggressive behavior) will jointly reduce inappropriate aggressive performance. A player who sustains physical abuse, either accidentally or on purpose, and does not respond in a hostile manner yet performs at an optimal level should be praised, especially in the presence of teammates.

10. Keep assertive behaviors, when they must be used, within the competitive environment. Verbally or physically abusing opponents before or after the contest only raises their anger and arousal to levels that may actually enhance *their* performance. It also wastes the players' energy that might otherwise be spent during the contest.

11. To reduce hostility, encourage interactions between opposing teams. As Cox (1995) suggests, "Sport is not combat. Sport is a highly significant event that promotes fitness and achievement. It's much easier to be aggressive against a feared enemy than against a respected and liked opponent" (p. 235).

12. The athletes' family members should be encouraged to attend contests and to reinforce at home what the coach communicates during competition: to play at one's best within the rules and with minimal or no hostility.

13. Coaches can discourage violent behavior during the contest in their pregame talk. If a talk before the contest is necessary—in some sports it is not—the content of such a message should encourage the use of skills and effort instead of convincing players to engage in previously learned behaviors that threaten physical well-being. Read an excellent editorial on this topic by Professor Shirl Hoffman (*The Chronicle of Higher Education*, Nov. 11, 1992, vol. 39, no. 12, p. A44).

Gender Differences and Aggression in Sport

Researchers have known for years that males are more competitive than females, at least among nonathletes (Gill 1992). But what about aggression and gender differences? Are male and female athletes similar in their aggression responses? In their review of the nonsport experimental literature, Frodi et al. (1977) concluded that the sexes can exhibit similar aggressive actions if females (1) do not feel empathy toward their opponent, (2) are not anxious about being aggressive, and (3) if an aggressive response appears justified.

What about gender differences and aggressive behavior in sport? In their review of this literature, Widmeyer et al. (2002) did, indeed, find that males, both athletes and nonathletes, demonstrated more aggressive behavioral tendencies than their female counterparts. Gender differences in nonsport studies were magnified in situations in which aggression produced pain or physical injury as opposed to situations in which aggression produced psychological or social harm. In sport, the authors cited previous studies in which: (1) male intercollegiate athletes felt more frustrated during competition than their female counterparts, (2) when feeling frustrated, male athletes, more than female athletes, became more angered and wanted to injure an opponent more frequently, whereas females wanted to try harder in response to their frustration, and (3) males rated behaviors that violated rules and could injure opponents as more acceptable than did females. The authors surmise that sport socialization may legitimize aggressive behavior that violates rules for males, but not for females.

What about the female athlete? Scientific studies are not conclusive, although personality studies (criticisms of their validity notwithstanding (see Chapter 2)) using inventories not designed for athletes indicate that female athletes score higher than female nonathletes on aggression as a personality trait. However, in my own interviews with numerous intercollegiate female athletes (in the absence of other research), they indicated that: (1) yes, aggression can be a legitimate response in sport under the proper circumstances (i.e., when it is warranted), but (2) there is no room for hostility or purposely injuring an opponent (goal aggression) at any time. Apparently, athletes tend to be uncomfortable with a coach's request to hit the batter with a pitch or in some way hurt the opponent. But this is even more true for females. Not unlike their male counterparts, the female competitors I interviewed vowed that they would never purposely injure another player, even if told to do so by their coach.

Aggression in sport will not go away, especially when hostility is sanctioned by sport administrators, team owners, and, of course, the coaches. This is often the case. For instance, John Ziegler, former president of the National Hockey League, defended violence in hockey, as reported in *USA Today*, May 13, 1987. Ziegler contended that "violence sells"; the fans want to see the players fight and use physical intimidation. Although *Sports Illustrated* writers have frequently criticized violence in sport, especially ice hockey, apparently NHL players and team owners are not listening. For example, an article appearing February 17, 1986, states, "Many NHL executives are scared to death that if fighting were banned from hockey, thousands of season-ticket holders who get their jollies from watching grown men in short pants do quasi-legal, bare-knuckle battle would bail out on the spot." This mentality still exists today. In a good example of this philosophy, a player from the Los Angeles Kings (NHL) hockey team was put on waivers—essentially cut from the team—because he refused to participate in a brawl on the ice with his teammates. This player was ostracized from his profession (no other team in the NHL signed him to play) because he did not follow the expected behavior. Even NHL referees have been accused by sportswriters in the media of being more tolerant of aggressive behaviors (resulting in fewer penalties) in the playoffs.

But many of the NHL hockey players would like to see more sanctions against overt aggression on the ice. Former Montreal Canadiens General Manager Serge Savard says, "Our club feels that fights should be banned from hockey. . . . Stop it altogether. After one fight, you're out of the game. If you fight in the last five minutes, you're out of the next game, too."

In the final analysis, athletes do what they are taught and required to do. The athletes themselves are not at fault, but the coaches, sport administrators, and even parents who dictate inappropriate behaviors are. Athletes respond to the expectations of others—as they must if they want to play. The adult leaders are responsible for separating assertiveness (instrumental aggression) from violence and hostility (hostile/reactive aggression) in sport.

Despite these conclusions, the area of aggression in sport is in tremendous need of additional research. The relationship that we observe between hostile behavior and the ability to learn and to perform sport skills is strictly correlational. That is, relatively higher hostility is related to lower learning and performing levels. However, researchers are not certain that aggression, especially of the goal or reactive nature, actually causes or directly leads to poorer performance. We also know very little about the factors that contribute to aggressive behavior in sport, why some participants have a greater propensity to aggress than others given the same sport situation. And we certainly know little about differences between male and female sport participants on this topic. What we do know, however, is that despite disagreement about the sources of aggression, coaches have the moral obligation to help overaggressive athletes redirect their energies and aggressive behaviors in a positive, self-fulfilling, and socially acceptable direction.

Mental Control of Anger

Is anger inevitable? Is it normal, healthy, even desirable? Can anger be controlled? Should it be? What are the implications for effective sport performance? Professors Dianne Tice and Roy Baumeister (1993) from Case Western Reserve University (Cleveland) have outlined two converging views about the "normality" of anger control, and self-induced cognitive strategies to help control it. One view is that anger cannot be controlled because emotions are passions, which are uncontrollable. This view is that people are unable to control their emotions, and that strong emotions prevent controlling one's actions. The second view is that anger should not be controlled. Withholding angry feelings can lead to poor physical and mental health, and, ostensibly, eventually lead to explosive anger. In their review of related research, however, Tice and Baumeister found that "dangers to health . . . appear to be associated with the presence of anger, not its absence or suppression" and that "reflective self-control of anger was consistently related to the lowest levels of blood pressure across all situations . . ." (p. 395). Apparently, being prone to undercontrolled anger is the strongest predictor of poor health. Further, bad moods, including anger, inhibit the processing of information, thereby reducing efficiency of short-term (temporary) and long-term (permanent) memory. In a sport context, the ability to analyze information, to strategize, and to make decisions can be markedly reduced. Anger, in particular, keeps the person focused on unpleasant, distressing thoughts. Angry outbursts result in a prolonged negative mood state. We do not typically "vent hostility" through our words or actions, then instantly feel better.

A third view is that anger can be completely controlled and, in fact, prevented. However, Tice and Baumeister (1993) have concluded that "the complete preventability of anger is a myth" and that "in practical terms, the complete elimination of anger has proven impossible despite sincere and strenuous attempts" (p. 396). Perhaps the greatest argument against this view is that if anger could have been eliminated, it would have been by this time. Most cultures hold disparaging views of anger. So, though anger can be controlled, regulated, and channeled, especially in sport situations, it cannot be eliminated. This is the reason we have programs called "anger management" rather than "anger prevention." How, then, can athletes, coaches, and sport psychology consultants work jointly in controlling anger?

Anger Management Strategies

Most anger management programs consist of several categories of techniques, as outlined by Tice and Baumeister (1993). *Relaxing activities* consist of taking steps to decrease arousal, such as taking deep breaths, lying down, meditating, taking a long walk, social isolation (a stress management technique called *social engineering*), or acting in a low-key manner that relaxes the person. A second group of anger control strategies is called *cognitive self-manipulations*. Examples include distracting oneself (e.g., watching television, observing a film, attending a sporting event), seeking to understand the angry person's reasons for acting in an angry manner (e.g., empathy, sensitivity to personal needs), reframing the problem in a way that reduces the negative emotion (e.g., "maybe they are just having a bad day" or "so-and-so is obviously very stressed"), and using humor (e.g., self-deprecating—"I can't believe I did that" or "boy, that was a good move"—or exposure to external humor).

Another approach to anger management is behavioral, as opposed to the cognitive approaches previously suggested. *Physical exercise*, for example, might remove anger by reducing arousal, distracting the person from unpleasant thoughts, and/or by inducing physical fatigue, which makes it increasingly difficult to generate and maintain thoughts that have highly negative properties.

Finally, there are two techniques for using or channeling anger. These techniques are based on the contention that sometimes anger is beneficial to meet goals. For example, sports coaches may argue with a game official, either to discourage the official from making further unfavorable calls or to increase the players' arousal level in the hope that they will perform better. In addition, self-induced anger might be needed to increase psychological readiness to perform, especially in contact sports, or, as Tice and Baumeister put it, for "mobilizing action for a cause" (p. 402). One technique for sustaining anger is to rehearse the basis for it, such as brooding about one's grievance (e.g., "I will not allow that pitcher to strike me out again" or "I have to be more aggressive to get the rebound"). Another anger preservation technique, reviewed by Tice and Baumeister, is called *crystallization of discontent*. Instead of viewing unpleasant or disappointing experiences in isolation, many similar, unpleasant instances may be observed over a period of time. For example, an opponent may be continually taking advantage of the athlete's perceived weakness, cheating, or performing in a highly aggressive manner, perhaps even resulting in an injury to the athlete. Instead of reacting impulsively to initial unpleasant experiences, it may be in the athlete's best interests to preserve anger over individual episodes to observe broader behavior patterns, which, in turn, may provide additional incentive to make significant changes in the player's emotions and performance.

An additional anger management strategy is called *channeling*. This technique is based on the long-known concept of displaced aggression, discussed earlier in this chapter. Whereas it is not productive to hurt, offend, or injure another person in place of the original source of angry feelings, aggression can be redirected (channeled) toward more desirable targets, such as sport opponents, overcoming unfairness, or exercising and training more vigorously.

Finally, one somewhat controversial anger control strategy is called *justification*. An angry person may feel justified in behaving aggressively, though this may depend on the severity of the provoking offense. For example, most instances of road rage occur when one driver feels that the "offending driver" performed a highly provoking maneuver. However, whether being cut off in traffic justified a hostile response, either verbally or behaviorally (as opposed to ignoring the "offending" driver), is what makes this method controversial. As a youngster, this writer attended a Chicago Cubs vs. Cincinnati Reds baseball game at Wrigley Field in 1964 when Cubs pitcher Jim Brewer threw a high, inside pitch to batter Billy Martin, just missing Martin's head. On the next pitch,

Martin swung lazily at and missed the pitch. The bat left Martin's hands and landed a few feet from the pitcher's mound. Martin then walked toward the mound where the pitcher was standing to retrieve his bat. However, instead of retrieving his bat, Martin planted his left fist into the pitcher's face. An all-out brawl between teams ensued. Pitcher Jim Brewer suffered severe facial injuries. Although considered highly unusual back in the 1960s, contemporary major league baseball is now replete with similar experiences in which the batter charges the pitcher's mound, ostensibly in defense of his perception that the pitcher intentionally hit the batter with a pitch. But was the pitch thrown intentionally at the batter? Was a retaliatory fistfight—with an almost certain financial penalty, possible suspension, and potential fight-related injury—sufficient justification following a pitch that may not have been intended? It is for this reason that justification as an outlet for anger control is questionable.

Most psychologists agree that anger is a normal emotion. The problem is its expression, and the extent to which it leads to aggression. The late clinical psychologist Haim Ginott (1965, 1969) has recommended that anger be expressed in "I," not "you" statements (e.g., "I feel very upset that you did such and such."). He also urges that statements reflecting anger address the behavior, not the personality, of the offending individual, and to separate one's expression of anger from providing information, a communication technique discussed in Chapter 9. Coaches would be more effective if they first expressed their anger (if they must), and then provided instructional information—even if the two components are separated by only a few seconds. Teaching strategy while remaining angry causes heightened anxiety in athletes, who will not process (remember) the instructional information. The effectiveness of anger management programs on mood state, aggression level, and sport performance among competitive athletes remains an area in need of much additional research.

Spectators and Violence in Sport

According to media reports, spectators at sporting events are becoming more and more aggressive in expressing their views about player performance and support for their team. Although no scientific studies have been conducted to confirm this observation, researchers have found that aggressive play and/or fierce competitiveness, combined with media coverage, tends to markedly enhance spectator interest. Based on Thirer's (1993) in-depth review of this literature, the best predictors of spectator violence (in no particular order) are crowd incitement to intimidate opposing teams and officials (sometimes engendered by the field announcer), availability of alcohol, lateness of the game, offensive rallies, warm weather, inexpensive seats, and violent behaviors by the athletes. In fact, Zillman and Paulus (1993) also contend that crowd noise may actually ignite more aggression from the athletes. This is because athletes enjoy exhibiting their skills in front of an enthusiastic and supportive audience; they want to satisfy the audience's expectations, including more aggressive behavior. This influence is especially powerful for athletes who are considered "low self-conscious," that is, individuals who are quite concerned with the reactions of spectators to their performance. In this way, spectator violence may trigger player aggression.

According to highly respected sport sociologist Jay Coakley (1990), however, spectator violence may occur less often than people think. Coakley contends, contrary to popular images and public perceptions, that attendees at sports events are usually subdued and orderly. He cites the rarity with which fans become aggressive while viewing *noncontact* sports. Even in contact sports, violent actions among spectators are unusual, Coakley notes. He points out that a high degree of noise and emotion, common among spectators, should not be confused with physical aggression, which is quite rare among viewers.

However, perhaps the greatest factor contributing to spectator violence in sport, not easily measurable, but clearly evident at the sport venue, is the general norms, conditions, and morals that encourage this type of behavior. It comes as no surprise that fans are more vocal and assertive at contact sports such as wrestling, rugby, and ice hockey matches than they are at noncontact sports such as tennis, baseball, and golf. Certainly the research is clear that observing aggression in sport increases spectator aggression and does not serve as an outlet for aggressive feelings and actions (Thirer 1993). As reviewed earlier in this chapter, this view—and numerous studies—contradict the catharsis hypothesis, which states that observing aggressive sport behavior actually decreases spectator violence.

What can be done to help prevent the onset of physical aggression among sport fans? First, sport administrators and parents can work toward changing the culture of sport violence by making it unattractive and intolerable. Sadly, however, at the elite sport levels, team owners and administrators cannot be expected to change game rules to limit violence among athletes. Why? Because violence among players increases game attendance. For example, for many years, owners of National Hockey League teams have stopped short of developing policies and penalties for fighting among players on the ice and have prevented their commissioner from instituting severe punishments, such as fines and suspensions, to abusive players (Smith 1988). This "license" for goal aggression during the game has fostered similar abusive behaviors among younger ice hockey competitors—behaviors that unfortunately have often been encouraged by their parents. This may be because of the "culture" of ice hockey that permits, even encourages, aggressive play and fighting to "gain respect" and intimidate opponents (Vaz 1972). Thus, the individual who supervises competitive sports clearly has a role in reducing spectator violence by improving the management of goal aggression by participants. As Thirer (1993) concluded from his review of relevant literature, player aggression fosters crowd aggression.

Other measures to curb spectator violence include reducing or eliminating availability of alcohol at the sport venue; starting contests at a time that encourages earlier completion times; generating and implementing harsh policies that punish abusive behavior exhibited by players and coaches; providing information to coaches, parents, game officials, and athletes about more constructive means of dealing with stress and frustration often experienced during the event; preventing parental abuse (a common problem); and banning parents from attending competitions. Other measures include having adequate security personnel on hand at events with large anticipated crowds and working with the local media to point out problems and possible solutions to crowd abuse in the community.

Perhaps any noticeable rise in spectator violence is a reflection of changes in contemporary society. Sports fans may be behaving in ways that they perceive as "normal" for their community or ethnic culture. Examples include the soccer referee who must occasionally run for his life from hostile fans following a loss by the home team; or the increasingly widespread use of profanity, drugs, and weapons, especially among preadolescents and adolescents. The rights of sports fans to express their feelings and emotions openly and constructively at competitive events must be retained in any free society. However, sport sociologists and psychologists also argue that constraints on unacceptable behaviors that endanger the safety and well-being of sports participants and fans are also needed to preserve these rights.

SUMMARY

Aggression is the intentional response a person makes to inflict pain or harm on another person. Two types of aggression have been identified. Instrumental aggression occurs when the athlete's intention is to meet a performance goal, whereas goal or reactive aggression is related to injuring or harming an opponent purposely. The concept of proactive assertion, often confused with aggression, means performing acts that are forceful yet acceptable—an integral part of the sport (such as blocking and tackling in football or checking in ice hockey).

Different theories attempt to explain aggression. Biological or instinct theories claim that human aggression is inevitable because it is a component of our survival instincts. According to the frustration-aggression hypothesis, aggression is a logical and expected consequence of frustration. The catharsis hypothesis indicates that human aggressive tendencies are related to available outlets for expressing it. Ostensibly, then, sports fans should be less aggressive than nonviewers of competitive sport. However, researchers have found just the opposite effect of viewing aggression in sport. Perhaps the most acceptable theory of aggression is based on social learning. Modeling and child-rearing experiences markedly dictate the extent to which a person possesses aggressive tendencies.

One area of sport in which aggression is increasing is among spectators. Not only are sports fans exhibiting more and more noise and emotion, but these emotions too often turn into physical aggression. For example, in 1995, upset New York Giants fans bombarded the football field with snowballs and injured a coach as a result. It is speculated that the current culture of sport, including norms, conditions, and morals, encourages this type of behavior. Only changing this culture by making it unattractive and setting strict limits on inappropriate behavior will change this situation.

Aggression is difficult to measure. Defining aggressive behaviors and measuring them directly are among the problems. Somewhat more certain, though in greater need of research, is that sport performance for each sport, skill, and individual athlete is related to an optimal degree of aggression. That is, some degree of aggressive or assertive behavior is good, but too much inhibits performance. This concept is similar to the inverted-U hypothesis pertaining to arousal. However, a method to measure and determine this optimal aggression level for a given sport or task is absent from sport psychology literature. The athlete's best interests would be served by the use of instrumental aggression or proactive assertion rather than goal or reactive aggression.

REVIEW QUESTIONS

1. How would you define and differentiate between *hostility* and *proactive assertion*? Which of the following terms are most similar: *violent behavior, instrumental aggression, proactive assertion, goal aggression,* and *hostility*? Explain why.

2. Two football players on opposite teams both reach for a pass. They collide, resulting in an injury to one of the players. What type of aggression has occurred, and why would it be classified as this type?

3. Are child athletes more likely or less likely to respond aggressively after observing violent behavior than other athletes? Defend your answer.

4. Briefly describe each of the three theories of aggression. How can aspects of each theory be supported and contradicted in a sport setting?

5. What is the catharsis hypothesis? Does research support it? In what way, or why not?

6. How are aggression and arousal related? Based on what you know about the effect of arousal on performing sport skills, how does aggression affect sport performance?

7. Should a coach ever want to promote aggression on the team? If so, under what conditions? When should aggression not be promoted?

8. What are some of the problems in measuring aggressive behavior? As a coach, how could you identify player aggression?

9. Describe two coaching strategies that should increase aggression in athletes and two strategies that should decrease it.

10. Describe five guidelines athletes should consider for using aggression in sport.

11. What are the primary causes of spectator aggression and what can sport administrators do to curb spectator violence?

CHAPTER 7

Team Cohesion and Group Dynamics

Coaches and sport psychologists agree that identifying a common purpose on which to focus the group's efforts is vital to success. The ability to "stick together" is a characteristic called *group cohesion* (Carron 1984a). The feeling of togetherness is considered important in satisfying player needs, deriving and making the effort to meet team goals, enhancing each player's loyalty to the team and coach, and gaining support among teammates. The purposes of this chapter are (1) to examine the extent to which team cohesion and the development of healthy player relationships contribute to group member satisfaction and sport performance, (2) to examine the roles that are common on sports teams and the coaching techniques that enhance some and diminish others, and (3) to suggest ways in which coaches can assess and promote a supportive and constructive team climate.

How a Group Becomes a Team

Sport teams are groups. However, it is wrong to assume that any group of individuals that gets together, shares the common goal of winning, and attempts to meet that goal is automatically a team. Carron (1994) defines a sport team as "a collection of individuals who possess a collective identity, have common goals and objectives, share a common fate, develop structure patterns of interaction and modes of communication, exhibit personal and task interdependence, reciprocate interpersonal attraction, and consider themselves to be a group" (p. 80). The last factor, that individuals perceive themselves as a group, separates *real* groups from a collection of individuals waiting at a bus stop or showing up at the same time for team tryouts. The perception of group members, then, is more important than previously recognized by researchers as well as by coaches.

A team of athletes, together with their coach, should seek the answers to eight questions posed by Francis and Young (1979).

1. What are we here to do? Learn skills? Improve performance? Win? Have fun? Some of each?
2. How shall we organize ourselves with respect to the playing position of each participant and formulating team policies?

3. What are the roles of the coach, coaching assistants, team captains, and other team members?

4. Who are our fans? To whom are we accountable? Members of the community? School officials? Parents of the athletes?

5. How do we work through problems? Does the coach have an open-door policy? Are team meetings held?

6. In what ways do we need to work together in order to perform successfully as a team?

7. What are the benefits of being a team member? Friendships? Affiliation? Recognition? Learning new skills? Having fun?

8. How, and under what conditions, should the team be included in determining team policies and punitive responses for breaking team rules?

Working through these issues will help team leaders to overcome potential blockages and build a cohesive unit of athletes. Clearing blockages is one task that separates successful teams from those that are less successful. This is because there is more commitment and identification within some teams than within others. One of the greatest challenges to coaches in sport is to ensure that all athletes are invested in the team's long-term success.

A group of athletes becomes a team via an evolutionary process. Although team development does not always follow a step-by-step sequence, a process exists by which a group of individuals comes together and, through a variety of actions and reactions, emerges as a cohesive unit—a team. Theorists refer to these normal evolutionary steps of team building as (1) forming, (2) storming, (3) norming, and (4) performing (Cartwright & Zander 1968). The coach's understanding of group formation in sport could lead to using strategies that promote harmony among team members.

Forming

The process of forming, referred to by Francis and Young as *testing*, is concerned with familiarizing group members with one another. At this time, the members of a team engage in social comparisons, assessing one another's strengths and weaknesses and the probability of playing. The first issue a person deals with is developing group identification: "Do I belong to this group? Should I be here? Do I want to be here? If so, what is my role?" The failure to address this issue may result in a participant's social isolation.

To help prevent introversion and feelings of isolation on the team, Carron (1984a) recommends that coaches try to limit the amount of turnover among team personnel. And for team newcomers, Carron suggests that established team members be assigned the tasks of introducing the new players to their teammates and engaging them in social exchanges. Still, the coach needs to be aware of the participants who do not feel group identification and who are unable to form positive relationships with other team members. Strategies should be enacted to facilitate group member familiarity and interaction at the early stages of team formation—even prior to the first practice if possible (Mechikoff & Kozar 1983).

Glen Patton, successful head swimming coach at the University of Iowa, engages in team-building sessions when the fall semester begins:

The swimming team has several social get-togethers to help members get to know each other. Picnics . . . soccer games . . . and other social nonswimming events. . . . Team members interview each other at length and then report to the rest of the team what they have learned about the individual. . . . The concept of [these] team building [sessions] is to develop team awareness, communication, and interdependence, so that when a fellow swimmer is feeling the pressure of competitive stress, he can obtain some psychological security by knowing that team members understand his responses to the situation (Mechikoff & Kozar 1983, p. 91).

Storming

The second stage of group formation is a bit less hospitable. Also called *infighting* (Francis & Young 1979), this level of functioning is characterized by polarization, conflict, and rebellion—not exactly components of team cohesion. Sometimes, though quite rarely, the conflict is physical. For example, during preseason tryouts and training periods, a relatively high incidence of aggressive acts tends to occur among teammates, each of whom is trying to make the team or the starting line-up. This is especially the case in contact sports such as football and ice hockey. But usually the issues are socially based. Athletes typically vie for control, for status, and for the coach's attention. The athletes are positioning themselves, or posturing, for recognition and approval. The amount of infighting is often related to the coach's ability to assess the strengths and weaknesses of each team member. When these assessments are objective and communicated to players, hostility tends to decrease because the participants are less concerned with the uncertainty of their role and status in the group (Carron 1984a). Although storming is often inevitable in group (team) formulation, coaches should communicate their displeasure with excessive, continuing intrateam rivalry. Often it creates dissension and lowers cohesion.

Norming

This is the "getting organized" stage in which the group comes together, resistance or "going your own way" is overcome, and cooperation among group members is improved. Teammates want to work together to establish success and improve satisfaction among team members. Whereas storming occurs most frequently in the early stages of a team's training period, norming is the quiet period after the storm. This stage is important because the concepts of group cohesion and team identity are defined here. The team needs the support and interest of all members. If members become preoccupied with personal needs, the team will not grow stronger. Mutual support and personal identification with the team will be compromised.

Norming is a function of the group's respect for each member's unique contribution to the team. Instead of competing against a teammate, players become more concerned with economy of effort and task effectiveness. Without a healthy norming stage, the team will become satisfied with mere adequate performance instead of striving for excellence. Further, team members will be more concerned with personal goals and needs than with what is best for the team. Coaches can facilitate the norming process by expressing public praise to team members for quality performance, effort, and improvement and by indicating realistic, yet challenging, team goals.

Performing

At this point, the group is prepared to direct its energy toward its goals. This fourth and final stage, referred to by Francis and Young as *mature closeness*, is characterized by a close rapport among group members. Roles of team members have been identified, and each person's contribution is distinct. Teammates sincerely want one another to succeed. Rather than feeling threatened by their teammates' success, they feel enjoyment and respect in response to each member's accomplishments. Group relationships are secure. Players interact informally with no artificial interpersonal behaviors, and there is a willingness to help a teammate if needed. In order to reach this stage, coaches should avoid, rather than promote, intrateam competition and interpersonal aggression. Instead, the value of each athlete's contribution to the team should be reinforced verbally by giving positive feedback and by publicly and privately recognizing the special role of every team member.

A Who's Who of Team Personnel

Almost every team member has a role. A role is a "set of behaviors that are expected from the occupants of specific positions within the group" (Carron 1993, p. 116). For example, we expect a coach to perform certain leadership functions, such as to structure and lead practice sessions, communicate with all team personnel, designate the team's starting and nonstarting players, and so on. The team captain may also have specific designated roles, such as to interact with the game referee during the contest, make certain decisions on the field or court, or foster communication between team members and the head coach. These are examples of *formal team roles*. Formal roles have been clearly indicated by the group or organization. *Informal team roles*, on the other hand, "evolve as a result of the interactions that take place among group members" (Carron 1993, p. 116). This is where members of sport teams, for example, are expected to assume certain tasks or exhibit particular behaviors based on their skills, previous experience, emotional maturity, personal preference, personality, or expectations of others. The team "enforcer" (often designated on ice hockey teams), "comedian," or "confidant" may be a function of certain personal characteristics or actions that foster his or her team role (see more on this topic later in this chapter).

A player's role may also stem from his or her relevance to the team's success. For example, substitute players rarely receive a similar amount of practice and instruction as starters, usually because of restrictions on the coach's time and energy. Thus, another way to look at team roles is to determine each player's contribution to the team. Francis and Young (1979) describe these contributions according to three levels: core team members, supportive team members, and temporary team members.

Core Team Members. The contribution of core team members is necessary over an extended period. This does not mean that core team members should receive superior treatment compared to the "less essential" participants. For example, Janice, a substitute, should not be punished for being late to practice while a starter, Ruth, is not. But it does mean that a coach needs to decide with whom to spend additional time in game preparation. Core team members should also serve as group leaders to help carry out team policies and demonstrate desirable behaviors, both on and off the field or court. Remember that a significant change in the content of core team members might occur if the team is consistently unsuccessful.

Supportive Team Members. These athletes, typically nonstarters, help the team to function more effectively. Rather than having a direct impact on game performance, they support and provide assistance or information based on their past experiences and observations to coaches and starters. They are very much needed, despite the infrequency of their participation in competition. In addition, the effect of their loss due to injury, poor school grades, or quitting should not be minimized. In fact, sometimes supportive team members carry even more "weight" with their peers than with the coach due to the high need of all athletes for affiliation, support, and recognition among teammates (Cratty 1983). Coaches should remember that supportive team members are only one injury away from becoming starters.

Temporary Team Members. The contributions of temporary team members are specific to tasks and the time available to perform them. These individuals usually bring a skilled service to the team based on their professional qualifications outside the sport domain. The team doctor, psychologist, publicist, academic counselor, and religious leader fall into this category. To have any one of these roles filled on a volunteer basis is not unusual, especially in a nonprofit organization such as a school or amateur sports program. Because of their prominence, unique skills, unpaid service, and low public profile, the coach must make temporary team members feel wanted, needed, and important. The best way to accomplish this is through recognition. Perhaps the coach should make it a point to express his or her appreciation and gratitude for their input, both privately and publicly. The person who knows that his or her advice is being heeded—that it is making a difference and affecting others in a desirable way—feels rewarded. This will go a long way toward keeping the services of temporary team members for the future and contributing to the team's effectiveness.

Traits of an Effective Team

A plethora of information exists describing the characteristics of "effective" groups that reach their goals consistently and efficiently while maintaining high member satisfaction and loyalty. Let's discuss the most critical of these traits in relation to sport teams.

Appropriate Leadership. Effective coaches use a variety of leadership styles to help athletes perform to their capability on a consistent basis. But one sign of a secure, effective leader is knowing when *not* to lead. Team personnel other than the head coach (assistant coaches and team captains, for instance) should be occasionally assigned leadership tasks. Sharing the leadership role may actually enhance the effectiveness of the head coach.

Suitable Membership. Effective teams consist of members who are proud of their affiliation and believe that their role will contribute in some way, large or small, to the group's success. Coaches need to be aware of specific strategies that facilitate the athletes' feelings of belonging on the team. For instance, the coach may place photos of outstanding former team members in highly observable places. This reminds current team participants of the team's elite history and the importance of maintaining the tradition of success.

Commitment of the Team. In sport, commitment means that each athlete makes the effort to learn skills and to support other team members. Members of effective teams feel a sense of belonging to the group and are proud to represent the team outside of the sport arena. Ideally, each member should find pleasure in the success of other teammates.

Concern to Achieve. Not only is the successful team aware of its objectives, but it is in total agreement with them. After all, if goal setting was conducted properly, the team should have had a role in establishing its objectives. Defining team standards is important so that performance levels and expectations can be set realistically, and, yet, be as challenging as possible. Team goals must take precedence over individual goals and achievements. The role that the athlete is asked to play in optimizing team success sometimes requires the modification of individual goals (Mechikoff & Kozar 1983). For instance, the team's strategy that prioritizes defense may supersede a player's desire to score a given number of points.

Effective Work Methods. The team should develop a systematic and effective way of solving problems jointly between coach and athletes. To establish a sense of personal commitment in each team member is desirable. One way to do this is to broaden the base for making decisions that affect team members. There are advantages to making team members responsible for decision making.

Well-Organized Team Procedures. Effective teams have clearly defined roles and well-developed communication patterns and administrative procedures. Players might be consulted before group goals are developed. However, the coach should make final decisions firmly and without equivocation. Yet, he or she should also show flexibility in examining alternatives and, perhaps, changing a decision that proves to be ineffective or unjust.

Critique without Rancor. An effective team consists of secure members. This means being receptive to feedback for improved performance. Team and individual errors and weaknesses should be examined objectively without attacking any person's character or personality. The correct policy is to learn from past mistakes in order to improve future performance.

Creative Strength. The effective team has the capacity and motivation to create new ideas through interactions with its members. Innovative risk-taking is planned and often accepted and rewarded. Athletes show that they are capable of thinking quickly and creatively during game situations, especially in making rapid, unrehearsed decisions. Less effective is total reliance on the coach for all decisions, task instructions, and strategies. Creativity, especially if shown by highly skilled athletes, has been shown to improve team satisfaction (Fisher et al. 1982).

Positive Intergroup Relations. Players should be aware that personal contact with other team members has its benefits. Sometimes assignments and strategies can be learned and remembered better under conditions of peer teaching (where the environment may be more relaxed) than if the coach provides the instruction. Teammates should be trusted to help one another.

Constructive Climate. When the atmosphere is relaxed and nonthreatening, athletes feel more comfortable in engaging in direct, honest communication with their coach and teammates. And they feel secure in taking logical risks in their performance, which is one component of success.

Developing an Effective Team Climate

Think of the various ways in which the weather is described: sunny, bright, cloudy, stormy, clear, warm, cold, fair, and dry. Some of these adjectives can be used to describe how people in a group interact, communicate, and feel about their affiliation. The terms portray what sociologists call a group's (team's) climate, atmosphere, or environment.

Team climate is a psychosocial construct, an internal representation of how a person perceives the conditions and interrelationships among group members (James et al. 1977). The key issue is the group (team) members' perceptions; it is not the coach who evaluates and determines the team's climate but rather the players. Athletes make an assessment, or a *value judgment*, based on their own needs and priorities, in identifying and categorizing the team atmosphere. What is so important about these perceptions is that they have a significant impact on each athlete's attitude about being a team member. Researchers refer to this feeling as *team member satisfaction*.

The coach, the person in the most powerful position on the team, has the greatest influence on establishing team climate and ensuring a healthy psychological environment (Fisher et al. 1982). Effective coaches, whose teams win and whose players have high group member satisfaction, follow certain guidelines that create a positive team climate. Much research has focused on determining these guidelines and strategies.

Factors That Most Affect Team Climate

DeCotiis and Koys (1980) found, based on their literature review in the area of organization and management, the use of 54 dimensions of the concept of group climate. Using only subjective measures (i.e., terms used and feelings described by group members in the different studies), clusterings of 8 dimensions of climate were uncovered. These were autonomy, support, pressure, recognition, trust, fairness, innovation, and cohesion.

For the athlete, *autonomy* is the opportunity to function independently of the group leader. Autonomous athletes might feel more satisfied if they were allowed to make decisions on their own—at least occasionally. For instance, many collegiate and professional athletes would prefer to plan and implement some of the plays themselves, without the coach making all of the decisions. One of the negative outcomes of always having the coach call the play is the possibility of blaming the coach for performance failure (e.g., "He called the wrong play. If only he had called 'this' play, we could have scored"). The players may not accept responsibility for the outcome. Also, occasionally allowing athletes to make their own decisions or, perhaps, to make them jointly with the coach can promote coach loyalty ("The coach trusts me and respects my opinion").

Perhaps no greater need exists for the athlete than emotional *support* from coaches and teammates, especially when the athlete's optimal effort in competition does not lead to success. This sense of "caring and sharing" provides participants with fundamental psychological needs such as recognition for a good effort and psychological comfort to help reduce the stress of nonsuccess (Fisher et al. 1982). Negative, inappropriate responses from group members, such as harsh criticism, sarcasm, nonrecognition of effort (ignoring the performer), and, in extreme cases, wishing physical harm or failure to a team member, can result in a cold, disloyal, nonsupportive team climate. The coach is the one agent in the group who makes a major impact on whether the atmosphere on a team is positive and supportive (Sage 1973).

The *pressure to succeed*, to meet the coach's expectations, and to reach predetermined goals is an integral aspect of competition. Tension and stress are often inevitable. The team environment may be "tight," meaning that athletes are afraid to make a mistake. Or the climate may be one that pressures performers to go beyond their ability to beat superior opponents. The athlete's perception of pressure inevitably heightens anxiety. The consequence of this additional tension may be poorer, not better, performance (Martens 1977). Two ways to reduce these undesirable emotions are to help athletes to feel competent and to focus on the athlete's performance improvement rather than only on between-player comparisons. According to one research study (Gill & Dzewaltowski 1988), elite competitors define success as improving on or matching previous attempts.

The coach's *recognition* of the athlete's efforts, improvements, and successes improves self-confidence, promotes feeling responsible for one's performance, establishes and maintains close personal friendships with peers, and fosters a supportive team climate. Further, the athlete's strengths are reinforced, which provides the participant with the personal security and confidence to be more receptive to critical feedback in order to improve weaknesses. The relationship between recognition and team climate is that more secure and satisfied athletes tend to be better prepared to support their teammates. Feelings of group member satisfaction and adequacy are heightened when athletes are given the proper recognition (Williams & Hacker 1982).

One of the most important components of team climate is *trust*. Each athlete on the team should feel that performing certain, perhaps risky, actions during competition is "allowed." The performer should not fear being emotionally and physically abandoned by teammates or losing group identity. The feeling of "You can count on me," "We're in this together," or "You gave it your best" is very motivating for most athletes. It creates a sense of fairness among teammates.

Fairness is in the eye of the beholder; it's based on the athlete's perceptions of the situation. This perception may be different from the coach's interpretation—and even different from reality. An athlete's interpretation of fairness is partly based on three issues:

1. The degree of compatibility between the coach's and the player's respective assessments of the performer's skills and contributions—or potential contributions—to the team. Why, for example, does the player not start or not receive more playing time?

2. The coach's manner in communicating—or not communicating—his or her views to the athlete.

3. Evidence of the coach's attempt to improve the athlete's skills and level of satisfaction as a team member.

The athlete's personal view of being treated fairly by the coach will have a strong and direct impact on the athlete's level of commitment, motivation, and satisfaction as a team member. This issue is capable of bringing a team very close together or driving its members far apart. Coaches rarely give much credence to the athlete's feelings of fairness, which is unfortunate given the degree to which these feelings transfer into action—even quitting the team. Therefore, an effective team climate must be based on the athlete's view of fair treatment. If this view differs from that of the coach, these two individuals must communicate directly to work it out.

One relevant issue in fostering *innovation*, or creativity, on the team is the group's and coach's willingness to tolerate—even to facilitate—adversity and change. Occasionally, athletes should have a chance to be creative in planning and executing strategies. (Effective coaches do not feel compelled to give directives and to know all the "right" answers.) Participants should be allowed to take risks. For instance, instead of the coach being responsible for calling all of the plays, the players are allowed to react to game situations independent of coach directives. Offering new and exciting alternatives to practice schedules and drills and teaching new skills and strategies during practice are other ways to improve team innovation. A positive, effective team climate is one in which change, creativity, input from athletes, and some risk-taking are encouraged. In this way, the participants are cognitively involved in all aspects of the team's performance, feel accountable for the outcome, and are mutually supportive—all key aspects of group cohesion.

Cohesion is a measure of a person's attraction to, sense of belonging to, and desire to remain a part of the group (Carron 1984a). A warm and enduring team climate reflects what Widmeyer et al. (1985) call high social cohesion, in that participants develop and maintain an atmosphere that members find attractive and desirable. In a high social cohesive team climate, members are communicating, and the members' collective personality is compatible with that of the coach. With high task cohesion, team goals reflect those of the individual members, and the roles of each member are clarified, understood, and agreed upon by all participants. Teams with the proper team climate provide players with the incentive to invest energy in meeting group goals. Social and task cohesion are discussed in more depth later in this chapter.

Is the proper team climate related to, or does it actually cause, desirable performance? Craig Fisher and his colleagues at Ithaca College (1982) studied the effects of coach-athlete interactions on team climate. They videotaped and tape-recorded three groups of varsity high school basketball athletes. Coaches and athletes completed questionnaires that measured their respective views on the degree of team member satisfaction, which they labeled "social climate." It was found that:

- The satisfied athletes received more verbal and nonverbal praise and acceptance from their coach and responded to the coach's instructions with more verbal and nonverbal initiative. Satisfied athletes, in general, were more verbal than their less satisfied counterparts.
- Coaches of satisfied teams asked their athletes more questions during instruction, but provided less feedback. The content, rather than the amount, of feedback appeared to be an important factor in promoting satisfaction.

- Athletes on less satisfied teams were more predictable and mechanical in their responses in drills and scrimmages. On satisfied teams, athletes had more freedom to experiment and to be creative.
- Coaches of less satisfied teams spent more time giving information and directions compared to coaches of satisfied teams. And much of it was negative. Feedback to dissatisfied players was excessive—70 percent more than with satisfied teams.
- Satisfied teams were more cohesive and received more support from their coach.
- The coaches of both satisfied and dissatisfied players perceived their team's climate as matching what they considered to be an ideal climate. However, less satisfied athletes perceived a less positive climate than did their coaches. The implication here is that coaches of less satisfied players may not be "in touch" with their athletes' feelings, nor do they apparently comprehend the manner in which they affect their players.

The Fisher et al. (1982) study showed a strong relationship between player satisfaction and team climate. Not only was the coach-athlete interaction in a positive climate more trusting, sensitive, and supportive, but it involved more productive and effective use of practice time and instructional techniques. In addition, coaches on satisfied teams appeared to be more accurate in perceiving the feelings and attitudes of the players than leaders of unsatisfied teams. These findings were supported in a study by Westre and Weiss (1991). Their examination of the relationship between team cohesion and U.S. football players' perceptions of their coaches' leadership style and behaviors indicated that coaches who were viewed by their players as giving the athletes extensive social support, training and instruction, and positive feedback, and who had a democratic leadership style, had teams who scored highest for task cohesion. In addition, players with higher perceptions of individual success revealed greater attraction toward group cohesion and felt their coach offered more positive feedback. It is clear that some degree of humanistic coaching favorably influences group climate.

Team Climate Checklist for Athletes

What is the best way a coach can assess his or her team climate? Ask the athletes. The purpose of a team climate checklist (see Figure 7.1) is to ascertain the players' feelings about being members of the team and their perceptions of the coach's behaviors and attitudes. Its usefulness is dependent on the coach's willingness to read, reflect on, and react to these opinions in a positive and serious manner. The checklist is derived from Francis and Young (1979) and is applied here in a sport context.

There are three guidelines for its use. First, the checklist is without norms; no scale defines a "warm" or "cold" team climate or a "satisfied" or "dissatisfied" competitor. Everything is relative, so coaches should be interested in changes in scores over time. Thus, the checklist should be administered periodically, preferably before and during the season, so that coaches can ascertain team climate and use the information. Second, the players should be told that the checklist is not a test; there are no right or wrong answers. And third, anonymity is essential! Athletes need to feel that they can respond to each question with complete honesty and without fear of repercussions from the coach. To avoid such fears, the coach might want to ask a player to distribute and collect the checklist to/from the athletes, whose identities would be coded—perhaps by using the birthday of a parent or by selecting a number from a hat. The coach can compare scores based on the coded number on the different administrations of the checklist.

Figure 7.1 Team climate checklist.

Please use the following code, and write in the appropriate number after each statement:

1 = never occurs   2 = sometimes occurs   3 = usually occurs   4 = almost always occurs   5 = always occurs

1.   I make many of the decisions that affect the way I play. _____
2.   I can count on the coach to keep the things I say confidential. _____
3.   People on the coaching staff pitch in to help one another out. _____
4.   I have enough time to do the things the coach asks me to learn and perform. _____
5.   I can count on my coach to help me when I need it. _____
6.   I can count on being told when I play well. _____
7.   I can count on a fair shake from the coach. _____
8.   The coach encourages me to create and develop my ideas about any aspect of the team. _____
9.   I have a role in selecting my physical conditioning procedures, especially during the off-season. _____
10.   The coaching staff tends to agree with one another. _____
11.   Practice sessions are relaxed places to learn and implement techniques. _____
12.   My coach is interested in me becoming the best player I can be. _____
13.   The feedback I receive from coaches is balanced (both positive and negative). _____
14.   The goals the coach feels I can reach are reasonable. _____
15.   The coach is open to alternative ways of getting the job done. _____
16.   I make decisions about my playing strategy—what to do and when. _____
17.   The coaching staff takes a personal interest in one another. _____
18.   I welcome having the coach observe me perform at any time. _____
19.   The coach is behind me 100 percent. _____
20.   The coach knows my strengths and lets me know it. _____
21.   The coach follows through on his or her commitments to me. _____
22.   The coach is honest with me in statements and actions. _____
23.   The coach recognizes me when I perform well. _____
24.   The coach is easy to talk to about personal or team-related problems. _____
25.   The coach understands the players' need to get away from the same sport occasionally rather than risk becoming burned out. _____
26.   I don't feel overworked and mentally drained. _____
27.   I have an important role in setting my own performance standards. _____
28.   The coach does not play favorites. _____
29.   The coach encourages me to find new ways around problems or strengths of our opponents. _____
30.   My teammates do not get burned out from the practices and length of the season. _____
31.   The coach talks to me (or the team) about new approaches to coaching. _____
32.   The coach criticizes only players (including me) who deserve it. _____
33.   The coach supports me and helps me learn after I make a mistake. _____
34.   I have a lot in common, and socialize, with my teammates. _____
35.   The coach is not likely to give me bad advice. _____
36.   The coach uses me as a positive example in front of other team members. _____
37.   I am aware of my role on the team. _____
38.   Practice sessions and drills change during the season to prevent boredom. _____
39.   The coach keeps in touch with my parents. _____
40.   The coach is supported by his or her supervisor (boss). _____

Total Score: _____

Higher scores represent warmer team climate, better player satisfaction.

Group Dynamics: The Roles and Interactions of Team Members

Coaches should be aware of the need of most athletes to belong—to affiliate with other team members. The process of making friends and developing into a cohesive, supportive group is best understood as a process of *group dynamics*. This is an analysis of the ways in which group members interact and the development of certain roles within the group. Coaches should be aware of common traits of group behavior, particularly at the beginning stages when team members make first impressions and judgments about others and begin to develop a level of group satisfaction.

Everyone Has a Role

Promoting or, in some cases, inhibiting the player's role on the team contributes to team cohesion. As you will see shortly, some roles actually dampen the proper team climate. The roles most commonly observed in most groups, including sport teams, include the positive leader, negative leader, follower, isolate, scapegoat, and clown. The following sections provide a description of each of these roles, their advantages and disadvantages, and the coaching strategies that can improve team harmony. It is important to note that much of this literature resides in social psychology; research in this area remains nonexistent in sport psychology.

The Positive Leader

The positive leader is a "dream come true" for the coach. Other terms used to describe him or her include *facilitator, encourager, supporter,* or *rescuer.* The positive leader is like an assistant coach among peers. He or she is among the more mature and supportive athletes on the team. One would expect this person to be the team captain, but this is not always the case. Sometimes the role of captain is awarded to the most popular player or to the team's most productive player. Positive leaders are well liked and respected by their teammates. This is because they tend to be good listeners, are sensitive and empathetic, have good communication skills, support team policies and rules, usually do well in academic subjects, and establish mature relationships with authority figures. Coaches are drawn to positive leaders by their good problem-solving and decision-making skills, their willingness to set high and challenging goals, and their tendency to persist at activities with optimal effort; they just don't quit.

The positive leader is "in touch" with the "pulse" of the team and is aware of the personal problems of some athletes. The positive leader can be a confidant in that he or she will not divulge private or confidential information to others if asked not to. The coach may ask this person to befriend a team member who seems withdrawn from the group or to discourage inappropriate behaviors such as drinking, smoking, or fighting.

The positive leader is not without problems, however. This athlete wants to affiliate with teammates just as much as any other team member. Yet, the coach might ask this person to assume responsibilities that appear authoritative and supervisory to fellow teammates—to take on the role of "pseudocoach." This person may lose friendships and acceptance by teammates if given too many supervisory responsibilities. The positive leader is still an athlete, not a coach, and should be perceived as one. However, the positive leader has talent that can be utilized by the coach—the talent to work and communicate with others. Sometimes athletes are more responsive to, and affected by, actions and statements of teammates than those of coaches (Bird & Cripe 1986).

The Negative Leader

Negative leaders are a coach's nightmare because they depress team morale and unity, among other reasons. This type of person tends to act against the coach, either personally (in an antagonistic relationship), philosophically (by not following team rules), or both. Psychologically, negative leaders often have personal problems with authority. They do not like to be told what to do and, consequently, resent an authoritarian leadership style. If their feelings were kept to themselves, this role might not be so potentially harmful to the team. But the real problem is that others tend to follow their lack of cooperation and testing (breaking) of rules.

Negative leaders perform numerous potentially destructive functions. Sometimes they solicit other team members in generating anticoach sentiment. What makes this person especially dangerous is his or her ability to succeed at these goals, at least with a few teammates. Negative leaders possess enough charisma to cause less mature teammates to follow them down the wrong path. Breaking curfew, illegal drug ingestion, and dishonesty are examples.

Benne and Sheats (1970) describe negative leaders as aggressors, blockers, or jokers. *Aggressors* deflate the status of others; express disapproval of the values, acts, or feelings of others; verbally attack group members or the group's objectives; joke aggressively (e.g., with pranks and other acts of hostility); or try to take credit for the contribution of other group members. *Blockers* are negativistic and stubbornly resistant; disagree with and oppose others without, or beyond, reason; and attempt to maintain or bring back a contentious issue after the group or coach has rejected, bypassed, or solved it. *Jokers* display a lack of involvement in the group through cynicism, horseplay, and apathy.

So what can the coach do about this negative influence? Before the coach dismisses this person from the team, he or she should remember that this athlete possesses leadership qualities and perhaps sport skills that a coach can use to the team's advantage. If the coach can turn these qualities into something more productive, such as supporting the team's starters or motivating teammates, then everyone wins.

Here are a few recommendations for dealing with the negative team leader:

Problem Recognition. The most important step is to identify this person's counterproductive behaviors. Does the person demonstrate a tendency toward testing rules, chronically making excuses for inappropriate behavior, or not following instructions? Testing team rules may be a way of communicating doubt in the coach's leadership ability or a technique for gaining group acceptance. Actually, some athletes believe that this is the only way they can gain respect.

Positive Confrontation. After certain behaviors or attitudes of the negative leader have surfaced, it's time for the coach to move quickly. The offending individual should be approached privately and quietly by the coach under relaxed conditions; no public confrontations. The coach should first inform the athlete about his or her (the coach's) observations. Whether or not the athlete denies his or her actions, the coach must engage in strong limit-setting as soon as possible. This means informing the athlete that the offending actions will not be allowed to continue. Positive confrontation, however, is a dialogue, not a lecture, as the next section indicates.

Conclusions and Agreements. The athlete may have feelings that underlie and help explain his or her behaviors. These feelings should be heard. The real objective of this meeting is to reach an agreement that the athlete stop the inappropriate behaviors immediately. For example (coach to athlete): "Having our friend buy alcohol for members of this team will not be tolerated, Jim. It's against team rules, and I want it stopped now!"

The conclusion from this meeting must be the athlete's agreement to stop counter-productive behaviors. But it doesn't end there. If this issue is handled constructively, then agreements for future behaviors should be negotiated and concluded. This is what some coaches refer to as "respecting the integrity of each athlete" (Mechikoff & Kozar 1983).

Sometimes athletes refuse to change their actions and the coach has no other choice but to suspend or dismiss the athlete from the team. Although giving the person an opportunity to make realistic changes in his or her actions is constructive, the athlete may not agree to the required changes in behavior or may not follow through on agreements. However, before athletes are dismissed from the team, they should be warned about the consequences of their actions. In this way, they make the choice and take responsibility for their own behaviors. An even more effective strategy is to announce before the season starts the possibility of dismissal from the team in response to committing certain acts.

The Follower

This person can play any one of several roles. He or she is extremely susceptible to the suggestions and actions of others. Often the person follows directions or imitates the actions and attitudes of leaders. Usually, the follower seeks friendship with more popular, influential members of the team. Followers are not inherently "bad." A team cannot perform optimally with too many "generals" and no "soldiers." A team needs athletes who will follow the leader without questioning every strategy and policy. But in a less desirable way, followers may select the wrong team members to emulate, have low self-confidence and self-esteem (which is often associated with being afraid to take risks and initiate actions that may help their performance), be a noncontributor to building team cohesion, avoid taking responsibility for their performance ("I just do what I'm told" or "It's not my fault"), and lack the ability to support teammates.

In describing individuals they call *help-seekers*, Benne and Sheats (1970) suggest that followers have the potential to drain the group's energy. They can solicit sympathy from other members through expressions of insecurity, personal confusion, or self-doubt. Followers, therefore, can possibly be a drain on the group.

Coaches can help the follower to mature by implementing strategies that develop leadership skills. These include (1) placing the follower in situations in which he or she will be seen by others as successful, (2) determining the follower's skills and using these skills to the team's advantage, (3) placing the competitor in a leadership role that the coach decides is within the follower's capability, (4) giving the person plenty of positive feedback on performance to build self-confidence, (5) offering comments or assigning tasks that help the person to feel that he or she is an important part of the team, and (6) publicly recognizing the follower's accomplishments to others. See the section on behavioristic coaching in Chapter 8 for more ideas.

The Isolate

If you were to ask a coach to describe the strengths, weaknesses, and personality characteristics of each player on the team, the people who would first come to mind would be those who get the coach's attention—leaders and starters. One type of individual who does not usually have a high profile on the team is the isolate. Isolates are, as suggested by the term, physically and mentally removed from other team members, at least more often than not. Sometimes this response is self-imposed; they choose to be alone.

However, isolates do not always want this role. Sometimes they demonstrate certain habits or communicate in a manner that seems peculiar to other players and that makes teammates feel uncomfortable. It's entirely possible that isolates are rejected by the team rather than the other way around. For example, a junior high school baseball player verbally announced to several teammates who were taking batting practice that he was the best hitter on the team. He further suggested that only he possessed the skills necessary to make the high school team. The immediate and long-term response of his teammates was to ignore him. The other players rejected his requests for affiliation, both on and off the ball field. A team isolate was "born." Despite the seemingly deserving nature of the team's response in this situation, isolates rarely deserve or appreciate this role.

Researchers have not actually studied the personality characteristics of isolates in sport. But I have gathered anecdotal evidence from observations and conversations suggesting that causes range from a mild case of social maladjustment to more serious psychological problems associated with feelings of revenge, hostility, and destruction. A social worker with extensive experience in detention centers for adolescents once described the isolate as "a negative leader waiting to happen."

Typically, isolates (especially child athletes) may:

- be less skilled as compared to other team members (but exceptions have occurred, particularly in professional sports)
- be disloyal to team goals and, instead, be more concerned with their own performance quality and psychological survival, even at the team's expense
- lack physical and psychological maturity for their age
- feel rejected by others and sometimes think that they deserve such treatment
- have a low self-image
- lack effective communication skills
- be critical of others (but may not typically voice this opinion except when asked by someone they consider nonthreatening)
- rarely smile (a partial display of low self-esteem)
- be chronic complainers
- test authority by breaking team rules (perhaps to gain attention or for revenge)

Since athletes, in general, are a particularly gregarious population (Iso-Ahola & Hatfield 1986), isolates, especially children and adolescents, should concern the coach. Children have a salient need for affiliation (Cratty 1983). It is the rare child who consciously chooses to remain alone, without the warmth and support of peers. Perhaps the most common and saddest result of the isolate's behavioral tendencies is dropping out of sport (Gould 1984).

Coaching strategies can be initiated that will make the isolate feel more wanted, motivated, and, most important, more connected—emotionally and behaviorally—to the team. The following true story includes several suggestions for dealing with the problem:

Martin was a 15-year-old who played outfield on his high school's baseball team. His models were professional athletes, and he dreamed of making it to the major leagues. He was tall and lanky for his age, appearing awkward and clumsy, a sign that his body was growing too fast for his neuromuscular development. He possessed a strong arm (was a good thrower) and had above-average total body movement speed. His most glaring weakness was batting; he simply could not get the bat around quickly; he swung late and missed fast pitches. But one of Martin's most obvious characteristics was that he did not associate with any team members. In fact, the other players indicated that they rarely noticed him interacting with others off the field. Martin was the team isolate.

An outside observer noticed Martin and discussed his social status with the baseball coach. Not surprisingly, the coach knew relatively little about Martin. Usually, the athletic skills of isolates are below average. Consequently, coaches tend to spend only minimal time with them.

Martin's coach agreed to let the observer study Martin as part of a research project concerned with identifying player roles and enhancing each individual's contribution to the team. The coach would help by implementing the following strategies over the next two weeks: He would (1) observe Martin's actions toward other teammates to determine whether he had any friends on the team, (2) include Martin in drills and offer instruction, (3) give him as much honest, performance-based, and positive feedback as possible, (4) ask one of the more mature, positive players on the team to befriend Martin, to get to know him and include him in activities in which other team members participated both on the field (e.g., playing catch) and off the field (e.g., going to a movie), (5) give Martin the responsibility of calculating the batting averages and earned run averages (i.e., a measure of pitching effectiveness) of each player each week, and finally, (6) engage Martin in verbal and nonverbal exchanges on an ongoing basis.

Follow-up observations of Martin's behavior two weeks after the implementation of these techniques revealed an incredible transformation. He started smiling occasionally at practice and, in a 180-degree change in demeanor, engaged in frequent conversations with his teammates. There was more. What surprised both the coach and the observer was the obvious increase in energy Martin exhibited on the field. This was a youngster who went from casual walking to running when going to the outfield to shag fly balls in batting practice. Martin's skills were still below average, and the coach and observer agreed that either he would make a better basketball player than a baseball player (he towered over his teammates) or he would need to receive more instruction and plenty of practice to gain the necessary expertise.

One more positive outcome emerged from this project. Three team isolates (of which Martin was the most obvious) were identified. The coach implemented a plan to deal with each one in a relatively short time span. After one month, it became apparent that eliminating the roles of team isolates translated into three additional team supporters; three more players who cheered for the starters and displayed team loyalty, energy, and enthusiasm in helping others prepare for games; and three individuals who grew as athletes and matured as young men. Although it could not be proven that this change also resulted in more team victories, clearly the lives of three individuals became more enjoyable, on and off the field, and the whole team benefited.

The Scapegoat

The term *scapegoat* is defined as "a person made to bear the blame for others or to suffer in their place." The concept of a scapegoat has a biblical derivation (Lev. 16:8–22) in which a goat was sacrificed as the symbolic object of the people's sins. In contemporary social psychology, scapegoating is described as a phenomenon in which "aggression toward a frustrator is suppressed and displaced upon some nonparticipant bystander" (Harari & McDavid 1974, p. 357). Apparently, scapegoating has been around a long time and occurs in many different settings, including sport. But this does not make it a constructive form of communication. Ginott (1968) refers to scapegoating (and sarcasm) as "sound barriers to learning" (p. 67).

Athletes might be teased by peers for a number of reasons (e.g., an awkward appearance, poor performance, peculiar habits, and just to be "funny"). Although a scapegoat by definition is a victim who does *not* warrant or seek out such treatment, sometimes a person may *appear* to deserve it, that is, a person who is teased by peers may have prompted this reaction through inappropriate or unfriendly actions. For example, the scapegoat might behave in a manner that is so upsetting to others that they actively reject the targeted person. In one example, Dale had the disturbing habit of constantly asking the coach to repeat information in team meetings. This player made it obvious that either he was not listening to the coach or was confused by the coach's message. Either way, the group grew impatient with his habit, which disrupted meetings. Eventually, Dale became the target of crude remarks and pranks.

Another possible reason for scapegoating behavior is the insecurity of team members. Some individuals, especially those who are relatively younger or less skilled, have a psychological need to blame others due to their own lack of self-confidence, self-esteem, and emotional maturity. Persons who are uncomfortable with themselves tend to blame others subconsciously for their own inadequacies. Scapegoating fulfills this need; the abuser perceives the victim as less competent. Preadolescent and adolescent age groups are especially susceptible to scapegoating. Peer pressure, the need for group affiliation and acceptance, and conformity are present during the preteen and teenage years to a greater extent than at any other time in a person's life (Ginott 1969). Other common reasons for teasing others include individual differences in physical appearance, a "foreign" accent, or other unique behaviors or characteristics.

Sadly, one possible instigator of scapegoating behavior in sport is the coach. Sometimes the coach will unfairly blame the athlete or a small group of players for the team's continual lack of success or, in some cases, the failure to win a major event. Despite the team's decisive loss, one participant might shoulder the blame for the entire team after failing to execute a single play successfully. Or in attempting to be popular or to improve the mood among the players, the coach may use "gallows humor"—invoking laughter at the expense of a person's character or self-esteem through sarcasm or teasing. The targeted individual does not find such comments humorous.

Scapegoating has a potentially negative impact on team success. First, the team climate lacks mutual support, trust, and warmth (Harari & McDavid 1974). Second, when a group of players scapegoats a teammate, it is likely that the players are not making accurate causal attributions for the team's lack of success. In other words, instead of taking responsibility for their own performance in explaining a poor team record, they are choosing to blame an "easy" target.

The coach can and should do everything in his or her power to prevent and stop scapegoating behavior. It is harmful and unneeded. The "victim" needs protection and, in sport situations, only the coach can supply it. This is why the coach should put a stop to scapegoating immediately when it's detected. Players should be warned that hurting the feelings of others will not be tolerated. But the coach's reaction shouldn't stop there.

Probably the most constructive approach is to try to understand the derivation of the scapegoating. Why is this particular athlete the victim? Who are the organizers, initiators, and leaders of this behavior, and what is their complaint or problem? Perhaps the coach can best handle the situation by getting at the root of the "attacker's" feelings. To avoid embarrassing the scapegoat and invoking hostile reactions from teammates, the coach's approach to the problem should be low key, an attempt to seek information rather than exhibit hostility.

The coach must be able to separate scapegoating behavior from legitimate and normal teasing and joking. It would be inappropriate to overreact to the players' statements of friendly banter, which reduce anxiety and help to relax the participants. However, destructive sarcasm is a different message. How can the coach tell the difference? Look at the targeted person's reaction to the statement. Is it genuine laughter? Does he or she return the teasing? Are statements accompanied by physical abuse or light playful interactions? Coaches must listen to the verbal and emotional messages of such responses. Does the teasing occur after successful performance or failure? How consistent is the teasing? Is it rare or chronic? Is there a pattern of its occurrence, or does it happen rarely? A problem is more likely if the teasing doesn't stop.

Coaches can also help the scapegoat to understand how the scapegoat's own behaviors and comments affect others if he or she is, in fact, doing or saying something that triggers teasing. In addition, the scapegoat can be informed about the emotional immaturity and undesirable personality traits of persons who engage in scapegoating (e.g., "They don't know any better"). This technique, called *psychological distancing*, helps the victim to gain perspective about the problem and to take the insults less personally. American journalist David Brinkley is quoted as saying, "A successful man is one who can lay a firm foundation with the bricks that others throw at him."

As noted, sometimes the coach is actually the cause of the problem. Coaches should never join the players in scapegoating anyone, as harmless as it may seem. The coach should never tease an athlete for the sake of gaining popularity with other players or to foster humor in the group. In one case, I was present when a coach walked in on a discussion among the players (ages 11 and 12 years) in which one person was being teased because of a spot on his uniform. The coach, thinking that such bantering was harmless, joined the laughter. The young athlete took one look at the laughing coach and immediately burst into tears; the frustration was too much to take. Tears were his only release.

The coach's job is to "save" a scapegoated athlete from the cruel remarks of others. A philosopher named Gough once said, "We constantly underrate the capacity of children to understand and to suffer." A primary role in coaching is to avoid this pitfall.

The Clown

Everyone on the team seems to need attention, but some are in far more need than others. In fact, certain team members seem to demand it—even if it means demonstrating behavior that is obnoxious, unpleasant, or perhaps humorous. The team clown (or clowns—many teams have more than one) has this need. What is it about the clown's personality that brings on the need to be so often "on stage"? Why does the person need attention and choose to obtain it in this manner?

Athletes who clown consistently do so for different reasons. The most salient of these is peer recognition (Ginott 1969). Any normal athlete needs recognition. However, this need should never be met at the expense of team goals. Athletes who continuously clown around likely have certain psychological needs that mandate these behaviors. They may (1) feel unsure of their skills and contributions to the team, (2) be masking a low self-image and insecurity, (3) need attention to feel adequate, (4) feel negative toward authority figures such as the coach, (5) feel physically unattractive, in which case humor would be used to cover up a poor body image, (6) display disloyalty toward the coach by using antics to disrupt the coach's goals and strategies, and (7) feel unwanted by others, in which case humor is used to gain love, recognition, and admiration.

Coaches must make accurate judgments about the timing and content of their reactions to clowning. They must take into account whether clowning behaviors are harmless, or even helpful in reducing tension; whether the clown's actions are at the expense of other's feelings; and the appropriate timing of such behaviors. For example, during practice and instructional sessions or before the contest, humor is rarely conducive to establishing proper arousal and concentration levels. Depending on the type of and the personalities of the athletes, some appropriate levity may improve the team's mood before a contest.

How does the coach deal constructively with the team comedian? First, coaches may circumvent having to deal with clowning by stating their expectations and regulations of inappropriate behaviors before the season, specifying when clowning is off limits and a more serious atmosphere is warranted. Second, the coach's reaction to clowning behavior should be appropriate for the situation. Overreacting may be less productive than no reaction at all. An explosive reaction will diminish the athletes' concentration and give the clown the attention and recognition that he or she seeks. The coach's reactions to the clown could range from selectively ignoring the behavior or comment (especially if it is displayed rarely by the individual or is ignored by or has minimal impact on others) to voicing disapproval immediately after the clowning action, followed by moving ahead to the task at hand. Coaches should make their point and get back on track as soon as possible.

In fact, seeking recognition from the coach is often the primary rationale behind clowning behaviors. Perhaps the best response is to provide positive attention on occasions when the athlete is not clowning, through skill instruction, feedback on performance, and mature conversation related and unrelated to sport—clowns often have difficulty in, or are incapable of, verbally communicating with others. Clowns seek approval. Coaches should try to give it to them in ways that motivate, not demean.

That group members take on roles is a natural phenomenon of human behavior. Because teams are groups, this practice similarly exists in sport. The coach's job is to deal with this natural occurrence in an insightful and productive manner so that the unique personality and ability of each athlete contributes to the good of the team and improves team cohesion.

Team Cohesion

For years coaches have assumed that positive feelings among team members result in better sport performance. Coaches contend that team unity is essential for success, and consequently, they have used techniques to help ensure an "esprit de corps" among the players. The pregame meal, physical conditioning programs, meetings, and pregame preparation traditionally occur as a group. Ostensibly, when the players interact and share team-related experiences, they develop closer interpersonal relationships and feelings of mutual support and trust. Although this outcome is intuitively appealing, researchers aren't certain that it is true.

For example, Carron (1984a) and Widmeyer et al. (1985, 1992) reviewed several studies in which teams that were highly cohesive also achieved superior performance outcomes and other studies that indicated a low relationship between cohesion and team performance. However, a study by Fiedler (1967) showed that poor team cohesion actually interfered with team success. Teammates on a basketball team who were very close friends chose to pass the ball to one another rather than to players in better shooting positions. In this case, team success was not a priority. Thus, coaches who try to promote cohesion might, under some circumstances, do more harm than good.

An example is the common strategy in team sports of requiring all athletes to be together and to follow the same protocol up to 24 hours before the contest. I found that collegiate and high school football players were actually annoyed at following this procedure (Anshel 1989a). My more recent consultation with professional athletes supports this finding. Many players preferred to be alone with their thoughts or to have the option of attending team activities that did not relate directly to game preparation such as viewing a commercial film, engaging in mental imagery, spending their "free time" with their position (assistant) coaches, spending the night before competition in a local hotel (and being assigned their roommate), or being with personal friends. Still, sport psychology researchers have found that this "we" feeling improves the level of interpersonal attraction and feelings among team members.

What Is Group Cohesion?

As indicated earlier, *cohesion* is a term used to describe feelings of interpersonal attraction and the sense of belonging to the group by its members. It also signifies the members' desire to remain in the group (Carron 1984a). Two different types of cohesion have been identified by researchers: social (or sociometric) cohesion and task cohesion (Widmeyer et al. 1992). *Social cohesion* is the degree of interpersonal attraction among group members, the extent to which the group allows a person to reach a desired goal. *Task cohesion* refers to the athletes' objective appraisal of their group's level of coordinated effort or teamwork. In other words, it is the degree to which the team and the individual members reach their respective goals. Acknowledging the differences between social and task cohesion is imperative in determining how each might affect a person's level of group satisfaction. For example, Carron (1994) concluded from his review of several studies that "athletes on teams perceived to be high in task cohesiveness readily accept more responsibility for team failure than athletes on teams perceived to be low in task cohesiveness" (pp. 94–95).

Several factors affect both social and task cohesion. As Table 7.1 shows, these include characteristics of team members, characteristics of the group, and situations experienced by the group (Widmeyer et al. 1985).

Table 7.1 Factors that contribute to cohesion on sport teams.

	Characteristics of Team Members	Characteristics of the Group	Situations Experienced by the Group
Social cohesion improved if:	1. Liking one another is a need among players	1. Small group size	1. Players perceive team is threatened
	2. Similar personalities exist among teammates	2. Democratic leadership style used	2. Athletes share blame for failure
	3. Athletes have similar social backgrounds	3. Team captains selected by team and have active role	3. Athletes make similar causal attributes for success and failure
	4. Being on team meets person's social needs	4. Structured to reward and recognize athletes equally	4. Group receives equal recognition and adulation for same achievement
	5. Players have become good friends off the field	5. Players choose to socialize among themselves	
	6. Each player feels accepted by teammates	6. Warm group atmosphere	
		7. Group leader supports each player	
Task cohesion improved if:	1. Players are satisfied with their performance	1. Members work together	1. Competition with another team
	2. Players feel their sport skills are improving	2. Players are aware of and accept team	2. Team has consistent success role
	3. Players demonstrate similar skill levels	3. Frequent practice helps players anticipate their teammates' movement patterns	3. Intragroup competition (team rivalry) for team status, position, skill development, etc.
	4. Each member perceives role on team as important to team's success	4. All athletes have similar work patterns	4. Social cohesion for independent-type sports detracts from intrateam rivalry, perhaps reducing individual optimal effort
		5. Team's goals are clear to each athlete	
		6. Team accepts group members	
		7. Path to meet team goals is clear	

Factors That Influence Group Cohesion

In developing their Group Environment Questionnaire, Widmeyer et al. (1985) reviewed the literature about the issues that most strongly influence group cohesion. These issues include group size, interaction among group members, clarity and acceptance of group roles, warmth of group atmosphere, clarity of members' roles, geographical factors, personal sacrifice and overcoming adversity, shared perceptions, and leaders' appreciation of members' performances.

Group Size. The larger the group, the less chance there is for task and social forms of group cohesion. The number of group members that most strongly affects cohesion differs because it depends on the type of task being performed and other factors listed below. However, Carron's (1980) review of literature indicated that a likelihood of group member conformity to expectations, rules, and norms of group behavior begins to decrease with more than three members in the group. In a rare study examining group size and cohesion in sport (basketball), Widmeyer et al. (1990) found that enjoyment and cohesion decrease as group size increases. In particular, "action units" (i.e., a group of individuals performing simultaneously to meet a common goal) of three and six performers are ideal. An action unit of 12, however, resulted in overcrowding, less enjoyment, and lower social as well as task cohesion.

Interaction among Group Members. Some sports require more interaction among team members than others. In team sports such as basketball, football, and soccer, performance success is directly linked to the ability to coordinate various roles and functions and interact with one another simultaneously. Other team sports such as rowing, tennis doubles, and, to some extent, baseball, in which performers are co-acting rather than interacting directly, do not require the same degree of group cohesion for team success. In fact, as discussed later, Lenk (1969) found that low group cohesion contributed to the success of his Olympic German rowing team. Further, media stories in the United States have reported on the relative lack of team unity among professional baseball teams with winning records. According to interviews conducted by author George Will (1990), professional athletes consider sport their job and perform it to the best of their ability, often with little regard for the success or friendship of team members. Finally, individual sports, even when performed on a team basis, such as swimming and track, require far less group cohesion for performance success.

Clarity of Group Goals. Teams that are highly focused on meeting team and individual goals perceive a greater task orientation than teams whose goals have not been stated or are unclear. The term *clarity* is important here because it represents two factors: (1) setting goals that are challenging and agreed upon by team members, and (2) the ability to measure (and hopefully observe) if goals have been met successfully. Under these conditions, the group's direction and focus for performance effectiveness strengthen its cohesiveness.

Acceptance of Group Goals. Goals are only as effective as the group's agreement with them. In 1987, the first-year head coach of a college (U.S.) football team made the grave mistake of informing the media before the team's first game that his team would go undefeated during the season, a virtually impossible goal, considering the team's losing record over the previous several seasons. Sure enough, the team lost its first three games of the season, drastically reducing the team's preseason cohesion level. Closer team cohesion is far more likely if all or at least most group members accept its goals. In their study of the psychological consequences of athlete involvement in team goal setting, Brawley et al. (1993) concluded that: (1) with greater participation in team goal setting, team cohesion is greater, and (2) when cohesion is high, athletes are more satisfied with their team's goals for practice and competition.

Warmth of Group Atmosphere. A hostile, authoritarian coaching style is less likely to foster team cohesion than a leadership style that balances the need for authority with a more humanistic, respectful approach. A study by Fisher et al. (1982) showed that a warm, supportive team climate not only heightens member satisfaction but also increases player motivation to improve performance.

Clarity of Members' Roles. Researchers have found that group members who understand their position and role in the group will more likely support its goals. This is not to say that the individual should perceive his or her role as unimportant for group success. For groups to function properly, some members must play a more prominent role than others in initiating and completing tasks that directly lead to meeting group goals; not everyone can be the team captain. The clarification of roles within the group fosters cohesion by increasing group identity, focusing on necessary tasks, and mutually enjoying the benefits of group success.

Geographical Factors. Group cohesiveness also reflects the physical proximity of group members (Carron & Hausenblas 1999). Athletes will bond more closely due to more opportunity to interact and communicate about sport-related and personal issues. Examples include playing positions that require frequent interaction (e.g., the shortstop and second baseman or pitcher and catcher in baseball), or locker location in the locker room.

Personal Sacrifice/Overcoming Adversity. Giving up something of personal value for the group's benefit, or overcoming barriers in meeting a group goal, each tend to improve cohesion and facilitate bonding among group members. Spending considerable time and energy in training, practice, and travel, often at the expense of one's personal life, or experiencing the loss of a team member (temporarily or permanently) tend to improve group member bonding.

Shared Perceptions. The extent to which team members share attitudes, beliefs, and motives will affect group cohesion. According to Carron and Hausenblas (1999), while "initial similarity in attitude increased the likelihood that individuals will come together and develop group cohesiveness," other factors such as time, the group's usual work (e.g., sport competition), common experiences, and cohesion will interact to encourage similar attitudes among team members.

Leaders' Appreciation of Members' Performances. Recognition is a basic social need. Group leaders and, to a lesser extent, other group members would improve social group cohesion measurably by providing positive feedback and, if needed, instructional input on some aspect of the member's performance (e.g., a positive attitude, good effort, skilled performance).

Collective Efficacy: The Group's Beliefs about Member Competence

For many years, sport psychologists and researchers have known that success in sport is closely tied to the performer's belief that he or she is capable of achieving certain short-term and long-term goals. The strength of this belief is called self-efficacy, a concept first developed by Bandura (1977). This concept is similar to confidence; however, whereas confidence refers to a general feeling about performing well in many types of situations (i.e., the "confident athlete"), efficacy is situation-specific. Thus, an athlete can feel certain of his or her capability during sports competition (i.e., high self-efficacy), but feel less certain about being successful in nonsport settings.

Bandura and, more recently, Zaccaro and his colleagues (1995) recognized that the concept of self-efficacy can be transferred to group situations, and developed the concept of *collective efficacy*. Groups, not unlike individuals, also have different perceptions, goals, and expectations of success. These shared perceptions are important because they influence the group's effort, selection of activities, and willingness to pursue participating in these activities, particularly when faced with adversity and other types of challenges.

Zaccaro et al. formally defined collective efficacy as "a sense of collective competence shared among individuals when allocating, coordinating, and integrating their resources in a successful concerted response to specific situational demands" (p. 309). When, for example, a team is more likely to anticipate success, it is more likely to set lofty, realistic goals, possess high group performance expectations, perceive group skills as sufficient to meet these goals, and to give 100% personal effort.

There are four primary components to collective efficacy, according to Zaccaro et al.: *shared beliefs, coordinative capabilities, collective resources,* and *situational specificity.* Collective efficacy does not influence mental or physical processes if only a few group members have the same attitude about the group's competence. All group members who have a role in fostering the group's high performance quality should have similar, positive feelings—shared beliefs—about the group's ability to meet its goals and expectations about successful outcomes. Coordinative capabilities refers to the ability of each group member to interact and to complete numerous functions in a timely, planned manner that meets group needs and leads to successful outcomes. A basketball player would strongly consider passing the ball to the "open" teammate rather than take a longer, riskier shot. Bunting in baseball is another example, in which the player sacrifices personal statistics (e.g., raising one's batting average) to move the runner into scoring position. Of course, in contemporary baseball, try asking a major league ballplayer making millions a year for his batting skills to bunt. Indeed, bunting is very rare in professional baseball, perhaps a partial reflection of low collective efficacy (e.g., "my statistics are more important than helping the team win").

Collective resources refers to the belief of each group member that the team has the skills necessary to be successful. This is why it is potentially so damaging when the media quotes a team member who expresses doubts about his or her team's ability to succeed. Team administrators and coaches must emphasize team competencies, strengths, and reasonably high expectations about the season ahead. More on this topic is covered in Chapter 4 on causal attributions, in which explanations about the causes of perceived "success" and "failure" have a significant impact on the performer's motivation. The last component of collective efficacy, situational specificity, refers to the instances in which a team has a strong belief about its competence in some, but not all, aspects of its performance. Hence, a team might feel very strong defensively, but have a lower perception of its competence on offense. The team may feel more likely to beat certain teams, but lose to others.

Where does collective efficacy come from? Bandura (1977) and Zaccaro et al. (1995) contend that the team's belief in its competence is derived from five primary sources: *prior performance, vicarious experiences, verbal persuasion, leadership,* and *cohesion. Prior performance* success is the strongest source of collective efficacy. Expectations of future success are usually dependent on previous success. For athletes, *vicarious experiences* consist of comparing one's own performance against the performance of other athletes in similar roles and positions—for instance, a basketball forward comparing his or her skills against those of other basketball forwards at the same level of competition. Live (actual athletes whose characteristics are similar to those of the viewer or to an opponent) or symbolic models (watching a training film or athletes who possess characteristics that far exceed those of the viewer, such as Olympians or professionals) are other sources of vicarious experiences. *Verbal persuasion* consists of encouraging and supporting others, primarily from sources of meaningful, credible information. Clearly, the group leader is the primary source of verbal persuasion that fosters collective efficacy. *Leadership* behaviors directly enhance group functioning. Leadership characteristics directly influence the athlete's performance level and team member satisfaction. Finally, high *cohesion* in teams directly and favorably affects collective efficacy. Inversely, teams that have higher collective efficacy also tend to be more cohesive.

The Disposition of Self-Handicapping (SH)

Self-handicapping, first introduced by Jones and Berglas (1978), is defined as strategies that people use to protect their self-esteem by providing excuses before events occur and explaining reasons for the anticipated lack of team success. Self-handicappers externalize or excuse failure and internalize (accept credit for) success. These individuals do not link failure with their low ability following failure, thereby protecting their self-esteem. Group cohesion is influenced by SH if any individual member feels, *before* the contest, that he or she will not be at fault for group failure, yet takes full responsibility for group success. In their study, Carron et al. (1994) found that *high social cohesion* (i.e., the extent to which team members interacted positively away from the sport venue) was related to *less* SH. In addition, *low task cohesion* (i.e., the degree of team harmony and effective interactions while executing performance skills during the game) was associated with *high* SH. Thus, SH enhances group cohesion because it improves members' sense of acceptance and support from others, increases the sharing of responsibility for team failure, and results in more acceptance by and support for other group members.

While an SH disposition may improve group cohesion, the problem is that it ensures low to moderate expectancies. Remember, SH is a proactive explanation of not being responsible for possible future team failure. Thus, athletes may use excuses, such as injury (imagined or real), lack of practice time, fatigue from travel, or lack of practice as possible (and plausible) reasons to attribute the reason(s) for losing the contest or not performing well. Conversely, as Carron and Hausenblas (1998) point out, "if the athlete is successful, his/her self-esteem is enhanced because the victory was obtained despite the presence of an injury and lack of practice" (p. 250). However, many coaches like the idea of each team member feeling responsible for the performance and well-being of others (as in the old saying, "There is no 'I' in TEAM"). In addition, self-confidence and motivation are protected by individuals' propensity *not* to blame themselves following failure or poor performance. According to Carron and Hausenblas (1998), use of SH strategies should be less necessary in cohesive groups. Responsibility for perceived failure is usually shared equally in cohesive groups, in which group support is readily available and there are fewer threats to self-esteem.

Social Loafing

Social loafing is a decrease in individual effort and performance due to the physical presence of other persons as opposed to performing the task alone (Anshel 1995a, Hardy 1990). Social loafing is evident only under conditions in which more than one person is performing the same task simultaneously. Examples include blocking by the offense in (U.S.) football or group tackling in contact sports. Usually social loafing occurs when subjects perceive the criterion task as unimportant, meaningless, not intrinsically motivating, or if it is performed by relative strangers, especially (though not always) under noncompetitive conditions. Social loafing has been explained as a motivational loss, because individuals are less likely to feel accountable for the quality of their performance if they are held *collectively* responsible for task success.

Anshel (1995a) examined social loafing among elite female rowers when subjects engaged in a simulated (laboratory) rowing task alone and in group conditions for periods of one stroke, 1.5 minutes, and 10 minutes. Results indicated a significant loafing effect only for the team/10-minute condition, but not when performing one stroke nor for 1.5 minutes under both individual and group conditions. An additional finding was that subjects' vigor decreased under all three group conditions, another loafing indicant. The results of this study suggest that social loafing may be strongly related to task duration; athletes may more likely loaf under conditions of fatigue, boredom, or prolonged repetition of the task.

The extent to which social loafing has been supported by researchers in several studies was examined by Karau and Williams (1993). Using a statistical process called meta-analysis, in which the results of many studies are examined simultaneously to determine the overall effect, the researchers concluded that social loafing occurs across many different types of tasks, including physical tasks, cognitive tasks, evaluative tasks, and perceptual tasks. It is evident in both males and females and across different cultures. However, Karau and Williams found that the degree of social loafing is less in women and for people of both genders in Eastern (e.g., Asian) cultures. The researchers concluded that the tendency to engage in social loafing *increases* when:

1. the performer's effort cannot be assessed independently of the group
2. the task is perceived by the performer as not meaningful
3. the performer views his or her contribution to the outcome as redundant
4. the performer's personal involvement in the task is low
5. the performer questions the relevance of his or her contributions to the outcome

6. the individual's co-workers/teammates are highly skilled and expected to perform well

7. a comparison against group standards is not available

Strategies for overcoming or preventing social loafing, according to Hardy (1990) and Karau and Williams (1993) include (1) identifying the performer's efforts (the coach would likely be the most powerful source of incentive here), (2) helping the individual form perceptions that he or she is making a unique and important contribution to the group's effort, (3) that the task being performed is difficult, (4) performing the task with friends as opposed to strangers or performing as a group high in social cohesion, (5) ensuring that the task personally involves the performer (i.e., that the individual has a personal stake in the task's outcome), and (6) making each performer's task unique to increase a sense of control over their efforts and personal responsibility for performance outcomes.

Measuring Team Cohesion and Player Roles

If it's so important to have a cohesive team, as is commonly assumed by coaches and sport psychologists, then we need to determine the extent of its presence on a particular team. Yet, the sport literature gives relatively little attention to measuring team cohesion.

The Sociogram.   Used primarily in sociology, a sociogram is an "illustration" of affiliation and attraction among group members. It reveals (1) the degree to which group members are valued by teammates, (2) the existence of clusters (subgroups or cliques) and social isolation of group members, (3) persons who are actively rejected by others, (4) friendship choices, and (5) the degree of similarity among team members about their feelings toward one another. A coach or researcher can obtain this information in two ways. One approach is to ask team members (preferably in written form to ensure privacy and confidentiality, although child athletes may require an interview format), and the other is through direct or indirect (videotaped) observation. In fact, to validate data accuracy, both methods can be used jointly.

The coach could create a questionnaire on which each athlete would indicate specific teammates with whom he or she would prefer to share a certain activity (e.g., tossing a ball) or situation (e.g., sharing a motel room on the road). Interpersonal attractions and repulsions within the team would be obtained. The data concerning "who chooses whom" would then be diagrammed as a sociogram in which individual team members and their choices are represented by the connection of circles by lines.

The coach could ask each athlete to respond in writing to a single question that best fits a particular situation. Sample items might include: "Name three people on the team whom you would most like to invite to your home and three people whom you would least like to invite" or "Name the one person on the team with whom you would most prefer to share a room when we're on the road and one person with whom you would least want to share a room." Sociogram questions, then, should be concrete, such as "a person with whom you would like to work," rather than abstract, such as "a person whom you like very much." They should also have real meaning and actual and direct consequences for the respondent. So, if the coach asks the players to select a teammate with whom they would prefer to share a room, it is best to assure them, if possible, that actual room assignments will be based on their replies.

Two other issues in gathering such information are confidentiality and honesty, especially when athletes are asked to indicate a person whom they do not like. Athletes must be told that all responses are confidential but not anonymous; after all, coaches must know who feels what about whom. Instead of saying, "Whom do you dislike on the team?" the question might read, "Whom do you like less than others on the team?" The coach can ask the athletes to rank order their responses to a predetermined number or to list as many teammates as they wish. A diagram of the players' responses might look something like that in Figure 7.2.

The sociogram in Figure 7.2 reveals that Peter is well liked and very popular among his teammates, at least by a subgroup of team members. Fred, however, appears to be an isolate. (The word *appears* is important because a sociogram reflects feelings, not actual behaviors. The coach should follow up these data with direct observations.) Bill is not liked by several teammates. But interestingly, he has positive feelings toward one of the players who reject him. Apparently Joe and Mike do not care for each other. Based on the information provided on just a few of the team members, it appears that (1) Fred needs some attention, (2) Bill, a possible scapegoat, appears to desire acceptance from others but is apparently not a welcomed group member, and (3) the conflict between Joe and Mike should be resolved by the coach. If a friendship cannot be developed, attempts should be made to reduce discord. Finally, the mutual attraction of Mike, Steve, and Xavier indicates the formation of a subgroup. The coach's direct observations of this threesome will indicate whether they need further attention.

The Sociometric Matrix. Here, the observer makes pluses and minuses in a given box when two or more persons interact positively or negatively. Rows indicate the outgoing choices of, and columns indicate the choices received by, each person as indicated in Figure 7.3.

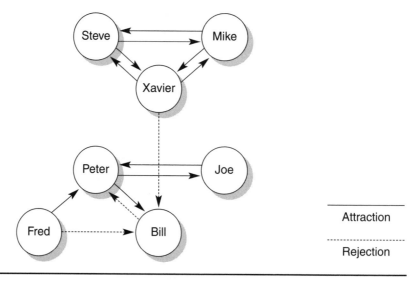

Figure 7.2 Sociogram illustrating types of feelings among group members.

	Susan	Janice	Gail	Maria	Renee
Susan		++++	– –		
Janice	+		+		
Gail		+		– – –	
Maria					
Renee					

Figure 7.3 Sociogram indicating frequency of attraction or acceptance and rejection among group members.

It can be seen in Figure 7.3 that Susan and Janice positively interact somewhat frequently, with Susan taking more initiative in the relationship. Gail, however, rejects the approaches of Maria. Sadly, Maria does not approach anyone else on the team. Renee interacts with no one.

Clearly, one limitation to the use of sociograms in the absence of other information is that the nature of the interactions is not explained. Taking this last example, does Renee become the group isolate by choice, or is this role imposed by her teammates? Does she behave in a manner that facilitates this role? How does Renee feel about the situation? Is she more comfortable keeping to herself? And of particular importance to the coach, is Renee's role detrimental to her performance? Only further observations and information gathered from others will help the coach to understand the dynamics of the relationships on the team.

Apparently only one study has used sociometry as a technique to measure group dynamics in elite sport. Weiller (1988) applied sociometric measures, in addition to interviews and a questionnaire, to identify leaders of the Dallas Mavericks 1985–86 basketball team in the (U.S.) National Basketball Association. The players and coaching staff were asked to identify the player or players whom they believed to be team leaders. Fans, sportscasters, and sportswriters also were asked to make these identifications in order to compare the perceptions of players with nonplayers. Weiller used the paired comparison technique, which estimates the possibility that a randomly selected subject (e.g., one of the Maverick players) will rank a particular object (e.g., a teammate) above another in all possible pairings (i.e., comparisons between other teammates) from the team. According to Weiller:

Paired comparison allows a subject to choose between two items and establish which of the two items is more important. Items are then ranked in order of importance, resulting in a numerical score which reflects the distance between the ranks. If the numerical distance between the two items is large, then it can be said that the subjects have a very definite preference about one item over another. If the distance is small, then it can be surmised the subjects have little preference about one item as the other (p. 163).

The results of the sociogram showed that the same player was identified as the positive leader by the players, coaching staff, and media personnel. However, the fans identified a different player as their top choice. The ability of sociometry to identify the team leader allowed all players and coaches to agree to whom they should turn to fill the leader role. In Weiller's study, the identified player did just that, which, in turn, improved team member satisfaction.

The Value of Sociometry. Sociograms are rarely used by coaches and sport psychologists, partly because most are not aware of their existence and because very few people are trained to use them. But they can be a valuable tool in sport to understand better the extent of team togetherness. Sociograms allow the coach to observe his or her players objectively and in the context of a sport environment—although information used in constructing sociograms could be gathered at team social events as well.

Sociometry is particularly valuable for teams with many members. Researchers have shown that as group size increases, the level of member satisfaction decreases proportionately (Fiedler 1967). So, it is possible that fewer satisfied members (or more players who express lower satisfaction) will exist in football than in basketball. Information derived from a sociogram could either improve team relations or work toward preventing a disruption in team cohesion. Sociograms can help the coach to answer some of the following questions:

- Who does and who doesn't have friends on the team?
- Is any one player being rejected by other team members? If so, could this be one reason for a player's lack of incentive, commitment, and effort?
- Who are the team leaders, and who's popular among the players?
- Who is and who is not a satisfied team member? Is everybody happy?
- Do subgroups (cliques) exist on this team? Who is in them? Do these friendships help, hurt, or have no effect on team morale?
- Are the players communicating? Does a player in a key position, a quarterback or goalie for instance, go his own way during practice? Are pitchers talking to each other or speaking with catchers about opposing hitters or pitching strategies? Does a particular player refuse to approach another player?

In summary, sociometric techniques measure (1) the ratio of friendship choices within or outside of the group, (2) group congeniality, (3) the presence or absence of cliques, (4) members' perceptions of group closeness, (5) the extent of group attraction, (6) social activity of the group, (7) the degree to which the athletes perceive interpersonal feelings and behaviors similarly, and (8) reciprocal sociometric choices (Widmeyer et al. 1985). There is debate in the literature as to the effectiveness of sociograms. They certainly alert the user to the manner in which group members interact and tendencies toward leadership, attraction, rejection, and isolation. However, according to Widmeyer et al. (1985), sociograms have some disadvantages.

Operational measures of cohesion based upon interpersonal attraction: (a) underrepresent the concept—there are other factors at work within the group in addition to attraction to other members which keep individuals in a group, (b) fail to account for cohesiveness in situations characterized by negative affect (i.e., dissatisfaction, dissension, hostility), (c) have not been supported empirically—interpersonal attractiveness has not been shown to correlate with other attractiveness measures in groups . . . and (d) do not totally account for the conditions necessary for group formation. In addition . . . interpersonal attraction may be synonymous with group cohesion in sociometric groups but be unrelated in task groups (p. 8).

Widmeyer et al. also criticized other inventories that purportedly measure group cohesion because they were not developed from a conceptual or theoretical model on which to make predictions and test hypotheses, were not tested extensively for psychometric soundness, or were specific to only one sport. Apparently, then, the coach should use as many tools as possible, particularly those with which he or she is most comfortable, in assessing the interactions and feelings of players.

Team Cohesion Questionnaires. The sport psychology literature includes four questionnaire methods for measuring team cohesion. The sociogram, described earlier, has been used primarily in social psychology research and to date has not been used in research in sport with the exception of Weiller's (1988) study. Nevertheless, it is included in this review because of its potential to contribute new information to assessing group cohesion not included in survey techniques, the ease with which it can be applied in field settings, and because it is the only approach to measuring cohesion that is not inventory based.

The inventories that have been used over the years to measure group cohesion in sports teams have been the Sports Cohesiveness Questionnaire (SCQ) (Martens & Peterson 1971), the Task Cohesiveness Questionnaire (TCQ) (Gruber & Gray 1981), the Sport Cohesion Instrument (SCI) (Yukelson et al. 1984) and, the most popular in recent years, the Group Environment Questionnaire (GEQ) (Widmeyer et al. 1985). (Note that the terms *inventory, survey, questionnaire, profile,* and *instrument* are all interchangeable in the literature. However, a survey can also refer to oral collection of information. Also, the word *test* makes many researchers uncomfortable because it infers "right" and "wrong" answers to questions, a result that is rarely required or intended.)

The SCQ has been used in at least 12 published studies. It consists of seven questions, measuring both social cohesion (five items) and task cohesion (two items). The primary criticism of this inventory is its lack of psychometric construction, that is, unproven reliability and validity. In addition, Widmeyer et al. (1985, 1992) assert that development of a psychological inventory should be derived from a conceptual model which, in turn, gives the inventory what statisticians call high predictive validity. This means that a score should measure what it claims to measure and is capable of predicting the person's thoughts, emotions, or behaviors. Although some inventories serve the purpose of examining or describing behaviors or feelings, most inventories have a predictive function. The usefulness of inventories that lack predictive validity is, at best, uncertain and, at worst, misleading.

In developing the SCI, Yukelson et al. (1984) found that four factors accurately depict team cohesiveness. They labeled these factors attraction to the group, unity of purpose, quality of teamwork, and valued roles. As did the developers of the SCQ, they lacked the preplanned model from which to develop their instrument, which, according to Widmeyer et al. (1985), makes it difficult to test the inventories predictions. In addition, the SCI was developed for the sport of basketball. Another inventory, the TCQ, was also developed for basketball teams.

To overcome these limitations, Widmeyer et al. (1985) constructed and validated the GEQ. This 18-item inventory measures group cohesion on four dimensions: *group integration-task* (GI-task; an individual's feelings about team members' similarity, closeness, and bonding within the team around the group's task); *group integration-social* (GI-social; the individual's feelings about team members' similarity, closeness, and bonding around the group as a social unit); *individual attractions to the group-task* (ATG-task; the individual's feelings about his or her personal involvement with the group's task, productivity, and goals); and *individual attractions to the group-social* (ATG-social; the individual's feelings about his or her personal involvement, acceptance, and social interactions with the group).

Examples of items for each of these dimensions are:

GI-task: "Our team is united in trying to reach its goals for performance."

GI-social: "Members of our team would rather go out on their own than get together as a team."

ATG-task: "I am not happy with the amount of playing time I get."

ATG-social: "I enjoy other parties more than team parties."

The authors have conducted several studies in an attempt to validate the GEQ. In a series of three studies, Brawley et al. (1987) examined the ability of the GEQ to separate the four different types of group cohesion among different types of sports for adult competitors. In general, the findings indicated that task cohesion scores correctly identified if athletes were from individual or team sports; GI-task was greater for team sport athletes, and ATG-task was greatest for individual sport athletes. Thus, the GEQ successfully separated athletes' membership in teams that differed in their level of required task interaction; teams that were highly task-focused scored higher on the ATG-task measure. An additional finding was that athletes who were labeled "longstanding" (i.e., veterans) were higher in GI-social than athletes from these teams labeled "new" (i.e., rookies). Thus, the GEQ successfully predicted social cohesion based on the length of time athletes participated with that particular team. The longer they were with the team, the more socially cohesive they became.

In another study, Carron and Spink (1993) examined changes in the effect of cognitive and behavioral techniques on group cohesion. Briefly, the intervention consisted of establishing group identity, developing goals and friendships (including assigning partners) among group members, and using music with exercise. Social cohesion was not affected by the treatment. The researchers concluded that group cohesion strategies should focus on the primary goals of group members—in this study, improving fitness. The intervention was effective because it targeted meeting this need. Thus, the GEQ can be used in both sport and exercise settings to monitor current levels of, and changes in, group cohesion.

Although the GEQ has provided researchers and educators with valuable insight into the group cohesion process, the instrument is not without its critics. Robert Schutz and his colleagues (1994) conducted additional statistical analyses on the GEQ using a new set of subjects, high school athletes aged 13–19 years. They were unsuccessful in replicating the GEQ's four-factor structure (ATG-social, ATG-task, GI-social, GI-task). They also found low internal consistencies—poor reliability—among items within each structure. This means, for example, that the items within the ATG-social factor, and within each of the other factors, were not highly related, an undesirable finding. The researchers concluded that "the findings . . . emphasize the need for continued refinement of the GEQ as a multidimensional measurement instrument of group cohesion in sport and exercise" (p. 235).

Does Cohesion Affect Player Satisfaction?

How important is it for athletes to like one another or to be close friends in order to win consistently? Can teams be successful if some (or even most) of the players do not get along or if they compete among themselves for playing status? Does the coach need to be concerned about the players' social interactions in addition to other coaching responsibilities?

Satisfaction is in the eyes of the beholder. Each individual athlete must define what he or she finds satisfying as a team member. Tennis professional and former college coach Bill Glaves contends that one important component of player satisfaction is being recognized for effort and talent (Mechikoff & Kozar 1983). One way in which he promoted this philosophy was to encourage the press to talk to the players rather than speaking only with him. In addition, he mounted press clippings on the team bulletin board and continually updated them. As Carron (1984a) asserts, "Whereas cohesion is a group construct, satisfaction is an individual one." Carron's review of related literature indicates "a strong positive relationship between cohesion and satisfaction" (p. 349).

If satisfied athletes feel closer to one another, does this mean that their level of satisfaction will also enhance performance success? Williams and Hacker (1982) asked female intercollegiate field hockey players to complete questionnaires to obtain cohesion scores. They found no evidence that satisfaction led to an increase in performance success. However, successful performance was related to improved satisfaction. They concluded that "performance success and cohesiveness lead to greater satisfaction but satisfaction, in turn, does not lead to anything" (p. 336). It is important to remember that this study does not imply cause and effect, that is, that success improves cohesion or vice versa, nor that cohesion causes satisfaction. Such conclusions would require a different type of research design. However, the high relationship between cohesion, success, and satisfaction implies that athletes who perceive their team as successful will more likely feel closer and happier as team members than athletes who do not view their team as successful. Along these lines, Weinberg and Gould (1995) suggest that "leaders do well in building group cohesion because being in a cohesive group is satisfying and also indirectly and directly enhances performance" (p. 191).

Does Cohesion Affect Team Performance?

Intuitively, we assume that cohesive teams win more games or, inversely, that teams lacking in cohesiveness (with more dissension and conflict) fail to live up to their potential. Research findings are equivocal on this issue. Some investigators have found that cohesion is related to team success—that there is a high relationship between team cohesion and winning—but that it does not necessarily cause success (Iso-Ahola & Hatfield

1986). Others have found that team success is not related to whether or not the players like one another but, rather, to the extent to which they can interact constructively during the contest to use proper skills and strategies (Carron 1984a). Making any definite conclusions about cohesion and performance is difficult because researchers have studied different types of sport populations. Generalizations about the results of these studies for all teams and sports would be unsound since most of the research on team cohesion has centered on university intramural teams.

Landers et al. (1982) examined the cohesion-performance relationship with collegiate intramural teams. They found a significant relationship between friendship and performance outcome. A particularly high relationship was found between friendships occurring in early to midseason and late-season performance. Specifically, the quality of play increased later in the season for the intramural athletes if their team was cohesive earlier in the season. Cohesion that was apparent before the season or near its end did not influence performance. Remember, this was a study of intramural teams (whose members are often recruited by personal friends), not of organized competitive sport leagues.

In another study of intramural (college) male competitors, Martens and Peterson (1971) found that highly cohesive teams (identified by how participants rated the value of team membership, teamwork, and closeness) won significantly more games than did low cohesive teams. Similar advantages for cohesive teams were found in examining team success on postseason performance; high cohesive groups won more games (Peterson & Martens 1972).

Also of interest is the extent to which the positive cohesion-performance relationship with intramural (recreational) competitors is replicated with intercollegiate athletes. In a review of related literature, Gill (1980) found that cohesiveness was positively related to team success (close teams won more games) in intercollegiate football, high school basketball, intercollegiate ice hockey, ROTC rifle teams, and women's intercollegiate volleyball. However, other studies have not only failed to show positive relationships, they have indicated just the opposite finding, that highly cohesive teams lost more games or had less satisfied members than did groups that were low in cohesion. One factor that may help explain these mixed findings is the type of sport skills being measured.

Mullen and Copper (1994) carried out the most extensive study, to date, on this topic. The researchers conducted a meta-analysis, described earlier as a statistical comparison of the results of many studies (in this case, 49 studies), on the extent to which group cohesion is related to, or predicts, performance. They reviewed sport and non-sport studies, and laboratory/contrived settings, as compared to real-life environments. The results were encouraging for sports teams. They found that the relationship between cohesion and performance quality was better for real groups than for groups in contrived (artificial) settings, and better in sport than in nonsport studies. The relationship was even slightly better among sports teams than in military groups. Of particular importance was the finding from their study that the group members' "commitment to task" was the most critical component of group cohesion that best predicted group success. Interpersonal attraction among group members and group pride, however, were not related to team success. It would appear, then, that task cohesion is of greater importance to desirable performance outcomes than social cohesion.

One possible reason for the lack of clarity between group cohesion and performance is that different sports place various types of physical and mental demands and interactions on their participants. Weinberg and Gould (1995) classify sports as interacting teams (e.g., basketball, field hockey, soccer), co-acting teams (e.g., archery, bowling, golf), and mixed co-acting-interacting teams (e.g., American football, baseball/softball, rowing, swimming, track and field). *Interactive* sports require that players work together and coordinate their actions in order to reach team goals and be successful. *Co-active* sports, on the other hand, do not require similar levels of team interaction to be successful. A *mixed* co-acting-interacting sport includes segments that require both co-acting (e.g., kicking the ball) and interacting (e.g., passing the ball). Cohesion may be more closely associated with team success for (interactive) sports that require ongoing interaction and coordination among players. Cohesion would be less related to team success among (co-active) sports that require no such extensive engagement among teammates.

In summary, cohesion does not appear to markedly improve sport performance, with the possible exception of collegiate intramural teams. However, team success appears to breed cohesion. As Williams and Hacker (1982) concluded, while coaches may not need to be concerned with building cohesiveness to enhance team success, cohesiveness still may be important since participation on cohesive teams appears to be more satisfying than participation on less cohesive teams. Thus, given a choice, perhaps coaches should consider the objective of establishing compatible, mutually enjoyable relationships among team members (social cohesion) and having all team members function harmoniously toward meeting both personal and team goals as highly desirable.

When Low Cohesion Is Better. German sport scientist Hans Lenk (1969) studied two high-caliber rowing teams over four years (1960–1964). One team (1960) represented its country in the Olympics. The second team (1962) became a world champion.

Lenk studied the interactions and interpersonal relationships and attractions among team members, as measured by sociometric analyses. His data were derived by directly observing the behaviors of the athletes and through self-report techniques. In his 1960 study, Lenk observed sharp conflicts among racing team members, especially between two unfriendly subgroups. He reported that the internal strife was so bad that the team was almost abandoned. Nevertheless, a performance deficit was not found as a result of group tension. Ironically, performance slightly improved as team members became increasingly combative toward one another over the two years of the team's existence. In fact, the team became an unbeaten Olympic champion. Lenk concluded that teams in sport are capable of achieving maximal performance outcomes despite strong internal conflicts.

The world champion rowers of 1962 were from a club team rather than a racing team. Lenk noticed a subgroup of four rowers that set itself apart from the others. Sociometric data indicated that the subgroup formed due to the mutual attraction of the team's four strongest rowers, leaving the remaining four members to affiliate among themselves. Moreover, the cliques resented each other for different reasons. Members of one subgroup thought of themselves as physically superior to the others, while the second subgroup resented the "second-class" treatment and one-upmanship attitude of their teammates. This led to infighting for team leadership. The intrateam rivalry intensified with time. Despite this lack of cohesion, the eight teammates won the European championship during the second year, the time at which intrateam rivalry was strongest. The level of performance had not suffered from the conflicts over the players' status.

Consider two important and unique circumstances that surrounded Lenk's studies: First, these were world-class athletes, not exactly players from the local high school or club. These men were highly skilled; had a history of past success; were self-confident about their ability; and were less reliant on teammates for recognition, support, and affiliation than less-skilled competitors might have been. Further, the team's relatively short life span—about two years—in which to train and compete combined with the unified purpose of representing its country successfully in international competition were likely more important in the team becoming successful than were team members' establishing close relationships.

The second circumstance was discussed earlier: rowing is a *co-acting* sport requiring less interdependence for team success than other types of sports. Other examples of co-acting sports are team (or doubles) versions of tennis, bowling, and golf. As Lenk readily admitted, co-acting group members can successfully meet their goals without extensively affiliating with others. On the other hand, *interacting* sports, like baseball, basketball, or soccer, require far more interdependence and therefore higher social cohesion. Further, Lenk never claimed that low cohesion in teams was desirable. He contended only that his study found no decrease in performance.

Factors That Inhibit Cohesion

Albert Carron (1993), from the University of Western Ontario, in Canada, a prolific researcher on group cohesion and dynamics in sport and exercise, designates several factors that can hurt team togetherness. These include:

- disagreement among team members about the group's goals (e.g., "Are we here to win by playing as a team or to help individuals score more points?")
- rapid or frequent changes in group members
- a struggle for decision-making power within the group
- poor communication among group members
- unclear task or social roles among team members (e.g., which player will tell the coach that early morning exercise is at an undesirable time of day)
- role conflict (e.g., when members usurp the team captain's authority)
- lack of a clear vision by the team leader (e.g., what does the team want to accomplish and how will it get there?)
- ongoing criticism of team members by the coach, blaming individuals for poor team performance
- a clash of personalities among team members (e.g., outgoing, loud, and talkative versus more inhibited and quiet, especially during times that require concentration)

Suggestions for Improving Team Cohesion

If having a cohesive team is important to the coach, several strategies can help to make it happen. Sport psychology researchers (Carron 1984a; Bird & Cripe 1986; Widmeyer et al. 1985) suggest the following.

1. *Acquaint players with the responsibilities of their teammates.* This will help to develop support and empathy among the players. This can be facilitated by having players

observe and record the efforts of other athletes at their positions. If subunits naturally exist on the team, which is common in many team sports, coaches will want to develop pride within each of these subunits. Players need the support of their peers, especially of the same positions and in team sports where the interaction among athletes is required for success.

2. *Use effective communication strategies.* The appropriate use of humor and praise in verbal and nonverbal forms is advantageous in generating feelings of mutual satisfaction and enjoyment. Athletes are especially responsive to recognition for special contributions.

3. *Know your players.* Coaches should be "in touch" with their players and should know something personal about each player. If a competitor has a problem that affects his or her play quality or, conversely, is celebrating some joyful event (e.g., a birthday or receiving a good grade in class), the coach can acknowledge it and perhaps respond to the athlete appropriately. How do the players feel about the team? What changes would they like to see? What explanations do they need that will help them to understand better the reasons for certain approaches to game preparation?

4. *Look for, and communicate, something positive after each game.* Playing effectively, yet losing, does not have to result in a hostile, negative response from other players and coaches. There should always be something to feel good about after the contest regardless of the final outcome.

5. *Provide feedback to players.* To promote motivation and team loyalty, players should be informed about their status on the team, given an explanation for this status, and told what they can do to upgrade or maintain it. Each athlete should feel that he or she has an important role with the team. Further, the value of every role should be expressed by the coach.

6. *Teach and require interpersonal player support.* Players should not be "allowed" to hurt the feelings of teammates. The coach has an obligation to the players to promote group support. Unhappy athletes are unproductive and demotivated. Scapegoating, blaming, and chronic teasing must be stopped quickly, or cohesion will dissipate.

7. *Be consistent when setting limits.* Discipline of players should be consistent for all team members. Starters or stars should not be treated differently from others with respect to setting limits.

8. *Try to inhibit player dropouts.* Excessive turnover of personnel is not helpful to cohesion. Establishing close rapport with a group is difficult when its members are unfamiliar with one another and are uncertain as to the longevity of their group. Individuals avoid risking being close to teammates when they perceive the relationship to be short term. So, when a new member joins the team or a player appears to be isolated from other team members, established players should be asked to integrate that individual into the larger established players' group and to help outline task expectations. The selected individuals should be warm, sensitive, mature, have good communication skills, be capable of establishing personal contact, and interact in a positive manner on and off the field or court.

9. *Elect and work with player representatives.* Group cohesion means, in part, open communication between coach and athlete. Therefore, it is wise to have player-selected team representatives (even from each subunit, if necessary) meet with the coach on a regular, prescheduled basis—perhaps weekly or biweekly—to discuss various issues.

10. *Leadership should be developed among team members.* Coaches are mistaken in assuming that they are (and should be) the only team leader. Athletes respond favorably to peer leaders. Perhaps player leaders can lead discussions among themselves about developing or maintaining team cohesion. Such feelings and needs should be communicated between coach and athlete. Ultimately, the result of such interaction may be to make appropriate adjustments in strategies for team management.

SUMMARY

A warm, supportive climate on sport teams, of which group cohesion is a relevant component, is highly desirable for group member satisfaction, performance, and team success. Other aspects of a healthy team environment include autonomy, recognition, mutual trust among coaches and teammates, the players' perception of fairness, opportunities for innovation, and the absence of social loafing.

The manner in which group members interact is referred to as group dynamics. Coaches should monitor the frequency with which players interact and the nature of these interactions. From this ongoing assessment, coaches can determine the role or roles of each player on the team. Group dynamics may be measured using a sociogram or sociometric matrix, both of which illustrate the feelings and interactions among group members. The common roles described in this chapter include the positive leader, negative leader, follower, isolate, scapegoat, and clown. After acknowledging these roles, coaches can (and should) initiate strategies to augment some (positive leadership, for instance) and attenuate others (such as isolates and scapegoats). The actions of negative leaders must be dealt with immediately, especially exposing the issues that caused these actions. The objective is to promote team cohesion, to develop the team's beliefs about the competence of its' members called collective efficacy, and to build team member satisfaction.

Self-handicapping (SH) is a disposition consisting of strategies that people use to protect their self-esteem by providing excuses before events occur and explaining reasons for the anticipated lack of team or individual success. High social group cohesion is related to less likelihood of self-handicapping.

For athletes to like one another appears to be desirable in terms of a warm, supportive team environment and the enjoyment of sport participation. Indeed, researchers have found that cohesiveness is associated with player satisfaction, a concept called social cohesion. What is less certain, however, is the extent to which social team cohesion influences performance. In Lenk's examination of elite rowers, less cohesiveness was related to better success. However, Lenk did not differentiate between social and task cohesion. Therefore, his rowers may have been low in social cohesion but quite high in task cohesion, that is, the extent to which group members share group tasks, productivity, and goals. Still, research has not yet been able to conclusively support the contention that team cohesion, even group member satisfaction, is significantly related to performance outcome. However, one motive for participating in sport is affiliating with peers and meeting new friends. More research is needed in this area, particularly in comparing age groups and skill levels—whether child athletes, for instance, are affected differently by these factors than older, better skilled competitors.

REVIEW QUESTIONS

1. The evolutionary stages of most groups include forming, storming, norming, and performing. Provide examples in which each of these steps is evident on a sport team.

2. Describe at least five factors that contribute to a proper team climate in sport. What techniques can the coach use to ensure that each of these factors will be present?

3. What is the difference between formal and informal team roles? Provide examples of each.

4. The chapter describes 10 traits of effective teams, or groups. Reflecting on your current or previous participation in sport, to what extent were each of these traits present or absent from your team? Provide examples.

5. Describe the six roles of team members discussed in this chapter. What are the advantages and/or disadvantages of each role? What can the coach do to facilitate or reinforce some roles while inhibiting or preventing others?

6. Do you feel that it is appropriate for coaches to become involved with the athletes' interactions with other team members away from the sport environment? Why or why not?

7. Describe the different types of group cohesion. Under which conditions is one type of cohesion preferable over another, if at all?

8. What is self-handicapping, and how does it influence group cohesion?

9. Does being a satisfied team member usually result in better sport performance? In other words, will the team play better if each member likes (or is friends with) other members?

10. Provide an example of using a sociogram to illustrate the degree of player affiliation or team cohesion using contrived information. For instance, assume that the players responded to a question about preferences or attraction toward another team member. What might their responses look like on a sociogram?

11. Should the coach request that certain athletes interact with other team members to improve team cohesion or to help change an athlete's role on the team? What are the advantages and disadvantages of this strategy?

12. What are the barriers to team cohesion? How can coaches improve team cohesion?

13. What is social loafing? Describe three techniques coaches can use to prevent or eliminate it.

CHAPTER 8

Leadership in Sport: A Matter of Style

A leader is a person who directs and coordinates activities of an organized group toward achieving specific goals (Murray & Mann 1993). If a leader is to be effective, he or she must be recognized as having the most influence on the behavior of group members. But a leader who is not capable of altering the behaviors and attitudes of group members (in other words, who has no influence) is not effective in the position.

This chapter is about predicting and describing effective leadership in sport with respect to a person's attributes and skills. Of particular concern in this chapter is the degree to which the coach actually makes a difference between winning and losing. Can the coach be held responsible for the team's (or a player's) performance? Can the contest's outcome be influenced by the coach's leadership skills? Is effective sport leadership really dependent on the team's win-loss record, as is commonly depicted in the media? Or, instead, is effective coaching more often a matter of having the better players?

After reading this chapter, the student should be able to identify characteristics and techniques of effective leaders, in general, and coaches, in particular. As the literature reviewed in this chapter will show, the coach *can* make a difference in the athlete's sport performance and team success; leadership skills count. Athletes are human beings, not machines. Consequently, they are affected by the coach's attitudes, behaviors, perceptions, and decisions. The team leader's job is to help each competitor to reach his or her potential. To do this, the coach must take on an array of roles.

Roles of the Coach

Being responsible for influencing the behaviors and actions of the many different individuals on a team, and usually at the same time, is no easy task. Athletes differ as to the type of personal approach with which they are most comfortable. Not all coaches are prepared to meet these individual needs. Coaches who are less effective say, "I can't do that; it's not me" or "Everyone gets treated alike, regardless of individual needs or preferences." Effective coaches, on the other hand, say, "I'll work at changing this behavior (habit)" or "I'm not good at doing 'that' so I'll ask someone with better skills in this area to do it." The best coaches are secure individuals. They recognize their strengths and limitations. Sometimes they'll attend workshops or seminars and read professional literature in an attempt to improve their skills or change a particular approach, or consult with specialists such as sport psychology consultants, educators, trainers, and researchers. The coaching profession demands the mastery of many personal and technical skills. Leaders in sport maintain a variety of roles to meet each of these skills.

Leader

When a group of individuals is attempting to meet a goal, usually someone has to be in charge. In sport situations, that's the coach. Perhaps some coaches practice this role too authoritatively. Nevertheless, competitors assume that their coach will provide a sense of leadership—direction with a purpose—to achieve group success. Some examples of effective leadership include taking responsibility for team failure; giving direction during practice; devising and communicating pregame, game, and postgame strategies; and articulating expectations to each team member.

Follower

If coaches are expected to provide strong leadership, how can they be followers? Because good leaders know when *not* to lead, when to respect and be sensitive to the needs and decisions of others, and when to respond sincerely and honestly to input from others. Following, when it's a conscious strategy, is not a weakness but rather a sign of strength and security. The group leader should not need to constantly demonstrate dominance, for the role is, by definition, the most powerful position on the team. The coach can be more effective by allowing assistant coaches and team captains to be responsible for certain team-related tasks. Examples include leading warm-up exercises, recommending and implementing strategies in practice and during the contest, and making decisions on selected issues, on and off the field or court.

Teacher

Effective coaches are educators. How else could participants learn and improve their skills? Athletes who make progress in developing their skills become more creative, self-assured, and successful. Part of the educational process in sport is to teach athletes to think independently of the coach's directions and to respond creatively to unanticipated actions of their opponents. Effective coaches are knowledgeable about the skills and strategies of their sport. But just as important is that they are able to communicate this knowledge to their players so that it can be applied proficiently in competitive situations. The best coaches also work at upgrading their expertise by reading relevant literature, attending seminars, and soliciting feedback from others as to their teaching effectiveness. The coach who is an effective teacher (1) asks athletes about the effectiveness of his or her teaching, (2) uses a variety of modes of communication, such as videotape to model skills and to provide a visual form of information feedback, (3) provides specific feedback that athletes can use in a relatively low-key, nonhostile manner, and (4) does not teach new, unrehearsed skills and strategies during the contest but, instead, rehearses them in practice until the participants can perform them comfortably and consistently.

Role Model

Model is defined in the *Random House College Dictionary* as "a standard or example for imitation or comparison." Coaches serve as models for their athletes in demonstrating proper behaviors. Coaches must be consistent in following the same rules and expectations in their own actions and attitudes that they expect of their players (Figure 8.1).

Figure 8.1 Good coaches are good teachers. Modeling is usually the most effective way to teach sport skills.

The rules that forbid profanity, alcohol abuse, and intake of illegal drugs, and that demand a 100 percent effort should hold true for coaches and athletes alike. To maintain a double standard in regard to team policies is to invite distrust and a loss of credibility. For example, if the coach requests that all team members refrain from berating game officials, the coach must express feelings and ask the official for decision interpretations in a low-key, mature manner. Similarly, the coach should keep a neat, professional appearance commensurate with the demands on each player.

Limit Setter

Effective coaches have realistic but high expectations of their athletes. Demands on athletes include maintaining proper training and conforming to team policies. Sometimes the coach must restrict and set limits on certain behaviors to ensure the proper preparation of players for maximal game performance. Guidelines, and specific procedures for monitoring the players' adherence to them, need to be developed and implemented. The coach has several choices as the limit-setter. He or she can decide to amend the rule, ask for more player input, promise to think about the matter, or explain why the issue is not negotiable. See Chapter 9 on additional strategies for setting limits.

Often, athletes find limit setting to be necessary—even desirable—in helping them to control certain actions. Peer pressure to test rules and to "go along with the gang" is sometimes overwhelming. One good example is the pressure to experiment with illegal drugs. Athletes have told me (Anshel 1991a) in confidence that social gatherings often provide the opportunity to take drugs. Accompanied by the intake of alcohol and a rather seductive environment, the temptation to "try it" is almost overwhelming. But athletes who are warned about the dire consequences of ingesting drugs and breaking other team rules (and the law) have "an excuse" for refusing the drug. "If my coach finds out ("If my drug test is positive"), I'll be dismissed from the team" is a face-saving and justifiable reason to "just say no" (see Anshel 1991b for suggestions related to limit-setting and drug-taking).

Psychologist or Counselor

Effective coaches are approachable. They are not threatening to their athletes, and the players, in turn, feel that they can risk communicating most thoughts to the team leader. In this atmosphere, the coach can listen and respond to the needs of each athlete, which is important if the coach wants players to perform without thoughts and feelings that interfere with performance preparation and participation. The "airing out" of feelings that might inhibit full concentration on the task at hand is desirable. In one typical situation, the coach may receive information that a player is struggling in class; the student's grades are low, and his or her future in this course looks ominous. The counseling coach would immediately seek to meet with the athlete's teacher to discuss the problem. The coach would then meet with the athlete to (1) decide jointly on selected strategies to overcome the poor classroom performance, (2) set specific, realistic goals for academic improvement, and (3) agree on regular meeting times to track progress. Chapter 9 includes specific strategies for providing counsel to players.

Friend and Mentor

Can a coach ever really be an athlete's friend? Should coaches and athletes relate to one another as though they are in the same peer group, have similar interests, and share the same friends? The answer is a simple "no," at least during the athlete's participation on the coach's team. Athletes want to admire and respect their coaches. The athlete views the older, more experienced coach in a very different light than a teammate or friend. The player's expectations of the coach's behaviors and attitudes differ from those of the player's peers. Athletes tend to be uncomfortable with the coach who tries to be "good friends" with the players.

However, an element of friendship does exist in a healthy player-coach relationship. It's called *mentoring*. Mentoring, unlike friendship, "occurs when a coach willingly invests time in the personal development of the athlete, when a trusting relationship evolves, when needs and interests are fulfilled, and when imitation of behavior takes place" (Bloom 2002, p. 441). The mentoring process is an integral component of learning to coach in sport. It's an ongoing process that teaches athletes, many of whom become coaches, coaching styles, strategies, and philosophy. The positive outcomes from mentoring are a primary reason why coaches should be available to interact with athletes in a meaningful way, even away from the sport arena. Jones and her colleagues (1988) suggest that "coaches can get players out of trouble, lend them money, pat them on the back, laugh, cry, and cheer with them, and not let anyone else talk about them" (p. 22). Thus, a relationship built on trust, honesty, disclosure of feelings, support, and, to a degree, nurturance can be a healthy friendship.

Parent Substitute

According to Jones et al. (1988), "Stable children must have someone who cares about them who is important in their life . . . one must have the love and concern of a significant other—someone who really matters" (p. 25). The coach's role is not to *be* the parent but rather to support the same goals that parents have for their athlete sons and daughters. As the role model for players, the coach carries out a host of parental functions. This role is magnified when the athlete has a single parent. After discovering academic problems with an athlete, the coach might act as a parent in meeting with school personnel to schedule tutorial sessions. After finding out that a team member has cut class, the coach might need to set limits on inappropriate player behavior by giving the athlete a choice between attending every future class session or leaving the team. No abusive language, embarrassing and insulting comments, or disclosures to the athlete's parents should be necessary. To build trust and mutual respect, agreements about future behaviors should be conducted exclusively between coach and athlete.

A good example of the parental role that coaches bring to their relationships with athletes is how Shaquille O'Neal, all-star center of the Los Angeles Lakers basketball team, views his coach, Phil Jackson. An article in *Sports Illustrated* magazine (Nov. 1, 1999, vol. 91, no. 17), entitled "Father Phil," quotes O'Neal as describing Jackson as "a white version of my father" (p. 84). Jackson has provided O'Neal, and the rest of the Lakers team, with stability, a sense of purpose, a vision about what they want to achieve, a mission about how to achieve their goals, values about what is—or should be—important to each player, opportunities to help players establish their respective role on the team (the role of leader, in O'Neal's case), respect for each player, and instilling a sense of team and individual integrity (be true to yourself, true to your standards and ideals, and keep promises). Yet, Jackson also sets limits. On who would be the team leader, Jackson said that "Shaquille would be the obvious choice, but because of his (poor) free throw (shooting percentage), he can't be the leader" (p. 85). "Look," Jackson asserted, "you've got to deliver in the clutch if you're going to be the leader, and if you can't make free throws. . . ." (p. 85). Instead of feeling humiliated or angry, O'Neal felt inspired and challenged to improve his free throw shooting percentage by over 60%. This is a good example of the parental role in coaching.

Family Member

The coach who has a spouse and, perhaps, children must acknowledge family responsibilities. Working a 60- to 70-hour week, as some coaches do, may be destructive to one's home life. Is team and professional success directly proportional to the number of hours spent per week in game preparation and player development? An analysis of the effectiveness of such extreme coaching behaviors is open to debate but goes beyond the purpose of this discussion. On the one hand, spouses of coaches have to be supportive of the required work that goes into the coaching profession, especially if recruiting is a job component; on the other hand, families should be a rewarding and pleasant component of a coach's life, a source of pleasure, and a means of preventing burnout and loneliness. The right perspective on sport leadership and home life is needed.

Theories of Leadership in Sport

What constitutes effective leadership? Several theories have been supported by researchers and educators. Some writers claim that effective leadership is an inherited skill, but others contend that it is learned. Still others assert that the combination of natural ability and an environment that nurtures this ability is required to lead successfully. The following sections explain a few of the more popular theories of effective leadership with reference to sport.

Fiedler's Contingency Model

Fiedler (1964) suggests that the effectiveness of any single leadership style is dependent on the type of situation. An authoritative approach might be more functional in some environments (e.g., the military) and situations (e.g., during a game or when leading exercise drills) than in others. Sometimes the appropriate leadership style depends on the skill level, age, and maturity of group members as well as on their expectations of "proper" or preferred leader behavior. For example, most athletes would typically expect their coach to make unilateral decisions during the contest, but they might also expect the coach to solicit their input when setting individual performance goals. The key to Fiedler's model is maintaining a favorable situation. The various components of such situations include (1) personal relations with group members, (2) the structure of the group's task, and (3) the power and authority inherent in the leader's position. Each of these components will be examined in the context of competitive sport.

Personal Relations with Group Members.   Fiedler contends that the personal relationships between the leader and key group members (e.g., team captains and starters) are an important factor affecting team performance. This view supports the findings of sport researchers that coaches of winning teams are viewed by their players as honest, receptive, good communicators, and effective teachers of sport skills (Anshel & Straub 1991; Mechikoff & Kozar 1983). Conversely, players may view their coach far less positively if the team consistently loses (Anshel 1989a). Hence, "The liked and respected leader does not need formal power. . . . [His or her] interpersonal attitudes influence group performance to a significantly greater degree than similar attitudes of a leader who is not accepted by his group" (Fiedler 1964, p. 159).

Task Structure.   The leader's job is easier when the task is highly structured, that is, when group roles and objectives are identified and accepted by members. However, when a group is given an unstructured task such as planning an event or jointly establishing group policies, the leader is relatively less able to affect group activity. What many leaders fail to realize is that this holds true even in situations where the leader holds considerable power. Think about it: How much cooperation will a boss (coach) receive if he or she makes overpowering, perhaps unfair, demands on employees (athletes)? The result may be poor, inefficient productivity.

An effective leader uses task structure to his or her advantage without coercion and without deceit toward subordinates. Task structure in competitive sport may be analyzed in four areas:

1. *Decision verifiability:* Determining the degree to which decisions are correct by examining the consequences of these decisions or by obtaining information feedback from persons who are directly affected by the decisions. For example, an injured starter is replaced by a substitute who demonstrates high performance success. The coach's dilemma is whether to continue to play the substitute when the injured starter is ready to compete again, a decision made even more difficult if the substitute shows high competence over several contests.

2. *Goal clarity:* The extent to which task requirements are clearly stated or known to group members. For example, did coaches explain to athletes the purposes for engaging in certain strategies and exercises in preparing for the contest?

3. *Goal-path multiplicity:* Is there only one way to meet goals and to become successful at the task? Could alternative approaches be discussed? In sport, a good idea might be to solicit the opinions of coaching assistants and selected players to establish a joint commitment to meeting team and individual goals.

4. *Solution specificity:* Is there more than one "correct" solution to a problem? Must the coach always have the answers (or be expected to)? Are other group members allowed to express different points of view? Is there room for disagreement and negotiation off the field or court, during practice, and even throughout the contest? For example, if players seek permission to execute a particular strategy, should the coach give it?

Position Power.   How much influence does the leader have over group members? It may be significant between workers and their immediate supervisor and between players and their coach. However, administrators, including athletic directors and the owners of businesses and sports teams, who "go over the coach's (supervisor's) head" in making team-related decisions are usurping the team leader's responsibility and effectiveness. Members of task- and goal-oriented groups, such as sport teams, should understand that the role of making decisions and influencing member behaviors and attitudes belongs to one person—the team leader.

There is little doubt that power is inherent in sport leadership. But the effectiveness of this power in a sport context is open to scrutiny. Fiedler's contingency model would not support the notion that more leadership power is always, or even usually, better.

The ideal situation, using Fiedler's model, would be one in which a trusted, respected leader interacts with a homogeneous work group (for instance, a team of skilled athletes who share common goals), and has a significant degree of influence over members' actions, in a program governed by standard procedures (e.g., conditioning, practice, and game schedules). The least favorable situation is where the coach (1) is disliked by a mixed group (say, for instance, team members who differ greatly in skills and goals, or do not like one another), (2) is managing an ill-defined task (e.g., directing a physical conditioning program or a practice session), and (3) has relatively little power to influence behavior. In this last situation, the coach would lack credibility and player loyalty.

Team sport leaders can use one of four alternatives to increase the probability of successful coaching:

1. *Use the appropriate style.* A coach's leadership style should be compatible with the situation. Citizens expect the head of their country to demonstrate strong decision-making capability, but the president of a labor union is expected to solicit the advice and voting participation of union boards, committees, and members. In sport, coaches of elite athletes, usually in high-pressure situations in which winning is an expectation or even a mandate to keep their jobs, should not use the same leadership style as the coach of a team consisting of younger, nonelite competitors. The needs and expectations of athletes in these situations differ.

2. *Meet situational needs.* Effective coaches can alter their behaviors to meet the needs of a given situation. In addition to age and skill level partly determining leadership style,

clearly effective leaders respond in a manner that is compatible with the situational demands. Attending to an injured athlete or a team member having personal difficulties requires a humanistic response. Reacting to many game situations may call for authoritarian decision making. It is *not* realistic, perhaps not even possible, for a coach to change his or her personality per se. But a person's actions are changeable. Developing the ability to change the content and manner of one's communication style to meet situational needs is feasible and a desirable characteristic of successful leaders.

3. *Make the job fit the person.* The leader should seek a position that is suitable to his or her personality or natural leadership style. Fiedler (1964) asserts that this may be the most realistic approach to being a successful leader or coach. If the coach's personality is more compatible with a smaller group of players or is better suited to the achievement of relatively fewer tasks than governing a large group of players, then coaching golf, archery, and other teams with relatively few participants might be a good choice.

4. *Learn to change styles.* Coaches can be trained to alter their styles. Seminars, conferences, in-service instruction, consultation with a sport psychologist, and published literature can promote professional and personal growth and can help one to upgrade leadership and administrative skills. A person's predisposition to act in a certain way need not necessitate nor predict his or her behaviors. People can choose to control their actions. The mentality of "I am who I am" rather than a willingness to adapt to various environments has very limited validity in effective leadership.

The Life Cycle Theory

Effective leaders perform two functions: They complete the group's goal or goals (task-oriented behavior), and they facilitate positive interaction among group members (people-oriented behavior). The main feature of the life cycle theory is the development of *task-relevant maturity* in the group, essentially the coordination of people-oriented and task-oriented behaviors (Hersey & Blanchard 1977).

The leader's actions are partially dependent on the maturity of group members, specifically job maturity and psychological maturity. *Job maturity* comprises three components: (1) the group's capacity to set and reach goals, (2) the group's willingness and ability to assume responsibility, and (3) the extent of group education and experience—in a word, competence. *Psychological maturity* indicates the level of self-respect, self-confidence, and self-esteem that each member brings to the group. As maturity increases, the need for task-structured behavior decreases. Leader behaviors go from a more directive style to placing an increased emphasis on developing the leader-subordinate relationship. In the latter stages of the life cycle (with extensive psychological maturity), the leader assumes a consultant role; people are allowed more independence to get the job done. Decisions tend to be more negotiable than directed.

Effective coaches, in implementing the life cycle approach, will:

- *Begin with a strict approach.* In the beginning stages of group development, before or early in the season, the coach should assess the maturity level of each performer prior to determining the needed leadership style. Typically, however, the team leader should maintain a relatively authoritative, structured posture, reducing the intensity level on selected occasions or when necessary. Expectations for player behaviors within and outside the sport setting should be communicated at this time.

- *Build self-confidence and mutual respect with each player*. Player achievement, constructive feedback on performance, honesty and sincerity, sensitivity to the feelings of others, and skill development for performance improvement are needed here.

- *Nurture team leadership*. The opportunity to develop and exhibit leadership is inherent in the team captain position. But coaches may want to give opportunities for leadership to other team members as well. To develop leadership qualities in all players is desirable. Leaders tend to be self-motivated, to take responsibility for their performance, and to remain loyal to group goals.

- *Establish trust*. To build the coach-player relationship, trust between these parties should be established as soon as possible because this is a time-consuming process. Strategies to gain trust are covered in Chapter 9 on communication. In a leadership context, the ability to establish trust with one team member has the advantage of spreading to others—athletes talk to one another. Conversely, athletes who mistrust their coach are more resistant to being influenced, and less loyal to their coach. Rarely is a leader trusted by some group members but not by others.

The focus of life cycle theory is on the situation created by the subordinates' maturity level. One limitation of this theory is taking into account the age and experience of group members. The life cycle may not begin and mature in the same way for different groups. After all, older, more experienced athletes have different needs and expectations of a leader than their younger, less experienced counterparts. This issue is addressed in the multidimensional model.

The Multidimensional Model

Athletes of different ages and skill levels do not have the same needs. Older, more experienced competitors differ from their younger counterparts with respect to their needs and their reasons for participating in sport. Chelladurai and Carron (1978) found that child competitors preferred a relationship-oriented coaching style rather than a task-related approach. In other words, kids need the coach's friendship as an integral part of the leadership role. College-age athletes, on the other hand, were found to have relatively low relationship needs and, instead, preferred more task-oriented coaching behaviors.

The multidimensional model, as depicted in Table 8.1, shows that professional athletes, persons whose careers and salaries are dependent on performance, have high task orientation. Although a positive relationship between the coach and player certainly contributes to effective performance, professionals expect a leader to exert marked influence on the team through insight, intelligence, and the ability to communicate knowledge. Notice that college competitors also have high needs for a task-oriented approach. However, the importance of getting along with the coach is more prominent for them than for professional athletes. High school athletes might mentally withdraw or even drop out if the relationship with their coach is unsatisfactory. The model predicts that child athletes will almost surely quit the team without warm coach-athlete interaction unless pressured by parents to do otherwise.

In an update of this model, Chelladurai (1990) views leadership effectiveness as a function of three interacting components, stable factors that precede leader behaviors, leader behaviors, and the consequences of combining these components for team member satisfaction and performance. The *stable factors* include (1) situational characteristics

Table 8.1 Leadership preferences by athletes of different maturation/age levels.

Leader Behavior Level	Task-Oriented	Relationship-Oriented
Professional	High	Low
College	Moderate to high	Moderate to low
High school	Moderate to low	Moderate to high
Elementary—youth sports	Low	Very high

(i.e., any constraints or observations of the situation that may influence the leader's actions, such as specific rules, game situations, behaviors of others), (2) leader characteristics (e.g., the coach's personality or behavioral tendencies), and (3) group member characteristics (e.g., varying degrees of assertiveness or other emotions, self-confidence, age, skill level).

Leader behaviors are categorized as (1) required (e.g., need to set limits or to encourage or discourage certain emotions, depending on the sport, skill level, or age of athlete), (2) preferred (e.g., athletes' desire for a spirited, "take-charge" coaching style or a highly sensitive, low-key approach), and (3) actual (e.g., often a combination of both required and preferred behaviors). High or low *team member satisfaction* and *team performance* are dependent on the degree of compatibility among the characteristics of the leader, team members, and the situation. According to Chelladurai (1990), *the best outcome of coaching performance, based on team performance and member satisfaction, is predicted when the leader's actions are appropriate for the situation, and the leader's actions match the athletes' preferences.* Thus, highly autocratic coaches are more likely to be effective team leaders if their athletes prefer this type of coaching style and if the type of sport (e.g., basketball, American football, and most other contact sports) is compatible with a more assertive approach. Another important situational factor in leadership effectiveness, correctly noted by Chelladurai (1993), is culture. He cites several studies in which preferences for certain leadership styles are a function of cultural backgrounds and ideologies.

Taken collectively, Chelladurai's (1993, p. 653) review indicates that athletes from certain cultures, and within particular types of sports, have different leadership preferences. For example, while Japanese physical education students in modern sports (e.g., basketball and volleyball) showed a preference for democratic behavior, Japanese in traditional sports (e.g., judo and kendo) preferred more autocratic leadership behavior. In contrast, Canadian physical education students in modern sports preferred more autocratic leadership. The Japanese athletes, in general, preferred more social support than the Canadians and perceived their coaches to be more autocratic than did their Canadian athlete counterparts. The Canadians, on the other hand, perceived their coaches to provide more training and instruction and to be more democratic and more rewarding than the Japanese. One conclusion, derived from these studies and others from Finland, Korea, and Portugal, is that cultural influences on leadership preference depend partly on the type of sport in question.

In their review of the research that has tested the multidimensional model of leadership, most of which is descriptive (i.e., relationships between variables rather than cause and effect), Chelladurai and Riemer (1998) found two general lines of inquiry.

One focus of researchers has been the influence of certain antecedent variables (e.g., gender, personality, age, experience, maturity, ability) on preferred and/or perceived leadership. Situational factors studied in relation to preferred/perceived leadership included organizational goals, type of task, culture, and team role (e.g., offensive vs. defensive players in football). Another approach of researchers has been to study the extent of similarity between perceived and preferred leadership in relation to the athletes' satisfaction with their coach, team performance, and/or individual performance. For example, will a significant difference between the coach's actual leadership style and the athletes' preferred style influence team, or player, performance or team member satisfaction? The authors have concluded that players' satisfaction is enhanced if their coach: (1) engages in training and instruction to improve the players' ability and coordinated efforts, and (2) rewards high-quality performance through the use of positive feedback. In addition, the authors concluded that any discrepancy between that coach's actual behavior and the players' preferred coach behavior was not related to sport performance, at least based on the results of very few studies.

In summary, the multidimensional model focuses on three aspects of leadership: (1) actual leader behavior, (2) leader behavior that is preferred by subordinates, and (3) required leader behavior—that is, behavior that is dictated by the organization or team. Chelladurai and Carron predict that performance outcomes and group member satisfaction will be positively related to the compatibility of these three components. Additional research is needed to test the model.

Measurement of Sport Leadership. To date, only one psychological inventory of coaching leadership that has been statistically validated has appeared in the sport psychology literature. The Leadership Scale for Sports (LSS) was developed by Chelladurai and Saleh (1980) and reflects the Multidimensional Model of Leadership. For a summary of the psychometric (statistical) properties of the LSS, and an updated review of studies using this inventory, see Chelladurai (1993). The LSS, translated into seven non-English languages, consists of 40 items representing five dimensions of leader (coaching) behavior:

1. *Training and instruction.* Behavior that emphasizes strenuous training, skill instruction, clarifying the relationship among teammates, and structuring and coordinating members' activities

2. *Democratic behavior.* Behavior that allows greater participation by athletes in decisions relating to team goals

3. *Autocratic behavior.* Behavior that limits independent decision making and emphasizes personal authority

4. *Social support.* Behavior in which the coach shows concern for the welfare of each athlete, positive group atmosphere, and warm interpersonal relations with members

5. *Positive feedback.* Behavior that recognizes and rewards good performance

While the LSS supports the multidimensional model, perhaps its most worthy applied function is to examine coach-athlete compatibility (Chelladurai 1993). Further information about the LSS may be obtained from P. Chelladurai, Ph. D., School of HPER, The Ohio State University, Columbus, Ohio, 43210, USA.

Mediational Model

Previous leadership models in sport (and in general psychology) are defined primarily on the coach's behavioral tendencies (e.g., types of interactions with team members, how group decisions are made, origins and maintenance of group control). Professors Frank Smoll and Ronald Smith from the University of Washington (Seattle), in their mediational model, recognize an array of personal factors—individual differences—in the way coaches and their athletes think (cognition) and feel (affect) that are similarly important as overt behaviors and situational factors that contribute to or explain leadership style and effectiveness. The authors claim "cognitive and affective processes serve as filters between overt coaching behaviors and [athletes'] attitudes toward their coach and their sport experience" (p. 1527). Figure 8.2 illustrates the mediational model.

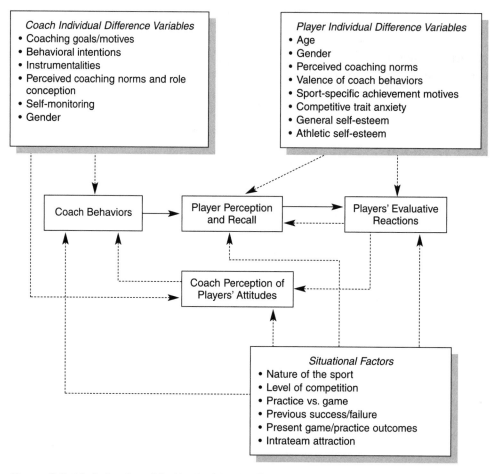

Figure 8.2 Mediational model of leadership (Smoll & Smith, 1989).

Note: From Smoll & Smith (1989). Reprinted with permission from *Journal of Applied Social Psychology*, Vol. 19, No. 18, pp. 1522–1551. © V. H. Winston & Sons, Inc., 360 South Ocean Boulevard, Palm Beach, FL 33480. All rights reserved.

The model consists of three primary components: coach behaviors, players' perception and recall, and players' evaluative reactions. The authors contend that the way in which players respond to their coach is a function of their perception (meaningfulness) and recall of the coach's previous behaviors. Thus, if a player views a reprimand from the coach in a positive, constructive manner, ostensibly the player will react in a more efficient and positive manner, emotionally, mentally, and physically, than if the player's perception of the coach's reprimand was negative and destructive. In addition, the coach's behaviors will result from his or her perception of player attitudes and the players' evaluative reactions to those coaching behaviors. For instance, if a coach feels that the players are undermotivated (perhaps exhibited by a clear lack of enthusiasm), not listening to instructions, or moving too slowly, the coach will react in a way to which he or she feels the players will respond favorably and respect. This reaction might range from a reprimand to a low-key request to demonstrate more desirable emotions and behaviors. Perhaps a brief philosophical speech or words of encouragement might improve the athletes' state of mind. Or the coach might solicit from selected players the source of the apparent undermotivation, then choose to either respond or not respond to this information.

There are numerous personal and situational factors that influence leadership and group member behaviors. For example, the coach's personal factors include the coach's goals/motives, behavioral intentions, gender, perceived coaching norms and coaching role, and self-monitoring. Player personal factors include age, gender, general and sport self-esteem, competitive trait anxiety, sport-related achievement motivation, and perceptions of the coach (i.e., normative beliefs about how the coach should act in this particular sport). Finally, the model includes situational factors that influence all other processes in the model. These include sport type, level of competition, practice versus game, previous success and failure, present game or practice outcomes and intrateam member attraction. Smoll and Smith call for additional research to examine the relationships among these factors. Chelladurai and Riemer (1998) concluded that the model needs further testing. Clearly, though the mediational model addresses characteristics in the sport leadership literature that have been previously ignored, and reveals an increasingly complex set of processes that influence effective coaching.

Theory X and Theory Y

McGregor (1967) asserts that individuals in leadership positions typically formulate one of two sets of basic assumptions (referred to as Theory X and Theory Y) about subordinates. The assumptions of *Theory X* are that:

- Workers inherently dislike their jobs and will avoid working whenever possible.
- Subordinates must be coerced, controlled, directed, and even threatened to work at optimal efficiency.
- Followers mostly prefer to be directed; they avoid responsibility and have relatively little ambition to achieve or in any way to get ahead.

In the opposite direction, *Theory Y* acknowledges workers who:

- Perceive physical and mental effort on the job as natural and necessary.

- Are capable of exercising self-direction and self-control to meet group objectives to which they feel committed.
- For the most part, learn to perform their jobs under appropriate conditions.
- Accept and actually seek responsibility.

Theory X is more comparable to an authoritative coaching style in which task completion comes first and warm relationships between coach and athlete are viewed as least critical to success. Personal concerns of subordinates almost always take a back seat to the objective at hand. The coach often believes, rightly or wrongly, that players want a tough leader who will direct and control all activity.

In fact, the leader's negative perception of team members is often fulfilled by the players' actions, a phenomenon called the Pygmalion Effect or the self-fulfilling prophecy (discussed throughout this text). The coach's typical behaviors and attitudes toward team members are condescending, insensitive, mistrusting, and disrespectful. The players then react to the coach in accordance with his or her expectations and perceptions, just as the coach predicted (Rejeski et al. 1979).

Theory Y reflects a more humanistic coaching style that is compatible with developing positive relationships and communication with players. Such "person-oriented" coaches are concerned about (1) team morale, (2) personal feelings—in addition to each player's attitude toward team goals, (3) relationships and affiliation among players, (4) discovering and attempting to meet the athlete's personal goals for participating, and (5) the general level of team member satisfaction.

Both Theory X and Theory Y have weaknesses. A firm hand in directing player behavior is often desirable, especially when the task is clear and player incentive is low (Chelladurai & Carron 1978). A coach who assumes a consistent posture of total domination will rarely be successful, at least in most cultures. However, a military drill sergeant might be able to get away with a continually authoritative style, at least during the training period. Many coaches are convinced about the need to be strictly task-oriented and are quite naive about the need to be sensitive to the emotional needs of players. Ignoring this component often leads to a lack of player loyalty toward the coach, and the motivation to exhibit high effort decreases over time. Leaders must interact with others in a respectful manner, no matter what the situation, if they are to have the credibility and loyalty of subordinates.

One disadvantage of Theory Y is that extraordinarily high concern for personal feelings might occur at the expense of meeting team goals and task productivity (Straub 1980). Because coaches are rarely all X or all Y in style, clearly there is a need for a balanced approach.

Tannenbaum and Schmidt's Model

Similar to Fiedler's theory, Tannenbaum and Schmidt's (1958) view of effective leadership comprises three areas: (1) forces in the manager, (2) forces in the work group, and (3) forces in the situation.

Forces in the Manager. The central issue here is the degree to which a leader has the power to make decisions on a continuum from leader-centered to group member-centered decision making. As illustrated in Figure 8.3, the coach slowly allows more and more

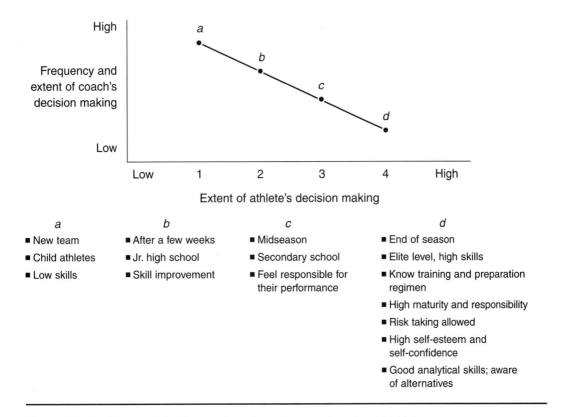

Figure 8.3 Continuum of decision-making role and power of coach and athlete.

player involvement in the decision-making process. The sequence indicates a maturation of player leadership skill based on time, age, maturity, and performance level of group participants. Older athletes, in particular, want to have, and feel that they deserve, additional freedom to at least partially determine team strategies and contest-related decisions that affect performance outcomes. Coaches of older, more advanced competitors tend to have the personal security and flexibility to take risks and to share power.

Forces in the Work Group. Effective leaders "tune in" to group members. Leadership style is determined after a coach ascertains the maturity and skill level of the team. Higher skilled, more mature players respond better to a laissez-faire approach with greater allowance for decision making and independence toward preparing for the contest than younger, less skilled performers.

Forces in the group include the following:

1. Member (athlete) expectations of the leader
2. Ability of members (athletes) to assume responsibilities (e.g., conducting themselves off the field/court in a mature manner)
3. Amount of instruction and learning needed for success

4. Group's (team's) emotional maturity (e.g., handling sport-related stress and anxiety)

5. Ability of the players to tolerate uncertainty and to initiate proper behaviors in the leader's absence

6. Level of team member satisfaction (i.e., sense of pride as team members)

Examining these issues will assist the coach in determining his or her expectations toward player behavior and the extent of monitoring, supervising, and guiding that will be necessary to lead effectively.

Forces in the Situation.   Only poor leaders are oblivious to their surroundings. One coach of a college team for whom I served as a sport psychology consultant for three years (Anshel 1989a) did not have the ability to stop, look, and listen to what his athletes were saying both verbally and nonverbally. Consequently, he couldn't possibly realize that his athletes were not responsive to his leadership. His words had no meaning because he was not trusted and had no credibility. Not surprisingly, he did not have their respect. Yet he maintained that the players were happy; he claimed that discussions about "team problems" were not necessary.

Intelligent managing is based on the ability to take an objective look at a situation, to gather information, and then to react accordingly. Understanding the group's immediate history (past successes and failures, for instance) and the backgrounds and current needs of group participants might partially dictate a certain leadership style.

Here are a few questions that coaches should ask when assessing forces in the situation:

- What is the nature of problems within the group? Are athletes getting along?
- What is the group climate? Do players support one another or are jealousy and criticism pervasive?
- Are there any time restraints that may require a certain leadership style? Preparing for a game in two days necessitates a different approach to some issues than resolving certain issues between seasons.
- Does the team or league have a philosophy or policy that dictates team behavior (e.g., forbidding drug use)? Youth sports leagues should require a relatively less intense atmosphere for winning than other levels of play. To what extent are school grades connected to further sport participation? The coach should communicate his or her philosophy so that the expectations of each athlete will be formed realistically.
- Are there any team traditions that promote enjoyment and positive feelings that should be maintained or, for that matter, any negative traditions that should be abandoned?
- Finally, is the group effective? Do players agree about meeting group goals? Is it best to leave well enough alone and avoid opening up certain issues? As former U.S. president Harry Truman said, "If the plumbing ain't broke, don't fix it."

What Leadership Theories Do and Do Not Tell Us

Effective leadership behavior is impossible to dictate for all situations and populations. Scholars who examine the interactions between a group leader and the group's members are unable to prescribe any single best leadership approach. This is particularly true in sport, where participants who differ in age, skill, maturation, expectations, and personality must interact. Various types of sport also require different approaches. Attempting to predict success based on certain leadership characteristics is extremely difficult. While one purpose of developing a theory is to be able to make accurate predictions, the very definition of "success" differs from situation to situation. Do we mean that a leader is successful if group members are satisfied? Or is the team's win-loss record a more accurate indicator of successful leadership? Nevertheless, several recommendations can be derived from these leadership theories.

- *There is no "best" way to lead for all situations.* Coaches in golf and basketball differ markedly as to the leadership style that best fosters athletic performance. Coaches should make critical assessments of their unique situations and surroundings prior to charging "head-on" into a style that may or may not be compatible with their players, assistants, administrators, their players' parents, and the community.

- *Effective managers of groups "tune in" to the needs of members.* In addition to making their own plans, decisions, and strategies, coaches have to take the time to listen and react to the feelings of their athletes. Members of any group—and sport is no exception—tend to feel greater identification with group goals if they have played a part, however minor, in creating and carrying out these goals, along with team rules, and expected behaviors. Athletes need not create and implement all of the rules and goals, of course. But they also have feelings, needs, and skills that team leaders should not ignore.

- *There is a balance between task- and relationship-oriented styles.* Members of sports teams could probably function to some extent if they did not like one another. But member satisfaction through affiliation—getting along and developing some degree of friendship—helps teammates to support one another. Receiving recognition, respect, and support from teammates is an important need for most athletes. Completing tasks to reach goals and maintaining healthy relationships among group members are not mutually exclusive. This is especially true for younger athletes who have a greater need to establish meaningful relationships with their coach as compared to older, higher skilled performers (Chelladurai & Carron 1983).

- *Coaches must teach skills.* Very few competitors come to the sport arena with the necessary sport skills and proper attitude and mental training to compete successfully and consistently. Effective coaches teach mental and physical skills, or at least provide skill learning situations by other instructors. They take the necessary time and exert the required energy to ensure each player's growth and maturation as an athlete.

- *There is a difference between a facilitator and a power broker.* Good coaches have skilled and motivated athletes. But such desirable outcomes do not happen on demand. A coach cannot simply command and expect to receive respect, loyalty, and credibility. As Fiedler (1964) asserts, "The liked and respected leader does not need formal power" (p. 159). In other words, leadership is not built on intimidation, fear, and the mere completion of tasks. Instead, effective leaders have earned the respect of their subordinates through honesty, sincerity, mutual respect, fairness, empathy, and the ability to teach skills.

The style that a leader projects is perhaps the single most important characteristic that influences how he or she is perceived by the group. According to Cribben (1981), the group's *perception* of their leader is more important than the effectiveness of the leader's behaviors. In sport, often the players' perception of their coach dictates loyalty and respect (whether the coach seems to be fair and to treat each athlete with dignity, for example). "Images, not people, interact," Cribben asserts (p. 82).

Successful versus Effective Leadership

Successful leadership has been defined as the ability to get others to behave as the manager intends them to behave (Zaleznik 1977). The job may get done, and the coach's needs may be satisfied, but the players' needs are ignored. Perhaps the coach attends only to starters while ignoring substitutes. In *effective leadership*, the athletes perform in accordance with the coach's intentions and, at the same time, find their own needs satisfied. As Cribben (1981) points out, "Success has to do only with getting the job done, whereas effectiveness adds the concept of satisfaction on the part of those who do the job" (p. 35). In this way, the positive feelings of subordinates usually contribute to long-term benefits such as team loyalty, support, and enjoyment of participation, an important component of intrinsic motivation. For instance, team captains might feel better about their role— and would be more helpful to the team—if the coach gave them a sense of importance, perhaps a significant responsibility such as leading a team meeting or gathering information from team members. In addition, resolving conflicts in the privacy of a coach's office rather than in the presence of teammates certainly contributes to team and coach loyalty. Thus, effective coaches are concerned with maintaining good relations with team members over several months, even years, rather than with just winning a specific contest.

Successful (but Ineffective) Coaches

Teams led by "successful" leaders may win more often than not, and they may even like or respect their coach. However, these leaders might intimidate or hurt the feelings of their players, thereby limiting the achievement of each player's potential. What these leaders have in common is the appearance of success. Usually team members are performing tasks in a manner intended by the leader, and desirable outcomes may be achieved. Often the missing link, however, is the somewhat low level of satisfaction by group members. Further, if the team begins to lose, it is extremely difficult for these leaders to motivate the players. Coach loyalty drops markedly—that is, if it was there in the beginning. Table 8.2 includes a few styles that fit the so-called successful leader who is not necessarily effective.

Mechikoff and Kozar (1983) interviewed 23 coaches with highly respectable winning records in various sports at the high school and collegiate levels. None of these coaches intimidated, ignored, deceived, or embarrassed an athlete to evoke some desirable mental state or to enhance physical performance. For example, former University of Nebraska head football coach Tom Osborne reinforced the importance of honesty and being "genuine" with athletes. Terry Donahue, former head football coach at UCLA, praised the use of nonverbal cues in effective communication. And John Robinson, currently head football coach at the University of Nevada at Las Vegas, suggested that coaches should "treat your players with respect."

Effective Leaders

The renowned scientist Albert Einstein once said, "I have received excessive admiration and respect from my fellow men through no fault of my own." This is a man who "made

Table 8.2 Leaders who are successful but not effective.

Style	Characteristics	Typical Behavior
Bureaucrat	Formal, disciplined, impersonal.	Product more important than process. Tasks necessary to win more important than family and personal needs of athletes.
Zealot	Impatient, outspoken, very confident, demanding, domineering.	Very task-oriented, little concern for meeting personal needs of others, aggressive, works best with weaker assistants who do not challenge authority.
Machiavellian	Self-oriented, devious, manipulative. Cold but can be charming.	Takes advantage of others' weaknesses; exploits others; must win at any price.
Missionary	Too concerned with people and what they think. Likable but tries too hard to be liked. Superb interpersonal skills but not highly respected.	Prizes harmony over conflict. Low task orientation, gets emotionally involved, does what is popular, ignores "tough" decisions, extreme humanist.
Climber	Striving, driving, energetic, self-oriented; polished and smooth but always aggressive; little or no loyalty to organization, team, or players; competent but is motivated by self-glory and own achievement.	Able to maneuver into the limelight; high task orientation but for self-serving purposes, not for the team's good. Relates well to others but has no interest in them.
Exploiter	Arrogant, insistent, abusive, demeaning, coercive, vindictive, domineering, rigid, prejudiced, makes snap judgments, yet competent. Exploits others' weaknesses.	Exerts constrictive control. Hurts anyone who is vulnerable. Uses pressure and fear to get things done. Demands subservience.
Glad-hander	Superficial, deceptively friendly, extroverted, top interpersonal skills, lacks depth and substance, minimally competent, good survival instincts, talkative, and humorous.	Sells him/herself very well. Low modest task orientation, gets by on "personality," unconcerned with people but excellent in dealing with them, seeks to impress others.

it" without stepping on the toes of others. He created, initiated, and produced. He led by example. Einstein was not only successful in meeting his own goals, he was an effective leader of the whole international scientific community. His scientific research made him a model others wanted to emulate. His hard work, determination, and incredible perseverance to gain knowledge were never at the expense of the "other fellow." In fact, Einstein is reputed to have assisted others in their work to help ensure their success.

It might be said about effective coaches that they receive excessive admiration and respect from their players because (1) they have a genuine concern for people, (2) they have the ability to teach, (3) they demonstrate their knowledge and intelligence in sport, and (4) they communicate well. They respect others and, in turn, get it back several times over. Phoniness and intimidation are not part of the profile. Relationships are based on a long-term commitment to the program and the desire to reach team and individual goals. Some examples of effective leadership styles are described in Table 8.3.

Horn (1992) conducted an extensive review of literature in examining the factors that most contribute to team leadership effectiveness. In these other studies, athletes had been asked to identify which decision style (e.g., autocratic, participative) and coach characteristics they

Table 8.3 Leaders who are effective.

Style	Characteristics	Typical Behavior
Entrepreneur	Extremely competent, forceful, dominant, self-confident, high need to achieve, can be very loyal, protective, and generous to team. Firm minded, innovative, often a loner. Creative.	Commands great loyalty, unable to function well in a subordinate position. Offers challenges and opportunities to succeed. Motivates by example, rewards, and fear.
Corporator	Quite directive but gives people freedom; cordial to others but keeps a certain distance.	Concerned about the good of the team; wins respect; high task orientation; polished and professional; makes people feel needed; delegates tasks and authority and consults, yet keeps effective control.
Developer	Trusts subordinates, wants to help them reach their potential, superb human relations skills; wins personal loyalty; builds a supportive achieving climate. Good counselor.	High people orientation; people considerations may take precedence over achievement, although is very productive. Supportive and emotionally involved with subordinates.
Craftsperson	Amiable, very conscientious, bright, highly task oriented, honest, straightforward, mild mannered, analytical. Proud of competence. Perfectionistic.	Likes to innovate, build, and try out new ideas. Not overly concerned with status; motivated by desire for excellence. Prefers to solve problems alone or in a small group. Supports subordinates.
Integrator	Excellent interpersonal skills; good insight into people. A team builder; prefers group decision making.	Shares the leadership role. Thinks in terms of associates rather than subordinates. Welcomes the ideas of others. Gives great freedom and authority to others.
Gamesperson	Fast-moving, flexible, very bright, skilled. Takes risks, assertive, intent on winning, but not petty; does not try to hurt or "get back at" others. Will not purposely hurt another player or team. Very ethical, but will take advantage of good opportunities to succeed.	Wants to win from good strategy; enjoys fair competition. A tough leader to outsmart who challenges and rewards a person's contributions. Eliminates the weak and nonachievers.

preferred in their coaches. She concluded that "situational factors and personal characteristics interact to determine the particular leadership behaviors that will be most effective in specific sport environments" (p. 191). Thus, a coach's tendencies will be more effective in some situations and sports than others. However, Horn also found that certain traits of effective leaders are relatively consistent and generalizable to most athletes, situations, and sports. In addition to characteristics listed in the previous paragraph, other coach behaviors linked to team member satisfaction include high frequencies of rewarding behavior, social support, and fairness in decision-making style (i.e., using input from athletes when it is warranted and beneficial).

All coaches in sport want to win. The coach's objective is to lead in a manner that not only will ensure a desirable outcome but also will ensure that the participants learn from, and are satisfied with, their sport experiences. The effective coach knows that *athletes are people*. These leaders are genuinely concerned about the human component—the feelings—of their athletes, in contrast to coaches who are "merely" successful (that is, their teams tend to win more games than they lose). Many well-known coaches with winning records have been known for their hot tempers and aggressive leadership styles. These coaches have maintained high winning percentages year after year, yet do not fit the description of effective coaches. Perhaps this is because they were able to recruit elite athletes who, like most top performers, could mentally overcome a more assertive, even abusive, communication style. However, it is quite likely that these coaches interacted with the players in a more mild and sensitive manner outside of the competitive arena. Therefore, the players did not take the occasional verbal assault personally. In this way, the level of compatibility between the personalities of athletes and their coach may be an important predictor of coaching and team success.

Leadership Styles

Most effective coaches use a variety of coaching styles at one time or another, sometimes in rapid succession. As indicated earlier, some styles are more appropriate in certain situations than others. This is why identifying the characteristics of at least some of these styles, describing their advantages and disadvantages, and determining the times at which each would be most appropriate are useful exercises. Many of the traits described in the preceding successful and effective categories are included in the four major leadership styles, described as authoritative, behavioristic, humanistic, and democratic.

The Authoritarian (Autocrat)

The authoritarian leader is characterized as achievement-oriented and impervious to criticism (he or she projects an image of knowing all the answers). He or she feels that athletes want and need a "tough guy" approach and rarely doubt their actions. Authoritarians have great confidence that they can finish what they start and that they can do so successfully. In all probability, autocrats were exposed to similar models either in their father or a former coach. "If it was good enough for me, it's good enough for my players" is their motto.

Sport psychologists Tutko and Ogilvie (1967) believe that authoritarian coaches have a need to control others and gravitate to a sport situation to satisfy this need. To date, no study conducted more recently has contradicted this assertion. But the authors also claim that athletes perceive the coach's role as an authority figure and, thus, expect authoritarian behaviors. Authoritarians believe that athletes actually seek dominance from the coach. According to Chelladurai and Carron's research (1983), this may at times be true.

Power, if used effectively, represents direction; it facilitates action, especially with relatively younger, less skilled performers. In the literature on management, Hersey and Blanchard (1977) found that when the level of group member maturity is low, a highly task-oriented leadership style is most effective. Thus, participants in youth sports or in physical education classes, for instance, need and prefer a high-task approach. In this way, power in leading others can have long-term benefits of facilitating action rather than inhibiting it. Fromm (1941) believes that persons who wish to be powerless do so to escape the responsibility that comes with independent thinking and decision making. Young, unskilled, less mature sport competitors might fall into this category. Fromm suggests that:

Most people are convinced that as long as they are not overtly forced to do something by an outside power, their decisions are theirs, and that if they want something, it is they who want it. But this is one of the great illusions we have about ourselves. A great number of our decisions are not really our own but are suggested to us from the outside; we have succeeded in persuading ourselves that it is we who have made the decision, whereas we have actually conformed with expectations of others, driven by the fear of isolation and by more direct threats to our life, freedom, and comfort (p. 200).

In Praise of Coach Bobby Knight.   Perhaps no college coach has been more controversial in recent years, and better depicts authoritative coaching, than Mr. Bob Knight, coach of the Texas Tech University men's basketball team, better known as the former basketball coach at Indiana University. The media has been extremely critical of Coach Knight. Undoubtedly, Coach Knight has, at times, acted in a highly emotional manner, intimidating athletes and offending spectators. Many athletes have not coped well with Coach Knight's communication style, while others have offered unending praise of his leadership, competence, and compassion. I have read the book, *Season on the Brink*, which describes the observations and experiences of writer John Feinstein as he accompanied Coach Knight's Indiana University basketball team through the entire 1985–86 season. One reason I read the book was to answer one important question. If Bob Knight treats his players in such a controversial, unpleasant manner, why do his teams continue to win? Why do so many of his former athletes sing his praises and talk about the very positive outcomes of playing on his team? After analyzing Feinstein's descriptions of Bob Knight's behavioral patterns, relationships with players, communication style, and features of his personality, I could understand why some players could not cope well with the intensity, expectations, and level of commitment of this man. Eventually, they would quit the team. Yet, others flourished and competed at levels that reached, perhaps went beyond, their potential. And all of the players who remained with his team graduated, a relatively rare outcome on college sports teams. I concluded that Coach Knight was a lightning rod for criticism for some individuals, particularly media reporters. Yet, few people were exposed to a different side of him.

So, why did his teams win? If he was so nasty and hostile to players, such an extreme autocrat, why did he continue to recruit so much talent, and, most important, why did so many players reflect on their experiences as a member of this team with such high regard? I cannot defend his frequent use of profanity, the wounding and often humiliating effect of his critical comments, which often chastise the player's character rather than behavior (see Chapter 9 for guidelines on providing criticism), his propensity to bring up the past when dealing with a current concern, and other shortcomings that contradict the applied sport psychology literature and have received widespread media attention. However, examples abound in *Season on the Brink* of a highly authoritative coach who was obviously perceived by his players (at least by most of them) as having high credibility and integrity, and engendering mutual respect among his players. A few direct quotes from Feinstein's book would provide the best evidence of this.

- "There are only three crimes an Indiana player can commit that will get him in serious trouble with Knight: drug use, skipping class, and lying" (p. 18).
- "Don't go out there *thinking* you're ready to play. Go out there *knowing* you're ready" (p. 129).
- This example is among my favorites: Coach Knight was speaking to his players in the locker room after practice. He lamented, "We always had players who wanted

to play and wanted to compete. I feel like with you guys that you are *required* to play. And I hate using that word: required" (p. 174). Knight went on:

"On Christmas night, all of you had dinner at [Indiana University President] Rink's house. I would imagine that Mrs. Rink spent the better part of three days cooking that dinner for you. What did you, as a team, do to thank her for dinner? Tell me. Did you all kick in a dollar to send her some roses? Did anybody write a thank-you note? Anybody? Speak up, anyone who did anything to thank Mrs. Rink."

He looked around the room. No one looked back. He turned to [starting guard Steve] Alford. "Steve, why do you think I was able to ask that question with absolute and complete confidence that no one had done anything?" "Because we're selfish," answered Alford. "Exactly. And that is reflected in the way you play basketball. The most selfish thing in the world is only worrying about guarding your man or only worrying about boxing out your man. . . . You just worry about yourselves. And as long as you do that, you'll continue to play selfish basketball, you'll continue to make the mistakes that cost us this game and you won't be able to beat anybody. Think about it" (p. 174).

Perhaps understanding any authoritative coach whose teams consistently win is to understand the concept of a *balanced* coaching style. Balance means that there are times for expecting strict adherence in carrying out team strategy, demonstrating full commitment and concentration in playing up to one's capability, taking responsibility for your performance, and never giving up. Coach Knight, like many coaches who spend so many hours trying to succeed in a highly competitive profession in which there is no silver medal for finishing second, is driven by a fear of failure. Fear drives negative emotion, such as anger, frustration, and worry. Yet, many of these autocratic coaches tend to have winning teams because their players realize that, at least away from the sport venue, their coach cares about them as people, as students, and as their parents' sons and daughters—and their parents have entrusted this coach with helping the athlete succeed in sport, in school, and in life.

In sport, power is a tool used by coaches to reach goals. But an authoritative approach to coaching need not always take the form of being a repressive drill sergeant. The alternative might be what Sabock (1985) calls "the benevolent dictator." This coach makes demands and decisions based on the athletes' best interests. A vigorous conditioning program to get everyone in shape, raising one's voice to increase the players' arousal level and attentional focus, and making sudden and important decisions during the contest are examples. Sabock believes that "a good leader will tolerate uncertainty only up to a point" (p. 106). As noted, the authoritarian approach is not necessarily bad (Figure 8.4) Tutko and Ogilvie have described four benefits of an authoritative coaching style.

1. *The athletes feel secure.* The insecure athlete may feel more protected with a strong leader, one who makes virtually all the decisions.

2. *Aggression can be redirected.* Theoretically, an authoritative approach may heighten aggression in the athlete, perhaps by increasing his or her frustration. This strategy reflects the frustration-aggression hypothesis that was more popular several years ago than it is in current thinking (see Chapter 6). The intended result of this strategy is to translate these feelings into heightened aggression, which in turn is redirected toward an opponent. One limitation of this technique is that many sport

Figure 8.4 An autocratic leadership style in sport is often expected and preferred by athletes, who depend on their coach's knowledge and experience to enhance team and individual performance.

performers require relatively low levels of arousal and aggression. Arousal can be too high, which hinders rather than improves effectiveness. Further, not all individuals react to frustration in the same manner; some persons pout or withdraw. Others do not enjoy such treatment, become unhappy, and may even quit the team. Sometimes a theory accurately predicts behavior, and sometimes it doesn't.

3. *The coach's needs are met.* An authoritative style can be an expression of the coach's needs and personality. As a result, he or she is most effective when these needs are met.

4. *The authoritarian is viewed as efficient and decisive.* Nothing is more expeditious than a one-person system of decision making. If coaches take responsibility for all decisions, then they also take responsibility for the outcomes.

Certainly authoritative behavior has a place in sport leadership. However, because power is literally inherent in the coaching position, there should be less reason to assert it than many coaches realize. Even effective authoritative coaches understand the importance of respecting the character and integrity of athletes. The expression of authoritative behavior, whether it is in making decisions or in reprimanding, is clearly more useful with only selected competitors and under certain conditions. One objective of effective coaching is to determine when and with whom this style is best suited.

The Behaviorist

Coaches who pat a player on the back after making a good play or express disappointment or anger after an unwelcomed performance are practicing a style of leadership called *behaviorism* or the use of a strategy referred to as *behavior modification*. This approach is based on the contention that human behavior is shaped or reinforced by its consequences. Reaching a goal or receiving a reward, then, is dependent on performing certain desirable behaviors. For example, an athlete who clearly gives a 100 percent effort during some task may be rewarded by the coach's words, "Nice going, Susan. Way to hustle." Ignoring the athlete who performs poorly, who is clearly not giving a 100 percent effort, or who behaves in an inappropriate manner is another example. This process is called *contingency management*. Desirable responses from the coach are contingent on expected, desirable performance. The desire to receive positive recognition, an integral part of human nature, is well understood by the coaching profession as a tool to influence sport performance and motivation.

A behavioristic approach in group leadership, including sport, can be a sophisticated science if conducted properly. Rather than merely giving orders and directing the behaviors of subordinates (more common with autocrats), the behaviorist sets up conditions in the environment that either (1) cause certain behaviors that have a desirable outcome (see Example 1) or (2) reinforce certain behaviors that can increase or decrease the probability of similar behaviors occurring in the future (see Example 2).

Example 1: A behavioristic strategy to improve group cohesion

The coach of a baseball team noticed that many of the players were forming their own subgroups (cliques) during their free time and ignoring other teammates. The cliques consisted of personal friends but, surprisingly, did not consist of only starters or only substitutes. Playing status was not an issue in forming these groups. The coach, worried that subgrouping would weaken the athletes' commitment to support one another and to reach team goals, planned two programs, one on the field and one off the field, designed to weaken the subgroups and to bring the team closer together.

The objective of the on-field strategy was to have the different cliques work together in fielding drills. Three practices were planned. The strategy, planned before the first practice, consisted of the following:

1. Writing down names of players who formed the various cliques.
2. Listing the athletes in each subgroup who would make up the practice groups (the coach was careful not to include the same subgroup members in any practice group). The practice groups comprised members of different racial and ethnic backgrounds, starters and nonstarters, players from different positions and of various skill levels, and leaders and less involved players.
3. Creating practice tasks that mandated interacting. Catching a fly ball and throwing it to the second baseperson would not allow players to interact with the desired intensity. The athletes had to actually depend on one another during the practice interaction. Each subgroup was assigned a different practice drill. The objective was to get players who normally did not congregate to interact around a common goal and literally to work together to meet that goal.
4. Offering verbal ("Excellent catch/throw/call") and nonverbal (smile, thumbs up, and so forth) congratulatory cues after each successful performance.

Due partly to this drill, players began to feel more comfortable with one another. In fact, they learned and used one another's first names. Further, the players helped one another to reach the desired outcomes. This carried over into games, where they supported teammates after errors, or striking out, as well as after making great plays and getting hits. The team grew closer.

The off-field strategy consisted of assigning athletes to committees that were responsible for meeting a certain goal. These goals included planning a team workout, leading a team meeting (without the coach's presence), arranging for a guest speaker, planning a team party, and forming a grievance committee to inform the coach about the athletes' feelings. Individuals who were usually quiet or tended to isolate themselves were invited to interact with other players who were more outgoing (positive leaders). In addition, to foster team member interaction among individuals who would normally not communicate (e.g., starters and nonstarters, or different racial and ethnic backgrounds), players were *assigned* to groups rather than volunteering for them, and every team member participated on one committee. Opportunities to meet were scheduled. Deadlines to provide information or to meet some objective from the group's activity were announced. The outcome of this strategy was that players became further acquainted with one another and, consequently, interacted in a more supportive, less "cliquish" (territorial) manner. The athletes actually enjoyed one another's company. Team harmony improved dramatically.

Example 2: A behavioristic strategy to improve risk-taking in basketball

A collegiate women's basketball coach was concerned about an athlete who played the forward position. He complained to the team sport consultant about the inability or unwillingness of this athlete to take open shots, to go after rebounds, or to maintain control of the ball. The player, in her first year with the team, was clearly tense. The coach asked her to see the consultant, and true to her word, she was on time for her appointment. The consultant asked her about her past successes in basketball and what she did to deserve this success. He also asked about her perceptions of the present situation; specifically about the coach's habits and personality characteristics, her relationships with other players, her general feelings about the nonsport aspects of her life (e.g., social relationships and academic status), and her adjustment to being a new team member.

Two things emerged from the conversation. First, this young woman was being pressured to do new things on the court that her previous coach did not require, such as scoring more points and exhibiting better ball control. Second, the coach's loud and aggressive manner made her uncomfortable and anxious. She realized that she was making mistakes on the floor and didn't need to be constantly reminded of this by the coach. However, the coach was openly critical of her errors on the court. His remarks carried over after the game. He was not hostile, but his loud, assertive manner made her feel uncomfortable. She was simply afraid of her coach. As a result, her strategy became, "If I don't try, I can't fail." This relatively talented athlete was in great need of success and complimentary feedback from her coach.

The consultant was given license in advance by the coach to make an agreement with the player concerning future behaviors. The coach agreed—also in advance—to abide by the contract. The agreement was that the athlete would relax, take more risks on the court, and try to have fun. In particular, she would shoot when she had the opportunity rather than pass the ball, and would be generally more aggressive on the court. This was to be carried out in both practice and game situations (she was not a starter and only entered the game when the outcome was not in jeopardy). It was understood that the coach would congratulate these new risk-taking behaviors regardless of the outcome. He would voice approval in response to the behaviors, whether or not they were successful. The coach and the athlete were to understand that all the parties were working on the process of establishing the player's mental set, not on the end product—at least not at this time.

The process established a risk-free environment in which the player could perform the skills that she was able to demonstrate during the preseason and in previous seasons as a superb high school athlete. The strategy was to let the player "be herself," to let her have fun as though the coach was not even watching. The coach and consultant decided to let the physical performance errors take care of themselves; with time and more opportunity to play, the athlete would gain confidence and improve. Meanwhile, the right time to criticize performance had not arrived. In fact, for the next few weeks, she received no critical feedback whatsoever. After three weeks, the coach began to suggest alternatives and to throw in a few reminders about technique. Not surprisingly, the athlete felt more relaxed and began to "play her game." Her performance improved dramatically, as did her happiness as a team member.

The use of behaviorism in this example served the purpose of extinguishing some feelings and behaviors while promoting others. The athlete's anxieties over the coach's actions and attitudes were real. Ironically, the coach didn't even realize that he was influencing the player in such an adverse manner (which, by the way, is not uncommon). The use of complimentary remarks after the athlete's change in performance (regardless of outcome) served to reinforce certain desirable behaviors, which increased the probability of their recurrence. In this example, by refraining from criticizing the athlete's performance outcome after she risked a more liberal playing strategy, the coach reduced and eventually extinguished her anxieties by dissolving the association between risking and failing. She began to relax, to have more fun, to perform up to her capabilities (and her coach's expectations), and to feel more comfortable with the coach's critique of her play—both positive and negative. Her ability to handle negative feedback was based on more successful experiences, which built up her confidence.

This example is supported by a similar set of behavior modification strategies conducted by Lynch and Stillman (1983) with a basketball athlete. The player was performing far below expectations and previous performances. In addition to poorer than expected performance (e.g., poor shooting percentage and poor rebounding), the athlete's abilities (e.g., reaction time, speed, and endurance) had dropped, and the athlete had gained considerable weight. The strategies used to change the situation were actually quite elaborate and more sophisticated than described in this summary. Briefly, however, the behavior modification program for weight loss consisted of (1) having the coach praise the player's gradual progress in weight loss and for her effort, (2) asking the player's apartment mates to provide support and encouragement, and (3) using a progress chart to provide immediate and frequent feedback as to how the athlete was progressing. The schedule of reinforcement in the skill development program included the coach's praise each time the athlete approximated the desired behaviors, including praise for improvement in shooting or rebounding, not only for performance outcome. Statistics and a progress chart were used to lend credibility to the coach's positive remarks, to help the athlete detect changes in her performance, and to serve as a source of immediate and frequent feedback. In addition, the schedule of offering positive remarks changed as the player's performance improved; the athlete had to be more efficient to receive the praise. Finally, the frequency of offering praise following desirable performance changed from practice to game behaviors, then to the practice session that followed each game. Significant changes in the athlete's performance and weight were noted during the season-long behavior modification program. The use of behavior modification gave the athlete a greater sense of control over the situation, inducing greater incentive to initiate and maintain changes from the status quo toward meeting targeted goals.

Improper and Proper Use of the Behavioristic Approach. The behavioristic approach in coaching can be used inappropriately, however. Two incorrect uses of behaviorism in coaching are *punishment* and *threatening statements*. Threatening statements such as "If you can't do 'such and such,' you'll sit on the bench" are supposed to increase the athlete's motivation and, perhaps, aggression level. In fact, they may—at least for a short time. But often, such statements have the opposite effect. Exposure to threats may result in withdrawal and diminished incentive. As Martin and Hrycaiko (1983) assert, punishment and negative statements may "cause tension and anxiety in the punished individual, which can interfere with desirable athletic performance" (p. 42). In addition, athletes may feel insulted, embarrassed, or angry at the source of this input—usually the coach. Risk-taking and effort may plummet. In the behaviorism literature, this is called *aversive stimulation* to modify a player's behavior.

The reason punishment may work, at least at first, is that threats and other unpleasant events usually cause a sudden increase in the athlete's level of arousal (a physiological response) and motivation (its psychological counterpart) as the athlete attempts to avoid unpleasant future consequences—similar to the fight or flight stress response. Because such techniques appear to result in desirable changes in player behavior, coaches are sold on their value and continue to use them. Of course, threatening someone's life will also result in very rapid behavioral changes. But does this make it an effective, long-term way to motivate people?

The aversive approach to behaviorism has a few potentially serious drawbacks. First, the fact that immediate changes in behavior are evident does not necessarily mean that future behaviors will be affected. Dickinson (1977), Martin and Lumsden (1987), and Rushall and Siedentop (1972) report that punishment (negative reinforcement) has an immediate effect on performance but that its impact fails to carry over to future situations. In fact, many athletes rebel at such treatment and, in response to their frustration, either quit the team or carry on at submaximal effort levels. A second problem is that aversive stimulation reportedly reduces risk-taking behaviors. The athlete is less inclined to attempt skills that do not virtually ensure successful outcomes. This is not desirable because good sport performers are risk takers (Orlick 1990; Vanek & Cratty 1970).

A third problem with punishment as a mechanism to control behavior is that it reduces the coach's ability to give positive reinforcement later on. The coach's effectiveness in positively arousing and motivating athletes is reduced because the team leader is perceived as a source of unpleasant input. Even the coach's nonthreatening suggestions become less credible (Dickinson 1977).

The behavioristic approach is based on (1) tangible performance-based achievement, (2) successful participation followed by reinforcement, and (3) responsibility for one's own actions. According to Anshel (1978), Dickinson (1977), Martin and Lumsden (1987), and Rushall and Siedentop (1972), the proper use of behaviorism in coaching entails using the following guidelines:

- Create a situation in which players are achieving desirable outcomes from their own efforts. Have athletes compete against individuals or teams of similar caliber, particularly in practice.

- Remain aware of the performances of all team members—starters and substitutes alike—especially in practice sessions. Successes should be reinforced through recognition, praise, and an occasional (intermittent) tangible reward—a reward that players find meaningful and desirable.

- Behavioral objectives of player performance should be (1) attainable yet challenging, (2) based on past experiences and performance outcomes, (3) realistic, (4) meaningful to the participant, (5) positively stated (what the athletes *should do* rather than what they shouldn't do), (6) both short term and long term, and (7) set jointly by coach and athlete. If disagreement about the goal exists between the coach and athlete and it can't be negotiated, the best course often is to let the player's goal be met first to optimize future motivation (if it is not detrimental to the team's success). Objectives should also be alterable. They're not written in stone. If the goal proves to be too easy or too difficult, it should be changed.

- The coach and team should agree on rules and regulations before the season starts to strengthen contingencies. For example, if the players understand that curfew is at a certain time and that breaking curfew will result in a particular unpleasant outcome, the contingency of maintaining this policy will be stronger. Players will be more responsible in supporting it.

The behaviorist coach may appear manipulative, but he or she can also be bright, insightful, goal-directed, and sincere. It's one thing to regulate the behavior of athletes both on and off the field or court based on a predetermined selection of rewards and punishments. But it's a feather in the coach's cap to be able to (1) understand the needs of each player or the team as a whole and (2) make sincere attempts to assist each person to meet his or her needs. Setting up environmental reinforcers that occur in a natural setting or situation is a complex procedure that entails planning and insight. Is it worth it? Authors Dickinson (1977), Martin and Lumsden (1987), Martin and Hrycaiko (1983), and Rushall and Siedentop (1972) contend that it can make the difference between the team's success and failure. This style has the added benefit of eliminating the authoritative, power-laden approach to directing the behaviors of athletes who rightfully feel that they deserve their coach's respect as human beings as well as sport participants. A sense of respect and sensitivity to the player's needs is the focus of the next leadership style, humanism.

The Humanist

The essential difference between authoritarianism or behaviorism and humanism is expressed by the contrast between viewing the athletes as a group and viewing the team as a group comprised of individuals who play a given sport. According to Sage (1980),

"The goal of school sports . . . for the humanist is the production of increasing unique-ness and independence, and this cannot be achieved in an autocratic atmosphere in which the team is built around an omniscient authority figure where all decisions are made by the coach while players are relegated to passive followers of orders" (p. 224). Humanism explains behavior in terms of the relationship between the individual and the environment. It implies the leader's desire to understand the athlete's emotional and psychological make-up and how these factors affect the player's sport performance. The thrust of this style is to treat each player in the way that the coach feels the player would like to be (and needs to be) treated (i.e., with respect, sensitivity, and fairness). Accord-ing to Sage, "The humanistic coach starts with the basic premise that the sport is for the players, not the coaches."

Mike Davis, Indiana University head basketball coach, had to teach his players to be more independent. According to a column by George Vecsey in the *New York Times* (March 24, 2002, Sec. 8, p. 3), "the leftover (Indiana) players had to remember they could be tough, resourceful, and improvisational without fearing the rages of Bob Knight. They had to be psychologically liberated. Davis did it by listening and sometimes even doing what they wanted. For example, if the players wanted to go right home after a game instead of going to a planned team event, Davis requested that they ask his per-mission." This is an example of humanistic coaching.

Mechikoff and Kozar (1983) describe the frequent use of humanistic strategies by former Western Illinois University head cross-country and track coach Dick Abbot:

> He was very concerned about his athletes as students and citizens as well as athletes. He tried to communicate with his athletes not just on the track but between classes, visiting them at the residence, etc. . . . He sought the help of other athletes in giving psychologi-cal and emotional help and guidance to the athlete. . . . One of the most important tech-niques he had . . . was his attempt to listen to athletes and allow them opportunities to vent their feelings . . . He feels the simple process of having someone care and providing them the opportunity to vent their concerns perhaps reduced some feelings of anxiety and tension and thus allowed them to perform well (p. 81).

The humanistic coach cares about meeting the competitor's needs as well as achiev-ing the outcome. In fact, the former should benefit the latter. Caring about the athlete's feelings and attempting to establish warm, trusting relationships with players should result in heightened loyalty, physical effort, and self-esteem. Smith et al. (1979) found that children who played for highly reinforcing and encouraging coaches had signifi-cantly higher levels of postseason self-esteem than did those who were exposed to coaches who did not behave in this manner.

Humanism may also be extended to coaching assistants. Head coaches have an obligation to solicit the input of assistants when making many team-related decisions. The sharing of authority and decision making gives assistant coaches a sense of mean-ingfulness and responsibility on the team. This aspect of humanism is referred to as the *participative approach*. In this way, the head coach uses the capabilities of each assistant and maintains "the congruence between [team] goals and the assistant's personal aspi-rations" (Magnotta 1986, p. 18). Thus, an important objective of humanistic coaching is to disprove a statement from the late baseball manager Leo Durocher that "nice guys finish last."

In summary, the characteristics of humanistic coaching include the following. The humanist:

- communicates in a sincere, honest manner with team members
- acknowledges, understands, and responds to individual differences among players
- is aware of the nature of relationships and interactions among the players and between player and coach (i.e., the group dynamics)
- shows a sincere interest in meeting the players' personal needs as team members (e.g., being successful, learning new skills, establishing meaningful relationships with teammates, and maturing as people) in addition to the ultimate objective of winning

In addition to these behavioral traits, the humanist is approachable. Players can confide in a humanistic coach and disclose their feelings to him or her. No question from a player is regarded as "stupid." The humanist understands that inquiries from athletes are desirable; they show interest and curiosity. Because this coach invests in the growth and learning of his or her players, typical responses from performers such as making mistakes, not remembering information, asking questions, and even having trouble making friends on the team are dealt with in a constructive and positive manner.

Humanism is the "fundamental concern for the human person . . . having a measure of autonomy, choice, and self-determination" (Sage 1980, p. 219). Humanistic coaches try to allow players the freedom to experiment, to take risks, to make decisions, and to learn from their decisions. The objective is personal growth.

Another aspect of enhancing personal growth in humanistic coaching is encouraging athletes to think at a higher level, to develop a sense of sophistication, maturity, and intelligence. For example, athletes tend to form closely knit peer groups that demand conformity to certain rules. Team members who do not conform are isolated rather than respected for their individuality, especially in the preadolescent and adolescent age groups. The humanistic coach, observing team members isolating or even scapegoating another teammate, would bring the parties together and help to resolve the conflict for the good of the team. More important, players would be encouraged to discuss their feelings about the pressures to conform to peer expectations. The coach would elaborate on the importance of accepting others, especially teammates who have the same goal of helping the team win. The coach can help competitors take an honest look at themselves—at their strengths, weaknesses, and aspirations, and what to do about them.

It is fair to say that many coaches and noncoaches have little patience for the humanistic style. To these individuals, effective coaching entails a "tough guy" approach: don't give the players an inch, or they'll take advantage of you. Perhaps. But if done right, the proper use of humanistic strategies can add significantly to the quality of team member satisfaction and performance. Consider these advantages of humanism in sport leadership:

1. *The athlete's internal (intrinsic) motivation improves.* The desire to play and improve comes from within, from personal gratification and feelings of competence and self-direction.

2. *The players' concentration and attention improve.* The humanistic coach helps players to resolve personal issues so that they can focus totally and clearly on performance-related tasks.

3. *Players experience personal growth.* Some coaches might not feel that furthering the athlete's personal development should be a concern. But hold on. Don't coaches (the same ones who want to win) also want to work with mature athletes? Don't coaches prefer athletes who will pursue many activities on their own without being told what to do? The humanistic coach can help develop each player's ability to deal with the more stressful aspects of competitive sport. Clearly, then, personal growth does transfer to the sport arena.

4. *Development of coach loyalty.* Let me discuss this issue with a tidbit about the late, successful (U.S.) football coach Woody Hayes. Hayes received considerable media coverage for his assertive behavior toward players. What is less well-known is the degree to which his athletes felt admiration and loyalty toward him. Why? Because he invested in each player's personal growth as well as in their athletic development. Hayes used to have long discussions with athletes, even sometimes in the stadium shower facility, about issues totally unrelated to football. He was very knowledgeable about contemporary U.S. history and politics, and often engaged in discussions with the athletes on such topics. He was also concerned about school grades and about their adjustment to life on the Ohio State University campus. The players believed in this man because they were correctly convinced that he believed in them. They wanted to win for Woody. Coach Hayes often followed an authoritarian coaching style on the field, but he was more of a humanist off the field than many would have thought.

5. *Leader charisma.* The term *charisma* is difficult to define and even more difficult to describe. Mitchell (1979) described the charismatic leader as one who is confident, dominant, and purposeful. He or she articulates goals and builds an image that fosters devotion and unquestioning support by followers. These qualities are also reflected in a humanistic leadership style.

Despite all of the positive outcomes attributed to humanistic coaching, this style of leadership still has its disadvantages. What, you might ask, can possibly be wrong with being sensitive to the feelings of players and wanting each performer to feel fulfilled as a sport participant? Not much, in fact. But no system is perfect. Here's why.

1. *It's not for elite performers.* Humanistic leadership might be incompatible with the requirements of advanced athletic competition. Chelladurai and Arnott (1985) found that when the coach is perceived by male and female collegiate basketball players as having the necessary information to make the best decision or when the type of decision to be made was based on a complex issue, the athletes preferred an autocratic leadership style. Relatively little time is available for meeting the personal (and often complex) needs of individual elite athletes.

2. *Outcome is not a priority.* The coach who practices humanism tends not to be consumed with achievement and winning, which seems incompatible with the nature and objectives of competitive sport. Concern for personal feelings and emotional problems will not, by itself, lead to successful game outcomes. Sage (1980), in reflecting the humanist philosophy in sport, asserts that "using victory as the only end, the goal of sport competition, is too limiting, confining, shallow, and short-sighted for humanism. . . . The end in sport is the joy, exhilaration, and self-fulfillment that one obtains from movement" (p. 226). For coaches who view the final score as the most important outcome of sport competition, the humanistic approach offers relatively little gratification.

3. *No success may lead to dropping out.* If meeting the personal needs of each athlete is more important to the coach than winning (an example is making sure that all players on the team play in every game, regardless of the score), and as a result the team tends to be unsuccessful, players might lose interest and quit the team. After all, everyone wants to win, especially at higher skill levels. Therefore, although being sensitive to individual needs is a part of winning, coaches should seek a balance between meeting individual needs and ensuring the positive reinforcement that comes with team success.

Here are a few coaching suggestions for using a humanistic leadership style:

- *Interact with the athlete in a warm, trusting manner.* This doesn't mean that less pleasant emotions should never be expected to enter the relationship, because after all, the parties are human. But mutual trust, respect, and sincerity result in mutual admiration.

- *Respect individual differences.* Effective coaches do not treat all players in the same way. They understand that some athletes are more sensitive and need more patience than others. Athletes also differ in the manner in which they prefer to prepare mentally for a game.

- *Engage in off-season interaction.* Humanistic coaches care about their players' welfare year round, not just during the season. Issues such as school grades, physical conditioning, and perhaps the player's social or family life might need input or reinforcement from the coach. The key here is a genuine concern for the total individual, a person who's more than just a sport competitor.

- *Take an active part in practice.* It's very common for coaches to "bark" their commands from a designated point and rarely become actively involved in the practice or conditioning program. Henderson (1971) suggests that, at least in the early part of the season, the coach should take an active part in practice. He or she might put on workout clothing and lift weights or run a few laps with the team. A closer identification with the performers results.

- *Promote mass participation.* Coaches and players alike want to win. To do so often means playing the team's best athletes. But it's clearly a mistake to ignore substitutes. To raise team morale, the humanist attempts to have as many team members as possible participating in the game. In fact, substitutes should be given tasks in practice as a technique to help them to feel more closely responsible for the team's game preparation and performance—and to improve their own skills if possible.

The Democrat

Any team with elected captains is exercising a democratic (also called delegative) leadership style. Holding team and individual player discussions prior to making rules that will affect the participants also employs a democratic philosophy. Is this an effective way to govern? It is, according to Litwin and Stringer (1968), who found that when group members desire participation in decision making, their performance and group member satisfaction is affected either positively or negatively, depending on whether this need is met. But whereas the authoritarian leader is efficient and decisive, the democrat is sometimes viewed as slow, inefficient, and confused. Slow because allowing a group of individuals to make decisions or policies takes time and patience. Inefficient because groups can make decisions that are counterproductive and not well thought out, decisions that meet short-term needs at the expense of long-term benefits. And confused because a coach who does not act decisively is not viewed by the players as "in control" or knowledgeable, which can cause player anxiety. Nevertheless, this leadership style can be inconspicuously effective.

The democratic leader need not leave all decision making to the team. Decisions may have to be made quickly and without input from players and assistants (for example, in the rapid deployment of game strategy). Chelladurai and Haggerty (1978) argue that in solving complex problems in sport the coach is more likely to make the best decision for the group. In fact, under certain circumstances, the players actually prefer that the coach make the decision, deferring to his or her apparent knowledge and past experience.

Chelladurai and Arnott (1985) examined when the democratic approach is most and least preferred by athletes, using a sample of 77 female and 67 male collegiate basketball players. They compared four styles of decision making: (1) autocratic (coach makes the decision alone), (2) consultative (coach makes the decision after soliciting input from players), (3) participative (coach and athletes jointly make the decision), and (4) delegative (coach asks one or more players to make the decision). The researchers then identified four factors that affect the choice of a decision style in a group context: (1) quality requirement, e.g., selecting players at certain positions, (2) information, e.g., coach knows weaknesses of opposition and decides on strategy based on this knowledge, (3) problem complexity, e.g., selecting plays to be used in competition, and (4) group integration, e.g., the cohesiveness of the group (it is better to involve a cohesive unit in decision making than a group with low interpersonal relations).

The study's results indicated that females were more oriented toward participatory decision making than males. The delegative style was uniformly rejected by all athletes, and the autocratic and consultive styles were substantially endorsed by both sexes. Members were prepared to sacrifice their influence in favor of the coach rather than in favor of teammates. Delegation to a few athletes was interpreted as unfair preferential treatment by other team members. The optimal situation for preferring an autocratic coaching style was when an important high-quality resolution was required and when the coach was perceived as being knowledgeable (i.e., when he or she had the information to make the best decision). However, for simple problems (e.g., what color to paint the locker room or whether to swing at a certain pitch), the athletes preferred to have more input. Finally, the athletes did not view group integration as an important factor in decision making, although groups that were highly cohesive felt more strongly about participating in decisions.

Examples of democratic strategies in coaching include allowing participants to nominate and elect team captains, members of the league's all-star team, and recipients of other individual player awards, or make decisions about certain team policies, which the coach is prepared to support. For example, whether the players can bring a partner to the team party might be a negotiable item, but whether team members should be allowed to smoke may not be negotiable.

The following are several advantages to using a democratic leadership style.

1. *It is nonthreatening to athletes.* The coach who follows a democratic style is typically more approachable and a better communicator to players than coaches who follow other styles. The reason is simply that democratic leaders are good listeners; they

respect the views—even the criticisms—of subordinates, and they offer advice only when it is either solicited or absolutely necessary. Consequently, this type of coach is perceived by players as being nonthreatening.

2. *Individual initiative.* Players feel that they have some control, either directly or indirectly, in the team's operation. Consequently, they are more apt to volunteer ideas, to demonstrate independence (presumably for the good of the team, although this is not always the case), and to feel less dependent on the coach in stressful situations. Athletes often cope with stress more successfully when they feel in control of a situation.

3. *Promotion of mature behavior.* All coaches desire maturity and personal growth in their players. By giving the players a role in decisions, the democratic approach helps to ensure that players take responsibility for performance outcomes. Few participants will abuse a coach's respect, which he or she shows by delegating decision-making powers.

4. *Greater flexibility and risk-taking.* When players are in the midst of game competition, sometimes they need to know that it's OK to take a chance. A batter can bunt if the third baseperson is playing deep, or a player can pass instead of taking the shot. Players adapt more quickly to new and different situations if the coach's style says, "Go ahead, take a chance—but also take responsibility for the outcome." Players should not be overprogrammed to perform in a certain manner because the obstacles that lie ahead can change.

Disadvantages of the democratic approach to leadership include the following:

1. *The sham democracy.* When is a democratic approach to governing a group not a democracy? When the group leader does not live up to his or her end of the bargain. Let's take voting as an example. Just because the team votes on a decision does not mean the process is democratic. The vote outcome must be supported and carried out by the leader. Even authoritarian leaders may use voting to support certain decisions. How democratic is it if the coach does not approve of the players' choice for team captain and appoints a different choice?

   Another factor that defeats the democratic style is intimidation. Using voting for team captain as an example again, what if the coach were to list all of the qualifications for team captain, thereby effectively eliminating 80 to 90 percent of the team? This is not a true democratic process. If the coach were to say, "This is what I believe" just prior to a team-related decision, the players will not feel comfortable in deciding against the coach's expectations or wishes.

2. *Watching others suffer.* Adherence to strong democratic principles demands a philosophy of noninterference. Interference might impede the progress of the group toward its goals. Thus, a democratic coach must have the ability to stand by and watch a degree of human failure and suffering without imposing on the situation. Democratic leaders must not be more loyal to one individual than to the group. For instance, a player or assistant with a violent temper might have to be rewarded or favorably recognized because of contributions in helping the team despite unpleasant personality traits. Examples include players who produce outstanding results, yet do not relate well to teammates or athletes who tend to argue with game officials. The democratic leader must consider decisions in light of their ramifications for the greatest number of team members.

3. *Slow decision making.* It's highly doubtful that a coach would call for a team vote with only seconds available to make a decision about game strategy while the game is in progress. For the most part, making decisions on a group basis is certainly slower than other leadership approaches. Thus, the coach should be careful that when a group decision is warranted, sufficient time is granted for this process.

Applying Different Coaching Styles in Sport

A considerable number of choices of coaching styles are evident. However, no single approach results in optimal success all the time. Situations dictate various ways of working with group members.

A number of criteria should be considered before a coach determines his or her fundamental leadership style:

- *The coach's personality.* Nothing is less effective than a team leader who tries to be someone he or she is not, or has a personality that is incompatible with the sport he or she is coaching. For instance, Claxton and Lacy (1986) compared the behaviors of 10 (U.S.) football and 5 tennis coaches, all of whom were "successful winners." They found that football coaches were more intense, directive, instructional, and critical than tennis coaches. No doubt the coaches' personalities and the sport type both contributed to these unique actions. In the final analysis, the coach's personality must be compatible with the sport and the situation, and the coach must be comfortable with himself or herself.

- *The athletes' characteristics.* Younger athletes need more direction, yet they are not favorably responsive to authoritative mannerisms. They are playing because it's fun, and the level of seriousness about competition for children must reflect this need. Hostile coaches need not apply. Older, higher skilled players (remember, age and skill level are not always equal) are more amenable to a firm, direct, task-oriented approach. Because of their superior skills, they are more susceptible to boredom and burnout. Innovation and creativity are important strategies here. As indicated earlier, Chelladurai and his colleagues found that elite athletes are more concerned with information and coaching knowledge than with establishing personal relationships. Younger, less skilled performers need more emotional support. When deciding on an appropriate coaching style, coaches should consider the athlete's particular emotional needs.

- *The situation.* Many events during the contest require firm leadership in which control, information, and guidance is required. The coach makes the final decision in most sport situations. During practice, perhaps when reviewing alternative strategies, or during breaks in the game, players can have more input. In addition, responding to an athlete's injury certainly requires a different leadership style than at other times. Good leaders adapt to situational requirements.

What We Don't Know about Sport Leadership

Although much research needs to be completed in the area of effective sport leadership, two very important questions must be answered: First, to what extent does the coach really influence player behavior? Coaches are using many different leadership styles currently in the sport world—many successfully. Does the use of any one style tend to benefit the players' performance more than another coaching style? Second, does the athlete's feeling of team member satisfaction have anything to do with his or her performance? In other words, does it really matter if an athlete relates positively (or for that matter, interacts at all) with his or her teammates? More research is needed to find answers to these questions.

Despite the frequent assumption that "good" coaches win and "poor" coaches lose, researchers have yet to support the existence of a coaching profile or "recipe" that will have a marked influence on the athlete's performance. The styles of coaches differ significantly. Lanning (1979) notes the "striking differences in the programs and personalities of coaches; but they all developed highly successful programs. . . . Each of [these very effective] coaches put together successful programs with certain *types* of athletes" (p. 265). Lanning's point is that perhaps the compatibility between the coach's and the athlete's personalities is what underlies effective leadership and quality sport performance rather than only the behaviors and techniques of the coach. All of the styles mentioned in this chapter have resulted in performance success at one time or another. But despite the descriptions, prescriptions, suggestions, and warnings about the "dos and don'ts" of certain coaching practices, researchers still aren't certain whether a coach's style really matters, as long as the performance-related areas of leadership—teaching skills and using game strategies effectively—are conducted correctly. In fact, there is mounting evidence that effective coaching behaviors that improve athletic performance may not be effective actions for increasing athletes' satisfaction and personal/psychological growth (Horn 1992).

For example, Horn concluded from her literature review that coaches who tend to prioritize positive interactions and feelings among team members or between the coach and players often do not have teams with high winning percentages. Put in more scientific terms, "Leadership behavior identified as social support was positively linked to satisfaction but negatively linked to win-loss records" (p. 195). Perhaps, then, of more value to the athletes' and the team's success is not so much that the coach and athlete like each other, but that the coach is an effective educator about sports skills and team strategies (Martin & Hrycaiko 1983). Athletes are learners; coaches are teachers. Effective coaches communicate team and player strategies that are clear, relatively simple to follow, repeated in practice under game conditions, and based on the team's strengths and the opponent's weaknesses.

Perhaps effective coaching is a function of the "right" person coaching the "right" athletes in the "right" situation. This means that team leaders (1) choose to coach sports that are compatible with their personality and past experience, (2) work with athletes who can respond effectively to the coach's style, and (3) use an approach to leadership that is most effective for the situation. As Kimiecik and Gould (1987) concluded from their interview with the highly successful former Indiana University swim coach, "Doc" Counsilman, coaches must "individualize their treatment of athletes" (p. 355). Mitchell (1979) concluded, based on his extensive review of the leadership literature, that "successful leadership is contingent upon a variety of factors and what we must determine is the best match between leaders and the situation" (p. 265).

The Workaholic Coach

Coaches in sport occasionally exhibit behavioral characteristics of work addiction, or workaholism. They fit the profile of the workaholic, as depicted in a book called *Chained to the Desk*, by Dr. Bryan Robinson (1998), a professor at the University of North Carolina (Charlotte). Workaholism, a term commonly used interchangeably with work addiction, is formally defined as "obsessive-compulsive disorder that manifests itself through self-imposed demands, an inability to regulate work habits, and an overindulgence in work to the exclusion of most other life activities" (Robinson 1998, p. 7). It is characterized as the absence of a work/life balance. The individual indulges in work-related tasks, either at the location of his or her work environment or at home, at the expense of doing things outside of work, such as pursuing recreational activities or hobbies, or interacting with family and friends. Other unpleasant side effects of workaholism include high levels of negative mood states, such as frustration, anxiety, defensiveness, anger, and impatience. Personal dispositions associated with work addiction include perfectionism (both normal and neurotic), fear of failure, trait anxiety, compulsiveness, low self-esteem, and depression.

I first became interested in work addiction while consulting with corporate clients, men and women who were very successful and skilled in their professional career, intellectually gifted, and extraordinarily committed to and self-motivated about their work. They had a very high need to achieve, yet rarely took the time to acknowledge their achievements. Sadly, there was no shortage of problems associated with their lifestyle. The most common example was a poor work/life balance, in which work virtually consumed their week. There was time for little else in their life. Despite disclosing strong family values, they tended to virtually ignore or give minimal attention to them. And their health suffered. These work addicts rarely exercised and exhibited poor nutritional habits, including consuming too much alcohol, caffeine, and fat food. Not surprisingly, many were overweight. Sadly, despite earning a high income, many of these individuals were not terribly happy in their work.

At the 2002 convention of the American Psychological Association, I presented a paper on interview data I had obtained from coaches in West Texas (Anshel 2002). The purpose of this qualitative study was to examine evidence of workaholism among male high school coaches in five sports (basketball, baseball, football, track and field, and soccer), to detect common psychological characteristics and behavioral tendencies, and to identify job characteristics and early life experiences that might contribute to this condition. Participants consisted of 28 male coaches, employed full time as physical education teachers and coaches from an independent high school system in the southwest U.S. Participants completed a sport version of the Work Addiction Risk Test (WART; Robinson 1998), a 25-item self-report, Likert-type inventory that measures a person's risk of work addiction via responses ranging from 1 (*never true*) to 4 (*always true*). Scores in the upper third (67–100), middle third (57–66), and lower third (25–56) are considered highly, mildly, and not workaholic, respectively. To determine the characteristics that were unique to high-level workaholics, a structured interview, with content analysis, was conducted. Since hours at work consisted of both teaching and coaching during the day (and some evenings), the total number of hours on all work-related tasks was used as one criterion for workaholism. Results revealed that high-scoring workaholics worked an average of 70.4 hours per week on coach-related tasks, whereas nonworkaholics averaged 40.2. Categories of responses were physical signs, behavioral signs away from the sport venue, behavioral signs at the sport venue, and mental and emotional signs.

Antecedents of workaholism were categorized as childhood experiences (e.g., parental expectations, criticism from others, and sibling rivalry, among others), history in sport (e.g., degree of experience as an athlete, successful vs. not successful, satisfying vs. not satisfying), and other personal characteristics (e.g., self-esteem, confidence, perfectionism, anxiety). High scorers for workaholism, in contrast to low scorers, were characterized as highly perfectionist, particularly reflecting signs of neurotic perfectionism, experienced frequent criticism from parents, had indicators of low self-esteem, low confidence, high anxiety, previous success as athletes in their youth, very high expectations of their high school athletes, a high degree of self-control, high importance that their team win, lack of acknowledgment of success and competence, a high degree of self-criticism, less time with family, and a short attention span. An unexpected finding was that feelings about the importance of family and job, attitude toward religion, and expectations of spouse about job demands did not separate levels of workaholism. None of the participants had ever attempted nor experienced counseling to reduce their workaholic tendencies. In fact, rather than perceiving their habits as related to workaholism, the coaches used euphemisms such as "total commitment to my job," "I do what it takes to win," and "high achiever" to describe the extensive number of hours devoted to their coaching. Apparently, behaviors associated with work addiction among sports coaches, at least in this study, are the norm, even expected.

Whereas work addiction is ubiquitous in the organizational and management psychology literature in reference to business and industry, it has apparently—and surprisingly—been ignored in sport psychology. Coaches are well-known for working well beyond anyone's definition of a "normal" week for work, and it is clear that many coaches, especially at the elite (college and professional) levels, are genuine workaholics. I want to briefly address this neglected area, because it is a negative habit that is very unhealthy with respect to maintaining physical health, mental health, work/life balance, and, of course, family relationships. One frequent outcome is burnout.

Simply working long hours, however, does not define workaholic habits. Instead, the workaholic ignores family and uses work as a means to escape intimacy or social relationships. Work provides the person with comfort and escape—an emotional sanctuary—while distancing the person from meaningful, close relationships. Work-related tasks fulfill self-esteem and the needs to feel competent and achieve. As Robinson (1998) explains, while healthy workers think about and enjoy whatever they are engaged in at the present moment, workaholics think about working a disproportionate amount of time, even during social activities or leisure times, when their minds wander and obsess about work. The workaholic behavior patterns in the corporate sector and the work habits of many coaches in elite-level sport are startlingly similar.

Robinson (1998) lists ten signs of work addiction. Work addicts:

1. Are usually rushed for time and "hyper busy," often multitasking (i.e., conducting two or three tasks at once).
2. Have trouble delegating, primarily because they have a need for control. Spontaneity and flexibility are forfeited.

3. Are perfectionists. They judge others harshly due to the "superhuman" standards they have of others, which reflects their high critical and judgmental nature about themselves: "It's never good enough; I can always do more."

4. Minimize the importance of relationships with others. Family rituals and celebrations are often ignored, forgotten, or simply unimportant because they interfere with work. The work addict assumes that family members "will understand."

5. Have a need to overachieve. They create personal deadlines and might require nonstop work patterns rather than spreading out tasks over a reasonable period of time.

6. Are restless and lack fun in their lives. Workaholics feel guilty and useless when they do anything that does not produce results.

7. Are impatient and irritable. Time is their most precious commodity; therefore, the work addict feels a "time famine." There is never enough time to meet self-imposed deadlines. Waiting in lines, for example, is sheer agony. Their fuse is short.

8. Judge themselves based on their last achievement. Very quickly after completing one task, they go on to the next one, taking hardly any time to reflect on deserved satisfaction and pride from their most recent accomplishment. Their self-worth is obtained only through successful performance outcomes, hence the strong emphasis on productivity with concrete results.

9. Experience memory loss of long conversations. They are so consumed with work that they tune out current situations and immediate information. Forgetting is not the problem; the information they were given was never processed and stored.

10. Have little time for self-care. Looking after their work rather than after themselves is a daily priority. Physical needs such as sleep, exercise, and nutrition are ignored or compromised. Self-destructive behaviors follow, such as smoking, missing meals or eating fast (high-fat) food, failing to monitor their health, caffeine abuse, and chronic fatigue.

Robinson (1998) makes numerous recommendations to combat work addiction, all of which have implications for coaches (and, for that matter, for athletes who overtrain and exhibit characteristics similar to those described above). Robinson, a licensed psychotherapist, clearly indicates that work addiction requires counseling. The antecedents and sources of this condition go back into the person's history, and are rarely changeable through self-help books and casual conversations. In my own private practice with corporate and sport clients, it was apparent that parental messages in one's childhood served as the primary source of work addiction, along with the dispositions listed earlier. Most therapies include two components: (1) cognitive therapy, in which the person works through the sources and antecedents of work addiction, and (2) a psycho-behavioral intervention, consisting of planned thoughts and actions that the client is required to perform, both related and not related to work. Although cognitive therapy goes beyond the scope of this section, Robinson (1998) offers the following suggestions.

Work-Related Tasks. (1) Do not let work dominate your life: Schedule time for fun, recreation, and family. (2) Delegate tasks to others, perhaps as part of a mentoring and supervision schedule, in which colleagues or subordinates are taught proper skills. (3) Learn the art of prioritizing your workload. Not everything has to be done *today*. Finally,

(4) take charge of your technology. Do not succumb to the trap of constant e-mails, beepers, and other forms of communication that literally consume the workday—and beyond, if you let it—without achieving desired results.

Mental Strategies. Work addiction reflects a person's thoughts and beliefs. According to Robinson: (1) Change how you think of yourself. Define your competencies beyond work-related achievements. (2) Learn to identify your feelings and to accept the fact that your frustrations and other unpleasant emotions may be based on flawed thinking. Acknowledge your lack of life satisfaction, happiness, and poor health, and the costs— mental and physical—of your current work habits. (3) Give yourself pep talks. Be aware of your achievements and feel proud of them. Then walk away and reward yourself with "time off" to have some fun and recover so that you have more energy to get back to work at the appropriate time. (4) Please yourself instead of pleasing others. You may have an inner voice telling you that "I can do more," or "It's not good enough, keep going." (5) Learn to accept your human limitations without feeling flawed. Often, you are more productive when you rest and recover from a challenging work schedule. (6) Recognize that less is more! (7) Work smarter, not longer.

Leadership Style: A Final Word

Effective leadership in sport is not learned exclusively in the classroom. Relatively few coaches ever take a school course in coaching and even fewer are familiar with the professional literature in sport psychology. Coaches learn their trade through participating in sport, first as athletes and then as coaching assistants. Many coaches have informed me that their techniques and strategies, even their leadership styles and personalities, are derived from models from their pasts—coaches they have known or observed. "If it worked for me, I guess it'll work for my athletes" is the common response. "If that coach (or school) is successful with this approach, why shouldn't I be?" is another frequent thought.

How receptive are coaches to recommendations based on sport psychology literature? In one investigation, while working as a team consultant, I studied the receptivity to sport psychology consulting of one collegiate football coach over three years (Anshel 1989a). Suggestions, both written and verbal, were based mainly on the professional literature (48 percent) and the feelings of the players (41 percent). I found that only 14 percent (27 of 165) of the suggestions were used. Of these, 22 suggestions were implemented in practice, not in the game. The coach's reasons for not using the recommendations were mainly that they were incongruent with the practices of other teams (48 percent) or that the coach lacked time to implement the suggestions (36 percent). Thus, regardless of the players' feelings or performance achievements, coaches tend to follow a traditional, somewhat conservative, path to leadership style. Many have remained obstinate in refusing to think about different, perhaps better, ways to do the job. There are many exceptions, of course. Most coaches invest in and actually learn from critical feedback, just as one invests in their training and education. These sport leaders are the real winners.

SUMMARY

Effective leadership in sport is a function of performing a variety of roles and in various styles to meet the needs of athletes and to reach team objectives. Coaches are leaders, followers, teachers, role models, limit setters, counselors, friends, and parent substitutes for their athletes. (They also have responsibilities as members of their own families.) These roles are conducted at different times and in various degrees with each team member. Leadership styles differ as a function of the sport situation, the nature of the coach-athlete relationship, and the preferences of the athletes. Sometimes the players desire a more dominant, authoritarian style, especially in task-oriented rather than relationship-oriented situations. Humanistic coaching, on the other hand, holds that positive sport experiences and the feelings of the athletes are priorities. Behavioristic approaches do not ignore the athletes' feelings; instead, they use environmental situations and selective reinforcement to guide the feelings and behaviors of the players. Finally, democratic leadership consists of a more laissez-faire approach in which athletes are able to make many team-related and some contest-related decisions. Although athletes often take greater responsibility for their actions when they make their own decisions, this approach is usually slower and less efficient than the other styles. The players may sense confusion or a lack of leadership on the team.

It would seem that a combination of these four leadership styles would provide the most effective means of working with athletes. For example, there are times when autocratic leadership is needed. Coaches need to make rapid decisions and dictate team policies and strategies. At other times, team members should be allowed to make decisions, or at least have input into the decision-making process—the democratic approach—especially when the decision is based on their own experiences and expertise, and if time allows for consensus building. In other situations, dealing with the athlete's feelings and well-being is needed. Examples include helping a competitor overcome pain or injury; dealing with a change in the player's team status, such as going from starter to substitute; and working through personal concerns and worries—a humanistic leadership style. If the coach wants to provide the athlete with a situation that will present an opportunity to exhibit his or her skills, or to facilitate a player's interaction with other team members, then a behavioral leadership style may be needed. In this way, effective leadership consists more of a dynamic and interrelated process among the different styles rather than of separate, discrete elements and strategies for coaching.

Workaholism, also called work addiction, is a common characteristic in the sports coaching profession. Typical manifestations include the inability to regulate work habits and an overindulgence in work-related tasks to the exclusion of most other life activities. There is an absence of work/life balance. Because family members are often ignored, marital strife and divorce are not uncommon. Causes of work addiction are psychological (e.g., low self-esteem and confidence, high work-related anxiety, perfectionism). Workaholics work far more hours per day and per week than is necessary to exhibit high quality performance. The roots of this condition go back to childhood. Professional counseling is usually needed to address and overcome this condition.

REVIEW QUESTIONS

1. Describe the various roles that a coach assumes and provide an example of each role.

2. Describe two ways in which each of the leadership theories described in this chapter are *similar* and two ways in which they *differ.*

3. You are the coach. Select a sport and apply one of the theories that explains effective sport leadership in two different situations prior to or during the contest.

4. Describe five differences between "successful" and "effective" coaches. As a coach, in what ways would you follow an "effective" coaching style?

5. Four leadership styles were discussed in this chapter. Provide an example of how a coach would implement each style.

6. Describe two advantages and two disadvantages of each of the four leadership styles.

7. What coaching style or styles would you employ as a leader of child athletes between the ages of 9 and 10 years? How might your style or styles differ if you were coaching relatively older (high school or college) athletes?

8. Power is inherent in coaching. The respective positions of coach and athlete dictate certain roles and expectations. Therefore, a coach can choose to make demands on athletes or to use authoritative means to influence behaviors. In this chapter, such an approach, if it is the only leadership style applied, is judged to be particularly unsophisticated and ineffective in the long run. Describe the potential disadvantages of exercising the power of the coach's position as the sole means of controlling the team and the individual players.

9. One coaching style not covered in this chapter was laissez-faire, a style characterized by a deliberate abstention from direction or interference. The leader allows group members to function almost independently of the leader's influence unless his or her input is solicited. This is quite rare in sport. However, certain circumstances might warrant such an approach. Given what you've read about the other leadership styles, in what ways and under what conditions could a laissez-faire approach be practiced in coaching?

10. Describe features of work addiction (workaholism). Where does it come from (its antecedents)? Describe five mental or behavioral strategies a person can use to combat, or prevent, work addiction.

CHAPTER 9

Communication and Counseling Techniques

Many fine coaches are geniuses at planning strategy, teaching techniques in performance, and knowing the details of their sport. But how effective and successful can such coaches be unless they can communicate their knowledge effectively? How important is communication in coaching? This brief story makes the point nicely:

A high-class sophisticate was crossing the river on a small boat. The sophisticate asked the uneducated boatman, "Tell me, sir, have you ever attended live theater?"

"No," said the boatman, "can't say that I have."

"You've lost one-third of your life," answered the high-class person. "Tell me," the sophisticate said again, "have you ever seen a ballet?"

"Can't say that I have," said the boatman.

"You have lost two-thirds of your life," said the high-class passenger. At that moment, the boat hit a large rock and started to sink.

"Tell me," the boatman said to the sophisticate, "can you swim?"

"No," said the passenger.

"Looks like you've just lost your *whole* life," said the boatman.

The point of this story is that unless a coach first masters the basic skills of communication—in this story, it was swimming—all of his or her knowledge about a sport will not be translated into improved athlete performance. No matter how brilliant a coach might be in planning strategy and knowing the technical aspects of his or her game, success depends on the coach's ability to communicate effectively with the athletes. Communication may be the essential skill without which the coach's efforts are doomed. Very little has been written in the sport literature about effective communication and counseling techniques. It is little wonder that coaches develop their style of addressing athletes through modeling—imitating the mannerisms and styles of their own coaches from the past.

The purposes of this chapter are (1) to offer guidelines about effective communication—the art and science of helping athletes feel good about themselves, raising the performer's self-image, effectively teaching sport skills, and gaining the athletes' respect and loyalty, since it doesn't happen automatically, and (2) to describe skills to engage with athletes at a deeper, more meaningful level, a technique called counseling. The techniques must be learned and used "naturally," or else the coach's statements will appear to be contrived and insincere. A coach cannot sound honest when his or her actions and words appear programmed and "stiff." We will review some of the most common situations in which communication becomes an integral part of coaching—and athlete—responsibilities. The examples we will review illustrate the need for dialogue in developing an effective communication style.

The Need for Dialogue

Consider all of the people with whom coaches must interact if they are to be successful: players, assistant coaches, coaches from other teams, parents of the athletes, referees, teachers of the athletes, the media, and the coach's own supervisor or employer.

Players. Communication with players can be both verbal and nonverbal. Teaching and practicing sport skills, presenting rules and team policies, interpreting strategies, disciplining the athletes, and using nonverbal techniques such as smiling, patting players on the back, and just noticing player performance are all examples of positive communication with athletes (Figure 9.1).

Assistant Coaches.   Soliciting information from assistants about the performance of various players on the team, as well as on opposing teams, developing game strategy, receiving feedback from assistants about the head coach's own performance, offering input to assistant coaches about their performances, and engaging in informal verbal exchanges in a social context off the field or court all require effective communication.

Other Coaches. Coaches on both sides of the court or field talk to one another about scheduling, defining rules for game play, exchanging team films, working out schedules,

Figure 9.1 High-quality coaching consists of clear, open dialogue with ahtletes.

attending seminars, and exchanging information on techniques and strategies. The coach who cannot communicate effectively will not be approached and will receive little more than a casual response from his or her peers.

Parents. Coaches are accountable only to their supervisors—legally, that is. But if the coach wants to gain the loyalty of the athletes and, in many instances, keep the athletes playing on the team, then communication with parents is both inevitable and a good idea. Speaking with a player's parents can be enjoyable. To know some background on each player is helpful, and this information is most easily attained by interacting with the parents. However, parental involvement can also be challenging to the coach. Explanations as to why the athlete is not playing or starting and other issues about his or her participation can test the patience of many coaches. The ability to deal constructively with the concerns of parents is important.

Referees. Constructive dialogue with the arbiter is both necessary and desirable. Coaches are models to their athletes and are responsible for conducting themselves in a manner that demonstrates maturity and logic. Contrary to the view of many coaches, evidence suggests that it is not an effective strategy to argue with the game official in order to excite and motivate the team. In fact, continued harassment of the official often fosters feelings of helplessness in the athletes. Their attitude becomes "if the referee is against us, why bother even trying?"

Teachers. For sports competitors who participate through their educational institution, eligibility to play depends on maintaining academic standards. It is imperative, even often required, that coaches interact with the athlete's teachers or professors to monitor the athlete's academic progress, and to respond quickly to concerns about his or her academic performance. Coaches who ignore this aspect of their job are acting irresponsibly and risk losing their player to academic eligibility. The ethical coach understands that the athlete's education is a priority, and helps the athlete feel responsible for, and commit to, life-long goals.

The Media. Newspapers, television, and radio form the link between the fans and players. Proper communication with the media is crucial because athletes are very sensitive about how they are perceived by others. Players typically read and hear about their coach's remarks concerning members of the team. Derogatory statements by the coach are usually demotivating and embarrassing to athletes, whereas complimentary remarks improve self-confidence and effort. Many elite sport organizations offer the following advice to their athletes about effective communication with the media.

1. *Don't be baited.* Remain calm at all times and be sure you are quoted accurately. Don't allow others to misinterpret your feelings or misstate the facts.
2. *Don't use jargon.* Use words that the general public can understand. It builds fan support and improves game attendance.
3. *Don't forget: you're always on.* If you can see a microphone, camera, or reporter's notebook, assume that your words and actions are being recorded.

4. *Be precise*. Avoid generalities. Use specific examples that clarify and make people care about your view.

5. *20-second rule*. Make your point in 20 seconds or less. Elaborate if there is time, interest, or need.

6. *Be yourself*. Don't appear stiff and uncomfortable. Relax and share your enjoyment in the sport. Be "human."

Supervisor.   Coaches can lose their jobs if they cannot get along with "the boss." Similarly, players can be cut from the team or benched due to a poor relationship with the coach. The use of correct communication techniques can help to eliminate any friction that may develop in these relationships. Some very fine coaches and athletes have lost their jobs or team status, respectively, because the two parties could not talk out or negotiate their differences. The proper use of verbal and nonverbal communication may prevent, eliminate, or at least minimize potential problems among team participants.

It is clear that effective communication is a necessary part of quality coaching. Based on my observations of coaches and discussions with athletes as a sport psychology consultant and researcher over the years, I have formulated a set of "dos and don'ts" in this area—what I call the 10 commandments of effective communication in sport (Anshel 1987b). The use of these guidelines on the style and content of communication with athletes separates the talented and skilled leader of a sports team from the less capable, inarticulate leader.

The Ten Commandments of Effective Communication in Sport

Effective communication consists essentially of 10 guidelines. These recommendations are so important in the process of affecting the athletes' attitudes, feelings, and behaviors that I refer to them as "commandments," or "must do" practices for effective communication. They are: (1) Thou shalt be honest, (2) Thou shalt not be defensive, (3) Thou shalt be consistent, (4) Thou shalt be empathetic, (5) Thou shalt not be sarcastic, (6) Thou shalt praise and criticize behavior, not personality, (7) Thou shalt respect the integrity of others, (8) Thou shalt use positive nonverbal cues, (9) Thou shalt teach skills, and (10) Thou shalt interact consistently with all team members.

I. Thou Shalt Be Honest

If coaches are to be effective, they must have credibility. They must be believed; otherwise, how can coaches do their jobs? Dishonesty destroys credibility. This commandment goes against the old adage "Never say never." The coach should never be dishonest. Sometimes dishonesty is used purposefully to make an athlete feel better (e.g., "Don't worry about the error; it wasn't your fault."). Being untruthful may also occur by accident. For example, a coach may make a promise that later cannot be kept due to a game situation or is simply forgotten. But in any case, the athlete often perceives this inconsistency as deceitful. Here are a few examples that actually happened. The names have been changed.

Example 1: Dishonesty ruins credibility

Bill was the starting first baseman on his high school baseball team. After he batted fifth and had difficulty hitting the ball, the coach moved him into the ninth batting position. The coach, trying to justify this decision, told Bill that he wanted his power at the end of the line-up. Bill knew differently. No one had to tell him that he was having trouble batting. Instead of telling Bill that the fifth batter in a line-up must hit the ball more consistently, the coach lied. The coach could have told Bill that together they would try to work out of the slump and that he was moving Bill down the order to take some pressure off. Bill had trouble believing the coach after that and, in fact, grew increasingly frustrated with his own lack of success. He hit a disappointing .191 that year and almost quit the team.

Example 2: A promise that was not kept

Frank, a punter on the college football team, injured his arm in a freak accident unrelated to sport. He lost the punting job to a first-year player. Into the fourth game of the year, the new punter was beginning to kick less and less consistently, which at times hurt the team's performance. In the meantime, Frank's arm was mending fast, but the coach decided to stick with the new punter. Finally, during practice after some poor punting in the fifth game, the coach told Frank, "If Joe kicks one more punt poorly, you're going in to do the kicking." Frank was excited and looking forward to his opportunity. Indeed, the new punter kicked the first one off the side of his foot, and it landed a very short distance away. The coach, caught up in the excitement of the game and carrying out his usual array of responsibilities, forgot about the promise. In this instance, a promise was made that was not kept. Frank was so heartbroken that he quit the team after the game in a very sad and angry confrontation with his coach. The team lost an athlete with potential to be among the best (as his statistics the previous year had indicated).

Example 3: The model

Susan was not starting on her volleyball team. She attended all practices and felt good about her progress. The coach was, in fact, providing very positive feedback to her on her fine play in practice. After the fourth game of the season, she went to the coach and said she felt like quitting because she never got a chance to play during games. "Even Jan gets to play ahead of me, Coach, and all the players know I'm better than she is," she complained. The coach responded, "Susan, I can understand your frustration. You've made tremendous improvements in your play, particularly on your passing. You have every right to feel frustrated, as I might be if I were in your shoes. I just want you to know that I'm really proud of the way you've been playing in practice and how you have supported the other players. I will do my best to give you a chance to play. Let's work together to help you become the best volleyball player you can be. I know you can help us win. Hang in there. I'm on your side."

Notice that the coach avoided referring to any other players. Instead, the coach reflected Susan's feelings of frustration and anger. The coach also was realistic in projecting the future. No promises were made about playing—promises that may have satisfied the athlete for the moment but would have led to an emotional disaster if they were not kept. The coach's honesty focused on realistic expectations for the immediate future—practicing, learning, and improving. The coach was not condescending (Susan's feelings were taken seriously), sarcastic ("If you were half as good with your hands as you are with your mouth, you'd be an all-star"), sexist ("Oh, my poor baby is sad"), or dishonest ("As soon as Jan makes a mistake, you're going in"). The coach was not defensive. Instead, the coach was compassionate, honest, and sensitive to the athlete's feelings.

Of course, honesty can be taken too far. Do coaches want to tell athletes what they really think at *all* times? Absolutely not! Imagine this conversation with an athlete whom the coach evaluates as having little chance of starting.

Athlete: Hey, coach, when do you think I'll get a chance to start?

Coach: Well, to be perfectly honest with you, Frank, I think you're about as good as you are going to get. I doubt you'll ever be as good as Ed. He just plays better than you do. So, if I were you, I'd forget about starting and just be happy to fill in when we need you.

Why is this form of communication destructive? When can honesty be taken too far? It is because the coach has an obligation to teach skills to athletes and to see to it that the participation of every athlete is as fulfilling as possible. The coach's role is not to predict an athlete's future level of performance, especially if the forecast is a pessimistic one.

Coaches are not prophets. They should avoid predicting any athlete's future or potential in sport because it is difficult to know to what degree an athlete will develop, grow, and improve. No one can predict the future about the athlete's growth and development. If all signs lead to the conclusion that this sport participant will never break into the starting line-up, never make it to a college team, to the pros, or to any higher level of play, coaches should not feel obligated to break the news. Voltaire said, "Truth is a fruit which should not be plucked until it is ripe." Honesty is necessary if the coach is to be credible (i.e., believable) and if he or she wishes to gain the athlete's loyalty. However, honesty is also a matter of timing and tact.

In my experience as a sport psychology consultant, I have never seen an athlete feel so distrustful, disloyal, and unmotivated as in response to a coach who has proven to be dishonest. Successful coaches can be honest without stepping on someone's toes or ego. One strategy is to be honest and verbalize thoughts for the purpose of making the listener feel better or improving performance. A second coaching technique is to avoid statements, even honest ones, that will hurt someone's feelings or will produce a sense of hopelessness (e.g., "I'd forget about starting if I were you"). In the words of the French philosopher Marquis, "Honesty is a good thing, but it is not profitable to its possessor unless it is kept under control."

II. Thou Shalt Not Be Defensive

Perhaps another way to word this commandment is "Thou shalt be a good listener" or "Thou shalt be receptive to the opinions of others." They all say the same thing. The literature, consisting mostly of research and opinion papers in sport psychology, counseling psychology, and management (coaches manage people), is filled with the notion that successful coaches and administrators have one thing in common: They are open to new ideas and receptive to feedback on their own performance. They are not defensive about who the expert is, being the know-it-all, or about who is "in control." The components of this commandment include (1) being open to the ideas and opinions of others—players, parents, assistants, and (naturally) supervisors, (2) engaging in active listening during discussions with other parties, and (3) soliciting the opinions of players and other coaches—getting assistance from your assistants.

Be Open to the Ideas and Opinions of Others. As an unpaid sport psychology consultant to a U.S. college football team for three seasons, I agreed to observe the behaviors of coaches and players during practice and at games, and then to submit written weekly reports on my observations. Included in these reports were recommendations on new and different strategies that coaches might want to use in teaching sport skills and in mental game preparation. I decided to collect data on the tendency of the coach to implement or to ignore the recommendations and his reasons for not using them (Anshel 1989a). The purpose of this case study, conducted over three years, was to see whether a college football coach would be generally receptive to the application of sport psychology research. Just to be sure that my suggestions were realistic and valid, I asked a high school football coach from another team and a physical education teacher who coaches high school football to review the suggestions. They thought that 192 of the 196 suggestions were justified. These suggestions, I might emphasize, were made at the invitation of the head coach.

The results indicated that of the 192 "valid" suggestions, 14 percent (27) were used and 86 percent (165) were ignored. Further, 22 of the 27 recommendations that were used were implemented during practice rather than before, during, or after a game, despite the fact that 64 percent (124) of the 192 recommendations were based on game-related observations. These results might be interpreted to mean that the coach was not very receptive to new and different approaches and, instead, conducted his job in the way he felt most comfortable: based on the coaches he learned from and techniques used in the past. Reasons for not using the advice related to the head coach's comparisons with other teams ("Winning teams don't do it that way"), a lack of time ("We don't have enough time to do what you are recommending"), not agreeing with the players' feelings ("The players here don't know what it takes to win"), and other reasons.

What do the results of this study say about being defensive? This coach chose to use poorly defensible excuses instead of innovative techniques that might have improved the morale and loyalty of the athletes. Essentially, he ignored the needs of the players because many of the suggestions were based on their input. The result was a team low in morale, loyalty, and success. Although not necessarily due to ignoring the suggestions, this team did not have a winning record for any of the three seasons it was studied. Sadly, this coach was fired after his third season.

Aside from attending to input from sport psychologists, even more important is for the coach to be receptive to the opinions and suggestions of assistants. This source is, perhaps, more knowledgeable about team personnel and strategies than anyone else. The inclusion of their opinions in the decision-making process will lead to greater collegial support and accountability for the outcome from those decisions. Coaching doesn't have to be "lonely at the top." The head coach does make the final decisions, but the use of all available resources to gather information before the decision is made will result in a more intelligent choice that assistants will support. Essentially, when leaders (coaches) are not defensive, they become active listeners.

Be an Active Listener.   Probably the best way to avoid appearing defensive and to succeed at appearing to be receptive to the feelings or attitudes of others is to listen to what others have to say before you answer. When a coach listens actively to a player, parent, referee, or an assistant, he or she shows sensitivity toward them. Sometimes, just sitting back and allowing the person to vent feelings is enough to solve part of, even the whole, problem. The failure to respond or to show attentiveness toward another's feelings is called *passive listening*. It doesn't work. *Active listening*, on the other hand, consists of being "concerned about the content, the intent, and the feelings of the message" (Rosenfeld & Wilder 1990, p. 3). Active listening occurs when someone engages in a dialogue with another person in response to what the person is saying and feeling. See guidelines on active listening later in this chapter.

Get Assistance from Assistants.   Coaches cannot win games by themselves. They need assistance from their assistants. Coaches who choose to "go it alone" or claim to have "all the answers" place themselves apart from the rest of the team. They do not receive the support of team members. Worse, others do not feel accountable for the team's success or failure because there is little sense of contribution. Still worse, some assistants and players want to see a coach who "knows it all" fail and may perform below par to see that it happens.

Doesn't a coach need to receive input from the people who are closest to the competition—the athletes themselves? Doesn't he or she need information from assistants who can offer insight into a player's physical or mental condition? Such information can help explain the reasons behind certain performance outcomes. Coaches should be interested in hearing the method a colleague would use in approaching the game, given his or her knowledge about the opponent or the team's mental state.

An important role for assistant coaches is to initiate and maintain close personal ties with the athletes. Mechikoff and Kozar (1983) found through interviews with successful coaches (i.e., coaches who had winning records) that successful coaches encourage their assistant coaches "to promote and nurture close personal ties with the players while (the head coach) cooperates in a critical objective manner during practice and games" (p. 10).

III. Thou Shalt Be Consistent

Fred was having a pleasant conversation with his tennis coach in the coach's office about the use of certain strategies against his next opponent. The conversation ended as the coach told Fred to see him anytime he had any questions or concerns related to tennis or anything else. Fred felt great, having a sense of closeness and trust toward his coach. Then two days later after practice, Fred asked the coach to look at a few of his serves with which he was having some difficulty that day. To Fred's utter shock, his coach retorted, "After the practice you had today, young man, you need to work on much more than your serve." Fred was devastated. Where was the coach whom he had visited in the office just two days earlier?

The confidence and security that athletes feel toward their coach can be destroyed by inconsistency. If athletes do not know how their coach will respond to an issue, most often they will choose to ignore the coach altogether. An important objective of coaches who are truly interested in fostering communication is to be consistent in the manner in which they come across. If coaches invite their athletes to visit them in their office yet close the door on them (literally or attitudinally) when they arrive, coaches are giving mixed messages. Perhaps the coach was being insincere to invite the athlete to visit in the first place. This tendency affects a coach's credibility. An inconsistent person might go out of his or her way to say "hello" to someone on Monday, then choose to ignore the same person on Tuesday. Such a person would be viewed as rather insecure, and most persons would prefer not to risk having a negative encounter with someone they could not trust. This is one possible reason why some athletes tend to ignore rather than communicate with their coaches.

Here are a few guidelines for showing consistency in coaching (remember, you can't coach effectively without it).

1. Avoid letting an opportunity pass to say a kind and encouraging word to or about someone. Praise good athletic performance. Even acknowledging the quality performance of opponents after (but not during) the game will confirm your admiration and respect for sport excellence.

2. Always recognize the greetings of others. Saying "Hi" with a smile or wave will help establish your reputation as a good, considerate person—and it costs nothing. Avoid being nice and friendly one day, then being stern, uncommunicative, and inconsiderate toward others the next. If your mood swings are extreme, people will avoid you like the plague.

3. If you have an open-door policy for your athletes and assistants (and you should, of course), show that you are sincere about it. Gil visited his coach during the office hours that were designated for athletes. Upon Gil's arrival, the coach looked up from his notepad with a look of annoyance and said, "Yeah, what can I do for you, son?" Gil was turned off immediately. "Sorry to bother you, Coach," he said. "See you later at practice. Bye!" Gil never felt comfortable about visiting his coach again. Naturally, a coach may excuse himself or herself if the time to talk to an athlete is truly not convenient. But the coach should tell the athlete that not meeting with him or her is due to an issue unrelated to the coach's interest in the individual. Restate your sincerity about having an open-door policy. Make an appointment to meet with the athlete again, soon.

4. Try to show the same compassion on the field as you do in the locker room or office. Yes, anger is a very natural, human response. But don't ask an athlete to play psychiatrist and try to figure out when and how to approach you and how to handle possible negative responses. No one is suggesting that coaches should not raise their voices or that they should never display irritation and frustration. However, such feelings can be both controlled and communicated nondestructively.

5. What about discipline? Here too, be consistent. If the team's policy is no smoking, and the punishment for smoking has been clearly communicated to the players, the coach must follow through with the punishment when players are found smoking. Again, what credibility can a coach maintain if rules and the results of breaking those rules are not carried out? Should the coach allow exceptions to a rule? In many situations, yes. Coaches must take on the role of judge and jury. Sometimes a verdict of "not guilty" or a warning is appropriate when the athlete has a legitimate reason to break a rule. It's a subjective call, and nothing short of common sense (as opposed to blind discipline) will succeed.

The bottom line on being consistent with one's behavior is really a function of respecting the feelings of others. Treat others as you would like to be treated, which leads us to the fourth commandment.

IV. Thou Shalt Be Empathetic

How many times have you heard the phrase, "How would *you* feel if . . . ?" Well, how do you think it feels to be ignored, lied to, rejected, blamed, teased, ridiculed, and injured? Inversely, how does it feel to be recognized, praised, accepted, depended upon, popular, and smiled at? The answers are obvious aren't they? Yet what do people, especially in roles or situations of power, commonly do to others? Exactly what we wouldn't want done to ourselves. Some individuals are not capable of putting themselves in the shoes of another. Such persons do not recognize that they can get so much more out of athletes who feel that they are important and that they contribute to the welfare of the team than from participants who feel worthless, unskilled, or neglected. The ability to both understand and respond to the feelings of others is a characteristic that will pay the coach many dividends. Sadly, this personality trait, called empathy, is often missing from the repertoire of techniques and strategies used by some team leaders.

Sharing and thinking about other people's feelings begins in childhood but does not come naturally to children, according to Seifert and Hoffnung (1994), child psychologists. They need to learn these traits from their parents. Children imitate the kind, joyful, loving manner of their parents. In homes in which such parental behavior is absent or scant, no learning of these types of responses occurs. Children who haven't learned by age 10 to share, to play by the rules, or to put themselves in another person's shoes usually are very troubled and not very well accepted by their peers, the authors assert, based on their review of this literature. Many adults do not know what it feels like to be on the receiving end of many of their comments, and, consequently, they make statements that hurt, offend, and even may destroy the aspirations and feelings of others.

Effective coaches remember how they felt when their feelings were hurt as athletes. The secure team leader says, "I don't want these athletes to be hurt and suffer the way I did as an athlete." Ineffective (insecure) coaches say, "If it was good enough for me, it's good enough for them." Was it really "good enough" then? Could it ever feel good to be emotionally distraught? We often get caught between celebrating our survival of tragic events from the past and thinking, often inaccurately, that such events actually allowed us to learn, to grow, and to become emotionally stable. The empathetic coach follows four guidelines: (1) do not attack the athlete's character, (2) be sensitive to the feelings of others, (3) do not allow peers or teammates to become verbally destructive toward one another, and (4) never embarrass anyone—athletes, assistant coaches, officials—in public. Public humiliation destroys trust, respect, and communication effectiveness. The key objective is loyalty to the coach and team. Empathy makes good sense, and one of the best ways to show it is to follow the next commandment.

V. Thou Shalt Not Be Sarcastic

A coach who has an acid tongue does not win. Why not? According to psychologist Haim Ginott in his book *Teacher and Child* (1972), adults who use sarcastic remarks erect a sound barrier to effective communication with children and athletes. "Sarcasm . . . destroys their self-confidence and self-esteem. Bitter irony and biting sarcasm only reinforce the traits they (coaches, teachers, and parents) attack" (p. 55). An athlete who is physically fatigued should not be called "lazy." A participant who asks a question about the team strategy must never be labeled "brainless."

As a team consultant, I overheard the following example of sarcasm. Coach Fred was observing his team run through several trials of a new play in football. He turned to his left and saw the team punter talking with a female student. "Hey, Lance," he yelled, "if you want to fool around with the ladies, do it on your own time. Pay attention to what we're doing on the field. Maybe you'll learn something." Lance was embarrassed, of course. Several players and other observers were also embarrassed for him. The coach, in the meantime, lost the respect of this athlete and diminished any chance of establishing a communication link for the future.

Here is another example of the destructive effects of sarcasm in coaching. Fran was running wind sprints with her softball teammates. Suddenly, she felt a sharp pain in her side and could not continue. "What's wrong, Fran, you out of shape?" the coach bellowed. "Too many pizzas, huh?" This sarcastic response from the coach angered the athlete because she was in pain and was not trying to remove herself from the drill. Fran, in fact, was in very good condition. Further, Fran perceived from the coach's remarks that her discomfort was not being taken seriously. "Perhaps she was faking," the coach might be thinking. In any case, sarcasm diminishes the chance for mutual respect and constructive dialogue between athlete and coach.

Have you ever heard someone make any of the following remarks? What do they have in common?

"Can't you even hold on to the ball?"

"Nice catch, Butterfingers."

"That was the wrong play, Joe. How did you ever make it through school?"

"You run as if you have cement in your shoes. Come on, move!"

Each of these sarcastic remarks has a common result. They destroy self-confidence and eliminate any existing respect between the speaker and the target of the statement. How can an athlete be expected to feel competent, motivated, and loyal to the coach after receiving messages whose contents serve to deflate his or her status as a person, athlete, and teammate? I have concluded, based on hundreds of conversations with athletes of all ages, that one of the biggest mistakes a coach can make, next to communicating the actual insult, is making a sarcastic statement to the player in the presence of other team members. That's a sin in the eyes of an athlete that is almost unforgivable and certainly unforgettable.

Two primary guidelines about the use of sarcasm are helpful. First, coaches, parents, and officials should avoid it at all times even when the intent is humor (called *gallows humor* in Ginott 1965). Such statements are never humorous, whether or not laughter follows the statement. In fact, the targeted person's laughter after a sarcastic statement usually serves as a defense against embarrassment. Laughter in this context is almost never genuine. The speaker of a sarcastic remark may think that he or she is entertaining the "victim" or other listeners, but often just the opposite is true. Respect, admiration, and loyalty toward the sarcastic speaker are never outcomes from such statements. It is true that sarcasm may not be harmful when the relationship between coach and athlete is built on trust. However, most relationships are not, and the self-esteem of most athletes is too fragile for a sarcastic remark to be taken lightly or humorously. While sarcastic remarks among peers is a common, informal way to communicate affection and to build rapport, adult (coach) to child (athlete) sarcasm is rarely taken lightly.

The second guideline is to use statements that convey sincerity. After observing a player fall and scrape her knees on the floor, the coach should simply ask the player if she is all right or initiate first aid procedures. The coach should not laugh and say, "Hey, nice balance," or make some other remark that would embarrass the person. After a coach explains the strategy for the second half, a player may ask the coach to repeat something. The coach should wisely comply, rewording his or her original statements so that the athlete is certain of the strategies. The coach should not say, "What's wrong, Al, can't you listen the first time?" Sincerity says, "I care about you," and it is inherent in effective communication. Sarcasm says, "I don't respect you." Such statements attack the individual's personality, a habit that is detrimental to open communication, as indicated in the sixth commandment.

VI. Thou Shalt Praise and Criticize Behavior, Not Personality

Ginott (1965, 1969) asserts that praising and criticizing character or personality is never constructive. Why? Because it offers the listener no information and, therefore, does not allow him or her to make a realistic judgment about his or her actions. Yet this is often the most common form of feedback that we give athletes.

The Correct Use of Praise. This is, perhaps, one of the most difficult skills to develop because, first, we don't offer praise as often as we should, and second, when we do offer praise, it's usually based on emotions of excitement and happiness, which means that we use statements that are hyperbolic. Examples include, "You're the *best* batter, the *nicest* kid, the *greatest* athlete," and so on.

The coach was very pleased about Bill's defensive skills in a recent basketball game. Certainly praise was in order, but it was not of a personal nature. The coach avoided saying, "Bill, you're wonderful. What a great ballplayer you can be." Instead, he described what Bill had accomplished: "I liked the way you stayed with your man, Bill. You prevented him from scoring at his average. Nice going."

Barbara hit a double in softball, scoring the runner at second base. After the game, the coach said to her, "Solid contact on that double, Barb. It's great that you were able to bring home that runner." The coach avoided: "Super hitting, Barb. I knew you could do it."

There are two types of praise that should be avoided. The first type is called *personally-based praise*. Praising the athlete's character or personality ("you are a great guy/girl," "what a good athlete you are") is vague, abstract, and may not be compatible with the athlete's own, personal view. Such statements may even be perceived by the player as insincere. Praising personality tells sport performers that they are accepted and liked only when they act in accordance with the expectations of others but are not deserving of such recognition when they don't. These expectations may be very difficult for the player to meet. Another reason statements that praise character are best avoided is because they create dependence on the coach for approval. The athlete might conclude, "If the coach says I'm good (or the best), then he (she) likes me." Inversely, if the coach does not give the athlete similar praise on a given day, the competitor might feel differently about the coach—"I guess the coach doesn't like me today." It may never be the coach's intention to use praise as a means of conveying subjective feelings about the athlete (e.g., "I like you because you're a good player"), yet this is often what happens when praise becomes personally based rather than behaviorally based. Personal feelings about an athlete should not be based on the person's sport skills; this disrupts team unity.

The second type of praise that should be avoided is called *judgmental praise*. Telling athletes that they (1) are "the best," (2) played a great game, (3) are better than someone else, or (4) did a "super" job might make an athlete feel good for the moment, but such statements fail to reinforce the *behaviors* that were responsible for the desirable outcomes. Judgmental praise creates anxiety and evokes defensiveness. It does not lead to the athlete's sense of self-reliance, self-direction, or self-control. Applauding the athlete's efforts with superlatives such as "great" or "the best" brings on feelings of discomfort, especially for younger competitors. The athlete gains little understanding about what he or she did to deserve such a comment. Praise of this nature also may be incompatible with the athlete's own self-image or perception of the situation. In this case, the athlete may actually behave or perform differently, in a manner more compatible with a lower self-concept. Ginott (1965) suggests, "Avoid praise that attaches adjectives to [an athlete's] character" (p. 106). He further states that avoiding praise that judges character or evaluates personality allows the person (athlete) to feel more secure in making mistakes and taking risks without fear. This, in turn, raises self-confidence.

The cardinal rules of praising are:

- Describe without evaluating.
- Report, do not judge.
- Let athletes evaluate themselves.

The correct use of praise has been demonstrated in a model by Smith et al. (1977a). Their "sandwich approach" is a model for offering praise while teaching skills and is especially effective when providing instructional feedback after an error. The underlying philosophy of this approach is to ignore the past mistake—or at least not to overemphasize it—and, instead, to focus on future performance.

The Sandwich Approach. This technique is used to offer constructive feedback to athletes in a sensitive, yet effective, manner. It consists of three elements that are verbalized in the proper sequence: (1) a positive statement, (2) future-oriented positive feedback, and (3) a compliment (as illustrated in Figure 9.2).

The positive statement. After an athlete makes an error, he or she typically anticipates a negative remark from the coach. To "survive" the predicted verbal assault, the player will usually avoid listening—will literally tune out the unpleasant message. It's the coach's job in using the sandwich approach to dispel this fear. Otherwise, the information feedback will never be heard. Instead of a negative message, the player needs to acknowledge a positive one. Once he or she is receptive to the opening (positive) statement, the athlete will also be listening to the next, instructional segment. Examples of appropriate positive statements are: "Good try, Gene." "Nice effort, Mary." "That was a tough ball to hit." "Not your fault, Barb." Notice the use of the player's first name. People are always more attentive to the speaker and less threatened when their first name is used. This also shows sensitivity toward the individual.

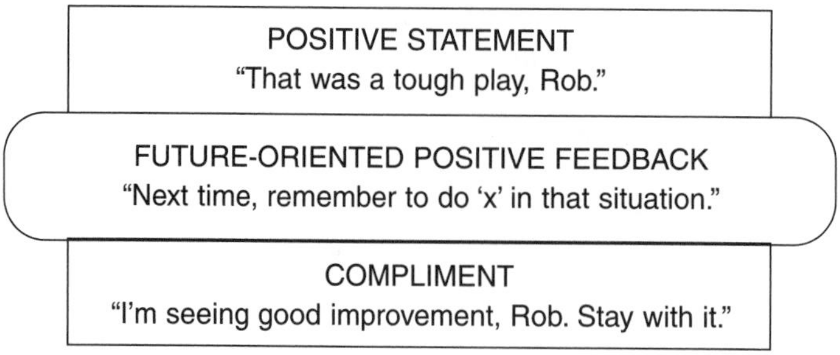

Figure 9.2 Elements of the sandwich approach for constructive feedback in sport.

Future-oriented positive feedback. The athlete should now feel no threat after the opening statement. At this time, the coach instructs the athlete about behaviors or strategies that should be attempted next time. The reason for keeping feedback positive and future-oriented is to avoid having the competitor think about the error (thinking about the mishap actually increases the chance of repeating it). The message should be positive in content. Learners remember positive information better than negative information. Coaches should say, in effect, "Next time, do this." No ridicule, guilt, threats, or anger. Examples include: "Next time the ball goes to your right, cross your left leg over the right leg" or "You'll have a better chance of catching the ball, Tanya, if you visually follow the ball into your hands."

The compliment. This reflects a phenomenon in cognitive psychology called the *recency effect.* It means that the most recent information is better remembered than messages presented before it. In the sandwich approach, it is important that the athlete reflect favorably on his or her interaction with the coach, especially when receiving constructive feedback on performance. To end the interaction on a positive note will (1) improve the retention of the information—we remember positive input better than negative input, (2) result in more trust and loyalty toward the coach and team, (3) reinforce actions that are being performed correctly—athletes need to remember what they are doing well, and (4) help the player to perceive learning skills as far less traumatic than if the coach's emotions got in the way. Examples of compliments include, "I like the way you ran that pass pattern," "Way to keep your eye on the ball," and "You almost got it. Good improvement, Doug."

Now let's put the three components together in a few imaginary examples.

Example 1

Jennifer bobbled a ground ball hit hard to her left. "OK, Jennifer. Good effort. That was a tough one. On those grounders, try to keep your glove down a bit more. I liked the way you kept your eye on the ball. Stay with it."

Example 2

Steve made an inaccurate pass in basketball. "Almost, Steve. Next time, pass closer to the basket. When your man is guarding you close, use a bounce pass. You gave it a good try. Stick with it."

Three additional suggestions about the sandwich approach are in order. First, do not say "but" before the future-oriented positive statement. "Nice try, Bob, *but* next time do 'this'" tells the athlete that the positive statement was insincere. It's like saying, "I really like you, Bob, but . . . ," which is another way of saying, "The truth is, I really *don't* like you, Bob."

The second recommendation is that statements to athletes must be honest. Insincerity is easy to spot. If the athlete really made a poor judgment in executing a task, then a stronger form of feedback might be in order. It's better to say nothing than to say something without meaning it.

The third recommendation is in response to many coaches who tell me that the sandwich approach is more applicable in practice than during the contest. I respectfully disagree—and so do the authors Smith et al. (1977). This technique should be a habit that is used consistently in most situations. In fact, the contest presents additional pressure for athletes. Making an error is more anxiety-provoking, embarrassing, and stressful than at any other time. What better opportunity to present information in a relatively calm, factual manner so that the athlete learns and adapts to new demands than during the contest? Coaches—indeed, all teachers—should practice this technique alone until it sounds natural.

Constructive Criticism. Sadly, most of us who criticize others do so for sinister reasons—usually to hurt the other person. We develop our vocabulary and our habits in offering critical remarks based on the models in our lives. We hear our parents, coaches, teachers, and friends criticize us and one another, and we, in turn, use similar messages in the way we criticize others. But rather than offer feedback, too often the goal is to hurt the feelings of another person, and we succeed in this goal frequently.

In coaching, criticism is often used to give feedback on performance or to express anger or frustration. It isn't that criticism is so bad in itself but, rather, that the manner in which it is communicated can have negative ramifications. Most critical remarks bring on anger, resentment, and a desire for revenge. When an athlete is criticized, particularly if the criticism is constant, he or she learns to condemn himself or herself and to find fault with others. The athlete becomes suspicious of others and trust dissipates. Ironically, the last thing an athlete needs is to have his or her character chastised; success in sport requires self-confidence. Consider the following incident.

Janice, a high school volleyball player, hit a spike stroke out of bounds, resulting in victory for the other team. The outraged coach reacted, "What the hell did you do that for, Janice? What a dumb mistake. If you can't hit the ball where you're supposed to, get off the court." The player's feelings were terribly hurt. This form of criticism condemned Janice's attempt to risk an offensive shot that could (and often does) score a point. In the future, she may well concentrate on merely returning the ball in bounds with a weaker, less risky shot. But winners are risk takers. Chronic criticism reduces risk-taking behaviors in sport.

As indicated earlier, the problem lies not so much in criticism, but, rather, in its content. The main function of *constructive criticism* is to indicate what must be done in the situation (Smith 1993). Helpful criticism never addresses itself to the player's personality. Remarks are aimed toward the conditions in the environment—what has to be done—while not attacking the person. There is a right way to criticize.

One technique for offering criticism in a nonthreatening manner is Miller's (1982) three-step sequence. The objective of Miller's approach is to express appropriate thoughts and feelings without injuring the athletes' self-esteem, that is, without demeaning others. The three steps include (1) describing the situation, (2) explaining how it affects the team, and (3) telling the other person what you think should be done. For example, if an athlete fails to perform a predetermined strategy, which results in a lost point or an error, the coach might say, "Your assignment was to do 'such and such.' When you follow your assignment, the other team can't move against us. I'd appreciate it if you would learn your assignment and follow the strategy correctly in this situation at all times."

Using Miller's model, statements are made without accusation. The situation is described without evaluation. Emotions such as anger and guilt do not get in the way. The message is received by the athlete clearly, and future tasks and expectations of the coach are identified. This type of approach to communication between coach and athlete brings about the trust and loyalty that coaches need from their players to be effective team leaders. Let's review what psychologists call the cardinal rule of constructive criticism: Talk to the situation, not to the person's (athlete's) character or personality.

Example 1

Melissa arrived 10 minutes late for the warm-up segment of practice. The coach said, "Melissa, all members of the team need to be here on time for the warm-up. If it's impossible, speak to me earlier in the day and tell me you will be late." The coach did not ridicule, engage in name-calling, or offend the athlete. The coach also did not ask the athlete her reason for being late. This conscious psychological ploy was designed to communicate to the participant the necessity of warming up. No damage was done.

Example 2

The coach, speaking to his starting forward in basketball, remarked, "Conrad, I want you to run the play we just practiced." The player looked down for a second, trying to remember whether he should pass to player "x" or player "y." He hesitantly asked the coach. The coach responded, "Your pass on this play should be thrown to the person closest to the free throw line." Conrad was relieved that the coach did not explode. No name-calling, no temper tantrum, and no guilt-ridden statements were used to undermine the athlete's intelligence and self-concept (e.g., "You should know better than to ask me that question"). The coach simply responded with the requested information.

What if the player forgot a play that was used in an earlier game and one that he should have remembered? The coach might want to offer constructive criticism after practice in this manner: "Conrad, I'm happy to answer your question about the play, but don't forget that you must remember the plays. Try to take some additional time to study them, and if you have any questions or want to review the plays before practice, let's do so. On this play, you are the leader of the offense out there." The coach communicated his feelings by dealing with the situation without attacking the player's character. No statements were made that said, "You're stupid."

Speaking of the word *stupid,* some words are so damaging to the listener that perhaps they should be deleted from vocabularies of all human language. Words such as *stupid, dumb, fool, idiot,* and *jerk* serve one purpose—to hurt the feelings and lower the self-image of others. They are terms that say nothing about the inappropriate behavior of the person but instead focus on degrading the individual's character and personality. They never serve the purpose of offering information. As Ginott (1969) suggests in his book *Between Parent and Teenager,* "When a person is drowning, it is not a good time to teach him to swim, or to ask him questions, or to criticize his performance. It is time for help." Criticizing personality is like performing surgery: The results always hurt, and at times they can be fatal.

In summary, the advice on criticism is:

- Don't attack personality attributes.
- Don't criticize character traits.
- Attend to the situation that faces you. Decide "Where do we go from here?"

VII. Thou Shalt Respect the Integrity of Others

The eighteenth-century German philosopher Johann Friedrich Herbart once said, "He that respects not is not respected." To be an effective communicator, the coach must show respect when interacting with the players. Respect entails an awareness of the athlete as a unique and distinct individual. This means respecting the athlete's feelings, opinions, privacy, and individual differences derived from both environmental and genetic sources. Dishonesty, pontification, sarcasm, and a lack of communication are examples of disrespectful ways of relating to others. If the coach communicates to the players with the same respect that he or she expects from them, loyalty toward the team leader and effort in performance should be optimal. Some of the feelings that are almost inherent in coaching include anger, frustration, and disappointment. An effective coach learns how to express those feelings without losing respect for the athlete.

Expressing Anger. Anger is a fact of life. Like the common cold, anger is a recurrent state that rarely feels good. Anger is used to "release" strong emotional feelings and tension, and this venting of feelings might relax the person. But usually, our response to anger is guilt, an upset stomach, or a headache. Of course, many coaches use anger as a technique to arouse, motivate, or condemn. Does it work? It may. The important point is that, as in giving praise and criticism, there is a right way and a wrong way to use and express anger.

It has been said that if people speak when they're angry, they will make the best speech they'll ever regret. Typically, anger is based on irrational statements and behaviors. A temper is lost; so is a little sanity. Coaches have been known to say and do things without thinking of the consequences, like anyone else. The angry coach will insult, "hit below the belt," fly into a rampage, swear, and perhaps (albeit very rarely) physically strike at the source of his or her irritation.

The good news about anger in coaching is that anger does have its time and place. In fact, failure to express anger at certain times during practice or a game would convey to the athlete indifference, not approval and reinforcement. Coaches who care about the athletes and about team success cannot altogether shun anger. This does not mean that sport competitors can withstand a deluge of violence and hostility. It only means that the athlete should expect the wrath of the coach that says, "There are limits to my tolerance toward the level of your play."

It is crucial to remember that the medication must not be worse than the disease. For example, many coaches believe that getting angry, particularly at an umpire or referee, has an emotional effect on the team that may have its time and place. But this inspirational technique is not a panacea to arouse the team. Anger should be used as an honest means of communicating feelings based on actual performance. In one example of using anger effectively, a coach was meeting with his basketball team at half-time. His team was not using the defensive patterns that they had practiced during the week. He was genuinely angry that the athletes seemed to forget what they had spent hours practicing in preparation for the game. The coach told them, in no uncertain terms, the following in this order:

1. The specific performances that he had observed so that the athletes were made aware of the same situations and events as the coach.
2. What he had observed during the first half of play that was contrary to what they had practiced.
3. His feelings of anger and frustration about the incongruence between what the team must do on defense to win and what it had been doing in the first half.
4. What the team had practiced in preparation for this game and how these plays related strongly to the necessary strategy during the game.
5. What the team had to do to counter the opponent's offense—sometimes position by position.

The coach did two things that made his half-time talk effective. First, his anger (which, by the way, was justified) was directed at specific behaviors of the athletes. He engaged in no name-calling and no hollering just for effect. Sometimes a coach will try to communicate feelings of sorrow and disappointment to make the athletes feel guilty, which the coach hopes will result in subsequent superior performance. Sometimes this approach works. A second problem with the "guilt approach" is that its effect, if it works, is short term. It does not breed self-confidence and team loyalty. Players may become quickly psyched up, but participants who are more concerned with not hurting the coach's feelings than with performing for personal satisfaction are quickly demotivated after the contest. Essentially, they are saying, "There, coach, I did it for you. Are you happy now?"

The second effective strategy used by the coach occurred after his expressions of anger. He told the athletes of his confidence in their ability to perform according to the plans. "I know you men can do it because I saw you do it beautifully this week in practice," he hollered. The players felt more confident leaving the locker room. His anger was expressed before he offered instruction and was not the last message he verbalized before the team left the locker room. Had the coach's message ended on a down note—that the players were doing a terrible job and had no business being out on the court or winning the game—the team would have been undermotivated, less confident, and more forgetful of the instruction.

Guidelines for the constructive use of anger are as follows:

- It's fine for the coach to express angry feelings provided the athlete's character and personality are not attacked. Sarcasm, name-calling, use of destructive adjectives, and physical abuse are never appropriate.

- The first step in handling emotional upheaval is to identify feelings verbally by name. "I am annoyed with you. I am very, very upset. I'm furious." Sometimes the mere statement of feelings changes behavior, according to Ginott (1965). Most athletes fully realize the rationale behind the coach's angry emotions.
- The next step, not always necessary, is to give the reason for one's anger by stating inner thoughts and wishful actions.

This takes some practice and control, but the following are a few true examples of the constructive use of anger. Also see the box following the examples for constructive ways of dealing with an angry person.

Example 1

A high school basketball team was making the same mistakes repeatedly during practice. It was obvious to the coach that her players were not concentrating, not motivated. After several more minutes of some less-than-inspirational play, the coach threw up her hands and said,

> *I've had it. You women are obviously not in the mood to play basketball. I can't stand what I'm seeing. Several of you are out of position. Jane, you're not guarding your opponent. Barb, you are simply not hustling. Elaine, if you knew where you were supposed to be on the play we just ran, you didn't show it. I'm extremely upset at your performance out there. I want to see "this" happen. I want to see "that" happen. I wish that you women had shown me that you wanted to practice today because that's the only way we can win. I just can't take your lack of concentration any longer. I'm leaving.*

And sure enough, the coach stalked out of the gym, leaving the stunned players feeling sorry that they had played so halfheartedly. The coach had a right to be upset. The players were very upset about their coach leaving practice. The team played magnificently during the rest of the week. Now that's player loyalty! The coach's refusal to attack the character of any athlete made a big difference in how her message was received. The players felt no bitterness toward the coach in this example, only remorse.

Example 2

The tennis coach noticed that a player on his team was using the wrong stroke on a few returns to his opponent during practice and said,

> *Leo, I am becoming very frustrated in trying to be a good coach. When you continue to use a lob instead of a drive when your opponent is playing deep, I feel like taking you off the court. I wish I could get you to realize that you have the ability to win if you use the right strokes and that your drive stroke is the best choice in that situation. If you refuse to follow instructions, perhaps you need more time to learn the game, and we'll let another player compete instead while you sit and watch.*

The key message in the above examples is that the coach is giving information instead of losing self-control. The coach in each case was attacking specific, identifiable behaviors of the athlete and told the player the reasons for the coach's emotions. In both examples, the coaches also identified wishful actions, changes in the athletes' behaviors that they'd like to see occur. It's best to conclude by expressing wishful actions. "I want to see 'such and such' happening out there" is far more constructive than "Can't you do anything right?"

Although the above examples are centered on the feeling of anger, feelings such as frustration and disappointment are also inherent in coaching. These feelings should be handled in a similar manner. If the coach wants the players to respond to his or her comments with enthusiasm, to retain the skills that they have learned, to support teammates, and to play with a strong desire to win, then constructive communication is the answer (Figure 9.3). For effective communication, the integrity of all individuals must be respected. Even in a state of anger, the coach must appear sensitive, informative, intelligent, and emotionally mature.

Dealing with Anger

One of the least pleasant and most intimidating experiences is being confronted by an angry person. The emotions that accompany anger make it difficult for the listener to perceive the message as sensible or sincere. Although the speaker may intend to send a message of deep, sincere feelings, his or her anger is often interpreted as meaningless and irrational, and the message is not effective. This is especially the case when the speaker is a subordinate (e.g., athlete, worker) and the receiver of the hostile message is in a superior position (e.g., coach, supervisor). Tragically, in recent years, subordinate anger has turned increasingly violent, even deadly, in business settings. Guidelines for dealing with angry workers have been published in the organizational and counseling psychology literature. Because emotions in sport sometimes, albeit rarely, result in coach-athlete confrontations, these guidelines, originally provided for supervisors in business settings, also appear to be relevant for coaches in responding to an angry athlete (or may be used with upset teammates). According to Keister (1984), targets of another person's anger should consider reacting in the following manner.

1. *Make eye contact.* This lets the angry person know that you take his or her feelings seriously and are prepared to deal with, and hopefully resolve, the issue. However, if the angry person is also aggressive and threatens you, eye contact should be avoided. If possible, under such circumstances, walk away quickly.

2. *Stop what you are doing and give your full attention.* The last thing an angry person wants is to be discounted. Again, show that you take his or her feelings and message seriously.

3. *Speak in a calm voice and create a relaxed environment.* This will also help diffuse the intensity of the speaker's emotions. It reduces tension and keeps actions under control.

4. *Be open and honest.* Angry individuals want respect for their feelings, and they want to resolve an important issue. In addition, failure to open up issues and communicate feelings honestly further increases the person's frustration and anger because he or she feels disrespected. The feelings are real, and the source of these feelings must be addressed.

5. *Let the person have his or her say.* Sometimes just having a chance to get something off one's chest, to speak one's mind, perhaps after weeks or months of keeping feelings inside, is all that is needed to resolve the problem. In addition to defusing a potentially violent situation, allowing for freedom

(continued)

of expression shows respect and interest in the other person's feelings.

6. *Ask for specific examples of what the person is upset about.* Examples of events, words, or individuals that illustrate the source of feelings places the issue(s) in concrete terms. The conversation turns from name-calling and criticizing a person's character to dealing with specific, concrete issues. After calming down, identifying specifics is the first stage of problem resolution. Another important reason for examples is to clarify misunderstandings ("I was only joking when I called you a 'such and such'"), misperceptions ("I took you out of the game because I thought you were tired, not because you played poorly"), or unintended messages ("You thought I was ignoring you, but actually I walked past you without saying hello because my mind was someplace else; I never saw you").

7. *Be careful to define the problem.* Try to put the issue into terms that all parties understand and agree upon. In addition to reflecting the "facts" of an issue, defining the problem also helps the parties decide about next steps.

8. *Ask open-ended questions and explore all sides of an issue.* This task entails asking the angry individual to provide more information, to clarify issues and feelings, and to show sensitivity about the conflict. Examples include: "Why did that upset you?" "Why do you think you received that evaluation?" "What would you have done in that situation if you were the supervisor?" "How can this unit function properly if you are continuously late to work (practice)?"

As stated earlier, the coach is not a trained psychologist—a topic that is addressed later in this chapter. Nevertheless, coaches (even athletes) are asked to help resolve conflicts and calm angry feelings before they get out of hand. The supervisor or coach, or any other target of verbal hostility, has to keep things in perspective and engage in constructive dialogue to resolve matters peacefully.

VIII. Thou Shalt Use Positive Nonverbal Cues

Over the years, there have been some great coaches in sport who would say relatively little to their athletes. Nonetheless, they were inspiring and produced a tremendous sense of player loyalty. How could this be? In many cases, the coaches with relatively poor verbal skills were able to communicate nonverbally and, thus, could produce in their players the desired psychological benefits and performance outcomes. The meaning conveyed by nonverbal communication and the proper use of its techniques are the issues here.

Martens et al. (1981) classify nonverbal communication (or what is sometimes called *body language*) into six categories:

1. *Body motion:* gestures or movements of body parts such as the hands, head, and feet. Tilting the head, shifting the eyes, or raising the eyebrows in the proper context can tell another person a great deal about what is on your mind.

2. *Physical characteristics:* physique, height, weight, body odors, and hairstyle. For example, fitness instructors must never be overweight, or they will lose all credibility toward what they are trying to teach. You can't preach cleanliness while looking sloppy.

Figure 9.3 Coaches of winning teams share the ability to communicate skillfully with their athletes.

3. *Touching behavior:* patting someone on the back or placing an arm around a player's shoulders. Studies have shown that cultures differ on habits of touching and maintaining a certain physical proximity while communicating verbally. Yet touching conveys one of the most sensitive, caring, and trusting messages that a coach can project to an athlete. One sad commentary on contemporary society, however, is that touching can convey the wrong message or be misunderstood by the person who is touched. In recent years, there has been heightened awareness of the sexual connotations of adults touching younger individuals. Coaches must use common sense about when, how, and where to make physical contact with an athlete.

4. *Voice characteristics:* Sometimes our messages to others are reinforced by the manner in which we send them rather than only by their content. The pitch, rhythm, resonance, inflections, and amplitude of our words and sounds often indicate the feelings that underlie them. "Nice play, Phil" can mean a sincere compliment when spoken with a smile or sarcasm when spoken with a stern, cold face.

5. *Body position:* How close do you stand to another person whether or not you are interacting? The personal space between you and others and position of your body offer an unspoken message about the intensity and importance of your information or the status and respect you feel toward the person.

6. *Eye contact:* Although missing from the list in Martens et al.'s (1981) book, the tendency to look the intended listener in the eye makes a different impact on the sincerity and intensity of the message than speaking to, while simultaneously looking away from, the person. Of course, eye contact can be a glance, a glare, or a gaze, each denoting a different message.

Of central importance is understanding how nonverbal communication can work either for or against the coach when he or she tries to send important messages to athletes. For example, the coach should not raise his or her voice in an angry manner when giving information to the athletes. The participant will become conscious of the coach's angry feelings and, either intentionally or more often unintentionally, will filter out the coach's message. Anger and information should be separated.

Another important behavior to consider is whether the coach surrounds himself or herself with starting players or "popular" team members. This habit sends messages to others about the status of certain individuals, which may lead to resentment by persons not selected. It's important to avoid showing favoritism on the team. According to media reports, coach John Thompson of the Georgetown University basketball team makes a habit of sitting among the nonstarters and, by interacting with those around him, is in a favorable position for instructing and motivating this group of players, who can have an important impact on the team.

Sometimes nonverbal communication can be even more effective than the use of words to get across a message. It is desirable for coaches to express themselves with feelings of sincerity, warmth, sensitivity, and sometimes assertiveness. A coach's smile can show empathy and understanding to an athlete whose feelings may be hurt due to an unsuccessful attempt or who feels "great" after performing admirably. A pat on the back tells the player, "Nice try, better luck next time. You did the best you could. I [the coach] still support you," among other messages. Use of a regular speaking voice, as opposed to a raised, excited vocal tone, communicates a sense of calm, sincerity, and realistic appraisal of performance, while offering valid information feedback or suggestions and mutual respect. The player concentrates on and remembers more of the message when it is communicated calmly than when it is communicated in a highly aroused manner. The key issue is to make the best use of nonverbal communication through positive rather than negative channels.

IX. Thou Shalt Teach Skills

Silva (1984) conducted a national survey of coaches (640 returned questionnaires) about which areas of sport psychology were viewed by coaches as most important and useful to them. Silva reported that the more current and fashionable areas of sport psychology, such as psychological preparation, anxiety management, and imagery, were not ranked highly. The need to use improved methods in teaching sport skills was highly ranked. It was found that "the interest in motoric processes indicates that motor learning-performance researchers with applied interests may find the coaching community more open to their inquiry than previously assumed" (p. 47). My own experience with numerous coaches concurs with Silva's findings. Many coaches are more interested in having a sport psychologist assist them in becoming more effective educators of sport skills than many sport psychologists realize. Coaches need, and many want, to become better teachers of sport skills.

Teaching sport skills and strategies is a science referred to in the literature as sport pedagogy (Anshel et al. 1991a). Techniques for teaching skilled athletes differs from instructing the novice, but less than one would think. Basic guidelines of effective instructional techniques must be applied if skills are to be learned, remembered, and applied in a game situation (see Anshel 1990d, 1990e). Some of these techniques include the following:

- Communicating the goal of the instructional session (what the athlete has to do).

- Modeling the skill in correct form so that a visual representation of the skill is used by the athlete during practice to compare his or her performance with that of the "perfect" model.

- Reducing the amount of information taught at one time, then allowing time for athletes to mentally rehearse, plan, and review their performance. Highly skilled athletes can learn and remember skills with which they are familiar better than the novice can, of course. But information overload is still possible when new information is transmitted, especially in verbal form.

- Allowing skills and strategies to be learned in practice before they are used in a game, a concept referred to as *game simulation* (Orlick 1980). It is necessary to allow for numerous repetitions to improve retention of the information or skill. Due to the athlete's psychological state during competition, entailing anxiety and high arousal, teaching new skills should not be attempted during the game.

- Giving learners feedback on their performance. Informing the athlete as to which skills are or are not being performed correctly is more than a matter of shouting, "Nice catch, Jack." The timing of such feedback, its content, the manner in which it is communicated, and allowance for repetition of the skill are just a few of the considerations that need to be applied for conditions of optimal learning.

Perhaps one issue that some coaches need to address and to do more thinking about is their tendency to make conclusive, long-term judgments about an athlete's skills and abilities based on initial, brief observations of performance with little regard to the benefits of skill instruction. All athletes need to learn and to improve sport skills, no matter at what level of play and expertise they begin the program. In addition, differences between individuals in their present skill levels, their desire to learn, and other psychological characteristics make it impossible to predict to what degree a player will improve or how he or she will perform during the competitive event.

Making judgments about the future of a person's sport performance is scientifically invalid, unreliable, and unfair to the aspiring athlete at best, and psychologically crippling to the athlete at worst. Researchers in the area of motor learning (see Magill 2001) agree that perfection is virtually impossible in sport performance due to the complexity and speed of neuromuscular and psychological demands on the human organism.

Although the experienced coach often has good judgment about the required "tools" to compete successfully in a given sport, one must not judge hastily. The commandment to teach skills says two things to the coach: (1) do not assume that "what you see is what you get" because athletes improve dramatically with quality instruction, and (2) improvement in performance often takes time and patience on the part of the coach, and due to developmental differences, some athletes will learn and greatly improve faster than others. Do not give up on them prematurely.

X. Thou Shalt Interact Consistently with All Team Members

Goethe, a philosopher, said, "Treat people as though they were what they ought to be, and you help them to become what they are capable of being." A coach will receive maximal effort, concentration, commitment, and loyalty from virtually all players on the team if those players believe that the coach is interested in them both as athletes and as people. Probably the best way for coaches to communicate these feelings is to interact with all team members—starters and nonstarters—on a consistent basis.

A few definitions of terms will help to clarify this recommendation. First, consistent and constant interaction are not the same thing. *Consistent* interacting in the present context refers to demonstrating an ongoing, predictable pattern of communication with others, whereas a *constant* communication style requires interacting with others on an almost nonstop basis. The coach should not attempt to speak with all team members (starters and nonstarters) all the time, particularly not with large teams as in football. This would not be the best use of a coach's time. What is suggested is that the coach "keep in touch" on a regular basis to (1) be aware of the strong and weak points of each athlete, (2) point out the ways in which the athlete has shown improvement, (3) acknowledge specific skills that have been demonstrated efficiently, (4) remind individuals of the skills that they need to improve further, and (5) offer compliments to performers based on some aspect of their play from the recent past or the same day. The contact may also be based on a more personal level. Discussing sport-related topics or the athlete's performance does not always have to provide a reason to interact.

Athletes feel greater loyalty to the coach who shows a personal interest in their lives. They resent "being used" by the coach to attain the coach's own objectives. Coaches who care only about player performance but have little regard for the human being will not develop the athlete's long-term commitment to succeed. How can a coach earn a sense of loyalty from players who do not perceive their coach to be caring, honest, respectful, or sensitive to their needs? How can the coach be aware of the unique needs and feelings of the team if players are ignored? Effective coaches commit time and energy toward interacting with nonstarters as well as starters, all of whom have had, and will continue to have, an impact on team success.

The Importance of the Nonstarter. It's no secret that many, sometimes most, players do not receive an opportunity to play in the contest, particularly at more advanced levels of competition. Nor can everyone have an opportunity to play in every game. Due to the extensive time required to teach and practice skills and strategies to athletes who will compete, coaches will often neglect the nonstarter. This is a terrible mistake and forms the rationale for the inclusion of this commandment.

It is wrong to ignore or to dismiss the importance of nonstarters on sports teams for several reasons. First, the nonstarter is only one injury away from becoming a starter. How many athletes enter a game and play as effectively as the starters? Not too many. Yet skill differences between starters and nonstarters are often relatively minimal, especially among elite performers. One possible reason why nonstarters do not perform at levels similar to starters may partly be due to differences in the time and effort coaches offer starting players relative to players who are not scheduled to play or start. The high relationship between the coach's expectations of player performance and actual performance outcome is a phenomenon known as the self-fulfilling prophecy (or Pygmalion effect). This phenomenon is partly dependent on the lack of attention and practice given to nonstarters for whom the coach expects—and gets—relatively lower skill execution than from starting players (Martinek & Karper 1984).

Other reasons the nonstarter should receive attention, respect, and consistent communication from the coach include (1) to avoid the appearance of a double standard between starters and nonstarters that, if perceived by the players, would divide the team, reduce team loyalty, and lead to feelings of helplessness about future game participation by nonstarters, (2) to allow the coach to observe improvements in skill and performance of a given athlete, and (3) to prevent the deterioration of team morale—a devastating psychological state that leads to the low self-image of participants, a lack or absence of motivation to learn and perform at optimal levels, and a conscious or unconscious desire by players to see their coach and, perhaps, their teammates fail. It is important to remember that members of sport teams are usually friends. Such friendships are not often composed of nor dictated by similar status on the team. If nonstarters are perceived by team participants as being treated unfairly, all team members are affected, with only rare exceptions. The coach must treat the team as a unit of individuals who jointly serve the common purpose of performing all the necessary tasks to win.

Many coaches have forgotten how they felt when they were sport competitors. It's important to remember the common feelings of many athletes: frustration, disappointment, the need to be recognized and to succeed, a desire to learn new skills, the need to affiliate with peers, and the desire to be accepted as a part of the team. The 10 commandments of effective communication, if applied consistently, will vastly improve the coach's ability to help each athlete find greater enjoyment in sport and to more closely approach their performance potential. Communication, however, is a two-way street. In the next section, we look at what athletes can do to foster the coach-athlete interaction.

Approaching the Coach

Perhaps asking coaches to use perfect communication techniques is an unfair expectation. Coaches are human, too. No doubt they can use some help from the athletes if the coach-athlete interaction is to remain strong and consistent. But an athlete may be confident of his or her own feelings yet hesitate about communicating them to the coach. Most athletes are, in fact, aware of the techniques that work best for them in the psychological preparation of sport competition. Athletes have specific preferences about choices of food in the pregame meal, their mood both hours and minutes prior to the game, the type of atmosphere with which they are most and least comfortable prior to the game, and the manner in which they are being utilized as an athlete (e.g., the position at which they play best or starting versus substitute status). However, the players can be intimidated or unsure of themselves when it comes to approaching the coach about their needs. Whether it is the coach's manner that intimidates a player, the athlete's lack of confidence, or a socialized fear of authority is a riddle. The obvious answer is that both parties need to develop communication skills and to use those skills if they are to resolve the issues that may potentially inhibit desirable performance outcomes.

The Athlete-Coach Interview

Athletes may want to follow all or some of the following guidelines on approaching the coach to discuss their feelings, whether positive or negative:

- *Make an appointment to see the coach.* Appointments allow the coach to plan the time to see you, thus creating a relatively relaxed environment free from interruption. In addition, taking the time to make an appointment sends a message to the coach. The coach will realize that your concerns or feelings are serious enough to warrant special attention. Although appointments to see the coach may be made indirectly through the coach's secretary or directly by asking the coach for a time to meet, requesting an appointment in writing has one advantage. It allows the athlete a chance to briefly describe the issue that needs to be discussed. This way, the coach might give the matter additional thought and this might help to produce a more meaningful discussion.

- *Plan an agenda.* Decide in advance on only one or two issues that you wish to discuss. Keep the agenda short. You, the athlete, may have a dozen issues that warrant discussion. However, an avalanche of concerns will only place most coaches on the defensive and convey the feeling that "nothing is going right." This is not the impression you want to make.

- *Be on time for your appointment.* If you're even a minute late, you are sending a message that your concerns are not that important. Further, you are showing disrespect to a person who has cleared his or her busy calendar for you.

- *Dress neatly and appropriately.* There is no need for a tie and coat, but a torn sweatshirt and blue jeans show a lack of respect for your audience. If you want to be taken seriously and respected, look like it.

- *Take notes.* Bring along a notepad and pen or pencil for note taking. You would not be wise to interview or interrogate the coach while recording every word. However, it makes sense to record agreements or statements about the tasks that need to be completed if the issues are to be resolved. Never bring a tape recorder. This shows distrust and will cut off communication immediately. Again, the purpose of the paper and pencil is to help you clarify and remember some of the coach's recommendations about or responses to your concerns. In fact, you may even be perceived as conscientious in your efforts to remember information.

- *Plan warm-up strategies.* Upon entering the coach's office, shake hands (this shows sincerity, warmth, and a willingness to communicate in a positive manner) and begin your conversation (if you have a choice) on a topic unrelated to the reason for being there. Warm up, but only for a few minutes. A good idea is to converse about other aspects of the coach's job: "Are you enjoying the health course you're teaching?" "That was a crazy road trip we took last week, wasn't it, Coach? It took forever to get there." Don't take up too much of his or her time. Get to the point rather quickly. Come across as low-key and sincere. Avoid making jokes.

- *Make the opening statement positive.* You (the athlete) make the first statement about the reason for coming. For example: "Coach, like everyone else, I'm really pleased about the way the team has been playing lately. I hope it continues. The reason I needed to speak with you is that I've been concerned about my role with the team. I feel that I can contribute and . . ." By beginning with a positive statement, you are tearing down the tendency of many coaches to anticipate criticism or to respond to a critical remark in a defensive manner. Persons who are defensive cannot communicate effectively because they are occupied with explaining their views while ignoring the feelings of the other party. Again, start out with something positive, something that is going well, or a good feeling you have about an issue. Then, bring up your concern.

- *Use "I" statements; avoid "you" statements.* Since the focus of your visit is to voice how you feel about something, state your feelings clearly and respectfully. Once you begin to say, "You did this" or "You said that," the coach will become defensive, stop listening, and show you the door. An example of a desirable approach is, "Coach, I'm a bit confused about our agreement last week. I heard you say that I would play in the games we had this past week. Of course, I didn't play, and I'm concerned about my role with the team and what ways I need to improve to play more often. Can you help me get a handle on this?"

- *Give specific, behavioral examples when making your point.* Avoid discussing general perceptions of the coach's attitude or behavior toward you. Instead, refer to the exact times and behaviors of the coach (or any other source of your feelings) that affected you. It's fine to have these thoughts written down in front of you so that you may refer to them for the purpose of accuracy. Failure to be precise with the use of performance examples will often result in denial of how you feel ("Oh, no, I don't ignore you" or "You have it all wrong. You shouldn't feel unneeded on this team"). Tell the coach exactly what events and behaviors took place that gave you your perceptions (e.g., "The reason I think you don't like me is because you ignore me when we pass each other").

- *Be agreeable.* Avoid challenging the coach's responses to your verbalized perceptions, at least in the initial meeting. Coaches who feel guilty or defensive about their behavior will, as a protective device, offer the best answer to get them off the hook. Their response might also be honest, to the point, and painful to hear. Even if you disagree with the coach's explantion, there is nothing to gain by statements that are antagonistic or that question the coach's honesty and integrity. Your point has been made. Expressing your feelings in a positive, mature manner may result in more desirable changes than you think. Be patient. Never raise your voice and always stick with the facts—behaviors, not perceptions.

- *Verbally review agreements or plans.* If agreements or verbal contracts are completed, verbally review them in summary form before leaving the coach's office and agree to meet again if the need arises. Write down the agreement or agreements for your own records as soon as you can (in the coach's office or soon after the meeting) to remember exactly what was said. If the agreement is not carried out as promised right away, do not remind the coach. Allow some time to pass, and give the coach the flexibility to fulfill his or her end of the bargain. The team leader may have a good reason for postponing or for not fulfilling the promise as soon as you expect.

- *Remember the "recency effect."* End your meeting with (1) a handshake, (2) a smile, (3) a statement of appreciation for the person's time and understanding, and (4) a positive statement about your future as an athlete. For example: "Coach, I'm really looking forward to doing everything I can to help us win. Thanks so much for taking the time to help me out."

- *Keep your conference confidential.* This may be the toughest part of all. If word were to spread about the nature and content of your discussion among the players, the coach might feel obligated to refrain from carrying out the agreement; some coaches are concerned about looking foolish or "weak" in the eyes of the other players and assistant coaches. Perhaps most important is that the meeting's purpose, content, and outcome is no one else's business and that maintaining confidentiality enhances the integrity and ethics of both parties. Even if teammates inquire about your meeting, avoid full disclosure. If you feel inclined to respond, talk in generalities, not specifics (e.g., "It went OK"; "It was a good meeting").

- *Have reasonable expectations about the meeting's outcome.* Try not to confuse the opportunity to communicate issues to your coach with the expectation of immediate conflict resolution or immediate decisions. Conflicts and decisions may or may not be addressed quickly. Often, sufficient time must pass to gain perspective and resolution of the issue or concern. Be patient.

From the coach's perspective, players may or may not respond in an expected, preferred manner. Rather than agree and promise to make suggested changes, they may be defensive or not respond at all. This is not the military; players should not be expected to "immediately follow orders." Coaching psychology reflects a more sophisticated approach, in that messages are communicated in a sincere, candid, yet sensitive manner. Yet, the athletes' integrity is respected by allowing them time to reflect on and contemplate the issues you have discussed.

Written Feedback

The content of this chapter has focused mainly on verbal communication with a small segment on nonverbal mannerisms. Not discussed as yet is the written form of communication. Figure 9.4 is a feedback sheet that has been used by a few coaches with athletes at the high school and college levels. They have found the results of the survey rewarding. The advantages of using the feedback sheet in written form include:

- Making available a vehicle for gathering input from the players that can be used at any time during the season as an expression of feelings or attitudes.

- Allowing players a chance to vent their feelings instead of keeping them inside, which could interfere with concentration and mental preparation for competition.

- Having an instrument that allows for anonymity so that the athlete can communicate feelings openly and honestly without fear of retribution.

- Giving the coach a chance to ask athletes questions in a nonthreatening manner without the potential of intimidation from the coach's presence.

- Allowing for the fact that some athletes prefer, and may be more effective in, writing rather than verbalizing their thoughts. The chance to write down one's feelings allows time for reflection and eliminates the possible inhibiting influence of trying to communicate sincere feelings nervously in the presence of another person.

Figure 9.4 Feedback sheet for sports teams.

Athlete Feedback Sheet

(This can remain anonymous. Signing your name is optional.)

To the athletes: The purpose of this form is to gather your input about how you feel as a member of this team so you can play your best and enjoy your experiences on the team. Thank you for your honesty and candor.

Circle the number that best describes your feelings, ranging from 1 (not at all) to 5 (very much). ALL INFORMATION WILL BE HELD STRICTLY CONFIDENTIAL BY THE HEAD COACH, WHO WILL THEN COMMUNICATE THE INFORMATION COLLECTIVELY TO THE ASSISTANTS WITHOUT IDENTIFYING THE SOURCE OF THE COMMENT.

I.   Feelings about being a member of the team:

    (a) I enjoy being on the team: 1   2   3   4   5

    (b) I understand the reasons behind our conditioning: 1   2   3   4   5

    (c) I understand the reasons for our training schedule: 1   2   3   4   5

    Please feel free to expand on your answers here:

    _____

    _____

    _____

    _____

II. About the coaches:

    (a) I understand the function of each coach, head coach,
        and assistants: 1   2   3   4   5

    What in particular do you *not* know?

    _____

    _____

    _____

    _____

    (b) The thing(s) I like best about the coaches or team are:

        (1) _____

        (2) _____

        (3) _____

    (c) The thing(s) that concern(s) me most about the coaches or team are:

        (1) _____

        (2) _____

        (3) _____

    (d) I would like my head coach to be *more:* _____

    (e) I would like the assistant coaches _____
                                    Names (optional)

        to be *more:* _____

    (f) I would like my head coach to be *less:* _____

(continued)

Figure 9.4 Feedback sheet for sports teams *(continued)*.

    (g) I would like the assistant coaches _____

                                       Names (optional)

      to be *less:* _____

III. About you—the athlete:

    (a) I am coached fairly: 1   2   3   4   5

    (b) I feel the coaches like me: 1   2   3   4   5

    (c) Generally, I like the coaches: 1   2   3   4   5

    (d) My performance has improved due to my
        relationship with the coach: 1   2   3   4   5

    (e) I am not playing the best I can: 1   2   3   4   5

    Please feel free to include additional comments here:

    _____

    _____

    _____

    _____

    If you were coaching *you*, what would you do differently from the way you are now being coached? That is, how would you coach yourself?

    Any other comments: _____

    _____

    _____

                   Thanks for taking the time to help create a better team.

The Ten Commandments of Effective Communication for Game Officials

A satisfying experience in competitive sport includes proper communication strategies by a group of dedicated individuals who must try to meet the most impossible of all expectations in sport—perfection. These individuals are the umpires, referees, and judges whose role it is to declare performance deficiencies and point out failure to every observer in the sport venue. Remaining popular among sport participants—the athletes and coaches—is impossible with this role. However, game officials can maintain their integrity and the respect of others if they do their best to follow a few communication guidelines during the contest. Readers may find an elaboration of this information in Anshel (1989b).

I. Keep Calm. Remember that players and coaches are "psyched up" during the contest. Heightened emotions promote frustration and aggression by participants in response to punitive sanctions by the official. Arbiters must remain calm and keep the proper emotional perspective, especially under such difficult circumstances.

II. Treat Participants with Respect. Quality officials do not patronize players and coaches by claiming, "I'm the referee; what I say goes, just play the game and keep quiet," or "Who do you think you are?" Not every call can—or should—be explained, nor is each inquiry legitimate and in need of attention. But there is no need to abuse or reinforce this power. Try to avoid calling the game in a highly demonstrative fashion; protect the player's/coach's integrity.

III. Use Positive Nonverbal Cues. Effective officials exhibit self-confidence. In order to avoid appearing threatening and intimidating to other game participants, a goal of every self-assured, skilled official should be to use nonverbal cues such as the occasional nod, smile, thumbs up, a gentle touch when explaining a call, and other nonverbal messages that indicate respect to others.

IV. Listen Actively. Effective arbiters listen to the words of individuals, especially during moments of intense emotion. The listening official may discover that the coach or player is voicing frustration about an issue unrelated to the official's call and merely wants a sympathetic ear.

V. Explain Decisions about Infractions. Coaches and athletes appreciate officials who are willing and able to explain their decision. Taking an extra few seconds to respond to an inquiry conveys sensitivity to the feelings of others, contributes to the perception that the official is in control of the contest, and reduces the chance of coach and player aggression.

VI. Do Not Embarrass Others. Some officials appear perpetually "on stage" and assume the role of star attraction and center of attention. This is called "hot-dog officiating." Verbalizing penalties in an assertive, animated, and boisterous manner is embarrassing to the targeted individual. The result often is heightened aggression by the athletes.

VII. Criticize Behavior, Not Character. Similar to the commandment for coaches, the rule here is to confine critical feedback to the *actions* of a coach or player, not the person's personality. An example of proper criticism is "I feel annoyed" (identify feelings); "Coach, I don't mind explaining my decision, but I get very upset when you start using abusive language with me. This I will not tolerate" (give the reason for your anger); "I expect adults to address me in a respectful manner" (state your wishful actions).

VIII. Selectively Ignore Comments. Sometimes in sports officiating, the best response is no response at all. Sometimes individuals make statements that serve only to vent feelings and that have nothing to do with the situation. If the comment is not directed at the official but, instead, at no one in particular, perhaps the best thing to do is ignore it.

IX. Avoid Sarcasm. Sarcasm from the person who regulates proper and improper behavior is unprofessional and unethical. Sarcasm lowers the "victim's" self-esteem and, for this reason, induces an angry response. It also reduces the respect of others toward the official. Avoid sarcasm at all costs.

X. Let "Them" Have the Last Word. Anger and frustration do not reflect mature, rational thinking in most instances. Angry coaches and players often "know" they are right and the call was "wrong." As long as their message is not insulting, let them have the last word and move on. The battle for "being right" has no winner.

Communication Techniques in Counseling Athletes

The concept of counseling might create anxiety in many sport leaders who contend that they know very little about counseling others. Yet, successful coaches counsel their players all the time, some more effectively than others. They offer guidance to the players about making personal decisions related and unrelated to the team, they listen to personal problems, and they offer advice on alternatives from which the athletes may choose. Coaches are quite able to use fundamental counseling skills to enhance communication with athletes. It is *not* the intention of this section to turn coaches into psychologists, but rather to offer guidelines about applying fundamental counseling skills and about knowing when to refer an athlete for professional counseling.

The role of counselor should be integrated into the coach's responsibilities. *It is important to remember, however, that coaches, and others without the proper credentials, are not licensed psychologists,* may not refer to themselves as "psychologists," and must not engage in the counseling process in areas related to the athlete's psychological well-being (see Singer 1993 for a review of this issue). There are many issues that athletes bring to the sport venue that require the aid of a trained clinical or counseling psychologist (see Anshel 1992a for a brief discussion of the differences in clinical and counseling psychology credentials). Examples include eating disorders, sleeplessness, chronic anxiety, stress, low self-esteem, chronic and severe depression, taking drugs, and many others (Nideffer 1981). Coaches, indeed even sport psychology consultants and licensed counseling psychologists, must know when to refer the athlete to a person trained in clinical psychology.

What Is Counseling?

Counseling is concerned with helping normal people to cope with normal problems and opportunities. It's a process—which is sometimes long term—that involves responding to the attitudes, feelings, and behaviors of each client. Also integral to the counseling process is the acceptance of the client's perceptions and feelings without personal prejudice and outside evaluation standards (Hackney & Nye 1973). This means that if the coach and athlete engage in an open, honest, and meaningful dialogue, the coach must accept the athlete's feelings ("I'm better than 'so-and-so'") and perceptions ("The coach doesn't like me") as real rather than denying that the athlete's feelings and perceptions are legitimate ("You can't feel that way" or "Your opinion is wrong").

Coaches may be better counselors than they think, even without professional training. Counseling is similar to interviewing, and coaches interview players (and assistant coaches) all the time. Tasks of the counselor include (1) gathering information, which requires good listening skills, (2) helping the athlete to solve problems by looking at alternative approaches and solutions to issues, and (3) giving information or advice. Counseling about problems such as drug abuse, eating disorders, emotional instability, personal problems, and quitting school might necessitate referral to professional counseling services and staff, depending on the severity of the problem and the type of relationship between the coach and the athlete. Issues in which the coach needs to become involved are usually related to the athlete's participation on the team. However, topics that are not directly related to athletics, such as school grades, the athlete's behavior away from the sport venue, and family concerns are certainly open—and sometimes necessary—to discussion.

Examples of topics with which athletes commonly confront the coach include: "I'm not playing up to my potential"; "What should my goals be?"; "Why am I not playing (starting)?"; "Will I ever get a chance to play?"; "I'm getting burned out"; "I've lost my confidence"; "I don't have any energy on the field (or court)"; "The players don't like me"; "I want to quit the team"; and "I broke up with my girlfriend (or boyfriend) and I can't concentrate."

In dealing with these and other concerns, the counseling coach must recognize that counseling can be risky, especially for athletes. First, it requires one to expose deep-rooted, private, sometimes negative, attitudes toward another person. For instance, an athlete may feel that disclosing negative feelings may result in a nonplaying status or even dismissal from the team. Athletes need to feel secure about the benefits and outcomes of "opening up" with the coach prior to risking self-disclosure. A second risk lies in being candid in comparing the athlete's perceptions of a situation with the coach's views. For example, if an athlete is upset and frustrated over his or her lack of playing time, the coach might feel compelled to be candid about the player's lack of necessary skills to start. The coach's role is to help players to feel secure about disclosing personal feelings and perceptions without risking their self-esteem or participation on the team. Such disclosures may benefit the athlete emotionally and may lead to improved performance.

What Is Mentoring?

While coaches (and parents) are not trained counselors, there is another role that is even more important and easily within their ability and training: the role of mentor. Mentoring is defined as "the complex process by which a trusted and experienced individual takes an interest in the personal and professional development of a younger or less experienced individual" (Hardy 1994, p. 196). The term *mentor* comes from the name of a character in Greek mythology who was a wise guide, advisor, and teacher (Hardy 1994). According to Bolton (1980), the essence of mentoring is sharing power, sharing competence, and sharing self.

Unlike counseling athletes, mentoring includes sharing values and modeling appropriate (desirable) behaviors: it applies to every facet of life—physical, intellectual, emotional, spiritual, and social. In his presidential address at a conference of the Association for the Advancement of Applied Sport Psychology (having direct implications for sports coaches), Hardy (1994) asserted that "If we fail to provide effective mentoring to our talented [athletes], they are likely to abandon their dream . . . to travel uncharted routes with limited skills and resources to cope with the challenges, risks, and ambiguities with which they will inevitably be confronted" (p. 197). Hardy's message resonates for sports coaches, because the failure to improve the quantity and quality of mentoring athletes will jeopardize the athletes' potential growth and development.

The Need to Counsel Athletes

Although it is commonly called "a game," participation in organized competitive sport is stress inducing. In school situations, for example, athletes are asked to follow training and practice schedules that reduce time for academic studies. Despite the long hours of practice and other tasks for game preparation, athletes in school settings are required to maintain an acceptable scholastic record. Traveling exacerbates the problem.

Athletes often need assistance in the areas of time management and study skills. Many athletes do not obtain desirable grades because they have not been trained to manage the time constraints placed on them, and given the time for study, relatively few athletes have developed proper study skills (Lanning 1982). These problems may inhibit concentration, sport performance, or academic pursuits. Coaches should counsel athletes about and provide resources for achieving academic as well as athletic success. Study time during the day and tutorial assistance are examples where coaches can favorably influence academic achievement. The coach should be empathetic about the daily pressures and time constraints with which athletes are confronted.

Sometimes athletes set their own lofty, sometimes unrealistic, goals of playing professional sports. This is unfortunate because available data suggest that fulfilling the dream of competing as a professional athlete in any sport is quite rare. For example, a report from the NCAA Intercollegiate Athletic, Physical Education, and Recreation *Progress of the Member Institutions*, Report No. 4 (1979), indicated that only 4.5 percent of high school football players will participate in college football, with only about 2 percent of those collegians going into professional ball. That means only about one of 10,000 high school football athletes realizes the dream of playing professionally. And if the athlete gets there, it likely won't be for long. The average career span for a player in the National Football League (NFL) is only 4.5 years. While similar data are available in other sports, more recent research in this area is necessary. The need to prepare athletes academically and psychologically for a life that is independent of participation in competitive sport is obvious. This is partly the coach's role.

The Need for Team Counseling

Winning is a team effort—and so is losing. If team members consistently need to resolve issues among themselves, they will have less energy and concentration available for competition. Coaches, based on their observations, need to ask questions such as: Do the players on the team get along? Do some members isolate themselves from the others? Do players spend time with one another while away from team-related gatherings or tasks? Do arguments break out among teammates, particularly off the field or court or during practice? Is anyone deliberately ostracized by the others or teased (scapegoated) excessively? These are issues about which the coach should be aware despite occasional claims that "how the players get along off the field (or court) is their own business."

Is it important for coaches to acknowledge each athlete's level of satisfaction? Absolutely! An unhappy player is an unmotivated and ineffective one. In visiting a women's collegiate volleyball team as a consultant, I recall the anxiety of one player who felt that she was being ignored by the team's setter. She lamented that this player rarely passed the ball to her and that her teammate disliked her because of her poor ability. This perception was affecting her incentive and performance. When I raised this issue privately with the setter, I quickly learned that personal feelings had nothing to do with her strategy. Instead, I discovered that the net player was left-handed, forcing a spike at an awkward angle. The insulted player's feelings quickly dissipated when she learned of the setter's perceptions. The net player then positioned herself differently, which, in turn, resulted in more passes and an improved frame of mind. The important issue was not so much the correctness of the setter's explanation but, rather, the debilitating effects of the net player's feelings on her motivation and performance, which were resolved with the explanation.

Team counseling is needed for other reasons in addition to responding to personal problems or problems with interpersonal relationships. Coaches agree that cohesiveness—what Widmeyer et al. (1985) call the athletes' feelings of "stick-togetherness" in the group—and high morale are team characteristics that improve performance. For players to feel high group satisfaction and to support one another mutually is desirable. When cohesiveness and morale are not at preferred levels, counseling with all or part of the team to gain insight into the issues that cause team dissension is in order. Coaches cannot dictate heightened cohesion, morale, and team member satisfaction. The primary objective of team counseling, then, is to facilitate player discussion on an individual or group basis to solve problems or to confront and deal with issues. Group cohesion was discussed in depth in Chapter 7.

Fundamental Counseling Skills for the Coach

People need not be licensed psychologists to be effective in helping other people. Research has shown that people who are often in a position to hear the concerns and feelings of others can be quite effective in the role of confidant. Examples include bartenders, hairstylists, and yes, coaches. How is this possible without proper training? The untrained "counselor" can be effective if he or she has the ability to (1) listen, (2) show concern, (3) be supportive, (4) be honest, and (5) keep conversations private and confidential.

Listening

Professional counselors call listening *attending behaviors,* comprising several techniques to facilitate the client's need to talk. This is probably the most critical aspect of the counseling process (Ivey 1983). The basic approach for the nonprofessional is to sit back and listen attentively—and actively.

Effective coaches are active listeners. They (1) maintain consistent eye contact, (2) face the speaker squarely with a slight forward trunk lean, (3) use encouraging gestures (such as a slight smile or nodding) or a reassuring "hum-mm" once in a while, (4) avoid distracting movements like manipulating an object or doodling on paper, giving full attention to the athlete, (5) avoid cutting off the speaker in midsentence or midthought, allowing the person to continue expressing his or her feelings, and (6) are nonjudgmental in response to the player's comments, at least initially.

Showing Concern

A coach must take the performer's feelings seriously regardless of any discrepancy between the coach's and the athlete's perceptions of the situation (Figure 9.5). If the

Figure 9.5 An important role of the coach is to show sensitivity and provide emotional support to distressed athletes.

athlete feels that the issue is serious, then it *is* serious, no matter what anyone else thinks. It is the athlete's perceptions that are important. Responses that incorrectly minimize the importance of the other person's feelings include "Don't give me that," "How can you think that?" and "It's your own fault, now get yourself out of it." Coaches who ignore or do not show sincere concern about helping the player cannot expect to receive the athlete's loyalty. Disloyal players do not tend to contribute to the team effort.

Being Supportive

Whereas showing concern is a part of the listening phase of communication, giving support is the response phase. It doesn't take a degree in counseling to show empathy and understanding toward the player's feelings. It's fine to disagree with the athlete's point of view on a matter, but don't make him or her feel inadequate as a person for having a different perception or opinion. "I disagree with you about that" is more constructive than "You don't know what you're talking about." Support means "I understand" and "Let's try to work things out so that the situation is resolved." Support can also mean helping the athlete to "face facts" (e.g., "Ruth, I hear what you're saying, but there is a team rule about this and you broke that rule").

Being Honest

Was it the player's fault that the defensive unit surrendered so many points and responded incorrectly to the opponent's offense? Were the communication between coach and athlete and the selection of strategies during game preparation accurate? In other words, is it fair to "fault" the athlete for the contest's outcome? Could the coach or other athletes have made an error in judgment or performance that contributed to the outcome? The coach should try to assess these issues honestly.

Respecting Privacy

Conversations between coaches and athletes should often be held in private, particularly if content is contentious and the tone is argumentative. Privacy also means *confidentiality*. The athlete's feelings are no one else's business. If an athlete comes into the office for a discussion and the coach fails to provide an environment that is free of interruptions and other listeners, the message is "What you have to say isn't important." Where is the trust—or the respect? Eventually, the coach will be asking, "Where is the athlete?"

The Microskills Approach to Counseling

A popular model in the counseling literature for identifying and using specific counseling skills is called the *microskills approach* (Ivey & Simek-Downing 1980). This technique is based on the premise that effective counseling requires using certain techniques that lie within broader types of skills. These broader skills are attending behaviors (listening) and influencing behaviors (speaking).

Attending behaviors involve three dimensions: (1) eye contact, (2) appropriate body language, and (3) verbal following (Figure 9.6). *Influencing behaviors* involve the coach in causing growth or change in the athlete. The coach needs to do more than listen and offer brief verbal exchanges if he or she wishes to influence a change in the player's behavior. At times, the coach will need to direct the interview process actively.

Figure 9.6 This coach exhibits proper attending behaviors (notice his eye contact) in providing emotional support to an athlete.

Attending Behavior Strategies

Not every coach is comfortable with the task of discussing another person's feelings or with discussing his or her own. Coaches who want to have nothing to do with counseling athletes in any form—those who resist listening and verbally responding to athletes' feelings—should avoid this role completely. Don't fake it. Athletes can clearly tell when a person is insincere, uncaring, or uncomfortable. However, it is very important that another responsible adult (an assistant coach or sport psychology consultant, for instance) maintain this role. Athletes need someone with whom they can talk, and if possible, who is in an influential position with the team.

One head coach of a university women's basketball team evenly divides the team of 12 players into three groups. Then he and two assistant coaches meet privately with each athlete several times before, during, and after the season. They rotate these subgroups on three occasions so that each coach eventually meets with all the players. They discuss performance goals; exchange views about the player's role on the team; offer feedback on athletic performance, academic performance, and potential concerns in these areas; and engage in verbal exchanges on personal and social topics (e.g., relationships, goals, and family matters). The players also have the opportunity to offer their views about the team, teammates, and coaching behaviors and decisions. All information is respected, open for discussion, and held confidential. The players are convinced that they are respected by the staff, and that they are perceived as students and adults in addition to their athletic roles and responsibilities.

In discussing types of counseling behaviors, Hackney and Nye (1973) identify three categories of erroneous communication patterns: (1) underparticipation, (2) overparticipation, and (3) distracting participation. *Underparticipators* have the image of incompetence or insecurity or both. They convey to the client an unwillingness or an inability to offer assistance. In a sport setting, this lessens the player's faith in the coach. The typical underlying cause of underparticipation may be the coach's fear of involvement either with the player or a particular topic. The counselor withdraws in both verbal and nonverbal directions. Nonverbal examples include (1) appearing stiff, with little body movement, (2) positioning the body away from the player, (3) directing the eyes downward, avoiding eye contact, (4) maintaining a stooped-shoulder position, frequently shrugging the shoulders during the conversation, and (5) using a very soft, weak tone of voice (responses sometimes trail off into silence).

Overparticipators may be covering up their anxiety, as evident in the person who always has to be the center of attention and who is constantly talking or clowning. Typically, this is descriptive of an insecure person who's afraid to lose control of the environment or who desperately needs attention to reinforce his or her self-worth and to overcome self-doubts. Overparticipating is a way of exerting control, which, in turn, reduces anxiety.

Coaches who overparticipate usually confront the athlete and jump to conclusions with little awareness of the player's feelings. Overparticipation also occurs when the "counselor" is doing most of the talking or does not let the "client" finish his or her statements. Examples of nonverbal traits common to overparticipators include creating much body movement, gesturing frequently, or fidgeting and talking in a very animated and expressive manner.

The *distracting participator* overresponds to irrelevant issues, sometimes with loud (nervous and contrived) laughter. At times, the issues may never be addressed because the conversation becomes bogged down in trivia. Coaches should not carry on and on about the weather, who's going to win the championship, and other irrelevant subjects. Use only the first minute or so to get comfortable and exchange pleasant comments. This tends to reduce nervousness and defensiveness. Then address the "gut" issues.

A second tendency of the distracting participator is to shift topics hastily before the primary issue has been resolved or at least dealt with at length. A frequent change in topics tells the player that the main issue has not been heard or is not being taken seriously by the coach or else has not been adequately communicated by the athlete. The counseling coach should get to the "nitty-gritty" and stay with the topic until a sense of closure is reached; summarizing key points and agreeing on future actions can be helpful.

Coaches want to be approachable so that they can favorably affect the emotions and actions of athletes. To foster openness and honesty, effective coaches use some of the following strategies:

- *Facial animation.* Show interest and active mental involvement in the conversation through facial expressions.
- *Good eye contact.* Avoiding eye-to-eye contact and glancing everywhere but at the athlete shows disinterest, a lack of seriousness or sincerity, or the coach's own low self-confidence in the situation.
- *Occasional head nodding.* This is used effectively to reinforce the player's commitment to talk. It also shows that the coach is interested in the topic.
- *Soft, firm tone of voice.* Effective communicators avoid appearing defensive and, instead, remain in control and relaxed, which fosters honesty and continued communication.
- *Occasional smiling.* This relaxes the athlete and makes the coach appear compassionate, understanding, and "human."
- *Occasional gesturing with hands.* This helps the speaker to make a point and maintains the listener's attention.
- *Moderate rate of speech.* This prevents the listener from "tuning out" the speaker and facilitates getting the message across without being overpowered by too much information.
- *Occasional use of minimal verbal reinforcers.* A brief "hum-mm" or "interesting" fosters continued conversation and informs the speaker (athlete) that his or her message is being heard. It can also indicate agreement with the message.

Any of the following optional responses would be appropriate as examples of proper attending skills.

Athlete: Coach, I don't feel I'm getting a fair shake with my lack of playing time.
Coach: (*Option 1*) Tell me about it.
            (*Option 2*) Could you tell me a little more about exactly what you feel is unfair?
            (*Option 3*) I can understand how you feel. Let's discuss what it will take to play more often.
            (*Option 4*) I've definitely noticed improvement in your skills. It's easy to see why you're frustrated.

The key element here is to address the player's feelings immediately. Athletes need to feel that the coach is listening and taking their feelings seriously. Here are a few examples of how *not* to respond.

Athlete: Coach, I'm really falling behind in my schoolwork. It seems that the hours of practice time are making it difficult to keep up. Any suggestions?

Coach: *(Inappropriate response 1)* Tell me your favorite subject in school.
(Inappropriate response 2) It doesn't look like you're any better at school than at remembering the plays.
(Inappropriate response 3) Go ahead, quit the team. It doesn't seem to be working for you.

In these examples, the athlete's feelings are not being taken seriously or the real issue of schoolwork is not being addressed. The player is not saying that he or she wants to quit the team, only that he or she is worried about the effect of participating with the team on his or her grades. Asking the athlete if he or she would prefer to leave the team may in some cases be appropriate, but the main issue is that the athlete needs help finding an alternative to quitting.

Proper Strategies for Influencing Behavior

Listening and verbally reacting are important. But what effect will these strategies have on the athlete's behavior? Influencing behavior is a function of the coach's making the "right" verbal responses. The counseling skill that will be discussed in this section is called *responding* (Carkhuff 1980). There are two types of responding: (1) responding to content and (2) responding to feelings.

Responding to Content. What is the athlete saying? What is his or her message? Responding to content means that the coach communicates his or her understanding of the athlete's experience. It involves imagining another person's world as though the coach is the player. Coaches can best facilitate this empathetic understanding by encouraging the player to be specific about experiences or feelings, and by not indicating (the coach's) personal attitudes to the player—at least not for the time being. Athletes should feel that they can explore their feelings without fear of retaliation. For example, if a player remarks, "Coach, running wind sprints is a waste of time," the coach can respond, "Those wind sprints can be tough, no doubt about it. The reason we do them is . . ." An inappropriate response would be: "Do them or leave the team" or "You don't know what you're talking about."

Responding to content also involves the coach's ability to show the player that he or she understands the player's situation or feelings. This is done by carefully listening to the details presented by the athlete and rephrasing the player's expression in a fresh way. Rather than "parrot" back the player's own words, respond with, "What I hear you saying is . . ." or "In other words . . ." For example:

Athlete: Coach, I'm really upset about being replaced in the second half just because I fumbled the ball one time in the second quarter. I thought I was playing really well, and I had a good week of practice. Then, all of a sudden, I'm on the bench because I made one mistake.

Coach: You're obviously upset and disappointed that you didn't play the whole game, especially after the fumble. And you feel that fumbling the ball was the reason you were taken out. I can understand your feelings. I'd feel uptight too in the same situation.

Responding to Feelings.   Athletes may express their feelings directly through their choice of words or indirectly by tone of voice, by describing a situation without stating their feelings, or by facial and body gestures. When a player says, "Hey, Coach, you wouldn't believe how tough my math course is," he or she may be asking for assistance. Perhaps the person needs tutoring in this subject. Or perhaps the athlete just needs reaffirmation from a significant other that they are capable of meeting high academic demands. Athletes who walk in a dejected manner with head down or who isolate themselves from others after being taken out of the contest might also be making a strong nonverbal statement about their feelings of disappointment. Whatever the form of expression, the coach's role is to respond to the speaker's underlying feelings.

The following true story actually occurs with some frequency. At the first practice, one athlete was particularly vocal about how easy it is to play the game and to perform a particular sport skill. The youngster was "mouthing off" before he even took the field. "Eh, this is easy," the youngster said. "I already know how to catch a fly ball." Which of the following responses should the coach make?

1. "Oh, yeah? You think you're better than everyone else, big shot? Let's see you try to catch a few of these." (Coach then hits a long, towering fly ball to the player, who naturally doesn't come close to catching it.)
2. "You're no better than anyone else. Everyone does what I say. I'm the coach."
3. "I'm sure you can do a fine job. Some of us have more experience than others, but we all want to improve on what we can already do. Even the major leaguers practice daily. So, let's all practice catching a few fly balls."
4. "Good for you. A real major leaguer, eh? Why don't you go out there and show us just how good you are."

The third response is the correct one. Many coaches become upset when a player claims to "know it all," without realizing that the bragging player is often masking low self-confidence or low self-esteem (not the same thing), or a need for recognition. What is important is listening to what the athlete is *not* saying. What he is not saying is, "If I boast and show how confident I am, I'll appear to be as good or better than the others; I'm scared to show my lack of skill to the others; I can use some attention and approval."

And what about the athlete who can play as well as she says but enjoys boasting? This youngster—and sometimes adults do the same thing—lacks general self-confidence (called *trait confidence* by Vealey 1986) and may not feel secure about her ability to make friends. Her approach to gaining respect from peers is to show off and demonstrate superior skills. Again, this person lacks a sense of security and needs to know that she will be accepted regardless of her skill level. And what about the coach's reaction? Criticizing the person only reinforces a low self-image. Instead, let the player know that good skills are evident and that she need not advertise them. Also, tell her, privately, that her bragging disturbs others and may prevent her from forming close friendships. For excellent instruction on this technique, see Ginott (1965, 1969, 1972).

Counseling Techniques for the Coach-Athlete Interview

Ivey (1983) suggests that counselors use three strategies to help clients. Each is applicable to the counseling coach in sport. He suggests (1) asking the right questions, (2) confronting, and (3) summarizing.

Asking the Right Questions

Effective questioning techniques encourage the client to talk more freely and openly. Questions serve various purposes. They can:

- Help to begin the interview ("What would you like to discuss today?" or "How have things been going since we last spoke?").
- Help the player to elaborate on issues ("Could you tell me more about that?" or "How did you feel when one of the other players criticized you?").
- Help to bring out concrete examples about the player's feelings ("Could you give me a specific example of what I did that upset you?" or "What do you mean when you say our team meetings depress you?").
- Provide a diagnosis and assessment of a problem. The coach might ask: Who is responsible for these feelings? What is the player's concern and the specific details of the situation? When does the problem come up? When did it begin? Where does the problem occur? On the field? In the dormitory? At home with your mom and dad? How do you (the athlete) react to the problem? How do you (the player) feel about the issue? Why does the problem occur? Are you (the player) doing something—intentionally or unintentionally—that is provoking the issue?

Different types of questions have their own purpose. Used harmoniously, the different types of questions open new areas for discussion, assist in pinpointing and clarifying issues, and aid in the player's ability to self-explore feelings, attitudes, and behaviors (Ivey 1983). The important point is to ask questions selectively and in a nonthreatening manner. There are two types of questions, open and closed.

Open questions are those that can't be answered in just a few words, whereas *closed questions* require a relatively short response. Typically, open questions begin with *what, how, why,* or *could.* For example, "Why didn't you bunt after I gave the bunt signal?" Such questions encourage others to talk. Closed questions often begin with *is, are,* or *do.* An example is, "Do you expect to start if you show up late for practice?" The advantage of a closed question is that it focuses the interview and elicits specific information from the client.

In the following examples of closed questions, the coach is asking for specific information. This approach is used when there is no time to get into long discussions.

Coach: Hi, Sue. Is your injured knee feeling better today?

Athlete: Well, it still bothers me. Seems that it gets inflamed after a few minutes of running.

Coach: Is the trainer aware of your discomfort?

Athlete: Oh, sure. I still see him for daily treatments.

Coach: Do you think you can practice with it if the trainer gives the OK?

Athlete: As of now, I might have to wait a day or two until the swelling goes down a bit. I can't seem to put too much pressure on it for more than a few minutes.

Coach: I'm sure it's best not to take a chance. I'll get a report on it from the trainer this afternoon. In the meantime, do you think you can attend and observe practice, or should you stay off the leg completely?

Athlete: Even if I'm walking with a cane, Coach, I'll be there.

Coach: That's great! Hang in there.

Now, let's take a look at the open-question technique with the same situation. Notice that the athlete is asked to express her feelings no matter which direction they take. There is also no time urgency; sufficient time is allowed for interacting with the player even though the topic is specific and answers are needed.

Coach: Hi, Sue. How's your injured knee today?

Athlete: Well, Coach, it's still a little tender. Seems to swell up on me after a few minutes of running.

Coach: How does it feel when you're not playing and just walking around on it?

Athlete: Not too bad. As long as I don't put too much pressure on it.

Coach: Our next game is in two days. What is your feeling about playing if we maintain treatment and the trainer says it's OK?

Athlete: I'll sure give it a try. In the meantime, I'll rest it until practice and continue to see the trainer for therapy.

Coach: That's all anyone can ask. We'll just take it one day at a time. Don't get too discouraged. No use in taking a risk. Just give it your best.

Questioning strategies, like all techniques, have certain limitations, especially when used by an untrained counselor. The following problems should be avoided:

- *Posing multiple questions (bombarding or grilling).* The coach may confuse the athlete by tossing out several questions at once. Too many questions tend to put the athlete on the defensive, especially delivered in a rapid-fire manner. And some individuals might feel it is an invasion of privacy.

- *Asking questions as statements.* For example, "Don't you think your contribution to the team would be more helpful if you remembered your assignment?" (which could be viewed as either sarcastic or condescending). Or, "What do you think of using imagery techniques every night?" (which traps the athlete because it is a suggestion cloaked in question form). As Ivey (1983) suggests, "If you are going to make a statement, it is best not to frame it as a question" (p. 47).

- *Asking "why" questions more often than necessary.* These questions often put people on the defensive, sometimes producing the feeling of being grilled or trapped.

Confrontation

What should the coach do when an athlete offers mixed messages, discrepancies, untruths, or is simply not making sense? Should the player be labeled a liar? Should the "truth" be communicated in no uncertain terms with crude candor (e.g., "You're not starting, Bob, because you don't have very good skills. You might as well know the truth"). Instead, a powerful tool called *confrontation* might be used very carefully and sensitively. It is a technique that allows the client to understand the issues more clearly without feeling undue stress, guilt, and inadequacy. It is usually applied to overcome a defensive person or someone who has not acknowledged the facts.

Confrontation involves three steps. First, the athlete's mixed messages, lies, and incongruities have to be identified by the coach. Second, the player's messages must be pointed out clearly to him or her. Third, the coach and athlete must jointly work through the issues to a constructive conclusion. No one should leave the coach's office in tears, in anger, or in frustration, although sometimes this can't be helped; each is a way of dealing with a stressful situation. Effective confrontation includes the use of questioning, reflective listening, and feedback.

Identifying Incongruities and Mixed Messages.
When athletes behave in a manner that is inconsistent with what they say, then incongruent, contradictory, and mixed messages are being conveyed. How to identify the incongruity is the trick. Here's an example:

Athlete: Coach, I think I should get more playing time.
Coach: Could you tell me why you think so?
Athlete: I've been on the team longer than Jeff, who's starting, and quite honestly, I think I can do a better job. I even know the plays better than he does.
Coach: Bill, do you think your feeling of having more talent and the desire to play more is consistent with the number of times you've arrived late to practice, run at half-speed during wind sprints, and failed to cheer on your teammates during games? How do these habits square with deserving to play more? Where's the evidence of dedication?
Athlete: I didn't realize that I was doing those things, Coach, but I hear what you're saying. I'll show you a different approach in the future.

In this contrived example, the obvious inconsistency was between the athlete's feelings versus his behaviors, which the coach was compelled to point out—quickly. There was no attempt to tell the athlete that he was a bad person, a poor performer, or simply wrong. The coach merely pointed out discrepancies between the athlete's wishes and his behaviors. Other ways in which a person can display incongruities and inconsistencies include these examples:

- *Between two statements.* An athlete might say at one point how much he or she supports the team, yet indicate later that reaching his or her own personal goals is most important. For example, "I'll do whatever it takes to help this team to win. But I want to keep up my scoring average."

- *Between what one says and what one does.* An athlete may voice full loyalty to the coach yet miss team meetings, clown around at inappropriate times, or not make the effort to support his or her teammates.

- *Between statements and nonverbal behaviors.* A player might claim to be motivated and excited at some point before the game but act withdrawn (not maintaining eye contact when communicating this "excitement") and show nervousness and tension. In another example, some coaches may talk to their players about the importance of having fun when they compete. However, they do so in a loud and serious tone of voice without smiling. The message and the manner in which it is communicated are not consistent.

- *Between two nonverbal behaviors.* The athlete may be breaking out in a nervous sweat or looking pale while smiling or telling the coach that everything feels fine when, in fact, he or she is limping, holding an injured area, or appears to be in pain.

- *Between statements and the context.* A player may claim that he or she will be the game hero when, in fact, the player may have neither the skill nor the playing opportunity to live up to this expectation. Or a team may feel confident of victory prior to playing a far superior opponent. This is not to suggest that the team should not show up at the game. But having unrealistically high expectations could augment the disappointment of losing.

- *Between statements in different contexts.* The coach may say positive things to a player but then make negative statements to others about the same player.

Techniques for Confrontation

How should the coach handle the apparent discrepancy between fact and fiction? The most blunt technique is simply to tell the athlete about the difference in perception between the parties. A more sophisticated approach would be to follow these four steps:

1. *Identify the incongruity clearly by leading the athlete to self-confrontation.* "You say you want 'this,' but you're doing 'that.' How do you match what you say with what you're actually doing?"

2. *Draw out the specifics of the conflict with the use of questioning skills.* Give attention to each segment of the mixed message without appearing judgmental. Aim for facts. "OK, John, you say you never forget your field assignment. Let's review what happened when they scored in the final quarter last week." The coach would then ask one or more of the following questions to gather information, establish facts, and clarify perceptions, not to instill guilt and cause embarrassment (the athlete must not be "grilled" as though a crime had been committed; tone of voice should be low key and nonthreatening): "Where were you lined up?" "What formation were they using on the play in which they scored?" "Where are you supposed to go on this play?" "Where did the videotape indicate that you went?" "Were you covering the correct man?"

3. *Periodically summarize the different dimensions of the discrepancy.* For instance, you can say, "On the one hand . . . but on the other hand . . . ." Then add, "How does that sound to you? Am I on target? What do you think?"

4. *Provide feedback with opinions and observations about the discrepancies.* Here's an example: Janice, it is becoming increasingly difficult for me to believe that you really want to play volleyball, given the way you're going about preparing for the game. When I speak to the team, your eyes start to wander and you appear to be bored. At least that's my perception. For example, I asked each player to submit to me suggestions for making practice more exciting, and I received nothing from you. The message I get from you is that you don't want to be here. If I'm wrong, then help me to be a better coach by understanding the meaning of your actions. Nothing would make me happier than to help you out because I think you can contribute to this team, but only if you want to be here.

In this example, the coach is fostering decision making by the player as to whether or not she stays with the team. But most important, the athlete is being confronted with the realities of her behavior. The coach is risking losing this player by going into an area that raises serious questions about the player's willingness to be there. The door is now left open for her to leave the team. But, if she does, she has probably wanted to leave for quite some time.

Summarization

The technique of gathering together the client's words, behaviors, and feelings and then presenting them to the client in outline form is called *summarization*. Its purpose is to review the significant content of the conversation, to clarify the issues, and to agree on the athlete's message—before the coach responds. Summarizing is similar to paraphrasing but covers a longer time span and more information. Whereas a paraphrase might reflect a sentence or a few minutes of conversation, summarizations might be used to begin or end a complete interview, to act as a transition into a new topic, or to clarify lengthy and complex client issues.

Summarizing techniques can be used at the beginning, middle, and conclusion of the interview. The following session between an athlete and the team's sport psychology consultant provides some examples.

Beginning a Session. "The last time we met, Brad, we discussed your not feeling motivated to give 100 percent. It is well into the season, and you said your performance has been uneven—some good games and some games not so good. You indicated you are a bit fatigued and seem to feel a bit bored by it all. You thought it could be a midseason slump and that others were feeling the same. However, you thought that the whole team would benefit by getting away from the game for a few days. Examples included taking a one-day field trip somewhere or even camping out for a couple of days. Having a social event, however, would not do the job. You needed a longer time period to get your mind off the game. Am I right so far?" (Assuming the summary is accurate, the player nods in agreement.)

"We discussed two strategies. First, you and the team captain were going to talk to the coach privately about these feelings and see if a trip could be worked out at a reasonable cost to the players. The second strategy was to get a few players to form a team meeting to discuss issues related to the team's lack of enthusiasm, asking players to discuss openly the team's current midseason status, concerns, and feelings. The meeting would have two objectives: First, to form a plan for what to do about these issues, and second, to get a commitment from everyone to continue giving 100 percent and not to give up. Did I hit the main issues of our discussion, Brad? How have things gone since our last meeting?"

At the End of the Session. "OK, Brad, let's review what we've discussed today. You approached the coach, but he was not keen on a field trip, saying there wasn't the time or money. Second, you asked the coach to call a team meeting, which he did, but you were disappointed that no one really spoke out about feeling bored or tired as they told you privately. Am I right so far?" (Player agrees.) "Understandably you have not been very happy about not meeting the goals of the original plan. The issue now is, where do we go from here?"

The counselor then works with the athlete to formulate an optional plan to get several players—with permission from their parents, since this is a team of adolescent athletes or younger—to take a one-day or overnight trip after completing a home game. Or a trip to the "city" to see a professional sports team might be an option. About the player meeting issue, another plan is to have the players meet without the coach's presence (but with the coach's knowledge, if possible).

Short-Term Team Counseling

A university (U.S.) football coach once told me that a team meeting should never focus on the personal feelings of players because "it turns into a gripe session." In fact, this coach contends that when one player voices a complaint, the atmosphere snowballs into a widespread negative feeling on the team that did not exist before the meeting. In other words, he contends that complaints in groups have a bandwagon effect. Is this coach's view accurate? Do team meetings in which feelings and future team directions are discussed undermine team morale and cohesion? It is the major premise of this section that group discussions about the feelings of players (on various issues) are essential to team cohesion and morale. Team-related unresolved issues must surface and be confronted with the proper attention of all concerned parties. Otherwise, the athlete's full and proper attention and concentration will be diminished and redirected away from game preparation and skill development.

Team (group) counseling involves meeting in relatively small groups to share concerns; to explore common problems; to gain insight, knowledge, or understanding about issues; and to share these thoughts with one another (Grayson 1978). In addition, attempts are made to meet the objectives of the sessions in relatively short order so that issues can be quickly resolved and team members can give their proper concentration to preparing for the contest.

Team counseling does not involve addressing individual or personal issues, although exceptions to this rule exist. One exception is when a player is unable to establish a positive relationship with any other team member, an issue that affects the attitudes or performances of others. A second exception is when an issue concerns relatively few team members, at which time it is better to interact in a small group or individually with the athletes involved. Drug abuse, academic problems, lack of social contacts, personal feelings of dissatisfaction, concerns about the team or coach, and questions about a player's role on the team are all examples of items that do not belong on the team counseling agenda.

However, examples of issues that are open for discussion on a group basis might include the pervasive use of drugs by team members, the development or changing of team rules and policies, choice of team captains, widespread feelings of dissension, displeasure, lack of motivation (boredom), the team schedule, and concerns about other facets of the team affecting more than just a few team members. Discussions may also involve positive topics, such as reviewing the best plays from the previous game (on video, if possible), planning a social event, or discussing strategies for continued success. In short, group counseling, in addition to individual counseling, provides another vehicle for delivering help to athletes who need it. The trick of using team counseling as a constructive, rather than a destructive, tool is structuring the sessions so that issues are addressed positively (try to avoid shouting) and are resolved to everyone's satisfaction.

The Short-Term Counseling Process

If the purpose of having a team meeting is to share feelings, discuss concerns, offer opinions, and exchange information, then the participants must feel secure in the meeting environment. Having an open group dialogue means that the opinions of every group member must be tolerated and communicated without judgment, vindictiveness, or recrimination. For instance, if an athlete feels that there should be no curfew or bed checks, the opinion should be respected, dealt with, and resolved during the meeting.

The player should not be criticized, nor should the recommendation be ignored. This is not to say that every suggestion is valid or should be followed. Nor does it mean that the team should have a role in making every team policy; the coach also has an obligation to set limits and rules that are nonnegotiable. But the feelings of the players need to be exposed, and concerns resolved. Sometimes the team should be informed about the reasons for a particular nonnegotiable policy (Figure 9.7).

An example of a team counseling session in youth sports involved a player who was disliked by all of his teammates. Not only was this player, aged 12, being unmercifully scapegoated, but other team members seemed to be giving more of their attention to criticizing and blaming him for the team's problems than to learning skills and improving their performance. The coach, noting the constant ridicule and lack of attention to game preparation, called a meeting to resolve the issue. I was brought in as an observer to offer feedback to the coach regarding the conduct of all parties during the meeting.

Figure 9.7 Sometimes team-related issues require the coach's immediate attention so that concerns can be quickly addressed and resolved.

The coach began the meeting by stating his observations of the players' scapegoating behaviors and their lack of full concentration in game preparation. The meeting's purpose, then, was to resolve these concerns. Each player was given a chance to state his feelings about the ridicule and the reasons behind it. Some of the accusations were simply unfair (e.g., "I don't like the way Bill wears his hat"). But others were based on valid points about inappropriate behaviors (e.g., "Bill swears every time he doesn't get a hit").

The coach reacted to the views of each player with respect, allowing the speaker to complete all statements before moving on to the next athlete. No player was interrupted, although occasionally statements were clarified and summarized. Further, no single issue was dealt with until all players had an opportunity to speak. Then the subject under discussion, the scapegoated player, had a chance to offer his input by responding to the issues and asserting his own feelings about how it feels to receive constant ridicule from his teammates.

After input from all of the players was completed, the coach addressed each issue separately without making any value judgments about "good" versus "bad" responses. He did indicate, however, how unfair it is to criticize other persons based on the way they wear their hats, or comb their hair, or any other aspect of physical appearance. The session ended with several agreements among the coach, the players, and the scapegoated athlete.

This meeting not only helped a young athlete to have a more pleasant experience in sport but also redirected the team's energy from ganging up on one youngster to preparing for and playing the game. The atmosphere of the meeting was devoid of fear of retribution, moral "preaching," threats, criticism of a point of view, and continuation of name calling. The meeting was not a forum for additional scapegoating. The box on the next page includes suggestions for providing the proper environment for a team meeting and suggestions for what not to do.

Group counseling has the dual role of (1) exposing and exploring the feelings of group members in an open atmosphere and (2) supporting those participants who need help coping with their current predicament. According to Grayson (1978):

> Another supportive potential in group counseling is derived from the possibility that, when a member feels uneasy, anxious or threatened, for whatever reason, he or she may take refuge in the group. He or she can . . . melt into the group mass and not venture forth until he or she feels ready and secure. A good [coach] will sense this and will seek to provide the encouragement and warmth that will motivate the person to venture forth and risk making a contribution to the group process (p. 24).

If the coach perceives the use of team counseling as meaningful and potentially effective, then the chance of a warm, cordial atmosphere will be highly probable. Here are some advantages of short-term team counseling.

1. *To gauge group feelings.* In team counseling, coaches can spot group problems before they have a chance to spread among the players and undermine morale. Ultimately, the honesty and openness that develops between coach and athlete can be transformed into a highly effective tool to enhance player loyalty to the coach and the team.

2. *To provide information and insight.* From group counseling sessions, the coach can obtain information on the thoughts, feelings, needs, motives, and problems of the

Dos and Don'ts for Creating a Healthy Meeting Environment

Do:

- Be at the meeting location at least a few minutes in advance.
- Inform all invited players of the meeting's correct time and location.
- Be warm to the arriving players. Let them see a coach who is relaxed, yet serious.
- Meet at a location that is familiar and easily accessible to the players and that encourages privacy.
- State the meeting's purpose and goals—and stick to them; don't be influenced by extraneous issues.
- Accept all points of view no matter how irrational. Remember that acceptance doesn't mean that you agree with others but, rather, that you respect the athletes enough to allow them to express their opinions freely.
- Allow for a free exchange of views.
- Solicit the opinions of all members present.
- Be patient. Let the athletes do most of the talking. Then respond in a relaxed, sensitive, and mature (nondefensive) manner. And hold off on reacting to an opinion unless it is more constructive and informative to deal with the player's statement immediately. When in doubt, it's best to keep quiet.
- Use nonverbal positive feedback to the players' input with signals that indicate understanding of the message.
- Write down important points on a chalkboard or other surface visible to the group, particularly if the input needs to be reviewed and discussed further.
- Communicate to everyone the purpose, objectives, and format of the meeting. Will players be allowed to "barge in" with their opinions at any time or must they wait until later? Some counselors feel that formal approaches to group sessions stifle a warm, free communication style.
- If held at an appropriate time and venue, serve a small snack at the beginning (not end) of the meeting. Food, even just cookies, improves mood and facilitates communication.

Don't:

- Show anger if a player arrives late; deal with the tardiness later.
- Become visibly upset if a player disagrees with your opinion.
- Dominate the conversation.
- Voice your own opinions first. This "cuts off" the comments of the players, especially if they disagree with yours.
- Raise your voice; it puts listeners on the defensive.
- Patronize the athletes. Instead, address them with the same respect as you would any other adult and use their first name in discussions.
- Try to be "one of the guys" or close friends with the players. Differences in age, responsibilities, and expectations make such attempts unnatural and may make athletes uncomfortable.
- Be sarcastic. There's no room for appearing to be funny at the expense of a person's feelings.
- Be humorous if the situation is serious, although professional counselors suggest that some humor, if it's handled in a mature manner, could facilitate discussion.
- Allow any group member to be insulted or offended in any way by another group member.

team members. The coach, therefore, becomes more effective because he or she understands "what's happening behind the scenes."

3. *To humanize player-coach relationships.* Coaches should welcome the opportunity to interact with the players on an informal, nonthreatening basis rather than only in a sport-related context. Athletes are markedly more loyal to coaches who relate to them in ways beyond the role of player. Many athletes have warm feelings toward a coach who treats them as a mature, thinking human being rather than as a "mindless jock" (Anshel 1989a). Group counseling is a process that allows a coach to be "human," to say "I don't know," or to look into previously undiscovered issues. Even more important, the players have a chance to disclose their insecurities, questions, fears, and feelings on a variety of issues.

Planning the Group Meeting

Surgeons don't walk into the operating room before examining the patient's condition. Lawyers never enter a courtroom without prior extensive preparation. And, just as effective coaches would never approach a contest without a game plan, neither should they approach a team meeting unprepared. Several questions should be addressed. What is the meeting's purpose? Does a specific topic need attention, or is this a gathering with an open agenda? What outcomes need to be derived from the meeting? Is there a time limitation on completing the agenda? Who will lead the meeting? What will be the roles of the players, coach, team captains, and assistant coaches? Is someone dictating information, or is the item open for discussion? Will this be a passive audience (listening only) or will they take a more active role (discuss, debate, decide)? If a follow-up session is necessary, will the coach be able to indicate the time and place before the meeting is adjourned? The following are a few specific considerations in planning a successful team counseling session.

For Whom Is the Meeting Intended?   Determine with other responsible parties (such as assistant coaches and team captains) the meeting's purpose and who will attend. Should it be for the full team or only for a subgroup of players? Does the agenda require that only particular players attend but not others? Is privacy and confidentiality among selected players required?

What's There to Discuss?   The coach should have a fair idea about the meeting's content before it starts so that the manner of presenting an issue and responding to verbal input from players is planned—or at least given some thought—in advance. This does not suggest that a coach should always anticipate his or her responses to projected questions and statements before the meeting. However, the meeting presents a golden opportunity for the coach to demonstrate that he or she is "in control" and comfortable with team policies, yet secure with discussing change. The coach should be knowledgeable about the alternatives available to him or her on any given issue. One response that players do *not* want to hear is, "We do it this way because *I'm* the coach, that's why."

Be Prepared to Be Put on the Spot.   It's not uncommon for coaches to be asked provocative questions—some of which do not require (indeed, should not receive) an answer. For example, during discussion of a no-smoking team policy, one high school athlete asked his coach, "Why can't we smoke if you smoke, Coach?" A college player quizzed her coach on the hypocrisy of a rule against smoking marijuana when the coach was accused of trying it in the past. How should the coach respond to such testing of authority (or challenging the double standard, as some have put it)?

Preplanning responses to challenging questions will help to prevent the coach from having nothing (or worse, the wrong thing) to say. According to most authorities in counseling, coaches should avoid talking about themselves; their role is to foster communication among group members and not allow the group to control the session. Asking or challenging the coach to defend his or her personal habits and behaviors places the coach on the defensive and leads the discussion away from the real issue. So, the first rule of thumb about responding to such personal questions is not to respond to the question at all. In other words, don't provide an answer beginning with "because." Here are a few suggested responses to such provocative questions:

- "Smoking marijuana is illegal, and it is my responsibility to prevent the athletes on this team from breaking the law."
- "Why do I smoke cigarettes? The issue here is *your* behavior, not mine. As an adult who is not involved in competitive sport, I understand the negative consequences of smoking and how bad it is for my health. It is a decision that I must live with, perhaps living a shorter and less healthy life."
- "I cannot give you permission to smoke for three reasons. First, it's bad for sport performance. You lose endurance. Second, I cannot allow you to maintain a habit that has proven to be so harmful to health while you are on my team, because I have a responsibility to protect your health. And third, most people of your age smoke because of peer pressure, because it's the "in" thing to do; it's "cool." Young men and women need protection from this pressure by someone in an authority position. This removes the pressure on you to conform. Now you can say, 'Hey guys, I can't smoke because the coach won't allow us' or 'The coach will kill me if he (or she) finds out.'"

What Is the Role of Team Captains? One of the surprises I've experienced as a sport psychology consultant is that some coaches are less knowledgeable than I thought about the role of team captains. One college football coach (with 10 years of experience as a high school coach) told me that "To this day, I don't know what a team captain should do beyond leading team exercises and working the coin toss before the game." Well, one very important role for a team captain is to lead team (or partial team) meetings—either in the presence of, or perhaps more comfortably, the absence of team coaches. Captains might lead sessions that partially determine the team meeting agenda.

Often, players are more apt to disclose feelings with their peers than in the presence of the coach. And they may more comfortably decide issues or determine policies that the coach has delegated to the team. For instance, should there be a team party after the season? If so, where will it be held, and should personal friends be invited? Of the list of videos the coach has provided, which one would the players like to see on the night before the game? Coaches should be cautious in living up to these agreements. Giving responsibility to and supporting the team and team captain's decisions on selected issues is critical. Preplanning is essential to effective control and content of team meetings. Coaches should not have the team meet without goals and an agenda that is well thought out. The next step is implementation.

Implementing the Meeting

One way to avoid having a meeting that no one wants or that elicits virtually no active participation by the players is to be clear and honest with the group at the start. Remember that the purpose of the meeting may be to address a need, either of the team, an individual player, a group of players, or the coach. As the players enter the meeting area, allow a brief time for "chitchat" among them. Informal interaction among group members before a meeting often serves to relax participants. Serving refreshments at this time may improve the players' moods and relax the atmosphere of the meeting. Perhaps the coach can also speak informally with a few players or with other team personnel. This is a time to loosen up. Anxious group members do not talk; relaxed, secure members do. The coach is now ready to open the session, one in which an exchange of feelings is planned. See Anshel (1992b) for additional guidelines in conducting group and individual meetings for coaches and other supervisors.

The Meeting's Purpose. Inform the players at the start about why you've gathered. Stating the meeting's purpose helps the participants to stay on track rather than trying to cover too much ground or discussing extraneous issues. For example: "The purpose of getting together is to review the strengths and weaknesses of our weekly practice schedule and to try to meet the needs of many of you who claim to need more time to study. If this meeting is going to be successful, it will require that the people in this room feel comfortable about voicing their opinions. That means each of you."

Expectations of the Meeting. What are reasonable expectations of the meeting? Can players and coaches expect to reach decisions on at least certain issues at the end of the gathering? Or is it more probable that the coaches will take the athletes' feelings (those generated in the meeting) into consideration and decide on a plan of action in the near future? To keep expectations about the meeting's outcome realistic and conservative is important. In most cases, change takes time, and deciding to make changes from previous habits or policies takes even longer. Rarely should the coach promise a change or decision before the meeting ends unless the meeting's primary objective was to resolve an issue. Then a decision is imperative.

Establishing the Ground Rules. If full participation is to take place, the players need to feel secure about several items. For instance, they should be made to feel that everything said in the meeting will remain *confidential*. To gain trust and credibility, the coach may need to promise not to tell parents that their son or daughter engages in some behavior of which they would not approve. If it is learned that a player broke the law, the promise of confidentiality means that the coach will not consult the school principal or law officers unless school policy dictates otherwise. Of course, it is also against the law to hide information about a past crime, and the coach does have an obligation to convince the athlete to approach school or legal authorities under extreme conditions. In extreme cases (e.g., assault, robbery, taking or selling drugs), the coach has a moral and legal obligation to consult the proper authorities.

Another ground rule is a promise not to use the athlete's words against him or her in future encounters. What would a player's perception be if he or she said something at the meeting that may have offended the coach and never or rarely played thereafter, especially if that player received more playing time in contests before the meeting? Could the coach keep the team's loyalty and trust? Could the coach again be viewed as credible? Unlikely! So, it might be prudent to tell the players, "This is the time to get those feelings off your chest" or "I will respect all points of view at this meeting without feeling insulted or upset, as long as we talk to one another in a mature manner and with respect." For many athletes, a preferable tactic would be to have the team captain or an assistant coach run the meeting rather than the head coach.

A third ground rule concerns the *choice of topics* under discussion. The coach may feel that it would be more productive to center the discussion on one or two issues at a given session and then discuss other issues at another meeting held at a later date. The coach might suggest: "Let's keep the discussion limited to your feelings about practice time and game preparation. In this way, there's a better chance of reaching an agreement sooner than if we were to go off in different directions. At the next meeting, we can discuss other issues."

Another rule is to encourage the participation of all team members present, but *not to force participation*. Players can be invited to send an anonymous note about their feelings at some future time if so desired. Also, participants should agree that one or more players may not dominate the conversation unless the players announce that one player is acting as the spokesperson for the group. However, the participation of relatively few players may defeat the purpose of a team meeting. Further, team counseling (expressing feelings, changing behavior, and so on) requires massive participation. Only in this way will each athlete feel responsible for fulfilling the agreement of the meeting.

Respecting the feelings of each participant is another ground rule. Before the meeting, members should agree that none of them will be insulted, teased, ridiculed, abused, laughed at, or threatened. Everyone should be entitled to and respected for his or her point of view.

Finally, the time limitation of the meeting should be announced before beginning. For example: "We will adjourn in one hour," "We need to conclude this meeting no later than 6 P.M. I will tell you when we have 10 minutes left," or "In another five minutes, we will bring the discussion to a halt, and I'll summarize where the group stands and then review our options."

The Meeting's Verbal Content. Coaches can assume that group participants are going to be initially cautious about becoming involved too quickly. They'll want to "test the waters" by observing how the coach responds to other participants. Group meetings foster self-consciousness which, in turn, inhibits free expression, at least initially. Therefore, it is crucial that the discussion leader be accepting of nearly all input, giving full recognition to all participants.

Grayson (1978) makes the following additional suggestions to keep the session moving:

1. Guard against going on unrelated tangents.
2. Give credit to individuals for all contributions, however minute.
3. Take time out at appropriate points in the session to summarize what has been said up to that point, being fair to each point of view.

4. Point out related areas or issues that the group might explore.

5. Encourage the expression of different points of view. Know the difference between inaccurate information and personal opinions. The latter should always be encouraged unconditionally (no "right" and "wrong" reaction), whereas the expression of misperceived or wrong information needs correction.

6. Tactfully discourage "soap box" oration, including that of the group leader.

7. Patiently help members to express themselves if they are floundering in the attempt.

Closing the Session. As indicated earlier, the length of the meeting and ending time should be determined and communicated to all group members at the start. The coach should remember several points about terminating the session:

- *Be prompt when ending the meeting.* If one hour is set aside for the meeting, stick with the schedule.

- *Summarize.* At the time of termination, review the highlights of the session with the group. The summary should include a brief restatement of all points of view expressed by team members. Were there any particularly interesting issues raised or statements made during the session that are deserving of further comment? Group participants will feel a sense of closure, purpose, and accomplishment if the numerous comments and issues are crystallized into meaningful units. In this way, the meeting's contents and decisions will be better remembered and the basis for the decisions better understood. This means more support for carrying out these decisions.

- *Suggest further exploration.* Certain points may need additional discussion at subsequent meetings. Perhaps more information must be gathered or more exploration of established policies is needed before a decision can be made. The coach, in his or her concluding comments, can point out these needs, which will be the basis for further discussion. Perhaps a committee can be formed whose responsibility it is to generate recommendations or obtain information about an issue. Name the committee members at the meeting and provide their objectives, task(s), and a deadline by which to provide their findings.

- *Thank participants and offer special recognition.* There's nothing wrong with expressing gratitude to group members for their attendance and participation. At this time, the coach might want to suggest that certain positive outcomes were derived from the meeting. These may include a sense of fulfillment and accomplishment in expressing feelings and making decisions, feelings of team togetherness, improved team morale, an optimistic view of the team's future, better team member satisfaction, learning and sharing new ideas that might improve team or individual performance, and, perhaps most important of all, the coach's sense of appreciation for the players' candor and honesty in expressing their sentiments. If possible, the coach should inform the group when the next session will be held and provide some information about the possible agenda for that session. This allows the players time to think about the issues, to plan their responses, and to begin to make observations and notations that may serve as topics or ideas for further discussion.

After the Session. When the meeting has concluded, the session leader should remain in the meeting area to discuss any personal or follow-up issues with group members.

Unless previously arranged and announced, the coach should not socialize with the players at a club or restaurant after the meeting. Players need the opportunity and the "space" to share their feelings about meeting content and to discuss ideas about future directions of the team without the presence of an authority figure. After all, the coach is not the players' "buddy" or best friend. The coach's job at this point is to ensure the proper follow-through on issues and decisions that were discussed. It is crucial that decisions from the session be carried out as soon as possible (or when agreed upon) to support the coach's credibility. In some cases, a written summary of the meeting's points and decisions might be distributed to the players within a few days after the meeting.

The coach should be consistent in his or her behavior toward the athletes between meetings. Imagine the players' confusion if the coach espouses in meetings the need for players to be open and sensitive to one another, yet tends to ignore or reject certain players. All the work it takes to gain the athletes' loyalty can go down the drain very quickly if coaches preach one set of actions yet demonstrate another set toward the participants.

Finally, on occasion participants can evaluate the session by having players complete an anonymous form in response to specific questions about the session (with room for additional comments). Alternatively, the team captain can get verbal feedback from several players. Perhaps the captain can offer the coach a summary. In this way, confidentiality and anonymity are ensured.

General Recommendations

No one said counseling athletes was easy. In fact, it's important to remember that a certain type of counseling expertise, called clinical psychology (or psychotherapy), requires additional training and legal recognition with a state board of licensed psychologists. But providing counsel to most athletes about sport does not require the same level of expertise. Here are some simple guidelines for the amateur counseling coach offered by Chappell (1984) and others in the literature:

1. Make personal contact with every athlete on the team—starters and substitutes. This includes establishing an open-door policy.
2. If the head coach is unwilling or unable to establish rapport with an athlete, make sure that at least one other member of the staff (even the coach's spouse) can. The important thing is that all performers need someone with whom they can speak.
3. Talk regularly with support staff (such as athletic trainers, medical personnel, consultants, counselors, even family members) about the athletes. Their impressions can help to support or dispel the head coach's perceptions.
4. Be genuine. Even youngsters are aware of insincerity. Be yourself and respond honestly—the athletes will respect this and will give you, their coach, more trust and credibility.
5. Be supportive and strive at all times to build the players' self-esteem and self-confidence. A positive self-image improves performance and other aspects of the players' lives. Criticisms related to skills and specific performance are necessary but can be done constructively, at the proper time and place.
6. Encourage outside interests and a balanced preparation for life beyond the sport experience. Coaches must communicate to the players that sport is only one facet of life, albeit an important one.

7. On a personal, one-on-one basis, do not treat all athletes alike. The psychological needs of each athlete differ. For instance, not all players respond to the same approach; some need—even expect—a stricter approach than others. Experts in industrial psychology suggest that managers think about treating others not so much the way they would want to be treated but, rather, the way they feel that their subordinates would want, or need, to be treated.

8. When it comes to team rules, however, all athletes should be treated alike. The starter should receive the same reaction for breaking a rule as the substitute. Inconsistency will affect the coach's credibility.

9. The individual's best interests should be put above the team's (though many coaches would find this suggestion controversial). Examples include not playing an injured athlete, allowing an athlete to practice less in order to study, or taking the pressure off a key player in the big game because of extraordinarily high stress. This approach may appear to reduce the team's chances of winning the next contest, but it will more likely pay off in the long run. Perhaps a player who stays qualified academically or stays healthy and well-adjusted will ultimately be of greater benefit to the team.

10. Be aware of the way in which athletes relate to one another. Discourage cruel, nonsupportive behavior. The coach sets the example; to allow (or model) such behavior is to condone it, and team member satisfaction will suffer.

11. Try to meet each athlete's parents or other family members. They can serve as excellent sources of support in the attempt to enhance the player's attitude and performance if they are convinced that the coach's priority is their child's well-being.

12. Finally, remember your responsibility as the team adult leader and supervisor. Sometimes this means setting rules and limits on player behavior. It also means that you do not need to justify every policy and action. Sometimes coaches need to help athletes overcome peer pressure to do the "wrong thing." Group (team) members feel more secure when they know their leader is in control. Coaches should demonstrate their knowledge, concern, and leadership by doing what they think is best without abusing the athlete's integrity.

SUMMARY

The amount of information and number of suggestions contained in this chapter may seem to be overwhelming. Coaches and sports officials may feel justified in concluding that "I just want to be myself and forget this 'stuff' about how to talk to athletes." Others might say that they have coached or officiated a long time without resorting to psychological techniques and still have been quite successful. It is not suggested that coaches, referees, umpires, and judges dismiss their present modes and styles of communication and switch to a new set of behaviors. Instead, the content of this chapter offers these individuals a chance to examine the emotional impact that they have on athletes. These insights can help make them more successful. Developing new communication strategies could mean the difference between success and failure to a team or to a particular athlete.

Questions that coaches might want to ask are whether their use of certain words or emotions are effective in helping the athlete succeed or whether they are actually inhibiting the athlete from performing at peak levels. They might also consider whether their intentions are being perceived accurately, whether something about their demeanor fosters or inhibits open dialogue with team members, whether conversations with players and assistants easily turn into arguments, and whether they usually force their point of view on others without hearing the other side. Do players or assistants take advantage of their coach, or do they tend to avoid confrontations at all costs? The answers to these questions, and others, will help coaches take a close look—perhaps for the first time—at how they are perceived by others, which in turn will help point out areas for further personal growth.

Effective communication is a difficult assignment. It's an art to translate thoughts and feelings into words and actions. And it's virtually impossible to fake being a sensitive human being. Communication also involves effectively using certain techniques that meet the speaker's objectives in affecting the listener. Coaches cannot affect the thoughts, feelings, and actions of athletes and other team personnel unless they are aware of the manner in which they communicate information—verbally and nonverbally.

This chapter includes 10 guidelines, or "commandments," that are very important to being an effective communicator in coaching sport. These include being honest, empathetic, and consistent with all team members; using positive nonverbal cues; teaching skills; praising and criticizing behavior and not personality; expressing feelings constructively; respecting the integrity of others; not being defensive; and avoiding sarcasm. The chapter also offers guidelines for athletes to use when communicating with their coach, verbally and in written form. In fact, coaches are urged to consider providing players and coaching assistants with an opportunity to express their views in writing in addition to face-to-face discussion. Sports officials will also benefit from using effective communication techniques.

Keeping calm, treating players and coaches with respect, explaining decisions, selectively ignoring comments, and not trying to have the last word are just a few suggestions for a more effective officiating performance.

Counseling is helping normal people to cope with normal problems and opportunities. In coaching, it involves responding to the attitudes, feelings, and behaviors of the athletes (and, for that matter, all other team personnel). Counseling is based on the counselor's sincerity, honesty, warmth, and sensitivity in the communication process, and consists of an array of techniques that are enacted to help clients (individual athletes or the team) to resolve issues and to meet personal goals.

Fundamental counseling skills include listening, showing concern, respecting privacy and confidentiality, and being supportive and honest. With the microskills approach to counseling, the coach's primary objective is to interact with the athlete by using an array of listening and speaking skills. The counseling coach moves toward confronting issues and, then, through the athlete's new insights, begins to help resolve these issues. The coach's role is to ask the right questions and respond appropriately to the player's answers on an individual and group basis.

Team counseling is somewhat different in terms of the types of issues that need to be addressed and the techniques used to resolve them. Although the same fundamental communication skills are necessary in team sessions, the coach is faced with additional challenges, such as dealing with team silence or confronting and resolving the feelings of several athletes. The players' feelings may or may not be compatible among all team members or with those of the coach on a given issue. Resolving (perhaps preventing) controversy involves the coach's use of strategies, from planning the meeting to preparing several approaches—in advance—for responding to the players' feelings. The fundamental imperative is that coaches respect the feelings of others during the counseling process, no matter how incompatible those feelings may be with those of the coach.

REVIEW QUESTIONS

1. Describe the three parts of the sandwich approach to effective communication and corrective feedback. Provide an example of a situation in which you would apply it.

2. In this chapter, honesty, loyalty, and credibility are three of the most important characteristics that coaches should possess if they want to be effective motivators, educators, and communicators. Describe three behaviors of the coach that help to promote these traits and three behaviors that diminish or eliminate each of these traits.

3. As a coach, how would you respond to an athlete who approaches you and expresses his or her negative feelings about not playing? He or she is certain that the teammate who plays his or her position is inferior. What strategies can a coach employ that would help to prevent the athlete from feeling this way in the first place? Remember to use some of the 10 commandments.

4. Describe the behavioral strategies an athlete might use in speaking with the coach privately.

5. Describe five guidelines game officials might use to promote effective communication with coaches and players. Indicate the circumstances under which each technique would be appropriate.

6. What are *attending* and *influencing* behaviors? Provide an example of each.

7. Describe the nonverbal behaviors that counselors can use to facilitate client communication. Which nonverbal behaviors inhibit communication?

8. Encouraging, paraphrasing, and summarizing are three strategies for effective individual counseling. Create a dialogue between coach and athlete—perhaps two or three paragraphs in length—in which the coach is using each of these techniques.

9. Asking the right kinds of questions in a sensitive manner is important in counseling an athlete. Name and give an example of the two types of questions. How can each type of question be used incorrectly? Create a discussion in which the coach is asking both types of questions in order (a) to gain further insight into the situation, (b) to help the athlete become aware of his or her behaviors, and (c) to seek alternatives to the situation.

10. What is confrontation? How can it be used by a coach in a sensitive way to help an athlete understand certain behaviors or habits?

11. Describe the steps a coach could take in preparing for a team counseling session.

12. How can the coach promote group interaction in a team meeting? What could a coach do if the interaction stalls?

CHAPTER 10

Coaching Youth Sports: Special Considerations

W hat is going on? The seriousness with which the adult world takes children's sports is getting out of control—in one recent case resulting in a homicide. On July 8, 2000, the Associated Press reported that "Mr. Michael Costin, a 40-year-old single father of four, was beaten into a coma . . . in front of some children at [an ice hockey rink at a Boston suburb]. He was declared brain dead [the next day]. . . . Thomas Junta, 42, had been conviction with assault and battery before Mr. Costin's death. 'We are now treating this death as a possible homicide,'" according to a District Attorney (*Dallas Morning News*, July 8, 2000, p. 6A). Mr. Junta is now serving an extended prison sentence on a conviction of manslaughter. Apparently, Mr. Junta did not approve of the strategy of Mr. Costin, who was his 10-year-old son's coach. Earlier in the year, the *Dallas Morning News* (March 17, 2000) reported another assault, this time by a "hockey dad who allegedly got mad when his son was benched in the final minutes of a game." According to reports, "Mr. Matteo Picca, 40, was indicted on a second-degree assault charge ... for breaking the coach's nose [with two hockey sticks]" (p. 2B).

The volunteer coach for the city league was meeting just before the game with his young athletes, boys aged 9 and 10 years. He was talking about how important it was for everyone to play well and win; this was a "big game." Then he asked whether anyone had any questions. A youngster raised his hand and asked, "Coach, will everyone get a chance to play?" "What's more important," the coach snapped back, "everyone playing, or winning?" In a nutshell, these actual stories illustrate two things: first, the problem with youth sport today, and second, the different needs and priorities of child athletes as compared with those of the "mature," grown sport competitor.

Youth sports typically include children aged 16 years and younger who are involved in adult-organized sport programs (Gould 1987). Adult-organized programs are characterized by an arranged schedule of contests for children in a competitive environment using prescribed rules (Martens & Seefeldt 1979). They may be held within or outside a school. This means that pick-up games and other free-play situations are not considered youth sport. About 20 million children and adolescents participate in organized sport programs in the United States (Brustad 1993).

The purpose of this chapter is to take a close look at child athletes, specifically at their needs as children, and how being a sport competitor can meet these needs; the reasons they participate in sport and why they drop out; how child athletes differ from older, higher skilled players; and finally, how coaches and parents of young performers should help the young athletes enjoy the experience of competitive sport. First, however, we will examine the social and cultural factors that influence sport participation, especially for females.

Sport Socialization

Socialization is the process by which society communicates to an individual the kind of person that he or she is expected to be. Individuals learn to play various social roles to be effective members of society. Over the years, these roles have been rather well defined for males and females in sport. In one study (Wittig et al. 1986), sports were judged to be more important for males than for females by both genders. As the researchers explained, females who choose to participate in sport step outside recognized social boundaries and confront a dilemma. It is easy to see the social and emotional limitations placed upon young girls who desire to engage in sport. Moreover, females who do engage in sport, particularly after reaching puberty and later, are exceptional in terms of overcoming societal barriers. These barriers are less restrictive of leisure activities but do discourage sport competition. How, then, do athletes and nonathletes differ in the socialization process?

Probably the most inclusive, extensive, and current explanation of socialization into sport and physical activity is derived from the General Model of Achievement and Activity Choice by Eccles and Harold (1991), which is illustrated in Figure 10.1. In their model, the authors assume that a person's decision to engage in particular activities is based on a variety of perceptions the individual has about his or her ability, expectations for success, and the value that sport holds in the individual's life. Eccles and Harold build their model "on the assumption that it is one's interpretation of reality rather than reality itself . . . that most directly influences activity choices" (p. 8). It is a person's socialization experiences that strongly influence these interpretations. Although a review of their model is beyond the scope of this chapter, it contains the four primary factors that influence involvement in sport and physical activity: (1) socialization factors, (2) situational and environmental factors, (3) family trends, and (4) personal factors.

Socialization Factors. Can you recall any person in particular who had a major impact on your decisions, attitudes, and habits? Did a coach, parent, friend, or professional athlete make a strong impression on you? Have you ever found yourself imitating or following the directions of another person? If you value the opinion or advice of an individual, you regard that individual as a *significant other*. And if a group of persons has a marked personal influence over you, you regard them as a *reference group*. Reference groups comprise several individuals who collectively direct or modify a person's attitudes, choices, and behaviors concerning what the person should become. Examples include the nuclear family (mother, father, and siblings), coaches in sport, the peer group, school personnel, the mass media, and neighbors. Females who have become athletes seem to be especially influenced in this decision by their reference groups.

Although female athletes have disproportionately more parents who were former athletes when compared to female nonathletes (Greendorfer 1992), biological explana-

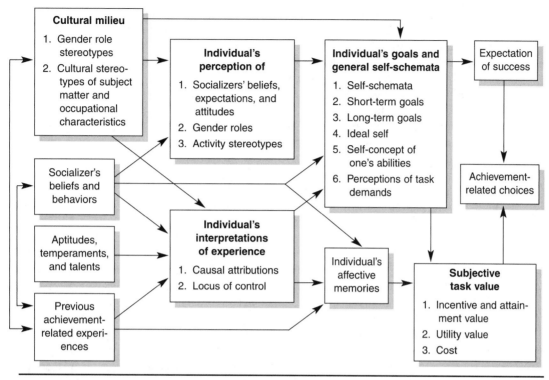

Figure 10.1 General model of achievement and activity choice.

From J. Eccles & R. Harold, "Gender differences in sport involvement: Applying the Eccles expectancy-value model." *Journal of Applied Sport Psychology*, *3*, no. 1 (pp. 7–35). Copyright © 1991 by Allan Press: Lawrence, KS. Reprinted with permission.

tions for engaging in sport have not been supported by researchers. For example, girls tend to select sports identical to those in which their mothers currently or formerly participated. Miller (1974) confirms this extensive parental involvement. In her review of related research, she found that female golf and tennis players tended to be reared in families in which at least one parent was an active sport participant. When this was not the case, the child athlete was surrounded by siblings, usually older, or other relatives with similar sport-related interests. It is likely that the home environment offers the support, incentive, and models for some young girls that makes a sport experience more attractive (Eccles & Harold 1991). In her reviews of research published 12 years apart, Greendorfer (1980, 1992) found that family influence continued to be the best predictor of sport involvement. This means that parental attitudes and preferences are also passed on to offspring.

If parents perceive a particular activity as more appropriate for a female and others as more restricted to males, the young female will tend to develop attitudes about which sports she may and may not choose to learn. This is referred to as *gender typing*, or sex typing (Greendorfer, Lewko, & Rosengren 1996). Mothers and fathers may worry about their son's attraction toward ballet or their daughter's willingness to play touch football. But it isn't usually the mothers who decide which sports are appropriate for their children. Researchers Lewko and Greendorfer (1977) found that fathers are the most "important others" in making these judgments, and that girls are more negatively affected by lack of a father's support than boys are. Thus, when a female desires to participate in a sport deemed more appropriate for males, she may receive more negative feedback—especially from her father—than if she were male and played a sport that was perceived as feminine.

Gender typing is supported by social learning theory. For example, according to Greendorfer et al. (1996), girls are rewarded less than boys for taking an interest in, and developing, motor skills. Girls are also discouraged from participating in vigorous physical activity, and are not provided with the same opportunities for sport skill instruction as boys. To Greendorfer et al., "these early socialization practices influence later sport involvement [resulting in] low rates of female participation," as compared with males (p. 89). The authors contend, however, that recent data suggest that "more females are engaged in sport and physical activity than during any other period in American history" (p. 89). The likely primary source of this change in female sport participation is that parents now view sports as an appropriate outlet of recreation and physical activity for both their daughters and their sons. Gender typing, then, results in gender role socialization, in which distinctions are made between what is and is not appropriate for each sex. These decisions are determined from the family's cultural ideology and from the characteristics of each individual family unit.

Siblings close in age, usually within three years, interact in play groups throughout the socialization years (Leventhal 1968). Leventhal's *sibling-similarity hypothesis* suggests that second-born children model much of their behavior on the male or female first-born sibling. Thus, girls with older brothers tend to identify more strongly with, and practice, activities in which boys typically engage. Several studies support this premise.

But does this mean that coaches should ignore female sport participants who have older sisters? Not according to the *social system balance theory* of Parsons and Bales (1955). The reasoning of this theory is that persons with opposite-sex siblings can identify more with the same-sex parent. With same-sex siblings, the opposite-sex parent is a more powerful model. Thus, females with sisters will tend to identify more strongly with their fathers and be overrepresented in sport. But contrary to the sibling-similarity hypothesis, females with male siblings will have a greater tendency to emulate their mothers. Research findings are less than conclusive in support of these hypotheses.

Eccles and Harold's (1991) model predicts that the individual's perceptions of the beliefs, expectations, and attitudes of significant others are important determinants of future sport involvement. The role of these individuals (i.e., parents, coaches, peers, school teachers, television and film actors, siblings, friends, and neighbors) is to be interpreters of experience and providers of experience. Interpretation of experiences includes defining success and failure, achievement, and satisfaction. The role of provider helps individuals have different opportunities "to discover their various talents and interests and, thus, [they] are likely to form different self-perceptions and task values" (pp. 13–14).

In summary, the approval for sport and exercise participation by parents and peers reinforces a child's willingness to become involved in these activities and to have the incentive to maintain participation and interest. Although the model also includes cultural values and stereotypes that influence the *type* of sport selected for involvement, any conflict between traditional cultural roles and the child athlete's internalizing of this conflict may be negligible (Allison 1991). In this way, personal factors such as high self-concept, self-confidence, and a personal belief in the child's ability to succeed appear to play a more important role than societal expectations.

The important points to remember about the role of significant others and reference groups for participation of children in sport and exercise include the following:

- Both male and female sport performers are more likely to come from families that are active in or support participation in sport.
- The interest in developing sport skills and maintaining athletic participation begins in childhood, but participation should not be restricted to one sport, unless this is the child's own wish. Specializing in some sports (e.g., tennis, swimming) need not occur until the adolescent years, whereas other sports (e.g., gymnastics) require childhood participation.
- Children are more likely to persist at sport involvement if they are surrounded by proper models with whom they can identify or from whom they receive reinforcement. Brothers and fathers in particular should encourage continued play and skill improvement.
- When examining the factors that contribute to a young athlete's desire to compete in sport, researchers find no differences between boys and girls. Both sexes experience similar socialization in the development of attitudes and feelings about becoming and remaining an athlete.

Socialization factors that influence involvement in sport go beyond family and friends. In recent years, several writers in sport psychology have recognized the importance of *culture* to help explain gender differences in sport. Krane (1994), for example, contends that coaches, teachers, and even parents differ in their beliefs about and expectations toward male and female sport participants, which in turn strongly influences the athletes' attitudes, dispositions, and performance. Krane states, "gendered beliefs affect the experiences of female athletes as they are expected to be at a psychological disadvantage and less adept at sport than their male counterparts." The source of these lower expectations is "cultural differences that lead boys to highlight their skills and girls to downplay their talents" (p. 404). The result, Krane argues, is reduced quality and quantity of skill instruction and less positive social reinforcement for females as compared with their male peers. These factors, taken together, may partially explain why females exhibit lower self-confidence and different attributional styles (i.e., tendencies in explaining the causes of performance outcomes) than males.

Krane's views have been supported in a study by Clifton and Gill (1994) on self-confidence among male and female university cheerleaders. The researchers found that gender differences in self-confidence depend on the extent to which subjects viewed the task as "feminine" or "masculine." First, cheerleading was perceived as more feminine among typical college students than by the cheerleaders, who rated cheering as more gender neutral. Second, even the cheerleaders indicated a gender bias toward different cheering tasks. Both male and female cheerleaders rated partner stunts as more masculine, whereas dance was rated as more feminine. A particularly interesting result of this study was that female cheerleaders were more self-confident than their male peers on all tasks rated by both groups as feminine or gender neutral. In only one area, partner stunts, rated as masculine by both genders, were males more self-confident. Clifton and Gill suggest that research on gender differences in self-confidence should consider the sport and the task within that sport when measuring confidence rather than simply examining one global confidence question.

Finally, studies indicate that both males and females want and need an opportunity to play competitive sport. Women who have received extensive exposure to sport situations during their growth and development are more inclined to have a positive attitude toward athletic participation than women who have been relatively isolated from such experiences (Allison 1991). Specifically, the home, neighborhood, school, role models, peers, and exposure to the mass media are influential agents of sport socialization. The importance of each agent and situation varies for different age groups and sports and for different societies.

Situational and Environmental Factors. Several factors that occur prior to, during, or following a sport experience may influence subsequent participation. For example, Eccles and Harold (1991) contend in their model that the person's long-term and short-term goals, perceptions of task demands, expectations of success, and causal attributions (i.e., explaining the causes of performance outcomes) all influence the choice to participate in sport and physical activity. The one factor that all these issues have in common is their motivational properties. It is because of this characteristic that these are labeled situational rather than personal factors. As indicated in Chapter 3, goal setting has long been known to have a motivational influence on initiating and persisting at a task. Female and male athletes will more likely engage in a task when standards toward which they strive are determined and viewed by the athlete as desirable. Perceptions that task demands are achievable and within the performer's ability are also motivational—and situationally specific.

Expectations of success, the next factor, should be positive and achievable. According to Gill et al. (1984), "Perceived ability and expectancies not only influence performance, but also mediate the interpretation of success or failure" (p. 340). That is, persons who expect to succeed tend to feel good about their ability and effort in response to their success—should they achieve it. This leads to the next factor, causal attributions. After the performance outcome is derived, the competitor searches for an explanation for the outcome (see Chapter 4). When athletes conclude that success was obtained because of their high ability or good effort, they will tend to remain sport participants. These "internal" causes of success are highly motivational. However, if the performer concludes that failure is due to low ability or that success is due to external factors, such as an easy task, low-skilled opponent, or good luck, the incentive to persist at the activity is diminished. Hence, how an athlete reacts to particular situations strongly influences the motivation to remain a participant and to find pleasure from the situation. Females do not differ from males on these situational characteristics; however, apparently, a combination of forces best explains if, how long, and at what skill level a female engages in sport. Situations and significant others interact. It is imperative that the opportunity to play sports is accompanied by the presence of others who act as reinforcers of her attraction to sport. Young girls would be unlikely to experience and to maintain their interest in sport if they did not receive the approval and reward (through positive feedback, successful performance, or both) from a parent, peer, or instructor (Oglesby & Hill 1993).

Family Trends. Contemporary society, in general, and the socialization process within the family unit, in particular, have evolved considerably in recent years, at least in North America. Two trends that may influence the sport involvement of boys and girls include increased levels of maternal employment and greater participation of fathers in child rearing. Conversely, a steadily increasing divorce rate and more single parenting potentially create greater demands on a single parent, in time and financial resources, to provide their children with organized sport experiences.

With respect to changing parental patterns among mothers, maternal employment may lead to increased maternal power in the family (Greendorfer et al. 1996). The working mother, in turn, may become an even stronger role model to her daughter(s). Greendorfer et al. surmise that "children of working mothers are more likely to receive fewer gender-stereotypic sport socialization influences; therefore, such children might make significantly different sport involvement choices than children of nonworking mothers" (p. 103). Fathers, on the other hand, have traditionally been the strongest influence on their children for sport involvement. A perusal of the literature indicates that, though fathers are more involved with their children than ever before, they remain far less involved than mothers. Evidence is still lacking about whether children, especially daughters, of highly involved fathers participate in sport or select certain types of sports at a different rate than children of less involved fathers (Greendorfer et al. 1996). Nevertheless, it is intuitively appealing to conclude that the extent of parental involvement with children, especially that of fathers, will influence their children's decisions—both sons' and daughters'—about participating in organized sport.

Personal Factors. The skills and dispositions that athletes bring to the sport milieu are a function of abilities and other genetically based physical attributes, in addition to early childhood experiences in which personal attributes, values, and attitudes are learned. The level at which abilities are demonstrated in performing sport skills is at least partially inherited (Singer 1980). This means that all people have their own unique capacity or optimal level of sport performance. Singer, in his review of this literature, has identified 11 motor abilities, based on earlier research by Edwin Fleishman. Examples of these abilities include speed of movement, reaction time, and hand-eye coordination. Abilities, which are different from skills, are enduring. Skills, on the other hand, are susceptible to short-term conditions such as fatigue, mood, and drugs (e.g., alcohol, caffeine, or tobacco intake). Early childhood experiences include opportunities to engage in motor activities and an activity-oriented environment. Abilities and social environment are important contributors to a person's success and enjoyment as a sport participant.

According to Maccoby and Jacklin in their book, *The Psychology of Sex Differences* (1974), "The path of development is somehow more fixed by biology for girls than it is for boys" (p. 69). Thus, female athletes may have a genetic disposition for superior motor abilities related to successful sport involvement. These abilities may include spatial ability, speed and coordination of gross bodily movements, visual-motor coordination, manual dexterity, and motor memory.

In their model, Eccles and Harold (1991) describe an array of personal dispositions, thoughts, and emotions that markedly influence involvement in sport and physical activity. The female's *locus of control* (see Chapter 4), her perceptions of her abilities, her personal values (i.e., the importance she places on participating in sport and physical activity), her perceptions about the proper roles for men and women in society, and her incentive to demonstrate competence and achieve goals are the primary personal factors that predict participation in sport. It is important to note that at no time do Eccles and Harold allude to the concept of personality traits as predictors of sport involvement. As indicated in Chapter 2, dispositions are more broad and encompassing ways of relating to situations than are traits, which are narrower in scope and dispose a person to react in certain ways (e.g., aggression) in given classes of situations (e.g., frustration or pressure).

Another personal disposition that influences sport participation starting in childhood is the female athlete's *fear of success*. It has been reported in literature reviews by Ogilvie (1979b) and Harris (1979) that women in sport may be inhibited by an above-normal fear of success, an issue discussed in Chapter 2. This might be due to a learned tendency resulting from social rejection and loss of femininity when successful behavior involves aggression or competition, particularly against males.

The findings of other research (Blucker & Hershberger 1983; McElroy & Willis 1979; Silva 1982) do not support the contention that women are intimidated as athletes. In fact, females in sport (as well as in academic and professional pursuits) are becoming more and more comfortable with setting high goals and working hard to achieve them, and doing so with less guilt. The sex-role conflict appears to be fading, but has not yet disappeared (Allison 1991).

Although female athletes of all ages appear to be "winning the battle" of sexism in sport, social norms die hard. Sport models at the elite amateur and professional levels help young women to feel more comfortable with participating competitively, winning, and deriving all the potential benefits accrued from being a sport participant. Yet, traditional images of the sporting life—toughness, aggressiveness, and even success—may conflict with societal images of females as submissive and passive. Allison (1991), in her extensive review of the literature, claims that the collision of these traditions, called *role conflict*, is more fiction than fact. She contends, in support of cited research, that female athletes have "a positive sense of self and a solid self-concept" that make them relatively impervious to internalizing these negative images and messages (p. 58).

Still, the female athlete, beginning in childhood and throughout the socialization process, must battle sex-role stereotypes that channel her into competing in certain sport activities (e.g., dance, tennis) and not in others (e.g., soccer, baseball). Apparently female sport participants of all ages must possess certain characteristics in order to overcome societal values and sex-role stereotyping and to achieve sport success. Young female competitors have the personal attributes (e.g., motivation, persistence, and the ability to overcome failure) to handle themselves in situations that nurture the desire to play competitive sport. Most have been raised since childhood to feel good about physical activity. Like males of all ages, the female athletes desire to feel competent on the court or field as well as in the classroom or in professional endeavors. In overcoming the obstacles that members of society place in her path, the female sport performer is likely to be as mature and motivated a competitor as her male counterpart, if not more so.

When Are Children Ready to Compete?

Pat McInally, newspaper columnist of youth sport and former professional football athlete, had this to say on "pushing" kids into sports prematurely:

> *I think parents should try to judge their children's talents objectively and avoid pushing them into sports they're either ill-suited for or unenthusiastic about. . . . Instead of pressuring your child into sports, which he might be unequipped for, perhaps you . . . should introduce him (or her) to other sports. . . . There are so many sports available to kids these days and you should help your child find the one or ones which will allow him to best express himself and enjoy the experience most.*

McInally goes on to suggest that parents should find out why their child is engaging in a particular sport. If it's just to make a parent happy instead of for the fun of it, then the parents should help their child to find another sport—or for that matter, another noncompetitive recreational activity—while giving him or her full emotional support. Inflicting feelings of guilt (e.g., "Make us proud of you") is inappropriate. A more difficult task for parents is to know when their child is physically and mentally ready to engage in competitive sport.

The word *readiness* implies that a person has reached a certain point of maturity and skill development that allows for the opportunity to succeed (Malina 1988). Malina contends that a match should exist between a child's level of growth, development, and maturation and the demands of the task. The use of a batting tee to replace a live pitcher in baseball, lowering the height of baskets in basketball, and lead-up games that make fewer complex physical and psychological demands on the players are three popular examples that facilitate this developmental match (Magill 1989). How do physical education teachers, coaches, and parents know when that point has been reached? According to Seefeldt (1988), specialists depend more on tradition than on developmental progressions: "[We] depend on the performer to tell us when the state of readiness exists" (p. 45). For many years, researchers have attempted to identify the primary factors that underlie a child's state of readiness (i.e., the abilities that allow for sport involvement) and to recognize the initial signs of readiness to learn and perform sport skills. This process occurs when a minimal degree of competence in entry behaviors, or "must have" skills that allow for successful participation, are demonstrated.

Primary Factors of Readiness

Maturation, the most important determinant of readiness (Gagné 1977), is one of three primary considerations indicating when to introduce a skill to a young participant. Through interacting with the environment, a child assimilates new information and new experiences into existing cognitive structures. The child's prior experiences through *learning* is the second consideration. Learning occurs with greater efficiency at some periods in life than at others (Magill 1989). According to Magill, the so-called critical period for learning sport skills is when sensory (mental) processing and motor responses are functioning at optimal levels. The child must be able to understand and to identify the demands of a task—the speed and trajectory of a ball in flight, for example—and respond accordingly for a successful outcome. The third consideration is *motivation*.

Learning theorists agree that skill acquisition is impossible unless the learner has the incentive to learn.

Thus, the child's greatest potential for achieving in sport is dependent on his or her maturation level, prior experiences through learning, and motivation. These factors, however, do not necessarily function independently of one another. For example, a youngster might have the incentive to play a competitive sport—perhaps to please parents or to emulate older athletes—but not have the mastery of skills or the experience to perform effectively. The result of premature participation could be inefficient performance and failure, with the subsequent dropping out of sport. Children who do possess the proper skills might be afraid to fail, feel "burned out" from too much participation or too much pressure, or for some reason not have the motivation to continue. Thus, all of the readiness factors must be present if sport skills are to be learned and performed successfully and consistently.

Competition and cooperation, both central to sport competition, are learned behaviors; they are not inborn (Malina 1988). Further, children learn to compete in stages. Veroff (1969) has shown that children at about age 4 years exhibit more cooperative than competitive behavior. They have learned to compete by about age 5 or 6. By 7 or 8 years, they compare themselves to others. This social-comparison process becomes increasingly intense with age. At about age 12 years, the child athlete associates losing with failure (Roberts 1993). Moreover, as indicated earlier, the young performer perceives the cause of this failure as his or her own lack of ability; the hope and desire to improve, to learn new skills, or to recognize the fun component in competitive sport is greatly diminished. The result is often dropping out of sport. However, participating in competitive sport need not produce such outcomes. In fact, competition can be quite beneficial to children.

Psychologists have contended for many years that central to a child's psychological development is the comparison of one's own skills to the skills of others in order to develop an appreciation of personal capacities (Coakley 1990). Sports games and contests, when conducted in the proper (i.e., constructive and supportive) atmosphere, offer an excellent opportunity for this normal and desirable process. Sport provides a way for children to seek and obtain information about their own qualities, as well as areas for improvement, thus creating the opportunity for raising self-esteem (Brustad 1993).

In summary, two important issues emerge at this point concerning readiness in sport: (1) that children are not likely to be ready to compete in sport until they have acquired the necessary skills to become successful and (2) that the likelihood of skill learning and performance is dependent on the individual's level of cognitive (perceptual and sensory) and physical (movement coordination) maturation.

Meeting the needs and limitations of children as sport participants requires instruction and adaptations in the environment that will lead to successful experiences. Wise choices need to be made about the type of sport in which a particular child should engage, about changes in rules and equipment, and even about the dimensions of the playing surface that will accommodate the youngster (Magill 1989). Examples of the "small is better" approach include fewer players per team, smaller fields, reduced equipment size (e.g., lower basketball goals, smaller and lighter balls), and less emphasis on competition outcomes and more emphasis on skill development and player achievement. Finally, for young children, in particular, equipment should be altered to promote fundamental motor skills such as climbing and throwing (Herkowitz 1984). Climbing equipment should accommodate children with limbs of all sizes; balls should not be too large, heavy, or hard to grasp. Striking movements should be aimed at stationary targets (bowling pins or a ball dangling from a string, for instance) rather than at balls in flight at high rates of speed.

Signs of Readiness for Learning Sport Skills

In order for a child to be ready to participate in sport, he or she must have the ability to learn and demonstrate competence in requisite skills. What "immediate signs" can parents look for before signing up their child in a sport program? One way to make accurate decisions is to determine the subordinate or prerequisite sport skills that must be effectively performed for the child to engage successfully in a particular competitive sport. A second sign of readiness is cognitive maturity.

Competition can promote mental health and emotional maturity when the individual has the capacity to understand his or her role in relation to the role of others within the competitive situation. Factors that accompany psychological development through competitive sport, usually starting at 8 to 10 years of age, include empathy (i.e., sensitivity toward another person's point of view) and understanding one's role and the responsibilities of each team member in the competitive environment (i.e., valuing cooperation and sacrifice, rather than competition and placing one's needs and interests above those of others). The appreciation of other perspectives is essential for cooperation and is especially important in the team-related activities of sport, in which each individual must understand the importance of cooperation for the good of the team (Brustad 1993).

Premature participation in sport does not foster team harmony due to the child's developmental inability to place the team's interests ahead of his or her own. Immature cognitive development is reflected by a "me first" mentality; sadly, some people never appear to outgrow this way of thinking. Psychologists indicate that the capacity to behave altruistically does not reach full maturity until age 10 to 12 years. However, as Brustad (1993) notes, "It is not possible to identify a specific chronological age at which it can be confidently stated that children are psychologically ready to engage in competitive sport" (p. 697). This conclusion is based on the high degree of individual variability in children's maturation. However, some researchers (e.g., Passer 1988) contend that involvement in competitive sport before age 7 or 8 years is not a good idea because these children will not have the cognitive and motor skills that produce the enjoyment and benefits derived from participation in sports.

Another approach parents and coaches can use to ensure that children are ready to participate in a sport program is to encourage youths to experience a variety of skills. Researchers have found it unwise to restrict a child's repertoire of skill development, for several reasons. First, children who start early in one sport and rarely engage in others tend to burn out by the time they are adolescents (Cratty 1983). Stories abound of famous athletes who quit or took a prolonged "breather" from sport competition (e.g., tennis and swimming), because as young competitors, they either were bored or were under too much pressure to be successful in the activity. Second, growth and maturation may dictate that the child is better suited for a sport other than the one that he or she experienced in earlier years. A boy who is an early maturer in junior high school may actually be too small to play contact sports by the time he reaches high school or college. Third, children should be allowed to participate in sports that they enjoy; otherwise, they may not persist very long at the activity. How are children to know whether they enjoy badminton or some other sport until they try it? And finally, children, like individuals of all ages, tend to maintain interest and incentive to participate in activities in which they succeed. Why not allow each person to experience willingly as many different sports as possible to increase the probability of success in as many sports as possible?

Perhaps the most important factor that underlies acknowledging a child's readiness to play competitive sport (aside from physical or anatomical limitations) is that of *competence*. How well can the young participant perform the fundamental skills of the sport? Is he or she able to catch a hard baseball without fear? Can a rapidly pitched baseball be visually tracked and the bat swung at sufficient speed to contact the ball? Can the ball be thrown at the proper speed or distance to ensure a successful outcome? How many youngsters are playing basketball who lack the physical maturity to shoot the ball into the hoop? And what about the young athlete's ability to learn and apply cognitive and performance strategies in competitive situations? The acquisition of primary skills associated with the particular sport, which often takes years rather than weeks or months, is an imperative, but often lacking, first step *before* children are involved in competition (Figure 10.2). When children are able to perform the necessary tasks successfully, then parents can consider enrolling them in a competitive sports program—given, of course,

Figure 10.2 Teaching sport skills should be the primary goal in youth sports programs, rather than physical conditioning and winning.

their wish to become involved in such a program. They may prefer to play the game but not participate in an organized league. In addition, learning is enhanced in a low-pressure, less win-oriented setting. Exactly why young athletes want to play competitively will be addressed in the following discussion.

Why Children Participate in Sport

Youth sport involvement is becoming more and more popular around the world, especially in North America. Unfortunately, equally common is the degree to which children drop out of sport. The pattern of involvement as discussed in most studies indicates an increase in youth sport participation up to the age of 13 years, with a marked decline after that (Brustad 1993). If we can identify the reasons for participation, then adult leaders of teams and organizations can more adequately meet the needs of child participants and significantly lower the dropout rate.

Many studies have examined the reasons for sport participation. The age of subjects in these investigations ranged from 6 to 18 years. In summary, the young athletes tended to rank their reasons for playing in the following order: (1) to have fun, (2) to learn and improve skills, (3) to be with friends and make new ones, (4) for excitement, (5) to succeed or win, and (6) to exercise and become physically fit (Weinberg & Gould 1999). A study by Wankel and Kreisal (1985) indicated that pleasing others, receiving rewards, and even winning the game—contrary to popular opinion—were consistently rated least important by their sample of 822 youth sport participants, aged 7 to 14 years. Of far greater importance were the excitement of the sport, personal accomplishment, improving one's skills, and testing skills against others.

Of great interest when reviewing children's responses about their reasons for participating in sport is the dichotomy between what adults *think* children want and what the children *really* want. The use of rewards, the importance of winning, the benefits of competition, and pleasing others (parents, for example) are viewed by adult leaders in youth sport programs as imperative for a successful program. "The kids *want* this," they seem to be saying. Program leaders insist on providing elaborate rewards to participants (sometimes only to athletes on winning teams), stress the importance of being in first place or winning the championship, and convince parents of the need for children to "build character" through competitive sport. And what do the kids say? "No thanks!"

Wankel and Kreisal (1985) found that "getting rewards" and "pleasing others" ranked very low in importance as reasons for enjoying sport. Instead, "fun," "improvement of skills," and "personal accomplishment" were rated high. Of more moderate ranking were "excitement" and "to compete." "Getting rewards" and "being on a team" are considerably more important for the enjoyment of younger participants but become less significant with age. Apparently young children react more strongly to material reinforcers (i.e., rewards and recognition from "important" adults) than older players who, with age and maturity, find these reinforcers less crucial. Further, younger players identify with being part of a team—for many their first organized team experience— more strongly than do their older counterparts. Wankel and Kreisal concluded that "winning and receiving rewards for playing, aspects that are frequently given considerable emphasis by parents, coaches, and the media, are of secondary importance to the participants' enjoyment and accordingly should not be heavily emphasized" (p. 62).

Sport Commitment Model

One apparent reason for the current and continued participation of youth sport athletes is their level of psychological attachment to their sport. The factors—psychological and social—that contribute to the athlete's attraction to sport have been outlined in a model proposed by Scanlan and her colleagues (1993). They define sport commitment as "a psychological construct representing the desire and resolve to continue sport participation" (p. 6). According to the researchers, the athlete's psychological attachment, or commitment to engage in a given sport, "reflects a motivational force for continued involvement, and consequently, reflects an important psychological underpinning of persistence" (p. 6). In other words, if the word motivation is derived from the Latin word, *motivum*, which means "a moving cause" (as described in Chapter 3), then sport commitment examines the sources of a young athlete's passion to engage—or not to engage—in sport competition.

There are five factors in the model that influence the young athlete's drive to compete: sport enjoyment, involvement alternatives, personal investments, social constraints, and involvement opportunities. *Sport enjoyment* refers to the amount of pleasure, liking, or fun that the child experiences in sport. *Involvement alternatives* reflect the attractiveness of continuing to engage in the current sport or activity. Greater enjoyment increases sport commitment. To Scanlan et al., "having more attractive alternatives is predicted to lower sport commitment" (p. 7). *Personal investments* consist of resources, such as time, effort, and money, that have supported participating in the activity and cannot be easily recovered if the child's sport involvement is discontinued. Greater personal investment fosters sport commitment. *Social constraints* reflect expectations that contribute to feeling obligated to remain in the activity. Examples include parental expectations, peer pressure, and coaches who recruit the athlete. The athlete's physical characteristics (e.g., height, body size, and musculature) might also promote involvement. According to Scanlan et al., "the more pressure to continue that an individual perceives from others, the greater his or her commitment" (pp. 7–8). Finally, *involvement opportunities* comprise the perceived benefits experienced from continued sport participation that are not provided through other activities. This dimension focuses on the athlete's *anticipation* of events or experiences rather than the expectation of a firm, concrete outcome from sport involvement. For instance, perhaps remaining in the program will improve fitness, enhance social relationships or recognition and status from peers, or lead to an athletic scholarship. Greater levels of perceived involvement opportunities will lead to more extensive sport commitment. Thus, the sport commitment model predicts that reduced involvement alternatives, combined with a higher degree of sport enjoyment, personal investment, involvement opportunities, and social constraints, will result in greater motivation for children to remain in sport.

Why Children Drop Out

Children approach the sport environment for different reasons and to meet various needs. These reasons are dependent on psychological factors (e.g., experiencing success), emotional factors (e.g., feeling competent), and social factors (e.g., affiliating with and meeting new friends). But regardless of the many characteristics of children that underlie their involvement in sport, for some reason (or reasons), they do not tend to "stick with it." The dropout rate in youth sport is soaring. Between the ages of 10 and 17 years, about 80 percent of all children in the United States who are enrolled drop out of organized sport programs (Roberts 1984, 1993). Similar dropout rates have been reported in other countries, including Australia, the U.K., and Canada. Why? Because the children's needs mentioned earlier are not being met. In his review of related literature, Gould (1984) found that the primary reason for quitting was an overemphasis on winning. A lack of success, not playing, involvement in other activities, and "other interests" were also rated highly. Other reasons, offered in more recent research (Gould 1987), include boredom, little skill improvement, and excessive competitive stress. Typical examples of reasons included in some studies were: "The coach yelled at me when I made a mistake," "I never got to play," and "I wasn't good enough."

Researchers have written extensively about the needs of young competitors and the factors that appear to be most responsible for discontinued involvement in sport. The causes of quitting sport fall into three areas: (1) comparative appraisal, (2) perceived lack of ability, and (3) low intrinsic motivation.

Comparative Appraisal

Children begin comparing themselves with others to determine their own relative status on motor ability starting at about ages 4 to 5 years; this increases in importance through the elementary years (Scanlan 1988). This process is called *comparative appraisal.* During grades 4, 5, and 6, both appraisal and the number of children engaged in youth sports interact optimally. This means that children in sport are comparing themselves with the abilities of others more often at this time than at any other. The reason for this is that children have relatively little past experience on which to base accurate self-appraisals. Consequently, they become dependent on others for information about their own adequacy.

The competitive sport arena is filled with many public situations in which coaches, parents, teammates, and spectators provide the young athlete with feedback on performance. The input comes in verbal and nonverbal forms—both positive and negative. Positive verbal statements reflect pleasure, recognition, and praise, while negative verbal communication includes ridicule, reprimand, and rejection. Nonverbal cues, both intentional and unintentional, are emitted continuously. Parents telegraph pride and approval, or embarrassment and annoyance, by facial expressions, body language, eye contact, or ignoring the youngster. It is easy to see how comparative appraisal, at first externally derived from others, then internally defined by the athlete, can lead to either the athlete's persistence or withdrawal from the competitive sport experience.

The primary objective of working with child athletes should be to provide them with information that promotes a feeling of success at performing sport skills. When this happens, other needs are also met (such as enhancing self-concept, the feeling of mastering one's environment, receiving recognition for effort and improvement, and gaining a sense of competence and achievement). The following suggestions indicate how coaches and parents can help young participants to deal constructively with the process of comparative appraisal.

1. *Avoid comparing children.* Every child has his or her own skill level, strengths, and weaknesses. The role of the adult is to inform participants about their adequacies and to help them learn skills and improve performance. Statements such as "If

Jimmy can do it, why can't you?" are unfair at best, and destructive to a child's character at worst. To realize that children excel at different sports and skills is important. Give them the credit they deserve so that they stay involved in sport.

2. *Help children to realize that "different" doesn't mean "better."* Because of the social pressures exerted by parents, children will compare their performances with the performance of others. However, when a child believes that love and recognition from "significant others" (persons whose opinions are valued) depend on favorable performance outcomes, such as getting a hit, catching a pass, or scoring a point, the youngster is apt to be more intense in the comparative appraisal process. Consequently, he or she will be more critical and will manifest insecure behaviors (Ginott 1968). One child might possess a set of skills different from that of another child. The important issue is that each young competitor has something to feel good about.

3. *Adults should be positive models for children.* If we expect our children to avoid criticizing peers, coaches and parents must do likewise. Children's performances should be critiqued, particularly during practice, and in private, not in public. Embarrassing a child in the presence of peers creates bitterness and resentment, as it does for older athletes as well. The desirable outcomes of sport, such as skill learning and fun, become nonexistent under too much criticism.

4. *Finally, help to prevent sport-related stress.* Adults can help children to make more positive appraisals of their sport experiences and to overcome stress in sport. The sport environment is filled with evaluative messages of approval and disapproval. Coaches and parents, aside from not being the source of negative messages themselves, can help children to deal with the unpleasant messages given by fans, opponents, and others. A pat on the back with a few kind words of support go a long way toward preventing depression—especially after the player has made an error or in some way contributed to an unfavorable team outcome (missing a shot, for instance). Teach children how to handle some of the unpleasant aspects of playing competitive sports such as receiving insulting or angry remarks from others. Better yet, give the young victim of such verbal abuse an immediate heavy dose of emotional support and, if possible, put an end to the negative remarks.

Perceived Lack of Ability

The best advice for leaders of youth sport programs is to focus on improvement and effort, not low ability. As indicated earlier, Roberts (1984, 1993) has concluded that the primary reason children drop out of sport is that they attribute failure (poor performance) to their lack of ability. Early in a child's athletic experience, successful performance is based on merely completing the task—just getting to the finish line in a 50-yard dash, for example. Later, however, social approval becomes an important goal. If the athlete is to maintain participation in sport, he or she needs the approval of significant others such as the coach, teammates, friends, and parents. The young player soon realizes that the approval of the coach is dependent upon effort. "If I try hard, the coach will like and accept me," he or she feels. Therefore, trying hard becomes the main criterion of success and failure.

Starting at about the ages of 11 and 12 years (and sometimes younger), "perceived ability" becomes of paramount importance as the motivating factor for playing sport. Instead of completing a task (the goal of the 6-, 7-, and 8-year-olds) or vying for social approval (common at the ages of 8, 9, and 10 years), the youths' primary source of motivation in sport becomes feeling competent. For example, an 8-year-old feels successful after completing a 50-yard (-meter) dash. A 10-year-old may reflect success if a coach, parent, or peer praises the runner's effort. An adolescent, on the other hand, is pleased if he or she is a first-place finisher. The outcome of winning takes on an increasing importance with age. The lack of competence is now attributed to low ability, instead of to a lack of effort or to task difficulty. Most kids who drop out of sport (as many as two-thirds, in some studies) think that they are "not good enough." The link between perceived ability and quitting sport is best documented in Nicholls' (1984) developmental theory of achievement motivation.

Lack of Achievement Motivation

As indicated in Chapter 3 on motivation, individuals have a need to feel competent. Nicholls (1984) contends that perceptions of competence or incompetence are the most critical factors that influence performance and persistence. The individual constantly strives to demonstrate high ability and minimize low ability. Thus, an athlete's perception of success is based on his or her interpretation of demonstrating high competence; an athlete's perception of failure is based on his or her interpretation of demonstrating low competence. It is important to point out that the athlete's actual success or failure (e.g., winning or losing, making an error, or demonstrating skill mastery) is not the important issue here. Rather, it is the individual's *perception*, or interpretation, of success or failure that determines the influence of competence on motivation and persistence.

This interpretation is a crucial factor in making decisions about maintaining sport participation or dropping out. To Nicholls, two factors contribute to persisting or dropping out of sport: (1) the individual's perception of his or her performance as successful or unsuccessful, and (2) the causes he or she attributes to this outcome. Attributing success to high ability or high effort has measurable reinforcement value (Duda 1987, 1992). Child athletes who make ability or effort attributions after success tend to be better skilled and remain active in sport. Sport dropouts, on the other hand, more often attribute success to an easy task or luck in achievement situations (such as competitive sport). Even more important, dropouts tend to attribute failure to low ability (Burton & Martens 1986). It is this low ability attribution following perceived failure that is of central importance to Nicholls' theory.

Nicholls contends that the criteria an individual uses to determine his or her level of competence change with age, personal factors, and situational factors. An extensive review of these factors goes beyond the scope of this chapter. However, the key point connecting these factors is that at age 7 to 9 years, children tend to attribute high or low effort as the cause of outcomes. But beginning at age 10 or 11 years, the child differentiates effort from ability. At this time, ability is perceived to be the person's "capacity." According to Duda (1987), "When ability is viewed as a capacity and a child perceives his or her competence to be low, he or she realizes there is only so much that trying hard can do when attempting to succeed at a normatively difficult task . . . perceiving oneself as able entails the comparison of one's demonstrated effort and performance outcomes with those of relevant others" (p. 134).

Thus, the critical component of Nicholls' theory is that in order to persist at a task (i.e., task-involved goals), an individual must have feelings of competence or perceived success. In the case of ego-involved goals, perceptions of success are defined by a favorable comparison of one's present athletic skill relative to that of other competitors. Therefore, to maintain motivation and task persistence in any achievement situation such as sport, it is important that athletes perceive their participation as generally successful and attribute this success to high ability. However, the athlete's conclusion that he or she is deficient in both will likely lead to termination of the activity, that is, becoming a sport dropout.

Sources of perceived competence for the young athlete change with age. In his review of this literature, Brustad (1992) concludes that younger children (ages 8 to 11 years) demonstrate a greater preference for external sources of information such as input from significant others, whereas older children (ages 12 to 14 years) are more dependent on social comparisons. Accomplishing these tasks should not be difficult. As long as the young athlete defines performance success as a function of improvement or high *effort* and obtains information that confirms these perceptions, he or she is likely to continue to participate in sport—or at least not drop out due to perceptions of low ability.

Coaches, in particular, can directly affect a child's feelings of competence in sport by helping the youngsters to interpret the causes of performance outcomes. Missing a shot or making an error can be interpreted as due to a lack of ability ("You don't have a good eye for hitting") or lack of effort ("With more practice, performance will improve; keep trying"). Coaches and parents, then, need to offer feedback to young players that indicates three things:

1. That doing the best they can—making the effort—is very important for success.
2. That their performance (any aspect of it that can be observed and identified) is, in fact, improving.
3. That lack of ability has nothing to do with poor performance outcome because they are capable of improving with practice and instruction.

Children should know that everyone is capable of improving. In youth sport, the accent should be on skill development and fun, not on winning contests. The game outcome is not an end in itself but merely a result of learning, performance improvement, and improved self-confidence. Once a player feels that he or she lacks the ability to be successful, the probability of dropping out of sport increases dramatically. Adults can prevent this by doing the following:

1. *Make within-individual comparisons.* Help to focus the child's attention on how he or she is performing in relation to previous performances and away from comparing himself or herself with other children. To do this, orient the child to the use of performance goals within the sport rather than to the outcome of winning or losing.
2. *Focus on strengths.* If assessing one's own ability is inherent in older children (about 10 years and up), then coaches can encourage a positive perception of ability through sport mastery. Reinforce the specific skills that each athlete can perform competently while emphasizing improvement on weaker skills.
3. *Set performance goals.* Youngsters might view themselves as skilled in some areas and unskilled in others. To help children develop accurate and stable views of their abilities, set performance goals for each individual that he or she is capable of achieving. Use performance (e.g., number of catches, tackles, or weight lifted in strength

training) as the standard for success and failure rather than winning or losing outcomes. The youths will be less apt to fail if goals are set realistically.

4. *Encourage children after failure.* Children tend to have global perceptions of their abilities after success or failure—particularly after the latter. Making an error translates into "I'm a terrible player." Children need to be reminded that a quality athlete can also experience performance failure. They need to be reminded of their competence.

5. *Stress individual differences.* Children need to know that people grow and mature at different rates. Comparing themselves to bigger, stronger peers may promote feelings of inadequacy and low self-esteem. In young males, low testosterone levels prior to puberty will minimize marked increases in strength and other physical development. This is why physical conditioning in youth sport should be secondary to building skills. Coaches should communicate to young athletes about what is happening to their bodies and assure them that they will grow, become stronger, and improve in the performance. The message should be, "Be patient."

Also, parents and coaches should never attempt to predict the young athlete's future in sport. Statements such as "You'll never do well at 'X' sport (or perform 'X' skill effectively)" are likely inaccurate and extremely demotivating. On the other hand, "You should make the pros" is equally detrimental to participation satisfaction. If given proper instruction and the opportunity to practice skills, the potential of any sport competitor is unknown.

Young athletes drop out of sport to avoid feeling incompetent and to save face in front of peers and parents. One way to help these children to deal with athletic competition is to teach them how to ask the right questions. Asking "How can I improve?" or "How can I improve this skill?" is a far more constructive strategy than "Can we win?" or "Am I good enough?" Children should be concerned with sport mastery and not ego-involving outcome assessments.

Low Intrinsic Motivation

As previously noted in Chapter 3, the main reason children want to participate in sport is to have fun. Conversely, the most common reason they offer for dropping out is "It's not fun." This fun component underlies the concept of intrinsic motivation. Motivation is having the desire and drive to move toward some goal (Magill 2001). Intrinsic motivation is the desire to do something because it's enjoyable; the experience itself is enough to feel good about performing some task. Outside rewards and ultimate goals are not necessary. Low intrinsic motivation plays a significant role in withdrawal from sport. Sadly, parents and coaches, often unknowingly, contribute to this predicament.

Adult leaders in sport typically claim that children want and need a reward system (trophies, for instance) to maintain interest in, and derive pleasure from, playing competitive sport. Researchers have not found this to be the case. Reliance on rewards, a form of extrinsic motivation, turns play into work. Activity that is intrinsically motivating is often play activity (Duda 1992; Siedentop & Ramey 1977). The important questions that adults should be asking are: (1) "What can I do to maintain or increase intrinsic motivation in child athletes and reduce or prevent the onset of extrinsic motivation?" (2) "Does the use of all rewards undermine intrinsic motivation?" and (3) "Do kids want and enjoy receiving rewards?" The good news is that the selective use of rewards in sport has been shown to benefit young athletes; rewarding play activity can actually increase intrinsic motivation under certain circumstances but can decrease it in others.

The effect of an award on intrinsic and extrinsic motivation is directly related to how the child perceives the *reason* for the award. Sometimes a child's motivation for engaging in an activity goes from internal (e.g., fun) to external (e.g., a trophy). This process has been termed the *overjustification effect* (Lepper et al. 1973). This occurs when the child receives an award that is expected and highly recognized—not just a pat on the back but a highly visible reward such as a trophy. The overjustification effect is based on adult assumptions that the child can't possibly want to participate in an activity simply for its enjoyment. "Doesn't every kid want a trophy?" they seem to ask. "Won't most-valuable-player awards and all-star team recognition motivate them to play better and have more fun?" The answer is an emphatic "no!" Sport leaders and parents of many child athletes "overjustify" the youngster's reasons for engaging in the activity by making an erroneous assumption: that kids can't possibly have the incentive to play sports in the absence of some tangible reward. Awards *can* increase intrinsic motivation, but only under certain conditions.

To increase intrinsic motivation through the use of rewards, consider the following suggestions:

1. *Rewards should reflect ability.* Remember that children seek information about personal ability through sport performance. Therefore, rewards should reflect some aspect of that performance. A trophy, ribbon, certificate, or positive verbal remark should recognize some accomplishment, improvement, or effort.

2. *Reward all players.* The reward should reflect some aspect of performance worth recognizing. Not every athlete can demonstrate efficient sport skills, but all athletes can exhibit improvement or effort. Recognize it.

3. *Don't coerce participation.* Let the motive for playing be self-determined. The motive should not be to gain their parents' love but should be because they want to play.

4. *Teach skills.* Children can improve only if they are taught sport skills. It's unfair to expect better performance simply as the result of repetition in practice.

5. *Promote social support.* Help the team members to support one another. Point out a good performance of one athlete to the team. Encourage mutual support by team members.

6. *Remember the modeling effect.* Often coaches are the models for desirable behaviors. As such, their statements and behaviors of positive verbal and nonverbal communication, support, and approval of others will facilitate similar responses by team members.

7. *Allow for team decisions.* Whenever possible, give players an opportunity to make decisions that affect their play or the game. Choosing one's position, developing team strategy, and making other decisions can help participants to meet their needs for self-determination.

8. *Ensure success.* Try to have each youngster experience some degree of success as soon as possible during the sport season. The need for competence is most salient at the early stages of involvement when youngsters have the most doubts about their skills and make rapid judgments about further participation.

9. *Awards should be unexpected.* Researchers (e.g., Lepper et al. 1973; Roberts 1993) have found that children who receive rewards unexpectedly maintain a stable level of intrinsic interest. Avoid promising some reward if they win, because not winning will be perceived by the athletes as failure, and they may feel resentful. After a well-played game or practice session, perhaps surprise them with a treat or social outing. The effect will be much longer lasting. The participant will receive the reward as an outcome of competence rather than playing for the treat; although the reward is external, it is noncontrolling.

10. *Use joint goal setting.* Establish individual goals jointly with the athlete based on realistic expectations of the person's performance.

11. *Keep practices and games fun.* Fun is the top-ranked reason most youngsters give for playing sport (Gould 1987). Highly regimented practices, lack of playing time, and verbal abuse destroy their primary motive for participating. Kids are not miniature adults, so keep it light.

Why do kids drop out of sport? The comparative-appraisal process, the lack of perceived ability, and lower intrinsic motivation are each—and in combination—primary causes. But the single condition that underlies each of these perceptual processes leading to withdrawal from competition is stress.

Competitive Stress

If competitive sport is a game, and kids participate in sport to have fun, why do so many children find the sport experience unpleasant and even stressful? The negative emotional reaction of a child when his or her self-esteem is threatened is referred to as *competitive stress*. Scanlan and Passer (1978) examined the topic of competitive stress in the child athlete. They found that competitive stress is based on the child's perceptions of inadequacy in meeting performance demands and his or her perceptions of the consequences of failure. Rather than actual performance level or game outcome, it is the child's own appraisal of the situation that determines whether his or her self-esteem is threatened. If the child predicts that not scoring a point will result in negative consequences (e.g., being ignored by peers, reprimanded by parents or the coach, or booed by spectators), then competitive stress is heightened. If the child feels comfortable that doing his or her best is all that's expected to gain the approval of others, the perception of threat (i.e., competitive stress) is greatly reduced.

Competitive stress can occur at any time: (1) before the competition in anticipation of poor performance or a superior opponent, or if preparation is considered inadequate; (2) during the contest if performance is viewed as inadequate, the opponent shows superior performance, spectators offer negative input, there is a "bad" call by the referee or umpire, equipment or facilities are poor, or the athlete is experiencing pain or injury; or (3) after the competition if the child has concluded that the completed performance or game outcome did not meet expectations.

Further, in her 1984 review of literature, Scanlan concluded that the most common cause of competitive stress, also referred to as *state anxiety*, is the threat of failure. State anxiety increases with age and is most prevalent at age 12 years and during adolescence, the time when dropping out of sport is highest. Children in sport fear failure because of the importance adults place on success and game outcome.

One factor that further contributes to state anxiety is the situation. Scanlan (1986) cites other studies indicating that individual sports are more stressful than team sports, more important events are more stressful than less important events, and critical game situations are more stressful than noncritical game situations.

What is apparent from these findings is that (1) child competitors are being placed under great pressure to succeed, and (2) adults (i.e., coaches and parents) need to help young athletes improve their mental preparation. Cognitive strategies, such as positive self-talk and mental imagery, behavioral techniques, such as emphasizing effort ("Just do your best and don't worry about winning and losing"), goal setting, and positive reinforcement ("Nice work; good job of hustling on that play"), are needed to reduce the unpleasant effects of competitive stress.

Other strategies to combat competitive stress include less emphasis placed on meeting performance expectations, winning the contest, and comparing athletes' abilities. At the same time, more attention should be given to teaching skills, emphasizing effort and performance improvement, training coaches to communicate with young athletes in a mature, nonthreatening manner, and deemphasizing championships and other forms of selective recognition that reward relatively few children, and that generate feelings of failure and inadequacy in a far greater number of child participants. Gould (1987) concludes that a greater perception of fun on the part of the young athlete is strongly related to lower stress levels, both before and after the contest.

According to Gould (1984), coaches and parents should ask the following questions to become more aware of the characteristic symptoms of competitive stress or anxiety: (1) Does the athlete consistently perform better in practice than in actual competitive situations? (2) Is the player having trouble sleeping, especially the night before competition? (3) Does he or she have trouble "getting loose" before an event? (4) Are there marked personality changes just before competition? (5) Does the athlete complain of illness or become ill the evening before, or the day of, a contest on a regular basis? This tendency is referred to as "Little League Syndrome," in which the stress of anticipating an unpleasant sport experience is so great that the child either feigns illness or experiences psychosomatic effects of stress (e.g., headaches, stomach aches, nausea, muscular pain). These are issues that need to be discussed and resolved, perhaps with a physician or counselor, should they become evident.

Based on a review of the youth sport literature, it is apparent that young athletes experience excessive stress when they:

1. Have little confidence
2. Make negative self-statements
3. Feel ill before competing
4. Have trouble sleeping the night before the event
5. Consistently perform better in practice than in games
6. Show observable changes in personality before the contest
7. Urinate frequently the day of the competition

Educators and researchers are uniform in agreement that although some degree of stress is inherent, even necessary, in sport, a chronically stressed child is an unhappy participant. If coaches and parents neglect their responsibility to promote young competitors'

A Study of Young Elite Athletes

Much of this chapter content has related to the needs and characteristics of young athletes at nonelite, lower skilled levels. The literature on elite younger athletes is quite rare. However, in 1993, Peter Donnelly, from McMaster University in Ontario, Canada, conducted in-depth interviews with 45 Canadian elite athletes, aged 19 to 35 years, about their childhood experiences as sport competitors. Subjects included 16 males and 29 females, all retired by age 19 years, who first became involved in sport during childhood or young adolescence. Sports represented included gymnastics ($n=12$), figure skating ($n=5$), swimming ($n=5$), synchronized swimming ($n=4$), track ($n=6$), martial arts ($n=3$), two subjects each from tennis, field hockey, and ice hockey, and one subject each from wrestling, downhill skiing, rowing, and football.

The subjects indicated some of the benefits of competing, including travel, prestige, attention from family and friends, and enjoyment of the sport. Other positives were improved fitness and health, and the pleasure from skill improvement. However, Donnelly noted that "subjects spent far more time [in the interview] on negative experiences" (p. 101). A review of these less pleasant outcomes from elite-level participants is of particular interest given the general, and perhaps false, belief that elite-level youth sport is relatively free of hardships.

Family relationships. Donnelly's results indicated that 65 percent of the athletes reported family problems. Examples included lack of family time, regret about missed family life, parental pressure, constant parental presence at practices, sibling rivalries and jealousies, and more attention received than siblings. Some families even split so that one parent and the athlete could live closer to a well-known coach.

Social relationships. Friendships were not a problem for some subjects, but others noted they had difficulty making time for meeting new people and maintaining an adequate social life due to their heavy involvement in sport. In a few cases, the competitive atmosphere at practices inhibited friendships with teammates. Athletes were victimized by jealousies of their peers (often due to being viewed as "different"), missed out on social events, and were unable to establish long-term or serious relationships.

Athlete-coach relationships. As Donnelly noted, "coaches can become quite controlling and manipulative" (p. 104). Although coach-athlete relationships among higher skilled competitors tend to be nurturing and supportive, the large amount of time spent together can create tension. In extreme cases, athletes reported emotional and sexual abuse. Coaches have tremendous inherent power because so much of the athlete's self-esteem is tied to his or her success in sport. Thus, statements about the need to lose weight, controlling the use of free time by requiring extra practice or other forms of preparation (e.g., reviewing performance videos), and greater reliance on criticism than praise add tremendous stress to being a talented competitive athlete. Particularly at the elite level, the coach's words are difficult to ignore.

Educational problems. Donnelly reported relatively little difficulty with academic pursuits, although the problems reported were usually attributed to the time committed to sport. Although sport did not usually impede progress in school, it was often a conflict. Most athletes needed flexibility from teachers and school administrators to miss classes, delay submitting assignments and taking exams, and be exempt from participating in required physical education classes. Some athletes regretted not developing skills in other sports.

(continued)

Physical and psychological problems. The majority of Donnelly's sample did not escape a malady common among elite-level competitors—overtraining. Gymnasts and contact sport athletes, who suffered the most serious injuries discussed in this study, also represented the highest dropout rate due to physical problems, such as mononucleosis, lack of sleep, and dietary problems. Donnelly also reported, however, that elite competitors usually understand and accept the risks and injuries of their involvement.

Excessive behavior. Donnelly found that about 40 percent of his sample admitted to temporary excessive or uncontrollable behaviors such as "bingeing," an eating disorder in which the person gorges on food or consumes alcohol well beyond previous, normal amounts. Other short-term behavioral changes include drug ingestion, engaging in physical fights, and vandalism. These actions would more likely occur after important competitions, at season's end, or after retirement. One explanation for this surprising lack of discipline among this elite group is an overreaction to the very strict and structured regimen with which most performers lived for so long. Donnelly stated, "All bingeing might result from the temporary or permanent removal of the daily structure of training" (p. 107).

Use of performance-enhancing drugs. Not surprisingly, Donnelly reported that the athletes in this study were reluctant to discuss doping in sport. No one admitted to drug use, although one track-and-field athlete felt that "his chances of success had been compromised by remaining drug free" (pp. 108–109). Surprisingly (or, perhaps, not surprisingly), several athletes admitted that their coaches actually suggested that some of them use drugs (e.g., steroids to build muscle tissue or laxatives for weight loss). Anshel (1991a, 1991b) contends that coaches have failed to play a bigger role in controlling drug abuse among competitors. Whether a true or false picture,

Donnelly concluded that, "in general, doping was not a serious issue with these subjects" (p. 109).

Dietary problems. This area was of particular concern to all females in this study. Many had suffered from conditions such as anorexia nervosa and bulimia, and had concerns about weight, appearance, and changing body shapes. Puberty was found to be the most difficult time. Athletes reported that their coaches expressed concern about changing body size and shape to their athletes, both directly (e.g., "Aren't you putting on a little weight?") and indirectly (e.g., overhearing coaches talking about athletes).

Internal politics. Issues such as team selection, subjective judging, and poorly trained coaches were common topics raised by the subjects. They contended that politics negatively affected their lives; decisions were made with lack of due process and no predetermined criteria or accountability. Other examples the subjects cited were judgments about making the team, skill level, determination of team status or position based on an athlete's race or other "hidden" criteria, decisions about receiving scholarships, and placement of coaches in responsible positions even if they had little apparent knowledge of or talent for the job.

Retirement from competition. Some athletes experienced difficulties when leaving sport behind them. As seen elsewhere in the literature, reasons for retiring in this study included injury, burnout, turning professional, and getting married. As indicated earlier, reactions to retirement included engaging in excessive behavior; missing the physical routine; and feeling bored, bitter, isolated, or lost. The most difficult reactions were from those who regretted not accomplishing their goals. Retirement was often involuntary. The Donnelly study clearly supports the need for counseling services for athletes immediately after their retirement from sport.

success and enjoyment of their sport experiences, then disinterest and quitting will soon follow. Based on one Canadian study by Donnelly (1993), explained in the following box, such problems are not restricted to nonelite sport levels.

Coaching Children: Positive Approaches to Avoiding Dropout

Effective coaches of young athletes help them to develop skills and positive attitudes about participating in sport. Successful experiences can improve each youngster's self-image and lead to a variety of other desirable personal attributes discussed earlier. However, the coach must understand the unique qualities of child athletes and learn appropriate ways to respond accordingly. One way that coaches can provide effective leadership to children is to understand the children's reasons for dropping out of sport and to address their concerns on an individual basis.

Reason 1: Not Getting to Play. Researchers have found that, given the choice, more children in sport would rather play on a losing team than remain on the bench of a winning team. Playing is valued much more than winning. Therefore, coaches should be sure that skills are taught so that all players on the team can participate successfully. If arranging for game participation is difficult, then coaches should ensure that all players receive plenty of attention and positive feedback during practice. Their affiliation with the team should remain meaningful.

Reason 2: Negative Reinforcement. Errors, for children and adults, are a normal part of learning, particularly with less skilled performers. Children are especially vulnerable to negative feedback and ridicule because it's so difficult for them to put the situation in perspective. To many children, being a "poor" player also means being an inadequate person. Kids believe what adults tell them. Eventually, if insults don't stop, self-esteem plummets, and the kids will drop out. Coaches should focus their comments (even critical comments) on performance, not character. Follow the "sandwich approach" discussed in Chapter 9. Also, keep errors in perspective. The coach's reaction to an error has a direct relationship to the amount of learning gained from it.

Reason 3: Mismatching. When kids are mismatched in size and skills, the underdog finds little about which to feel successful and motivated. Boys of the same chronological age may differ by as much as five years anatomically. Try to provide a safe and enjoyable environment for each child. Each player should enter a program and be assigned a team that is compatible with his or her physical maturity and approximate skill level.

Reason 4: Psychological Stress. Kids should not have to feel anxious before games. The competitive process should be challenging but also rewarding and fun. The more closely practice situations simulate actual games, the more easily athletes will be able to adjust to game conditions. Also, coaches should avoid telling the players about the importance of winning or reminding them of who's watching them—both tactics raise anxiety and pressure needlessly, and contribute to high dropout rates.

Reason 5: Failure. Failure is a perception—a label we give to performance outcomes. If children want to derive a sense of satisfaction and fun from playing sports (it is, after all, a game), then chronic perceptions of failure will diminish interest, generate anxiety, and lower feelings of self-worth. This is particularly true as children move closer to adolescence. Perceptions of failure occur only when coaches and parents send messages indicating such. For example, an error can be interpreted as failing, making a good attempt, improving, or just being human. The positive aspects of performance should be emphasized. Errors can be minimized by teaching skills and engaging in efficient practice sessions. Coaches must know the correct skills and how to teach them in order to avoid dropout.

Reason 6: Overorganization. Some studies show that children can receive more exercise in unorganized sports around the neighborhood than in structured programs. The kids simply do not get the chance to become physically active, particularly nonstarters. Even practices are often too regimented and lack opportunities for physical exertion. When practice is boring and physically inactive, the fun component has been effectively removed. Coaches should follow the principles of effective skill instruction. In other words, talk less and do more. Keep the kids moving. Also, be creative. Avoid engaging in the same drills constantly. Simulate game conditions. Have contests among team members that utilize game-related skills. Promote fitness, but don't overwork them. Child athletes need skill development more than bigger muscles and aerobic fitness. In fact, muscular development is minimal in the absence of hormonal changes that accompany adolescence. Aerobic training usually occurs in response to the child's daily physical activity.

A significant contribution to the youth sports literature by Ron Smith, Frank Smoll, and their colleagues from the University of Washington concerned the role of coach communication on the psychological development of the young athlete. Smith, Smoll, and Hunt (1977b) developed the Coaching Behavior Assessment System (CBAS), which showed that 12 coaching behaviors influence the psychological growth of young athletes: encouraging an athlete after a desirable performance, encouraging an athlete after an error, failing to respond to positive behavior, offering technical instruction after an error, negatively responding to undesirable behavior, punitive technical instruction, ignoring mistakes, keeping control, general technical instruction, general encouragement, organization, and general communication.

The CBAS was developed to code coaching behaviors during the contest and has been used to offer the coach feedback on his or her coaching effectiveness. In later research (Smith et al. 1979), the CBAS revealed that players of coaches who gave more technical instruction praised their coach more than did players of coaches who exhibited more general communication and general encouragement. In addition, coaches who provided more reinforcement and encouragement after player mistakes were rated higher by their players than coaches who rarely or never performed these actions. Finally, the coaches' use of positive reinforcement (e.g., "Stay with it, Ann, it's looking better"), especially after an athlete committed an error, was highly related to improved player self-esteem; liking their teammates, their sport, and their coach; and remaining active in youth sport. This research clearly indicates that coaches' behaviors influence the attitudes and mental growth of their players. Ironically, coaches are rarely given the proper training to perform these actions.

Government-generated and -regulated coaching certification courses in countries such as Canada, Australia, and England have markedly improved coaching effectiveness and the satisfaction of young participants. Similar procedures have been adopted in the United States by private enterprise (e.g., the Coach Effectiveness Training Program, Human Kinetics Publishers) rather than by government sponsorship.

Gender Differences: Implications for Coaching Females

What do the physical differences between males and females tell the coach about working with female athletes? Before puberty, girls are similar and in many instances superior to boys anatomically and physiologically. Thus, at or before this time, coaches, teachers, and parents should feel comfortable in coaching girls and boys in a similar manner and in encouraging co-ed sport competition in which boys and girls can engage jointly, with the exclusion of contact sports, in which *no* child should engage before puberty (Astrand 1986; Eckert 1973). No evidence supports the use of a double standard in sport where girls are automatically assigned substitute roles or asked to play positions of less importance, or worse, not given the same opportunities as boys to learn and improve their sport skills.

Although female athletes have psychological attributes similar to those of male performers, clear physiological differences emerge at puberty. Some of these differences lead directly to superior performance for males in many competitive sports (Wells 1985). Thus, coaches should realize that even mature female athletes have physiological limitations. This is not to say that training and conditioning are of less importance or should be less vigorous for females. But anatomical characteristics unique to women should result in different expectations for training.

For example, women have a higher percentage of body fat than men. So coaches should not mandate that female athletes keep a total body weight or fat percentage at dangerously low levels. Coaches have been known to make such demands, especially in gymnastics and swimming (Anshel 1991b; Harris 1987). This strategy is dangerous to good health. Physical training often adds weight to any person owing to an increase in muscle tissue. At the same time, body fat may decrease because more calories are being burned in exercise than are ingested on a day-to-day basis. The overall effect is a possible *increase* in body weight but a decrease in body fat. This is highly desirable and is much healthier than excessive dieting.

Women *typically* have lower increments in muscular strength with weight training because they have fewer muscle fibers and less muscle mass than men (Astrand 1986). Individual differences in muscle mass, both within and between genders, are genetically determined. This means that there are limitations as to the additional strength and size of the female physique that can be achieved with weight training. The genetically determined nature of muscle mass also means that *some* females will have more muscle mass than *some* males. For these reasons, the average female cannot compete with males of equal ability after puberty.

Nevertheless, it is mentally and physiologically healthy for men and women to remain physically active, even jointly where possible. As discussed earlier, parents, teachers, and coaches should promote sport involvement for females, particularly at relatively young ages when women are less conscious of culturally based gender-role stereotyping and engage in sport because it's fun. This is when they possess sport skills similar or superior to those of boys. Attitudes about sport involvement later on are developed and nurtured early in life.

In general, performance comparisons between males and females should be avoided by coaches. There are skilled as well as unskilled female sport performers just as there are different skill levels among males. Despite scientific evidence of superior physiological performance in males when compared with females, there's little doubt that the development of skills and relatively limited participation in sport by women is a cultural, rather than a genetic, outcome. Coaches, educators, and parents have an obligation to develop healthy attitudes, mental well-being, and physical stature for both genders. It makes good sense to give both men and women, boys and girls, the opportunities to reach these objectives. To do so makes winners of *all* sport participants.

Menarche

Strenuous physical activity before puberty can delay the onset of menarche. This is especially common in sports where reduced body weight is preferred, such as gymnastics and long-distance running (Harris 1987). A young female athlete may be concerned with this delay and worry about her normality. This increases her awareness of being "different" from most of her female peers; doubts about her femininity may emerge. A visit to a gynecologist may be a good idea to alleviate her anxiety and ensure that she is "normal." Consequently, it may be the athlete's heightened anxiety that harms performance rather than her very normal medical condition. Decisions about the type of menstrual protection, alteration of training routine, and her training schedule may need to be made.

Contraception

Athletes need to be informed about the various types of contraception available in order to avoid pregnancy and sexually transmitted diseases. Harris (1987) recommends that education should include separating myths and truths about sexual behavior and pregnancy, taking the proper precautions before engaging in sexual activity, regularity of menstrual period, and personal values and convictions. The issue of contraception is more relevant for female than male athletes due to hormonal changes that accompany many contraception methods which, in turn, negatively affect physical performance (e.g., side effects from some birth control methods). Harris correctly suggests that athletes experiment with contraception during training so any individualized response can be determined and adjustment made well in advance of competition. To reduce performance distractions, the use and method of contraception should not cause anxiety or concern about its effectiveness or its use.

Pregnancy

The research literature is controversial on the effects of vigorous chronic exercise and training on pregnancy. Naturally, consultation with one's personal physician is imperative to ensure proper activity patterns, especially during the first trimester to ensure proper implantation (Harris 1987). Researchers strongly recommend against intense physical activity during the last trimester of pregnancy. In addition to meeting physical needs, "the pressure of competition and the desire to perform well may alter an athlete's sensible judgment about listening to her body" (p. 111). Possible deleterious effects of exercise on a pregnancy may be due to high body temperature accompanying exercise and the shunting of the blood flow from the fetus to the working muscles. Otherwise, there is evidence that regular aerobic exercise throughout most of a woman's pregnancy can actually be beneficial (Wells 1985).

The Role of Parents

The coach may have a primary role in how much younger competitors play, in helping determine their perceived success or failure, and, to some degree, whether the athletes continue or quit sport involvement. It is their parents, however, who are mainly responsible for providing initial opportunities to engage in sport, maintaining their involvement, and influencing their children's withdrawal from sport (Greendorfer et al. 1996). In recent years, researchers have become increasingly interested in the extent to which different parenting styles have affected various psychological factors of younger competitors. For example, it is of interest whether parents who are highly involved in their child athlete's sport participation—escorting and attending most practices and contests, providing instruction and feedback, having high expectations of their child's performance—influence their child's self-perceptions of success and failure, motivational characteristics, emotional experiences, and long-term decisions differently from parents who are relatively less intense and involved. Brustad, Babkes, and Smith (2001) provide an extensive review of this literature.

Child Athletes' Self-Perceptions and Motivation. Children's self-perceptions will be heavily influenced by adults with extensive involvement in youth sports who are thus able to provide considerable information to child athletes about the athletes' current and potential skills. In addition, younger children tend to use information obtained from adults as the primary source of information about their competence and level of success. Parents, in particular, are the primary source of a child's self-perceptions of competence and control. Self-esteem, positive emotion, and intrinsic motivation levels are particularly affected.

The nature of parental involvement in children's perceptions of their sport experiences can be particularly poignant, as shown in a study by Babkes and Weiss (1999). The researchers asked young soccer players, ages 9–11 years, and their parents to assess the player competence, performance expectations, extent of positive feedback on performance, and level of parental involvement in the child's sport. They found that children who perceived their parents as supportive and holding positive beliefs about their child athlete's competence also had a more favorable perception of their own competence and higher intrinsic motivation, as opposed to child athletes who thought their parents had less positive perceptions. Further, children who thought they were competent in soccer viewed their fathers as more involved in their soccer participation, but did not exert a high degree of pressure on their children, as opposed to children who possessed lower perceived soccer competence. Finally, children of high-pressure fathers reported lower intrinsic motivation compared with children of low-pressure fathers. The results of this study suggest that the quality of parental involvement has a marked influence on the self-perceptions and motivation of young athletes.

Child Athletes' Emotions. This area of research has explored children's emotional responses, primarily trait and state anxiety and enjoyment, to their perceptions of parental pressure, expectations, and evaluations. Brustad and Smith (2001), from their review of this literature, have concluded that: (1) children's perceptions of parental pressure to participate in sport, concerns about their parents' negative evaluation, and concerns about meeting their parents' expectation levels have been linked to heightened child anxiety; (2) parental behaviors that their children perceive as positive and supportive are associated with favorable emotions reactions by child athletes, and (3) parents may influence their child's need and motivation for achieving challenging goals when they provide their child with competence-related information.

Despite serious concerns about parental behavioral patterns while attending youth sports events, without the support of parents, no program would exist. Youth sport program administrators sometimes think that the presence of parents at contests adds stress to an already anxiety-filled situation. It's true that some parents are sources of stress to their children (and to other players and coaches, too). In some leagues parents have been barred from appearing at games; the kids play quite happily without spectators. However, to prevent parents from observing their children as they engage in sport competition is counterproductive; it does not resolve the issue of the overzealous parent spectator. The real issue is how can league officials get more cooperation from parents who receive considerable satisfaction from observing their child participate? In fact, many children enjoy having family members watch them play; the need for parental recognition is very real to these kids. What, then, can coaches and program administrators do to turn the situation around? How can parents become sources of strength and support for the participants?

The Parent Orientation Meeting

Clearly, the first priority for league officials should be to educate parents about the league's goals and priorities in providing an enjoyable and quality sport experience for their children. Parents want and need information about the program's philosophy and approach to sport. In addition, parents also need to be informed about their role in supporting the league's goals. Examples include supporting coaches and game officials; eliminating unpleasant remarks or actions that may occur at the sport venue; and providing their child with unconditional love, acceptance, and emotional support. The exchange of information is even more productive if it flows in both directions: Parental support is more forthcoming if opinions are solicited and if meetings are held to exchange information.

Youth sport league administrators need to understand that parents have a right to know as much about the program as possible. In fact, parents will be far more supportive of program objectives (and will conduct themselves accordingly) if the program is discussed before the season begins. The best way to communicate this information is through the parent orientation meeting. Here are a few guidelines:

1. The meeting should be at a time and location convenient to all concerned.
2. Children should not be prohibited from attending for two reasons: (a) content of the meeting should not be inappropriate for children anyway, and (b) many parents are unable or unwilling to pay for child supervision and, if required to do so, will not attend.

3. Be sure free refreshments are available and mentioned on all written advertising. Studies show that food and nonalcoholic beverages enhance mood and facilitate communication.

4. League officials should dress appropriately to project a professional image. Someone once said, "You have just one chance to make a good first impression." Sloppy dress says to the audience, "I don't respect you."

Developing the Meeting's Agenda. The meeting's content should be planned in advance and include the following items:

Introductions. The administrator, coach, and team sponsor should be introduced (including their business and/or home telephone numbers). A plan to introduce parents to one another would also be helpful. The purpose of the meeting should be described and any handouts distributed at this time.

Understanding the sport. Parents need to have an understanding about the basic rules of the game as well as what may be realistically expected of the young players. It would be useful at this time to demonstrate the techniques and perhaps show a film depicting the particular skills of the sport. A coach or referee (umpire) might be the best source to lead this segment of the meeting.

Dangers and risk of injury. Let parents know if a medical examination is required before participation. What are the common injuries of the sport, and how should they be treated? Who pays for medical care? Is there a league accident insurance policy? What are the safety rules for games and practices, and what can parents do to promote these rules in the home?

Equipment needs. What equipment does the league provide, and what must the players supply? Parents may need advice on the type and brand of equipment to purchase and the approximate cost of these items.

Coaching philosophy. The goals of the program and of the coaches should be articulated. Is winning the most important thing? If having fun and learning skills take priority, it is crucial that parents realize that winning and losing are mere by-products of the child's involvement—not ends in themselves. Other rules concerning who starts; who plays; discipline; expectations about showing up for practice; and the rationale for, or existence of, awards, an all-star team, most valuable player, a postseason banquet or awards event, and other forms of recognition should be discussed now. What are the criteria for selection and how is it conducted? If rewards are offered, are they contingent upon performance, or are they given to all participants regardless of achievements? Does the team or league have a drug policy? If so, what is it? What are the penalties for smoking or drinking alcohol, especially if the athletes are under age? What are the penalties for ingesting or selling anabolic steroids, marijuana, and other banned substances? Setting a policy both verbally *and in writing* will ensure parental support in carrying out the policy away from the sport environment. If no policy exists, generate one (perhaps with parental representation on a "Drug Policy Committee") as soon as possible in consultation with league officials and community members.

Emergency procedures. Obtain a list of the names, addresses, and telephone numbers of parents, family physicians, and other adults if parents cannot be contacted in case of an injury or other emergency. This information should be distributed to all parents of each team to facilitate contact between families. Emergency procedures should be outlined.

The child's responsibilities. If children are to mature due to their sport experiences, they must assume certain responsibilities. These include (1) reporting promptly to practice and games, (2) cooperating with coaches and teammates, (3) wearing the proper uniform and equipment at games and practices, (4) following team rules, (5) making the proper effort to condition their bodies and learn sport skills, and (6) conducting themselves in a mature manner before, during, and after team-related functions. Parents should be asked to support these behavior expectations at home.

The parents' responsibilities. All of the programs related to effective youth sport programs agree on the importance of parental involvement as an integral part of the child's experience in competitive sport. Parents should help to ensure that their child meets the responsibilities that are entailed in program participation.

In addition, parents should:

1. Learn what their children want from the sport—why they are participating in the first place. If the child does not want to participate, especially after meeting the coach and team members, parents should not force it. Maybe after observing a few games or maybe even next year, the hesitant youngster will feel more comfortable participating. Perhaps they prefer to play a different sport. If children are playing only to please their parents rather than to enjoy themselves, they should be allowed the freedom to say "no thanks, at least for now."

2. Have realistic expectations and help their children to understand the time and effort that goes into quality sport performance.

3. Help their children to understand the causes and meaning of winning and losing, the probable outcomes from high versus low effort, the importance of personal improvement, and the disadvantages of comparing themselves with others.

4. Not interfere with their children's coach during the contest, but solicit information about the child's progress or offer to assist the coach at practice or after the contest. Negative interactions such as blaming and arguing should be avoided.

5. Conduct themselves in a mature, supportive manner at games and practices.

The competitive event presents a relatively tense atmosphere even without the presence of parents. What the children need is support and recognition in both verbal and nonverbal forms. What they do not need is ridicule, pressure to succeed, reprimand, blame, threats, and isolation. Often it is the parents' response to the athletic event that determines the type of experience sport will provide: fun or misery.

The season's schedule. At the parent meeting, provide written documentation of the locations and times of all games, practices, and other events that are scheduled before, during, and after the season.

Written Input.   Not everyone is able to attend meetings, nor are they comfortable expressing themselves verbally. There should also be a written outlet for expressing opinions and providing feedback during and after the season. In this way, parents begin to feel a sense of ownership toward program policies and activities. A follow-up to this input is advised, either a written response acknowledging the feedback or by making actual changes in some aspect of the operation that reflect their suggestions.

Scheduling Parent Meetings. There are good reasons to offer opportunities to meet with parents before, during, and after the season. As indicated earlier, preseason meetings introduce the parents to the program. Interaction with parents should not stop there, however. Meeting during the season provides a forum to offer feedback that can result in immediate changes or, at least, discussion about concerns from program experiences. After the season, it's time to reflect and discuss what went well and what did not; what to keep for next year and what to change. In addition to meeting times, it would be a good idea to hand out suggestion/feedback forms with a mailing address indicated. The league may even want to invest in using self-addressed, stamped envelopes to ensure a greater return. This would allow each parent or player an opportunity to communicate his or her feelings—both positive and negative—rather than holding them inside, which, under some circumstances, could be frustrating and raise the chances of future hostilities among parents, coaches, and administrators.

Postseason Evaluation

Evaluating events from the season is very important in examining the beneficial and detrimental effects of the season and in determining how coaching can ensure that the positive effects outweigh the negative effects. Beneficial and detrimental effects of sport, as determined by Vogel (1987), are listed in Table 10.1.

What Should Be Evaluated?

Vogel recommends that four objectives be assessed at both the beginning and the end of the season. Using baseball as an example, these include: (1) skill (e.g., hitting, running to first, running extra bases, fielding), (2) knowledge (e.g., warm-up, rules of play,

Table 10.1 Beneficial and detrimental effects of sport.

Beneficial Effects	Detrimental Effects
1. Develop proper skills.	1. Develop improper skills.
2. Develop fitness.	2. Injury, illness, or loss of fitness.
3. Acquire knowledge of proper conditioning techniques.	3. Acquire incorrect or no knowledge of conditioning techniques.
4. Acquire knowledge of rules and strategies.	4. Acquire incorrect knowledge of rules and strategies.
5. Develop realistic and positive self-esteem.	5. Develop unrealistic or negative self-esteem.
6. Facilitate a lifetime of participation in activity.	6. Avoid future participation in activity for self and others.
7. Develop a respect for rules that foster fair play.	7. Learn to misuse rules for the purpose of winning.
8. Enjoyment and recreation.	8. Lack of enjoyment or fear of failure.
9. Develop beneficial personal, social, and psychological skills.	9. Develop detrimental social skills or psychological injury.
	10. Loss of time available for other activities.

player positioning), (3) fitness (e.g., abdominal strength, aerobic capacity, grip strength), and (4) attitude (e.g., persistence, cooperation, best effort, self-esteem). It is important that the participants and their parents be aware of the evaluation process before the season begins. This will assist in focusing effort toward achieving these goals during the season.

Who Should Evaluate?

Certainly the coach is the primary agent in assessing player progress. To ensure that all intended evaluation issues are covered and communicated to the players, a coach's *evaluation form* should be constructed (see Vogel 1987 for examples). For better reliability and objectivity, Vogel recommends that a second party also evaluate the players. Input from parents, an assistant coach, and/or from the assessed athlete are sources of evaluation. Players should be viewed in comparison to preseason objectives, not relative to other team members. As stated earlier, comparisons between players show a lack of sensitivity to initial skill level and tend to cause stress. Instead, Vogel's suggestion is based on the need to assess player competencies to establish starter status and criteria for improvement. Each of these two assessments (from the coach and one other source) requires two separate evaluation forms.

Evaluation Steps

Vogel recommends four steps in the evaluation process: (1) identify the outcomes of the season, (2) collect evaluation data, (3) analyze the evaluation data, and (4) implement the needed changes.

Identifying season outcomes entails listing the specific skills, knowledge, fitness capacities, and attitudes that the coach intends to teach to the players. The important point here is to select objectives that can be measured and, in the case of skills and attitudes, observed. For example, an objective that meets these criteria might be, "By the end of the season, Jill will show enthusiasm (sportsmanship) during games and practices." Some authors question how sportsmanship can be measured or observed directly. Enthusiasm, support of teammates, and cooperation might be indirect measures of sportsmanship, yet are observable and therefore measurable. A poor objective might be "Jill will improve during the season."

Collecting the evaluation data requires evaluators to set a standard that represents the answers "yes" or "no" or that defines each number from 0 (not at all) to 5 (very much). Does "yes" mean that proper defensive skills were demonstrated 50 percent of the time? More? Less? In practice sessions? In games? What does the number 3 mean? Only 50 percent of the time? Setting standards informs the player and his or her parent(s) of the criterion for this measure and the basis on which to judge future improvement. When rating the entire team, evaluators might indicate if the player is in the top 25 percent, mid-50 percent, or bottom 25 percent for each performance area.

Of critical importance in collecting and interpreting data is knowing player performance levels at the beginning of the season. Vogel contends "it is the change in the performance levels of the players resulting from participation in the season that provides insight into your coaching effectiveness" (p. 368). Here it is also important to obtain input from the players on their perceptions of their own skills. Although the primary focus of the evaluation process is to offer feedback to players, coaches must always be open to feedback on their own performance and determine their strengths and weaknesses. A coach who does not recognize or cannot identify areas for further personal improvement is either dishonest or insecure. As Vogel asserts, "Although obtaining 100% of the responses in the "yes" category would be nice, it is the "No's" that are most helpful in identifying needed coaching improvements" (p. 371). A rate of 100 percent "yes" is not a statement of perfection; it's a statement of dishonesty.

Analyzing the data consists of obtaining a percentage of "yes" and "no" responses for each objective or any dimension (e.g., subskills) of the objective. To do this, total the number of "yes" responses entered for each player across all objectives. Then divide the number of "yes" responses by the total number of season objectives. Enter the percent of "yes" responses to obtain a total for each player. Similarly total the number of "yes" responses across players for each season objective for a team assessment. To identify objectives in which your coaching is most and least effective, Vogel recommends that coaches "force themselves to use 25% 'Yes' and 25% 'No' responses for each season objective (and for each player)" (pp. 371–372).

Finally, Vogel recommends that coaches implement needed changes by planning new approaches and strategies for the next season. In fact, if this evaluation plan is enacted at midseason, there is time for needed change before the season ends. The key words here are "planning a strategy" for using the information obtained in the evaluation process.

Should parents allow their children to engage in organized competitive youth sport? The answer appears to be, based on accumulated research evidence and the conclusions of medical and psychological experts, *yes*—but with conditions. The box on pages 372 and 373 includes a review of the most important issues surrounding healthy versus unhealthy participation in youth sports.

Bill of Rights for Young Athletes

The National Association for Sport and Physical Education's Youth Sports Task Force prepared a set of guidelines to help adults provide quality youth sport programs (Martens & Seefeldt 1979). The primary component of the guidelines was a Bill of Rights for Young Athletes that adults should acknowledge and implement as leaders of youth sport programs. The ten rights include (1) the right to participate in sport, (2) the right to participate at a level commensurate with each child's maturity and ability, (3) the right to have qualified adult leadership, (4) the right to play as a child and not as an adult, (5) the right of children to share in the leadership and decision making of their sport participation, (6) the right to participate in safe and healthy environments, (7) the right to proper preparation for participation in sport, (8) the right to have an equal opportunity to strive for success, (9) the right to be treated with dignity, and (10) the right to have fun in sport.

Right to Participate in Sport

Competitive sport should be available to every child, regardless of skill level. Why should only the gifted play while the unskilled are eliminated from the sport arena? In community youth sport, why should only the "best" be selected to participate, as in the professional and school models, while others are "cut" from the team? *All* children

Youth Sports: The Good, the Bad, and the Ugly

In 1990, the American Orthopaedic Society for Sports Medicine held a workshop in Peoria, Illinois, that included the top experts from North America in the area of intensive training and participation in youth sports. Psychological, sociological, physiological, and clinical areas were addressed. This section highlights the potential benefits and possible problems that can come from overintensive involvement in youth sport. The material reflects the observations of Rainer Martens (1993), a participant at the workshop, who explored the psychosocial aspects of competitive sport.

Workshop members agreed that competitive sport has the *potential* to enhance the psychological and social development of children and to enable children to continue to lead an active lifestyle and enjoy physical activity. However, whether the benefits will outweigh the costs depends on the quality of supervision among coaches, parents, game officials, and organization administrators. Martens (1993) addressed the following areas.

Sport-related stress. Life is inherently stressful, and youth sports provide ample opportunities for child athletes to cope effectively with sport-related stress. As Martens (1993) writes metaphorically, "competitive stress . . . may serve as an inoculation to build antibodies in children against the more harmful stress viruses they will encounter later in life" (p. 10). The downside of child sport is that the psychological stress experienced may be so high that the resultant chronic anxiety, burnout, or even depression may lead to dropping out of sport. Children may develop negative lifelong attitudes toward sport and physical activity, leading to an inactive lifestyle.

Self-esteem. Sport may build children's self-esteem by helping them to develop self-confidence (e.g., perform skills successfully,

promote team success) and social skills (e.g., meet new friends, gain respect from others). The key to reaching these desirable outcomes is to encourage young competitors to view success as achieving their own realistic goals, rather than depending on winning as the main criterion for success. Self-esteem suffers, not surprisingly, when children perceive repeated failure in sport as due to their own actions. When adult leaders send messages that equate success with winning and failure with losing, self-esteem usually suffers.

Motivation. The athlete's perception that he or she has obtained personal goals creates further incentive for achievement. Kids who interpret their involvement on a task as successful persist and their motivation to be involved remains high. However, persistent failure may lead to expectations of future failure, setting up a self-fulfilling prophecy: "I've failed before, no doubt I'll fail again." Young athletes who fail repeatedly ask themselves, "Why bother even trying?" The children are then less motivated and often drop out.

Competitiveness. Although sport has the potential to teach children to use competitive and cooperative behaviors in order to reach both personal and group (team) goals, the competitive process of sport can also produce undesirable outcomes. Sadly, child athletes can learn to be "irrationally competitive, a by-product of the adult-induced pressure to win at all costs" (Martens 1993, p. 11). These children learn that competitive behaviors are always necessary or desirable, when actually cooperative behaviors may be more effective and appropriate to meet goals and attain personal satisfaction.

Moral development. Sport provides a vehicle for learning socially approved moral behaviors. This occurs through observing positive role

(continued)

models and being recognized for performing appropriate actions (e.g., "It was nice of you to shake hands with the other team after the game"). The flip side of such preferred outcomes is that child participants may observe or experience unsportsmanlike actions, such as cheating, violence, and intimidation of opponents and game officials as part of "game strategy." If these actions are condoned by adults (i.e., coaches and parents) and lead to performance success, then children learn that these immoral behaviors are acceptable because they are "a part of the game."

Unhealthy attitudes. One benefit of sport involvement is that it encourages physical activity and other recreational pursuits. These are long-term benefits because children grow to enjoy sport as recreation throughout life. However, similar to any other activity, routine unpleasant experiences in sport may result in negative attitudes that may inhibit future participation. For example, exercising as a form of punishment, being criticized and embarrassed by others, and messages of failure, particularly messages of low ability, create unhealthy attitudes among children and may preclude their further involvement.

Development of responsibility. When participants are allowed to share in decision making or are given messages that help them to take responsibility for their actions, then young competitors learn the value of accountability. As Martens (1993) states, "they perceive that they are the origin of their own behaviors and thus are responsible for the outcomes of their actions" (p. 13). The other side of this tendency is not accepting responsibility for their own actions, partially due to the absence of decision making, and partially based on coaches and parents who foster external causal attributions (e.g., absence from practice that contributes to flawed performance, not following the coach's directions, or not remembering game strategies).

Social development. Sport sociologists refer to the social cost of overintensive participation in sport as "the lost childhood." Sadly, many elite athletes, particularly in tennis, gymnastics, and swimming, have questioned whether the years they put into developing their talent had cost them the experience of a "normal" childhood or adolescence. The downside of sport involvement is the failure of some individuals to develop well-rounded, emotionally and socially mature personalities. Because of the extreme psychological demands and social isolation that come from developing sport skills and preparing for competition, some athletes become very self-centered and lack the ability to interact with others in a comfortable and mature fashion. On the other hand, sport can provide young athletes with many opportunities to socialize with others. Interpersonal, verbal, and leadership skills often develop because of the nature of participation in the sport domain.

should have the right to choose whether to participate and the opportunity to learn and apply their sport skills, regardless of gender, race, or ability level.

Right to Participate at a Level Commensurate with Each Child's Maturity and Ability

According to the guidelines, "The use of age and sometimes weight as the only criterion for classifying children often denies late-maturing children the right to participate at a level commensurate with their maturity" (Martens & Seefeldt 1979, p. 18). The task force recommends that a greater variety of sports be offered to match children to the sport that best fits their physical statures, maturities, and abilities. Also, offering varying levels of competition within a sport will group children of comparable ability and maturity more homogeneously.

Right to Have Qualified Adult Leadership

Qualified leaders (1) understand children, (2) organize and conduct efficient practices where children learn, (3) keep it fun, (4) do not abuse their power, (5) understand the basic skills and strategies of the particular sport, (6) do not abuse children, and (7) have no need to seek their own recognition.

Right to Play as a Child and Not as an Adult

Because children define success differently than adults, it is unnecessary to seek victory as the primary objective of youth sport. For many child athletes, simply contacting the ball is a far more important criterion for success than scoring runs. A quality soccer kick carries more weight than whether the ball goes into the goal. For children under 10 years of age, just completing a 50-yard dash is the measure of success, not arriving first at the finish line. Sport is an experience or, better yet, a set of experiences that allows a youngster the opportunity to explore, experiment, and risk. Let them try.

Right of Children to Share in the Leadership and Decision Making of Their Sport Participation

This is a difficult objective for coaches who are consumed with the power to make decisions, dictate strategies, and control the environment. Such persons should *not*, in fact, be leaders in youth sport programs. A quality youth sport experience should include the development of independence and accountability for one's own (the young player's) behavior. Giving children the choice of whether to play sports, and the opportunity to decide the sports in which to participate, to establish goals of their play jointly, and to share their opinions with the coach about practices, games, and other aspects of their involvement helps to meet program objectives.

Right to Participate in Safe and Healthy Environments

Parents are rightfully concerned for the safety of their children when participating in sports. Coaches must do whatever possible to prevent injuries from occurring and use correct first aid procedures when they do occur. In addition, coaches must know how to contact parents (or another person) in case of emergency. Safe equipment, safe facilities, and safe activities must be guaranteed components of the program. Equipment in disrepair should be discarded and unsafe facilities rejected. Participants must learn performance techniques and, to the extent necessary, engage in conditioning programs that reduce the probability of injury.

Right to Proper Preparation for Participation in Sport

Physical and mental readiness is an integral part of the sport experience. Tell the children what is expected of them and what they can expect from their efforts. Tasks such as obtaining a medical clearance for participation, leading proper physical conditioning (making it fun, not torture), and teaching skills are responsibilities of the coach.

Children should not be thrust into competition prematurely. Understanding the rules and performing skills at even minimal levels are requisites for sport competition. Parents also have a role in ensuring that their child pursues proper nutrition and sleep habits so that engaging in athletics becomes a pleasant, healthy experience.

Right to Have an Equal Opportunity to Strive for Success

The issue here is not having a right to success, but the right to strive for it. Martens and Seefeldt (1979) contend that "children must be taught (and so must some adults) that success is not synonymous with winning, nor failure with losing. They must be helped to see success as progress towards achieving their potential" (p. 29). Children are denied an opportunity to strive for success when they are given little or no instruction, when criticism of errors replaces constructive coaching, when they have little opportunity to practice skills or perform those skills in contests, and when they are thrust into competition at levels for which they are not prepared. Although winning constantly is impossible, all children can succeed when success is viewed as progress toward meeting one's potential.

Right to Be Treated with Dignity

Children want and need respect. There is no place for the humiliation of children, particularly in an activity in which participation is voluntary and meant to be fun, such as sport. Sadly, the competitive sport arena is fertile territory for abusive treatment, disparaging remarks, intimidation, and criticism owing to (1) the requirement of performing complex tasks successfully and consistently and (2) the inherent component of athletes that always compares performers, viewing one as more skilled (the winner) than the other (the loser). Adults must always be self-conscious about prohibiting abusive treatment of the players. Even some forms of punishment, if necessary, can be carried out without destroying the child's dignity. "Through sport, adults need to help children build self-respect, not destroy it" (Martens & Seefeldt 1979, p. 30).

Right to Have Fun in Sport

It is "fun" to feel comfortable risking attempts at new skills without fear of unpleasant ramifications such as rejection or ridicule. In fact, if the nine previous rights are obtained, then these fun components are virtually ensured. If fun is lacking in sport involvement, then the child has every right to withdraw from the situation and to seek fun elsewhere. Too often this is exactly what happens. Ideally, adults should prevent stress from becoming a predominant component of the sport experience and respond immediately to overly stressful situations. In sport, it is the responsibility of each adult leader (and parent) to ensure that these experiences are as successful and pleasant as possible. Children learn what they live.

According to Seefeldt (1980), youth sport is too stressful when:

1. Children aren't having fun in practice and games.
2. Winning becomes the most important element of the competition.
3. Children return from practice or games emotionally upset because of what their coaches or teammates have said to them.
4. Practices or games interfere with scheduled meals or sleep.

5. Participation causes a negative change in the child's overall personality or attitude (e.g., frequent emotional outbursts, chronic complaining, belittling others).

6. Children within an eligible age group are eliminated because of their gender, inadequate motor skills, or body size.

7. Children are asked to practice or play one position and are prevented from trying out for others that they prefer.

8. Children are asked to concentrate on one sport for the greater part of the calendar year, thus depriving them of learning the skills that are essential for other sports.

9. Parents coerce or compel children to participate in sports.

Concluding Thoughts

What is going on out there? What in the world are we—the adult community—doing to our kids? For many years, participating in youth sports has defined our childhood memories, has developed healthy habits (e.g., training and fitness, skill learning) and ways of thinking (e.g., commitment, responsibility, teamwork), has provided us with models that have formed our aspirations and dreams, and has given us a sense of achievement and happiness. We survived adolescence with reasonably healthy self-esteem. The opportunity to compete in sports has given kids a sense of hope, and has taught us to link our goals with the effort and hard work to achieve those goals. The French playwright, Joseph Joubert, said, "Children need models rather than critics" (*Thesaurus of Quotations*, 1970, p. 78). Being a child athlete has also prevented a lot of kids from going in the wrong direction in life. Just ask many of today's professional athletes who would be dead or sitting in prison instead of performing their extraordinary sports skills and receiving more compensation than they had ever dreamed of.

It is very possible, even likely, that a culture that does not look after the welfare of its children compromises its future. Creating an unpleasant environment in which to play sports has led to less physical activity—creating a culture of couch potatoes, reducing opportunities to improve and maintain healthy self-esteem, and forcing kids to engage in alternative activities that are unhealthy and even illegal.

When discussing the role of adults—parents and coaches—who are primarily responsible for this dilemma, it is easy to become cynical and pessimistic. After all, who is responsible for the approximate 80 percent dropout rate in youth sports, a figure that is reported in the U.S. and many other countries? What drives adult behavior toward child athletes that can be labeled irresponsible, abusive, immature, and even emotionally dysfunctional? In a word: *fear*! To sport and clinical psychologist Jim Loehr (1997), "fear . . . stems from perceived threats to our physical or psychological safety," and anger is the behavioral manifestation of that fear (p. 174). While it is true that anger is a normal response to concern (Ginott 1969), clinical psychologists tell us that often what drives adult anger, especially in sport settings, is fear of failure, fear of humiliation, and seeing in someone else what we like least in ourselves. Let's try a few clinical explanations of why adults react to child athletes with over-the-top aggressiveness.

Clinicians might explain a father's anger in response to his child's error as due to reminders of his own inadequacies, childhood failures, or even reflections of poor parenting. Coaches who chronically respond to disappointing athletic performance with anger also fear failure and humiliation—the fear that the athlete's lack of success reflects poor coaching. For the coach who derives a significant degree of self-esteem from the team's success, performance failure can be devastating. Fear also explains the athlete's temper tantrums following performance outcomes perceived as failure by the athlete. An athlete's fears of failure and humiliation are usually derived from early child-hood, in which parents shower their child with recognition, approval, praise, and love following perceived success, while responding to their child very differently—with dis-appointment, reprimand, or lack of communication—when their child does not meet their expectations. The athlete's anger is a reflection of deep disappointment and embar-rassment from associating perceived failure with the loss of parental approval (see Chap-ter 9 on communication).

These explanations may be interesting, but where do we go from here? Should every parent and coach sit down with a psychologist before attending his or her child's sports event? Or, as sportswriter (and former youth sports coach) Rick Reilly suggests, remove parents from the equation by not allowing them to attend their child's contest? In his *Sports Illustrated* column (2/28/00, vol. 92, no. 9, p. 88), Reilly suggested just that—and more. He reported on the new policy in Jupiter, Florida, that parents were required to sign a youth sports code of ethics, which included such pledges as "I will remember that the game is for youth—not adults" and "I will do my very best to make youth sports fun for my child." Breaking the code would lead to immediate banishment from further attendance. Reilly claims that the code did not go far enough. He suggests that sports organizations add the following (paraphrased):

- If my kid looks happy, I'll shut up.
- I won't dump my kid off 20 minutes late to practice and then honk the horn when I pick him up 20 minutes early. And I'll call the day before if my kid has to miss a game.
- Since my kid's game is not a national championship series, it's unlikely the game's content and its outcome will be remembered by suppertime. So, I'll just settle down and be thankful my youngster is involved in sport.
- I won't give the umpires and referees a hard time, since they have a tough enough job as it is, and I doubt that they've received professional training.
- I won't complain about the coach, either, unless I want to give up 20 hours a week to volunteer to do what he or she is doing. Oh, yes, at least once during the year I'll actually thank the coach.
- I won't rupture my larynx hollering nonstop directions or giving critical feedback. I'll leave judging to the court system (my words, not Reilly's). In fact, since I really don't know what I'm talking about anyway, I'll stop pretending I'm an expert.
- "Win or lose, I won't make the ride home the worst 20 minutes in my kid's life" (p. 88). "Great effort" should about cover it.
- One season a year, even if it kills me, I won't coerce my kid into playing every sport that's available to the free world. Sports camps and neighborhood recreation also have their place in childhood.
- Finally, Reilly suggests that "most important, I promise I'll do everything in my power, no matter what, to remember to arrive at games with the single most impor-tant thinking of all . . . the orange slices" (p. 88). Let the fun begin.

SUGGESTED READINGS IN YOUTH SPORT FOR PARENTS, COACHES, AND STUDENTS

Engh, Fred (1999). *Why Johnny hates sports*. Garden City Park, NY: Avery Publishers. (Fred Engh is President of the National Alliance for Youth Sports, West Palm Beach, Florida.)

Murphy, Shane (1999). *The cheers and the tears*. San Francisco, CA: Jossey-Bass Publishers. (Dr. Shane Murphy is a clinical psychologist and academic in Connecticut.)

SUMMARY

Socialization is concerned with how a person's environment communicates socially expected roles and behaviors. Socialization into sport refers to a society's specific expectations of individuals' participation in sport. According to Eccles and Harold (1991), an individual's decision to engage in sport is based on several types of factors, including socialization, situational, environmental, and personal factors, and family trends.

Once they choose to participate in sport, children should not be treated as miniature adults. Child athletes have needs that differ from their older, more mature, and higher skilled counterparts. First, children mature at vastly different rates. This means that at a given age, some youngsters will be better prepared to develop and perform sport skills more proficiently than others. A second need of child athletes is to learn sport skills prior to the time that these skills are executed in competitive situations. Unlike older players, children are significantly less physiologically affected by vigorous physical training for strength and endurance. Another important need of child athletes is to participate in an environment that includes equipment size and dimensions that are commensurate with their smaller physical size, strength, and skill.

The primary reasons children participate in sport are to have fun, followed by learning new skills, being with friends or making new ones, having excitement, succeeding, and maintaining physical fitness or exercise. Participation is optimal when children are intrinsically motivated. The primary reasons they quit sports are due to a lack of fun, having something else to do, boredom, and not feeling competent. Winning is among the least important reasons for participating. Rather, the coach's emphasis on winning is a primary factor for leaving the sport experience. Probably the most important issue that underlies withdrawal from sport is the determination of low ability: "I'm not good enough" or "I'm not successful." To have a successful youth sport program, league administrators must be able to articulate their philosophy to coaches and parents, train coaches in skill instruction and team management, and evaluate their operation on a regular basis.

Although boys and girls perform similarly up to the time of menarche, differences in their ability to perform motor skills arise after this time. Taken together, these gender differences in physical maturation suggest that males and females should not compete jointly in all sports, at least those in which strength, size, and speed are major components. However, in other types of sports (e.g., golf, tennis, swimming), interaction between genders at subelite levels appears harmless—even enjoyable.

Finally, a youth sports task force in the United States has generated a "Bill of Rights for Young Athletes" that adults should implement in their youth sport organizations. Meeting these rights will almost certainly reduce the high dropout rate from youth sport dramatically.

REVIEW QUESTIONS

1. Describe the *main* socialization factors that contribute to participation in competitive sport. How do family members *encourage* and *discourage* sport involvement of young females?

2. What psychological and physical factors indicate when a child (under age 13) is ready to compete in sport?

3. What are the most important reasons that children give for engaging in sport? In what ways are the needs of children *not* met in many competitive sport programs?

4. Why do children drop out of sport? How can coaches and parents help to prevent this?

5. If you were a parent, what issues would you consider before allowing your child to engage in competitive sport? (Hint: Focus on the areas of physical and mental maturity.)

6. From the section on the role of parents, what can parents and coaches do to foster "healthy" participation in sport for children?

7. How does coaching children differ from coaching older athletes? What can coaches do to create and maintain a healthy psychological environment in youth sports?

8. Combining the information provided in Chapter 3 with the information in this chapter, describe what adult sport leaders can do to increase intrinsic and decrease extrinsic motivation in young athletes.

9. You are the administrator of a youth sports league. How would you develop and implement strategies to (a) involve and work with parents, (b) train coaches, and (c) receive evaluative feedback on your program?

10. Name 5 of the 10 rights of children participating in youth sports, and describe how each should be protected in a sport setting.

11. Should boys and girls be coached differently? Why or why not? Consider physical and psychological maturation issues in your answer.

CHAPTER 11

Applied Exercise Psychology: An Emerging Area in the Field of Sport Psychology

Chapter 1 included an overview of the dimensions of sport psychology, one of which was exercise and rehabilitation psychology. I have included a new chapter on this topic in the fourth edition because it has taken on increased importance in the field of applied sport psychology. In partial support of this point, in 1988 the *Journal of Sport Psychology* was renamed the *Journal of Sport and Exercise Psychology*. The journal's editor, Dr. Diane Gill, explains the change in the journal's title this way: "Given the increasing prominence of exercise in such contexts as corporate fitness, wellness, and preventive and rehabilitative health programs, and the increasing attention to the psychological aspects of such programs, it seems appropriate to include the word exercise in the title rather than assume everyone knows such activities are implied in our definition of sport" (Gill 1987, p. 1). It is not my intention in this chapter to provide readers with an exhaustive review of the growing literature in this area. Instead, this chapter is concerned with linking theory in exercise psychology to application in attempting to help individuals—healthy and unhealthy—to develop and to maintain exercise habits.

What Is Exercise Psychology?

As discussed in Chapter 1, exercise psychology is defined as "the study of psychological factors underlying participation and adherence in physical activity programs" (Anshel et al. 1991, p. 56). Exercise psychology differs from sport psychology in several ways: the nature of the population—athletes versus exercise participants; the type of physical activity—sport versus exercise; and the goals of that activity—improved health and fitness versus optimal athletic performance and successful outcomes. Both areas attempt to explain, describe, and predict behavior. Exercise psychology, as a subdiscipline of sport psychology, is comprised of several components.

According to Berger, Pargman, and Weinberg (2002), exercise psychology includes the ways in which exercise alters mood, reduces stress, is a partial treatment in reducing the effects of mental disorders, enhances self-concept and confidence, and can lead to positive or negative addiction/dependence. Other effects from increased aerobic training include reduced acute and chronic anxiety, reduced chronic depression, improved acute and chronic pain tolerance, and improved quality of life. In an expansion of this description, Buckworth and Dishman (2002) also include "psychobiological, behavioral, and social cognitive antecedents and consequences of acute and chronic exercise" (p. 17). By "antecedents," the authors include factors that will predict who will engage in an ongoing habit of exercise and who will quit. The term "consequences" reflects the study of exercise outcomes, that is, the ways in which exercise (both short term, also called acute, and long term, also referred to as chronic) influences mental and emotional processes. The effect of mental skills on exercise performance is also included in this definition. For example, as discussed later, thinking positive thoughts (e.g., "I feel good" or "stay with it") will result in better endurance than thinking negative thoughts (e.g., "I don't like this" or "when will this be over?"). Although there is a growing body of research in exercise psychology, a neglected aspect of this field has been to examine the effectiveness of research findings, theories, and models in exercise settings. It is this area—applying the exercise and sport psychology literature in exercise settings, and going beyond the theories and research findings—that is the focus of this chapter.

An extensive review of the literature (e.g., Berger et al. 2002; Buckworth & Dishman 2002) reveals the following areas that define the field of exercise psychology:

- Designing specific exercise programs for experiencing psychological benefits
- Examining positive addiction and commitment to exercise
- Understanding the causes and antecedents of negative addiction to exercise, in which excessive physical activity leads to injury, eating disorders resulting in excessive weight loss, social isolation, exercising when sick, or feeling depressed or anxious (worried) if an exercise session is missed
- Studying the psychological predictors (dispositions and personality profile) of who will and will not engage in regular exercise
- Determining the effects of short-term (acute) and long-term (chronic) exercise on changes in mood state
- Measuring changes in selected personal dispositions due to exercise, such as various dimensions of self-esteem, confidence, optimism, and anxiety
- Identifying the psychological benefits of regular exercise
- Exercising to improve quality of life
- Prescribing exercise as a tool in psychotherapy (e.g., for depression, anxiety, or emotional disturbances) for specific populations, such as children, the elderly, or the physically disabled
- Using exercise in rehabilitation settings (recovery from injury, or for those with cardiac or pulmonary disease)
- Predisposing factors that explain the exercise high, flow, and peak experience and how to facilitate these feelings
- Studying the effectiveness of mental skills that improve exercise performance
- Examining the effectiveness of cognitive and behavioral techniques that promote exercise participation and adherence
- Predicting exercise adherence and dropout
- Prescribing exercise as a stress management strategy

The principles, concepts, and theories that describe, explain, and predict sport performance also apply to all forms of human performance, including exercise. There are now more research studies, articles, books, and job opportunities related to exercise participation and nonparticipation, partly due to the existence of an increasingly overweight, inactive, unhealthy population. The need to understand the reasons for these very unhealthy trends, particularly related to explaining a person's sedentary lifestyle and studying effective interventions that promote exercise behavior, is growing.

Exercise Motivation: A State of Mind

During my early career, prior to graduate school, as a Director of Physical Education and Fitness in the community recreation field, I would often hear people who led a sedentary lifestyle say, "Every time I think about exercising, I lie down until the feeling passes." The late comedian, Milton Berle, was quoted as saying about exercise, "The doctor said it would add 10 years to my life, and he was right. I feel 10 years older already" (*Orlando Sentinel*, March 31, 2002, p. C2). To exercise or not to exercise is clearly psychological. Even individuals who choose to lead a sedentary lifestyle know the benefits of exercise. Yet, they do not exercise. Bring on the TV, high-fat foods, weight gain, and poor health. The reasons some individuals make the choice to exercise and others do not, and why a person chooses to quit his or her exercise program constitute a major area of study and practice in the field of exercise psychology.

Without question, helping a person initiate and maintain a regularly scheduled exercise program is a challenge to all health and fitness professionals. One reason walking programs have become so popular in recent years is because the more intense aerobic programs that elicited a very high (training) heart rate and extreme physical fatigue in the 1970s and 1980s resulted in widespread injuries and exercise dropouts. People would return to a sedentary lifestyle rather than submit to an exercise regimen perceived as grueling, difficult, and unpleasant. In order to get more people exercising and overcoming dropout, researchers started examining the benefits of brisk walking and other forms of low-intensity physical activity, especially for adults who are older, overweight, have joint problems, or lead a sedentary lifestyle. It was found that a highly intense aerobic workout was less necessary than previously thought in order to obtain the benefits of exercise (Marcus et al. 1998). For example, walking at least three miles an hour for at least 20 consecutive minutes can improve cardiovascular fitness (Anshel & Reeves 1998).

Perhaps one of the most convincing reasons to exercise comes from a published paper about exercise and weight control by Drs. Steven Blair and Suzanne Brodney (1999) from the Cooper Aerobics Institute in Dallas. The authors reviewed 24 studies that examined links between the effects of aerobic exercise on physiological outcomes and morbidity (disease) and mortality (death). The results of these studies, all conducted on males only, indicated that individuals who were overweight or obese received physiological improvements and health-related benefits in response to aerobic and strength-training exercises very similar to those of their normal-weight counterparts. It was important to restrict the reviewed studies to one gender because there are too many biological factors (e.g., hormones, bone density, body type, normal rates of morbidity and mortality) related to gender that might influence the conclusions of a review of mixed-gender studies. Clearly, as the authors conclude, a similar review of studies on women only is warranted.

The specific conclusions from their study were as follows:

1. "Overweight and obese individuals who are active and fit have lower rates of disease and death than overweight and obese individuals who are inactive and unfit" (p. S659).

2. "Overweight or obese individuals who are active and fit are less likely to develop obesity-related chronic diseases and have early death than normal-weight persons who lead sedentary lives" (p. S659).

3. "Inactivity and low cardiorespiratory fitness are as important predictors of mortality as being overweight or obese" (p. S660).

The researchers found that a person's decision to exercise should not be associated with weight loss. This is because exercise itself, even if not accompanied by a loss in weight or body fat, results in physiological benefits very similar to those for persons who are not overweight or obese. Thus, engaging in aerobic forms of exercise is the most important factor contributing to good health and lower rate of disease (rather than being consumed with weight control, especially through dieting but not exercising). Since losing weight is among the more motivating reasons to exercise, and since the failure to lose weight is a primary reason individuals stop exercising, promoting the health-related benefits of exercise reduces a very common tendency to quit exercising. Determining a person's motives for exercising, including weight loss, has been addressed in recent years using the Exercise Motivation Scale.

Measuring Exercise Motivation

Professors David Markland and David Ingledew from the University of North Wales generated, validated, and published the Exercise Motivations Inventory in 1993 (in the *Journal of Personality and Individual Differences*), but revalidated the inventory, using additional data analyses (EMI-2), in 1997 in the *British Journal of Health Psychology* (see reference list). The EMI-2 measures a person's motives for exercising. The inventory categorizes 12 sources of exercise motivation: stress management (e.g., "to release tension"), weight management (e.g., "to stay slim"), revitalization (e.g., "because it makes me feel good"), social recognition (e.g., "to gain recognition for my accomplishments"), enjoyment (e.g., "because I enjoy the feeling of exerting myself"), challenge (e.g., "to help me explore the limits of my body"), (social) affiliation (e.g., "to spend time with friends"), competition (e.g., "because I enjoy competing"), health pressures (e.g., "because my doctor advised me to exercise"), ill-health avoidance (e.g., "to avoid heart disease"), positive health ("to help me live a longer, healthier life"), and appearance (e.g., "to have a good body"). Attempts to begin an exercise program and to avoid the probability of dropping out should consist of structuring a program and providing an environment that addresses the individual's exercise motives. Figure 11.1 contains the Exercise Motivations Inventory.

Figure 11.1 The Exercise Motivations Inventory - 2 (EMI-2)

The Exercise Motivations Inventory - 2 (EMI-2)
Scoring Key

Scale scores are obtained by calculating means of the appropriate items.

Scale	Items			
Stress Management	6	20	34	46
Revitalization	3	17	31	
Enjoyment	9	23	37	48
Challenge	14	28	42	51
Social Recognition	5	19	33	45
Affiliation	10	24	38	49
Competition	12	26	40	50
Health Pressures	11	25	39	
Ill-Health Avoidance	2	16	30	
Positive Health	7	21	35	
Weight Management	1	15	29	43
Appearance	4	18	32	44
Strength & Endurance	8	22	36	47
Nimbleness	13	27	41	

On the following pages are a number of statements concerning the reasons people often give when asked why they exercise. *Whether you currently exercise regularly or not,* please read each statement carefully and indicate, by circling the appropriate number, whether or not each statement is *true* for you personally, *or would be true* for you personally is you did exercise. If you do not consider a statement to be true for you at all, circle the '0'. If you think a statement is very true for you indeed, circle the '5'. If you think the statement is partly true for you, then circle the '1', '2', '3', or '4', according to how strongly you feel that it reflects why you exercise or might exercise.

Remember, we want to know why *you personally* choose to exercise or might choose to exercise, not whether you think the statements are good reasons for *anybody* to exercise.

(continued)

Figure 11.1 The Exercise Motivations Inventory - 2 (EMI-2)

It helps us to have basic personal information about those who complete this questionnaire. We would be grateful for the following information:

Your age _____ years   Your gender   male/female

	Not at all true for me					Very true for me

Personally, I exercise (or might exercise) . . .

1. To stay slim	0	1	2	3	4	5
2. To avoid ill health	0	1	2	3	4	5
3. Because it makes me feel good	0	1	2	3	4	5
4. To help me look younger	0	1	2	3	4	5
5. To show my worth to others	0	1	2	3	4	5
6. To give me space to think	0	1	2	3	4	5
7. To have a healthy body	0	1	2	3	4	5
8. To build up my strength	0	1	2	3	4	5
9. Because I enjoy the feeling of exerting myself	0	1	2	3	4	5
10. To spend time with friends	0	1	2	3	4	5
11. Because my doctor advised me to exercise	0	1	2	3	4	5
12. Because I like trying to win in physical activities	0	1	2	3	4	5
13. To stay/become more agile	0	1	2	3	4	5
14. To give me goals to work toward	0	1	2	3	4	5
15. To lose weight	0	1	2	3	4	5
16. To prevent health problems	0	1	2	3	4	5
17. Because I find exercise invigorating	0	1	2	3	4	5
18. To have a good body	0	1	2	3	4	5
19. To compare my abilities with other people's	0	1	2	3	4	5
20. Because it helps to reduce tension	0	1	2	3	4	5
21. Because I want to maintain good health	0	1	2	3	4	5
22. To increase my endurance	0	1	2	3	4	5
23. Because I find exercising satisfying in and of itself	0	1	2	3	4	5
24. To enjoy the social aspects of exercising	0	1	2	3	4	5
25. To help prevent an illness that runs in my family	0	1	2	3	4	5

(continued)

Figure 11.1 The Exercise Motivations Inventory - 2 (EMI-2)

	Not at all true for me				Very true for me
26. Because I enjoy competing	0	1	2	3	4	5
27. To maintain flexibility	0	1	2	3	4	5
28. To give me personal challenges to face	0	1	2	3	4	5
29. To help control my weight	0	1	2	3	4	5
30. To avoid heart disease	0	1	2	3	4	5
31. To recharge my batteries	0	1	2	3	4	5
32. To improve my appearance	0	1	2	3	4	5
33. To gain recognition for my accomplishments	0	1	2	3	4	5
34. To help manage stress	0	1	2	3	4	5
35. To feel more healthy	0	1	2	3	4	5
36. To get stronger	0	1	2	3	4	5
37. For enjoyment of the experience of exercising	0	1	2	3	4	5
38. To have fun being active with other people	0	1	2	3	4	5
39. To help recover from an illness/injury	0	1	2	3	4	5
40. Because I enjoy physical competition	0	1	2	3	4	5
41. To stay/become flexible	0	1	2	3	4	5
42. To develop personal skills	0	1	2	3	4	5
43. Because exercise helps me to burn calories	0	1	2	3	4	5
44. To look more attractive	0	1	2	3	4	5
45. To accomplish things that others are incapable of	0	1	2	3	4	5
46. To release tension	0	1	2	3	4	5
47. To develop my muscles	0	1	2	3	4	5
48. Because I feel at my best when exercising	0	1	2	3	4	5
49. To make new friends	0	1	2	3	4	5
50. Because I find physical activities fun, especially when competition is involved	0	1	2	3	4	5
51. To measure myself against personal standards	0	1	2	3	4	5

Thank you for completing this questionnaire.

Source: D. Markland, SSHAPES, University of Wales, Bangor, January 1997.

Psychological Benefits of Exercise

Though it has been well-known for many years that exercise has a strong, favorable effect on physiological processes, similar benefits have been found to have a bearing on mental and emotional factors, including changes in personality. It is important to point out that these benefits are not typically experienced after a brief period of time, but accrue after several weeks or even months (Berger et al. 2002; Buckworth & Dishman 2002).

Stress Reduction

After extensively reviewing the related literature, Buckworth and Dishman concluded that "aerobic exercise programs lasting at least a few months seem best for reducing reports of chronic stress" (p. 79). The mechanisms by which this positive effect occurs seems to be the short-term distraction from unpleasant thoughts and/or increasing feelings of control or commitment that buffer the impact of stressful events. Stress-reducing properties are more likely if each exercise session lasts for at least 30 minutes.

Anxiety Management

While stress reflects a person's sense of immediate danger, anxiety reflects an individual's perceptions of worry and threat about *future* harm. As reviewed in Chapter 5, anxiety can be further defined as *trait*, defined as a feature of personality in which an individual is predisposed to perceive apparently harmless situations as threatening, or *state*, defined as an immediate emotional state to perceive an approaching situation as threatening. In addition, there exist acute (short-term) anxiety and chronic (long-term) anxiety, upon both of which exercise, particularly *aerobic* exercise, has a favorable influence. Exercise benefits only state, not trait, anxiety, however. The finding in numerous research studies, reviewed by Petruzzello and his colleagues (1991), is that even a single bout of aerobic exercise, as well as involvement in a longer term aerobic exercise program, will markedly reduce state anxiety. Aerobic exercise has also benefited patients with various anxiety disorders (e.g., panic disorder, posttraumatic stress disorder) and clinical depression. These findings were similar for individuals with varying initial fitness levels. Exercise of any type, however, is not likely to influence trait anxiety because of its permanent, unchanging nature. Personality traits such as trait anxiety are simply not susceptible to short-term treatments. Reasons for the positive effects of exercise on state anxiety include favorable changes in the exerciser's biochemistry, "time out" or distraction from the sources or symptoms of anxiety, a heightened sense of competence and achievement, improved self-concept, and increased social support (see Buckworth and Dishman 2002 for a review of this literature).

Mood Effects

Because mood is usually measured as a state characteristic, research on the effects of exercise on mood have focused on immediate, rather than long-term, effects. Perhaps the most recent and comprehensive review of the research literature related to the effects of exercise on mood was conducted by Berger and Motl (2000). The authors examined studies over the past 25 years in which mood was measured specifically by the Profile of Mood States (POMS), described in Chapter 2. They concluded that there is unequivocal support for the mood-enhancing effects of exercise, specifically on improved vigor and reduced tension, depression, anger, confusion, and fatigue. The authors attribute changes in mood following exercise to psychological mechanisms, including "enhanced self-concept, feelings of self-efficacy, enjoyment, expectancy of psychological benefits, 'time out' from one's routine and daily hassles, and an increased sense of control" (p. 84). Physiological mechanisms (e.g., cortisol, endorphins, monoamines), reflecting biochemical changes, may also partly explain mood alteration during and after exercise. With respect to exercise intensity, the authors recommend that unless a participant prefers low or high exercise intensity, optimal conditions for mood changes occur at a moderate intensity level. In summary, exercise, in particular moderate-intensity aerobic exercise, reduces negative mood and improves positive mood state.

Self-Esteem Support

Self-esteem, highly similar in meaning to a concept called self-worth, is typically defined as the degree to which an individual likes or approves of himself or herself. These concepts are multidimensional, meaning that there are different sources of self-esteem. These include knowledge (academic) self-esteem, physical/somatic self-esteem, sport self-esteem, social self-esteem, religious self-esteem, family self-esteem, and work self-esteem. Buckworth and Dishman (2002) describe self-esteem as a function of physical self-worth, with subdimensions of sport, physical condition, body, and strength. Does exercise alter any of the dimensions of self-esteem, especially given the fact that it is a relatively stable, long-term disposition? Buckworth and Dishman's (2002) extensive review of the literature concluded that "positive associations between exercise and self-esteem have been found, but effects are stronger for individuals initially lower in self-esteem" (p. 168), and that "exercise has more potent effects on physical self-concept and self-esteem than on general self-perceptions" (p. 168). The authors also found that, among females, exercise is especially tied to body/physique self-esteem. Concomitant changes in other forms of self-esteem (e.g., family, academic, sport) were not noted. In summary, any behavior such as exercise that induces a sense of competence and achievement, and that is perceived as enjoyable and produces desirable changes in a person's physical characteristics (e.g., weight/fat loss, increased strength), will positively influence self-esteem, particularly in the physical dimension. Although other dimensions of self-esteem, such as academic, work, family, and so on, do not seem to be affected similarly, as Buckworth and Dishman conclude, "positive self-esteem is associated with good mental health, so linking exercise with improvement in physical self-concept and thus with better self-esteem offers another reason for adopting and maintaining a physically active lifestyle" (p. 174).

Theories and Models in Exercise Psychology

In order to provide effective programs that will foster a deep sense of responsibility and long-term commitment to exercise, we must first understand the processes and factors that contribute to a person's decision to engage in and persist at exercise behavior. Exercise-related theories and models help us gain this understanding so that practitioners can initiate more effective programs and interventions. To date, the fitness industry has not obtained and applied this information, hence one reason for the massive percentage of individuals who do not exercise or who begin a program and then drop out within three to six months. We will now describe the most common models in exercise psychology, and then discuss ways in which each can be applied in exercise settings.

Health Belief Model

If a person believes that certain behaviors are healthy, will that person more likely engage in those healthy behaviors? The answer is "yes," according to the health belief model (HBM). Becker and Maiman (1975) propose that anticipating undesirable health outcomes will lead to behaving in a way that avoids these outcomes or at least reduces their impact. Thus, a person who feels that starting an exercise program will prevent or control the experience of poor health, overweight, and other undesirable outcomes will likely exercise. Furthermore, to initiate an exercise program, the HBM states that individuals must be concerned about their health, feel threatened about being susceptible to or be currently experiencing health problems, perceive that they can prevent or control the health problem, believe that exercise will reduce the likelihood of becoming ill or unhealthy, and experience cues that raise their awareness about the need to improve health (e.g., genetic predisposition based on health of family members, getting older, exposure to news stories or advertising campaigns, initiative by a friend or family member to exercise, poor mental or physical health, recommendation by a professional, positive feelings about attending an exercise facility). As Buckworth and Dishman (2002) assert, the HBM is an illness avoidance model. The HBM is based on perceptions of disease (health behaviors) rather than exercise. Health is only one reason people exercise. Other reasons include social interaction, enjoyment, stress reduction, competition, and improved physical appearance.

The HBM has received moderate support by researchers. In their review of literature, Berger et al. (2002) concluded that HBM components (i.e., perceived barriers to exercise, perceived benefits of exercise, and perceived susceptibility to disease) accurately predicted health-related behaviors. The authors warn, however, that "most of these studies focused on younger populations and more research is needed with middle-aged or elderly persons whose ability to engage in vigorous physical activity may be limited" (p. 176). In a test of the HBM to predict dropouts and compliers among cardiac rehabilitation patients, Oldridge and Streiner (1990) found that the HBM correctly classified 80 percent of the patients. The most important factor that predicted exercise behavior (dropout versus compliance) was perceived exercise effectiveness, followed closely by feeling motivated by improved general health. Thus, if patients felt that their exercise routine significantly improved their health, they were more likely to continue their exercise regimen. Clearly, the HBM can predict exercise participation only to the extent that an individual links exercise habits with improved health. This is quite a challenge, however, when individuals do not perceive that their health is at risk. Adolescents and young adults, for example, are known to engage more frequently in high-risk behaviors, such as tobacco, drug, and alcohol use and faster driving habits. More research is also needed to test the model among older people, both healthy and unhealthy populations.

According to the HBM concepts, motivating individuals to exercise includes *providing educational materials* that address the benefits of exercise and the costs of leading a sedentary lifestyle, *modeling proper exercise habits and routines* (this is where hiring a physical trainer and receiving instruction is so valuable), *enhancing the exerciser's perceived competence* (e.g., "I can do this," "I have good technique"), *improving perceived exercise effectiveness* (e.g., "I'm improving," "My health is improving"), *elevating self-efficacy, or confidence* (e.g., "I feel comfortable exercising; it is becoming easier"), *developing set exercise routines* (e.g., "I know exactly when, where, and how I will exercise"), and *establishing easy access to an exercise facility* (preferably within a short distance of work, home, or between these locations). Quitting an exercise habit tends to be far more common when the person relies only on home exercise equipment, since we associate our home environment with relaxation and recreation, not with the challenging levels of physical exertion, sweating, and physical fatigue commonly experienced with exercise.

Theories of Reasoned Action and Planned Behavior

The theories in this section are discussed together because one theory is an extension of the other (Ajzen 1988; Ajzen & Fishbein 1974). The primary question addressed by both the theory of reasoned action (TRA) and the theory of planned behavior (TPB) is "What influences people's decisions about their behavior in social settings?" According to the TRA, people make proper decisions about their behavior based on information and beliefs about their actions, the outcome they expect from their actions, and the value they place on these outcomes. The most important component of this theory, however, is that an individual's *intentions* form the best predictors of actual behavior. The intention to perform certain actions reflects the person's *attitudes* about the behavior and about *subjective, social norms* of that behavior. The attitude toward exercise, for instance, reflects the individual's beliefs about the benefits and consequences—positive and negative evaluations—of engaging or not engaging in regular exercise. One limitation of the model's attitude component, pointed out by Buckworth and Dishman (2002), is that a person may believe that exercise is very healthy, yet conclude that there is a lack of time in the day to exercise regularly. I hear this excuse constantly from corporate clients who work well over 60 hours a week, and tend to be overweight and lead a sedentary lifestyle.

The second component of TRA consists of subjective, social norms about the behavior. This reflects the individual's perceptions about the importance that others place on the behavior and the person's incentive to meet others' expectations. Thus, a person who is surrounded by one or more friends or family members who habitually exercise is more likely to exercise regularly than an individual whose friends and family do not. It is understandable, then, that developing social links as part of an exercise program (e.g., hiring a physical trainer, working out with friends, socializing at fitness clubs, training with teammates) often results in better exercise adherence. As Ajzen and Fishbein (1974) conclude, sometimes attitude is the primary predictor of intentions, while other times the social norm component is.

In his modified follow-up of TRA, Ajzen (1985) added a third component to predicting exercise behavior: perceived behavioral control—that is, an individual's perception that he or she has the resources (i.e., skill and ability) and the opportunity to perform the behavior or to attain the goal. Thus, an individual with unrealistic expectations, such as a large improvement in exercise performance or fitness level (exercise outcome) and a significant reduction in percent body fat (or weight) as a result of the exercise habit, especially within a predetermined (often unrealistic) time period, will likely experience low perceived control. Unmet expectations will lead to disappointment and feelings of helplessness (i.e., low self-control) about their apparent inability to meet their fitness-related goals. Subsequent low expectations about future success may result in quitting future exercise participation. Implications for supporting TRA and TPB through higher perceived behavioral control include setting realistic performance (exercise) goals and experiencing perceived skill and performance quality early in the exercise program (e.g., perceptions of improvement and using proper technique).

How effective are TRA and TPB in predicting exercise behavior? Hausenblas, Carron, and Mack (1997) conducted a meta-analysis, a statistical technique that analyzes the results of many published studies within a specific research area, to determine the extent to which each of these theories (TRA and TPB) successfully predicted exercise behavior. They concluded that exercise behavior does, indeed, result when a person develops the intention to exercise. Secondly, attitude strongly influences intention to exercise, while the subjective norm factor has only a moderate effect on intention to exercise. Thus, intention is strongly related to attitude with respect to exercise behavior. But that's not the complete picture. The researchers found that TPB (Ajzen 1985) provided greater insight into the underlying reasons that intention and attitude form strong predictors of exercise behavior. The individual's perceived control over his or her behavior must be assessed to markedly improve the accuracy of linking intentions with behaviors.

The overall conclusion of Hausenblas et al. (1997), based on the results of their study, was that the strength of an exerciser's feelings that attaining a behavioral goal is under an individual's volitional control is strongly related to the person's intention to actually perform the behavior. This finding might explain the decision by many athletes to discontinue exercise habits when their sport careers end. It is understandable that the combined factors of low perceived control over exercise behavior (as an inherent part of their training, directed by their coach) and the attitude that exercise serves the sole purpose of performing optimally during sport competition (rather than to improve health, avoid illness and disease, reduce stress, and other exercise motives) would result in a lack of interest in exercise when a person's sport career has ended. Consequently, when competitors have the opportunity to regain control over the decision to exercise, their decision is often not to exercise.

A final conclusion of their findings was that "individuals have the greatest commitment to exercise when they hold favorable beliefs about exercise and believe that they can successfully perform the behavior" (p. 45). This is commonly referred to as perceived competence. Lack of perceived competence is one cause of dropping out of organized exercise programs. In fact, about 50 percent of individuals who join fitness clubs drop out within six months due to their feelings of no progress or lack of skill in performing the exercise program (Marcus et al. 1996).

The three clear components of TRA offer ways to encourage exercise participation and maintenance: attitude and subjective norm, which, taken together, form the person's intention to exercise, and perceived behavioral control. First, a person must develop a favorable attitude toward exercise. More specific suggestions to accomplish this goal are described later in this chapter. It is important to remember that fulfilling personal needs motivates people. A person who is informed about the advantages of exercise is more likely to have a positive attitude about participating in exercise. Understanding the benefits of exercising and the costs of not exercising will help promote a desirable attitude toward initiating and maintaining an exercise program. Second, it would be helpful if exercisers developed social support, perhaps exercising with a friend, receiving positive feedback about their exercise habits (e.g., "it's great that you are exercising") and information about the desirable outcomes from their exercise participation (e.g., "you are looking great"), or having a social component to their exercise program, perhaps by developing friendships at their fitness club. Third, the exerciser should be in control of all decisions surrounding the exercise program, including the time (days of the week and time of day), location, duration, and program content. This is where a commitment to working with a physical trainer would be helpful, at least during the initial stages of an exercise program.

Self-Efficacy Theory

Self-efficacy is a set of beliefs and expectations about how capable a person feels in performing the necessary behaviors to achieve a desirable outcome (Bandura 1977). Self-efficacy is specific to a behavior and situation. A person can feel high self-efficacy about his or her ability to gain strength through weight training, yet feel low self-efficacy when it comes to performing aerobic exercise. High self-efficacy about the activity results in a higher likelihood that the person will engage in that activity, but this feeling will not necessarily be generalized to other types of tasks (e.g., competitive sport versus exercise) or situations (e.g., a running competition). Not surprisingly, an individual who believes that he or she is capable of performing the required actions to meet situational demands will more likely engage in those actions. These expectations affect the person's selection of those activities, the degree of effort expended on the activities, and the extent to which a person will persist at the activities, especially after experiencing failure and the unpleasant consequences of not meeting expectations. For instance, persons who eat a particular diet that consists of foods they would not ordinarily eat, then quickly put on weight (or, more accurately, fat) soon after quitting the diet, will often give up on their desire to take off pounds. Similarly, exercisers who do not experience rapid success—that is, meet goals quickly—will presume that the task is of insurmountable difficulty and will quit exercising, perhaps due to low self-efficacy.

McAuley and Mihalko (1998) reviewed over 100 studies on the effects of self-efficacy theory on exercise behavior. They concluded that self-efficacy is higher, leading to greater likelihood of exercise participation and maintenance, if the individual: (1) selects the type of exercise behavior undertaken, a concept called *perceived choice*, (2) possesses certain *thought patterns*, such as optimism, intrinsic motivation (i.e., exercising for pleasure and enjoyment, under conditions of high self-determination and competence; see Chapter 3), and heightened self-control, (3) *expends optimal effort* and feels capable of redoubling efforts in the face of barriers and challenges, and (4) has *reasonably high expectations* of successful performance and desirable outcomes. To McAuley and Mihalko, the strongest influence of self-efficacy on exercise behavior is performance accomplishments. Mastering tasks perceived by the performer as difficult markedly increases self-efficacy. The ways in which mastery occurs could include observing a model perform the desired task, getting encouragement from significant others, and observing other persons with similar characteristics to oneself succeed through effort and get rewarded as a result of their success (a process called vicarious experience). Using performance data that indicates improvements, such as minutes of aerobic work, resistance, repetitions, percent body fat, flexibility, and heart rate (maximal oxygen uptake, or max VO^2) will improve self-efficacy and, consequently, exercise adherence.

Not surprisingly, the authors acknowledge that even when self-efficacy beliefs about exercise are high, "the decision to embark on an exercise program . . . is fraught with challenges especially when individuals are sedentary, older, or recovering from a life-threatening disease" (p. 372). For many people who live a sedentary lifestyle, engaging in physical activity at the correct level of intensity, duration, and frequency to obtain sufficient health and medical benefits is simply too unpleasant. These individuals conclude that the "benefits" of remaining sedentary and not exercising (e.g., having more time to do other things, not experiencing the discomfort associated with vigorous exercise) are greater than the "costs" of remaining sedentary (e.g., weight gain, poorer health, reduced life span). Perhaps only when these costs are greater than the benefits and are perceived by the person as unacceptable will the person decide to exercise. The decision to both initiate and maintain an exercise program, then, is more complex than each of the preceding theories and models suggests. Perhaps changing behavior from sedentary to active, rather than consisting of one determinant, consists of a series of stages, as suggested in Prochaska and DiClemente's (1982) transtheoretical model, originally applied to addictive behaviors and later modified to exercise by Prochaska and Marcus (1994).

Transtheoretical Model

According to the transtheoretical model, the decision to begin and maintain a habit of exercise—behavior change—occurs over a long period of time. Because the decision to change one's behavior is not always permanent, such as attempts at dieting, quitting the habits of smoking or drug taking, and continuing to exercise, the model is cyclical, not linear. Behavioral patterns occur again and again. The model's five stages are precontemplation, contemplation, preparation, action, and maintenance.

Precontemplation. At this stage, the inactive person has no intention of exercising, at least not in the next six months. This person is a typical "couch potato." The person does not feel the need to exercise, or perhaps has not had positive experiences with previous attempts at exercise. Perhaps there are social pressures not to exercise, such as lack of approval from family and friends, self-consciousness about exercising in a public facility in the presence of others who might be more fit or younger, not being able to afford exercise equipment or fitness club memberships, or living too far away from available programs and facilities. There is never a shortage of excuses to avoid exercising, if that's a person's intention. Even reading about the advantages of exercise is often avoided.

Contemplation. At this stage, the person now intends to start exercising within the next six months. The person might have become enlightened about the advantages of exercise; perhaps a physician has cautioned about the need to exercise or face undesirable health consequences; or the person's current state of mental or physical health virtually "requires" starting an exercise program. The "costs" of not exercising are now beginning to become excessive and the benefits are increasingly attractive. "Thinking" about exercising can take considerable time, even two years, before it's acted upon. Prochaska and Marcus (1994) report that "on the average, individuals stay in this relatively stable stage for at least 2 years, telling themselves that someday they will change but putting off change" (p. 162). The authors refer to individuals who substitute thinking for acting as *chronic contemplators*.

Preparation. At this stage, individuals intend to take action in the near future, usually within a month (e.g., "I'm going to join a fitness club and start a regular exercise routine"). Typically, an action plan is formulated, although the plan may not be carried out to obtain the optimal benefits (e.g., exercising only on the weekend rather than at least three times a week). Finally, the individual is not yet fully committed to the plan because the disadvantages of exercising (e.g., not enough time, cost of a fitness club membership, lack of space for exercise equipment in the house) still outweigh the advantages.

Action. The person has finally initiated an exercise routine, though for less than six months. Although an extensive amount of activity (e.g., scheduling exercise, thinking about its advantages, working with a partner or personal trainer, even packing the gym bag) is now under way, "it is the least stable stage and tends to correspond with the highest risk for relapse" (Prochaska & Marcus 1994, p. 163). This stage endures for about six months. One uncertainty about this stage concerns the criteria that constitute action. Unknown is whether a specific exercise program three times per week (e.g., at a given intensity and duration) defines "action," or whether this stage refers to any general, consistent, and enduring change in exercise behavior. As Prochaska and Marcus (1994) conclude, "problems exist in areas for which there [are] no agreed upon criteria" (p. 163).

Maintenance. After a period of six months, there is now less risk that the person will quit the new behavior. Similar to the previous ("Action") section, there is uncertainty in the literature about the operational definition of maintenance. Writers in the medical literature (e.g., Rand & Weeks 1998) have used terms such as "partial adherence," "ideal adherence," "appropriate adherence," "erratic adherence," and "involuntary adherence" to mean that a person's decision to maintain a prescribed behavior reflects the criterion under which the behavioral change was originally intended, planned, and most important, would result in the desired (anticipated) outcome. Thus, if a person started on a three-day-per-week exercise program, and after a few weeks exercised only one day per week, the health benefits from exercise would be compromised. Yet, because the person went from no exercise to once per week, this could reflect partial, not full, adherence. Prochaska and Marcus consider five years of continuously maintaining an exercise habit as the time interval in which a person will not return to their previous, nonexercise lifestyle.

Termination. At this stage, there is no temptation to engage in the old behavior and 100% confidence about overcoming previously tempting situations (e.g., "Whenever I feel like exercising, I'll just lie down until the feeling passes"). However, there remains uncertainty about whether a previously sedentary person who has maintained a regular exercise program will ever return to a life of no exercise. A review of the addiction literature, however, from which the transtheoretical model was derived, reveals that reverting to previous habits is always possible, given the presence of some factors (e.g., high demands on time, injury, one or more unpleasant exercise-related experiences, poor weather, breakage of equipment, other, more tempting, activities that replace exercise) or the absence of others (e.g., lack of social support, failure to meet goals, increased exercise difficulty due to weight gain or aging, lack of financial resources to afford a fitness club membership). In their review of this model, Berger et al. (2002) suggest matching treatment (intervention) strategies to the individual's stage of change, progressing one stage at a time. Thus, a person who is in the contemplation stage needs a personal invitation to work out, preferably by someone with whom he or she feels comfortable, education about the benefits of exercise, and a high degree of structure in preparing for and scheduling an exercise routine.

A person at the preparation stage needs considerable positive reinforcement about the initial outcomes of exercise, social support, perhaps some work with a personal trainer, and baseline testing that allows the person to observe desirable changes in exercise performance. An exerciser at the action stage might prefer structured exercise sessions (e.g., an aerobics class), positive reinforcement (e.g., praise from significant others), and, again, test data that show improvement on various dimensions (e.g., improved cholesterol measures, reduced percent body fat, improved cardiovascular functioning, strength gains). Although the transtheoretical model as applied to exercise has been criticized (see Buckworth & Dishman 2002, pp. 222–223, for a brief review), another review of this literature by Berger et al. (2002) reveals a more supportive interpretation. According to the model, for example, people think and behave differently across various time periods related to changing their behavior. At the precontemplation and contemplation stages, the case against exercise is stronger than the case in favor of it. However, at the preparation stage, the benefits of exercise begin to outweigh the costs. In the action and maintenance stages, the advantages of exercise over an inactive lifestyle are clear and consistent. Another advantage to the transtheoretical model is that it forms a coherent structure from which to understand the reasons that underlie a person's decision to change or not change behavior, and to construct interventions that facilitate desirable changes—in this case, to engage in a long-term exercise program.

There is one problem associated with all of these models that researchers have not addressed, at least not consistently. How does the public define exercise? Ask individuals who walk a mile a day if they exercise, and they say "yes." Others will categorize themselves as exercisers if they lift weights or engage in flexibility exercises. However, the general mental and physical health benefits of exercise are minimal unless a person engages in *aerobic* exercise. The validity of theories and models in explaining and predicting exercise behavior is clouded by the failure to recognize what *type* of exercise we are trying to encourage. Perhaps it's best to simply encourage people, especially if they are elderly, overweight, or recovering from sickness or injury, to engage in any type of exercise habit they view as possible, safe, and mentally stimulating. If our standards for exercise participation consist of reaching our target heart rate or engaging in aerobic exercise at the exclusion of other forms of exercise that also improve health, we—researchers, writers, and practitioners—might be setting the bar too high and actually inhibiting a more active lifestyle in our society.

Exercise Adherence and Compliance

Beginning an exercise habit is challenging, but maintaining it is even more difficult. The tendency of a person to maintain participation in any behavioral regimen—exercise, in this case—once the individual has agreed to undertake it is called (exercise) adherence. In the medical literature, Rand and Weeks (1998) broadly define adherence as "the degree to which patient behaviors coincide with the clinical recommendations of health care providers" (p. 115). Other definitions of adherence include sticking to or faithfully conforming to a standard of behavior in order to meet some goal, and long-term behavior changes associated with preventing undesirable symptoms or outcomes. *Compliance*, on the other hand, although used interchangeably with adherence, is not the same thing. It refers to behaviors related to following immediate or short-term advice, a direct prescription to improve health or well-being, or a sense of coercive obedience to order. In calling for more compliance research in the health care industry, Nancy Miller and her colleagues (1997) define compliance simply as "the extent to which recommendations are followed and defined" (p. 1085). Thus, persons who initiate and maintain an exercise program *of their own volition* are adhering to rather than complying with their program. However, persons who are given instructions about what exercise to do and how to do it and who carry out these instructions are *complying* with the exercise program. If they permanently stop exercising (again, of their own free will), they are not adhering, and if they do not fulfill the wishes of an authority figure to carry out an exercise regimen (let's say, a personal trainer or a cardiologist who prescribed postcoronary exercise for rehabilitation purposes), they are noncompliant. Despite differences in how adherence and compliance are operationally defined, most authors in this literature continue to use the terms interchangeably.

Rand and Weeks address a common problem in the adherence literature: the lack of specific criteria that provide the "gold standard" for determining adherence. What is acceptable adherence in one study or for one exerciser might be nonadherence in another study or for someone else. As indicated earlier, adherence may be classified as "appropriate," "erratic/partial," "ideal," "voluntary," or "involuntary." Though a complete review of this area goes beyond the purpose of this section, three points are worth noting from an applied perspective in working with exercise clients. First, labeling someone as an exercise dropout (i.e., a nonadherer) has consequences for long-term, intrinsic motivation to persist at future attempts at exercising. The person will conclude, "I once tried that and quit." The person will less likely feel secure and motivated to try again. Instead, it might be more motivating to point out limitations in someone's current exercise habit (i.e., erratic or partial adherence) and to build on that person's strengths (e.g., "You are off to a good start; keep trying, because exercise gets easier as you get fitter").

Second, while exercise adherence is usually determined by the extent to which the person is maintaining the original exercise plan, there are often fair reasons for not continuing. One example is the lack of proper instruction, leading to poor exercise technique, higher perceived exertion (i.e., feelings associated with exercise intensity and effort), and greater difficulty in completing the planned routine. Other reasons include sustaining an injury, self-consciousness about one's appearance in an exercise facility, engaging in an exercise activity that one finds overly strenuous, failure to quickly meet goals (which may be unrealistic), and the lack of social support. Researchers have also determined that the absence of an exercise facility located near home or work, job-related travel, physical and mental fatigue, lack of interest, poor weather, family demands, and perceived lack of time may all lead to discontinuing an exercise plan.

The third point worth noting is the tendency of researchers to collect and publish their data based on formal group exercise programs, as opposed to a person's preference to exercise alone, perhaps at home. In other words, though some individuals might decide against continuing to exercise in a structured setting, they could continue to engage in a program of vigorous physical activity on their own. This does not mean they have dropped out, but rather that they have selected another type of venue and structure within which to exercise. To refer to such people as nonadhering to exercise would be incorrect. Sadly, approximately 50 percent of exercise participants discontinue exercising in structured programs within the first six months of starting, although researchers are uncertain if any of these individuals exercise on their own. More research is needed on exercise habits and adherence rates outside of formal exercise program settings.

Why Exercisers Quit

With all of the attention given to fostering lifelong exercise habits in a society that prefers to move as little as possible, it's sad when a person finally commits to exercise and then quits. Why does this happen? Even when a doctor prescribes a formal, supervised exercise rehabilitation program to heart or pulmonary patients, some individuals will simply not maintain this life-saving habit. Is the fitness industry to blame? Have researchers and practitioners not detected the "true" reasons for discontinuing one's exercise habit? Is there inadequate attention to monitoring the progress of a novice exerciser? Although the lack of continuous encouragement to the novice exerciser certainly contributes to quitting (discussed later), exercisers may also make several errors in technique that increase discomfort and exertion, and reduce progress.

How Novice Exercisers Can Avoid
Common Errors That Lead to Quitting

I am always saddened when I observe a person wander around a fitness facility appearing "lost" about what to do and how to do it, and then attempt to use an exercise machine for an all-too-brief time, with improper technique. Within a relatively short time, off they go to the locker room, having done only a fraction of the proper routine needed to experience the mental and physical benefits of exercise. Rather than providing instruction as part of a membership fee, fitness clubs ask members to pay an additional, optional fee to receive instruction by a physical trainer. While input from a trainer is helpful, it's no wonder that the lack of proper initial instruction and ongoing monitoring has contributed to an alarming dropout rate. Elements that contribute to exercise program success are discussed below. Attention to them may help prevent some common errors made by exercisers that compromise experiencing the full benefits of fitness programs.

Proper Attire. Proper foot gear and clothing will make the workout more pleasant and reduce the chance of injury. For example, high-quality exercise shoes are important to prevent lower-limb injury and promote aerobic exercise performance. And, since your body produces a tremendous amount of heat, clothing that allows for the evaporation of perspiration will have a cooling effect. "Sweating off pounds" is an old, very unsafe myth linking exercise to weight loss. This is because sweat, which is water being excreted by the body during intense work, is rapidly replaced by the body's need for water consumption due to thirst. Drinking water cools down the body's internal temperature, preventing heat-related illnesses, among other biological outcomes.

Warm Up Properly. Starting slowly increases the body's temperature, improves blood flow to muscles, and improves flexibility, making the person better prepared to meet greater exercise demands. The result is less chance of injury and, due to more oxygen being delivered to muscles, reduced exertion and better aerobic performance.

Stretch Properly. It is now understood that stretching *before* engaging in vigorous physical activity creates better flexibility for muscles and tendons to perform efficiently. Stretching technique should be *static*—in which the person holds the stretched position for several seconds—*not ballistic,* in which there is a "bouncing" motion to try to stretch the muscles to their maximum. Bouncing actually signals the muscle to contract rather than relax, resulting in less flexibility, not more. Furthermore, the timing of stretching is important. Exercisers should stretch on two occasions during their exercise session, before and immediately following vigorous physical activity. The sequence of exercise should be: (1) mild aerobic activity for 3–5 minutes as a low-intensity aerobic warm-up, which results in slightly raising the internal body temperature, (2) a series of static stretches, (3) vigorous aerobic activity, (4) reducing the heart rate by cooling down, usually with walking, and (5) a final series of static stretching. Strength (resistance) training, through lifting weights, is also recommended as part of an exercise regimen. Two reasons to resistance train include reducing the likelihood of injury and strengthening muscles, which increases metabolism and results in burning more calories at rest. There is no conclusive evidence about the best time to strength train in relation to aerobic activity. Some individuals prefer to lift weights before engaging in aerobic exercise, while other prefer to weight train after aerobic activity. Still others engage in resistance and aerobic training on alternate days. It's a matter of personal choice.

Interval Train for Improving Aerobic Fitness. An important objective of aerobic exercise is to attain training heart rate (THR). This is an easy calculation: heart rate (HR) should reach from 60 to 70 percent of the person's predicted maximum HR (220 minus age). For a 20-year-old person, then, THR would be: $220 - 20 = 200 \times 0.70 = 140$ beats per minute. The best way to reach one's THR is through a series of work/rest intervals, rather than engaging in nonstop (continuous) exercise. This is because HR will reach training level when exercise is conducted in a series of relatively brief (2 to 3 minutes), highly intense exercise bouts. Reaching THR strengthens the heart muscle and improves efficiency of the cardiovascular system.

One schedule, for example, would include exercising on a series of work/rest intervals, each consisting of 3 minutes of work (e.g., fast jogging, rapid walking, rapid bicycle pedaling) and 1 minute of rest (not total stopping, but rather significantly reducing work speed and intensity). The interval should continue over a period of 20 to 30 minutes because researchers have found that this is the minimum time period needed to strengthen the cardiovascular system. THR will be achieved after a couple of work bouts.

Think Minutes, Not Miles. Time goals are far easier to achieve than distance goals because the units are far more attainable in time (minutes) than distance (segments of a mile). It is important to reach pre-determined goals for improved motivation, a sense of achievement, and as a reflection of training. In addition, the exercise physiology literature addresses time, not distance, as an indicator of improved fitness because time can be controlled and measured much more easily than distance. It is also easier to examine progress against published tables and standards.

Cool Down Properly. A common error among exercisers of aerobic work is to stop too suddenly before the next task. The heart has been pumping blood at a furious pace in order to deliver oxygen to the muscles and prevent or reduce fatigue. Stopping suddenly will pool the blood in the legs, reducing the blood flow back to the heart (a process called venous return, the return of blood to the heart via the veins). The result can be dizziness. For individuals with advanced heart disease—perhaps as-yet undetected— the result can be fatal. The lack of blood supply returning to the heart can trigger a myocardial infarction (heart attack), according to the medical literature. Proper cooldown will also deliver more blood to the fatigued muscles, "flushing out" the fatigue chemical, lactic acid, thereby promoting recovery.

Resistance (Strength) Training. This form of exercise should not be ignored for reasons described earlier. Strength training is less about increasing muscle size than improving bone density, increasing metabolism (the rate of burning calories at rest), and protecting joints from injury. Improper resistance training, usually by lifting weights that are too heavy or performing it too quickly, can induce physical discomfort or injury. Proper instruction is a must.

Stretch Last. Muscles contract like an old radio antenna, and do not always return to their original length. Therefore, in order to avoid muscular stiffness, it's necessary to slowly (statically, not ballistically) stretch all muscle groups at the *end* of the exercise session.

Increase Water Intake. Most of us are in a state of dehydration and don't know it. We are simply not drinking enough water. Detectors in the brain are not properly developed to indicate the need to increase water consumption, a condition that has contributed significantly to many heat-related deaths in sports. This condition is exacerbated when exercising vigorously. Exercise induces extensive sweating and a concomitant rise in body temperature. Proper water intake is essential to maintain internal body temperature and to replace the normal, but extensive, loss of body fluids. Water—much better than the so-called "sports drinks," which have sugar and other ingredients that increase calories—should be consumed in small amounts *before and during* the exercise session, in addition to after completing the workout.

Strategies for Enhancing Exercise Adherence and Compliance

There is a huge fitness industry that depends on its members to maintain their interest in exercise, and that has made numerous attempts to promote exercise adherence. My own discussions with numerous owners of fitness facilities around the U.S. indicate that from 40 to 60 percent of members do not renew their club memberships. While the guidelines for promoting exercise participation and performance—applied exercise psychology— are discussed later, there are six primary guidelines for encouraging individuals who have started exercising to continue to do so. These are: (1) addressing the exerciser's dispositions that may prompt dropping out, such as anxiety, self-consciousness, perfectionism, need achievement, intrinsic motivation, fear of failure, and even clinical issues (e.g., depression, mood disorders, eating disorders, effects of medications), (2) "ensuring" perceived success and improvement in setting and meeting realistic exercise-related and personal goals, preferably supported by performance data, (3) providing instruction and feedback—both positive and constructive, (4) encouraging social support, (5) providing educational materials related to proper exercise techniques, exercise benefits, and improved nutrition, and finally, (6) working with the exerciser in creating and maintaining a healthy lifestyle that is dependent on proper exercise habits.

Addressing the Exerciser's Dispositions. As discussed in Chapter 2, all individuals possess a set of psychological characteristics, called dispositions, which differ from more permanent, stable personality traits, and that result in certain behavioral tendencies. There are certain personal features that predict a person's willingness to begin and adhere to exercise habits. For example, a highly anxious individual is more likely to feel threatened about engaging in a program that might prove disappointing in meeting personal goals, not be able to show competence in performing exercise tasks, or may not perform certain exercises as well as others in view. The effects of these feelings on adherence is magnified when the person is also highly self-conscious (heightened awareness of how one is being perceived by others), has a high need to achieve, fears failure, sets extremely high standards and is very self-critical when these standards—which are often unrealistic—are not met (i.e., perfectionism), and has very high self-expectations of rapid success. Competence and results are expected quickly. When the reasons for exercising are based on approval from others or some other source of reward, rather than from personal enjoyment, then the person is said to be extrinsically, rather than intrinsically, motivated. Finally, clinical issues, such as depression, social anxiety, mood disorders, eating disorders, and the effects of medications each work toward inhibiting one's energy to commit to a permanent change in exercise habits. Though the fitness industry is not expected to employ clinical psychologists to deal with the personal issues of fitness club members, it would be in the best interests of the exerciser to seek counseling and determine the sources of the habit of starting and then quitting new programs and of learning new skills. Though there is apparently no publication that focuses on counseling issues with exercise participants, the reader is referred to a book edited by Richard Ray and Diane Weise-Bjornstal (1999) that addresses many of these issues in sports medicine settings.

Ensuring Perceived Success and Improvement (Intrinsic Motivation). People are, by nature, attracted to activities that they perform well. Conversely, people tend to avoid activities that they perceive as too difficult and that lead to perceived failure outcomes. The word "perceived" is important, here, because it is the individual's own interpretation of success and failure that influences continued participation, rather than an externally imposed standard or the views of others that is the indicator of competence or incompetence. Of primary concern, then, is that novice exercisers experience and gain a sense of competence—success or improvement—from their participation in exercise, however these concepts are identified to the individual. Setting realistic goals that are not too challenging at first provides a sense of comfort and security about engaging in exercise tasks that might be viewed as very challenging. The goal, then, is to give novices a sense of "can do" about their ability to engage in exercise routines successfully, with minimum discomfort and optimal benefits.

Providing Instructional Feedback. Instructional feedback meets a number of needs and provides exercisers with a feeling of growth and development in exercise and social support by a specialist. There is a heightened sense of hope and optimism about overcoming physical and mental barriers (self-doubt, low confidence). Feedback also leads to improved performance quality and better results.

Ideally, the source of feedback would be data based (quantitative), such as improved fitness test scores (e.g., minutes of aerobic exercise, pounds of resistance lifted, degrees of flexibility improved, training heart rate reached and maintained). However, qualitative feedback (e.g., positive verbal praise) is also a reliable source of improved perceived competence if the person offering the information is credible (e.g., a fitness instructor, physician, or other specialist) and the information is based on concrete, specific performance—not the usual, more general and abstract, "nice job" that lacks specificity and identifiable performance (Figure 11.2). Heightened perceptions of competence increase intrinsic motivation (a person's self-determined drive to perform a task due to feelings of competence and satisfaction).

Figure 11.2 Providing instruction and feedback on correct exercise technique will improve fitness and adherence.

Encouraging Social Support. While some individuals prefer to exercise alone and are highly self-motivated, others rely on friends, family members, or groups with whom to exercise or from whom to receive encouragement. Being acknowledged by others often has very motivating properties. Individuals who encourage others act as a primary source of motivation.

Providing Educational Materials. For many individuals, additional information about their involvement in exercise contributes to its meaningfulness and might work to favorably influence desirable outcomes. For example, as Gauvin and her colleagues (2001) point out, individuals who learn the benefits—psychological and physical—of exercise are more likely to adhere to their exercise habits because they feel greater control over influencing their health. Consequently, these individuals take more responsibility for maintaining their exercise regimen while anticipating the benefits. The authors also suggest that exercise specialists work with employers to develop ways to educate their workers about delivering the many benefits of exercise and other health issues. Educational materials also have high positive reinforcement value, which improves adherence, because this information provides additional, credible support for the value and desirable outcomes accrued from exercise.

Developing a Healthy Lifestyle. Finally, exercisers are more likely to adhere if their habit is ritualized as part of a new, healthy lifestyle that encompasses nutrition, stress management, and positive thoughts and emotions. Rather than being an end in itself, exercise becomes part of a new set of routines and healthy habits that improves the person's energy, facilitates a desirable change in selected dispositions (e.g., greater optimism, confidence, coping skills; reduced anxiety and other negative mood states), and expands functional capacity to socialize with others and to engage in required life skills efficiently.

Finally, Miller et al. (1997) make several recommendations to providers and health care organizations to increase patient compliance. Though these authors are describing patients in cardiac rehabilitation programs, the same recommendations have implications for healthy exercisers, too.

Providers should:

1. Communicate clear, direct messages about the importance of a particular course of action or therapy (e.g., provide verbal and written instructions, including rationale for treatments)
2. Include patients/clients in decisions about prevention and treatment goals (e.g., use contracting strategies, anticipate barriers to compliance and discussion solutions, negotiate goals and a plan)
3. Include behavioral strategies in the counseling process (e.g., use active listening techniques, incorporate both cognitive and behavioral strategies)
4. Assess patient compliance at each office visit (e.g., use self-report or electronic data)
5. Develop reminder systems to ensure identification and follow-up of the patient's/ client's status (e.g., telephone calls for follow-up)
6. Be proper models of good health by engaging in proper exercise and nutritional habits

Health care organizations should:

1. Develop an environment that supports prevention and treatment interventions (e.g., preappointment reminders, telephone follow-up, schedule evening and weekend office hours, provide group and individual counseling for patients and their families)
2. Provide tracking and reporting systems (e.g., develop computer-based systems to locate electronic medical records)
3. Provide education and training for providers (e.g., require continuing education courses in communication and behavioral counseling)
4. Encourage providers to maintain a healthy lifestyle (e.g., exercise, nutrition) in attempting to reduce the likelihood of obesity, a condition of epidemic proportions in the United States (providing exercise equipment at or near the worksite or working with exercise facilities to reduce the cost of memberships would be helpful)
5. Provide adequate reimbursement for allocation of time for all health care professionals (e.g., develop incentives tied to desired patient and provider outcomes)

In summary, exercise leaders and organizations are challenged to overcome a culture that promotes the least amount of physical activity and the highest level of food intake in the world. It is imperative that the U.S. address its growing obesity epidemic, or face skyrocketing health care costs in coming years. Vastly reduced physical activity in childhood and adolescence has not helped. Greater use of computers, more access to television alternatives, increased displeasure with participating in youth sports, and a culture obsessed with fast, high-fat food are all having a detrimental effect on our health and well-being.

Exercise Addiction/Dependence

The antithesis of the problem of getting people to exercise—and adhere to their exercise habit—is the problem of people who become dependent on it. The concept is called exercise addiction or dependence. Originally referred to as positive addiction by Glasser (1976), the terms "exercise dependence" or "compulsion to exercise" have become more common recently. Is being an exercise addict necessarily a bad thing?

Although researchers and psychologists debate whether any addiction can be positive, most agree that addictions, in general, tend to be unhealthy and undesirable (Cockerill & Riddington 1996). This is because, by definition, addictions represent behaviors that are beyond the person's control or that reflect psychopathology, such as low physique self-esteem, an eating disorder, the need for social isolation, or represent some other compensation that requires treatment (Berger et al. 2002). For example, Berger et al. cite other studies in which the motivation for running or weight training serves the purpose of improving body image. Though it is normal to enhance one's physical features, a huge amount of time devoted to exercise, at the expense of other normal daily routines and social interactions, borders on abnormal or dysfunctional behavior. Although the compulsion to exercise may have a positive, anabolic (tissue-building) effect on the body—positive addiction—exercising excessively, whether it is a conscious decision or a behavioral habit driven by routine and a perceived personal need, has a catabolic (tissue-destroying) effect on the system. Negative consequences result (hence the term *negative addiction*) such as injury, illness, or exercising while injured or ill. Hausenblas and Symons (2002) have published the *Exercise Dependence Scale*, which measures evidence of negative addiction to physical activity (Figure 11.3).

Figure 11.3 Exercise Dependence Scale

Exercise Dependence Scale

Introduction

The *Exercise Dependence Scale* operationalizes exercise dependence based on the Diagnostic and Statistical Manual of Mental Disorder-IV (DSM-IV) criteria for substance dependence (APA 1994) and provides the following information:

1. Mean overall score of exercise dependence symptoms.

2. Differentiates between: (a) at-risk for exercise dependent, (b) nondependent-symptomatic, and (c) nondependent-asymptomatic.

3. Specifies whether individuals have evidence of physiological dependence (i.e., evidence of tolerance or withdrawal) or no physiological dependence (i.e., no evidence of tolerance or withdrawal).

Consistent with the DSM-IV criteria for substance dependence, exercise dependence was operationalized and measured as a multidimensional maladaptive pattern of exercise, leading to clinically significant impairment or distress, as manifested by *three or more* of the following:

(1) *Tolerance:* which is defined as either a need for increased amounts of exercise to achieve the desired effect or diminished effect with continued use of the same amount of exercise

(2) *Withdrawal:* as manifested by either the characteristic withdrawal symptoms for exercise (e.g., anxiety, fatigue) or the same (or closely related) amount of exercise is taken to relieve or avoid withdrawal symptoms

(3) *Intention Effect:* exercise is often taken in larger amounts or over a longer period than was intended

(4) *Lack of Control:* there is a persistent desire or unsuccessful effort to cut down or control exercise

(5) *Time:* a great deal of time is spent in activities necessary to obtain exercise (e.g., physical activity vacations)

(6) *Reductions in Other Activities:* social, occupational, or recreational activities are given up or reduced because of exercise

(7) *Continuance:* exercise is continued despite knowledge of having a persistent or recurrent physical or psychological problem that is likely to have been caused or exacerbated by the exercise (e.g., continued running despite injury).

The *Exercise Dependence Scale* items were based on the aforementioned 7 criteria.

The *Exercise Dependence Scale* can be administered in individual and group settings and has been used with respondents 18 years and older. Participants indicate their responses to each of the 21 items in the blank space provided after each item. They indicate their responses on a Likert scale anchored at the extremes with never (1) and always (6). The *Exercise Dependence Scale* requires approximately 5 minutes to complete.

Scale Scoring

The proposed scoring procedure for the *Exercise Dependence Scale* is computer based, which allows for immediate and accurate scoring. The computer scoring of the *Exercise Dependence Scale* is based on the SPSS (Statistic Package for the Social Sciences System). A syntax file has

---

(continued)

Figure 11.3 Exercise Dependence Scale

been developed (see below) by the authors that enables immediate feedback to the *Exercise Dependence Scale* responses once the items are entered into SPSS. The syntax enables:

1. Computing a total and subscale mean scores for *Exercise Dependence Scale*. A higher score indicates more exercise dependent symptoms.

2. Categorizing participants into either at-risk for exercise dependent, nondependent-symptomatic, or nondependent-asymptomatic groups. The categorization into one of the three groups is generated by a scoring manual that consists of flowchart decision rules, in which items or combinations of items determine if an individual would be classified in the dependent, symptomatic, or asymptomatic range on each of the 7 DSM criteria. Individuals who are classified into the dependent range on 3 or more of the DSM criteria are classified as exercise dependent. The dependent range is operationalized as indicating a score of 5 or 6 for that item. Individuals who scored in the 3 to 4 range are classified as symptomatic. These individuals may theoretically be considered at-risk for exercise dependence. Finally, individuals who score in the 1–2 range are classified as asymptomatic.

Exercise Dependence Scale

Instructions. Using the scale provided below, please complete the following questions as honestly as possible. The questions refer to current exercise beliefs and behaviors that have occurred in the *past 3 months*. Please place your answer in the blank space provided after each statement.

1	2	3	4	5	6
Never					Always

1. I exercise to avoid feeling irritable. _____
2. I exercise despite recurring physical problems. _____
3. I continually increase my exercise intensity to achieve the desired effects/benefits. _____
4. I am unable to reduce how long I exercise. _____
5. I would rather exercise than spend time with family/friends. _____
6. I spend a lot of time exercising. _____
7. I exercise longer than I intend. _____
8. I exercise to avoid feeling anxious. _____
9. I exercise when injured. _____
10. I continually increase my exercise frequency to achieve the desired effects/benefits. _____
11. I am unable to reduce how often I exercise. _____
12. I think about exercise when I should be concentrating on school/work. _____
13. I spend most of my free time exercising. _____
14. I exercise longer than I expect. _____
15. I exercise to avoid feeling tense. _____
16. I exercise despite persistent physical problems. _____
17. I continually increase my exercise duration to achieve the desired effects/benefits. _____
18. I am unable to reduce how intensely I exercise. _____
19. I choose to exercise so that I can get out of spending time with family/friends. _____

(continued)

Figure 11.3 Exercise Dependence Scale

20. A great deal of my time is spent exercising. _____
21. I exercise longer than I plan. _____

Scoring:

Component	Item Numbers		
Withdrawal Effects	1,	8,	15
Continuance	2,	9,	16
Tolerance	3,	10,	17
Lack of Control	4,	11,	18
Reduction in Other Activities	5,	12,	19
Time	6,	13,	20
Intention Effects	7,	14,	21

Positive Addiction to Exercise

As Glasser (1976) originally described, positive addiction is characterized by withdrawal symptoms within 24 to 36 hours without exercise. These symptoms include irritability, quick temper, anxiety, feelings of bloatedness, muscle tension, and sleeplessness. In extreme cases, the long-term cessation of regular exercise might result in changes in personal dispositions such as confidence, self-esteem, the ability to cope with stress, and self-control until the person resumes normal exercise habits. As long as a person's exercise compulsion is beneficial to his or her health and psychological well-being, the addiction (dependence on) to exercise may be called positive. However, when exercise deprivation has a deleterious effect on the person's physical or mental well-being, then the person may be manifesting negative addiction (dependence).

Negative Addiction to Exercise: A Mental Disorder?

The change from positive to negative exercise addiction occurs when the person becomes compulsive about an exercise routine at the exclusion of other daily activities. There are two mental conditions that likely drive a negative exercise addiction, obsessions and compulsions. According to the *Diagnostic and Statistical Manual of Mental Disorders* (4th ed., 1994), "obsessions" are any persistent, recurring, and disturbing thoughts, desires, impulses, or drives that control a person's behavior, and are viewed by the person as intrusive and inappropriate, causing significant anxiety or distress. "Compulsions" are repetitive ritualized behaviors or thoughts that persons are driven to do in order to relieve the anxiety caused by their obsessions. Obsessive-compulsive disorder (OCD) is present when the attempts to exert control over inner and outer worlds have become uncontrollable. One example is a person's tendency to wash his or her hands until the skin is raw in response to obsessive concerns about contamination in a distorted perception about staying clean. One sign of OCD is that the person is bothered by his or her obsessions or compulsions, and that the activities are time-consuming (typically, more than one hour a day) or interfering in the person's life.

Some individuals who suffer from negative exercise addiction feel compelled to exercise, even at the expense of working, socializing, or being involved in other important activities. Exercise is controlling their lives. Thus, a negatively addicted exerciser concludes that he or she "must" exercise, rather than exercising for improved health, relaxation, or other forms of enjoyment, and that exercise is the central point of life, even at the expense of health and life satisfaction. Other manifestations of negative addiction include exercising with a serious injury, when in pain, in poor health, exercising to lose weight when, in fact, the person's weight is normal or below normal, and exercising at the expense of attending to family responsibilities or developing social relationships.

Rather than a mental disorder, exercise-deprived individuals might be exhibiting short-term disturbances in mood state and other undesirable emotions. For instance, a study conducted at the University of Wisconsin by Gregory Mondin and his colleagues (1996) examined the psychological effects of no exercise for 3 consecutive days on males and females who exercised 6 to 7 days a week for a minimum of 45 minutes per session. The researchers, using the Profile of Mood States and State-Trait Anxiety Inventory, found that decreased vigor, and simultaneous increases in tension, depression, confusion, and state anxiety occurred within 24 to 48 hours of exercise deprivation. These mood disturbances improved when exercise was resumed.

In their review of related literature, Cockerill and Riddington (1996) claim that compulsive exercisers (1) are dissatisfied with their body or with themselves, (2) will exercise to have control, but become controlled by the activity, (3) do not enjoy having free time, (4) become dependent on the euphoric and calming benefits of exercise, (5) are avid goal setters, and (6) become socially withdrawn. The authors claim that committed exercisers differ from their compulsive counterparts by feeling invigorated and strengthened by exercise. Compulsive exercisers, on the other hand, perceive exercise as work and no longer enjoy the pleasure that it once provided. Negatively addicted exercisers are not happy about it and require counseling.

How to Avoid Negative Exercise Addiction

Berger et al. (2002) provide guidelines to try to prevent negative exercise addiction. These include: (1) keeping the exercise regimen to 3 to 4 times a week, and not more than 30 to 60 minutes in each session, (2) interval training, in which some days are harder than others, alternating high and low intensity, (3) finding a partner with whom to work out who is not obsessed with exercise, (4) scheduling rest days as part of the exercise program, (5) if injured, ensuring full recovery before starting to exercise again, and (6) setting realistic short-term and long-term goals, and a realistic time frame in which to meet those goals.

Other ideas to prevent negative addiction include alternating types of exercises so that certain muscle groups are not overtrained, engaging in a balanced exercise program that includes aerobic, resistance (strength), and flexibility training and relaxation strategies, developing firmly entrenched routines that indicate the type of exercises to be performed and the time of day they will be scheduled, and planning other activities in the day and week that promote a balanced lifestyle.

Spiritual Fitness: Linking Values to Exercise Habits

Dr. Jack Groppel (2000), in his book *The Corporate Athlete*, has a very interesting perspective on the way to ignite an individual's desire to start and maintain an exercise program. He calls it "spiritual fitness," and it is totally unrelated to religious practice. To Groppel, spirituality involves moral, ethical (and, yes, religious) attitudes, feelings, and values. Loehr and Schwartz (2001) include a spirituality component in their corporate program in attempting to get corporate clients to change habits that negatively affect health and quality of work. The authors define spiritual capacity as "the energy that is unleashed by tapping into one's deepest values and defining a strong sense of purpose" (p. 127). This capacity, they claim, "serves as sustenance in the face of adversity and as a powerful source of motivation, focus, determination, and resilience" (p. 127).

The individual is asked probing, personal questions, such as "to what extent are your values consistent with your actions? If you value your health, for instance, do you have habits that are not good for you, and therefore, inconsistent with your values? What about your family? Do you value your spouse, children, or parents? If you lead a sedentary lifestyle and are not involved in a program of exercise, yet one of your deepest values is to maintain good health, to what extent is your value inconsistent with your behavior? Is there a 'disconnect' between your beliefs about good health and your unhealthy behavioral patterns?"

Groppel also asks us to determine the benefits of our negative habits, such as lack of exercise (e.g., more time to do other things, not experiencing the discomfort of physical exertion, avoiding fitness club membership costs), and then to identify the costs of our sedentary lifestyle (e.g., weight gain, reduced mental health, low physique self-esteem, higher level of "bad" cholesterol). Are these costs acceptable? If they are, then the negative habit (i.e., lack of exercise, in this case) will likely continue. However, if the costs are far greater than the benefits, and the person finds these costs unacceptable, then a change in behavior is far more likely. Groppel calls this process expanding spiritual capacity. Figure 11.4 illustrates the process by which a person feels compelled to make a significant change in his or her life, partly reflecting concepts from Groppel, Loehr, and Schwartz.

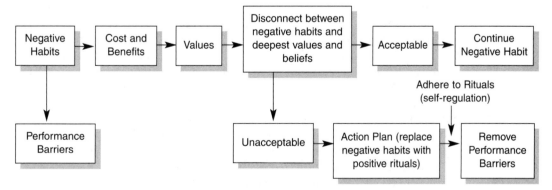

Figure 11.4 The change process to high performance

Exercise Interventions:
Applying Exercise Psychology

The Issue of Title: Who Is an Exercise Psychologist?

If practitioners in sport psychology are called sport psychologists, sport psychology consultants/counselors, or mental skills coaches, do similar titles apply to individuals who work in exercise settings? Are there exercise psychologists/counselors/coaches? Berger et al. (2002) use the terms "exercise psychologist" on numerous occasions. Yet, this title may not be correct. Let's start with the title "psychologist." As the authors duly note, the title "psychologist" is legally protected, and requires that the professional be licensed by a State Board of Licensed Psychologists (each state may have a similar, but not identical, board identification) to practice psychology in the state of residence and practice. In addition, graduate psychology programs that result in licensure do not include courses in the exercise sciences, so a graduate of such a program probably would not have completed a course in exercise psychology. Thus, licensed psychologists are rarely trained to work in exercise settings, and are unlikely to have mastered the professional literature in providing counsel to promote participation in and adherence to exercise programs, at least in the normal population. Any such experience is more likely to have been gained from working with a clinical population, in which exercise is a vehicle that provides a desirable treatment to overcome mental illness or some other psychopathology. Until university programs are in place to provide course work and clinical training for working with clients in exercise settings or who wish to engage in exercise, the term "exercise psychologist" is not very practical. Perhaps more common, and valuable, is a person trained in the exercise sciences who is familiar with the sport and exercise psychology literatures and can provide guidance and nonclinical interventions, perhaps under the title of exercise (or mental skills) counselor, consultant, or coach.

The Exercise Novice: Going from Contemplation to Action

The decision to start exercising, whether it is in a group setting at a local fitness club or privately at home, does not come easily. Our society provides constant, daily reminders to reduce physical activity—notice how many people stand still going *down* an escalator, for example. The less we move, the better. If we did not have to walk to the car, perhaps we would not move our body all day! Perhaps the most important impediment to exercise is our culture's negative attitude toward it. It was never pleasant—remember those physical education classes at school, often led by unfit, overweight teachers and coaches who were not exactly perfect role models for fitness and good health? When you combine an inactive lifestyle with a cultural tendency to overeat (particularly food high in fat), it is easy to understand why the resultant weight gain would make it harder for people to willingly face the challenges that exercise provides. It simply does not feel good to stress our body through vigorous physical activity.

Faced with the uphill battle to create a comfortable, secure environment in which to face the exercise challenge, there are still numerous things that fitness clubs, personal trainers, spouses/partners, and, most important, the individual himself or herself can do to begin and maintain a lifelong habit of exercise. Based on my reviews of this literature by Anshel and Reeves (1998), Berger et al. (2002), Gauvin, Levesque, and Richard (2001), Marcus et al. (1998), and Sallis and Owen (1999), these strategies will be classified as behavioral—observable actions of the exerciser or exercise leader—and cognitive—meaning the participant's use of mental skills.

Behavioral Strategies

A body of literature by researchers and practitioners is emerging on ways to promote exercise participation and adherence by adopting behavioral techniques. This section will discuss environmental influences that encourage continued exercise participation, based on the recommendations of several references (e.g., Anshel & Reeves 1998; Leith 1998; Sallis & Owen 1999).

Physical Location. Numerous studies have shown that a person is far more likely to exercise—and adhere to his or her exercise habit—if the exercise facility is located within three miles of home or work. Try to find a location either close to where you spend a part of your day or that is located on the way from home to work. Should you exercise at home? Since we associate home with relaxation and recovery, rather than with hard physical effort, it is not surprising that people tend to purchase, then stop using, exercise equipment in the home. It is preferred that exercise be performed in an atmosphere that provides incentive in the form of a "high-energy" environment (e.g., bright lights and colors, personal interactions with other exercisers and staff).

Scheduling. We are creatures of routines (not unlike others in the animal world) that get us through the day. There is a far greater likelihood of exercising if it is planned in advance. The more specific that plan, the better chance it will happen. Choose the time of day that an exercise session is most available and when it feels best—physically and emotionally—to do. However, it is best not to exercise aerobically within two hours of bedtime, according to several sleep studies. Aerobic work reduces time spent in deep (dream) sleep, according to the National Sleep Foundation (1522 K Street, NW, Suite 500, Washington, D.C. 20005; Web site: www.sleepfoundation.org/publications).

Introductory Consulting Issues. For the novice, in particular, exercise creates both stress and anxiety. The individual brings to a new program thoughts of previous exercise attempts, and fears about experiencing injury, fatigue, and how the body will respond to new exercise demands. There may be worry about his or her appearance and fitness level—fitting in—in a facility that may usually attract younger, fitter individuals. There is often heightened self-consciousness and concern about performing the exercises correctly and knowledge about proper use of the exercise equipment. But most important of all is the set of personal dispositions that each of us brings to new, challenging situations, especially when in the presence of strangers.

Novice exercisers need to be welcomed, comforted, and informed. What are their concerns and how might the staff help to reduce them? How can participants be taught to use proper exercise techniques, to set realistic goals, and to feel secure in an environment filled with uncertainties, intimidation, and physical and emotional challenges? How can people be helped to feel comfortable with their present state of fitness and their current physical characteristics, especially if these do not match those of other participants who may be younger, thinner, and fitter? Exercisers need a sense of belonging to the club; they need to establish relationships with the people they trust, starting with staff, and to feel comfortable and secure. The failure to connect with people personally will almost certainly lead to nonattendance.

Goal Setting.   Guidelines for setting goals, reviewed in Chapter 3, is particularly relevant for the exercise novice. One primary reason for dropping out is the failure to meet goals and expectations, particularly within the first six months of starting an exercise program. This is why it is so important to help individuals have realistic expectations about exercise outcomes, and to understand the need to be patient in overcoming years of leading a sedentary lifestyle. Short-term, performance-based goals that are minimally challenging are best to lift confidence and encourage a person to adhere to a program. Otherwise, a person may conclude that he or she is incapable of meeting the demands of carrying out a proper exercise program. Dropping out is preceded by thoughts of helplessness, low self-control, and the lack of perceived success. Sample goals in exercise settings include, "I will complete 20 minutes nonstop on the treadmill," "I will complete 3 sets of my upper-body resistance routine," or "I will reach my training heart rate during interval training." Notice that these goals are performance (process) goals, rather than outcome (product) goals (e.g., "I will lose 3 pounds" or "I will decrease 2 percent body fat"), which are long-term, not short-term, goals and are under less self-control.

Social Contacts and Interactions.   While some exercisers are quite happy to be left alone and to exercise in isolation, most novice performers need to feel connected to others during their routines. The need for social support is especially important in instances when the individual is self-conscious about physical features, and lacks confidence and knowledge about carrying out the exercise routine. Among the first goals of staff should be to introduce themselves to the participant, to instruct participants on exercise equipment, and to develop an exercise protocol. Introducing novices to other exercisers is also helpful, especially when the program consists of exercising in a group. If the person exercises at home, his or her family or friends should express complete support of the exercise habit. Several studies have shown that social support significantly improves exercise adherence.

Rewards.   According to positive social reinforcement theory, rewards have information value about competence. A reward—for example, a t-shirt that reflects achieving a certain level of competence (e.g., 500-mile club) or membership in a group (e.g., the YMCA Running Club)—enhances a sense of accomplishment and group member identification. Both outcomes markedly improve participation satisfaction and adherence. In order to build intrinsic motivation, it is best if the reward is linked directly to a desirable performance outcome or achievement, rather than being a response to participation perceived as automatic and expected. The latter loses its value as a reinforcement of competence.

Educational Materials.   The written word is a powerful tool in helping people to understand the value of what they do—in this case, exercise. While it is best to avoid providing complicated research journal articles to the public for information, other sources such as magazine articles, segments of books, and even materials that list credible sources of information and are created by staff provide exercisers with a deeper understanding of and justification for their exercise habits. Monthly newsletters with featured articles that address different types of exercises, techniques, and findings from recent studies all have great motivational value.

Clubs, Organizations, and Programs. Humans have a deep need to belong to a group or attend programs in which groups and friendships flourish. These provide comfort and security, and meet social needs. The greater the extent to which individuals feel emotionally attached to an exercise program or facility, the more likely they are to return and maintain their involvement. Running clubs, weekly lecture and reading groups, banquets that recognize exercise achievement, exercise-related events (e.g., Sunday morning jog), company- or individual-sponsored contests (e.g., "The John Smith Annual Run"), outdoor activity clubs, an annual guest speaker's event, a health-related conference, weekly seminars, and exhibitions by skilled exercisers (e.g., power lifting, aerobic dance) are sample activities that create excitement and motivation to exercise.

Personal Trainer/Instructional Opportunities. This growing area of service in the fitness industry is a welcome addition to facilitating exercise participation. Though fitness clubs tend to supply instructors to provide basic instruction and answer member questions, most individuals require more extensive, consistent training. The personal trainer meets this need. High-quality trainers have full mastery of fitness science, exercise technique, and nutrition; they know how to help each individual set and achieve individual goals; and they possess the ability to show compassion and genuine interest in their clients. While clients are exercising, the trainer should be located near the client and his or her eyes should be focused on the client's technique. The trainer should assist the client to keep fitness-related records and even phone the client if the latter has been absent from the facility after a week. The absence of proper exercise technique leads to injury and discomfort. Demotivation and quitting further exercise often result.

Environmental Features. Exercise facilities can create an environment that is exciting, intimate, and motivating for participants. In addition to the usual colorful walls and pleasant and upbeat music, facilities must ensure that their equipment is clean and functions properly. Broken equipment should be fixed within 24 hours, if at all possible. This includes television sets, sources of music, and torn fabric. Broken equipment communicates insensitivity ("we don't care about you"), poor management ("we are not in touch with program needs"), and reduced credibility on the part of management that does not take the necessary steps to provide high-quality equipment to promote fitness. Carpets, workout areas, showers, locker rooms, and all floors should be cleaned daily. Soap and shampoo in both men's and women's showers should be checked at least twice daily, and there should be separate facilities for confidential meetings with members (e.g., to discuss personal information about a member's health or feelings, membership information, or personal training instruction). Towels (if provided by the club) and refuse should be picked up and placed in containers constantly. In addition, important information should be easily accessible at the front counter, such as reprints on fitness-related articles and other educational materials, business cards of staff (including the club's manager), and club information (e.g., hours of operation, membership costs). But most important is the atmosphere that staff members create by their friendliness, sincerity in helping others, and professional conduct.

Proper Equipment. While the need to monitor, clean, and fix broken equipment on a constant basis was discussed in the previous section, it is also important that the facility have equipment available that meets the needs of all members. Resistance training requires different weight machines for the novice as well as the advanced power lifter. There are many types of equipment for aerobic training, and as many of these as possible should be made available, and in good working order. Finally, staff should be taught how to work each piece of equipment so as to be able to do so not only during the introductory session, but also at any time such instruction is requested.

Professional Counseling. Should a licensed psychologist or counselor be available at a fitness club? This is a novel idea, but given the overweight epidemic, terrible physical condition of most communities, and the large dropout rate at most facilities, perhaps this is an idea whose time has come. What would be the counselor's role and responsibility? What issues would be addressed? How could exercise participants gain access to the person? What would this service cost? Can confidentiality be guaranteed, especially if the service is offered on site? Where would this service be provided? In the facility? Close to a separate entrance to the club? At the counselor's private office? And perhaps most important, how would this person function differently from physical training staff? Though it is clear that clinical services are sometimes needed to address an individual's needs in order to feel more comfortable in an exercise program, it is less certain if this service should be provided on site.

But wait a minute. What if we changed the title and focus of this service to mean "mental skills coach" or "performance consultant," and the professional dealt with performance-related topics rather than psychotherapy? And what if this person worked in coordination with personal trainers, who would work jointly with the clients and refer clients to each other? This could change the whole perception of this type of service so that it was similar to the concept of "sport psychology consultant" adopted by the Association for the Advancement of Applied Sport Psychology (AAASP). AAASP has its own certification procedures and certified consultants do not refer to themselves as sport psychologists. Issues addressed with exercise clients are performance related, and would include: (1) building confidence, (2) managing anxiety related to exercise participation, (3) teaching clients how to use exercise as a means of stress reduction, (4) providing intervention information to improve client motivation, (5) helping clients set and achieve goals, (6) teaching the proper use of mental skills that enhance exercise performance (psyching up, imagery, and others discussed later), (7) providing social support, (8) linking the strengths of each personal trainer with the unique needs of each client, and (9) being the anchor point for participants who need to communicate with club staff or management, or who need someone to whom they can turn for advice.

Record Keeping. The importance of having exercisers keep records gets at the heart of intrinsic motivation: perceived competence. It is important that exercise leaders and physical trainers work with clients to record baseline measures of various dimensions of fitness, then monitor progress through maintaining those records. In this way, exercisers can detect indicators of improvement and achievement, which are important sources of intrinsic motivation (discussed in Chapter 3). Performance data should be recorded, updated, and monitored in quantitative form, reflecting numbers, rather than general comments such as "Susan did a good job today" or "Sid is feeling better about his exercise progress." Examples include minutes and seconds of aerobic activity, weight lifted, number of repetitions, degrees of flexibility (stretching), changes in percent body fat, number of laps or amount of distance jogged, and even frequency of attending the fitness venue or a particular program. To Sarafino (1994), "seeing on paper how far they have progressed can be very reinforcing" (p. 267).

Exerciser Checklist/Self-Monitoring. Developing an exercise habit requires learning a vast array of new skills and initiating many new routines to ensure a successful and pleasant experience. To many individuals, starting a new exercise program is intimidating and stressful, both mentally and physically. Perhaps it is not surprising that so many people quit exercise programs, given the amount of energy expended in finding the time to exercise, preparing for and engaging in the actual exercise activity, and then dealing with the physical challenges of overcoming a sedentary lifestyle. The novice exerciser needs help—and plenty of it. This is the value of an exerciser checklist, which I have developed while working with exercisers for many years. The technique, called *self-monitoring* in the sport psychology literature, entails listing the thoughts, emotions, and actions that should be part of the exerciser's weekly and daily protocol. There are no "right" or "wrong" answers. This is not a "test" of knowledge, but rather a set of guidelines about making exercise as pleasant and performed as efficiently as possible. Thus, answers as close to "5" as possible are always desirable. Items that are answered 1 through 3 require attention about the source(s) of this low score. *The goal in completing this checklist is to improve (increase) the total score for each segment.*

The checklist should be reviewed regularly by the exerciser's personal trainer or performance consultant—for novices, once per week, and less often after the first month. My experience is that after four to six weeks of constant monitoring, the checklist serves as an occasional reminder of things to do, but is less important in fostering exercise adherence than at earlier stages of developing exercise routines. Finally, selected items on the checklist may be irrelevant to some individuals. For example, an exerciser may prefer to exercise alone rather than exercising with others. Therefore, the item that addresses exercising in a group setting can be eliminated from the checklist. Figure 11.5 is a typical exerciser checklist.

Feedback on Performance. Providing information to exercisers, particularly about their level of competence and improvement, raises their level of confidence and enhances intrinsic motivation. Information that is critical, yet constructive, also has this effect, because constructive criticism serves the purpose of improving skills, knowledge, and performance outcomes. The key guidelines for performance feedback are identified in Chapter 9 on communication and counseling techniques. Briefly, however, all information feedback—in both positive and critical forms—should reflect observable and measurable behavior (e.g., "great effort on staying on task"), rather than reflect more abstract content (e.g., "you're looking better" or "nice going"). Giving feedback intermittently is more effective than giving it constantly. The important issue here is that

Figure 11.5 Self-Monitoring Exerciser Checklist

Self-Monitoring Exerciser Checklist

Please indicate how much you agree or disagree with each of the following statements concerning your exercise routine. The ratings go from **1** (the statement is *not at all like me*) to **5** (the statement is *very much like me*). Higher scores are viewed as more desirable than lower scores. You want to improve your score over time.

1	2	3	4	5
Not At All Like Me		Somewhat Like Me		Very Much Like Me

I. Lifestyle Habits (Exercise Preparation)

1. I think about exercising with enthusiasm.	1	2	3	4	5
2. I look forward to the next exercise session.	1	2	3	4	5
3. I do not make excuses for avoiding exercise.	1	2	3	4	5
4. I view exercising as a challenge, not a chore.	1	2	3	4	5
5. I feel healthier and happier for exercising.	1	2	3	4	5
6. I like to receive feedback on my exercise technique.	1	2	3	4	5
7. I am confident in my ability to exercise.	1	2	3	4	5
8. My family and friends support my exercise habit.	1	2	3	4	5
9. My spouse/partner encourages me to exercise.	1	2	3	4	5
10. I have a weekly exercise schedule.	1	2	3	4	5
11. I know the physical and psychological benefits of exercising regularly.	1	2	3	4	5
12. I think about the positive outcomes from exercising.	1	2	3	4	5
13. I would describe my lifestyle during the week as generally healthy.	1	2	3	4	5
14. I usually enjoy the company of others when I exercise.	1	2	3	4	5

Subtotal: _____

II. Day of Exercise

1. I look forward to exercising with great enthusiasm.	1	2	3	4	5
2. I am committed to my scheduled exercise time.	1	2	3	4	5
3. I have prepared a proper diet and fluid intake today.	1	2	3	4	5
4. I am feeling positive about exercising.	1	2	3	4	5
5. I am aware of the benefits of my exercise program.	1	2	3	4	5
6. Within 2 hours of exercising, I will not have any food, coffee, or alcohol.	1	2	3	4	5
7. If I feel sick, I will not exercise today.	1	2	3	4	5
8. I have a planned route to the exercise venue.	1	2	3	4	5
9. I have prepared my exercise gear in advance.	1	2	3	4	5
10. I have organized my day to accommodate my exercise session.	1	2	3	4	5

Subtotal: _____

(continued)

Figure 11.5 Self-Monitoring Exerciser Checklist

III. Pre-Exercise Activity (at exercise venue)

1. I arrive at the exercise venue on time/with enthusiasm.	1	2	3	4	5
2. I remember my goals and plan to meet them.	1	2	3	4	5
3. As I prepare to exercise, I feel energetic.	1	2	3	4	5
4. I feel confident in my ability to give 100%.	1	2	3	4	5
5. I plan to have adequate water intake when I exercise.	1	2	3	4	5
6. I have an exercise plan.	1	2	3	4	5
7. I remember the reasons that exercise is good for me.	1	2	3	4	5
8. I will do as much of the exercise session as I can.	1	2	3	4	5
9. I use positive self-talk just before I exercise ("I can do it," "I'm ready," "Stay with it!")	1	2	3	4	5

Subtotal: _____

IV. During My Exercise Session

1. I really enjoy my exercise session and give 100% effort.	1	2	3	4	5
2. I feel good during my stretches.	1	2	3	4	5
3. I warm up and cool down properly.	1	2	3	4	5
4. I use positive self-talk before and during exercise.	1	2	3	4	5
5. I will complete as much exercise as possible.	1	2	3	4	5
6. When I exert myself, I use a psyching up strategy.	1	2	3	4	5
7. My exercise performance is improving.	1	2	3	4	5
8. I don't care what I look like to others during exercise.	1	2	3	4	5
9. I try to perform up to my potential.	1	2	3	4	5
10. I do not compare myself to other exercisers.	1	2	3	4	5
11. I try to complete as many repetitions as possible of each exercise.	1	2	3	4	5
12. I view each exercise bout as a challenge, not a threat.	1	2	3	4	5
13. If I feel uncomfortable during exercise, I ignore my feelings, and focus externally.	1	2	3	4	5
14. I remember and try to reach my performance goals.	1	2	3	4	5
15. If I get tired, I rest, but then I continue.	1	2	3	4	5

Subtotal: _____

V. After the Exercise Session

1. I am generally pleased with my exercise performance.	1	2	3	4	5
2. I feel that my performance has improved since last time.	1	2	3	4	5
3. I take responsibility for my performance success.	1	2	3	4	5
4. I do not blame others (e.g., poor instructor, noise).	1	2	3	4	5
5. I have (physically or mentally) recorded my progress.	1	2	3	4	5
6. I am open to advice and feedback on my performance.	1	2	3	4	5

(continued)

Figure 11.5 Self-Monitoring Exerciser Checklist

7. I plan to keep exercising and return next time.	1	2	3	4	5
8. I feel a sense of accomplishment.	1	2	3	4	5
9. I replace my bodily fluids with water.	1	2	3	4	5
10. My exercise form has improved.	1	2	3	4	5

Subtotal: _____

GRAND TOTAL: _____

exercisers need to hear and observe positive messages about their performance or about outcomes derived from their efforts.

Monitoring Client Attendance. It is important to keep tabs on who is present and who is absent from the exercise venue. Absences are the first warning sign of quitting. While it is possible that individuals are deciding to exercise in locations other than formal programs and clubs, a person's commitment to an ongoing program of physical activity is strongly tied to developing relationships with individuals at the exercise venue. If clients have not attended the venue in a week, they should be contacted to determine the reason for their absence. This strategy will markedly improve adherence.

Using Small, Attainable Units to Reflect Progress. As indicated earlier, building intrinsic motivation to perform any task is strongly linked to building perceptions of competence. This is best accomplished when the exerciser detects increments of improvement, however small. The exercise program, then, should contain measures that are somewhat easy, or moderately challenging, to attain and that reinforce the performer's perception of moving toward achieving goals. This is why using the relatively small unit of time (minutes, for example) is more likely to reflect competent performance than measuring performance by the relatively larger unit of distance (miles, for instance).

Social Support. As discussed earlier, the likelihood to adhere to an exercise program increases significantly if a friend or family member accompanies the exerciser, or if the exerciser receives emotional support (e.g., praise, recognition, approval) for his or her efforts or on the positive outcomes of exercise participation. Nonverbal social support comes from providing ways to facilitate the exerciser's habit, such as driving a person to the exercise venue, giving a fitness club membership as a gift, or supervising or monitoring the exerciser's responsibilities (e.g., babysitting, performing work-related tasks, or recording a favorite TV program). As Sarafino (1994) confirms, "people are more likely to start and stick with an exercise program if these efforts have the support and encouragement of family and friends" (p. 267).

Perceived Choice. It makes no sense to force a person to engage in a certain type of exercise, or to use a certain piece of equipment if the person has negative feelings about it. For example, overweight individuals often dislike treadmills. This is understandable, since a treadmill forces the person to perform aerobically while attempting to overcome additional sources of discomfort (e.g., body weight, sore knees, bad back). The best approach would be to give exercisers choices about the types of activities they can perform that will have similar health and fitness benefits. At first, the novice should develop proper technique before attempting to be challenged physically. Tasks should be kept relatively easy at first, then slowly increased in difficulty. To Sarafino (1994), "people are more likely to stick with the program if it includes exercises that they enjoy doing" (p. 267).

Social Engineering. What can we do—how can we physically change our environment—to reduce external demands on us? Perhaps we can drive down a less traveled road, go to a restaurant at a less crowded time (e.g., an early lunch or dinner), or attend a fitness facility at a less busy time. The concept of social engineering comes from the stress management literature, in which persons will experience less stress if they locate themselves in a place in which fewer environmental sources of stress are present. If possible, the novice should exercise at a time when equipment is more likely to be available and when the staff can offer more attention and instruction. Even more important for the highly self-conscious exerciser is that fewer people in attendance means less likelihood of being observed by others (at least, that may be the exerciser's perception).

Music. It is well-known, according to scientific studies (e.g., Anshel & Marisi 1978) and from empirical observations, that more intense music has an arousal-inducing effect on exercise performance. Exercise facility operators acknowledge this, of course, and often have music playing throughout their facility. Some exercisers prefer their own brand of music and wear headsets or a "Walkman." Music has the advantage of distracting the exerciser from boredom and from the physical manifestations of vigorous physical activity (e.g., fatigue, sweating, high effort). Music also improves the exerciser's mood state. However, music can also reduce concentration on the task at hand, resulting in lower performance quality. Exercising to music is a matter of personal preference.

Modeling. Rather than feeling intimidated by highly fit exercisers, one source of motivation is to observe the high-level performance of another exerciser. The goal, here, is to emulate expert exercise techniques and to use high performance quality as a source of inspiration and motivation to pursue fitness and health-related goals.

Time of Day. Not surprisingly, each of us differs as to the time of day we prefer to exercise. This is due to both personal choice—feeling more like exercising at a certain time—and to the time that is available to us. Does time of day make a difference in how the body responds to exercise and to exercise outcomes? Not according to a study by O'Connor and Davis (1992), who confirmed the findings of several earlier Swedish studies. While the benefits are similar no matter the time one exercises, it is best not to exercise within three hours of going to sleep. Studies indicate that high-intensity aerobic exercise close to bedtime will reduce time spent in deep sleep.

Lifestyle Management.   The effects of exercising and improved fitness are not experienced in a vacuum. The goals of weight control, fat reduction, and gains in strength, firmness, and cardiovascular fitness must be accompanied by other healthy habits, such as proper nutrition and diet, sufficient sleep, and maintaining a work/life balance. The workaholic who exercises vigorously, yet neglects other important behaviors and ignores his or her family and friends is often lacking personal happiness, remains highly stressed, and is likely to succumb to sickness or disease. Exercise becomes just one more thing to have to do, rather than being a form of recovery and enjoyment. Fitness should be one segment, albeit an important one, of an overall lifestyle that creates a source of joy and life satisfaction. The following box provides a summary of ways to improve exercise adherence.

Guidelines for Maintaining Exercise Adherence

Almost 50 percent of people who start an exercise program will quit within three months. The most common reasons for dropping out of an exercise program include not meeting (very high) expectations, lack of enjoyment, injury, and lack of time. Maintaining an exercise program is called *adherence*. You can adhere to an exercise regimen if you follow a few important guidelines.

Have Realistic Expectations. It takes time to become overweight and out of shape. Fortunately, it takes less time to become more fit. This is because muscles were made to move; we need exercise. A sedentary lifestyle means that exercise is a struggle. Don't be impatient about experiencing the benefits of physical activity. Over time, usually within six weeks, exercise will improve your fitness level, self-esteem, and even your mental health. At the same time, your body weight may not decrease dramatically (see next point). Do not quit. Be patient.

Do Not Concentrate on Body Weight. Your weight scale is not telling you the truth, especially after you begin an exercise program. It fails to disclose how much of your weight is *fat* and how much of your weight is *muscle*. Because muscle weighs more than fat, and you gain muscle through exercise, your body weight may or may not change. But your fitness has improved dramatically and you are much healthier. The scale, which reflects weight loss, can certainly be a motivator to continue an exercise program. But remember that weight loss is not usually the primary purpose of exercise. Your health should be the main reason. According to a study published in the journal, *Medicine and Science in Sport* (1999), people who are overweight or obese experience similar physical and mental benefits from exercise to individuals of normal weight.

Receive Instruction on Proper Ways to Exercise.   Proper exercise technique must be learned. Invest in a personal trainer (not just anyone, but someone who really cares about helping you) and learn to exercise properly. This way, you will exercise more efficiently, with less effort, and you will improve your fitness more quickly. Also, remember to warm up and cool down properly, drink water before and during your exercise session, and stretch *after* your exercise session.

Schedule Your Exercise Times and Places. So many of us feel there is insufficient time to exercise during the day. *Plan your exercise times in advance*; prepare your exercise gear the night before (store it in your car, leave it by the door on your way out, or rent a locker at your gym). Joining a fitness club has its advantages, if you can afford it. Rarely do we feel motivated to exercise at home. This is because we associate home with relaxation and recreation, and rarely with engaging in vigorous physical activity. This is why exercise equipment usually sits unused in so many homes. It might be better to join a fitness club where the atmosphere is motivating to exercise, where you might meet friends, get support for your exercise program, and use high-quality equipment.

Seek Social Support. Exercise with a friend, or at least make sure your spouse/partner or family supports your exercise habits. Several studies have shown that surrounding yourself with others who encourage you to exercise significantly improves exercise adherence. Many people cannot do it all alone. Who doesn't need encouragement once in a while? It's normal to need our friends, spouse, and family to recognize and support us in our exercise habit. Social support can come from exercising with a partner or in a group setting, getting to know others at the fitness club who exercise at the same time, working with a personal trainer, or telling a friend about your exercise habits and progress (just don't make it a one-way conversation).

Combine Aerobic and Strength Exercises. If you want to benefit from exercise, don't forget two areas that need your attention, aerobic work (for the cardiovascular system) and strength training. Both have enormous benefits to good mental and physical health. Aerobic exercise, in particular, leads to improved self-esteem, reduced anxiety, and heightened tolerance to stress. Stretching exercises improve joint flexibility and helps reduce the onset of injury and discomfort.

Feel a Sense of Achievement and Competence from Exercising. Central to internal motivation is a sense of satisfaction, achieve-

ment, and competence derived from your exercise program. Use data—numbers such as changes in exercise time (speed), resistance, repetitions, frequency, distance, and so on—to indicate improved change over time.

Control Anxiety. Anxiety consists of feelings of worry or threat about the future. "Will I succeed?" "I hope I can lose weight," "What if I look ridiculous in front of all those people?" Sources of exercise anxiety include worry about meeting goals, our physical appearance, being accepted by others (especially strangers), and using time to exercise instead of doing something else ("I could be watching TV or finishing a report instead of going to the gym"). Incredibly, exercise reduces anxiety, both short term (acute anxiety) and long term (chronic anxiety). Exercise is what the doctor ordered for improved *mental* health.

Monitor High Self-Expectations. Too many people quit exercise programs when their unrealistic expectations (e.g., losing 20 pounds in a month, being able to keep up with the fitness instructor, eliminating excessive fat from the tummy or thighs) are not met. *You want improvement!* Favorable outcomes from exercise take time, so please be patient.

Work Against Low Perceived Competence. We rarely persist at anything about which we feel inadequate. Conversely, we are attracted to and engage in tasks at which we feel competent. Learn and practice the proper exercise techniques.

Do Not Indulge in Negative Self-Talk. It is impossible to remain motivated and "on task" if you are saying to yourself, "I don't like this," "I feel terrible," or "I'm tired." Turn those thoughts around. Stay optimistic and enthusiastic. Positive self-talk includes "I can do this," "I feel good," "just three more minutes to go," and "hang in

(continued)

there." You cannot be unhappy and enthusiastic at the same time.

Curb Perfectionism.   For some people, it's never good enough. It can always be better. Psychologists suggest elimination of that "little guy on your shoulder" reminding us that it's "still not good enough." Perfectionists are high achievers, no question. They persist longer on task and improve and achieve more with time and effort than do nonperfectionists. Good! However, the downside of being a perfectionist—called neurotic perfectionism—is the tendency to set goals that are unachievable and about which the person is unlikely to feel satisfied. Perfectionists' expectations of others are also excessive. Be careful. Set reasonable goals and recognize when you achieve them, especially in exercise. Have *indicators* of success. Don't try to look like someone from a magazine cover or like a movie star. Be you—just try to get better.

Cognitive Strategies

This section concerns the use of mental skills that favorably influence exercise performance. Most of these have been established in the sport psychology literature and used successfully in sport, yet they have a direct impact on exercise performance. All of these strategies have been discussed earlier.

Visualization/Imagery.   As discussed earlier, visualization, also referred to as imagery, consists of thoughts that form mental representations of physical performance. While the use of visualization, or mental imagery, is a common and effective technique in improving sports performance, the exerciser can also use this strategy for numerous reasons to gain confidence, to learn new exercise routines, to reduce tension and anxiety prior to exercising, to increase excitation and psychological readiness, and to improve motivation. The exerciser should find time and a location that is free of visual or auditory distractions, then take a few minutes to relax; relaxation causes the image to become more vivid and realistic. Then, think through the environmental features, specific exercises, and sensations and feelings experienced during the exercise routine in a highly desirable, positive manner. Mentally rehearse the activity, as performed in perfect form and followed by a desirable outcome.

Bizarre Imagery.   While normal imagery is a mental representation of *real life situations*, bizarre imagery is a mental representation of nonrealistic events. For example, cancer patients are sometimes asked to imagine their tumors being shrunk as they receive chemotherapy. Cardiac or pulmonary patients might imagine rapid changes in their circulatory system that are medically impossible during an exercise bout. An overweight person might imagine fat being dissolved or arteries being widened while exercising. The purpose of bizarre imagery is to heighten exercise motivation and to distract the person from the challenges presented by the exercise task.

Association/Dissociation.   During physical exertion, should you focus your attention on the muscles being used or ignore bodily sensations and become distracted from the task at hand? A conscious attempt to link the mind and body is called association. An example of properly using association is during strength training. The focus of attention should be on the muscle group being used to lift the weight. Dissociation, on the other hand, is used when the exerciser wants to ignore bodily responses. Examples include distance running, or someone undergoing exercise rehabilitation in which therapy requires movements that are uncomfortable.

Thought-Stopping. A common dilemma in exercise is engaging in self-statements that reveal unpleasant feelings about the task at hand. Unpleasant feelings, especially if continued during an exercise bout, may lead to demotivation, reduced effort, and even dropping out of further participation. The suggestion here is that in response to negative feelings, exercisers should say to themselves "STOP!" The effect is that the negative thoughts will go away. This is because the command to "stop" will remind the exerciser of the unpleasant effects of the negative, self-induced messages and allow the person to regain the proper mental set for a more positive, uplifting message. Thoughts go from irrational to rational.

Positive Self-Talk. After the negative self-talk (e.g., "This is terrible," "I feel awful," or "I can hardly wait until this is over"), the exerciser wants to engage in a more uplifting, motivating message. The result will be more effort and intensity, better concentration, and greater enjoyment of the task. Examples in exercise settings include, "Let's do it," "I feel good," and "Stay with it." The use of one or two words that influence mood are also effective, such as "Go," "Focus," and "Get it!"

Anticipation. The ability to predict a movement before performing it increases momentum, improves preperformance readiness, and reduces the amount of information the person must process quickly. This strategy is especially important when performing fast-paced, coordinated activity, common in aerobic workouts.

Psyching Up. For some activities, in which high arousal and energy are required (e.g., physical exercise), the performer's thought processes must be upbeat and "active." A cognitive technique called psyching up consists of thinking about the task at hand and having thoughts of excitation, challenge, spiritedness, engagement, connectedness, and high energy. Psyching up can be experienced in either physical or mental form. Physically, the person can engage in tasks that require increased energy and heightened somatic responses (e.g., higher heart rate, respiration rate, muscle tension). Mentally, psyching up usually consists of thoughts that increase confidence, motivation, and concentration. Examples of psyching up thoughts include "let's do it" and "I'm ready."

Location Cues. This mental skill is more for exercises that have predetermined starting and ending points, such as stretching, weight training, and yoga. It can also be used for certain aerobic activities that consist of specific steps and motions, such as foot or hand placements, in completing the move. A sample location cue would be to tell a person to have a 45-degree angle at the elbow before performing a lift, or planting one's foot "at 2 o'clock," indicating the angle at which the foot should be placed or pointed when hitting the floor. Tennis players, for instance, are asked to strike the ball "at 2 o'clock," using the clock face as a reference.

Attribution Training.   This strategy, reviewed extensively in Chapter 4, has strong implications in exercise settings. An exerciser, particularly a novice, will be physically challenged to complete one or more exercises despite a significant increase in effort, sweating, and fatigue. Exercisers should interpret their attempts as successful, and then attribute this success to high effort. Linking effort to success has very high motivational value and gives feelings of competence and self-control. Even experiencing fatigue and not meeting performance expectations can be attributed to task difficulty, and sometimes to low effort, if this is an accurate cause. Low performance quality should rarely be attributed to low ability. On the other hand, a few individuals who find it very difficult to move in a coordinated manner during an aerobics class might accurately conclude that a poor sense of coordination is responsible for less than desirable performance.

Building Intrinsic Motivation (IM).   Although building IM is not, in itself, a cognitive strategy, it is a necessary component of a long-term commitment to exercise. Chapter 3 includes several specific strategies for improving IM. For promoting exercise, it is important that the two main components, self-determination (high self-control) and information (high perceived competence), be addressed. Thus, the exerciser should make his or her own decision about the need to exercise, choose the type of exercise program and the location, feel confident about his or her ability to engage in exercise, and, finally, receive positive feedback about exercise success and competence.

Examining Personal Values and Beliefs.   Finally, based on the work of Dr. Jack Groppel (2000), in order to feel compelled about the long-term commitment and sense of responsibility to exercise, it is important to examine one's deepest values and beliefs—what is really important to oneself. If good health and family are important values, then a person should behave in a way that is consistent with these values. People often wish to live a long time because their family is depending on them. In addition, no doubt such people would like to live and remain healthy in order to see their children grow up. Those who value integrity should be keeping promises and being true to their standards and ideals. The person should be reminded of the cost/benefit trade-off, that is, the benefits versus the costs of not exercising. Are these costs acceptable? If they run counter to the individual's deepest values and beliefs, hopefully not.

SUMMARY

Despite the plethora of advantages to maintaining an active lifestyle that includes engaging daily in vigorous physical activity, a huge number of people in the U.S. live an overweight, sedentary lifestyle that is reducing quality of life and increasing health care costs. Researchers and practitioners in the field of exercise psychology have studied the causes of this problem and ways to help overcome it. Exercise psychology is defined as the study of psychological factors underlying participation and adherence in physical activity programs. The field consists of exploring the psychological factors that help explain a person's decision or refusal to participate in a continuous exercise program. Researchers are also examining the reasons that so many individuals who begin regular fitness programs, both individually and in group settings, tend to discontinue their involvement. Theories that help explain exercise participation include the health belief model, theory of reasoned action, theory of planned behavior, self-efficacy theory, and the transtheoretical model. A main feature of this chapter is to address ways of developing strategies that foster exercise participation and adherence. There are numerous cognitive (thoughts and emotions) and behavioral (actions) strategies that exercisers can use that will promote exercise performance and adherence. Examples of cognitive strategies include visualization, positive self-talk, psyching up, and thought-stopping. Behavioral examples include record keeping, social support, short-term (in small increments) and long-term goal setting, and perceived choice. Many of these can be applied to exercise settings, and are used by high-quality athletes in sport competition. The primary focus of these exercise-promoting strategies is to provide the exerciser with a sense of enjoyment, improvement, competence, and benefit from continued participation in physical activity.

REVIEW QUESTIONS

1. What are the advantages of three different types of exercise, aerobic, resistance (strength) training, and flexibility? Describe three ways in which this information can be communicated to exercisers.

2. In what ways does exercise influence self-esteem, mood, stress, anxiety, and mental health, in general?

3. What is exercise adherence? How does it differ from exercise compliance? How could a physical trainer, fitness instructor, or individual exerciser enhance exercise adherence/compliance?

4. Briefly describe the health belief model, theory of reasoned action, theory of planned behavior, self-efficacy theory, and the transtheoretical model. Describe how each of these can be used to promote exercise adherence.

5. Define exercise addiction, or dependence. What are the properties of positive and negative addiction? What are the signals that indicate that a person's positive addiction to exercise has become negative?

6. Define a cognitive strategy that can be used to facilitate exercise performance. Describe three cognitive strategies and how they might be applied.

7. Define a behavioral strategy that can be used to enhance exercise participation and adherence. Describe three behavioral strategies and how they would be applied.

8. Describe ways in which personal trainers and fitness instructors can enhance an exerciser's intrinsic motivation in continuing an exercise program.

CHAPTER 12

Athletes Speak for Themselves

In the final analysis, it is the athletes who play the games, score the points, and serve as the primary sources of victory or defeat, not the coach. Perhaps the often-heard phrase "winning coaches" should be replaced with "coaches of winning teams." The athletes' feelings, attitudes, and performances dictate the extent of individual and team success. The focus of this book has been on acknowledging the importance of the "mental game" on performance outcomes. Certainly, using X's and O's, planning game strategy, and engaging in physical conditioning are inherent aspects of game preparation and success. But, as the Peggy Lee song from the 1960s goes, "Is that all there is?"

As a consulting sport psychologist, I've had the opportunity to talk with hundreds of athletes of various ages and skill levels in different countries. Other sport psychologists and journalists have also published their observations or presented this information at professional conferences. From these personal and documented conversations, one thing appears to be clear: *The athlete is a powerful, but often untapped, source of information to the coach for the team's benefit.* Powerful because of the information's validity. This is not just any spectator or fan who is giving the respected and experienced coach advice. This particular informant is a team member, the target of the coach's behaviors, the person whose performance and attitudes lead directly to the contest's outcome (Figure 12.1). But this rich source of information is often left untapped; his or her views, perceptions, experiences, and dreams are—as they say in the movie industry—left on the cutting room floor. What the athletes have to say is simply not often taken into account. Let's look at just a few examples of input from a player that might be valuable.

Coaches do a superb job of observing, critiquing, analyzing, and strategizing. Based on their observations, sometimes from optimal vantage points, assistants forward recommendations to the head coach, who, in turn, directs changes in the team or player performance strategy. But wait. Is there something the athlete knows, based on his or her own experiences on the field, that would offer new insight to the coach? Is an opponent doing something that is making a certain skill difficult to carry out? Is the opponent showing certain tendencies that coaches may not have picked up or that was not practiced as part of the game preparation? And perhaps most risky, is the athlete free to articulate his or her uncertainties about the opponent's strategies or skills? In U.S.

Figure 12.1 Given the mental, emotional, and physical demands of competitive sport, the coach's insights into their athletes' needs would likely improve performance outcomes.

football, for example, does the defensive back lack the receiver's speed, making him susceptible to the long pass? If so, should a double coverage defensive strategy be planned and used more often?

The baseball coach orders the pitcher to walk the batter intentionally. But the catcher remembers that this hitter has shown virtually no skill in making contact with the pitcher's curve ball. Given the catcher's insight, is an intentional walk the best strategy?

And what about injuries? Can an athlete feel secure about telling the coach that he or she is injured (before the game) and is, therefore, unable to play at 100 percent effectiveness? Shouldn't the coach condone such total honesty without the athlete fearing retribution?

The purpose of this chapter is to hear what the athlete has to say concerning his or her perceptions of their coach and how the coach's actions influence their sport performance. The reader may get a slightly different perspective about effective coaching, about what works and what doesn't. What do athletes need, and how can these needs be met? Just as important is understanding the degree to which coaches and athletes observe the same situations differently. Statements of athletes will reinforce the crucial importance of communication between coach and athlete and, as depicted in Figure 12.1, will often improve the athlete's concentration and motivation.

The content of this chapter is based almost exclusively on personal interviews with athletes of different ages and skill levels and on my own empirical observations and informal discussions with players and coaches. Other information was obtained from the media and from the applied sport psychology literature. Athletes of all ages and skill levels—even the professionals, as indicated by a major league baseball coach—seem to have similar needs.

Athletes have personal needs, and the coach has the responsibility of determining and meeting these needs, if possible. The following sections deal with the feelings and attitudes of athletes that affect their motivation, commitment, energy, and, ultimately, their game performance. The players' comments also reflect certain coaching behaviors that either enhance or detract from their mental readiness. Their opinions are grouped into five time periods during which coaching behaviors in some way affected the athlete's feelings, attitudes, or performance: practice, pregame, game, postgame, and off the field or court.

About Practice

Performers and coaches agree that the primary purposes of practice are to learn and improve upon skills and to perform game strategies that simulate game conditions. Many of the athletes interviewed, high school and collegiate, felt that both objectives were either unclear or unmet. Many of the comments centered on the manner in which coaches and players interacted:

- "I'm afraid of my coach. He's very critical. The more he yells at me, the more nervous I get and I make more mistakes. I need compliments once in a while."
- "My coach is always hollering. Sometimes I get tired of listening to him."
- "It seems the only reason we do wind sprints is for punishment after losing. It would be nice to know why we do certain things during practice."
- "I give my coach credit for trying to teach us things. But he talks very fast, and I don't always understand and remember everything he says. So I mess up and get him mad."
- "The biggest problem I have with practice is that it's boring. Why can't it be more fun? If it was, I bet the team would try harder and we'd be better prepared to play the game."
- "My coach doesn't say much to me. He's really quiet, and I don't know what he's thinking."
- "I know I'm better than the guy starting ahead of me, but the coach won't tell me why he's starting and I'm not. I wonder sometimes if this is all worth it."
- "My coach is a great guy. The only concern I have is that he expects us to hurt our opponents. I have trouble with that."

- "I'm just not psyched when we're practicing during the off-season. The coach works us just as hard, but with no game coming up, I'm not as motivated. I think he expects us to go at 100 percent every minute all year, but that's impossible for most of us. And he gets real mad if we don't."

- "The one word that describes practice to me is 'boredom.' We do the same thing all the time. I'd love to try some new and different things or even have some time off to study once in a while."

- "I wish I knew the basis on which the coaches evaluate me in practice. I'm told I'm an average player, but no one tells me what that means."

- "We sure do a lot of sitting around."

- "I get real uptight when the coach yells at me after I make a mistake. I know I made the error. What I need is encouragement, not put-downs."

What these players are saying is that they have needs that are not being met, which is detracting from their motivation to persist, learn, improve, and help the team succeed. Players are saying, "Hey, Coach, be honest with me. Tell me what I need to do to be successful. What are my limitations? What am I doing well? Be patient with me while I learn new skills and improve; this takes time. Treat me with the same respect that you expect from me, and I'll give you all I've got. I can't play my best after I've been insulted or embarrassed in front of the team."

Practice is the time for learning, improving, taking risks, and, yes, making mistakes. At this time, attitudes of self-confidence, self-image, positive player relationships, trust between coach and athlete, and motivation are developed. It's the time for coaches to establish rapport, communicate openly, and use strategies that enable performers to be mentally and physically prepared.

Based on the players' views, a coach who is interested in meeting as many of the athletes' needs as possible would do the following:

1. *Be discreetly honest with the players.* The coach can be candid about the player's weakness in a constructive manner in the hope that improvement in future performance is possible, even likely. Statements such as "There's no way you'll ever be a starter with your slow speed" are destructive, unmotivating, and unnecessary.

2. *Make practice exciting.* Repetition breeds boredom. Change practice procedures and content on occasion. In fact, follow the strategy of a few teams in the National Hockey League and take a few days off in the middle of the season to get away from the sport. This means no practice. Maybe an affordable trip can be planned that will entertain or relax the athletes. This will help to prevent burnout.

3. *Provide player roles.* Be sure that all team members have a significant role in every practice period. This is the time to teach skills, attempt new strategies, and fail. Coaches sometimes say that it is impossible to work with all the athletes equally. One coach indicated a split of 80 percent with starters and 20 percent with non-starters. This approach alienates a large number of team members who feel excluded from the coach's attention and instruction. Further, substitutes are only one injury away from starting or playing. It makes good sense to work with them as much as possible for better team morale and more skilled athletes.

4. *Realize that athletes can't go all-out all the time.* Coaches should not want to maintain the same level of intensity in all team-related situations. Sometimes it is a good idea

to use a relaxed, low-key approach, especially in practice or during the off-season. In this way, players will respond more enthusiastically when conditions warrant it.

5. *Separate anger from instruction.* Athletes do not integrate information when they are tense and anxious. But these are exactly their feelings when the coach reprimands an athlete in offering instruction or feedback on performance. Nothing sinks in. The suggestion for coaches is simple: *Don't teach and be angry at the same time*, especially during practice, when instruction is most appropriate.

An often-quoted adage in sport is that players play in the game as they practice. An athlete who has worked hard and performed optimally in preparation for the game is predicted to play better than if practice sessions were uninformative, unstimulating, and poorly planned. The best way to prepare an athlete to play at optimal levels under game conditions is to *practice* under game conditions; simulate the competitive situation. Game-simulation techniques need to be instituted during practice. Coaches should try to imitate game conditions as closely as possible so that athletes are better prepared to make appropriate responses during the game.

For example, take the quarterback aside and tell him what play to call. The quarterback then calls out the play in the huddle. After the ball is snapped (assuming that all players are dressed for contact), have everyone perform at full speed. Research clearly indicates that artificially slow movement does not prepare participants to meet the demands of actual game conditions.

In baseball, simulate game conditions when a runner is on first base contemplating "stealing" second base. The batter tries to bunt when the pitch is in the strike zone. Infielders must decide where to go: either ensure against the stolen base or field the bunt. The batter is required to guess the type of pitch to hit, a curve or fast ball, as he or she would during a game. Pitches are thrown at gamelike velocity. Team members should act the role of spectators using both positive and negative (i.e., realistic) verbal messages to the batter in an intrasquad game. Thus, hitters can practice filtering out potentially obtrusive noise as they would need to during an actual game. This suggestion should *not* be used during the first few weeks of practice, until players are conditioned and have mastered fundamental skills.

In gymnastics, some practices should occur in a noiseless environment, similar to a gymnastics meet. Gymnasts are given the opportunity to perform their complete routine without interruption—errors included—then receive assessments by "judges."

The focus of practice behaviors is game preparation. The closer an athlete is able to mimic a game condition during practice, the closer he or she will replicate successful practice performance during the contest. The coach's job is to provide these opportunities. Another aspect of coaching that helps to prepare the athlete for competition—and an area about which athletes had much to say—is related to behaviors and strategies before the game.

Pregame Issues

The day of a sport contest is usually filled with a set of preplanned routines devised by the coach. How does the coach determine this schedule? From interviews with 35 high school and college coaches and one major league baseball coach, I found that coaches carry out their pregame strategies based on one or all of the following: (1) techniques used by their coach when they were athletes, (2) discussions with colleagues at different programs, (3) readings in coaching publications, or (4) "tradition." Not one coach indicated that the needs of, or input from, his or her players were a factor in deciding pregame strategies. Nor was it indicated that consulting a sport psychologist or reading related literature influenced pregame protocol. Here is what the players had to say:

- "I prefer not to eat meat at the pregame meal. It's too heavy for me and makes me feel sluggish. The coach feels a pregame steak is necessary."
- "The day of a night game is usually boring. But one thing my coach makes us do is spend time with him or an assistant coach during the day. Usually we just relax and watch TV, but I'd rather be alone or study."
- "When my coach tells me to relax and don't be nervous, I get *more* uptight. I'd rather no one would say anything to me."
- "I'd prefer to prepare for the game alone rather than be with the team the whole time. I value my private time."
- "I don't enjoy hearing a lot of false chatter—stuff that coaches and players say that is supposed to motivate me. I need honesty. Coaches should talk from the heart."
- "My coach is a good guy, but he says the same thing all the time. [His message] doesn't affect me anymore."
- "I'm uncomfortable when my coach loses control before the game. It gets me nervous because if anyone has to remain cool, he does."
- "Sometimes I want to hear other players and team captains talk to the team rather than the coach. I like hearing what my teammates are thinking."
- "I'm glad the coach has banned music in the locker room before the game. It drove me nuts. Now, players have a choice of using headsets if they want music."
- "I don't want to hear how important this game is to us. I already know that. We all want to win. I don't need to be reminded. My advice is [to have the coach] say nothing to us or just review a few things."
- "I saw the movie *Bear* about Bear Bryant [the legendary University of Alabama football coach]. He reminded his players that 'Mom and Dad were watching, so have a good game.' I'd rather not hear that. I'm nervous enough without thinking about who's watching me."
- "I'm not in favor of the pregame warm-up ritual. We spend too much time going through the motions and using up energy, especially when it's hot outside. I also think we warm up too early before the game. By the time the game gets going, we're not as psyched. It takes us a while to get the adrenaline going again."

These athletes are saying things that go against the traditional practices of coaching in sport. The pregame meal is an example. Although many coaches think that the value of food intake on game day is in the player's minds, researchers are not so sure. True, the "placebo effect" is alive and well in sport. Players who *think* they'll do better if they eat steak just might perform less effectively if denied a pregame meat meal. On the other hand, meat has been found to take significantly longer to be digested and used for energy as compared to complex carbohydrates. Many college teams, for instance, eat pancakes or spaghetti four to six hours before game time, as indicated by sports medicine literature.

Other examples of a disparity between tradition in pregame coaching procedures and player preferences include (1) having all team members stay together as though team unity and morale will be negatively affected if the athletes go their separate ways hours before game time, (2) following an exhaustive pregame warm-up procedure despite air temperature and research that contraindicates the need for prolonged warm-up, (3) in the pregame talk, reminding players about the importance of winning the game and who's watching them from the stands (an attempt to motivate that usually results in more tension), and excessive hollering, (4) relying on only the coach for pregame verbal communication instead of using captains or other team leaders to communicate information or deliver messages to heighten incentive, and (5) failing to respect individual differences and needs among athletes. Some performers enjoy and even need intensive group affiliation, while others are less gregarious and prefer more solitude, particularly on game day.

It is virtually impossible for coaches to please every member of the team. Sometimes athletes need to adjust to situations that are not to their liking. Further, some situations warrant a certain protocol. For instance, golfers and basketball players would not prepare for their respective contests in the same manner. But if coaches were to follow many of the suggestions offered by athletes in my interviews, the "greatest good for the greatest number" might be accomplished. Here are some procedures that should seriously be considered.

1. Try to give the athlete a choice as to the type of pregame meal that he or she would prefer. Or read the scientific literature and discuss with the players your rationale for choosing a particular team meal. If they believe you, performance will likely increase—due to the placebo effect, self-fulfilling prophecy, or valid science.

2. Treat all players alike. Avoid giving starters more time and attention on game day than other participants. The use of a double standard when interacting with players backfires. It sends a message that the support that substitutes offer starters is minimal and unimportant, and that substitutes are less important.

3. Ask the players about their feelings toward game day procedures. Would they rather be left alone than go to the coach's house to relax? Do they need more study time? Are they more comfortable in their own home or room than somewhere else? Some structuring of the day's events is necessary, but how much is too much?

4. In general, players seem to prefer a more subdued approach to the game than a boisterous, highly vocal style. The low-key locker room allows athletes to save their energy, think about their playing assignments and team strategies, and communicate voluntarily instead of feeling compelled to "make noise." Of course, certain games and situations may warrant a highly aroused response from players. It's the coach's job to set the tone and to know which direction—from highly intense to low key—will enhance performance.

5. Perhaps one of the most discussed and overrated coaching strategies in sport is the pregame talk. For years, coaches followed the style portrayed by popular films and military commanders, and often modeled by their own coaches, in which athletes were given a highly emotional verbal message just prior to the event. This was especially the case with team sports. However, after discussing the appropriateness of this strategy with athletes and reading many articles appearing in popular sports magazines, books, and applied research journals, the fact emerges that often athletes prefer just the opposite style of pregame talk—less emotion, more relaxed, and low key. The "less is more" approach often allows the athletes to save their emotion and energy for the contest, to relax and concentrate on their game strategy, or to

mentally practice their skills. An uplifting talk by the coach, if warranted, may be more effective if used at halftime, between periods, or during timeouts when the team needs a higher level of arousal, especially in contact sports. Chapter 3 discusses effective and ineffective content and styles of the pregame talk.

6. Finally, try not to fatigue your players prematurely during the pregame warm-up period. Valid reasons exist for following a certain warm-up procedure, particularly physiological reasons such as raising internal body temperature and providing more flexibility and range of motion. But in warm temperatures or high humidity, the length of warm-up time should be reduced. Moreover, the mental advantages of the warm-up, which include increasing arousal and lowering anxiety, have a threshold beyond which arousal becomes too low. The incentive to play at optimal levels is reduced.

During the Game

Well, sports fans, the time to separate the teams according to talent, preparation, and readiness is here. It's game time. Players interviewed for this book had much to say about the strengths and weaknesses of their coach's behaviors during the game. I was not surprised to learn that certain coaching behaviors led directly to less effective performance, and yet sometimes they didn't. The most salient and typical player complaint was based on the coach's use of anger and other negative communication during the game. Often, this had a devastating impact on the athlete's tendency to take risks, relax, attend to proper cues, follow the coach's directions, and play in a highly motivated state. Here are some of the more typical comments from players:

- "Don't yell at me to motivate me. It makes me nervous and ruins my concentration."
- "I don't like to be criticized. It makes me nervous. I mean, I get blamed for something I couldn't help. It wasn't my fault."
- "My coach is very patient with me, and that's just what I need."
- "The worst thing a coach can do to motivate me is yell and scream. I absolutely 'freak out.' I need to be respected. Straightforward, honest talk is all I ask."
- "Every quarterback has to learn to accept criticism . . . the one thing that has to be within your personality is that you don't let criticism affect you or it will affect you all year."
- "I think my coach is an honest guy, but when he says I'm going to play and I don't, I stop believing him. This may be wrong to say, but whether we win or lose, I won't be happy if I was promised a chance to get in [the game] and don't."
- "Our team has two co-captains, but they never say anything. I don't think they were ever told what to do. Captains should lead, but they don't."
- "I think an effective coach knows how to treat us before the game and at half-time [in football]. If we've been lazy, he should give us a tough time about it. But if only a few players are messing up, or the first half wasn't too bad, then I don't think he should get angry at the whole team. If we've been doing our job, it just gets the rest of us down."
- "I wish my coach would ask the players for our input during the game. One time, I was having trouble defending against one of [my opponent's] plays. Instead of asking me to explain the problem I was having, he jumped all over me. In fact, I could have used some instruction at that point."

- "I get uptight when the coach argues with the referee all the time. If he [the coach] is out of control, I start to lose my concentration. The team seems disorganized. I need a coach who remains cool, especially under pressure."

- "My coach is a super bright lady. She really knows the game. The only thing that drives me up the wall is when she threatens us if we mess up. Then we start to choke. And the game isn't fun anymore. I just don't think we play our best when we are afraid to lose. Being threatened with punishment turns me off. The odd part is that even if we win, I feel anger toward the coach, who made some pretty terrible statements as her way to motivate us."

- "I learn a lot from my coach. She's made me 10 times the player I was last year. My only gripe is her tendency to embarrass individual athletes in front of the team instead of speaking to them privately. I don't want to hear one of my teammates get yelled at and put down. It could be me next time. I'd respect her a lot more if she knew when to go behind closed doors."

- "You know what a double standard is? Well, we have double standards on our team. When an important player [makes a mistake], the coach doesn't get angry. He just tells him to watch it and do better next time. But when a nonstarter messes up, look out. The coach explodes. That isn't fair. If I had one wish on this team, it would be that all players are treated equally—with respect."

- "I notice something interesting about our team. The subs rarely cheer for the starters. That's too bad because we need the support of our teammates. The reason for this lack of support is because nonstarters don't feel they're contributing to the team. They can't identify with the uniform. If they have to get in the game, I don't think they'd know what to do because the coach doesn't include them in many of the drills. They get very little of the coach's attention."

- "The problem with getting too psyched before and during the game is that after we blow it, our mental state falls flat. We get so down, so disappointed, that it's tough to come back."

- "The most upsetting thing my coach ever did to me was complain about my weight right in the middle of the [tennis] match. There I was, down two games to one, and he tells me during the break that I need to lose five pounds. I was frantic. Of course, I lost the match."

A British philosopher named Buckle once commented: "Society prepares the crime; the criminal commits it." A similar situation exists in sport. The coach creates the atmosphere from which players respond accordingly. In doing so, the team leader must ask a very important question: What am I (the coach) doing that is promoting or inhibiting the type of attitude and performance skills necessary to have a successful team? The answer to this crucial question will allow the coach to reflect on his or her attitudes and actions that produce player attitudes. What the coach finds might be surprisingly different from what he or she would have predicted.

The coach may want to ask a second very important question: "What do my players want and need?" In fact, it may be better to pose this question to the players directly (or through intermediaries such as captains, assistants, supportive parents, or the school counselor). Although it is unfair and unrealistic to expect that all of the players' needs will be satisfied, at least the opportunity to communicate feelings to the coach will go a long way toward bringing important issues out into the open where they can be worked on and resolved.

Several coaches I've interviewed on the issue of "open" discussions do not agree that players should have an opportunity to speak their minds. Instead, they feel that athletes must learn to do what they are told and to follow directions. "By creating a free-for-all discussion, you open up a Pandora's Box," one coach told me. My discussions with players of all ages indicate otherwise. A performer with unresolved feelings loses the most important thought processes related to success in sport: inner motivation, persistence, concentration, and loyalty to coach and team alike. The message these players repeatedly offered during my interviews was: "Coach, don't be afraid to ask us what we think. What we have to say can make a difference."

Postgame Behaviors

Well, the contest is over. What is there left to say? Should the coach say anything and, if so, how should he or she say it? The events and words that follow the game or match will leave a lasting impression in the minds of all athletes, starters and substitutes. Should players feel guilty after losing a game? Responsible for their victory? Embarrassed for committing an error? Proud to be a member of the team? Clearly, some coaches make more effective and positive postgame impressions than others, as indicated by comments from the players.

- "Often after we lose, my coach cries. I can't blame him for being upset, but he's trying to make us feel guilty with his tears."
- "I like the way our coach handles losing. He just says, 'The game's over and I think we've all learned something from it. We gave it our best shot, so I'd like all of us to feel proud. Let's talk about what we learned from the game before Monday's practice when we're more relaxed, less fatigued, and can reflect on the game less emotionally.'"
- "My coach is at his worst after losing. He's not the same person. He gets so violent it scares me. I stay out of his way."
- "It's funny; I never feel depressed after a game, win or lose. Maybe it's because I've given it my best shot. Or maybe it's because I really have fun playing. But I'll be darned if the coaches on this team don't want the players feeling depressed. I mean, if they see one smile or hear someone utter a single word, they give that player a long glare. We've all learned to keep quiet and stay out of their way."
- "A strong coach should not take everything so personally. If we lose, his feelings are hurt. He's insulted. I'm uncomfortable with that."
- "Men shouldn't think that a woman athlete's tears are a sign of weakness. Tears help me express how I feel. It's OK to feel—and appear—upset. Tears are my way of dealing with feeling down, but they don't say I'm out."
- "If my opponent was too easy, I don't feel very satisfied after winning."
- Sometimes I wish I received more criticism from my coach. I feel responsible for how I perform, so being criticized will help me. Don't go soft on me."
- "If I succeed, I feel it was due to my skills which I worked so hard to perfect. I don't feel my victory was due to a poor opponent—not at this level."
- "If there's one thing I need after the game, it is to be left alone. I have a hard time talking about the game over and over again. I just wish we could go home and put it behind us. Reviewing the game is depressing."

- "My coach has a split personality. After we win, he's friendly, warm, smiling, and happy. After we lose, he's ready to tear our heads off. It's so predictable that I lose respect for him. I try just as hard after a win as after a loss. If I had my wish, he'd be consistent after all games regardless of outcome."

- "I have a lot of respect for my coach. But he has two habits after we've lost that make me lose that respect. One is swearing. It's unbecoming of the team leader. And besides, he tells us not to swear. The second is doing physical damage to the locker room. Throwing and kicking things won't make us a better team. The game is over. Time to move on."

- "My coach tends to insult us after we lose, especially the players who made an error during the game. The worst time occurs when he singles out players by name and embarrasses them. It's uncalled for."

- "Win or lose, my coach reminds us what we did right during the game. We never leave the locker room feeling defeated as people. He puts sport in perspective. Sport is not life; it's a part of life. We respect him for showing us that."

- "My coach is a nice person, but he thinks the team should be together *after* the game [at home games]. Wrong! We need to get away and have some freedom. I like the guys on our team, but all of us can use a break. The worst part is that he [the coach] wants to party with us. Like I said, he's a good guy but I wish he'd simply leave us alone when the game's over."

These players are making very simple requests of their coach when the game is over. "Don't put us down," they seem to be saying. Essentially, that's all they ask. Ignore them if you *must*. Provide positive verbal or nonverbal feedback if you'd like. Even display emotion if it's necessary. But placing blame, pointing fingers, invoking guilt, and embarrassing team members clearly have deleterious effects on the players' attitudes and future performances. According to the interviews, players respond best to the following postgame coaching strategies:

1. *Negative responses.* Players understand anger. Many even feel that it's justified if the team did not play well, although mature players feel more comfortable with the coach's hostility than do child athletes. In general, it is not anger in itself that upsets the athlete. It's the purpose and content of it that does so much damage. It's one thing for the coach to exclaim: "I'm really upset about how we played today. We could not carry out our plan. . . ." It's quite another thing to say something like the following, especially in the presence of teammates: "Bill, you blew it. Why didn't you do as you were told? Your fumble cost us the game. If you would have made those free throws, we would have won. Why didn't you catch the darn ball?" Insults breed contempt and disloyalty toward the coach and even the team. Players begin to think twice about the reasons they're participating. "Who needs this?" many begin to think. The result is either physical withdrawal (quitting) or mental withdrawal (a lack of effort).

2. *Consistency.* Players want their coach to react in the same respectful, constructive manner, win or lose, whether it is after the game or the next day. They do not respond well to a "Jekyll and Hyde" type of personality who expresses warmth and sensitivity after winning, but just the opposite responses after losing. Developing a postgame routine will facilitate consistent behaviors. Reviewing team/player performance ("What did we do well, and not do so well?") and plans/goals for future performance will help.

3. *Placing the blame.* As indicated in Chapter 4, the accurate use of attributions to explain the probable causes for winning or losing leaves a very important impression with the athlete. Athletes are asking their coach to use proper attributions: Was it their ability, effort, opponent, or luck that was the primary cause of the game outcome? The accurate and *sensitive* use of attributions will help players to learn from the game—as a reflection of their mistakes as well as from skilled performance and positive outcomes.

The coach is a model for his or her players. As such, there is an image the coach should project if player loyalty and credibility are to survive. In two words, that image is stability and maturity. Someone associated with the team must bring everyone together and maintain a sense of purpose, composure, and direction. That job belongs to the team leader. But even if coaches and athletes agree on this, they do not appear to share the same perceptions about what are appropriate behaviors away from the sport setting.

Behaviors Off the Field or Court

Coaches have told me that sometimes they feel responsible for their (high school and college) players 24 hours a day, seven days a week, especially during the season. This feeling reminds me of the writing of Haim Ginott (1969) in his book *Between Parent and Teenager*. It's common knowledge that conflict between parents and their children is most intense during the adolescent years. This is because, Ginott explains, the primary need of parents is to be needed, to guide behaviors of their children so that growing up is as constructive and as painless as possible. Unfortunately, the number-one need of the adolescent is independence. Teenagers are struggling to identify themselves as responsible adults and to escape the control of parents. The inevitable result is conflict. Athletes have similar needs. They yearn to be independent and to enjoy the company of friends—not only because they are expressing normal needs of peer affiliation, but because they need distance from authority.

What this means is that athletes need time away from their coach off the field or court. But there are also times when meeting the coach away from the sport situation to discuss personal concerns is important. Thus, there is a balance as to the coach's availability to the players in a nonsport setting, as indicated by these comments:

- "My coach says he has office hours, but when I try to see him, he's always too busy."
- "My coach shares an office with another coach. The lack of privacy prevents me from being open with him about how I feel."
- "My coach wants to be my drinking buddy. He asks me where I go for entertainment and would I go with him. I sure don't want to."
- "I wish the coach would avoid talking to my parents about me. He could just ask me for the same information he discusses with them. Quite honestly, I love my folks but what I do at school and on the team is between the coach and me."
- "The coach wants to know what we [the players] do in our free time. I don't think it's his business."
- (From a college athlete): "I see the coach at the bar every week. For some reason, I'm uncomfortable with his drinking and dancing at the same place the players go."

- "My folks wanted to speak to the coach after the game, and he was nice enough to take the time and do it."

- "This might sound weird, but I view the coach as an authority figure. He's a lot older than me, and I don't feel we should be buddies. He's got his job and I have mine. But I still want to respect him for being a good coach."

- "I really enjoy talking to my coach about things that have nothing to do with football. I mean he actually showers with us and talks politics, history, and other stuff. It shows he respects us as people, not just football players."

- "Joking around is important for me. Competing has its pressures, so I need to unwind and have fun sometimes. Coaches should always have a sense of humor."

- "Before he left the school, my coach tended to flirt with his favorite players. That wasn't right."

- "I respect my coach because he shows respect for me. I like the adult type of relationship even though I know he's still the coach."

- "My coach shows favorites. That's bad."

- "I've never heard my coach make a sexist remark, which I respect. If he did, the team would stop going all-out."

Coaching has many roles. It's no easy task playing all of them—and at the right time. Athletes want stability and dependability from their coach. The leader who does not live up to this image will not gain the respect and loyalty necessary to influence the athlete's behaviors, feelings, and attitudes. According to input from the players, coaches should think about the following:

1. Coaches and athletes are not in the same peer group. The coach is invariably older and more mature than the players. Therefore, a coach can never be a true friend of an athlete. Such relationships are uncomfortable at best, and they conflict with roles on the team. Socializing between the two parties should be avoided except at team-related functions. As the baseball pitcher Billy Southward used to say back in the 1950s, "Never fall in love with your ballplayers."

2. Athletes need and want private time with their coach. It is absolutely necessary for coaches to set aside the opportunity for players to engage in private conversation. If a coach shares an office, one of two strategies should be used: An arrangement could be made to have exclusive use of the office during certain hours of the week, or another facility could be scheduled that would allow private meeting time. The attitude that "My office colleague can be trusted" may be true, but this does not allow the performer to speak openly and without intimidation. Coaches who ask for open communication with their players should show that they mean it.

3. Do coaches have the right to drink at a bar frequented by their players (or their players' parents)? Yes, they do. But should they? It depends on the type of image a coach wants to project and the effect of this image on the ability to be an effective coach. Athletes do not want to see their coach in any role that will erode the image of a mature, responsible team leader. Bars, with or without entertainment, license certain behaviors that are not compatible with desirable images of a coach. The advice? It's probably better to choose drinking establishments (if you must) that are *not* in the local area.

Another disadvantage of associating with the players "after hours" is that it places the burden of feeling responsible for the players' behavior on the coach's shoulders.

Coaches realize that there is a time to ignore certain behaviors of their players. This is not to condone these inappropriate actions. However, the coach cannot assume the roles of parent, police, and friend of players in situations unrelated to the team. That would be unfair—both to the player and the coach. Further, the coach is an important model for his or her athletes and, as such, is in a position to influence the behaviors and attitudes of athletes in a positive manner.

4. This suggestion should be almost unnecessary to mention except that it is imperative that it be followed. Coaches should never become romantically or sexually involved with their athletes. Their respective roles and the image such involvement would project to others would impede coaching effectiveness. One female athlete disclosed to me that her male coach became inappropriately friendly during a road trip. She felt guilty and confused about rejecting her coach as an intimate companion, yet needing his guidance and friendship as a mature team leader. She was uncomfortable with his flirtation and hoped that her rejection of him would not result in a change in her playing status. This player's concerns illustrate just some of the many reasons why coaches and athletes must not confuse sensitivity and dependency with excitement and personal relations. Ultimately, no one benefits.

In the final analysis, off-the-field or off-court actions of the coach can either augment or reduce effectiveness in team-related situations. Coaches are correctly concerned with image—their own image and that of the team. What all members of the team—including the coach—do and say away from the sport environment reflects the maturity, stability, and quality of team leadership. Effective coaches ensure that their own positive self-image is compatible with the way they want their players to perceive them: as intelligent, articulate, knowledgeable, and motivated leaders of skilled athletes. But, as we'll see in the next section, coaches and their players often see the same thing differently.

Differing Perceptions between Coach and Athlete

Sport psychologists try to understand the perceptions and roles of coaches and athletes. The objective is to help both parties to become increasingly compatible in meeting personal needs and in achieving performance and team success. Although both parties want success, they do not always agree on the best ways to achieve it. Even more surprising is the frequent lack of communication between them; people who desire the same thing should talk to each other, not necessarily to teach skills and game strategies, but to develop trust and loyalty—and to monitor and adjust each person's perceptions about issues that influence attitudes and performance.

For example, one common area of concern for athletes is whether or not the coach likes them. Participants of all ages and expertise feel various degrees of anxiety about the coach's personal feelings about them. If the coach is not attending to, or reprimands, the player, the coach is perceived as "not liking me." Often, in the participant's mind, coaching decisions are based on the athlete's personality instead of on his or her sport skills. Yet, coaches say just the opposite. They want to win, of course. So they strongly refute the notion that decisions about who plays or for how long are based on anything but the performer's skills. "I want to field my best players," they often say. But what coaches rarely realize is that the athlete's perceptions must not be ignored. If a player feels unwanted or disliked by the coach, he or she will be less attentive, less loyal, less motivated, and less supportive of the coach and the team.

One purpose of this section is to illustrate just how dissimilar are the views of athletes and their coaches about the same situations in sport, specifically the coach's behaviors. It is partly based on a research study carried out over a three-year period (Anshel & Straub 1991). Because the nature of coach-athlete relationships differs from sport to sport, we restricted our sample to football.

Twenty-two football coaches were interviewed, including 12 at the collegiate level and 10 from secondary schools. The athletes in the study, randomly chosen starters and nonstarters, consisted of 58 and 23 college and high school players, respectively ($n = 81$). The players and their coaches represented schools in the southeastern, southwestern, and midwestern United States. Thus, because of the selective sources of the data as opposed to totally random procedures, the findings of this study cannot be representative of the total population.

A total of 31 undesirable coaching behaviors were depicted by the players and grouped into seven categories. They are ranked from the complaints expressed most commonly (1) to those that were mentioned less often (7), followed by behavioral examples of each:

1. Lack of effective communication between coach and athlete
   a. Athletes are not allowed to express feelings to coach
   b. Lack of praise
   c. Coach makes statements that embarrass athletes in the presence of peers
   d. Lack of sincerity and honesty
2. Not explaining to players rationale for strategies
   a. Reasons for running wind sprints
   b. Rationale for the game plan
   c. Benefits of learning and practicing performance techniques
3. Expression of anger toward athletes
   a. Coach is angry when he gives me feedback
   b. Coach is upset with me when he teaches a skill
4. Not defining the role or status of nonstarters (reported by starters and substitutes alike)
   a. Coach ignores nonstarters
   b. Coaches interact less with nonstarters than starters
   c. Athlete does not know the criteria for starting status or why he or she doesn't start
   d. Athlete feels that coach does not like him or her
5. Inappropriate content in pregame and half-time talk
   a. Coach says the same thing every game
   b. Coach berates athletes
   c. Coach *requires* athletes to use imagery minutes before the game

6. Failure to treat players as individuals
   a. Whole team admonished or praised regardless of individual performance
   b. Coach disregards an athlete's pain, injury, frustration, or depression
7. Ineffective use of assistant coaches
   a. Assistants are "puppets" for head coach
   b. Head coach is always taking over
   c. Assistants do not seem to be motivated

The next step was to ask the coaches their opinions about data gathered from the players. Here's what they said:

- Five of twenty-two (22.7 percent) denied affiliation with any of the seven traits.
- Thirteen of twenty-two (59 percent) identified with one of the seven behaviors.
- Four of the twenty-two (18 percent) agreed that they practiced two of the seven traits.
- None of the twenty-two coaches identified more than two of the traits as their own.

Which of the behaviors did the coaches admit were theirs? Seventeen admitted to expressing anger toward players, three said that they had not defined the nonstarters' roles, and one acknowledged using assistants ineffectively. Apparently all of the 22 coaches felt that they communicated effectively, and only one coach confessed that he didn't meet at least one of the players' needs. The coach's perceptions were in stark contrast to those of their players.

Coaches and athletes differed significantly as to the ways in which they assessed coaching effectiveness. The survey revealed that an incredible 87 percent of the players felt that their coach did not communicate effectively. Yet none of the 22 coaches agreed with this assessment. Only one coach admitted that he did not explain the reasons for using particular strategies with the players. But a whopping 79 percent of the athletes said otherwise.

In contrast to the coaches' perceptions, the athletes claimed that their coaches expressed anger (77 percent), that they did not define the team role or status of nonstarters (68 percent), that players were not motivated by their coach's comments at halftime or before the game (47 percent), that coaches did not treat athletes as individuals (42 percent), and that they did not work with assistants effectively (36 percent).

From the results of this investigation, two conclusions can be made: First, a tremendous disparity existed between the perceptions of athletes and their coaches on the use of effective techniques in football. Second, the coach and his players viewed his coaching and personal behaviors very differently. Essentially, the players said, "Coach, you're not doing such and such, and we need that." But he said, "Yes, I am doing such and such, and in fact, I'm quite good at it." What seems to be the problem? Why is it that coaches and players viewed the same situation—even the identical behaviors—differently?

Mechikoff and Kozar (1983), based on their interviews with 22 "winning" collegiate coaches in various sports, concluded: "All coaches indicated that athletes needed to be aware of themselves, their abilities, limitations, anxiety levels, wants, needs, etc., yet few had developed a structured system to help the athlete in these areas" (p. 122). In all due respect to many bright, articulate, experienced, and hard-working coaches, I heartily agree. It is one thing to list the qualities of successful coaches and athletes, but quite another to set up situations and carry out the activities that ensure meeting the athletes' needs. Yet this is what athletes say they want when they have the opportunity to speak for themselves.

Psychologists have known for years that our images of our environment are colored by various factors. These include expectations, past experiences, how persons perceive their role in a situation, selective use of feedback from external sources, the influence of others, and even genetic disposition, among others. Possible explanations of apparent misperceptions in sport are that:

1. Coaches are consumed by many tasks related to skill development and game preparation. Consequently, they do not actively attend to the area of players' feelings. In other words, coaches might be far more concerned with giving information than they are with receiving it.

2. Players tend to be too shy to "risk" communicating with their coach openly and honestly. Fear of retribution (e.g., not playing), intimidation, and a socialized fear of authority are likely reasons why athletes choose not to approach their leader to disclose feelings.

3. Coaches are selective about from whom they obtain feedback. Thus, the team captain, certain starters, or coaching assistants become more valuable and credible sources of feedback than other team members. Of course, this limits the reliability of information to which the coach is exposed.

4. Coaches may not view athletes' feelings as valid. As more than one coach has told me, "What do these athletes know about what it takes to win?" Consequently, coaches are prepared to risk "turning off" and not meeting the personal needs of their athletes in the anticipation that team success (winning) will justify their behaviors and techniques. In other words, actions will speak for themselves.

5. Some coaches may not be comfortable with allowing players to offer input. As indicated by several coaches, team leaders would prefer that the players' negative feelings be kept to themselves. That way, meetings do not become "gripe sessions," and team members do not "feed off" of one another's complaints.

6. Coaches typically view themselves as successful or are imitating the behaviors and techniques of other coaches who are successful. Their philosophy is, "If it worked for so and so, it can work for me."

7. The coach may be, in fact, meeting the needs of selected participants but inaccurately perceiving that all players are receiving the same treatment. For instance, when I've asked coaches to give me examples of explaining to players the reasons for performing certain tasks, invariably they name two or three individuals with whom they have interacted. And that's it. The rest of the team has not heard his rationale.

8. Coaches may not feel obligated to meet certain needs of players. In fact, many coaches feel that they are using the type of leadership style that athletes want. Perhaps. However, some athletes, especially at higher skill levels, prefer a more authoritative, "take charge" leadership style, a concept supported in the literature (Chelladurai 1984; Sandler 1981). Other athletes, especially at younger, less skilled levels, prefer a more humanistic approach.

9. Some coaches simply do not have a personality that is conducive to healthy relationships with athletes. School principals and athletic directors do not observe and evaluate the coach's performance. No personality assessments are made on a coach before he or she is hired. In addition, sport competitors are a captive audience; they participate voluntarily. Consequently, players have the choice of either doing it the coach's way or leaving the team—which, of course, is no choice at all.

SUMMARY

The literature in sport psychology and coaching is primarily concerned with suggested strategies, usually based on research or previous experience in coaching, to optimize sport performance. Researchers tend to gather information about athletes from questionnaires or, in fewer cases, structured interviews, while coaches develop their techniques in response to conversations or materials from other coaches. Rarely do athletes have direct input into the contest strategies or motor skill development that will be executed in practice and competitive situations. Consequently, it is not surprising that coaches and athletes perceive the same situations in sport differently and that the techniques and leadership styles that coaches commonly use are often incompatible with the preferences and needs of their players. This chapter focused on articulating these differences with specific reference to pregame, during-game, and postgame issues. Specific coaching recommendations were offered *that encourage coaches to be more sensitive to the value of communicating with athletes about their needs and desires*. Every need cannot be met, but coaches can at least become aware of, and sensitive to, them. In this way, athletes would likely become more responsive and loyal to their team leader, and coaches could go about their business with their eyes wide open. This can only happen when athletes have the opportunity to speak for themselves.

REVIEW QUESTIONS

1. Describe two coaching behaviors used prior to, during, and immediately following the sport contest that athletes claim are inappropriate or disturbing. What is the basis for these feelings? Do you agree or disagree with the players, and why?

2. Name five concerns athletes have about coaching behaviors in practice settings. Describe five techniques the coach can use in practice (for any sport) that will meet players' needs and overcome their concerns.

3. Image—how the team leader is perceived by his or her players—is a crucial aspect of effective coaching. Based on the input from athletes as depicted in this chapter, what can a coach do to improve his or her image? What can he or she do to hurt it?

4. In what ways do coaches and athletes differ about how they perceive the coach's actions and attitudes toward the players? What would you tell athletes and coaches to do to narrow this discrepancy?

5. According to player interviews, in what ways are coaches doing their jobs correctly? What do the athletes feel are desirable coaching behaviors?

CHAPTER 13

Conclusions and Future Directions

There are two purposes for writing this book. One purpose is to share the accumulating body of knowledge in sport psychology with participants—athletes (and their parents), coaches, and sports officials—beyond the common one-hour seminar format. The second purpose is to bring "life" to this very exciting and interesting area of study and practice. I was impatient with traditional textbooks that offered relatively bland accounts, laden with theory and prolonged reviews of research studies, with very limited implications for actually using this information. For this reason, this book contains numerous examples, some of which were taken from media stories and from my 20 plus years of professional experience as a sport and exercise psychology consultant, to support research findings and to provide real-world instances of theories and models. By including the theoretical foundations and review of selected research studies in sport psychology, I have attempted to give this field the academic respect and credibility it richly deserves. This approach, combining research with application, is what Smith (1999) calls the Scientist-Practitioner Model, linking theory, research, and intervention. To gain credibility among practitioners, Smith contends that "intimate relations should exist between theory development, research, and application as the field of sport psychology continues to mature." Further, Smith contends, "applications should be based on soundly designed basic research, and accountability demands that interventions be rigorously evaluated" (p. 31).

In my research for writing this book, I was surprised by two discoveries. First was the relatively small number of competitive athletes and coaches who understand the psychological factors that contribute to quality sport performance. Consequently, the *art* of mental preparation and using psychological-behavioral skills (e.g., cognitive strategies, goal setting) that improve the ability to manage anxiety, cope with stress, and reach preferred arousal and motivational levels is ignored. Second, I was surprised by the lack of understanding of proper instructional techniques by coaches, an area within the sport sciences called *sport pedagogy*. Without the use of quality instruction, the coach's expertise is only minimally used by participants.

Coaches and athletes are not trusting—at least initially—of psychological techniques such as imagery, progressive relaxation, centering, meditation, and cognitive self-control. With the exception of most competitive tennis players (see Figure 13.1) and golfers, sports which have embraced sport psychology interventions, most sports competitors are often suspicious of anything they can't feel, physically experience, or observe—and so are their coaches. This is not a criticism but rather a reflection of their training and past experiences. Nor are they particularly trusting of a person who may refer to him or herself as a sport *psychologist* or *consultant*. The basic philosophy of many participants is, "I've been successful up to this point, so why try something new?" Athletes would far prefer to listen to another athlete or coach whom they respect. To most athletes, the effect of listening to a present or former great athlete is far more powerful than that of listening to any researcher, educator, or psychologist, perhaps to the chagrin of many sport psychology consultants who would "give their right arm" for such respect.

Figure 13.1 The future acceptance of sport psychology by coaches and athletes is dependent on the proven effectiveness of mental skills in enhancing sport performance.

Surprisingly, and sadly, too many coaches are using the same militaristic tactics and strategies to motivate their athletes as was the case decades ago. Despite the abundant availability of research indicating the advantages of using different, more effective, approaches to leadership, athletes are still running laps for punishment, being told what to do without explanation, having relatively little input into the development of team strategies or policies, and being motivated through threats and other aversive, unpleasant means. The application of mental skills to manage stress and anxiety both before and during the contest is often nonexistent. Where is the recognition and use of new approaches in affecting human behavior and emotion? With obvious exceptions, especially among Olympic athletes, advances in the field of sport psychology are going relatively unnoticed. A library full of information that could help sport participants become more successful has been sadly ignored more often than not.

What are some of the problems that are preventing sport leaders from "coming in from the cold" and applying (not to mention even reading) the sport psychology literature? Based on numerous conversations with coaches at different levels of competition, I have concluded that these problems are based on at least five factors:

1. *The lack of credibility and trust of resource personnel outside the profession.* As one coach said, "You folks [sport psychologists] might know your area, but can you coach?" A related problem is that early attempts to use psychological techniques by "experts" proved ineffective at best and destructive at worst. Personality inventories that purportedly could predict future success in sport were later found to lack statistical validity and reliability. The initial experiences of "sport psychologists" with athletes were usually unsuccessful, invalid, and occasionally even fraudulent. See Ogilvie (1979a), Nideffer (1981), and Anshel (1992a, 1993) for further discussion of this issue.

2. *The coach's fear of "losing control" over players.* While there are many very fine, personally secure, highly confident individuals in the coaching profession, others find the role of sport psychology consultants very threatening. Reasons vary, but examples include a clash of philosophies in working with athletes, the consultant's examination and critique of the coach's performance, and concerns that the consultant would receive credit that the coach really deserves should team or individual performance markedly improve. The key issue—and challenge—in developing a proper relationship is establishing trust. Ravizza (1988, 1990) provides guidelines for overcoming resistance to sport psychology consultation.

3. *The reliance on replicating the tactics of coaches whose teams are chronically successful.* "If so-and-so does it and wins, so should we" is a common feeling among coaches, which doesn't take into account the unique needs of each situation. For example, I consulted with one college coach who was insistent on using, with his relatively less skilled team, the identical psychological and behavioral tactics practiced by his former team of highly talented athletes. His approach didn't work, and the team was never consistently successful.

4. *The mistrust of using an approach that is unobservable.* "Don't talk to me about mental techniques; I just want solid effort and good performance" I was told (Anshel 1989a). So much for believing in the importance of psychological skills. This sentiment was echoed in an interview with well-known (and successful) (U.S.) football coach Bill Parcells, who said, "I believe in the psychology of results" (*USA Today*, Aug. 11, 1995, p. 1c).

5. *The absence of applied material that is accessible and understandable.* "I can't understand the stuff in journals." This excuse is easy to understand. Many sport psychology practitioners complain that the quality of research journals with their academic jargon is usually judged by the scientific community according to the sophistication of the research design and statistical analyses. Little credence is given to influencing the behavior of practitioners. However, the publication of applied journals such as *The Sport Psychologist* (USA) and *Sports Coach* (Australia) and attempts in recent years by sport psychology researchers to write "hands-on" books for coaches and athletes help to overcome this problem. There must be quality scientific research with which to develop and test theories and models, examine the effects of interventions, and discover new techniques. However, in doing so, the field must not omit the practitioners who offer sport psychology the service, public recognition, and profile it deserves.

Another recent evolution in sport psychology has been the improved credibility of psychological and behavioral techniques based on published research. Yet more research is needed in examining the effects of various psychological techniques and interventions on desirable changes in emotion and performance. Many newer approaches to sport and exercise performance have replaced the earlier techniques and recommendations. As more professionals in the field receive the proper educational training, the use of applied sport psychology will gain an increasing foothold among sport leaders. Following are some developments and predictions in sport psychology.

1. The field has become more applied in the attempt to gain credibility and recognition from the scientific, educational, and sport domains.

2. University faculty who specialize in sport psychology will be required to perform more community service (e.g., direct or advise the governance of youth sport leagues) and publish more and higher quality research.

3. There will be an increase in private consulting and counseling in sport psychology. This tendency will contribute to the orientation of an applied, as opposed to a strictly theoretical, approach to research in the field.

4. The certification of sport psychologists will gain increased recognition by professional organizations.

5. Due to the current rise in demand for and interest in sport psychologists, especially by coaches of elite athletes (ironically, coaches of less skilled, younger participants appear to be slower to recognize the field's potential), sport psychologists will become more formally involved with professional and elite national sports teams. Eventually, sport psychologists will become accepted as permanent experts working full-time with teams.

6. Sport psychologists have become increasingly involved with the parents of young athletes and with community sports organizations by advising and developing sport programs. Through this relationship, child athletes have a more fulfilling and rewarding experience.

In recent years there has been extensive recognition of professional services, a proliferation of published written materials, and a vast increase in the number of college preparation programs, courses, and academic positions in sport psychology. The area is flourishing. For example, more sport psychologists than ever before report at conferences and in the professional literature about their experiences counseling individual elite athletes, sports teams, and coaches. In addition, a number of countries that participate in the Olympic Games now include full-time sport psychologists in their respective training centers. The governments of many countries, including the United States, Australia, Hong Kong, England, Israel, Korea, and others, employ sport psychologists on a full-time basis in their respective elite sports training centers or institutes. This illustrates the increased importance placed on providing psychological services for athletes and coaches. In addition, national psychology organizations in several countries have recently recognized sport psychology as an area of academic credibility.

Two other areas in human performance psychology have also become more popular—exercise and rehabilitation. Sport psychologists and consultants have a role in promoting physical activity and adherence to exercise programs in schools, industry, and health settings. Other job descriptions include providing psychological support for individuals engaged in postcardiac and weight control exercise therapy programs and working with therapists to help enhance compliance with prescribed therapies through use of cognitive strategies, facilitating recovery from injury, and teaching proper coping skills in response to stress and pain. Two popular books, *Psychological Bases of Sport Injuries* (2nd ed., 1999) edited by David Pargman, and *Psychology of Sport Injury* (1993) edited by John Heil, provide detailed descriptions of this new area of professional practice. In this way, the sport psychology profession has generated strong links to the field of health psychology and exercise psychology.

With regard to areas of competence, Nideffer et al. (1980) have identified six areas that sport psychologists should master.

1. *Developing performance improvement programs.* The purpose of techniques such as biofeedback, self-hypnosis, progressive relaxation, and attention control training is to give the athletes greater control over both cognitive and physiological arousal and concentration.

2. *Using psychological assessment techniques.* Numerous psychological inventories, interviews, and behavioral (observational) assessments have been used for the purpose of selecting, screening, and counseling athletes. The ability to predict the quality of an athlete's performance or the likelihood of becoming successful in sport has had only limited success. Assessment tools are best used to describe behavior or emotion, not predict them.

3. *Improving the communication among participants.* Through the use of personal consultation and behavioral group techniques, sport psychology counselors and educators are trying to enhance personal interaction among coaches and athletes.

4. *Providing crisis intervention services.* What happens when the stress of sport virtually immobilizes an athlete—or, for that matter, a coach? Team sport psychology consultants can sometimes help the participants quickly regain control of their emotions and cope effectively with the situation so that they can continue to be productive.

5. *Consulting with coaches, athletic and fitness trainers, and others who work directly with athletes.* Sometimes team leaders and administrative personnel prefer to work with a sport psychology consultant directly rather than allow athletes to have contact with the consultant. Some coaches feel that a sport psychologist can disrupt the coach-athlete relationship. Or, time constraints and other professional interests do not allow the consultant to have direct contact with athletes. In fact, some consultants believe

that their input will be more effective if they work through coaches, who have far more interaction with and influence on players than the consultant will ever have.

Working through coaches has its advantages and disadvantages. On the plus side, the sport psychology consultant may be more helpful to the team when advising coaches on the use of certain techniques. In most situations coaches have already established the necessary credibility and trust with athletes to suggest the use of certain mental strategies. On the minus side, the sport psychologist often needs direct contact with participants to determine individual needs, to suggest alternative approaches in meeting those needs, or to provide an opportunity for the player to disclose personal information that he or she might otherwise withhold from the coach. In the final analysis, sport psychology consultants must function in the athlete's world and have "hands-on" experience in working directly with players and coaches if they are to understand the role of sport psychology in competitive athletics.

6. *Functioning as a therapist or clinical psychology consultant.* A sport psychologist might be asked to provide clinical rather than educational services. The term *psychologist* is protected by law in most countries and states. Only persons with proper academic training in a program certified by their national psychology association and who are full members of their state psychology association may be called psychologists. If a person has completed a program in clinical (as opposed to counseling) psychology, this person is also certified to treat severe psychological problems. The challenge in the field of contemporary sport psychology is determining what constitutes a "psychological problem" requiring the services of a licensed psychologist. The certification program suggested by the Association for the Advancement of Applied Sport Psychology (AAASP) suggests that sport psychology consultants who are not licenced psychologists should learn how to detect psychopathological problems (e.g., chronic anxiety, eating disorders) and when to refer their client to a clinician. Not to do so is unethical (Anshel 1992a; Nideffer 1981; Sachs 1993). For an extensive review of this topic, readers should consult the journal *American Psychologist*, published by the American Psychological Association. Readers may also consult the AAASP Web site for more information on certification and contacting certified consultants: www.aaasponline.org.

Let's put sport psychology in perspective. Much research and trial-and-error experience lie ahead before established, functional techniques are effectively employed. The field must avoid the "Eureka" complex, the need to declare that "the answer" is at hand. It's this rush to make superlative, hyperbolic statements about linking mental techniques and interventions to positive performance outcomes, and to draw final conclusions based on relatively minuscule evidence that has drawn the ire of researchers, coaches, and even a few practicing sport psychology consultants. Based on the advice of some of our most respected and well-published sport psychology researchers, here are a few recommendations about how the field can grow and mature.

1. *Be supportive of professional colleagues.* Intelligent people can differ as to what constitutes quality research, the validity of using certain techniques in education and sport, and the general direction in which an academic discipline should go. Not only should coaches and sport psychologists recognize one another's strengths, limitations, and mutual interests, but so should researchers in the sport sciences. The various interests, challenges, and professional pursuits are what make the fields of psychology, physical education, and sport science fascinating. Given the vast

amount of knowledge we have not as yet acquired, scientists and practitioners can ill afford to diminish the importance of what others are doing. We have much to learn from each other. And in a democracy, no one is about to dictate what form this learning should take.

2. *Use a multidisciplinary approach.* Attempts to maximize sport performance often go beyond social/psychological factors. Sometimes a performance limitation is a function of improper movement mechanics, poor teaching techniques, inadequate physical conditioning, or a poor understanding of the needs and limitations of the participants. Sport psychologists either need to work with scientists from the other sport sciences (such as exercise physiology, biomechanics, and motor learning and development) or master the fundamental knowledge base in these areas themselves.

3. *Avoid the "quick fix."* The field of sport psychology is still paying a heavy price for the "snake oil" salespeople of past years. It's one thing to generalize about the effects of certain techniques on meeting a particular objective. But it's quite another to "know the answer" and "sell" the coach on an unproven "formula" for success. We need to be cautious and to make promises to no one. An applied sport psychologist should have a menu of alternative treatments and strategies that are warranted in a given situation. No single approach works for every athlete or in all situations. As one character used to say each week on the television police program *Hill Street Blues*, "Be careful out there."

4. *Do not take public credit for player or team success.* Coaches and athletes must take center stage when it comes to their success, and if a sport psychologist had a role with that success, this must not become public knowledge. Any publicity surrounding the "bag of tricks" that sport psychologists bring to the coach or athlete might diminish the public's proper recognition of and respect for that performer. The tangible benefits of observing clients improve their mental disposition or use psychological strategies to enhance performance are the consultant's best reward.

5. *Remember that "research" is not a four-letter word.* Some practicing sport psychology consultants and coaches are "turned off" by the word *research*. For the practitioner, it represents an area that is unfamiliar, insecure, and disconnected from providing any benefit to the competitive situation. Nothing can be further from the truth. To encourage the use of research by coaches and sport practitioners, researchers and educators need to do two things. First, more studies are needed that are field-based, have an applied dimension, and that establish stronger links between theory and practice. Second, useful research findings need to be translated into forms accessible to nonresearchers, such as coaches and athletes, most of whom are not familiar with the scholarly jargon found in most research journals. See Martens (1987) for a discussion of this topic that remains relevant today.

6. *Consider the pros and cons of certification.* The Association for the Advancement of Applied Sport Psychology (AAASP) has put considerable time and energy in developing a program that certifies sport psychology consultants, since the organization's creation in 1986 (see the AAASP Web site for details and the application: www.aaasponline.org). The program was formally adopted by AAASP in 1990 (*AAASP Newsletter*, Winter, 1990, pp. 3–8). Some professionals contend that as the field continues to grow and become more diverse in its areas of investigation and practice, a measure of quality control is needed. The easy part is to convene a group of sport psychologists and compose a set of guidelines that dictate the criteria for certification. If a person does not meet the criteria, he or she is not allowed

to practice sport psychology. Scholars, researchers, and practitioners do not agree on the criteria or the need for certification as a sport psychology consultant. This complex, inconclusive issue goes well beyond the purpose of this chapter. There are many pros and cons to certification, not the least of which is gaining agreement among researchers, educators, and practitioners as to what constitutes the competencies to consult. For further discussions on this issue, see Anshel (1992a, 1993), Danish and Hale (1981), Dishman (1983), Harrison and Feltz (1979), Zaickowsky and Perna (1992), and Singer (1993).

7. *"Allow" access of sport psychology literature to the practitioner.* When an academic discipline understandably yearns for acceptance from professional colleagues, there is a tendency to demonstrate academic competence through the publication of sophisticated, esoteric research. This often means testing the efficacy of theories and using complex statistical analyses to answer the research question. Somewhat more problematic is that this struggle for academic identity has resulted in depriving the practitioner, to a large degree, of using the wealth of knowledge that has accumulated in the sport psychology literature. Fortunately, as indicated earlier, new journals are now being published to help solve this problem. One area of future involvement for sport psychologists is to provide more written materials that coaches and athletes find palatable and exciting as a reference for applied sport psychology strategies.

8. *Ensure "hands-on" field experiences and supervision.* The field of sport and exercise psychology would enhance its recognition as an area of unique expertise by ensuring that two criteria are met: (1) that its practitioners (with graduate degrees) experience working with athletic competitors and/or others who engage in physical activity or rehabilitation in their graduate program and (2) that the individual receives supervision by a person qualified—however the university or state defines "qualified"—in sport psychology or health counseling. In a study on assessing the skills of sport psychology supervisors covering 79 sport psychology internship programs worldwide, Andersen et al. (1994) found that 56 percent of 71 supervisors never received supervision of their work with athletes. This figure should improve markedly in coming years, especially if academicians who teach sport psychology want to overcome the perception of many registered psychologists that training in general psychology is sufficient training as a sport psychologist, even without taking a single course in sport psychology.

The Emergence of Exercise and Sports Injury Psychology

Sport psychology is no longer restricted to sport. A new area of research called exercise psychology has emerged in recent years. The addition of a chapter on applied exercise psychology (Chapter 11) is testimony to this fact. Any discussion of the future of sport psychology must recognize the significant expansion of research in the exercise area. Thus, whereas sport psychology concerns the study of psychobehavioral factors related to participating in sport competition, exercise psychology research is usually linked to the study of similar factors related to physical activity and rehabilitation from sports injuries. For this reason, the study of sport psychology usually also includes examining the exercise psychology and rehabilitation psychology literatures. Psychological factors related to physical activity have been recognized by some journal editors and publishers. For example, as of

1988, the *Journal of Sport Psychology* was renamed the *Journal of Sport & Exercise Psychology*. Much of the sport psychology literature in several journals and presented at conferences now includes psychological factors related to exercise and injury rehabilitation.

Jobs for Sport Psychologists and Consultants

Although many students who enter sport psychology graduate programs profess to work with athletes and coaches, these ambitions are more likely to be part-time than full-time employment options. The *real* job market for these individuals is in *fitness, health, rehabilitation,* and the *corporate sector*. Opportunities to work as sport psychologists in non-sport settings will expand. Working in hospitals, sports medicine clinics, fitness (health) clubs, and in business and industry offers a far bigger market. The application of human performance psychology research fits well here, especially if the individual is a licensed counseling or clinical psychologist (Singer 1996).

Final Commentary: A Critique of the Strengths and Concerns in Applied Sport Psychology

In trying to create the proper climate for this section, I am reminded of a 1980s song entitled "The Future's So Bright I Gotta Wear Shades." Despite the many reasons to celebrate the growth and development of this field, certain areas of concern that require considerable attention still remain. In this final section, I'm going to offer a rather candid overview of the field, with particular emphasis on what should be a very optimistic and exciting future. This commentary comes from teaching, practicing, researching, and writing in the field for over 20 years. My perspective reflects employment in the university (as a professor) and private sectors (as a consultant), living in the U.S. and overseas, and my communication and interactions with colleagues at home and abroad. I also want to recognize a superb chapter on the topic of future directions in sport psychology by Williams and Straub (2001).

One fact is apparent: We all have much to learn from each other. The second apparent fact is that no one individual or group of individuals—scholars, educators, or practitioners—has all the answers. No one has a monopoly on the truth. Without researchers, studying both applied and theoretical issues, sport psychology would have no credibility, no basis on which to deliver service effectively. Without educators, the field could not entrust its future to students who provide a legacy and a future of the field. And, without recognizing the importance of practitioners, the efficacy of our research could not be tested in real-life settings, and the field would gain only scant recognition among sports participants.

I will briefly address three key points in this critique. Since each of these areas can consume far more material and scope than is intended in the final section of this book, my purpose here is simply to have readers give some thought to topics that may be provocative and even controversial, requiring much more time and reflection in future discussions. These topics are (1) defining—or redefining—the field of sport psychology; (2) the education and training of sport psychology consultants, and finally, and the most controversial, (3) candidly examining the issues concerning "ownership" of sport psychology education and training, currently disputed by the sport and exercise sciences/physical education versus the field of psychology.

Redefining the Field of Sport Psychology

First, the good news. As reviewed in Chapter 1, the field of sport psychology is evolving in very favorable, exciting directions. Examples include the publication of reputable journals reporting sophisticated scientific research, the availability of more books, representing both college textbook and trade (applied) markets, an increase in the number of undergraduate courses and graduate programs, improved membership rates among sport psychology organizations, increased international links among these organizations, expansion of the field to include recognition of other human performance areas, such as exercise for healthy (e.g., fitness clubs) and unhealthy populations (e.g., cardiopulmonary exercise rehabilitation), sports medicine/injury rehabilitation, and serving corporate clients, and finally, from an applied perspective, more recognition of sport psychology services from sports teams and organizations—elite and nonelite—than ever before. Many of these changes have been fueled primarily by the prolific publication record and marketing efforts of two publishers, Fitness Information Technology (Morgantown, WV; www.fitinfotech.com) and Human Kinetics (Champaign, IL; www.humankinetics.com).

Limitations and areas for future growth remain, however. The English playwright and philosopher, George Bernard Shaw, said, "We grow in relation to the limitations we must overcome." In order to grow, then, it is important to recognize the field's limitations, at least through my perspective.

The Training and Employment of Graduates. The first limitation concerns the area of future training and employment for graduates from sport psychology programs. An expanding job market has not accompanied the increased use of sport psychology services. Full-time employment in sport psychology, counseling athletes and coaches, remains a rare achievement, despite a graduate degree in sport psychology. Part-time consulting opportunities remain the norm, and even those are highly competitive. As an academic and applied discipline, far more emphasis must be placed on expanding expertise to include related areas of human performance, such as consulting in exercise, dance, rehabilitation (medical), and corporate settings. Given the widespread obesity in epidemic in the U.S., clearly there remains much that can be done to motivate individuals to begin and adhere to exercise programs. The use of cognitive strategies that improve exercise performance is another area of intervention. Numerous professionals in private practice work with corporate clients, as illustrated by Dr. Shane Murphy's book, *The Achievement Zone* (1996) or Dr. Jim Loehr's book, *Stress for Success* (1997). However, we need to improve our ability and effort to provide graduate students with the necessary education and training to pursue this area of service. To be trained to work in sport psychology will require student opportunities to complete graduate courses and experience internships in various areas of human performance.

Attention to Individual Differences. The second limitation in our field is our neglect of examining individual differences with respect to race, ethnicity, and culture throughout the sport psychology literature. Fortunately, a plethora of female sport psychology scholars have overcome early limitations in our field concerning research on the female athlete population. More attention in the literature to women in sport has been accompanied by a significant commitment to sport psychology services by female coaches and athletes. Similar attention to examining the African-American athlete, in particular, has been surprisingly scant. I published two research articles in 1990 (reported in Chapter 2) in *The Sport Psychologist* and the *Journal of Sport Behavior* in which I examined differences between Caucasian and African American athletes on their perceptions of experiences competing in college-level sport. There has been a paucity of research on racial differences since that time. Books such as *Black and White: Styles in Conflict* by Thomas Kochman (1981, University of Chicago Press) and *Darwin's Athletes: How Sport Has Damaged Black Americans and Preserved the Myth of Race* by John Hoberman (1997, Mariner Books) give credence to recognizing how racial differences among competitive athletes require heightened understanding and sensitivity among all athletes, coaches, and sports administrators. Because generalizing many research findings to both genders is now viewed as invalid, why do we feel that the factors that affect an athlete's thoughts, emotions, and performance would be consistent across race? Given the high percentage of African American athletes who compete in sport, vastly more study is needed in this area. Cross-cultural comparisons have also been lacking, despite a call for greater research efforts in this area by Duda and Allison (1990).

The Use and Misuse of Psychological Inventories.   A third limitation is the questionable use of inventories used in sport psychology research and practice. In preparation for my address at the 13th Asian Games Scientific Congress (November, 1998), I examined the ways in which inventories were used in sport psychology research, with particular attention to the basis on which researchers were selecting, using, and reporting inventory-generated data. I was surprised to find numerous limitations that need to be addressed in order to improve the generation and selection of research and counseling tools. For example, despite distinct differences in defining personality, dispositions, orientations, personal characteristics, and behavioral tendencies, research articles tend to define and measure these concepts interchangeably (see Chapter 2 for a discussion of this topic). Because personality is stable and far less susceptible to change through interventions, as opposed to orientations and behavioral tendencies, it is important to know what is and what is not being examined and measured in a study.

Another concern was using inventories in sport psychology research that were not intended for sport populations. It is exactly this tendency—making sweeping generalizations about predicting athlete behavior and success based on personality inventories that were generated for nonathletes (with some of these inventories developed for abnormal mental conditions)—that gave our field a bad name in the 1950s and 1960s. Fortunately, sport-related inventories have become more common in recent years, yet this issue remains problematic. There is also the concern of using inventories for diagnostic or clinical purposes that did not receive the required psychometric development. Validating an inventory requires numerous procedures, from defining the construct to be measured, generating the items that will measure the construct, and engaging in multiple attempts at data collection, each attempt followed by sophisticated statistical analyses. Researchers must clarify the purposes for the inventories they use. Is the purpose to create an instrument that measures a construct to diagnose and predict that is intended for samples beyond the immediate study (which requires extensive psychometric scrutiny), or is the inventory's purpose restricted to describing selected characteristics for a particular sample (requiring different statistical procedures)? In addition to reporting research findings correctly, practitioners need to be cautious about the ways in which inventories are used to assess psychological characteristics of clients. What do the inventory's scores represent? While the procedures for inventory development go far beyond the scope of this book, we need to be cautious about the purposes and interpretations of the inventories we use to report our research findings. Readers may consult a superb chapter on the topic of inventory use in sport psychology by Gauvin et al. (1993).

Professional Conferences.　Finally, a fourth limitation concerns the content of the field's most prestigious and well-attended conference, the annual conference of the Association for the Advancement of Applied Sport Psychology. With all due respect to the extraordinary commitment in time and energy to AAASP conference program staff, conference content needs a better balance between presentations on elite athletes and nonelite athletes, particularly youth sport participants. There is a particular dearth of content on psychology of exercise, sports injury, and rehabilitation. Perhaps the exercise and injury psychology researchers and practitioners are reporting their work at other conferences. However, sport psychology students need far more exposure to areas in which they are more likely to find jobs (e.g., health, fitness, and rehabilitation settings), but often lack expertise.

The Education and Training of Sport Psychology Consultants

There is both "good" news and "bad" news about the education and training in sport psychology. On a positive note, more undergraduate and graduate courses are being offered in sport psychology than ever. I applaud the many programs that now include additional areas of needed mastery such as counseling, psychological testing, exercise and rehabilitation/health psychology, field supervision, and internships that prepare students to apply their knowledge. But sport psychology training at the graduate level appears to be lacking content from the exercise sciences, beyond psychology. The sport psychology consultant would markedly benefit from understanding the literature in sport pedagogy, exercise physiology and fitness, motor behavior/learning, and athletic injuries. I have consulted with athletes and coaches on numerous occasions in which knowledge from each of these areas was applied. There also remains a need to establish joint programs between departments in psychology and exercise and sport sciences. There is a lack of consistency, however, among graduate educational and applied programs from various universities. Fortunately, AAASP is now working to establish standards for graduate programs in sport psychology. One particular area of concern, addressed shortly, is that individuals may legally refer to themselves as sport psychologists, yet have limited formal training and education in sport psychology.

Mentoring.　Mentoring—or rather, the absence or poor quality of mentoring—continues to be a problem in the field. The word "mentor" is formally defined in Webster's dictionary as "a wise and trusted teacher or guide." Hardy (1994) defines mentoring as the complex process by which a trusted and experienced individual takes an interest in the personal and professional development of a less experienced, often younger individual. Academic mentoring, according to Bloom (2002), occurs when a faculty member willingly invests time in a student's personal and professional growth and development, when a trusting relationship evolves, when needs and interest are fulfilled, and when imitation of behavior takes place.

With more and more pressure being applied to faculty to write grants, conduct and publish their research, teach (sometimes three to four courses per semester), and supervise graduate students, perhaps it's understandable—though not excusable—that the mentoring process has not received the attention and energy it deserves. We fail to mentor our graduate students at our peril.

There are four categories of mentoring, formal and informal, general and specific. *Formal mentoring* is time-limited, focused on particular outcomes, and less emotionally intense. *Informal mentoring* consists of the faculty member and students sharing their interests, needs, and values. *General mentoring* consists of providing education and information, with developing scholarship, helping students to develop a vision, a mission, and an action plan, to motivate, encourage, and build confidence, and to develop trust. *Specific mentoring* reflects the specific skills needed to succeed in an academic setting (e.g., writing and oral presentation skills, understanding the research process, providing feedback on academic performance, providing sources for career options, providing references).

Faculty in sport psychology should act in a manner that is consistent with their deepest values and beliefs. Failing to take the time and effort necessary to mentor graduate students who have been assigned to the faculty member, or whose supervision faculty have agreed to, shows disrespect for the student's time, compromises the student's financial investment in his or her education, and depletes the field of future resources for its growth and development. As Hardy (1994) correctly says, "If we fail to provide effective mentoring to our talented students, they are likely to abandon their dream, thereby impeding the constructive development of our field" (p. 197). There is a Chinese proverb that says: "The only thing we can take with us when we die is what we give away when we live."

One inventive approach to the mentoring process was decribed in a book by Dr. Gary Brannigan, *The Sport Scientists: Research Adventures* (see references). In it, he asked selected researchers in sport and exercise psychology to write personal accounts of their careers, focusing on the factors that ignited their research interests and "gave life" to their strong work ethic in helping to develop the field. The value of this book to graduate students and professional colleagues is to provide insight into the level of commitment, effort, and prolonged self-motivation that is needed to "light the fire inside" and to succeed in achieving one's goals. As Hardy (1994) concluded, "The most effective mentoring is about the development, nurturing, and sustainment of lifelong relationships. It is only within the context of relationships that the fundamental human needs of security and significance can be met. In sum, mentoring is about developing roots as well as wings through the sharing of oneself" (p. 202).

"Ownership" of Sport Psychology: The Sport and Exercise Sciences or Psychology?

This serious and contentious issue concerning the academic discipline that governs education, training, and practice of sport psychology is not about to go away. Without presenting this issue as combative, there is a clear political and philosophical "battle" for territory and ownership in representing sport psychology. Arguments in favor of one field having a greater identification with sport psychology over another field goes beyond the scope of this section. There are two fields of study, or academic disciplines, that have valid claims to maintaining a strong influence on the development of sport psychology. One area is sport and exercise science, also referred to as departments entitled physical education, health and human performance, kinesiology, and human movement. The second discipline is psychology.

Neither field is going to "own" or be the sole representative of sport psychology. There is much to be said for the fact that both disciplines bring to the field, and to students, complementary needs and skills. My attempt at examining how each discipline contributes to the growth and development of sport and exercise psychology is not intended to polarize the field. I have just the opposite intention—to recognize the importance of bringing together both disciplines in an effort to provide the optimal quality of education, research, and practice of our field.

In Favor of Sport and Exercise Sciences. A perusal of the *Directory of Graduate Programs in Applied Sport Psychology* (2002, 6th ed., Fitness Information Technology Publishers) clearly indicates that sport and exercise science (also referred to as departments of physical education, kinesiology, human movement, or health and human performance) is the primary area from which sport psychology programs are offered. It is the rare psychology department that includes a course or specialization in sport psychology. This is understandable, given the strict requirements placed on psychology departments in order to have a program approved by the American Psychological Association (APA). In most states, psychologists can be licensed only if they graduate with a Ph.D. from an APA-approved program. Course requirements and many hours of field supervision do not easily allow graduate students to complete additional courses, such as sport psychology. Consequently, it is the graduate students from an exercise and sport science background who register for courses in sport and exercise psychology and complete internships and practicum related to human performance psychology (sport, exercise, rehabilitation, dance, corporate). It is also students from these departments who train to conduct research in sport and exercise psychology when writing their master's theses or doctoral dissertations. From a political perspective, perhaps it is not surprising that 14 of the 17 presidents of AAASP (I am including the president-elect for 2003 at this writing) have their doctorate from sport science-related areas, with the remaining three former presidents from the field of psychology. Moreover, every editor of the scientific journals in sport psychology—the *Journal of Sport & Exercise Psychology, The Sport Psychologist,* the *Journal of Applied Sport Psychology,* and the *International Journal of Sport Psychology*—have doctoral degrees from the sport and exercise sciences rather than psychology. The exception to this tendency is the current editors of the *Journal of Sport Behavior,* who, at this writing, are professors in a department of psychology.

Further testimony to the origins of sport psychology comes from the sport psychology literature, which acknowledges the "father" of sport psychology as Dr. Coleman Griffith, a professor of physical education. The point here is that sport and exercise science/physical education educators and researchers appear to have given birth to the field. Perhaps it is not surprising, then, that AAASP has created and maintained the only certification program in applied sport psychology, although Division 47 (Exercise and Sport Psychology) within the American Psychological Association is currently developing its own set of criteria for recognition as a sport psychologist for licensed psychologists.

Finally, as discussed in Chapter 1, AAASP has recognized the importance of providing appropriate interventions based on the development and mastery of requisite skills and knowledge. While the field is embroiled in an ongoing debate about current certification content (see Chapter 1 for a brief overview on this topic), members of the sport and exercise science community contend that the practice of sport psychology warrants a level of sophistication that goes beyond traditional training in psychology. They are right.

In Favor of Psychology. The three main strengths of the field of psychology linked to sport psychology include the legal title of "psychologist," the status of licensure that allows clinicians/counselors/therapists to receive third-party payments (i.e., from the client's health insurance), and, of course, the training in counseling or clinical psychology that provides experience in administering and interpreting psychological tests that are available only to licensed psychologists and conducting various forms of psychotherapy on their athlete-clients.

The student's decision to seek graduate training in sport psychology should be primarily determined by professional aspirations. If the student plans on an academic career, then the sport and exercise sciences are more likely to have courses in sport psychology, and therefore, require a professor to teach and supervise graduate students in this area. If, however, private practice is the student's goal, then he or she should follow the road for licensure as a psychologist. Paid consultancies in sport psychology without licensure are difficult to find because a licensed psychologist is eligible to collect third-party payments from health insurance. This means two things. First, the client can be financially supported, perhaps paying only a fraction of the psychologist's fee. Second, licensure means that the psychologist can be covered by the organization's insurance policy, a requirement to guard against a possible lawsuit. Sport psychology consultants who are not licensed psychologists can gain employment if paid out-of-pocket by clients or by organizations for which the consultant is not—repeat, not—engaging in counseling or any form of psychotherapy. The consultant's content is restricted to performance enhancement techniques.

And then there is the small matter of who "owns" the title of *sport psychologist*. This issue is frustrating for those in academic circles who have spent their entire careers in sport psychology, yet may not legally use the title "sport psychologist" because the title *psychologist* is legally protected by State Boards of Licensed Psychologists. Using the title "psychologist"—sport, clinical, or anything else—requires licensure from the state board, meaning a Ph.D. from an APA-approved program in psychology and passing three national examinations: an oral exam, and two written exams, Examination for the Professional Practice of Psychology (EPPP) and the jurisprudence exam concerned with ethics and the law. Each state has its own set of rules and its own licensure board that arbitrates who may become or remain licensed, so there are exceptions to these criteria, including a master's-degree-level certification program in psychology that will also allow for third-party payments. However, only earning a doctoral degree will allow use of the title "psychologist," including sport psychologist. Some sport science professionals are not concerned about titles because, they say, the title "psychologist" is threatening for many athletes and coaches. Therefore, it is best to avoid that title, anyway. Alternative titles include mental skills coach, performance coach/consultant, or performance counselor.

To be fair, psychologists make a valuable contribution to sport psychology by their sophisticated published research describing clinical issues among competitive athletes, individuals who often require psychological intervention due to deep-rooted issues that cannot be addressed effectively by applying mental skills (just think of a few professional athletes who are in clear need of a psychologist, according to media reports) and through their support and collaboration with sport and exercise science departments in the education and training of sport psychology graduate students.

On the other hand, however, the field is replete with psychologists who have never taken a course in sport psychology, have not read and mastered the literature, and do not have a sport background (they are nonathletes), yet lay claim to the title of, and market themselves as a, sport psychologist. Is this unethical, or a misrepresentation? Depends who you ask. Our training and experience often dictate what we do and how we do it. Thus, trained psychologists will rely on their clinical training in representing the field, and sport psychology consultants with a sport science background will rely on mental skills training. What is apparent, however, is that many individuals, primarily academics, in the sport sciences perceive psychologists as intrusive and undertrained in sport psychology, and hence, a threat to the integrity of the field. It is an area of contention that is still being debated by scholars, writers, and practitioners. Who, then, "owns" sport psychology? In a capitalistic, open market society, it is the individual who delivers the most effective, highest quality product.

To overcome the initial mistrust or misunderstanding by many athletes of sport psychology interventions, I tend to begin my sport psychology seminars with this question: "How many people here are convinced that they are performing at their capacity and are as good as they will ever get? How many of you really feel that your performance can't get better?" In over 16 years of asking this question, no one has ever raised a hand. "Okay," I continue, "then we can agree that everyone in this room feels capable of performing at better than the present level, right?" "The purpose of sport psychology," I explain, "is to bring you from your present level of functioning to coming closer to what you are capable of doing." Now at least there's an improved chance my audience wants to hear what I have to say. Although researchers have known for many years that our capacity to perform motor skills is genetically fixed, "the purpose of sport psychology," I tell them, "is to come closer to playing up to your capability."

I want to end this section—and the book—on a very upbeat note. It has been an honor for me to be associated with such dedicated, committed colleagues whose vision of the future of applied sport psychology is matched in magnitude only by that of their time and energy. The result has been unparalleled growth and recognition in an area of scholarship and application that has changed the lives of many people, from youth sports players to those at the professional and Olympic levels of competition. The emergence of related areas of study and practice in other areas of human performance (e.g., exercise, sports medicine, rehabilitation, obesity and weight control, corporate/work performance, the arts) is testimony to the extent to which sport psychology has gained recognition, credibility, and sophistication over the years. This book is intended to be a celebration of this rewarding field, one in which the vast network of researchers, educators, and practitioners can come together and deliver an array of services that will ultimately improve the lives of others. To repeat the Chinese proverb stated earlier, "The only thing we take with us when we die is what we give away when we live." Here's to giving all students, practitioners, educators, and researchers every available opportunity to contribute to the growth and prosperity of sport psychology.

Research and Measurement in Sport Psychology

How would you like to be defended in court by a lawyer who hasn't read any professional literature since law school and, therefore, is unaware of the latest legal decisions and laws that could help your case? If you had to have surgery, would you mind being operated on by a surgeon who hadn't read about the latest medical tests and surgical techniques? In sport, how many coaches are using techniques that have been around for decades (no doubt implemented by their own coaches), yet have proven to be ineffective by scientific studies (and often by the team's poor record)? And how many athletes are not aware of or refuse to use mental strategies that have been shown in the literature to improve performance measurably? In many professions, refusing to read professional literature might result in poor evaluations of performance at best and, at worst, a lawsuit, job termination, or revocation of a license to continue practicing. Individuals who desire to become and remain effective in what they do, be it professional or amateur activities, obtain and maintain one common habit—they read and learn.

To their credit, professional coaches in sport are typically avid readers of the coaching literature. Several publications written for practitioners have served the noble purpose of sharing information about new strategies, equipment, and other professional issues of mutual interest.

In recent years, sport psychology consultants have become increasingly involved in applying the literature to athletes. The purpose of this appendix is to help the student of sport psychology—the athlete, prospective coach, or future scholar—become familiar and comfortable with the voluminous amount of resource material that exists in sport psychology journals. Ultimately, readers should be able to apply the findings of studies to their benefit as successful sport participants. It is also hoped that the basis for using certain approaches to coaching or competing will be scrutinized and either voided or validated by sport scientists. In sport, as in all competitive situations, knowledge is power.

Myths and Realities

An important reason to become familiar with the research literature in sport psychology is to know the difference between fact and fiction, myth and reality, truth and rumor. Some sport psychology consultants contend that relatively little coaching behavior is based on research. Instead, coaches tend to repeat the actions of other, relatively successful coaches through observations, seminars, published articles, discussions, and from their own experiences as athletes. When certain actions and beliefs are based on "what everybody is doing" or "the way it's always been done," quite often factual information gives way to myth. Here are a few examples of myths in sport that have been dispelled by research.

Myth: Punishment is the best way to discipline, teach, and motivate athletes.

Reality: Athletes frequently become intimidated, disloyal, angry, and demotivated by disciplinary actions such as running laps (associating exercise with punishment results in a dislike for all forms of exercise), being ridiculed in front of teammates (they'll never forgive a coach for embarrassing them), and increasing the time and intensity of practice (often the players need time off away from the sport arena).

Myth: Athletes need an arousing pregame talk to prepare them for competition.

Reality: Athletes differ as to their optimal pregame arousal. Some players, particularly in certain positions and in particular sports, want and need to relax before the contest and not get "psyched up."

Myth: Players who prefer to be alone or not to maintain strong group affiliation are not good "team players." Teammates who do not socialize outside the sport arena or do not like each other on a personal basis cause poor team cohesion and a lack of team success.

Reality: In fact, researchers have found relatively little relationship between team success and *social* team cohesion; a team can win without having teammates like one another or affiliate off the field or court. *Task* team cohesion is more important for team success.

Quantitative Research

Much can be learned from reading sport psychology research. Many often-used but ineffective coaching strategies would go by the wayside if coaches were taught the skills to read research and were exposed to the proper literature. Using a question-and-answer format, let's look more closely at quantitative sport research. Then we will examine qualitative research techniques in sport psychology.

Q. What exactly is research?

A. Research is a systematic, planned way of solving problems (e.g., Will this mental technique increase self-confidence and sport performance?), testing theories and models (e.g., the validity of Bandura's self-efficacy theory, that is, an individual's conviction that he or she is capable of producing a desired outcome in a given sport or sport situation), and explaining or predicting behavior (e.g., the effect of trait anxiety, a disposition to be anxious, on the athlete's emotions in tense situations). Taking the anxiety example further, researchers might determine that participants tend to get uptight under certain circumstances before or during competition. Perhaps through a player's score on a certain psychological inventory a coach can actually predict the player's state of anxiety under tense conditions based on measuring the athletes' trait anxiety, that is their disposition to feel anxious. Some players, after all, can cope better under pressure than others.

Q. How does one go about conducting research?

A. Researchers need to first find a problem that needs further study, a research question that needs answering. Research, by definition, consists of finding answers to problems.

Q. Where are such problems found?

A. Usually in the professional literature. That's why researchers must be avid readers. It's also true that in some instances a research idea stems from practical experience. For example, areas such as the "runner's high," the apparent benefits of exercising to music, and the high dropout rate in youth sports received extensive research attention because of everyday experiences. But most of the time, research actually creates the need for further investigations, delving deeper into an area or trying to answer additional questions that need examination. Authors of studies almost always suggest exactly what direction these future studies should take toward the end of a research article. The ideas are in the journals. That's why it's important for students of sport psychology, including coaches who seek answers to valid questions, to read research articles.

Q. Are we now ready to conduct a study?

A. Not quite yet. First, a research study needs a purpose and a direction. Remember, research is defined as an exercise in problem solving and not a matter of gathering information. The study's direction is formed by a published model or a theoretical framework. Models and theories describe and predict behavior. Therefore, examining a phenomenon within the confines of a model or a theory allows researchers to predict or generalize the results of their study to other populations (athletes or teams). Without the ability to predict, investigators cannot know if they have come closer to "solving" their research problem. To make a prediction, you need a hypothesis.

Researchers create testable hypotheses that indicate *predictions* of the study's results. The hypotheses can be *directional* (e.g., "It was predicted in this study that subjects who were exposed to relaxation procedures would perform better under tense competitive conditions than persons who did not experience this treatment,") or *null* (e.g., "No significant difference between the groups was predicted").

Q. When do you collect performance scores?

A. Hold on, we're getting there! After making their hypotheses (which are always made prior to a study), researchers must be sure that all relevant terms have been defined so that the results can be generalizable to other studies and subjects in which the same problem has been examined. For example, terms such as *stress, anxiety* (both state and trait), *fear,* and *arousal* have been used interchangeably in the literature. This is not such a good idea. Imagine if a researcher concluded that a certain treatment had a particular effect on state anxiety when, in fact, the test used to determine anxiety actually measured arousal? Or what if an inventory that measures trait anxiety (a stable, unchanging personality disposition) was used to measure state anxiety (a feeling that changes under various conditions)? And what is the difference between imagery and mental practice? Some scientists recognize no difference, while for others it's night and day. In fact, mental practice and imagery have been defined and used differently in the recent literature.

Q.   What happens next?

A.   Before data are collected, two additional steps are necessary: The subjects and instrumentation to measure performance must be selected. *Participants* are obtained based on the aim of the study. If a researcher is comparing high- versus low-skilled basketball players, for example, then obviously participants must have or not have extensive competitive playing experience. But quite often, individuals who have had no experience with the research task are preferred. In this way, no bias exists as to the participant's previous experience, which could mask the effects of the treatment.

With respect to *instrumentation*, or equipment, it is very important that the materials or equipment in the study meet two standards: They must be valid, that is, measure what they are supposed to measure and they must be reliable (consistent). For example, if a researcher wants to measure *state* anxiety, does the paper-and-pencil inventory assess it rather than *trait* anxiety or any other mental state? Is the measure consistent?

After research participants and instrumentation are ready to go, the procedures must be planned. Researchers must be sure to standardize the actual data-collection phase so that factors such as noise, lights, instructions, and other procedures faced by all participants in the study are the same. Often researchers complete what is called a *pilot study* that serves to "iron out the kinks" before data for the actual study are collected.

Q.   What happens after the data are collected?

A.   First of all, researchers must be sure, at least in studies in which behavior, feelings, or emotions are being measured, that there are enough participants—*at least* 10 per group are commonly recommended for most experimental investigations, but the more the better. Just a few participants will not be enough for valid (the test or instrument measuring what it's supposed to measure) and reliable (consistent) performance measures. Statisticians strongly recommend computing a power analysis to determine the proper sample size.

After the data are collected, the appropriate statistics are used to determine whether the treatment under investigation was effective or that the research question was answered. Were the scores for each group significantly different? The types and uses of these statistics differ based on many factors, some of which include (1) the type of data being collected (e.g., accuracy, speed of movement, observations), (2) the best way to answer the research question and each hypothesis (prediction), and (3) the number of subjects in each group.

After the data have been analyzed, the results are compared to each hypothesis. Hypotheses are either supported, partially supported, or rejected, and the researcher draws conclusions about the effect of the treatment on performance. Why, for instance, were these results different from those in past studies? How do the present data support or contradict previous studies? What has been learned from this study that can be applied in future research? Perhaps most important to the coach or athlete, how can the study be used in coaching or sport performance, if at all? What does the author view as an important direction for future research in this area? All of these questions can be answered in the last section, the discussion, of the research paper.

Q. Who are researchers?

A. Typically, persons who conduct research are professors in a university, graduate students who are required to demonstrate research skills as partial fulfillment of a master's or doctorate degree, and sometimes teachers or coaches who want to find the answer to problems they currently face in their jobs. Business and industry also hire scientists to improve a product or create a new one.

Q. I'm convinced that reading sport psychology research is important, but how difficult is it to understand? I mean, do I have to be a professor to read and interpret what a sport scientist examines? If I were a coach or an athlete, I'd want to be able to use this information.

A. You're touching upon a very important issue that has concerned physical educators, sport psychology consultants, and coaches. One reason coaches are not using more of the sport psychology literature in their practice is because they have not been trained to read scientific studies. This is no fault of their own. Further, researchers tend to write in a style that is not compatible with the nonscientist. Research journals are not magazines. It is the rare person who can understand the research literature without a university course in research methods and a basic knowledge of statistics. There is little question that a void exists in the professional sport literature for the person who wants to apply scientific sport studies in a competitive athletic environment. Some professional publications exist to partially bridge this void (e.g., the *Journal of Physical Education, Recreation, and Dance* [USA]; *Sports Coach* [Australia]; and various sport-specific magazines). Perhaps the most widely read applied journal in sport psychology that serves the primary purpose of bridging theory to practice through articles on applied research and professional practice is *The Sport Psychologist* (available from Human Kinetics, Champaign, Illinois, USA).

Any quality research article is going to include a certain style of writing, use of terms, and a format that is acceptable to the scientific community so that it is viewed as suitable for publication. In fact, to ensure accuracy of its content, such publications are *refereed*. This means that at least two or three respected scholars, usually members of the journal's editorial board, review a paper when it is submitted for consideration as a publication and judge it as either (1) acceptable for publication (i.e., it's accurate, professionally written, and contributes valid information to the professional literature), (2) acceptable for publication but only after the author has made certain changes in the manuscript, or (3) rejected for publication in the particular journal to which it was sent for reasons that the editor explains in writing to the author.

Qualitative Research

Not all research efforts consist of collecting data on athletes using numerical values to evaluate their attitudes, emotions, and performance—this method is called *quantitative research*; it was described in the preceding section. Sometimes the researcher wants to ask a group of athletes questions about their experiences that are best reported more openly and directly—straight from the athlete's mouth, in a manner of speaking—rather than from items on a psychological inventory or from performance measures. *Qualitative research* is based on three types of data collection: in-depth (open-ended interviews in which the subject speaks at length about a given topic), direct observation (detailed descriptions of people's activities, behaviors, actions, and interactions), and written documents (excerpts, quotations, or entire passages from records, correspondence, publications, personal diaries, and open-ended written responses to questionnaires). The most common form of data in published sport psychology research has been the open-ended interview, and the type of data analysis most often used has been inductive or deductive content analysis.

For example, Scanlan et al. (1991) wanted to identify the sources of stress among former elite figure skaters, an understandably small sample ($n = 26$), using oral interviews. The interviews, consisting of open-ended and follow-up questions, provided an in-depth understanding of the athletes' sources of stress. Inductive content analysis was used to categorize subjects' responses into common raw data themes and then higher order themes. Examples of raw data themes were "questioning if I am prepared/ready," "worrying about performing poorly," and "not wanting to let others down if performing poorly." These themes were then classified according to the higher order theme "experiencing competition worries," which in turn resulted in the source of stress "negative aspects of competition." Other sources of stress in their study were "negative significant-other relationships," "demands or costs of skating," "personal struggles," and "traumatic experiences."

In another study, Anshel (1991a) used deductive content analysis to determine the causes of athletes' drug use. Prior to interviewing athletes, Anshel divided drug use into performance-enhancing and mind-altering types, and then he further divided these categories, based on his review of the literature, into the following subcategories: physical ("steroids will help me bulk up"), psychological/emotional ("I feel on top of the world by using them"), and social ("all the pros do it and it doesn't hurt them"). The subjects' responses were then assigned to one of these predetermined categories. Responses from 126 male and female athletes representing nine sports indicated, perhaps not surprisingly, that the reasons for using performance-enhancing drugs (e.g., "to be competitive," "to increase strength," "to reduce pain") differed from the reasons for using recreational drugs (e.g., "to overcome boredom," "to cope with stress," "to have fun"). More insightful, however, were the psychological, emotional, and social explanations athletes gave for drug use in sport. Examples for taking steroids included fear of failure ("I'll be at a disadvantage"), building self-confidence ("I feel on top of the world"), meeting the expectations of others ("The coach expects me to . . ."), and most disturbingly, what psychologists call "the Superman Complex" ("I'm strong and healthy; steroids won't hurt me"). Recreational drug use was attributed to boredom ("It's boring doing the same thing over and over"), coping with stress off the field ("I'm trying to get my mind off of . . . "), peer pressure ("Everyone has drugs at team parties"), and experimentation ("I just wanted to try it"). What is apparent from the results of this study is that both performance-enhancing and recreational drugs are ingested by athletes for various reasons. If coaches are serious about reducing drug use on their team, then interventions should address these explanations.

Jackson (1995) reports several advantages of using qualitative research. First, rather than following a straightforward "a-to-z" sequence of classic experimental research, the researcher has considerable flexibility and decision-making power based on the study's purpose, focus, and research question(s). Second, it offers a depth and richness of findings and the potential to understand individual experiences. Qualitative research also identifies individual differences and examines between-case consistencies. For example, Gould et al. (1992) investigated the emotions and thoughts before and during the match of elite (U.S. Olympic) wrestlers that separated their "winning," highly successful performances from "losing," very unsuccessful performances. The researchers' extensive interviews reveal that high-quality performance is accompanied by extensive mental preparation plans and routines, high confidence, optimal focus on relevant tasks, and optimal arousal. Feelings before unsuccessful matches are opposite to these findings. This type of information, from a unique and relatively small sample of elite athletes about their thoughts and actions before and during competition, would have been difficult to obtain using traditional statistical (quantitative) techniques, which require a much larger sample size and would have failed to answer the research questions. As Jackson (1995) concludes, "qualitative research may be the method of choice when the interest is in understanding subjective experience, when the individual matters, when depth and richness of data is a priority, and when understanding the total picture counts" (p. 590). There are several excellent books on steps for conducting qualitative research. *Qualitative Evaluation and Research Methods* (3rd ed.) by M. Q. Patton (2002, Sage Publishers) has been cited frequently in sport psychology research.

Reading Sport Psychology Research

The purpose of this section is to take you through a typical research article in a journal. It's important to know that not all articles are research based. Some include a discussion or debate of the issues in the sport psychology literature. Other articles might deal with development or testing of a model that explains or predicts a phenomenon in sport or might examine the effect of an intervention technique that can influence an athlete's emotions and enhance sport performance. Research articles in psychology journals follow the writing style recommended by the *Publication Manual of the American Psychological Association* (5th ed., 2001), published by the APA, Washington, D.C.

Introduction

This section of a journal article (1) makes the topic meaningful to the reader, (2) describes the basis or purpose for which the study was conducted (the point of the study), (3) defines important terms so that the reader is clear about the issues under investigation, (4) briefly reviews previous literature (mostly research based) to provide the reader with a history of the issue under investigation, and (5) usually, depending on the research design, offers predictions (hypotheses) about the outcome of the study. Let's analyze the content from the introduction of a study that appeared in the *Journal of Sport Psychology* (1982, pp. 354–363) written by Brown, Morrow, and Livingston and titled "Self-Concept Changes in Women as a Result of Training."

1. *To attach meaningfulness.* "Although case study and self-report accounts of changes in psychological variables as a result of involvement in physical conditioning programs exist, definitive quantification of these changes is generally lacking."

   Translation: Participants of exercise claim to experience changes in one or more psychological factors believed to be the result of the physical activity. However, these changes have rarely been scientifically measured and documented.

2. *The basis and purpose of the study.* "Self-concept is a personality variable that has begun to receive considerable attention in the literature. These studies illustrate the fact that varied results have been obtained on self-concept changes associated with physical training. . . . The purpose of the present investigation, then, was to determine if self-concept changes in college-age females occur as a result of involvement in a 14-week physical conditioning program."

Translation: The topic of self-concept has recently become relatively popular. But no one knows for sure how or if physical training affects a person's self-concept. However, what is known is that personality characteristics such as self-concept are rarely alterable. If, in fact, self-concept can be changed (i.e., improved) due to an exercise program, this would be a very important finding. So the reason behind this study was to see if such a change was possible.

3. *Defining terms.* Although Brown et al. did not define any terms in their introduction, they did define a few factors that they used to measure changes in the subjects' fitness level. For example, "aerobic capacity as measured by the time to complete a 1.5 mile run, and . . . body composition characteristics as determined from skinfold measurements." Also, the authors justified the use of the instrument to assess self-concept: "the [Tennessee Self-Concept Scale] is among the better measures combining group discrimination with self-concept information."

4. *Brief review of literature.* The authors cite numerous studies and quote researchers to support the validity and need for their study. Why, for example, would they attempt to change the relatively stable personality trait of self-concept? Because while Kostrubala (1976) identifies the fact that psychologists are using training programs as therapy for some of their patients, Browman (1981) suggests that "personality and mood are essentially independent of exercise and fitness alone except in borderline normals" (p. 355).

Translation: Exercise can change some components of personality in the normal population. The authors go on to cite other research articles in which changes in self-concept as a result of physical training were sometimes found using the Tennessee instrument.

5. *Predictions.* Based on the findings of earlier research, what does the investigator expect to result from the study? A hypothesis can be one of two types, *directional* (also called a research hypothesis) and *null.* The directional (research) hypothesis says that there will be a significant difference, or relationship, between groups, conditions, or characteristics. The null hypothesis predicts no differences or a very low (nonsignificant) relationship between groups; any observed difference or relationship is due to coincidence or measurement error rather than the treatment.

Brown and her colleagues hypothesized in their study "that the completion of the conditioning program will be a significant event for participants, and that the significance will be related to the physiological changes that occur during the program."

Translation: Exercise participants will consider finishing the 14-week program a major accomplishment, and they will both feel better and demonstrate marked improvements on various fitness measures. What about predicted changes in self-concept? The authors say, essentially, that self-concept will improve, but only in the area related to these physiological changes. In other words, because there are different dimensions of self-concept, only the selected dimension most related to the treatment, in this case, changes in physiological characteristics, would be favorably affected by the program. Thus, they hypothesize "that significant differences will occur in . . . [physical self-concept but not social, knowledge, academic, or sport self-concept] as a result of completion of the [exercise] program."

The hypotheses of a study are very important because they help to define the research problem. How would researchers know if their treatment was effective if they could not compare their results with an educated guess (which is based on past literature) as to the likely or predicted outcome? And since hypotheses are often based on the findings of similar past research, it is important to compare the present results with those of other studies in the long-term attempt to answer, or at least better understand, the research problem.

Method

Now that the required background information has been presented, it's time to inform the reader how the present study was conducted. The method section should be detailed to the extent that the reader could reproduce the same experiment. The detail also allows readers to determine (1) if the manner in which the study was carried out was valid, which, in turn, may help explain the partial causes of the experiment's results, and (2) to whom the results can be generalized (e.g., only males or females, only with certain types of tasks, restricted to particular situations, and so on). The method section usually, but not always, consists of three sections: a description of the subjects, the equipment or materials used in the study, and the procedures.

Participants.   Participants in the study must be described in order to generalize the results. How many participants were there and what was their age range? How were they selected? Were they competitive athletes? What skill level? Volunteers? Required to participate? How many males and females participated, and what geographic location were they from? If a study is to be reproduced at some future time or the findings applied to other populations, the writer must describe in detail the participants' characteristics and *why* they were selected for this study.

Equipment and Materials.   The objective of this section is to tell the reader about the devices used to record performance. If thoughts, feelings, or emotions were obtained, which inventories were used? If the writer developed his or her own inventory for this study, then all the steps for constructing and validating the inventory must be reported. On what equipment did the participants perform? Was the equipment obtained from a commercial establishment? If so, usually only the firm's name and model number is written. Otherwise, the author describes the equipment's dimensions so that a reader could reconstruct the equipment to carry out a future, similar study. Reliability and validity measures of all inventories should also be reported.

Procedures.   As indicated earlier, this section includes a step-by-step description of the participants' assignment to different groups or treatments, and how the data were obtained. In this section, all aspects of the procedures are written out in case the reader would like to attempt a similar experiment.

After the method section, some studies include a section on data analysis, research design, or both. Usually this is done to (1) clarify the procedures, (2) transform (preanalyze) data into some other form for further statistical analysis that will eventually answer the research question, or (3) explain the purpose of using various sophisticated statistical procedures.

Results

After the data were collected (described in the procedures section), how were they analyzed? What were the statistical methods used and what was found? Did the treatment work? Were differences or relationships between groups statistically significant? For the person who lacks an enriched background in research, the sections on data analysis and results may be difficult to follow. A significant amount of technical jargon is often employed in these sections. Some educators object to the extensive use of specialized jargon on the grounds that such language denies nonspecialists access to research findings, but researchers often counter that the use of specialized language is necessary for precision of meaning and for effective communication between researchers in the same field. Either way, the language may pose a challenge for the uninitiated. Quite candidly, the nonresearcher or untrained reader could ignore the results section without losing the meaning and application of the study and instead focus on the discussion section where the results are summarized and explained. It would be fair to say that understanding a results section requires considerable training in statistics. The *true* audience of results sections is other academics, or perhaps some graduate students who want to gain expertise in this area. Scientists find the results section important for interpreting and understanding the treatment's outcome. In fact, occasionally an informed reader will disagree with the type of analysis that was used and replicate the study using different procedures and/or a different statistical analysis. For the undergraduate student, athlete, or practitioner, however, the results section is simply unnecessary to read.

One key issue that needs clarification before leaving the results section is understanding two very important words when reading a research article. The words are *significant difference*. If a certain treatment or condition affected the subjects' scores within each group or treatment consistently, then group differences should be sufficient to be "significant." In behavioral research, it is believed that *significant findings* means being able to predict the effect of some treatment or condition at least 95 percent of the time. So the probability that differences between groups will not be due to the treatment or condition and will instead be due to chance cannot be predicted to occur more often than 5 times out of 100; the differences between groups are then said to be consistent, or reliable, due to the treatment. This conclusion is represented in the literature by the term "$p < .05$" (representing 95 percent accuracy). The term "$p > .05$" means that the probability of an outcome occurring by chance and *not* because of the treatment will occur more often than 5 times out of 100 (no significant difference).

How does the researcher know whether the group averages are statistically different? First, the proper analysis is computed and reported—such as a t (a comparison between two group averages) or F value (comparing more than two group averages). This value is then compared to a number on a chart called the *critical value*. If the final analysis score—a t or F value, for example—is equal to or greater than the critical value, the researcher concludes that group averages were "adequately" apart; in other words, the groups were significantly different (as in the case of t or F value). By the way, there is no such thing as "almost" or "a little" significant, although researchers have occasionally referred to their results as "highly significant" or "approaching significance." Still, most statisticians contend that a statistical test has either reached the level of significance or it has not, that it supports or fails to support the study's hypothesis (or hypotheses).

As indicated earlier, most research articles—in sport psychology and other disciplines—are written for other researchers rather than for the untrained reader (athletes and coaches, for instance). This is understandable given the need for academicians to communicate with one another using widespread, acceptable scientific terms. After all, researchers contend, here and elsewhere, that sport psychology is a reputable area of scientific inquiry. On the other hand, the individuals who are in a position to apply this literature are unable to do so because they do not understand it. This conflict in the field is the primary reason for writing this book. Still, a coach or any untrained reader of research can understand and apply the findings of some investigations. One way to be familiar with the scientific literature is to become acquainted with the use of statistics. Here is a brief description of some of the more common statistical terms used in sport psychology research.

Correlations: Relationships between Factors

1. *Pearson product moment correlation.* This statistic, which uses the symbol r, is used to determine the relationship between two scores on each subject. Relating a score on a paper-and-pencil inventory to a performance score on a sport task is common in sport psychology. For example, I wanted to examine the extent to which mental arousal, as measured by a questionnaire, was related to physiological arousal, or heart rate (HR). Specifically, are the subjects' feelings of excitation related to more common physiological techniques used to measure arousal? I found that "the correlations were .76 and .88 for the first . . . and second . . . recordings, respectively. The subjects' feelings of arousal and HR were highly related. The psychological and physiological bases for arousal were thus assumed to be similar in this study" (Anshel 1985, p. 6).

2. *Regression.* Regression is used to predict future performance or some other psychological response. Predictions are based on relationships between factors under investigation. High regression correlations, usually considered .80 or above, are more accurate predictors of future behavior or feelings than relatively low correlations, for example, .30 or below.

3. *Multiple regression.* This statistic is used to increase the accuracy of prediction. To use it, the researcher must have one set of performance scores (collectively called the *dependent variable*) and two or more sets of *predictor* (or *independent*) *variables*. Actually, coaches conduct an informal form of this evaluation in their minds during team tryouts. Coaches who want to predict basketball playing ability, for example, would get a more accurate prediction using various tests of basketball skill than just one test. It would be helpful to collect data on performance and to calculate the probability of future sport success rather than relying on the typical "gut feeling."

For example, Scanlan and Lewthwaite (*Journal of Sport Psychology*, 1984, pp. 208–226) examined factors that best predicted sport enjoyment experienced by male wrestlers, aged 9 to 14 years. They found "the intra-personal variables, age and perceived wrestling ability, and the significant adult factors, Adult Satisfaction

with Season's Performance and Negative Maternal Interactions, emerged as significant predictors of enjoyment" (p. 223). The analysis indicated that younger children
and those who perceived themselves as more skilled felt relatively more enjoyment
than the others. In addition, greater enjoyment was experienced by boys who
thought that their parents and coaches were pleased with their wrestling performance and who felt less pressure from and had fewer negative interactions with
their mothers.

Experimental Research: Differences among Groups

1. *t-tests.* The purpose of this statistic is to determine whether the differences between
   two group averages (means) are significant. As indicated earlier, the researcher
   compares the obtained *t* value with the critical value, typically located in a table in
   the Appendix of statistics textbooks. If the calculated value is at or above the number in the table, it can be concluded that either the treatment (condition) in the
   study was effective in altering performance or some state, or that groups differed
   from each other on some characteristic before or after the treatment.

   There are two types of *t*-tests that are most commonly used in sport psychology:
   independent (unpaired) and dependent (paired). The *independent test* is a comparison between two separate sets of subjects, whereas the *dependent test* examines differences between the same set of subjects in two different conditions. If a scientist
   obtains significant differences in any *t*-test, how is it known which group is superior? Simply look at the two group means.

2. *Analysis of variance.* Frequently depicted by the acronym ANOVA, this is probably the
   most common statistic found in behavioral research. Whereas the *t*-test is a comparison of the means of two groups, ANOVA is computed to determine differences
   among three or more group means. Its numerical value is the symbol *F*. As with *t*,
   the scientist would compare the *F* value with the critical value located in an *F* table.
   If the computed *F* is equal to or greater than the critical value, then differences
   between at least two of the group means are statistically significant. Significant
   between which of the groups? It isn't known until a *post hoc comparison* is made. The
   post hoc test (there are several from which a researcher can choose) indicates which
   of the group means are statistically different from each other.

3. *Factorial ANOVA.* It's very common to read, "a 2 × 2 × 3 ANOVA was calculated to
   determine . . ." Translation: More than one factor (independent variable) is being
   analyzed simultaneously. An example is in order.

   Landers, Min Qi, and Courtet (*Research Quarterly for Exercise & Sport,* 1985, pp.
   122–130) compared high- and low-skilled rifle shooters on their ability to perform
   under different levels of stress. To determine if stress level caused differences in
   shooting performance as a function of the shooter's ability, the authors computed a
   2 (high versus low experience) × 3 (high, medium, and low stress levels) ANOVA
   with repeated measures on the stress condition. The repeated measures design
   means that the same subjects at both skill levels experienced *each* of the three stress
   conditions. Among other results, the authors found no significant differences
   between the groups or among the conditions. Although, as expected, higher skilled
   shooters scored significantly better than their lower skilled counterparts, skill level
   did not separate the subjects from their ability to perform under stress.

Thus stress, at least of an auditory nature as was used in this study, doesn't seem to upset even lower skilled shooters. The application of these results indicates that a quiet environment is not required for novice shooters to reduce or manage stress. It's also possible that shooters may not need to use stress-reducing strategies to the same degree as other athletes, perhaps because the nature of this sport (e.g., direct confrontation is absent and the competitor controls the pace of performance) does not elicit the same stressful responses as other types of sports.

4. *Multivariate ANOVA (MANOVA).* Multivariate research includes the simultaneous analysis of two or more dependent variables (e.g., performance speed, accuracy, and decision time). For example, how do persons determine whether speed or accuracy is more important when performing a motor skill? Do the instructions they receive before attempting the task correspond to the strategy they adopt? That's what researchers Gross and Gill (1982) wanted to know. They predicted that when subjects are given instructions that emphasize speed, they are faster but less accurate than when instructions emphasize accuracy. And how would speed and accuracy be affected with both types of instructions? The MANOVA was used so that speed and accuracy, two different sets of scores (two dependent variables), could be simultaneously compared. They found that receiving instruction influenced the subjects' performance priorities. When told to emphasize speed or to emphasize accuracy, the subjects did so while deemphasizing accuracy and speed, respectively.

5. *Discriminant analysis.* This approach is used to predict one independent variable based on a combination of two or more dependent variables. The researcher is interested in knowing which factors are most important in predicting the desirable outcome.

   For example, in their book *Research Methods in Physical Activity* (5th ed.), Thomas and Nelson (2001) offer an example in which 84 varsity football players were classified into three groups: offensive and defensive backs, offensive and defensive linemen, and linebackers and receivers (24 players per group). The athletes were tested on the 40-yard dash, 12-minute run, shuttle run, vertical jump, standing long jump, bench press, and squat. The objective was to determine the relationship among these seven test scores. Discriminant analysis was computed to find how many of the seven dependent variables (test scores) were important to separate the three groups of players and predict the players' skill in each group. It was found that three tests—the bench press, 40-yard dash, and vertical jump—separated the players by position. The remaining four tests did not significantly contribute.

6. *Significant interactions.* An interaction is possible only when two or more independent variables are being compared simultaneously. Specifically, it means that one of the factors is different from the rest, that is, they are statistically significant only in combination with a second factor (two-way interaction) or both second and third (three-way interaction) factors. This is almost always a desirable outcome in behavioral research. It is desirable because most often researchers predict that a certain treatment will affect performance of attitude, usually in a positive manner, under at least two conditions, not just one. The key is meaningfulness of the results.

   For instance, it's one thing to say that less skilled competitors suffer a higher rate of dropping out of sport than higher skilled performers. However, the results are far more meaningful if a skill level (high and low) × feedback (positive, negative, and none) interaction was significant. It could be that it's not the level of skill that causes athletes to drop out, but rather their ability to persevere under conditions of negative feedback. The researcher would examine group means to determine the direction of these differences (e.g., which groups were higher vs. lower, more vs. less, better vs. worse). Thus, if this was the actual finding, then it can be implied that less skilled, particularly younger, athletes are less able to tolerate negative feedback than their higher skilled peers.

Discussion

This is perhaps the most important section for the reader who wants an interpretation of a study's findings. The writer tries to answer the following questions: Have the findings agreed with my hypothesis (predictions)? Why or why not? To what extent do my results support or contradict the results of other studies? What have I contributed to the knowledge base in this area? To what degree have I answered my research question? What conclusions and implications can I draw from my study? What are some of the needs for future research in this area?

The writer can take the liberty of making a few guesses as to what it all means, but he or she had better justify this guesswork with previously published research. Some research articles combine the results and discussion sections. This is usually because there are relatively few results to report (making a separate section unnecessary) or the results are clearer if a brief explanation follows or accompanies each analysis. In fact, the "readability" of the discussion section contributes greatly to the reader's understanding of the study and the application of its results. The ability to read and interpret recent research findings and new techniques, and to apply this information, is a good reason for coaches to be better acquainted with the research literature.

A Final Word about Statistics and Research Results

Reading and understanding research is a skill. Readers should not approach a scientific journal with the feeling that information for direct application in sport will be crystal clear. In many studies, findings have no application. Not every study is applied, or is intended to be. Perhaps the purpose of the study was to test a theory or model. The results would support, partially support, or reject the theory or model. It may not be possible or desirable for potential users of this information to take an academic course that explains research. Nevertheless, a person can obtain plenty of useful material from certain sections of a research article. Primarily the introduction and discussion sections, for example, offer explanations of the topic and the implications of the findings without requiring knowledge of research and statistics. It is also important to know that the purpose of some journals is to publish *applied* research or reviews of literature, while other journals are primarily devoted to reporting nonapplied, theoretical research. There is a need for reporting both types of work in our field. Even applied, or field, research is theory driven. Sport psychology consultants and psychologists who work with athletes would represent sport psychology with far more sophistication and expertise if they read and used the vast resources of information published in our journals.

Imagery and Progressive Relaxation Sessions

The effective use of mental imagery is an art and a science. It is an art because some individuals are better able than others in their ability to imagine themselves performing in sport situations. Imagery is a science in that it requires specific techniques and skills in conducting an effective session. There are a few elements to consider before attempting this technique. First, this is a skill that, like any skill, requires practice and patience. Second, change in the athlete's performance, emotions, or any desirable outcome will not happen immediately. It may take weeks or months of using and mastering imagery skills to observe or feel change. Third, imagery or any other cognitive strategy will not help an athlete who has reservations about its effectiveness. The competitor who contends that imagery "doesn't work for me" can be assured that it won't, just as he or she predicted. For the athlete who is committed to using imagery, there are two requirements before the session: a quiet environment, and deciding on a "trigger." A quiet environment is needed to ensure prolonged relaxation and concentration; this means no disruptive noise and disturbances. The trigger consists of thinking of an inanimate object, usually a color or a pleasant scene, that will quickly relax the individual. For example, many athletes think of the color light blue as their trigger to relax and, soon thereafter, begin their imagery session.

Examples of Imagery Programs
Objective: To Learn a New Skill or Strategy

Use your trigger to relax. Now think of yourself slowly learning the new skill. Feel confidence in your ability to learn and perform it with success. You're excited about performing it. It will help you to become a better athlete. Hear the coach give you instructions. At the same time, see yourself perform the skill slowly during practice. First, feel your body go through the motions without any other athletes involved. Just you and the equipment. First in slow motion over several attempts, then, when you get the feel of it, go at full speed. Picture perfect performance and the desired outcome every time. Now include your opponent. Is he or she guarding you in basketball or soccer? Is he or she the pitcher in baseball? Include your opponent in the image and continue feeling confident in your ability. Continue to demonstrate perfect performance and success. Do this for the next few minutes, and repeat two or three times a day.

Objective: Gaining Self-Confidence

Think of your trigger to relax. Now, for about half a minute, think about the reasons you wanted to play this sport: the fun, the chance to compete, and all the other reasons sport is important to you (short pause). Now think back to a single event in one contest in which you were very successful—something that really stands out in your mind that was a very successful, very rewarding experience. Think of the enjoyment you felt from that event, the feeling of success, the recognition from teammates, the coach, spectators, and friends. Try to remember everything about that event (a home run, scoring a goal, winning a race, etc.). Relive the emotions you felt when the event was over. Think of how much fun it was. For the next few minutes, think of two or three very successful events that occurred during the contest and how confident you felt when it was over.

Objective: Overcoming a Slump

After getting completely relaxed, you should think of your performance problem. Actually go back and see yourself make the same mistakes you've been making for about half a minute. Let's get it out into the open. OK, now say to yourself, the time to turn it around is right now, and here's how you're going to do it. First, recall from your past performing this skill successfully. Picture a perfectly executed skill—the one that's been causing you some problems recently. See yourself go through the motions with perfect form. Recall what it felt like to perform it perfectly. Now, in slow motion, mentally review the skill, keeping in mind all of its parts you practiced when you first learned it. At this point, look through your mind's eye and perform the skill in slow motion. Observe the ball and opponents just as you've seen them during actual performance— just as if there's a camera on your head getting the picture of what it looks like. Now, in slow motion, track the tossed baseball, thrown football, kicked soccer ball, or observe the golf ball sitting on the tee, the target you're aiming at, or your wrestling opponent as he makes his move. See perfect performance. Excellent ball contact, accurate reactions, a perfect response, and a successful result. After a few minutes of slow motion imagery, speed up the action—the same play, the exact skill, a repeat of the slowed version—so that you are now performing perfectly at regular speed. For the next few minutes, review in your mind perfect performance at regular speed with full confidence of success each time.

Progressive Relaxation

Progressive relaxation was first developed by Edmund Jacobson in the early 1930s. The term *progressive* refers to the method of progressing from one muscle group to another as the person becomes more and more relaxed. The technique consists of inducing as much tension as possible into one muscle group then, after a few seconds, relaxing the muscle group so that all the tension is released. Hence, the objective of progressive relaxation is reducing muscular tension. This is accompanied by reduced heart and breathing rate. Although this technique is superb for lowering anxiety and unwanted thoughts and emotions, it should not be conducted before performing sport skills. Progressive relaxation is relatively easy to learn, yet is a skill that requires repeated practice for mastery. Based on his interviews with successful major league baseball players, Will (1990) concludes that "relaxation is, paradoxically, a form of baseball concentration. Relaxation must be *willed*. It is the necessary unclenching of the mind. It is a form of discipline" (p. 81). Use the following guidelines in practicing the progressive relaxation technique.

The First Relaxation Session[1]

1. Select a quiet, dim room and ensure that no distractions or interruptions will occur.

2. Check to see that the athletes are warmly clad and that the clothes that they wear are dry (not damp or sweat laden).

3. Spread the athletes around the room so there is at least three feet (one meter) between each of them.

4. Explain the principle behind relaxing:

   "Relaxation is important. What we are going to learn will help you to rest and sleep when it is necessary. To get you to relax we are going to do a set of exercises. There is a scientific reason for this because when you contract a muscle and then relax it, it returns to a state that is more relaxed than before the contraction took place. So, to get you to relax you need to do a series of exercises that contract and then relax all the muscles in your body. This first session will take about 30 minutes."

It should be noted that the verbal instructions given here are for example only. For the coach to give this training session it is best that he or she expresses the content in his or her own way.]

5. "Lie on your back with your arms at your side. Check:

   The middle of your head is touching the mat so that you are looking straight up

   Your shoulders are exerting equal pressure on the mat

   Your buttocks are exerting equal pressure on the mat

   Your calves are pressing equally on the mat

   Your heels are pressing equally on the mat

   You should be lying straight on the mat. Your spine should be straight, your thighs and calves close together touching lightly and your arms extended by your side with your palms facing slightly up. Check for the last time that you are straight, relaxed, and that the pressure of your body parts on the mat is equal on both sides of your body. You will probably find the exercises easier if you (lightly) close your eyes." The coach should then walk among the athletes to see that their position is correct. It is preferable that no head pillows be used and that no shoes be worn."

6. "We are now going to do a series of exercises. Each exercise will contain a very hard contraction—hold—and then release sequence. The hold is for a period of four to five seconds. Then relax to the position that you are in now. When you do the exercises, contract only the muscles that are involved in them."

7. It is good practice to do a preliminary exercise involving the arms. "Slowly move your arms to a position where your hands are together, fingers straight, and palms

---

[1] Reprinted with permission from the National Coaching Certification Program, Level Two, Coaching Association of Canada, Ottawa, Ontario (1979).

touching as if you were praying. When I say contract I want you to push your hands together as hard as you can and hold that force for five seconds. Then slowly let your arms sink back to your side as you were before."

"Ready! Contract! Only tighten your hands, arms and shoulders—nothing else—three-four-five-relax slowly to your side. Feel your arms relax; they may tingle a little, they may feel heavy, they may feel warm."

8. It may be necessary to give some pointers to the athletes at this stage. "During that exercise some of you tightened your legs, others your faces. Remember, contract only the part of your body that is being exercised."

"The exercise we have just done is always the first that you do. Let's do it again for practice. Slowly move your arms to the prayer position. Ready! Contract-two-three-four-five-relax and slide them to your side. Feel your arms heavy, feel them pressing on the mat, relax."

9. After the preliminary exercise involving the arms (palm press), the exercise routine progresses from the toes to the top of the head. After the following two toe curl exercises there is an introduction to concentrating on breath control. By the time the exercises are completed, the emphasis should be on breath control and total heaviness.

10. "The first exercise is a toe-curl backwards. Moving only your toes and not your ankles, curl your toes back to the tops of your feet. Ready, contract-two-three-four-five-relax. Let your toes go to the position that seems the most natural for them."

11. "The next exercise is the opposite of what you have just done, a toe-curl under. Remember, do not move your ankles. Curl your toes under your feet. Ready, contract-two-three-four-five-relax. Let them return to where they feel most natural."

12. This is the stage where there is an introduction to breathing control.

"From now on when you contract do not breathe. When you relax let all the air in your lungs out so that any breathing you do after an exercise is very regular and the very minimum that is necessary. I should be able to hear you all breathe out when I say relax. After each exercise do six breaths where you concentrate on making them even and very slight; six identical, hardly noticeable, breaths."

"The next exercise is an ankle bend. Pull your feet back to your shins as much as you can. Ready! Contract-two-three-four-five-relax and breathe out. Breathe it all out, settle into a steady even breathing pattern. Do six identical breaths."

13. "The next exercise is the opposite of the previous one. This is an ankle stretch where you point your feet as much as you can. Ready! Contract-two-three-four-five-breathe out, even breathing."

"Feel that your feet are heavy, they may even tingle slightly when compared to the rest of your body. See that there is no tension in your toes or ankles and that your heels are pressing on the mat with exactly the same pressure. Keep your breathing even."

14. "The next exercise is to press your knees together. If your knees are not touching move them slowly together. Press your knees together as hard as you can. Ready! Contract-two-three-four-five-breathe out, steady even breaths. Count your breaths and make them as small as possible."

15. "The next exercise requires you to contract your thighs. Make your thigh muscles as small and as bunched as possible. Ready! Contract-two-three-four-five-breathe out; steady even breathing."

"Feel your legs heavy. The pressure on the mat should be equal behind your heels, your ankles, and your thighs. Breathe evenly."

16. "The next exercise requires that you make your buttock muscles as small as possible. Make them rock hard and little. Ready! Contract-two-three-four-five-breathe out. Breathe evenly."

"That completes your leg exercises. We have reached what is called a *check point*. At this stage go back and check each segment of your legs for the same feeling of heaviness, the same loss of sensation, the same pressure on the mat. If there still is some tension in a muscle group, repeat the exercise for that group.

Check that your toes are loose.

Check that your ankles have no tension—they are hanging in a natural position.

See that your calves are totally loose.

Your thighs should feel heavy and droopy.

Your buttocks should be very soft.

Check that you have the same feeling of heaviness in your feet, your lower legs, the tops of your thighs.

Feel where your legs touch the mat. Make sure they feel super heavy where they touch. There should be the same amount of heaviness in each leg. You should feel that the mat is pressing against your legs.

Concentrate on the heavy, dead feeling. If you wanted to move your legs you could not because they are so heavy.

Do 12 even, easy breaths while your legs are totally motionless."

17. "The next exercises concentrate on your torso and shoulders. As you do these keep your legs totally relaxed. Also after each exercise do eight controlled minimal breaths."

"Press your stomach muscles into your abdomen as hard as you can. Do it as if your spine can show through to the front. Ready! Contract-two-three-four-five-breathe out, let out all the tension. Concentrate on your breathing."

(Leave sufficient time to get in more than eight, very even, controlled breaths.)

18. "The next exercise requires you to contract all the muscles in your back toward your spine. Pull your shoulder blades together and push the points of your shoulders into the mat. Remember only to contract your back muscles, do not rise up off the mat. Ready! Contract-two-three-four-five-breathe out. Let the tension in your back go. Breathe evenly."

19. "Now we do the opposite exercise. Compress your chest muscles together and round your shoulder points together. Ready! Contract-two-three-four-five-breathe out. Let your shoulders slide back to the most relaxed position. Breathe shallowly and steadily."

20. "The next exercise requires that you raise your shoulders up toward your ears; a mighty big shoulder shrug. Keep everything else still, only move your shoulders. Ready! Contract-two-three-four-five-breathe out. Let it go. Feel your body getting very heavy and losing its sensations. Do eight very shallow, hardly noticeable breaths."

21. "There is one more exercise to do for your body. That requires you to pull your shoulders toward your feet. This is done by pointing as hard as you can with

your fingers and reaching down your thighs as far as possible. Ready! Contract-two-three-four-five-breathe out, relax."

"Concentrate on using as little air as possible when you breathe."

22. "That completes your body exercises. This is the second check point. Here you check your body and leg segments for the same feeling of heaviness, the same loss of sensation.

Check your shoulder looseness and heaviness.

The middle of your back.

Your chest and stomach should be very relaxed.

Your buttocks very loose.

Your calves, ankles, and thighs very loose.

See that the mat is pressing evenly on each side of your body

—your shoulders

—your buttocks

—your thighs

—your calves

—your heels

Concentrate on feeling heavy.

Count 12 very, very small even breaths."

23. "The last section of your body to relax is your head. There are many muscles in your neck and head so this is very important."

"The first exercise requires you not to move except to pull your jaw down into your neck. Ready! Contract-two-three-four-five-breathe out. Relax. Count those eight breaths."

24. "Next, press your head directly into the mat. Do not arch your neck. Press directly down. Ready! Contract-two-three-four-five-breathe out. Since these exercises use small muscles they require small amounts of energy. Consequently, your breathing should not change much and it should be hardly noticeable."

25. "The next exercise requires that you jut your jaw forward as much as you can. Ready! Stick it out-two-three-four-five-breathe out. Relax your jaw. Breathe."

26. "Next clench your teeth. Bite them together as hard as you can. Ready! Contract-two-three-four-five-breathe. Eight even breaths."

27. "Keeping your teeth lightly together, spread your lips apart (as if smiling) as much as possible. Ready! Contract-two-three-four-five-relax. Breathe."

28. "Press your tongue against the roof of your mouth as hard as you can. Make your tongue as big as possible. Ready! Contract-two-three-four-five-breathe out. Eight even breaths. Feel heavy like lead, all over your body."

29. "Your eyes need to be compressed as much as possible. Pull your cheeks up and your eyebrows down as hard as possible to compress your eyes back into your head. Ready! Contract-two-three-four-five-relax. Let your face go smooth. Smile slightly."

30. "The last exercise requires you to make your forehead as wrinkled as possible while keeping your eyes closed. Ready. Contract-two-three-four-five-relax. Let that tension go right out of your head."

"Feel your face as being smooth, drowsy, very, very relaxed. Your jaw should just hang there. Do 12 very small, slow, rhythmic breaths."

31. "Since that is the last exercise check your whole body once again for heaviness.
    —your legs: heels, calves, thighs, buttocks.
    —your body: stomach, chest, lower back, shoulders.
    —your head: neck, jaw, tongue, eyes, forehead.
    See that all pressure points on the mat are even and very, very heavy. Do 12 very slow breaths."

32. At this stage the coach can terminate the first training session. However, it is worthwhile to allow the athletes to remain in this relaxed state for five minutes or so. Some of them may be asleep.

33. To arouse the athletes be very gentle in your commands.
    "After you have relaxed for a while it is important that you do not suddenly jump up. Gradually bring yourself back to normal by doing the following things:
    —wiggle your toes
    —wiggle your fingers
    —move your feet
    —move your hands
    —open your eyes very slowly
    —smile
    —move your elbows
    —move your knees
    —roll over onto your stomach and stretch lazily
    —slowly rise to a sitting position
    —move to a kneeling position
    —stand
    —have another good stretch"

Subsequent Relaxation Sessions

1. Subsequent relaxation sessions will be shorter in duration since explanations will rarely be required.

2. This procedure will usually take at least 15 minutes even when set to a bare minimum of commands.

3. It is not necessary to follow all the steps in the relaxation sequence all the time. If you find that you are pressed for time, conduct a shortened version by skipping some of the steps.

4. The athletes should learn the whole process so they can control themselves and relax when needed. It should be emphasized that this procedure is just one of many procedures which exist. The contraction-relaxation action has several advantages for athletes who have been exercising. It affords them the opportunity of gaining control over the relaxation process more quickly.

Learning to Relax

The fastest way to learn the relaxation technique described above is to do a number of sessions very close together. A schedule of practices that has proven successful is outlined below. Adapt it as needed to meet your particular situation.

Day 1   First session under coach control.

Second session by self as going to sleep.

Day 2   Third session under coach control.

Fourth session by self as going to sleep.

Day 3   Fifth session by self but in presence of coach and other athletes.

Sixth session by self as going to sleep.

Day 4   Seventh session under coach control.

Eighth session by self as going to sleep.

Day 5   Ninth session by self during day.

Tenth session by self as going to sleep.

Day 6   As for day 5.

Day 7   As for day 4.

Day 8   As for day 5.

Day 9   As for day 5.

Day 10 As for day 4.

The frequent sessions led by the coach are more for motivational purposes than for teaching. They are used to stress the importance of the process and to impress it upon the athletes. The coach should periodically inquire as to how athletes are relaxing and encourage them to practice in various situations (at home, before exams, at practice, at competitions). He or she should also hold "booster" sessions—coach-directed sessions held at varying times.

Suggested Relaxation Audiotape for Athletes

Ievleva, L. (1997). *Inner sports: Mental skills for peak performance*. Champaign, IL: Human Kinetics. Audiocassette: Running time: 133 minutes. ISBN: 0-88011-744-3.

Abramson, L. Y., Seligman, M. E., & Teasdale, J. D. (1978). Learned helplessness in humans: Critique and reformulation. *Journal of Abnormal Psychology, 87,* 49–74.

Adrian, M. (1973). Sex differences in biomechanics. In D. V. Harris (Ed.), *Women and sport: A national research conference* (pp. 389–400). University Park, PA: Penn State University Press.

Ajzen, I., & Fishbein, M. (1974). Factors influencing intentions and the intention-behavior relation. *Human Relations, 27,* 1–15.

Ajzen, I. (1985). From intention to actions: A theory of planned behavior. In J. Kuhl and J. Beckman (Eds.), *Action control: From cognition to behavior,* pp. 11–39. Heidelberg: Springer.

Allison, M. T. (1991). Role conflict and the female athlete: Preoccupations with little grounding. *Journal of Applied Sport Psychology, 3,* 49–60.

American Psychiatric Association. (1994). *Diagnostic and statistical manual of mental disorders* (4th ed.). Washington, D.C.: American Psychiatric Association.

American Psychological Association. (1992). Ethical principles of psychologists and code of conduct. *American Psychologist, 47,* 1597–1611.

Andersen, M. B., Van Raalte, J. L., & Brewer, B. W. (1994). Assessing the skills of sport psychology supervisors. *The Sport Psychologist, 8,* 238–247.

Anshel, M. H. (1978). Behaviorism versus humanism: An approach to effective team leadership in sport. *Motor Skills: Theory into Practice, 2,* 83–91.

Anshel, M. H. (1979). Effect of age, sex, and type of feedback on motor performance and locus of control. *Research Quarterly, 50,* 305–317.

Anshel, M. H. (August 1981). Effect of sexual activity on athletic performance. *The Physician and Sportsmedicine, 9,* 64–68.

Anshel, M. H. (1985). Effect of arousal on warm-up decrement. *Research Quarterly for Exercise and Sport, 56,* 1–9.

Anshel, M. H. (March/April 1986). Bridging the gap through research and a major league baseball coach. *Coaching Review, 9,* 59–63.

Anshel, M. H. (1987a). Psychological inventories used for sport psychology research. *Sport Psychologist, 1,* 331–349.

Anshel, M. H. (October 1987b). Ten commandments for effective communication. In *Fundamentals of coaching and understanding sport.* Ottawa, Ontario: Coaching Association of Canada.

Anshel, M. H. (1989a). Examination of a college football coach's receptivity to sport psychology consulting: A three-year case study. *Journal of Applied Research in Coaching and Athletics, 4,* 139–149.

Anshel, M. H. (1989b). The ten commandments of effective communication for referees, judges, and umpires. *Sports Coach, 12,* 32–35.

Anshel, M. H. (1990a). Exercise psychology: An emerging area of study in therapy, rehabilitation, and human performance. *Proceedings of the 27th National Scientific Conference of the Australian Sports Medicine Federation.* Alice Springs, Northern Territory. Belconnen, ACT (Australia): Australian Sports Medicine Federation.

Anshel, M. H. (1990b). Toward development of a model for coping with acute stress in sport. *International Journal of Sport Psychology, 21,* 58–83.

Anshel, M. H. (1990c). Perceptions of black intercollegiate football players: Implications for the sport psychology consultant. *The Sport Psychologist, 4,* 235–248.

483

Anshel, M. H. (May/June 1990d). An information processing approach to teaching motor skills. *Journal of Physical Education, Recreation, & Dance, 61,* 70–75.

Anshel, M. H. (Autumn 1990e). Strategies for improving the retention of sport skills for young athletes. *Australian Council for Health, Physical Education, Recreation & Dance National Journal,* No. 127, 22–26.

Anshel, M. H. (1991a). A survey of elite athletes on the perceived causes of using banned drugs in sport. *Journal of Sport Behavior, 14,* 283–308.

Anshel, M. H. (1991b). Cognitive-behavioral strategies for combating drug abuse in sport: Implications for coaches and sport psychology consultants. *The Sport Psychologist, 5,* 152–166.

Anshel, M. H. (1991c). Effectiveness of selected coping strategies in responding to acute stress in gymnastics. *Journal of Physical Education & Sport Sciences, 3,* 21–38.

Anshel, M. H. (1992a). The case against certification in sport psychology: In search of the phantom expert. *The Sport Psychologist, 6,* 265–286.

Anshel, M. H. (1992b). Cognitive-behavioral strategies: Effective staff supervisory meetings and performance evaluation. *Journal of Managerial Psychology, 7,* 11–16.

Anshel, M. H. (1993). The case against certification of sport psychologists: A response to Zaichkowsky and Perna. *The Sport Psychologist, 7,* 344–353.

Anshel, M. H. (1995a). Examining social loafing among elite female rowers as a function of task duration and mood. *Journal of Sport Behavior, 18,* 31–41.

Anshel, M. H. (1995b). Examination of self-regulatory characteristics and behavioral tendencies of elite and nonelite male Australian swimmers. *The Australian Psychologist, 25,* 109–125.

Anshel, M. H. (1995c). Anxiety. In T. Morris and J. Summers (Eds.) *Sport psychology: Theory, applications, and issues.* New York: John Wiley & Sons.

Anshel, M. H. (August 2000). *The use of psychological assessment in sport psychology consulting.* A paper presented at the American Psychological Association Convention, Washington, D.C.

Anshel, M. H. (2001). Drug abuse in sport: Causes and cures. In J. M. Williams (Ed.), *Applied sport psychology* (4th ed., pp. 416–444). Mountain View, CA: Mayfield.

Anshel, M. H. (August 2002). *The workaholic sports coach: Psychological characteristics and antecedents.* Paper presented at the 2002 American Psychological Association Convention, Chicago.

Anshel, M. H., Freedson, P., Hamill, J., Haywood, K., Horvat, M., & Plowman, S. (1991d). *Dictionary of the sport and exercise sciences.* Edited by M. H. Anshel. Champaign, IL: Human Kinetics.

Anshel, M. H., Gregory, W. L., & Kaczmarek, M. (1990). Effectiveness of a technique for coping with criticism in sport. *Journal of Sport Behavior, 13,* 194–218.

Anshel, M. H., & Hoosima, D. E. (1989). The effect of positive and negative feedback on causal attributions and motor performance as a function of gender and athletic participation. *Journal of Sport Behavior, 12,* 119–130.

Anshel, M. H., Kim, K. W., Kim, B. H., Chang, K. J., & Hom, H. J. (2001). A model for coping with stressful events in sport: Theory, application, and future directions. *Inter-national Journal of Sport Psychology, 32,* 43–75.

Anshel, M. H., & Marisi, D. Q. (1978). Effect of music and rhythm on physical performance. *Research Quarterly, 49,* 109–113.

Anshel, M. H., & Sailes, G. (1990). Discrepant attitudes of intercollegiate athletes as a function of race. *Journal of Sport Behavior, 13,* 87–102.

Anshel, M. H., & Reeves, L. H. (1998). *Aerobics for fitness* (5th ed). Paramus, NJ: Pearson Publishers.

Anshel, M. H., & Straub, W. F. (1991). Congruence between players' and coaches' perceptions of coaching behaviors. *Applied Research in Coaching and Athletics Annual,* 49–66.

Anshel, M. H., Brown, M., & Brown, D. (1993). Effect of a program for coping with acute stress on motor performance, muscular tension and affect. *Australian Journal of Science and Medicine in Sport, 25,* 7–16.

Anshel, M. H., Weinberg, R. S., & Jackson, A. (1992). Effect of goal difficulty and task complexity on intrinsic motivation and motor performance. *Journal of Sport Behavior, 15,* 159–176.

Ardrey, R. (1961). *The territorial imperative.* New York: Atheneum Press.

Arnold, R. K. S. (1981). Developing sport skills: A dynamic interplay of task, learner, and teacher. *Motor Skills: Theory into Practice* (Monograph 2).

Astrand, P. O. (1986). *Textbook of work physiology* (3rd ed.). New York: McGraw-Hill.

Atkinson, J. W. (1957). Motivational determinants of risk-taking behavior. *Psychological Review, 64,* 359–372.

Atkinson, J. W. (1966). Motivational determinants of risk-taking behavior. In J. W. Atkinson & N. T. Feather (Eds.), *A theory of achievement motivation* (pp. 11–30). New York: John Wiley & Sons.

Babkes, M. L., & Weiss, M. R. (1999). Parental influence on children's cognitive and affective responses to competitive soccer participation. *Pediatric Exercise Science, 11,* 44–62.

Bandura, A. (1973). *Aggression: A social learning analysis.* Englewood Cliffs, NJ: Prentice-Hall.

Bandura, A. (1977). Self-efficacy: Toward a unifying theory of behavioral change. *Psychological Review, 84,* 191–215.

Bandura, A., & Huston, A. C. (1961). Identification as a process of incidental learning. *Journal of Abnormal Social Psychology, 63,* 311–318.

Bandura, A., Ross, D., & Ross, S. A. (1963). Imitation of film-mediated aggression models. *Journal of Abnormal Social Psychology, 66,* 3–11.

Bandura, A., & Walters, R. (1959). *Adolescent aggression.* New York: Ronald Press.

Baumeister, R. F. (1984). Choking under pressure: Self-consciousness and paradoxical effects of incentives on skillful performance. *Journal of Personality and Social Psychology, 46,* 610–620.

Baumeister, R. F. (October 1985). *Performance under pressure: A self-attention model of choking.* Paper presented at a conference of the Canadian Society for Psychomotor Learning and Sport Psychology, Montreal, Quebec, Canada.

Baumeister, R. F., & Steinhilber, A. (1984). Paradoxical effects of supportive audiences on performance under pressure: The home field disadvantage in sports championships. *Journal of Personality and Social Psychology, 47,* 85–93.

Beilock, S. L., & Carr, T. H. (2001). On the fragility of skilled performance: What governs choking under pressure? *Journal of Experimental Psychology, 130,* 701–725.

Bem, S. L. (1974). The measurement of psychological androgyny. *Journal of Consulting and Clinical Psychology, 42,* 155–162.

Benne, K. D., & Sheats, P. (1970). Functional roles of group members. In C. G. Kemp (Ed.), *Perspectives on the group process* (2nd ed.) (pp. 271–275). Boston: Houghton Mifflin.

Berger, B. G., & Motl, R.W. (2000). Exercise and mood: A selective review and synthesis of research employing the Profile of Mood States. *Journal of Applied Sport Psychology, 12,* 69–92.

Berger, B. G., Pargman, D., & Weinberg, R. (2002). *Foundations of exercise psychology.* Morgantown, WV: Fitness Information Technology.

Berkowitz, L. (1969). The frustration-aggression hypothesis revisited. In L. Berkowitz (Ed.), *Roots of aggression* (pp. 1–29). New York: Atherton.

Berkowitz, L. (1970). Experimental investigations of hostility catharsis. *Journal of Consulting and Clinical Psychology, 35,* 1–7.

Berkowitz, L. (1989). Frustration-aggression hypothesis: Examination and reformulation. *Psychological Bulletin, 106,* 59–73.

Biddle, S. (1993). Attribution research and sport psychology. In R. N. Singer, M. Murphey, & L. K. Tennant (Eds.), *Handbook of research in sport psychology* (pp. 437–464). New York: Macmillan.

Biddle, S., Bull, S. J., & Seheult, C. L. (1992). Ethical and professional issues in contemporary British sport psychology. *The Sport Psychologist, 6*, 66–76.

Biddle, S. J. H., Hanrahan, S. J., & Sellars, C. N. (2001). Attributions: Past, present, and future. In R. N. Singer, H. A. Hausenblas, & C. M. Janelle (Eds.), *Handbook of sport psychology* (2nd ed., pp. 444–471). New York: John Wiley & Sons.

Bird, A. M., & Cripe, B. K. (1986). *Psychology and sport behavior*. St. Louis: Times Mirror/Mosby.

Birrell, S. (1978). Achievement related motives and the woman athlete. In C. A. Oglesby (Ed.), *Women and sport: From myth to reality* (pp. 85–112). Philadelphia, PA: Lea & Febiger.

Blair, S. N., & Brodney, S. (1999). Effects of physical inactivity and obesity on morbidity and mortality: Current evidence and research issues. *Medicine and Science in Sports and Exercise, 31*, S646–S662.

Bloom, G. (2002). Coaching demands and responsibilities of expert coaches. In J. M. Silva & D. E. Stevens (Eds.), *Psychological foundations of sport* (pp. 438–465). San Francisco: Benjamin Cummings.

Blucker, J. A., & Hershberger, E. (1983). Causal attribution theory and the female athlete: What conclusions can we draw? *Journal of Sport Psychology, 5*, 353–360.

Bolton, E. B. (1980). A conceptual analysis of the mentor relationship in career development of women. *Adult Education, 30*, 195–207.

Bond, C. F., & Titus, L. J. (1983). Social facilitation: A meta-analysis of 241 studies. *Psychological Bulletin, 94*, 265–292.

Bond, J. W., & Nideffer, R. M. (1992). Attentional and interpersonal characteristics of elite Australian athletes. *Excel, 8*, 101–110.

Boutcher, S. H. (1992). Attention and athletic performance: An integrated approach. In T. S. Horn (Ed.), *Advances in sport psychology* (pp. 251–266). Champaign, IL: Human Kinetics.

Brawley, L. R. (1980). *Children's causal attributions in a competitive sport: A motivational interpretation*. Unpublished doctoral dissertation, Pennsylvania State University, University Park, PA.

Brawley, L. R. (1984). Attributions as social cognitions: Contemporary perspectives in sport. In W. F. Straub & J. M. Williams (Eds.), *Cognitive sport psychology* (pp. 212–230). Ithaca, NY: Sport Science Associates.

Brawley, L. R., Carron, A. V., & Widmeyer, W. N. (1987). Assessing the cohesion of teams: Validity of the group environment questionnaire. *Journal of Sport & Exercise Psychology, 10*, 199–213.

Brawley, L. R., Carron, A. V., & Widmeyer, W. N. (1988). Exploring the relationship between cohesion and group resistance to disruption. *Journal of Sport & Exercise Psychology, 10*, 199–213.

Brawley, L. R., Carron, A. V., & Widmeyer, W. N. (1993). The influence of the group and its cohesiveness on perceptions of group goal-related variables. *Journal of Sport & Exercise Psychology, 15*, 245–260.

Brawley, L. R., & Roberts, G. C. (1984). Attributions in sport: Research foundations, characteristics, and limitations. In J. M. Silva & R. S. Weinberg (Eds.), *Psychological foundations of sport* (pp. 197–213). Champaign, IL: Human Kinetics.

Brennan, S. J. (June 1986). *Intrinsic motivation of intercollegiate male-female athletes in team and individual sport groups*. Paper presented at a national conference of the North American Society of Psychology of Sport and Physical Activity, Scottsdale, AZ.

Branigan, G. G. (1999). *The sport scientists: Research adventures*. New York: Addison Wesley Longman.

Brewer, B. W., Van Raalte, J. L., Linder, D. E., & Van Raalte, N. S. (1991). Peak performance and the perils of retrospective introspection. *Journal of Sport & Exercise Psychology, 13*, 227–238.

Brustad, R. J. (1992). Integrating socialization influences into the study of children's motivation in sport. *Journal of Sport & Exercise Psychology, 14*, 59–77.

Brustad, R. J. (1993). Youth in sport: Psychological considerations. In R. N. Singer, M. Murphey, & L. K. Tennant (Eds.), *Handbook of research in sport psychology* (pp. 695–717). New York: Macmillan.

Brustad, R. J., Babkes, M. L., & Smith, A. L. (2001). Youth in sport. In R. N. Singer, H. A. Hausenblas, & C. M. Janelle (Eds.), *Handbook of sport psychology* (2nd ed., pp. 604–635). New York: John Wiley & Sons.

Buckworth, J., & Dishman, R. K. (2002). *Exercise psychology*. Champaign, IL: Human Kinetics.

Bunker, L., Williams, J. M., & Zinsser, S. (1993). Building self-confidence in sport. In J. M. Williams (Ed.), *Applied sport psychology: Personal growth to peak performance* (2nd ed., pp. 225–242). Mountain View, CA: Mayfield.

Burton, D. (1989). Winning isn't everything: Examining the impact of performance goals on collegiate swimmers' cognitions and performance. *The Sport Psychologist, 2*, 105–132.

Burton, D. (1992). The Jekyll/Hyde nature of goals: Reconceptualizing goal setting in sport. In T. S. Horn (Ed.), *Advances in sport psychology* (pp. 267–297). Champaign, IL: Human Kinetics.

Burton, D. (1998). Measuring competitive state anxiety. In J. L. Duda (Ed.), *Advances in sport and exercise psychology measurement* (pp. 129–148). Morgantown, WV: Fitness Information Technology.

Burton, D., & Martens, R. (1986). Pinned by their own goals: An exploratory investigation into why kids drop out of wrestling. *Journal of Sport Psychology, 8*, 183–197.

Burton, D., Naylor, S., & Holliday, B. (2001). Goal setting in sport: Investigating the goal effectiveness paradox. In R. N. Singer, H. A. Hausenblas, & C. M. Janelle (Eds.), *Handbook of sport psychology* (2nd ed., pp. 497–528). New York: John Wiley & Sons.

Bushman, B., Stack, A., & Baumeister, R. (1996). Catharsis, aggression, and persuasive influence. *Journal of Personality and Social Psychology, 76*, 367–376.

Carkhuff, R. R. (1980). *The art of helping*. Amherst, MA: Human Resources Development Press.

Carron, A. V. (1980). *Social psychology of sport*. Ithaca, NY: Mouvement.

Carron, A. V. (1984a). *Motivation: Implications for coaching and teaching*. London, Ontario, Canada: Sports Dynamics.

Carron, A. V. (1984b). Cohesion in sport teams. In J. M. Silva & R. S. Weinberg (Eds.), *Psychological foundations of sport* (pp. 340–351). Champaign, IL: Human Kinetics.

Carron, A. V., & Dennis, P. W. (2001). The sport team as an effective group. In J. M. Williams (Ed.), *Applied sport psychology: Personal growth to peak performance* (4th ed., pp. 120–134). Mountain View, CA: Mayfield.

Carron, A. V. (1994). Group dynamics in sport. In S. Serpa, J. Alves, & V. Pataco (Eds.), *International perspectives on sport and exercise psychology* (pp. 79–101). Morgantown, WV: Fitness Information Technology.

Carron, A. V., & Hausenblas, H. A. (1998). *Group dynamics in sport* (2nd ed.). Morgantown, WV: Fitness Information Technology.

Carron, A. V., Prapavessis, H., & Grove, J. R. (1994). Group effects and self-handicapping. *Journal of Sport & Exercise Psychology, 16*, 246–257.

Carron, A. V., & Spink, K. S. (1993). Team building in an exercise setting. *The Sport Psychologist, 7*, 8–18.

Cartwright, D., & Zander, A. (1968). *Group dynamics: Research and theory* (3rd ed.). New York: Harper & Row.

Carver, C. S., & Scheier, M. R. (1981). *Attention and self-regulation: A control theory approach to human behavior*. New York: Springer-Verlag.

Chappell, A. J. (January/February 1984). Counseling your athletes. *Coaching Review, 34*, 46–48.

Chelladurai, P. (1984). Discrepancy between preferences and perceptions of leadership behavior and satisfaction of athletes in varying sports. *Journal of Sport Psychology, 6*, 27–41.

Chelladurai, P. (1990). Leadership in sports: A review. *International Journal of Sport Psychology, 21*, 328–354.

Chelladurai, P. (1993). Leadership. In R. N. Singer, M. Murphey, & L. K. Tennant (Eds.), *Handbook of research in sport psychology* (pp. 647–671). New York: Macmillan.

Chelladurai, P., & Arnott, M. (1985). Decision styles in coaching: Preferences of basketball players. *Research Quarterly for Exercise and Sport, 56,* 15–24.

Chelladurai, P., & Carron, A. V. (1978). *Leadership.* (Monograph). Ottawa, Ontario: Canadian Association of Health, Physical Education, and Recreation.

Chelladurai, P., & Carron, A. V. (1983). Athletic maturity and preferred leadership. *Journal of Sport Psychology, 5,* 371–380.

Chelladurai, P., & Haggerty, T. R. (1978). A normative model of decision styles in coaching. *Athletic Administrator, 13,* 6–9.

Chelladurai, P., & Riemer, H. A. (1998). Measurement of leadership in sport. In J. L. Duda (Ed.), *Advances in sport and exercise psychology measurement* (pp. 227–253). Morgantown, WV: Fitness Information Technology.

Chelladurai, P., & Saleh, S. D. (1980). Dimensions of leader behavior in sports: Development of a leadership scale. *Journal of Sport Psychology, 2,* 34–45.

Clarke, K. S. (1984). The USOC sports psychology registry: A clarification. *Journal of Sport Psychology, 6,* 365–366.

Claxton, D. B., & Lacy, A. C. (1986). A comparison of practice field behaviors between winning high school football and tennis coaches. *Journal of Applied Research in Coaching and Athletics, 1,* 188–200.

Clifton, R. T., & Gill, D. L. (1994). Gender differences in self-confidence on a feminine-typed task. *Journal of Sport & Exercise Psychology, 16,* 150–162.

Coakley, J. (1982). *Sports in society: Issues and controversies* (2nd ed.). St. Louis: C. V. Mosby.

Coakley, J. (1990). *Sport in society.* St. Louis: Times Mirror/Mosby.

Cockerill, I. M., & Riddington, M. E. (1996). Exercise dependence and associative disorders: A review. *Counseling Psychology Quarterly, 9,* 119–129.

Connelly, D. (1988). Increasing intensity of play of nonassertive athletes. *The Sport Psychologist, 2,* 255–265.

Conroy, D. E. (2001). Progress in the development of a multidimensional measure of fear of failure: The performance failure appraisal inventory (PFAI). *Anxiety, Stress, and Coping, 14,* 431–452.

Coté, J., Salmela, J. H., & Russell, S. (1995). The knowledge of high-performance gymnastic coaches: Competition and training considerations. *The Sport Psychologist, 9,* 76–95.

Cottrell, N. B. (1972). Social facilitation. In C. G. McClintock (Ed.), *Experimental social psychology* (pp. 185–236). New York: Holt, Rinehart & Winston.

Courneya, K. S., & Carron, A. V. (1992). The home advantage in sport competitions: A literature review. *Journal of Sport & Exercise Psychology, 14,* 13–27.

Cox, R. H. (1995). *Sport psychology: Concepts and applications* (3rd ed.). Dubuque, IA: Wm. C. Brown.

Cratty, B. J. (1973). *Psychology in contemporary sport.* Englewood Cliffs, NJ: Prentice-Hall.

Cratty, B. J. (1983). *Psychology in contemporary sport. Guidelines for coaches and athletes.* Englewood Cliffs, NJ: Prentice-Hall.

Cratty, B. J. (1984). *Psychological preparation and athletic excellence.* Ithaca, NY: Mouvement.

Cribben, J. J. (1981). *Leadership: Strategies for organizational effectiveness.* New York: AMACOM.

Csikszentmihalyi, M. (1990). *Flow: The psychology of optimal experience.* New York: Harper & Row.

Danish, S. J., & Hale, B. D. (1981). Toward an understanding of the practice of sport psychology. *Journal of Sport Psychology, 3,* 90–99.

Danish, S. J., Petitpas, A. J., & Hale, B. D. (1992). A developmental-educational intervention model of sport psychology. *The Sport Psychologist, 6,* 403–415.

Deaux, K. (1984). From individual differences to social categories: Analysis of a decade's research on gender. *American Psychologist, 39,* 105–116.

Deci, E. L. (1975). *Intrinsic motivation*. New York: Plenum.

Deci, E. L., & Ryan, R. M. (1985). *Intrinsic motivation and self-determination in human behavior*. New York: Plenum

DeCotiis, T. A., & Koys, D. J. (August 1980). *The identification and measurement of the dimensions of organizational climate*. Detroit, MI: Academy of Management Proceedings.

Deshaires, P. (May 1980). *The interactional model of anxiety in a sport competition situation*. Paper presented at the North American Society for the Psychology of Sport and Physical Activity, Boulder, CO.

Dickinson, J. (1977). *A behavioral analysis of sport*. Princeton, NJ: Princeton Book.

Diener, C. I., & Dweck, C. S. (1978). An analysis of learned helplessness: Continuous changes in performance, strategy, and achievement cognitions following failure. *Journal of Personality and Social Psychology, 36*, 451–462.

DiFebo, J. E. (1975). Modification of general expectancy and sport expectancy within a sport setting. In D. M. Landers (Ed.), *Psychology of sport and motor behavior* (vol. 2). University Park: Pennsylvania State University Press.

Dishman, R. K. (1983). Identity crises in North American sport psychology: Academics in professional issues. *Journal of Sport Psychology, 5*, 123–134.

Dollard, J., Miller, N., Doob, L., Mourer, O. H., and Sears, R. R. (1939). *Frustration and aggression*. New Haven, CT: Yale University Press.

Donnelly, P. (1993). Problems associated with youth involvement in high-performance sport. In B. R. Cahill & A. J. Pearl (Eds.), *Intensive participation in children's sport* (pp. 95–126). Champaign, IL: Human Kinetics.

Duda, J. L. (1987). Toward a developmental theory of children's motivation in sport. *Journal of Sport Psychology, 9*, 130–145.

Duda, J. L. (1992). Motivation in sport settings: A goal perspective approach. In G. C. Roberts (Ed.), *Motivation in sport and exercise* (pp. 57–91.) Champaign, IL: Human Kinetics.

Duda, J. L. (1993). Goals: A social-cognitive approach to the study of achievement motivation in sport. In R. N. Singer, M. Murphey, & L. K. Tennant (Eds.), *Handbook of research in sport psychology* (pp. 421–436). New York: Macmillan.

Duda, J. L., & Allison, M. T. (1990). Cross-cultural analysis in exercise and sport psychology: A void in the field. *Journal of Sport & Exercise Psychology, 12*, 114–131.

Duffy, E. (1957). The psychological significance of the concept of arousal on activation. *Psychological Review, 64*, 265–275.

Dweck, C. S. (1975). The role of expectations and attributions in the alleviation of learned helplessness. *Journal of Personality and Social Psychology, 31*, 674–685.

Dweck, C. S. (1980). Learned helplessness in sport. In C. H. Nadeau, W. R. Halliwell, K. M. Newell, & G. C. Roberts (Eds.), *Psychology of motor behavior and sport–1979* (pp. 1–11). Champaign, IL: Human Kinetics.

Dweck, C. S., & Reppucci, N. D. (1973). Learned helplessness and reinforcement responsibility in children. *Journal of Personality and Social Psychology, 25*, 109–116.

Easterbrook, J. A. (1959). The effect of emotion on cue utilization and the organization of behavior. *Psychological Review, 66*, 183–201.

Eccles, J. S., & Harold, R. D. (1991). Gender differences in sport involvement: Applying the Eccles expectancy-value model. *Journal of Applied Sport Psychology, 3*, 7–35.

Eckert, H. M. (1973). Age changes in motor skills. In G. L. Rarick (Ed.), *Human growth and development* (pp. 155–175). New York: Academic Press.

Endler, N. N. (1977). The interaction model of anxiety: Some possible implications. In D. M. Landers and R. W. Christina (Eds.), *Psychology of motor behavior and sport* (pp. 332–351). Champaign, IL: Human Kinetics.

Feinstein, J. (1986). *A season on the brink*. New York: Macmillan.

Feltz, D. L. (1988). Self-confidence and sports performance. In K. B. Pandolf (Ed.), *Exercise and sport science reviews* (vol. 16) (pp. 423–457). New York: Macmillan.

Fiedler, F. E. (1964). A contingency model of leadership effectiveness. In L. Berkowitz (Ed.), *Advances in experimental social psychology* (vol. 1) (pp. 149–190). New York: Academic Press.

Fiedler, F. E. (1967). *A theory of leadership effectiveness.* New York: McGraw-Hill.

Figler, S. K. (1978). Aggressive response to frustration among athletes and nonathletes. In F. Landry & W. Orban (Eds.), *Motor learning, sport psychology, pedagogy, and didactics of physical activity* (pp. 289–296). Miami: Symposium Specialists.

Finn, J. A. (1978). Perception of violence among high-hostile and low-hostile women athletes and nonathletes before and after exposure to sport films. In F. Landry & W. Orban (Eds.), *Motor learning, sport psychology, pedagogy, and didactics of physical activity* (pp. 283–288). Miami: Symposium Specialists.

Fisher, A. C. (1976). Psych up, psych down, psych out: Relationship of arousal to sport performance. In A. C. Fisher (Ed.), *Psychology of sport* (pp. 136–144). Palo Alto, CA: Mayfield.

Fisher, A. C. (1977). Sport personality assessment: Facts, fallacies, and perspectives. *Motor Skills: Theory into Practice, 1,* 87–97.

Fisher, A. C., Mancini, V. H., Hirsch, R. L., Proulx, T. J., & Staurowsky, E. J. (1982). Coach–athlete interactions and team climate. *Journal of Sport Psychology, 4,* 388–404.

Fisher, A. C., & Motta, M. A. (1977). Activation and sport performance: Some coaching guidelines. *Motor Skills: Theory into Practice, 1,* 98–103.

Francis, D., & Young, D. (1979). *Improving work groups: A practical manual for team building.* San Diego, CA: University Associates.

Frederick, C. M., & Ryan, R. M. (1995). Self-determination in sport: A review using cognitive evaluation theory. *International Journal of Sport Psychology, 26,* 5–23.

Friedman, E., & Berger, B. G. (1991). Influence of gender, masculinity, and femininity on the effectiveness of three stress reduction techniques: Jogging, relaxation response, and group interaction. *Journal of Applied Sport Psychology, 3,* 61–86.

Frodi, A., Macaulay, J., & Thome, P. R. (1977). Are women always less aggressive than men? A review of the experimental literature. *Psychological Review, 34,* 634–660.

Fromm, E. (1941). *Escape from freedom.* New York: Holt, Rinehart & Winston.

Fuoss, D. E., & Troppmann, R. J. (1981). *Effective coaching: A psychological approach.* New York: John Wiley & Sons.

Gagné, R. M. (1977). *The conditions for learning* (2nd ed.). New York: Holt, Rinehart & Winston.

Garari, J. E., & Scheinfeld, A. (1970). Sex differences in mental and behavioral traits. *Genetic Psychological Monographs, 81,* 123–142.

Garfield, C. A., & Bennett, H. Z. (1984). *Peak performance: Mental training techniques of the world's greatest athletes.* Los Angeles: Jeremy P. Tarcher.

Gauron, E. F. (1986). The art of cognitive self-regulation. *Clinics in Sports Medicine, 5,* 91–101.

Gauvin, L., Levesque, L., & Richard, L. (2001). Helping people initiate and maintain a more active lifestyle. In R. N. Singer, H. A. Hausenblas, & C. M. Janelle (Eds.), *Handbook of sport psychology* (2nd ed., pp. 718–739). New York: John Wiley & Sons.

Gauvin, L., & Russell, S. J. (1993). Sport-specific and culturally adapted measures in sport and exercise psychology research: Issues and strategies. In R. N. Singer, M. Murphey, & L. K. Tennant (Eds.), *Handbook of research on sport psychology* (pp. 891–900). New York: John Wiley & Sons.

Gerson, R. (1978). Intrinsic motivation: Implications for children's athletics. *Motor Skills: Theory into Practice, 2,* 111–119.

Gill, D. L. (1980). Cohesiveness and performance in sport teams. In W. F. Straub (Ed.), *Sport psychology: An analysis of athlete behavior* (2nd ed., pp. 421–430). Ithaca, NY: Mouvement.

Gill, D. L. (1987). Journal of sport and exercise psychology. *Journal of Sport Psychology, 9,* 1–2.

Gill, D. L. (1984). Individual and group performance in sport. In J. M. Silva & R. S. Weinberg (Eds.), *Psychological foundations of sport* (pp. 315–328). Champaign, IL: Human Kinetics.

Gill, D. L. (1992). Gender and sport behavior. In T. S. Horn (Ed.), *Advances in sport psychology* (pp. 143–160). Champaign, IL: Human Kinetics.

Gill, D. L. (1995). Women's place in the history of sport psychology. *The Sport Psychologist, 9,* 418–433.

Gill, D. L., & Deeter, T. E. (1988). Development of the sport orientation questionnaire. *Research Quarterly for Exercise and Sport, 59,* 191–202.

Gill, D. L., & Dzewaltowski, D. A. (1988). Competitive orientations among intercollegiate athletes: Is winning the only thing? *The Sport Psychologist, 2,* 212–221.

Gill, D. L., Gross, J. B., Huddleston, S., & Shifflett, B. (1984). Sex differences in achievement cognitions and performance in competition. *Research Quarterly for Exercise and Sport, 55,* 340–346.

Ginott, H. (1965). *Between parent and child.* New York: Avon.

Ginott, H. (1969). *Between parent and teenager.* New York: Avon.

Ginott, H. (1972). *Teacher and child.* New York: Avon.

Glasser, W. (1976). *Positive addiction.* New York: Harper & Row.

Gould, D. (1984). Psychosocial development and children's sport. In J. R. Thomas (Ed.), *Motor development during childhood and adolescence* (pp. 212–236). Minneapolis, MN: Burgess.

Gould, D. (1987). Promoting positive sport experiences for children. In J. R. May & M. J. Asken (Eds.), *Sport psychology: The psychological health of the athlete* (pp. 77–98). New York: PMA.

Gould, D. (2001). Goal setting for peak performance. In J. M. Williams (Ed.), *Applied sport psychology* (4th ed., pp. 190–205). Mountain View, CA: Mayfield.

Gould, D., Eklund, R. C., & Jackson, S. A. (1992). 1988 USA Olympic wrestling excellence II: Competitive cognition and affect. *The Sport Psychologist, 6,* 383–402.

Gould, D., & Krane, V. (1992). The arousal-athletic performance relationship: Current status and future directions. In T. S. Horn (Ed.), *Advances in sport psychology* (pp. 119–142). Champaign, IL: Human Kinetics.

Gould, D., & Pick, S. (1995). Sport psychology: The Griffith era, 1920–1940. *The Sport Psychologist, 9,* 391–405.

Gould, D. & Weinberg, R. S. (1999). *Foundation of sport and exercise psychology* (2nd ed.). Champaign, IL: Human Kinetics.

Gould, D., Weiss, M., & Weinberg, R. (1981). Psychological characteristics of successful and nonsuccessful Big Ten wrestlers. *Journal of Sport Psychology, 3,* 69–81.

Grayson, E. S. (1978). *The elements of short-term group counseling.* College Park, MD: American Correctional Association.

Greendorfer, S. L. (1980). Gender differences in physical activity. *Motor Skills: Theory into Practice, 4,* 83–90.

Greendorfer, S. L. (1992). Sport socialization. In T. S. Horn (Ed.), *Advances in sport psychology* (pp. 204–218). Champaign, IL: Human Kinetics.

Greendorfer, S. L., Lewko, J. H., & Rosengren, K. S. (1996). Family and gender-based influences in sport socialization of children and adolescents. In F. L. Smoll & R. E. Smith (Eds.), *Children and youth in sport: A biopsychosocial perspective* (pp. 89–111). Dubuque, IA: Brown & Benchmark.

Groppel, J. (2000). *The corporate athlete.* New York: John Wiley & Sons.

Gross, J. B., & Gill, D. L. (1982). Competition and instructional effects on the speed and accuracy of a throwing task. *Research Quarterly for Exercise and Sport, 53,* 125–132.

Gruber, J., & Gray, G. (1981). Factor patterns of variables influencing cohesiveness at various levels of basketball competition. *Research Quarterly for Exercise and Sport, 52,* 19–30.

Hackfort, D., & Schwenkmezger, P. (1989). Measuring anxiety in sports. In D. Hackfort & C. D. Spielberger (Eds.), *Anxiety in sport* (pp. 55–74). New York: Hemisphere.

Hackfort, D., & Schwenkmezger, P. (1993). Anxiety. In R. N. Singer, M. Murphey, & L. K. Tennant (Eds.), *Handbook of research on sport psychology* (pp. 328–364). New York: Macmillan.

Hackney, H., & Nye, S. (1973). *Counseling strategies and objectives.* Englewood Cliffs, NJ: Prentice-Hall.

Hall, E. G., & Purvis, G. (1980). The relationship of trait anxiety and state anxiety to competitive bowling. In W. F. Straub (Ed.), *Sport psychology: An analysis of athlete behavior* (2nd ed., pp. 250–256). Ithaca, NY: Mouvement.

Halliwell, W. (1980). Intrinsic motivation in sport. In W. R. Straub (Ed.), *Sport psychology: An analysis of athlete behavior* (2nd ed., pp. 85–90). Ithaca, NY: Mouvement.

Hanin, Y. L. (1980). A study of anxiety in sports. In W. F. Straub (Ed.), *Sport psychology: An analysis of athlete behavior* (2nd ed., pp. 236–249). Ithaca, NY: Mouvement.

Hanson, T. W., & Gould, D. (1988). Factors affecting the ability of coaches to estimate their athletes' trait and state anxiety levels. *The Sport Psychologist, 2,* 298–313.

Harari, J., & McDavid, J. W. (1974). *Psychology and social behavior.* New York: Harper & Row.

Hardy, C. J. (1990). Social loafing: Motivational losses in collective performance. *International Journal of Sport Psychology, 21,* 305–327.

Hardy, C. J. (1994). Nurturing our future through effective mentoring: Developing roots as well as wings. *Journal of Applied Sport Psychology, 6,* 196–204.

Hardy, C. J., & Rejeski, W. J. (1989). Not what, but how one feels: The measurement of affect during exercise. *Journal of Sport & Exercise Psychology, 11,* 304–317.

Hardy, L. (1990). A catastrophe model of performance in sport. In J. G. Jones & J. Hardy (Eds.), *Stress and performance in sport* (pp. 81–106). Chichester, UK: John Wiley & Sons.

Harris, D. V. (1979). Female sport today: Psychological considerations. *International Journal of Sport Psychology, 10,* 168–172.

Harris, D. V. (1987). The female athlete. In J. R. May & M. J. Asken (Eds.), *Sport psychology: The psychological health of the athlete* (pp. 99–116). New York: PMA.

Harris, D. V., & Harris, B. L. (1984). *The athlete's guide to sports psychology: Mental skills for physical people.* Champaign, IL: Human Kinetics.

Harrison, R. P., & Feltz, D. L. (1979). The professionalization of sport psychology: Legal considerations. *Journal of Sport Psychology, 1,* 182–190.

Harter, S. (1978). Effectance motivation reconsidered: Toward a developmental model. *Human Development, 21,* 34–64.

Harter, S. (1981). The development of competence motivation in the mastery of cognitive and physical skills: Is there still a place for joy? In G. C. Roberts & D. M. Landers (Eds.), *Psychology of motor behavior and sport–1980* (pp. 3–29). Champaign, IL: Human Kinetics.

Hausenblas, H. A., Carron, A. V., & Mack, D. E. (1997). Application of the theories of reasoned action and planned behavior to exercise behavior: A meta-analysis. *Journal of Sport & Exercise Psychology, 19,* 36–51.

Hausenblas, H. A., & Symons, D. A. (2002). How much is too much? The development and validation of the Exercise Dependence Scale. *Psychology and Health, 16,* 387–404.

Hays, R. D., Hayashi, T., & Stewart, A. L. (1989). A five-item measure of socially desirable response set. *Educational and Psychological Measurement, 49,* 629–636.

Heil, J. (Ed. 1993). *Psychology of sport injury.* Champaign, IL: Human Kinetics.

Henderson, B. (April 1971). The intangibles of baseball coaching. *The Coaching Clinic, 2–4.*

Henschen, K. (1991). Critical issues involving male consultants and female athletes. *The Sport Psychologist, 5,* 313–321.

Herkowitz, J. (1984). *Motor development during childhood and adolescence.* New York: Macmillan.

Hersey, P., & Blanchard, K. H. (1977). *Management of organizational behavior* (3rd ed.). Englewood Cliffs, NJ: Prentice-Hall.

Highlen, P. S., & Bennett, B. B. (1979). Psychological characteristics of successful and nonsuccessful elite wrestlers: An exploratory study. *Journal of Sport Psychology, 1,* 123–137.

Hoehn, R. G. (1983). *Solving coaching problems: Strategies for successful team development.* Boston: Allyn & Bacon.

Hokanson, J., & Burgess, M. (1962). The effects of three types of aggression on the vascular process. *Journal of Abnormal and Social Psychology, 64,* 14–24.

Hokanson, J., Burgess, M., & Cohen, M. (1963). Effects of displaced aggression on systolic blood pressure. *Journal of Abnormal and Social Psychology, 67,* 38–51.

Horn, T. S. (1992). Leadership effectiveness in the sport domain. In T. S. Horn (Ed.), *Advances in sport psychology* (pp. 181–200). Champaign, IL: Human Kinetics.

Horner, M. S. (1968). *Sex differences in achievement motivation and performance in competitive and noncompetitive situations.* Unpublished dissertation, University of Michigan, Ann Arbor, MI.

Hull, C. L. (1943). *Principles of behavior.* New York: Appleton.

Husman, B. F. (1980). Aggression: An historical perspective. In W. F. Straub & J. V. Daniel (Ed.), *Sport psychology: An analysis of athlete behavior* (2nd ed., pp. 211–219). Ithaca, NY: Mouvement.

Husman, B. F., & Silva, J. M. (1984). Aggression in sport: Definitional and theoretical considerations. In J. M. Silva and R. S. Weinberg (Eds.), *Psychological foundations of sport* (pp. 246–260). Champaign, IL: Human Kinetics.

Iso-Ahola, S. E., & Hatfield, B. (1986). *Psychology of sports: A social psychological approach.* Dubuque, IA: Wm. C. Brown.

Ivey, A. E. (1983). *Intentional interviewing and counseling.* Monterey, CA: Brooks/Cole.

Ivey, A. E., & Simek-Downing, L. (1980). *Counseling and psychotherapy: Skills, theories and practice.* Englewood Cliffs, NJ: Prentice-Hall.

Jackson, S. A. (1995). The growth of qualitative research in sport psychology. In T. Morris & J. Summers (Eds.), Sport psychology: Theory, applications, and issues (pp. 575–591). New York: John Wiley & Sons.

Jackson, S. A., Marsh, H. W. (1996). Development and validation of a scale to measure optimal experience. The flow state scale. *Journal of Sport & Exercise Psychology, 18,* 17–35.

Jackson, S. A., & Eklund, R. C. (2002). Assessing flow in physical activity: The Flow State Scale-2 and Dispositional Flow Scale-2. *Journal of Sport & Exercise Psychology, 24,* 133–150.

James, L. R., Hartman, E. A., Stebbins, M. W., & Jones, A. P. (1977). An examination of the relationships between psychological climate and VIE model for work motivation. *Personal Psychology, 30,* 229–254.

Jones, E. E., & Berglas, S. (1978). Control of attributions about the self through self-handicapping strategies: The appeal of alcohol and the role of underachievement. *Personality and Social Psychology Bulletin, 4,* 200–206.

Jones, B. J., Wells, L. J., Peters, R. E., & Johnson, D. J. (1988). *Guide to effective coaching: Principles and practice* (2nd ed.). Boston: Allyn & Bacon.

Jones, G., & Swain, A. (1995). Predispositions to experience debilitative and facilitative anxiety in elite and nonelite performers. *The Sport Psychologist, 9,* 201–211.

Kane, M. J. (1982). The influence of level of sport participation and sex-role orientation on female professionalization of attitudes toward play. *Journal of Sport Psychology, 4,* 290–294.

Karau, S. J., & Williams, K. D. (1993). Social loafing: A meta-analytic review and theoretical integration. *Journal of Personality and Social Psychology, 65,* 681–706.

Kelley, G. (1955). *The psychology of personal constructs* (vol. 1). New York: Norton.

Kerr, J. H. (1985). The experience of arousal: A new basis for studying arousal effects in sport. *Journal of Sports Sciences, 3,* 169–179.

Kerr, J. H. (1990). Stress and sport: Reversal theory. In G. Jones & L. Hardy (Eds.), *Stress and performance in sport* (pp. 107–134). Chichester, UK: John Wiley & Sons.

Kiester, E. (July 1984). The uses of anger: Winning athletes turn rage into motivation and concentration. *Psychology Today, 17,* pp. 19–24.

Kimiecik, J., & Gould, D. (1987). Coaching psychology: The case of James "Doc" Councilman. *The Sport Psychologist, 1,* 350–358.

Kirschenbaum, D. S., & Wittrock, D. A. (1984). Cognitive behavioral interventions in sport: A self-regulatory perspective. In J. M. Silva & R. S. Weinberg (Eds.), *Psychological foundations of sport* (pp. 81–97). Champaign, IL: Human Kinetics.

Kirschenbaum, D. S., Wittrock, D. A., Smith, R. J., & Monson, W. (1984). Criticism inoculation training: Concept in search of a strategy. *Journal of Sport & Exercise Psychology, 6,* 77–93.

Klavora, P. (1979). Customary arousal for peak athletic performance. In P. Klavora & J. V. Daniel (Eds.), *Coach, athlete, and the sport psychologist* (pp. 155–163). Champaign, IL: Human Kinetics.

Korzybski, A. (1933). *Science and sanity.* Lancaster, PA: Lancaster Press.

Krane, V. (1994). A feminist perspective on contemporary sport psychology research. *The Sport Psychologist, 8,* 393–410.

Krohne, H. W. (Ed.). (1993). *Attention and avoidance.* Seattle, WA: Hogrefe & Huber.

Krohne, H. W. (1996). Individual differences in coping. In M. Zeidner & N. S. Endler (Eds.), *Handbook of coping: Theory, research, applications* (pp. 381–409). New York: John Wiley & Sons.

Krohne, H. W., & Hindel, C. (1988). Trait anxiety, state anxiety, and coping behavior as predictors of athletic performance. *Anxiety Research, 1,* 225–234.

Kroll, W. (1979). The stress of high performance athletics. In P. Klavora & J. V. Daniel (Eds.), *Coach, athlete, and the sport psychologist* (pp. 211–219). Champaign, IL: Human Kinetics.

Kroll, W. (1982). Competitive athletic stress factors in athletes and coaches. In L. D. Zaichkowsky & W. E. Sime (Eds.), *Stress management in sport* (pp. 212–229). Reston, VA: AAHPERD.

Kroll, W., & Lewis, G. (1970). America's first sport psychologist. *Quest, 13,* 1–4.

Kroll, W., & Peterson, K. H. (1965). Personality factor profiles of collegiate football teams. *Research Quarterly, 36,* 441–447.

Kyllo, L. B., & Landers, D. M. (1995). Goal setting in sport and exercise: A research

synthesis to resolve the controversy. *Journal of Sport & Exercise Psychology, 17,* 117–137.

Landers, D. M. (1970). Psychological femininity and the prospective physical educator. *Research Quarterly, 4,* 164–170.

Landers, D. M. (1980). The arousal-performance relationship revisited. *Research Quarterly for Exercise and Sport, 51,* 77–90.

Landers, D. M. (1983). Whatever happened to theory testing in sport psychology? *Journal of Sport Psychology, 5,* 135–151.

Landers, D. M. (1988). Sport psychology: A commentary. In J. S. Skinner, C. B. Corbin, D. M. Landers, P. E. Martin, & C. L. Wells (Eds.), *Future directions in exercise and sport sciences* (pp. 475–486). Champaign, IL: Human Kinetics.

Landers, D. M. (1995). Sport psychology: The formative years, 1950–1980. *The Sport Psychologist, 9,* 406–417.

Landers, D. M., & Arent, S. M. (2001). Arousal-performance relationships. In J. M. Williams (Ed.), *Applied sport psychology: Personal growth to peak performance* (4th ed., pp. 206–228). Mountain View, CA: Mayfield.

Landers, D. M., Wang, M. Q., & Courtet, P. (1985). Peripheral narrowing among experienced and inexperienced rifle shooters. *Research Quarterly for Exercise and Sport, 56,* 122–130.

Landers, D. M., Wilkinson, M. O., Hatfield, B. D., & Barber, H. (1982). Causality and the cohesion-performance relationship. *Journal of Sport Psychology, 4,* 170–183.

Lanning, W. (1979). Coach and athlete personality interaction: A critical variable in athletic success. *Journal of Sport Psychology, 1,* 262–267.

Lanning, W. (1982). The privileged few: Special counseling needs of athletes. *Journal of Sport Psychology, 4,* 19–23.

Larsen, O. N. (1968). *Violence and the mass media.* New York: Harper & Row.

Lazarus, R. S., & Folkman, S. (1984). *Stress, appraisal and coping.* New York: Springer.

Leddy, M. H., Lambert, M. J., & Oles, B. M. (December 1994). Psychological consequences of athletic injury among high-level competitors. *Research Quarterly for Exercise and Sport, 65,* 347–354.

Lefcourt, H. M. (1976). *Locus of control.* Hillsdale, NJ: Erlbaum.

Leith, L. M. (1988). Choking in sports: Are we our own worst enemies? *International Journal of Sport Psychology, 19,* 59–64.

Leith, L. M. (1998). *Exercising your way to better mental health.* Morgantown, WV: Fitness Information Technology.

Lenk, H. (1969). Top performance despite internal conflict: An antithesis to a functional proposition. In J. W. Loy & G. S. Kenyon (Eds.), *Sport, culture and society: A reader on the sociology of sport* (pp. 224–235). New York: Macmillan.

Lepper, M. R., Greene, D., & Nesbitt, R. E. (1973). Undermining children's intrinsic interest with extrinsic reward. *Journal of Personality and Social Psychology, 28,* 129–137.

LeUnes, A. D., & Nation, J. R. (1995). *Sport psychology: An introduction* (2nd ed.). Chicago, IL: Nelson-Hall.

Leventhal, G. S. (1968). Sex of sibling as a predictor of personality characteristics. *American Psychologist, 20,* 783.

Lewis, B. P., & Linder, D. E. (1997). Thinking about choking? Attentional processes and paradoxical performance. *Personality and Social Psychology Bulletin, 23,* 937–944.

Lewko, J. H., & Greendorfer, S. L. (1977). Family influences and sex differences in children's socialization into sport: A review. In D. M. Landers & R. W. Christina (Eds.), *Psychology of motor behavior and sport* (pp. 434–447). Champaign, IL: Human Kinetics.

Litwin, G. H., & Stringer, R. A. (1968). *Motivation and organizational climate.* Boston: Graduate School of Business Administration, Harvard University.

Locke, E. A., & Latham, G. P. (1985). The application of goal setting to sports. *Journal of Sport Psychology, 7,* 205–222.

Loden, M. (1986). *Feminine leadership, or how to succeed in business without being one of the boys.* New York: Times Books.

Loehr, J. E. (1982). *Mental toughness training for sports: Achieving athletic excellence.* New York: Penguin Putnam.

Loehr, J. E. (1991). *The mental game: Winning at pressure tennis.* New York: Penguin Putnam.

Loehr, J. E. (1994). *The new toughness training for sports.* New York: Penguin Putnam.

Loehr, J. E. (1997). *Stress for success.* New York: Three Rivers Press.

Loehr, J. E., & Schwartz, T. (January 2001). The making of a corporate athlete. *Harvard Business Review,* 120–128.

Lorenz, K. (1966). *On aggression.* New York: Harcourt, Brace & World.

Lynch, A. R., & Stillman, S. M. (1983). Behavior modification in coaching basketball: A case study. In G. L. Martin & D. Hrycaiko (Eds.), *Behavior modification and coaching: Principles, procedures, and research* (pp. 239–245). Springfield, IL: Thomas.

Maccoby, E. E., & Jacklin, C. N. (1974). *The psychology of sex differences.* Palo Alto, CA: Stanford University Press.

Magill, R. A. (2001). *Motor learning: Concepts and applications* (6th ed.). Dubuque, IA: Wm. C. Brown.

Magill, R. A. (1989). Critical periods: Relation to youth sports. In R. A. Magill, M. J. Ash, & F. L. Smoll (Eds.), *Children in sport.* (2nd ed., pp. 411–452). Champaign, IL: Human Kinetics.

Magnotta, J. R. (1986). Positive motivational techniques: A key to teaching excellence. *Journal of Sport Psychology, 5,* 8–20.

Mahoney, M. J., Gabriel, T. J., & Perkins, T. S. (1987). Psychological skills and exceptional athletic performance. *The Sport Psychologist, 1,* 181–199.

Malina, R. M. (1988). Growth and maturation of young athletes: Biological and social considerations. In F. L. Smoll, R. J. Magill, & M. J. Ash (Eds.), *Children in sport* (3rd ed., pp. 83–101). Champaign, IL: Human Kinetics.

Malone, C. (1985). Risk-taking in sport. In L. K. Bunker, R. J. Rotella, & A. S. Reilly (Eds.), *Sport psychology: Psychological consideration in maximizing sport performance* (pp. 264–281). Ithaca, NY: Mouvement.

Mandell, A. J. (October 1974). A psychiatric study of professional football. *Saturday Review/World,* 12–16.

Marisi, D. Q., & Anshel, M. H. (1976). The effects of related and unrelated stress on motor performance. *New Zealand Journal of Health, Physical Education and Recreation, 9*, 93–96.

Marcus, B. H., Bock, B. C., Pinto, B. M., & Clark, M. M. (1996). Exercise initiation, adoption, and maintenance. In J. L. Van Raalte & B. W. Brewer (Eds.), *Exploring sport and exercise psychology* (pp. 133–158). Washington, D.C.: American Psychological Association.

Marcus, B. H., King, T. K., Bock, B. C., Borrelli, B., & Clark, M. M. (1998). Adherence to physical activity recommendations and interventions. In S. A. Shumaker, E. B. Schron, J. K. Ockene, & W. L. McBee (Eds.), *The handbook of health behavior change* (2nd ed., pp. 189–212). New York: Springer.

Markland, D., & Ingledew, D. K. (1997). The measurement of exercise motives: Factorial validity and invariance across gender of a revised Exercise Motivations Inventory. *British Journal of Health Psychology, 2*, 361–376.

Martens, R. (1971). Anxiety and motor behavior: A review. *Journal of Motor Behavior, 3*, 151–179.

Martens, R. (1975). *Social psychology and physical activity.* New York: Harper & Row.

Martens, R. (1977). *Sport competition anxiety test.* Champaign, IL: Human Kinetics.

Martens, R. (1979). About smocks and jocks. *Journal of Sport Psychology, 1*, 94–99.

Martens, R. (1980). The uniqueness of the young athlete: Psychologic considerations. *American Journal of Sports Medicine, 8*, 382–385.

Martens, R. (1987). Science, knowledge, and sport psychology. *The Sport Psychologist, 1*, 29–55.

Martens, R. (1993). Psychological perspectives. In B. R. Cahill & A. J. Pearl (Eds.), *Intensive participation in children's sports* (pp. 9–18). Champaign, IL: Human Kinetics.

Martens, R., Christina, R. W., Harvey, J. S., & Sharkey, B. (1981). *Coaching young athletes.* Champaign, IL: Human Kinetics.

Martens, R., Gill, D., Simon, J., & Scanlan, T. (October 1975). Competitive anxiety: Theory and research. *Mouvement: Proceedings of the Seventh Canadian Psychomotor Learning and Sport Psychology Symposium* (pp. 289–292). Quebec City, Quebec, Canada: Association of Professionals of Physical Activities of Quebec.

Martens, R., & Peterson, J. A. (1971). Group cohesiveness as a determinant of success and member satisfaction in team performance. *International Review of Sport Sociology, 6*, 49–61.

Martens, R., & Seefeldt, V. (1979). *Guidelines for children's sports.* Reston, VA: AAHPERD.

Martens, R., Vealey, R. S., & Burton, D. (1990). *Competitive anxiety in sport.* Champaign, IL: Human Kinetics.

Martin, G., & Hrycaiko, D. (1983). Effective behavioral coaching: What's it all about? *Journal of Sport Psychology, 5*, 8–20.

Martin, G., & Lumsden, J. A. (1987). *Coaching: An effective behavioral approach.* St. Louis, MO: Times Mirror/Mosby.

Martin, K. A., & Hall, C. (1995). Using mental imagery to enhance intrinsic motivation. *Journal of Sport & Exercise Psychology, 17*, 54–69.

Martinek, T. J., & Karper, W. B. (1984). The effects of noncompetitive and competitive instructional climates on teacher expectancy effects in elementary physical education classes. *Journal of Sport Psychology, 6*, 408–421.

McAuley, E. (1992). Self-referent thought in sport and physical activity. In T. S. Horn (Ed.), *Advances in sport psychology* (pp. 101–118). Champaign, IL: Human Kinetics.

McAuley, E., & Duncan, E. T. (1989). Causal attributions and affective reactions to disconfirming outcomes in motor performance. *Journal of Exercise & Sport Psychology, 11*, 187–200.

McAuley, E., Duncan, E. T., & Tammen, V. V. (1989). Psychometric properties of the Intrinsic Motivation Inventory in a competitive sport setting: A confirmatory factor analysis. *Research Quarterly for Exercise and Sport, 60*, 48–58.

McAuley, E., & Gross, J. B. (1983). Perceptions of causality in sport: An application of the causal dimension scale. *Journal of Sport Psychology, 5*, 72–76.

McAuley, E., & Mihalko, S. L. (1998). Measuring exercise-related self-efficacy. In J. L. Duda (Ed.), *Advances in sport and exercise psychology measurement* (pp. 371–390). Morgantown, WV: Fitness Information Technology.

McClelland, D. C. (1961). *The achieving society.* Princeton, NJ: Van Nostrand.

McCord, J., McCord, W., & Thurber, E. (1962). Some effects of parental absence on male children. *Journal of Abnormal Social Psychology, 64,* 361–369.

McCutcheon, L. E., & Mitchell, M. F. (1984). The prediction of running-related attitudes and behaviors from the androgynous model. *Wellness Perspectives, 1,* 31–34.

McElroy, M. A., & Willis, J. D. (1979). Women and the achievement conflict in sport. *Journal of Sport Psychology, 1,* 241–247.

McGregor, D. (1967). *The professional manager.* New York: McGraw-Hill.

Mechikoff, R. A., & Kozar, B. (1983). *Sport psychology: The coach's perspective.* Springfield, IL: Thomas.

Meichenbaum, D. (1985). *Stress inoculation training.* New York: Pergamon.

Miller, D. M. (1974). *Coaching the female athlete.* Philadelphia: Lea & Febiger.

Miller Lite/Women's Sports Foundation Report on Women in Sports (Dec. 12, 1985). *USA Today,* pp. 1A and 3C.

Miller, T. W. (1982). Assertiveness training for coaches: The issue of healthy communication between coaches and players. *Journal of Sport Psychology, 4,* 107–114.

Miller, N. H., Hill, M., Kottke, T., & Ockene, I. S. (1997). The multilevel compliance challenge: Recommendations for a call to action. *Circulation, 95,* 1085–1090.

Mitchell, T. R. (1979). Organizational behavior. *Annual Review of Psychology, 30,* 243–281.

Mondin, G.W., Morgan, W. P., Piering, P. N., Stegner, A. J., Stotesbery, C. L., Trine, M. R., & Wu, M. Y. (1996). Psychological consequences of exercise deprivation in habitual exercisers. *Medicine and Science in Sports and Exercise, 28,* 1199–1203.

Montagu, M. F. A. (1968). The new litany of "innate depravity," or original sin revisited. In M. F. A. Montagu (Ed.), *Man and aggression* (pp. 3–17). New York: Oxford University Press.

Morgan, W. P. (1979a). Prediction of performance in athletics. In P. Klavora & J. V. Daniel (Eds.), *Coach, athlete, and the sport psychologist* (pp. 173–186). Champaign, IL: Human Kinetics.

Morgan, W. P. (1979b). Anxiety reduction following acute exercise. *Psychiatric Annals, 9,* 141–147.

Morgan, W. P. (1980). Sport personology: The credulous-skeptical argument in perspective. In W. F. Straub (Ed.), *Sport psychology: An analysis of athlete behavior* (2nd ed., pp. 330–339). Ithaca, NY: Mouvement.

Morgan, W. P. (1985). Affective beneficence of vigorous physical activity. *Medicine and Science in Sports and Exercise, 17,* 94–100.

Morgan, W. P. (1988). Sport psychology in its own context: A recommendation for the future. In J. S. Skinner, C. B. Corbin, D. M. Landers, P. E. Martin, & C. L. Wells (Eds.), *Future directions in exercise and sport psychology* (pp. 97–110). Champaign, IL: Human Kinetics.

Morgan, W. P., & Pollack, M. L. (1977). Psychological characterization of the elite distance runner. *Annals of the New York Academy of Science, 301.*

Morris, D. (1967). *The naked ape.* New York: McGraw-Hill.

Mugno, D. A., & Feltz, D. L. (1985). The social learning of aggression in youth football in the United States. *Canadian Journal of Applied Sport Sciences, 10,* 26–35.

Murphy, S. M. (Ed.). (1995). *Sport psychology interventions.* Champaign, IL: Human Kinetics.

Murphy, S. (1996). *The achievement zone.* New York: J. P. Putnam & Sons.

Murray, M. C., & Mann, B. L. (1993). Leadership effectiveness. In J. M. Williams (Ed.), *Applied sport psychology: Personal growth to peak performance* (2nd ed., pp. 82–98). Mountain View, CA: Mayfield.

NCAA Intercollegiate Athletic, Physical Education, and Recreation. (1979). *Progress of the member institutions* (Report No. 4.). Manhattan, KS: National Collegiate Athletic Association.

Neal, P. E., & Tutko, T. A. (1975). *Coaching girls and women: Psychological perspectives*. Boston: Allyn & Bacon.

Nicholls, J. (1984). Achievement motivation: Conceptions of ability, subjective experience, task choice, and performance. *Psychological Review, 91*, 328–346.

Nideffer, R. M. (1979). The role of attention in optimal athletic performance. In P. Klavora and J. V. Daniel (Eds.), *Coach, athlete, and the sport psychologist* (pp. 99–112). Champaign, IL: Human Kinetics.

Nideffer, R. M. (1980). The future of applied sport psychology. *Journal of Sport Psychology, 2*, 170–174.

Nideffer, R. M. (1981). *The ethics and practice of applied sport psychology*. Ithaca, NY: Mouvement.

Nideffer, R. M., DuFresne, P., Nesvig, D., & Selder, D. (1980). The future of applied sport psychology. *Journal of Sport Psychology, 2*, 170–174.

Nideffer, R. M., Feltz, D., & Salmela, J. (1982). A rebuttal to Danish and Hale: A committee report. *Journal of Sport Psychology, 4*, 3–6.

O'Block, F. R., & Evans, F. H. (1984). Goal setting as a motivational technique. In J. M. Silva & R. S. Weinberg (Eds.), *Psychological foundations of sport* (pp. 188–196). Champaign, IL: Human Kinetics.

O'Connor, P. J., & Davis, J. C. (1992). Psychobiologic responses to exercise at different times of day. *Medicine and Science in Sports and Exercise, 24*, 714–719.

Officer, S. A., & Rosenfeld, L. B. (1985). Self-disclosure to male and female coaches by female high school athletes. *Journal of Sport Psychology, 7*, 360–370.

Ogilvie, B. C. (1968). The unconscious fear of success. *Quest, 10*, 35–39.

Ogilvie, B. C. (1979a). The sport psychologist and his professional credibility. In P. Klavora and J. V. Daniel (Eds.), *Coach, athlete, and the sport psychologist* (pp. 44–55). Champaign, IL: Human Kinetics.

Ogilvie, B. C. (1979b). The personality of women who have dared to succeed in sport. In J. Goldstein (Ed.), *Sports, games and play*. Hillsdale, NJ: Halsted.

Oglesby, C. A. (1978). *Woman and sport: From myth to reality*. Philadelphia, PA: Lea & Febiger.

Oglesby, C. A., & Hill, K. L. (1993). Gender and sport. In R. N. Singer, M. Murphey, & L. K. Tennant (Eds.), *Handbook of research in sport psychology*. (pp. 718–728). New York: Macmillan.

Oldridge, N. B., & Streiner, D. L. (1990). The health belief model: Predicting compliance and dropout in cardiac rehabilitation. *Medicine and Science in Sports and Exercise, 22*, 678–683.

Orlick, T. (1986). *Psyching for sport: Mental training for athletes*. Champaign, IL: Human Kinetics.

Orlick, T. (1989). Reflections of sportpsych consulting with individual and team sport athletes at summer and winter Olympic games. *The Sport Psychologist, 3*, 358–365.

Orlick, T. (1990). *In pursuit of excellence* (2nd ed.). Champaign, IL: Human Kinetics.

Orlick, T., & Botterill, C. (1975). *Every kid can win*. Chicago: Nelson-Hall.

Orlick, T., & Partington, J. (1986). *Psyched: Inner views of winning*. Ottawa, Ontario, Canada: Coaching Association of Canada.

Ostrow, A. C. (Ed.). (1996). Directory of psychological tests in the sport and exercise sciences (2nd ed.). Morgantown, WV: Fitness Information Technology.

Oxendine, J. G. (1970). Emotional arousal and motor performance. *Quest, 13*, 23–32.

Paige, R. R. (1973). *What research tells the coach about football*. Reston, VA: AAHPERD.

Pargman, D. (Ed.). (1999). *Psychological bases of sport injuries* (2nd ed.). Morgantown, WV: Fitness Information Technology, Inc.

Parsons, T., & Bales, R. F. (1955). *Family, socialization, and the interaction process*. Glencoe, IL: Free Press.

Partington, J., & Orlick, T. (1987). The sport psychology consultant: Olympic coaches' views. *The Sport Psychologist, 1*, 95–102.

Passer, M. W. (1983). Fear of failure, fear of evaluation, perceived competence, and self-esteem in competitive-trait-anxious children. *Journal of Sport Psychology, 5,* 172–188.

Passer, M. W. (1984). Competitive trait anxiety in children and adolescents. In J. M. Silva & R. S. Weinberg (Eds.), *Psychological foundations of sport* (pp. 452–461). Champaign, IL: Human Kinetics.

Passer, M. W. (1988). Psychological issues in determining children's age-readiness for competition. In F. L. Smoll, R. A. Magill, & M. J. Ash (Eds.), *Children in sport* (3rd ed., pp. 67–78). Champaign, IL: Human Kinetics.

Pelletier, L. G., Fortier, M. S., Vallerand, R. J., Tuson, K. M., Briere, N. M., & Blais, M. R. (1995). Toward a new measure of intrinsic motivation, extrinsic motivation, and amotivation in sports: The sport motivation scale (SMS). *Journal of Sport & Exercise Psychology, 17,* 35–53.

Pemberton, C. L., & Petlichkoff, L. (1988). Sport psychology and the female Olympic athlete. *Journal of Physical Education, Recreation and Dance, 59,* 55–58.

Perna, F., Neyer, M., Murphy, S. M., Ogilvie, B. C., & Murphy, A. (1995). Consultations with sport organizations: A cognitive–behavioral model. In S. M. Murphy (Ed.), *Sport psychology interventions* (pp. 235–252). Champaign, IL: Human Kinetics.

Peterson, J. A., & Martens, R. (1972). Success and residential affiliation as determinants of team cohesiveness. *Research Quarterly, 43,* 62–76.

Peterson, S. L., Weber, J. C., & Trousdale, W. W. (1967). Personality traits of women in team sports vs. women in individual sports. *Research Quarterly, 38,* 686–689.

Petruzzello, S. J., Landers, D. M., Hatfield, B. O., Kubitz, K. A., & Salazar, W. (1991). A meta-analysis on the anxiety-reducing effects of acute and chronic exercise. *Sports Medicine, 11,* 143–182.

Phares, E. J. (1976). *Locus of control in personality.* New York: General Learning Press.

Prapavessis, H. (2000). The POMS and sports performance: A review. *Journal of Applied Sport Psychology, 12,* 34–48.

Prapavessis, H., & Carron, A. V. (1988). Learned helplessness in sport. *The Sport Psychologist, 2,* 189–201.

Prochaska, J. O., & DiClemente, C. C. (1982). Transtheoretical therapy: Toward a more integrative model of change. *Psychotherapy: Theory, research, and practice, 20,* 161–173.

Prochaska, J. O., & Marcus, B. H. (1994). The transtheoretical model: Applications to exercise. In R. K. Dishman (Ed.), *Advances in exercise adherence* (pp. 161–180). Champaign, IL: Human Kinetics.

Rand, C. S., Weeks, K. (1998). Measuring adherence with mediation regimens in clinical care and research. In S. A. Shumaker, E. B. Schron, J. K. Ockene, & W. L. McBee (Eds.), *The handbook of health behavior change* (pp. 114–132). New York: Springer.

Rasch, P. J., & Kroll, W. (1964). *What research tells the coach about wrestling.* Reston, VA: AAHPERD.

Ravizza, K. (1984). Peak performance. In J. M. Silva & R. S. Weinberg (Eds.), *Psychological foundations of sport* (pp. 452–461). Champaign, IL: Human Kinetics.

Ravizza, K. (1988). Gaining entry with athletic personnel for season-long consulting. *The Sport Psychologist, 2,* 243–254.

Ravizza, K. (1990). Sportpsych consultation issues in professional baseball. *The Sport Psychologist, 4,* 330–340.

Ray, R., & Wiese-Bjornstal, D. M. (Eds.) (1999). *Counseling in sports medicine.* Champaign, IL: Human Kinetics.

Régnier, G., Salmela, J., & Russell, S. J. (1993). Talent detection and development in sport. In R. N. Singer, M. Murphey, & L. K. Tennant (Eds.), *Handbook of research in sport psychology* (pp. 290–313). New York: Macmillan.

Reilly, T. (1979). *What research tells the coach about soccer.* Reston, VA: AAHPERD.

Reis, H. T., & Jelsma, B. (1980). A social psychology of sex differences in sport. In W. F. Straub, (Ed.), *Sport psychology: An analysis of athlete behavior* (pp. 276–286). Ithaca, NY: Mouvement.

Rejeski, W. (1980). Causal attribution: An aid to understanding and motivating athletes. *Motor Skills: Theory into Practice, 4,* 32–36.

Rejeski, W. J., & Brawley, L. R. (1983). Attribution theory in sport: Current status and new perspectives. *Journal of Sport Psychology, 5,* 77–99.

Rejeski, W., Darracott, C., & Hutslar, S. (1979). Pygmalion in sport: A field study. *Journal of Sport Psychology, 1,* 311–319.

Roberton, M. A. (May 1984). *The weaver's loom: A developmental metaphor.* Presentation at the R. Tait McKenzie Symposium on Sport, University of Tennessee, Knoxville, TN.

Roberts, G. C. (1975). Win-loss causal attributions of Little League players. *Movement, 7,* 315–322.

Roberts, G. C. (1978). Children's assignment of responsibility for winning and losing. In F. L. Smoll & R. E. Smith (Eds.), *Psychological perspectives in youth sports* (pp. 145–171). Washington, DC: Hemisphere.

Roberts, G. C. (1984). Achievement motivation in children's sport. In J. Nicholls (Ed.), *Advances in achievement motivation, 3* (pp. 251–281). Greenwich, CT: JAI.

Roberts, G. C. (Ed.). (1992a). *Motivation in sport and exercise.* Champaign, IL: Human Kinetics.

Roberts, G. C. (1992b). Motivation in sport and exercise: Conceptual constraints and convergence. In G. C. Roberts (Ed.), *Motivation in sport and exercise* (pp. 3–29). Champaign, IL: Human Kinetics.

Roberts, G. C. (1993). Motivation in sport: Understanding and enhancing the motivation and achievement of children. In R. N. Singer, M. Murphey, & L. K. Tennant (Eds.), *Handbook of research in sport psychology* (pp. 405–420). New York: Macmillan.

Roberts, G. C., Keiber, D. A., & Duda, J. L. (1981). An analysis of motivation in children's sport: The role of perceived competence in participation. *Journal of Sport Psychology, 3,* 206–216.

Roberts, G. C., & Treasure, D. C. (1995). Achievement goals, motivational climate and achievement strategies and behaviors in sport. *International Journal of Sport Psychology, 26,* 64–80.

Robertson, I. (1986). Youth sport in Australia. In M. R. Weiss & D. Gould (Eds.), *Sport for children and youths* (pp. 5–10). Champaign, IL: Human Kinetics.

Robinson, B. E. (1998). *Chained to the desk: A guidebook for workaholics, their partners and children, and the clinicians who treat them.* New York: New York University Press.

Rosenfeld, L., & Wilder, L. (March/April 1990). Communication fundamentals: Active listening. *Sport Psychology Training Bulletin, 1,* 5.

Rosenthal, R., & Jacobson, L. (1968). *Pygmalion in the classroom: Teacher expectations and pupil's intellectual development.* New York: Holt, Rinehart & Winston.

Rotella, R. (1983). Motivational concerns of high level gymnasts. In L. E. Unestahl (Ed.), *The mental aspects of gymnastics* (pp. 67–85). Orebro, Sweden: VEJE.

Rotella, R. J. (1985). The successful coach: A leader who communicates. In L. K. Bunker, R. J. Rotella, & A. S. Reilly (Eds.), *Sport psychology: Psychological considerations in maximizing sport performance* (pp. 19–26). Ithaca, NY: Mouvement.

Rotella, R. J., & Heyman, S. R. (1993). Stress, injury, and the psychological rehabilitation of athletes. In J. M. Williams (Ed.), *Applied sport psychology: Personal growth to peak performance* (2nd ed., pp. 338–355). Mountain View, CA: Mayfield.

Rotella, R. J., & Murray, M. (1991). Homophobia, the world of sport, and sport psychology consulting. *The Sport Psychologist, 5,* 355–364.

Rotter, G. C. (1966). Generalized expectancies for internal versus external control of reinforcement. *Psychological Monograph, 80* (Whole No. 609).

Rushall, B. S. (1976). Three studies relating personality variables to football performance. In A. C. Fisher (Ed.), *Psychology of sport* (pp. 391–399). Palo Alto, CA: Mayfield.

Rushall, B. S. (1979). *Psyching in sport.* London: Pelham.

Rushall, B. S. (1984). The content of competition thinking. In W. F. Straub & J. M. Williams (Eds.), *Cognitive sport psychology* (pp. 51–62). Lansing, NY: Sport Science Associates.

Rushall, B. S. (October 1986). *On-site intervention techniques for athlete preparation.* Paper presented at a conference of the Association for the Advancement of Applied Sport Psychology, Jekyll Island, GA.

Rushall, B. S., & Siedentop, D. (1972). *The development and control of behavior in sport and physical education.* Philadelphia, PA: Lea & Febiger.

Russell, D. (1982). The causal dimension scale: A measure of how individuals perceive causes. *Journal of Personality and Social Psychology, 42,* 1137–1145.

Russell, G. W. (1981). Spectator moods at an aggressive sports event. *Journal of Sport Psychology, 3,* 217–227.

Ryan, E. D. (1976). Perceptual characteristics of vigorous people. In A. C. Fisher (Ed.), *Psychology of sport* (pp. 432–446). Palo Alto, CA: Mayfield.

Ryan, E. D. (1979). *Athletic scholarships and intrinsic motivation.* Paper presented at the North American Society for Psychology of Sport and Physical Activity Conference, Trois-Riviere, Quebec, Canada.

Ryan, E. D. (1980). Attribution, intrinsic motivation, and athletics. In C. Nadeau, W. R. Halliwell, K. M. Newell, & G. C. Roberts (Eds.), *Psychology of motor and sport behavior* (pp. 19–26). Champaign, IL: Human Kinetics.

Ryan, R. M., & Deci, E. L. (2000). Self-determination theory and the facilitation of intrinsic motivation, social development, and well-being. *American Psychologist, 55,* 68–78.

Ryan, R. M., Mims, V., & Koestner, R. (1983). The relationship of reward contingency and interpersonal context to intrinsic motivation: A review and test using cognitive evaluation theory. *Journal of Personality and Social Psychology, 45,* 736–750.

Sabock, R. J. (1985). *The coach* (3rd ed.). Champaign, IL: Human Kinetics.

Sachs, M. L. (1993). Professional ethics in sport psychology. In R. N. Singer, M. Murphey, & L. K. Tennant (Eds.), *Handbook of research in sport psychology* (pp. 921–932). New York: Macmillan.

Sachs, M. L., Burke, K., & Butcher, L. A. (2002). *Directory of graduate programs in applied sport psychology* (6th ed.). Morgantown, WV: Fitness Information Technology.

Sage, G. H. (1973). The coach as management: Organizational leadership in American sport. *Quest, 19,* 35–40.

Sage, G. H. (1980). Humanistic psychology and coaching. In W. F. Straub (Ed.), *Sport psychology: An analysis of athlete behavior* (2nd ed., pp. 215–228). Ithaca, NY: Mouvement.

Sallis, J. F., & Owen, N. (1999). *Physical activity and behavioral medicine.* Thousand Oaks, CA: Sage.

Sandler, R. L. (May 1981). Coaching style and the athlete's self-concept. *The Athletic Journal: 46,* 66.

Sarafino, E. P. (1994). *Health psychology: Biopsychosocial interactions* (2nd ed.). New York: John Wiley & Sons.

Scanlan, T. K. (1984). Competitive stress and the child athlete. In J. M. Silva & R. S. Weinberg (Eds.), *Psychological foundations of sport* (2nd ed., pp. 274–305). Champaign, IL: Human Kinetics.

Scanlan, T. K. (1986). Competitive stress in children. In M. R. Weiss & D. Gould (Eds.), *Sport for children and youth* (pp. 113–118). Champaign, IL: Human Kinetics.

Scanlan, T. K. (1988). Social evaluation and the competition process. In F. L. Smoll, R. A. Magill, & M. J. Ash (Eds.), *Children in sport* (3rd ed., pp. 135–148). Champaign, IL: Human Kinetics.

Scanlan, T. K., & Leuthwaite, R. (1984). Social psychological aspects of competition for male youth sport participants: I. Predictors of competitive stress. *Journal of Sport Psychology, 6,* 208–226.

Scanlan, T. K., & Passer, M. W. (1978). Factors related to competitive stress among male youth sport participants. *Medicine and Science in Sports, 10,* 103–108.

Scanlan, T. K., Simons, J. P., Carpenter, P. J., Schmidt, G. W., & Keeler, B. (1993). The sport commitment model: Measurement development for the youth sport domain. *Journal of Sport & Exercise Psychology, 11,* 65–83.

Scanlan, T. K., Stein, G. L., & Ravizza, K. (1991). An in-depth study of former elite figure skaters: III sources of stress. *Journal of Sport & Exercise Psychology, 13,* 103–120.

Schafer, W. (1996). *Stress management for wellness* (3rd ed.). New York: Harcourt Brace.

Schneider, J., & Eitzen, D. S. (1986). The structure of sport and participant violence. In R. E. Lapchick (Ed.), *Fractured focus: Sport as a reflection of society* (pp. 229–244). Lexington, MA: Lexington Books.

Schutz, R. W., Eom, H. J., Smoll, F. L., & Smith, R. E. (1994). Examination of the factorial validity of the Group Environment Questionnaire. *Research Quarterly for Exercise and Sport, 65,* 226–236.

Schutz, R. W., & Gessaroli, M. E. (1993). Use, misuse, and disuse of psychometrics in sport psychology research. In R. N. Singer, M. Murphey, & L. K. Tennant (Eds.), *Handbook of research in sport psychology* (pp. 901–917). New York: Macmillan.

Seefeldt, V. (October 1980). When are competitive athletics too stressful for children? *Family Forum.* Cooperative Extension Service, Michigan State University.

Seefeldt, V. (1988). The concept of readiness applied to motor skill acquisition. In F. L. Smoll, R. A. Magill, & M. J. Ash (Eds.), *Children in sport* (3rd ed., pp. 45–52). Champaign, IL: Human Kinetics.

Seifert, K. L., & Hoffnung, R. J. (1994). *Child and adolescent development* (3rd ed.). Boston: Houghton-Mifflin.

Seraganian, P. (Ed.). (1993). *Exercise psychology: The influence of physical exercise on psychological processes.* New York: John Wiley & Sons.

Siedentop, D., & Ramey, G. (1977). Extrinsic rewards and intrinsic motivation. *Motor Skills: Theory into Practice, 2,* 49–62.

Silva, J. M. (1979). Changes in the effective state of guilt as a function of exhibiting proactive assertion or hostile aggression. In G. C. Roberts & K. M. Newell (Eds.), *Psychology of Motor Behavior and Sport—1978* (pp. 98–108). Champaign, IL: Human Kinetics.

Silva, J. M. (1980). Understanding aggressive behavior and its effects upon athletic performance. In W. F. Straub (Ed.), *Sport psychology: An analysis of athlete behavior* (2nd ed., pp. 177–186). Ithaca, NY: Mouvement.

Silva, J. M. (1982). An evaluation of fear of success in female and male athletes and nonathletes. *Journal of Sport Psychology, 4,* 92–96.

Silva, J. M. (September 1984). The status of sport psychology: A National Survey of Coaches. *Journal of Physical Education, Recreation, and Dance, 55,* 46–49.

Silva, J. M., Hardy, C. J., & Crace, R. K. (1988). Analysis of psychological momentum in intercollegiate tennis. *Journal of Sport & Exercise Psychology, 10,* 346–354.

Simon, J. A., & Martens, R. (1979). Children's anxiety in sport and nonsport evaluative activities. *Journal of Sport Psychology, 1,* 163–169.

Singer, R. N. (1967). *Motor learning and human performance.* New York: Macmillan.

Singer, R. N. (1972). *Coaching, athletics, and psychology.* New York: Macmillan.

Singer, R. N. (1973). Motor learning as a function of age and sex. In G. L. Rarick (Ed.), *Physical activity: Human growth and development* (pp. 176–200). New York: Academic Press.

Singer, R. N. (1977). Motivation in sport. *International Journal of Sport Psychology, 8,* 1–21.

Singer, R. N. (1980). *Motor learning and human performance* (3rd ed.). New York: Macmillan.

Singer, R. N. (1984). *Sustaining motivation in sport.* Tallahassee, FL: Sport Consultants International, Inc.

Singer, R. N. (1988). Psychological testing: What value to coaches and athletes? *International Journal of Sport Psychology, 19,* 87–106.

Singer, R. N. (1993). Ethical issues in clinical services. *Quest, 45,* 88–105.

Singer, R. N. (1996). Future of sport and exercise psychology. In J. L. Van Raalte & B. W. Brewer (Eds.), *Exploring sport and exercise psychology* (pp. 451–468). Washington, DC: American Psychological Association.

Smith, M. D. (1980). Hockey violence: Interring some myths. In W. F. Straub (Ed.), *Sport psychology: An analysis of athlete behavior* (2nd ed., pp. 187–192). Ithaca, NY: Mouvement.

Smith, M. D. (1988). Interpersonal sources of violence in hockey: The influence of parents, coaches, and teammates. In F. L. Smoll, R. A. Magill, & M. J. Ash (Eds.), *Children in sport* (3rd ed., pp. 301–313). Champaign, IL: Human Kinetics.

Smith, R. E. (1984). Theoretical and treatment approaches to anxiety reduction. In J. M. Silva & R. S. Weinberg (Eds.), *Psychological foundations of sport* (pp. 157–170). Champaign, IL: Human Kinetics.

Smith, R. E. (1993). Principles of positive reinforcement and performance feedback. In J. M. Williams (Ed.), *Applied sport psychology: Personal growth to peak performance* (2nd ed., pp. 25–35). Mountain View, CA: Mayfield.

Smith, R. E. (1999). The psychologist as scientist-practitioner: Reciprocal relations linking theory, research, and intervention. In R. Lidor & M. Bar-Eli (Eds.), *Sport psychology: Linking theory and practice* (pp. 15–34). Morgantown, WV: Fitness Information Technology.

Smith, R. E., Smoll, F. L., & Curtis, B. (1977a). Coaching roles and relationships. In J. R. Thomas (Ed.), *Youth sports guide for parents and coaches*. Reston, VA: AAHPERD.

Smith, R. E., Smoll, F. L., & Curtis, B. (1979). Coach effectiveness training: A cognitive-behavioral approach to enhancing relationship skills in youth sport coaches. *Journal of Sport Psychology, 1,* 59–75.

Smith, R. E., Smoll, F. L., & Hunt, E. (1977b). A system for the behavioral assessment of athletic coaches. *Research Quarterly, 48,* 401–407.

Smith, R. E., Small, F. L., & Schutz, R. W. (1990). Measurement and correlates of sport-specific cognitive and somatic trait anxiety: The sport anxiety scale. *Anxiety Research, 2,* 263–280.

Smoll, F. L., & Smith, R. S. (1989). Leadership behaviors in sport: A theoretical model and research paradigm. *Journal of Applied Social Psychology, 19,* 1522–1551.

Sonstroem, R. J. (1984). An overview of anxiety in sport. In J. M. Silva & R. S. Weinberg (Eds.), *Psychological foundations of sport* (pp. 104–117). Champaign, IL: Human Kinetics.

Sonstroem, R. J., & Bernardo, P. (1982). Intraindividual pregame state anxiety and basketball performance: A re-examination of the inverted-U curve. *Journal of Sport Psychology, 4,* 235–245.

Spence, K. W. (1956). *Behavior theory and conditioning.* New Haven, CT: Yale University Press.

Spielberger, C. D. (1972). *Anxiety: Current trends in theory and research* (vol. 1). New York: Academic Press.

Spielberger, C. D., Gorsuch, R. L., & Luschene, R. E. (1970). *Manual for the state-trait anxiety inventory* (self-evaluation questionnaire). Palo Alto, CA: Consulting Psychologists Press.

Sternberg-Horn, T., Lox, C. L., & Labrador, F. (2001). The self-fulfilling prophecy theory: When coaches' expectations become reality. In J. M. Williams (Ed.), *Applied sport psychology: Personal growth to peak performance* (4th ed., pp. 63–81). Mountain View, CA: Mayfield.

Straub, W. F. (1980). How to be an effective leader. In W. F. Straub (Ed.), *Sport psychology: An analysis of athlete behavior* (2nd ed., pp. 382–391). Ithaca, NY: Mouvement.

Straub, W. F. (1982). Sensation-seeking among high- and low-risk male athletes. *Journal of Sport Psychology, 4,* 246–253.

Suinn, R. M. (1987). *The seven steps to peak performance: Manual for mental training for athletes* (2nd ed.). Ft. Collins: Colorado State University.

Sullivan, J., & Hodge, K. P. (1991). A survey of coaches and athletes about sport psychology in New Zealand. *The Sport Psychologist, 5,* 140–151.

Summers, J. J., Miller, K., & Ford, S. (1991). Attentional style and basketball performance. *Journal of Sport & Exercise Psychology, 13,* 239–253.

Swartz, B., & Barsky, S. F. (1977). The home advantage. *Social Forces, 55,* 641–661.

Tannenbaum, R., & Schmidt, W. H. (May/June 1958). How to choose a leadership pattern. *Harvard Business Review, 36*, 95–101.

Taylor, J. A. (1953). A personality scale of manifest anxiety. *Journal of Abnormal and Social Psychology, 48*, 285–290.

Terry, P. (1995). The efficacy of mood state profiling with elite performers: A review and synthesis. *The Sport Psychologist, 9*, 309–324.

Thirer, J. (1978). The effect of observing filmed violence on the aggressive attitudes of female athletes and nonathletes. *Journal of Sport Behavior, 1*, 28–36.

Thirer, J. (1993). Aggression. In R. N. Singer, M. Murphey, & L. K. Tennant (Eds.), *Handbook of research in sport psychology* (pp. 365–378). New York: Macmillan.

Thomas, J. R. (1980). Acquisition of motor skills: Information processing differences between children and adults. *Research Quarterly for Exercise and Sport, 51*, 158–173.

Thomas, J. R. (1984). Children's motor skill development. In J. R. Thomas (Ed.), *Motor development during childhood and adolescence.* (pp. 91–104). Minneapolis, MN: Burgess.

Thomas, J. R., & Nelson, J. K. (2001). *Research methods in physical activity* (4th ed.). Champaign, IL: Human Kinetics.

Tice, D. M., & Baumeister, R. F. (1993). Controlling anger: Self-induced emotion change. In D. M. Wegner & J. W. Pennebaker (Eds.), *Handbook of mental control* (pp. 393–409). Englewood Cliffs, NJ: Prentice-Hall.

Tresemer, D. (1976). The cumulative record of research on "fear of success." *Sex Roles, 2*, 217–236.

Tutko, T., & Bruns, W. (1976). *Winning is everything and other American myths.* New York: Macmillan.

Tutko, T. A., & Ogilvie, B. C. (1967). The role of the coach in motivation of athletes. In R. Slovenko & J. A. Knight (Eds.), *Motivations in play, games, and sports.* Springfield, IL: Thomas.

Vallerand, R. J. (1997). Toward a hierarchical model of intrinsic and extrinsic motivation. In M. P. Zanna (Ed.), *Advances in experimental social psychology: Vol. 29* (pp. 271–360). New York: Academic Press.

Vallerand, R. J., & Perrault, S. (1999). Intrinsic and extrinsic motivation in sport: Toward a hierarchical model. In R. Lidor & M. Bar-Eli (Eds.), *Sport psychology: Linking theory and practice* (pp. 191–212).

Vallerand, R. J., & Reid, G. (1984). On the causal effects of perceived competence on intrinsic motivation: A test of cognitive evaluation theory. *Journal of Sport Psychology, 6*, 94–102.

Vallerand, R. J., & Rousseau, F. L. (2001). Intrinsic and extrinsic motivation in sport and exercise: A review using the hierarchical model of intrinsic and extrinsic motivation. In R. N. Singer, H. A. Hausenblas, & C. M. Janelle (Eds.), *Handbook of sport psychology* (2nd ed., pp. 389–416). New York: John Wiley & Sons.

Vanden Auweele, Y., DeCuyper, B., Van Mele, V., & Rzewnicki, R. (1993). Elite performance and personality: From description and prediction to diagnosis and intervention. In R. N. Singer, M. Murphey, & L. K. Tennant (Eds.), *Handbook of research in sport psychology* (pp. 257–289). New York: Macmillan.

Vanek, M., & Cratty, B. J. (1970). *Psychology and the superior athlete.* New York: Macmillan.

Vaz, E. (1972). The culture of young hockey players: Some initial observations. In A. W. Taylor (Ed.), *Training—Scientific basis and application* (pp. 222–234). Springfield, IL: Thomas.

Vealey, R. S. (1986). Conceptualization of sport-confidence and competitive orientation: Preliminary investigation and instrument development. *Journal of Sport Psychology, 8*, 221–246.

Vealey, R. S. (1988). Future directions in psychological skills training. *The Sport Psychologist, 2*, 318–336.

Vealey, R. S. (1992). Personality and sport: A comprehensive view. In T. S. Horn (Ed.), *Advances in sport psychology* (pp. 25–99). Champaign, IL: Human Kinetics.

Veroff, J. (1969). Social comparison and the development of achievement motivation. In C. P. Smith (Ed.), *Achievement-related motives in children.* New York: Russell Sage.

Vogel, P. G. (1987). Post season evaluation: What did we accomplish? In V. Seefeldt (Ed.), *Handbook for youth sports coaches* (pp. 355–379). Reston, VA: AAHPERD.

Waitley, D. (1978). *The psychology of winning.* Chicago: Human Resources.

Wankel, L. M., & Kreisal, P. S. J. (1985). Factors underlying enjoyment of youth sports: Sport and age group comparisons. *Journal of Sport Psychology, 7,* 51–64.

Watkins, C. E. (1983). Counseling psychology versus clinical psychology: Further explorations of a theme. *The Counseling Psychologist, 11,* 76–92.

Weiller, K. (1988). Identification of leaders of a professional basketball team. *Journal of Applied Research in Coaching and Athletics, 3,* 158–171.

Weinberg, R. S. (1988). *The mental advantage.* Champaign, IL: Human Kinetics.

Weinberg, R. S. (1989). Anxiety, arousal, and motor performance: Theory, research, and applications. In D. Hackfort & C. D. Spielberger (Eds.), *Anxiety in sports* (pp. 95–115). New York: Hemisphere.

Weinberg, R. S. (1992). Goal setting and motor performance: A review and critique. In G. C. Roberts (Ed.), *Motivation in sport and exercise* (pp. 177–197). Champaign, IL: Human Kinetics.

Weinberg, R. S., & Gould, D. (1995). *Foundations of sport and exercise.* Champaign, IL: Human Kinetics.

Weinberg, R. S., & Hunt, V. V. (1976). The interrelationships between anxiety, motor performance, and electromyography. *Journal of Motor Behavior, 8,* 219–244.

Weinberg, R. S., & Jackson, A. (1990). Building self-efficacy in tennis players: A coach's perspective. *Journal of Applied Sport Psychology, 2,* 164–174.

Weiner, B. (1974). *Achievement motivation and attribution theory.* Morristown, NJ: General Learning Press.

Weiner, B. (1985a). An attributional theory of achievement motivation and emotion. *Psychological Review, 92,* 548–573.

Weiner, B. (1985b). Spontaneous casual thinking. *Psychological Bulletin, 97,* 74–84.

Weiner, B. (1986). *An attributional theory of motivation and emotion.* New York: Springer-Verlag.

Weiner, B., Frieze, I., Kukla, A., Reed, L., Rest, S., & Rosenbaum, R. M. (1971). *Perceiving the causes of success and failure.* Morristown, NJ: General Learning Press.

Wells, C. L. (1985). *Women, sport and performance: A physiological perspective.* Champaign, IL: Human Kinetics.

Wells, K. F., & Luttgens, K. (1976). *Kinesiology: Scientific basis of human motion* (6th ed.). Philadelphia, PA: Lea & Febiger.

Westre, K., & Weiss, M. (1991). The relationship between perceived coaching behaviors and group cohesion in high school football teams. *The Sport Psychologist, 5,* 41–54.

White, R. W. (1959). Motivation reconsidered: The concept of competence. *Psychological Review, 66,* 297–331.

Widmeyer, W. N. (1984). Aggression-performance relationships in sport. In J. M. Silva and R. S. Weinberg (Eds.), *Psychological foundations of sport* (pp. 274–286). Champaign, IL: Human Kinetics.

Widmeyer, W. N. (2002). Reducing aggression in sport. In J. M. Silva & D. E. Stevens (Eds.), *Psychological foundations of sport* (pp. 380–395). San Francisco: Benjamin Cummings.

Widmeyer, W. N., Brawley, L. R., & Carron, A. V. (1985). *The measurement of cohesion in sport teams: The group environment questionnaire.* London, Ontario, Canada: Sports Dynamics.

Widmeyer, W. N., Brawley, L. R., & Carron, A. V. (1990). The effects of group size in sport. *Journal of Sport & Exercise Psychology, 12,* 177–190.

Widmeyer, W. N., Brawley, L. R., & Carron, A. V. (1992). Group dynamics in sport. In T. S. Horn (Ed.), *Advances in sport psychology* (pp. 163–180). Champaign, IL: Human Kinetics.

Widmeyer, W. N., Dorsch, K. D., Bray, S. R., & McGuire, E. J. (2002). The nature, prevalence, and consequences of aggression in sport. In J. M. Silva & D. E. Stevens (Eds.), *Psychological foundations of sport* (pp. 328–351). San Francisco: Benjamin Cummings.

Widmeyer, W. N., & McGuire, E. J. (1997). Frequency of competition and aggression in professional ice hockey. *International Journal of Sport Psychology, 26,* 57–60.

Wiggins, D. A. (1984). The history of sport psychology in North America. In J. M. Silva & R. S. Weinberg (Eds.), *Psychological foundations of sport* (pp. 9–22). Champaign, IL: Human Kinetics.

Wiggins, D. A. (1986). From plantation to playing field: Historical writings on the black athlete in American sport. *Research Quarterly for Exercise and Sport, 57,* 101–116.

Will, G. F. (1990). *Men at work.* New York: Macmillan.

Williams, J. M. (1980). Personality characteristics of successful female athletes. In W. F. Straub (Ed.), *Sport psychology: An analysis of athlete behavior* (2nd ed., pp. 353–359). Ithaca, NY: Mouvement.

Williams, J. M., & Hacker, C. M. (1982). Causal relationships among cohesion, satisfaction, and performance in women's intercollegiate field hockey teams. *Journal of Sport Psychology, 4,* 324–337.

Williams, J. M., & Straub, W. F. (2001). Sport psychology: Past, present, future. In J. M. Williams (Ed.), *Applied sport psychology: Personal growth to peak performance* (4th ed., pp. 1–12). Mountain View, CA: Mayfield.

Willis, J. D., & Campbell, L. F. (1992). *Exercise psychology.* Champaign, IL: Human Kinetics.

Wittig, A. F., Balogh, D. W., & Butler, F. (June 1986). *Importance of sports for young women: A social dilemma.* Paper presented at a national conference of the North American Society for Psychology of Sport and Physical Activity, Scottsdale, AZ.

Wrisberg, C. A. (2001). Levels of performance skill: From beginners to experts. In R. N. Singer, H. A. Hausenblas, & C. M. Janelle (Eds.), *Handbook of sport psychology* (2nd ed., pp. 3–19). New York: John Wiley & Sons.

Yerkes, R. M., & Dodson, J. D. (1908). The relation of strength and stimulus to rapidity of habit formation. *Journal of Comparative and Neurological Psychology, 18,* 459–482.

Yukelson, D. P. (1984). Group motivation in sport teams. In J. M. Silva & R. S. Weinberg (Eds.), *Psychological foundations of sport* (pp. 229–240). Champaign, IL: Human Kinetics.

Yukelson, D., Weinberg, R., & Jackson, A. (1984). A multidimensional group cohesion instrument for intercollegiate basketball teams. *Journal of Sport Psychology, 6,* 103–117.

Yukelson, D., Weinberg, R. S., West, S., & Jackson, A. (1981). Attributions and performance: An empirical test of Kukla's theory. *Journal of Sport Psychology, 3,* 46–57.

Zaccaro, S. J., Blair, V., Peterson, C., & Zazunis, C. (1995). Collective efficacy. In J. Maddux (Ed.), *Self-efficacy, adaptation, and adjustment* (pp. 305–328). New York: Plenum.

Zaichkowsky, L. D., & Perna, F. M. (1992). Certification of consultants in sport psychology: A rebuttal to Anshel. *The Sport Psychologist, 6,* 287–296.

Zajonc, R. B. (1965). Social facilitation. *Science, 149,* 269–274.

Zajonc, R. B. (1972). *Compresence.* Paper presented at the Midwestern Psychological Association Conference, Chicago, IL.

Zaleznik, A. (May/June 1977). Managers and leaders: Are they different? *Harvard Business Review,* 67–68.

Zillman, D., Johnson, R. C., & Day, K. D. (1974). Provoked and unprovoked aggressiveness in athletes. *Journal of Research in Personality, 8,* 139–152.

Zillman, D., Katcher, A., & Milavsky, B. (1972). Excitation transfer from physical exercise to subsequent aggressive behavior. *Journal of Experimental Social Psychology, 8,* 247–259.

Zillman, D., & Paulus, P. B. (1993). Spectators: Reactions to sports events and effects on athletic performance. In R. N. Singer, M. Murphey, & L. K. Tennant (Eds.), *Handbook of research in sport psychology* (pp. 600–619). New York: Macmillan.

Zuckerman, M. (1984). Experience and desire: A new format for Sensation-Seeking Scales. *Journal of Behavioral Assessment, 6,* 101–114.

PHOTO AND ILLUSTRATION CREDITS

Chapter 1: Figure 1.2, University of North Carolina, Chapel Hill, NC; Figure 1.4, LGE Performance Systems.

Chapter 2: Figure 2.1, Reprinted with permission from *Psychology Today* magazine, copyright © 1980 (Sussex Publishers, Inc.); Figure 2.2, University of North Carolina, Chapel Hill, NC; Figure 2.6, LGE Performance Systems; Figure 2.7, *The Signal*, The College of New Jersey, Trenton, NJ.

Chapter 3: Figure 3.1, *The Signal*, The College of New Jersey, Trenton, NJ; Figure 3.4, Illawarra Academy of Sport, New South Wales, Australia; Figure 3.5, Vallerand, R. J., & Perreault, S. (1999). Intrinsic and extrinsic motivation in sport: Toward a hierarchical model. In R. Lidor & M. Bar-Eli (eds), *Sport psychology: Linking theory and practice* (pp. 191–212). Morgantown, WV: Fitness Information Technology; Figure 3.7, Illawarra Academy of Sport, New South Wales, Australia.

Chapter 4: Figure 4.2, University of North Carolina, Chapel Hill, NC.

Chapter 5: Figure 5.1, *The Signal*, The College of New Jersey, Trenton, NJ; Figure 5.2, From Theory and research on anxiety (1966). In C. D. Spielberger (ed.). *Anxiety and Behavior* (p. 17). New York: Academic Press. Reprinted with permission; Figure 5.3, Illawarra Academy of Sport, New South Wales, Australia; Figure 5.7, From P. Klavora (1979). Customary arousal for peak athletic performance. In *Coach, Athlete, and the Sport Psychologist* (pp. 155–163). Published by the School of Physical and Health Education, University of Toronto. Reproduced with permission; Figure 5.8, *The Signal*, The College of New Jersey, Trenton, NJ.

Chapter 6: Figure 6.1, *The Signal*, The College of New Jersey, Trenton, NJ; Figure 6.2, Illawarra Academy of Sport, New South Wales, Australia; Figure 6.3, University of North Carolina, Chapel Hill, NC.

Chapter 8: Figure 8.1, Illawarra Academy of Sport, New South Wales, Australia; Figure 8.2, From Smoll & Smith (1989). Reprinted with permission from the *Journal of Applied Social Psychology*, Vol. 19, No. 18, pp. 1522–1551. © V. H. Winston & Son, Inc., 360 South Ocean Blvd., Palm Beach, FL 33480. All rights reserved; Figure 8.4, Australian Sports Commission.

Chapter 9: Figure 9.1, © Jack Hollingsworth/CORBIS; Figure 9.3, *The Signal*, The College of New Jersey, Trenton, NJ; Figure 9.5, © CORBIS; Figure 9.6, Australian Sports Commission; Figure 9.7, Illawarra Academy of Sport, New South Wales, Australia.

Chapter 10: Figure 10.1, From J. Eccles & R. Harold. Gender differences in sport involvement: Applying the Eccles expectancy-value model. *Journal of Applied Sport Psychology*, 3, no. 1 (pp. 7–35). Copyright © 1991 by Allan Press: Lawrence, KS. Reprinted with permission; Figure 10.2, © Bob Daemmrich/The Image Works.

Chapter 11: Figure 11.2, LGE Performance Systems; Figure 11.2, Hausenblas, H. A., & Symons, D. A. (2002). How much is too much? The development and validation of the exercise dependence scale. *Psychology and Health*.

Chapter 12: Figure 12.1, Illawarra Academy of Sport, New South Wales, Australia.

Chapter 13: Figure 13.1, University of North Carolina, Chapel Hill, NC.